7½″

MASK FOR OVERHEAD TRANSPARENCIES

The area enclosed within the black rule gives the outline of the mask to be used with an overhead projector (proportion 4 × 5).

9½″

Planning, Producing, and Using Instructional Technologies

Seventh Edition

Jerrold E. Kemp
Professor Emeritus, San Jose State University

Don C. Smellie
Utah State University

With the assistance of
Ron Carraher
Art
University of Washington

Richard F. Szumski
Photography
Placerville, California

HarperCollins*CollegePublishers*

Acquisitions Editor: Christopher Jennison
Project Coordination and Text Design: Proof Positive/Farrowlyne Associates, Inc.
Cover Design: Kay Petronio
Text Art: Ron Carraher
Production Manager: Kewal Sharma
Compositor: Weimer Graphics, Inc.
Printer and Binder: Courier Corporation
Cover Printer: The Lehigh Press, Inc.

PLANNING, PRODUCING, AND USING INSTRUCTIONAL TECHNOLOGIES

SEVENTH EDITION

Library of Congress Cataloging-in-Publication Data

Kemp, Jerrold E.
Planning, producing, and using instructional technologies / Jerrold E. Kemp, Don C. Smellie ; with the assistance of Ron Carraher, Richard F. Szumski, photography. — 7th ed.
p. cm.
Rev. ed. of: Planning, producing, and using instructional media. 6th ed. c1989.
Includes bibliographical references (p.) and index.
1. Audio-visual materials. 2. Audio-visual equipment. 3. Educational technology. I. Smellie, Don C. II. Kemp, Jerrold E. Planning, producing, and using instructional media. III. Title.
LB1043.K40 1994
371.3'3—dc20 93-5844
CIP

93 94 95 96 9 8 7 6 5 4 3 2 1

Brief Contents

Contents

Preface and Acknowledgements

Through the six previous editions of this book, we have treated media resources for instruction primarily as separate entities—slides, overhead transparencies, motion pictures, video recordings, and so on. Each one required its own preparation methods and specific equipment for use.

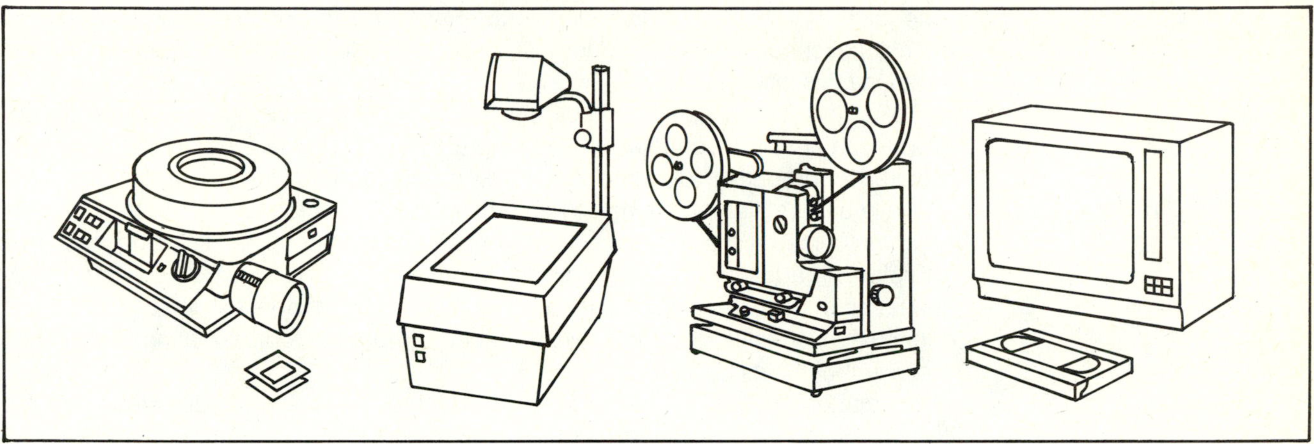

Now, the world of media and the new technologies for successful learning are undergoing fundamental changes—both in preparation and coordinated uses. Two major developments are affecting this transformation.

One is the application of digital technology—the use of a binary system to express words, numbers, and images—as opposed to the conventional analog system. Digital technology allows for their manipulation, enhancement, combination, transfer, storage, or duplication, conveniently and quickly.

The other development is the major spin-off from digital technology. Through the use of computer technology, we are able to converge all media forms to provide either a synchronous stream combining many forms of media (known as multimedia), or use a non-linear approach consisting of multiple paths involving the integration of various media forms.

The opportunities to design, create, and present information, allowing for a smooth orchestration, flexibility, and learner interaction, are both challenging and exciting. With these technologies, we are now able to accomplish many communication and instructional goals more effectively and efficiently than formerly. They can even open up possibilities we have not as yet come to realize. The purpose of this book is to provide the information and skills necessary to serve these goals.

Even though your major interest may be in the production aspects of specific media technologies, and their integration, as treated in Sections 3 and 4 of the book, do recognize that there is useful knowledge, based on research and pratical experiences, that should be studied prior to the start of production. The chapters in Section 1 provide this information.

Then there is the need to give careful attention to the planning and design of your chosen materials. The chapters in Section 2 are devoted to the specific planning steps required as preparation for production of all media forms.

While each of the technologies has an impact on how ideas and information may be communicated, the dynamics of delivery affects the effectiveness of the message. Therefore, in addition to the background information, planning aspects, and production techniques, carefully consider matters that can contribute to the successful use of each media technology form. Section 5 treats important topics relating to utilization of the technologies for instruction.

No matter which of the resources are selected, the vision of your ideas and the objectives you set, combined with the knowledge and skills offered in this book, can guide you to successfully produce and use any learning technologies.

We wish to thank the many colleagues who have assisted us with requested information and their reviews of specific topics.

From Utah State University
- Matt Dirks for information on video formats
- Dr. M. David Merrill for information on instructional translation theory
- Robb Russon for his review of audio related materials
- Dr. Steve Soulier for his general review of the manuscript and particular help with computer related topics
- Dr. Charles Stoddard for his input on photographic topics and development of a chart on photographic films
- Dr. Ron Thorkildsen for his review of videodisc content and recommended sources for services
- Dr. Linda Wolcott for her review of the materials and sources on evaluation and selection of instructional materials

From San Jose State University
- Betty Benson for her suggestions concerning distance learning content
- Sharon Englehardt for her review of sources for commercially available instructional materials
- Romaldo Lopez and Tom Tutt for their suggestions concerning the photography topic and preparation of new photos
- Dick Mills for assistance with developments in the graphics area and the preparation of some new computer-based materials
- Dr. Don Perrin for alerting us to new developments in multimedia and interactive techniques
- Bob Reynolds for his review and suggestions relating to video recording procedures

In addition, we would like to thank the following reviewers whose valuable comments helped shape the final product: Ronald Bouverat, Syracuse University; Alex Carter, Eastern Michigan University; William A. Carter, Texas A&M University; Paul H. Denton, Andrews University; Dilawar Edwards, California University of Pennsylvania; Richard Johnson, California State University—Long Beach; D. Franklin L. King, Alabama State University; Gary R. Morrison, Memphis State University; Amos C. Patterson, The University of Toledo; Robert V. Price, Texas Tech University; Steven M. Ross, Memphis State University; Roberta Lynn Ruben, Western Illinois University.

Finally, our thanks to Barry Willis of the University of Alaska for his materials on distance education, to colleagues who reviewed the early plans for this new edition, and to Dr. Scott Grabinger at the University of Colorado, Denver, for his particularly thoughtful suggestions for this edition.

Jerrold E. Kemp
Don C. Smellie

PART 1

Background for Planning, Producing, and Using Instructional Technologies

CHAPTER

1

Contributions of Instructional Technologies to the Instructional Process

Designing for Instruction

Patterns for Teaching and Learning

Media in the Instructional-Design Process

Levels of Instructional Materials Production

Learners and Instructional Materials Production

Instructional Technologies for Education and Training

When skillfully combined, pictures, words, and sounds have the power to evoke emotions, change attitudes, and motivate actions. Examples of this power can be seen every day on television: the commercial that motivates the viewer to buy a product, the political spot that attempts to sway a voter's choice of candidate, or the emotional appeal for donations to a charity. We have become accustomed to living in a world of mediated impressions. The impressions that are created by combinations of pictures, words, and sounds have been shown to be retained by viewers significantly longer than when they are only heard or read (Wilkinson).

Instructional technologies also make use of the power of pictures, words, and sounds to compel attention, to help an audience understand ideas and acquire information too complex for verbal explanation alone, and to help overcome the limitations of time, size, and space.

Contributions of Instructional Technologies to the Instructional Process

While the advantages of using the technologies of instruction have been recognized for a long time, their acceptance and integration within instructional programs have been slow. Recently, there has been increasing evidence of the effectiveness of carefully designed, high quality instructional media used either as an integral part of classroom instruction and training or as the principal means of direct instruction. These practical outcomes are often realized:

- ***The content of a topic can be more carefully selected and organized***—When planning a production or examining resources prior to selecting media for use, a person must give detailed attention to the subject matter. The process allows one to thoughtfully choose and structure the content for ease of understanding and use.
- ***The delivery of instruction can be more standardized***—Each learner seeing and hearing a technology-based presentation receives the same message. Instructors may interpret subject content in different ways, but by using media the variations can be reduced and the same information can be communicated to all learners as the bases for further study, practice, and application.
- ***The instruction can be more interesting***—A technology-based presentation tends to keep members of an audience alert. The clarity and coherence of a message, the attractiveness of changing images, the use of special effects, and the impact of ideas that can arouse curiosity cause an audience to laugh or be thoughtful; all factors contribute to the motivational and interest-creating aspects of instructional media.
- ***Learning becomes more interactive through applying accepted learning theory***—When designing media, consideration can be given to principles such as learner participation, feedback, and reinforcement to actively engage the learner in the learning experience. The continual interaction between the learner and the materials can result in more effective instruction and promote learning at a high intellectual level.
- ***The length of time required for instruction can be reduced***—Most media presentations require a short time to transmit their messages. But during this brief period, a large amount of information can be communicated to and absorbed by the learner. This can lead to greater efficiency in the use of time for both the instructor and the learner during an instructional session.
- ***The quality of learning can be improved***—When there is a careful integration of pictures and words, instructional media can communicate elements of knowledge in a well-organized, specific, and clearly defined manner. As a result, with adequate effort on the part of the learner and appropriate follow-up activities, learning can be expected to reach an acceptable competency level. Additionally, learning with media can be retained longer than reading or verbal learning.
- ***The instruction can be provided when and where desired or necessary***—When instructional media are designed for individualized use, then a learner can study at a time and place that is personally convenient. This flexibility is particularly important when individuals must integrate study activities with vocational and personal responsibilities.
- ***The learning needs of individuals can be effectively and efficiently met***—By using the capabilities of the computer, along with such developments as integrated multimedia presentations and the flexibility of hypertext/hypermedia, topics can be explored in many ways, leading to understanding and satisfactory learning.
- ***The positive attitude of individuals toward what they are learning and to the learning process itself can be enhanced***—Learners frequently express preference for using media as a means of studying. This may be due to both the motivational aspect and the contributions that media can make to a person's success in learning. Individuals find learning with instructional media both enjoyable and satisfying.
- ***The role of the instructor can be appreciably changed in positive directions***—While most benefits of instructional media are directed to the learner and to his or her accomplishment in learning, there are also advantages for the instructor. First, much of the burden for repeated explanations of content and skills can be eliminated. Second, by not having to present as much information verbally, other, possibly more important, aspects of a course can be given attention. Third, the instructor has increased opportunity to fulfill the role of consultant and advisor.

Taken together, these ten outcomes indicate that instructional technologies can enhance both the efficiency of learning and positive attitudes toward learning. Each person must decide which of these contributions should receive attention when planning and producing materials for instruction.

To satisfy the outcomes specified above, instructional materials have to be not only of high quality but also should be selected or designed, produced, and used as an integral part of an instructional program. They must make a definite contribution to the achievement of the program's objectives. For this reason, a person interested in planning, producing, and using instructional media should also become acquainted with the process of systematic instructional planning within which instructional technologies are to function.

DESIGNING FOR INSTRUCTION

Traditionally, plans for instruction most often are made in an intuitive fashion and may be based on ambiguous goals. Subject content is the basis for planning, and only casual attention is given to other details. It is now recognized that the instructional process is complex and that attention must be given to many interrelated factors if outcomes are to be successful.

For an instructional program to be successful, the following should occur:

- Satisfactory learning takes place so that learners have acquired necessary knowledge, skills, and attitudinal behavior patterns, and after training, perform productively in their assignments.
- The learning is accomplished with due regard for reasonable expenditures of money and time.
- The learning experiences are meaningful and interesting so that individuals are encouraged to continue with their studies.
- The planning and implementation of an instructional program prove to be a satisfactory set of experiences for the instructor and support staff.

The term **instructional development** applies to the broad process of designing an instructional program—whether a single module, a complete unit, or a total course—using an objective, systematic procedure. This method starts with answers to four questions:

1. For whom is the program being developed? (nature of the **learners**)
2. What do you want the individual to learn or be able to do? (**objectives**)
3. How is the subject content or skills best learned? (teaching/learning **methods** and **activities** with **resources**)
4. How do you determine the extent to which the learning has been achieved? (**evaluation**)

Four elements—learners, objectives, methods, and evaluation—form the framework of instructional development procedures. In addition, there are other factors that either support or relate to these four elements. Taking all these pieces together, we can develop a plan, termed **instructional-design plan,** consisting of these interrelated components (Kemp and others):

1. Assess **learning needs** for designing an instructional program; state **goals, constraints,** and **priorities** that must be recognized.
2. Select **topics** or **job tasks** to be treated and indicate **general purposes** to be served.
3. Examine **learner characteristics** that should receive attention during planning.
4. Identify **subject content** and **analyze tasks** relating to the topic and job.
5. State **learning objectives** to be accomplished by learners in terms of subject content and job tasks.
6. Through **pretesting,** determine preparation of learners for studying the topic.
7. Select a **teaching/learning method** and design **activities** to accomplish learning objectives.
8. Select **resources** (including instructional technologies) to support the activities.
9. Specify **support services** required for developing and implementing activities and acquiring or producing materials.
10. Prepare to **evaluate learning** as the program is developed (**formative evaluation**) and then judge **program outcomes** (**summative evaluation**) in terms of the accomplishment of objectives, with a view to revising and reevaluating any phases of the instructional plan that need improvements.

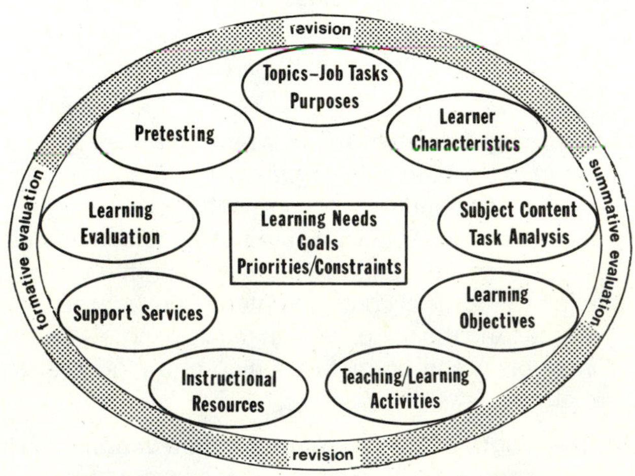

The ten elements of this instructional-design plan can be illustrated by a diagram. The diagram is circular in format because not all designers will start their plan-

EXAMPLE: Elements Within an Instructional Design

SUBJECT

Solar Energy

TOPICS

Collecting solar energy
Storing the energy
Using the energy for heating

GENERAL PURPOSE

To understand how solar energy can be used

OBJECTIVES

1. To explain how four scientific principles are applied for creating heat in a solar collector
2. To identify four parts of a solar collector and the functions of each
3. To assemble a solar collector when provided with the four essential parts

TEACHING/LEARNING ACTIVITIES	INSTRUCTIONAL RESOURCES
A. Presentation: Instructor to learner group Scientific principles applied to collecting solar energy	Overhead transparencies Video recording (animation) Printed worksheets
B. Self-paced Learning Parts, placement, and use of solar collectors	Slides/tape recording Worksheet review Self-check test
C. Group Activities 1. Visit local solar collector manufacturer and installer 2. Make plans for projects	

[NOTE: The slides and tape recording for B above are planned in detail in the chapters of Part 2.]

ning with the same element. One person might start with a consideration of the learner and another with one of content or objectives. Note the location and relationship of the instructional resources item to other elements of the instructional-design plan. You will discover in Part 2 of this book that a design procedure similar to that shown above is also applied when planning for the production of instructional materials.

As used here, the expression **instructional technologies** refers to **audiovisual, electronic media,** and **related materials** that serve instructional functions in education and training. As you will see in Chapter 4 (page 42), instructional technologies are also useful for *informational* and *motivational* purposes. Thus, their value extends beyond the "instructional" intent of the label *instructional technologies.* If your interest is in developing a type of instructional material for informational or motivational purposes, much of this background and the planning procedures in Part 2 will still merit careful attention.

One important consideration when planning and producing instructional media is the audience mode in which the technology might be used. You should recognize the possible alternatives that are available within instructional situations along with their advantages and limitations.

PATTERNS FOR TEACHING AND LEARNING

There are three broad methods within which most learning takes place: (1) **presentation** of information to groups of learners; (2) **self-paced study,** or individualized learning, with each learner working on his or her own; and (3) small-group **interaction** between instructor and learners or among learners. There is a gradual shift through innovative instructional methods away from complete dependence on group teaching to more emphasis on self-paced learning procedures. While instructional technologies do provide many necessary learning experiences within each of the three patterns, the technologies have essential functions in the newer, nontraditional instructional formats.

By recognizing the features of these three methods, you should be better able to decide on appropriate instructional media for use in any of them, and then to design the materials to fit the requirements of the pattern.

Instructor Presentation to Groups

This presentation method is typified by one-way communications from instructor to learners, as in a lecture. Information is presented at the instructor's rate of delivery. Individuals are physically passive, although listening, taking notes, or completing related worksheets. In this pattern, learners do not have the flexibility of individual pacing and choice of study methods and materials.

The purposes served by this pattern are changing. The current trend is toward reducing the time an instructor spends in conventional presentation of subject content. More attention now is given to self-paced study of content by individuals. Often, for efficiency, essential information may be transmitted to numbers of learners, in regular classes or in large groups, to serve these needs:

- Introduce new topics and provide orientation to activities in a unit of study.
- Provide motivation for studying a subject or topic, possibly through a videotape recording or a multi-image presentation.
- Illustrate relations or integration of one topic with another.
- Point out special applications or new developments in a topic that may be too recent for inclusion in the self-paced study materials.
- Provide special enrichment materials and experiences, such as a videotape recording or a guest speaker who cannot be available to small groups or to individual learners.

To complement or possibly replace an instructor's usual verbal presentation, instructional materials such as overhead transparencies, slides, a video recording, a film, or a multi-image presentation may be selected to serve one or more of these instructional needs relative to a topic. The usual video recording or other media formats, consisting of 10- to 30-minute presentations, can be modified to more succinct structures in terms of specific objectives to be treated. Also, the value of learner participation during a presentation can be increased by providing learner activities that may include responding periodically to questions on an exercise sheet or allowing the selection of items for follow-up work.

Self-paced or Individualized Learning

When an individual takes responsibility for his or her own learning, the study activities can take various forms. In a basic program, all learners follow the same track, using the same materials, with only their individual pace of study being different. Each person reads, views instructional material, and frequently is directed to respond to a question or complete other worksheet activities. Feedback on answers is provided. The media designed for such self-paced learning would be for **reactive learning.**

In sophisticated programs, learning is more individualized. Students may choose their objectives and alternative methods for study may be available. Then, depending on responses to questions, a student may be directed to remedial or review instruction, or to advanced study. This procedure is called **interactive learning.**

When systematic instructional development is applied to the design of self-paced or individualized learning programs, these elements are often included:

- Learning objectives and required levels of learner knowledge or performance are clearly stated.
- Pretesting permits the learner to skip study of one or more objectives if competency is demonstrated.
- Alternative procedures for accomplishing the objectives are specified.
- Participation activities and required responses for the learner are included.
- Confirmation or correction of performance or response is immediately available to the learner.
- Opportunities are provided for the learner to self-check understanding, progress, and performance against the objectives.
- The learner decides when he or she is ready to have knowledge or performance evaluated by the instructor.
- If the results of tests or other evaluation methods do not indicate a satisfactory competency level, the learner may restudy and be retested.
- Follow-up applications or projects permit the learner to use the knowledge or skill learned.

An individualized or **self-paced learning** program consists of study units often called **modules.** Each module treats a topic (examples: *The Tablesaw, Cardiogenic Shock, The Cold War*). The supporting resources, such as learning aids or other printed material, slides, an audiocassette recording, a short video recording, a computer-based program, or an interactive videodisc, are specific to the topic. This means that selected instructional materials must be in a form suitable for self-paced study, should be brief in serving one or only a few objectives, and should be carefully integrated with other activities.

Instructor-Learner Interaction

The third pattern for teaching and learning provides opportunities for instructors and learners to work together in small groups to discuss, to question, to report, to perform, to be evaluated, or to engage in other forms of personalized interchange. In light of the shift toward individualized learning, with the individual spending more time working on his or her own, it is necessary to provide opportunities for direct contact with instructors and with other learners. This pattern provides such experiences.

Some of the resources used in presentations and for individualized learning may be available for reference during small-group discussion. Also, special materials can be prepared for the purposes of motivating discussion, illustrating concepts, presenting problem situations for group consideration, and evaluating learning. A real need exists for instructional materials imaginatively designed for use in group activities.

A prime advantage of small-group interaction is the opportunity it offers for encouraging learner participation for socialization, leadership development, and peer recognition purposes. One of the best methods of providing experiences that lead to accomplishing one or more of these important purposes is to guide and assist individuals to plan and produce their own instructional materials, then present the results to their group. This can be a very practical experience for learners in all settings.

The three patterns we have examined—instructor presentation to groups, self-paced learning methods, and instructor-learner interaction activities—provide the framework within which experiences for learning can be planned. Many of these activities rely on the use of appropriate instructional media.

MEDIA IN THE INSTRUCTIONAL-DESIGN PROCESS

The newer technologies, particularly computer-based instruction, interactive video, and multimedia forms, are powerful resources that can have impacts on learning beyond what has been realized from conventional media. With careful planning and development, instructional designers can design these technologies so that learners can progress according to their own abilities and needs. Individually selected and self-paced activities will aid learners to develop clear understandings rather than simply absorb information as it is presented. This can significantly change the instructor's role from that of a presenter of information to that of a *facilitator* and *counselor.* Such a shift has been predicted for some time. It now can become a reality.

Instructional materials of any type should be carefully planned and produced, whether they will be part of an application of an instructional-design plan or discrete entities. The techniques described in subsequent chapters apply to materials being prepared for any purpose.

Media to be used within the instructional design are determined by the requirements of learners, objectives, content, and instructional methods. Media are *not* supplementary to or in support of instruction, but *are* the instructional input itself. In this light, the old concept of audiovisual *aids* as supplements to teaching can no longer be accepted. Determination must be made as to which media, in what form, and at what time, will most effectively and efficiently provide the most relevant experiences for learners.

Just as various instructional objectives require different kinds of learning, appropriate instructional resources should be matched to required tasks. This approach to teaching and learning is developed around *specificity*—specificity in terms of learning objectives to serve the needs of particular learners.

Each separate concept to be taught requires a separate consideration of resources. Certain media (sound or print, motion or still pictures) can best serve certain purposes. In other cases, available equipment, convenience, costs, and such factors may determine the choice. See page 56 for further discussion of a media-selection method and for an example of media selected for teaching/learning activities within a unit on Solar Energy.

LEVELS OF INSTRUCTIONAL MATERIALS PRODUCTION

The local production of instructional materials can take place on any of three levels.

Mechanical Level: Preparation

First, there is the *mechanical* level. Here the concern is solely with the techniques of preparation. Mounting pictures on cardboard or cloth, copying pictures on film for slides, recording a speech or other presentation on audio- or videotape, and running a printed page or clipping through a copy machine to make a transparency are examples of the mechanical preparation of materials. Even though the individual has a purposeful use in mind, little planning is required, and the actual preparation follows a routine procedure. Many persons start at this level in instructional media production and go on to other levels of activity.

Creative Level: Production

A step above the mechanical level is the *creative* level. Here, materials being considered for production require decisions; planning accordingly becomes an important forerunner of production. *Production* implies an order of activity beyond *preparation,* with its more routine connotations. The production of an instructional bulletin board, of a slide series with a recording, of a filmstrip for self-instruction, of a set of thoughtfully designed transparencies to teach a concept, of a videotape recording that illustrates a process, or a multi-image presentation as the motivational introduction to a topic—all are examples of materials produced on the creative level. The skills developed on the mechanical level become tools for use on this level.

Design Level: Conception

As previously explained, the production of instructional materials that can be carefully integrated into learning activities to serve specific instructional objectives and to meet the needs of individuals or a specific group of learners may be part of a *design for instruction.* The design of a slide/tape presentation or of an interactive computer/video program, as part of a self-paced learning module, are examples of this third level. Now *instructional materials* are conceived within a carefully designed instructional framework for group or individual uses. During the planning for materials on this level attention must be given to factors such as *specificity* in serving objectives, *adaptability* for certain individuals or groups, *flexibility* in method of use, and *integration* with other experiences. The skills developed on both the mechanical and creative levels serve important functions here.

While your interest in using this book may start with the mechanical level, it is hoped that you will find potentials for developing materials on either the creative or design levels.

On each level of production you can prepare appropriate materials to serve personal or instructional purposes of your own. Or, you might develop materials for other persons to use in satisfying their motivational, instructional, or informational communication needs.

However, there is another group showing increasing

interest in activities involving instructional technologies—learners on all levels, from nursery school to graduate school, including trainees in business and industry. Many instructors plan specific activities that will involve learners in the preparation of photographs, slides, video recordings, multi-image presentations, or computer-based multimedia programs. Others find that individuals, on their own, are ready to engage in such enterprises. Whatever the base, this increasing interest and enthusiasm on the part of individuals for planning and producing instructional materials should be recognized and encouraged. There are definite educational benefits for learners who engage in such activities.

LEARNERS AND INSTRUCTIONAL MATERIALS PRODUCTION

The recognition of the need to involve learners with instructional technologies in an active and productive way is a recent thrust in education and training. Its purpose is both to allow individuals to produce materials for projects and reports and to make learners more visually literate. Developing the skills to understand and use visual communication techniques is especially important in our society since so much information is transmitted in nonverbal modes—graphic design, still photography, motion pictures, and television. Learners need opportunities to become perceptive and analytical of the visual world in which they live so as to make their own judgments and choices of what may be appropriate and aesthetically pleasing in a situation. To do this, individuals must develop the skills needed for interpreting the messages they receive in visual form and must also become fluent in expressing their own ideas visually.

This visual awareness, comprehension, and expression can be obtained first by developing an intimate familiarity with design principles and visual tools (page 116) and elements of composition (page 97), and then by manipulating these items through involvement with a variety of graphic, pictorial, and other nonverbal communications media.

The skills an individual develops in interpreting, judging, responding to, and using visual representations of reality (i.e., a visual intelligence) result in what is called **visual literacy.** For learners on all levels, the process of becoming visually literate requires experiences that allow them to:

- Recognize and "read" graphic and photographic illustrations that represent objects, events, places, and people.
- Sort and organize such visual representations into patterns and relationships that apply a "vocabulary" of nonverbal visual expression.
- Produce visual materials as their own interpretations of actual objects, events, places, and people.

One of the best ways for individuals to become literate in this visual sense is by actively selecting an idea, developing it by planning as described in Part 2 of this book, and then translating the written words and

1

2

3

4

sketches into an audiovisual form. This can be done by learners individually or in groups.

When individuals work together to plan and produce a photographic picture display, a slide series, or a videotape recording of a community activity, they take part in a vigorous mental process. The planning phase requires that individuals in the group assume responsibilities, do research work, express and organize ideas, and structure the visual presentation to communicate the intended ideas. Then follows the hard but exciting work of production, which brings the verbal thoughts to visual life in a logical sequence. For learners of any age, such an activity can stimulate personal growth as well as promote visual intelligence.

What You Have Learned in This Introduction to Instructional Technologies:

1. Return to page 3 and number in order the ten *effects of instructional technologies on the learning process.* Use those numbers in answering this question: To which effect does each of the following relate?
   a. On a rating scale learners complete at the end of the course, they overwhelmingly indicate a preference for using media for learning.
   b. After seeing the visual report on the benefits of the children's program, many people volunteered their services.
   c. Technicians using computer-based materials completed their recertification in less time than when using only the manual.
   d. While developing the instructional materials, the planning team came up with ideas for additional teaching activities in the unit of instruction.
   e. As a video program is planned, careful attention is given to specifying the facts that support the concepts to be illustrated.
   f. All individuals in each of the three classes learned the procedures for equipment assembly in the same way.
   g. For upgrading skills, staff members were able to study, with the instructional materials, when they had free time while on duty.
   h. The instructor found more time to spend with individual learners when they used the media to study on their own.
2. What *four* elements form the basis of instructional design?
3. Why is a knowledge of instructional design important to a person interested in developing media for instructional uses?
4. What are the three patterns within which teaching and learning activities can be placed?
5. To which teaching and learning pattern does each situation apply?
   a. Individual studying at a computer terminal
   b. Instructor showing videodisc segments to a class
   c. Team of learners working together to edit their videotape
   d. Instructor using transparencies before a training group
   e. Salesperson listening to an audiocassette tape containing examples of sales methods while driving a car
6. What are the *three* levels on which instructional materials may be produced?
7. To which level of materials production does each of the following relate?
   a. Audiotaping a discussion session
   b. Developing transparencies in terms of objectives for a lesson
   c. Making a multi-image slide presentation
   d. Mounting a set of magazine pictures on cardboard
   e. Scripting and then shooting a how-to-do-it videotape recording
   f. Applying the knowledge learned to problem situations after each individual completes the computer program
8. Define *visual literacy.*

9. What are some benefits to learners who engage in instructional material production activities?

See answers on page 375.

REFERENCES

MEDIA IN THE INSTRUCTIONAL PROCESS

Gagné, Robert, ed. *Instructional Technology: Foundations.* Hillsdale, NJ: Lawrence Erlbaum, 1987.

Heinich, Robert; Molenda, Michael; and Russell, James D. *Instructional Media: The New Technologies of Instruction.* New York: Wiley, 1992.

Knirk, Frederick G. and Gustafson, Kent L. *Instructional Technology: A Systematic Approach to Education.* New York: Holt, Rinehart, and Winston, 1986.

Kozma, Robert B. "Learning With Media." *Review of Educational Research,* 61 (Summer 1991): 179–211.

Wilkinson, Gene. *Media in Instruction: 60 Years of Research.* Washington, DC: Association for Educational Communications and Technology, 1980.

INSTRUCTIONAL DEVELOPMENT AND DESIGN

Briggs, Leslie J. and others. *Instructional Design: Principles and Applications.* Englewood Cliffs, NJ: Educational Technology Publications, 1991.

Dick, Walter, and Carey, Lou. *The Systematic Design of Instruction.* Glenview, IL: Scott Foresman, 1991.

Gagné, Robert M.; Briggs, Leslie; and Wager, Walter. *Principles of Instructional Design.* Englewood Cliffs, NJ: Prentice-Hall, 1988.

Gustafson, Kenneth L. *Survey of Instructional Development Models.* Syracuse, NY: ERIC Clearinghouse on Information Resources, 1991.

Kemp, Jerrold E., Morrison, Gary M. and Ross, Stephen M. *Designing Effective Instruction and Learning.* Columbus, OH: Merrill, 1993.

Leshin, Cynthia and others. *Instructional Design Strategies and Tactics.* Englewood Cliffs, NJ: Educational Technology Publications, 1992.

Nadler, Leonard. *Designing Training Programs.* Reading, MA: Addison-Wesley, 1982.

VISUAL LITERACY

Lloyd-Kolkin, Donna and Tyner, Kathleen R. *Media and You: An Elementary Media Literacy Curriculum.* Englewood Cliffs, NJ: Educational Technology Publications, 1991.

Milheim, William D. *Visual Literacy: A Selected Bibliography.* Englewood Cliffs, NJ: Educational Technology Publications, 1991.

Wileman, Ralph. *Exercises in Visual Thinking.* New York: Hastings House, 1980.

INSTRUCTIONAL TECHNOLOGY JOURNALS AND PERIODICALS

British Journal of Educational Technology
Council for Educational Technology for the United Kingdom
3 Devonshire Street
London W1N 2BA, England

Canadian Journal of Educational Communication
Association for Media and Technology in Education in Canada
500 Victoria Road
North Guelph, Ontario N1E6K2, Canada

Educational Technology
Educational Technology Publications, Inc.
700 Palisade Avenue
Englewood Cliffs, NJ 07632

Educational Technology Research and Development
Association for Educational Communications and Technology
1025 Vermont Avenue, NW—Suite 820
Washington, DC 20005

Instruction Delivery Systems
Society for Applied Learning Technology
50 Culpepper Street
Warrenton, VA 22186

Performance and Instruction
National Society for Performance and Instruction
1300 L Street, NW—Suite 1250
Washington, DC 20005

Technology & Learning
Peter Li, Inc.
2451 East River Road
Dayton, OH 45439

TechTrends
Association for Educational Communications and Technology
see above

Training: The Magazine of Human Resources Development
Lakewood Publications, Inc.
50 South Ninth Street
Minneapolis, MN 55402

CHAPTER

2

Perception, Communication, and Theories of Instruction and Learning

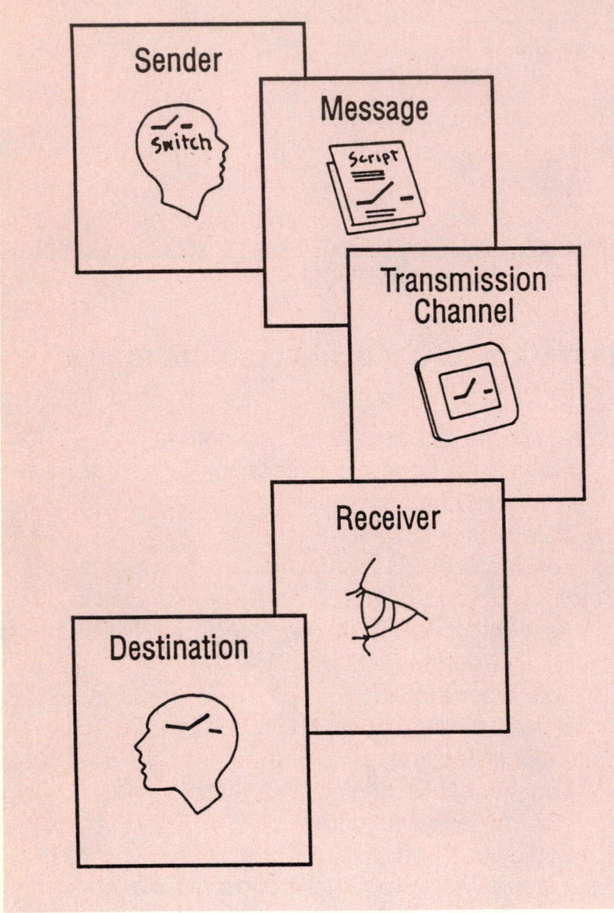

Slides, overhead transparencies, video recordings, and other instructional technologies have been in use for many years. While some of these materials do an excellent job of informing or instructing, of teaching skills, of motivating, or of influencing attitudes, others are less effective, and are of poor quality or may even be detrimental to the purposes they were made to serve.

Too often the production of a videotape recording or the planning of a multi-image presentation is based on intuition, subjective judgment, personal preferences for one's own way of doing things, or even on a committee decision. These, unfortunately, are ineffective bases for ensuring satisfactory results.

How can you be more sure that the materials you plan and produce will be effective? Is there evidence from research and some general principles to guide you?

Three areas should be of particular concern. One is the logical steps of developing objectives, of planning, and of getting ready to take or draw pictures and to make recordings. These procedures will ensure some degree of success for your instructional materials. Part 2 of this book presents the planning steps you should consider using.

The second area from which you can obtain help in designing effective instructional media includes reports on experimental studies measuring the effectiveness of such materials. In these studies specific elements that affect production have been controlled, thus providing evidence for handling various elements in media productions. Summaries of these research findings are reported in the next chapter.

Third, and fundamental to both media research and careful planning for materials production, is the need to know how people perceive things around them, how people communicate with each other, and how people learn. Therefore, our immediate concern is to examine evidence from the fields of psychology and communication.

The discussions that follow have one purpose—to make the reader aware of (or to review) some generalizations from the areas of perception, communication, and learning theories that can be applied to make instructional technologies effective. Admittedly the treatment of each topic is greatly simplified, and only the minimum essentials are presented. But even these can be useful to you as you plan your materials and consider the place of your materials for motivating, informing, or teaching in an instructional sequence.

PERCEPTION

Perception is the process whereby one becomes aware of the world around oneself. In perception we use our senses to apprehend objects and events. The eyes, ears, and nerve endings in the skin are primary means through which we maintain contact with our environment. These, and other senses, are the tools of perception; they collect data for the nervous system. Within the nervous system the impressions so received are changed into electrical impulses, which then trigger a chain of further electrical and chemical events in the brain. The result is an internal awareness of the object or event. Thus, perception precedes communication. Communication leads to learning.

Two aspects of perception are of major importance. First, any perceptual event consists of many sensory messages that do not occur in isolation but are related and combined into complex patterns. These become the basis of a person's knowledge of the world. Second, an individual reacts to only a small part of all that is taking place at any one instance. The part of an event to be experienced is "selected" by a person on the basis of desire or what attracts his or her attention. Hence, one must first design materials that will attract the attention and hold the interest of the learner, and then make certain that in this sampling procedure the learner gets the "right" sample, relevant to the learning task. The experience of perception is individual and unique. It is not exactly alike for any two people. A person perceives an event in terms of individual past experiences, present motivation, and present circumstances.

While any one perceptual experience is uniquely individual, a series of perceptions by different persons can be related to become nearly identical. If you walk around a statue, its shape will constantly change as you change the angles at which you look at it. If someone else then walks around the same statue and looks at it from the same angles, this other person will have different individual experiences but the ultimate result will be much the same as it was for you. Thus a succession of individual experiences enables us to agree upon what we have experienced, even though the individual experiences are somewhat different.

The instructional technology field rests on the assumptions that people learn primarily from what they perceive and that carefully designed visual experiences can be common experiences and thus influence behavior in a positive way.

A useful summary of research-based principles from the behavioral sciences that can be applied to the design of instructional media has been prepared by Fleming and Levie. In it over 200 principles and corollaries relate to areas of perception, memory, concept formation, and attitude change. Here is a selection of the major conclusions, concerning perception, that Fleming and Levie present:

- ***Basic principles***
  1. Perception is relative, rather than absolute.
     a. Provide reference points to which unknown objects or events can be related.
     b. Present a difficult concept through small steps.
  2. Perception is selective.
     Limit the range of aspects being presented to essential factors, presented a step at a time.
  3. Perception is organized.
     Use numbering and verbal cues ("next," "either-or") to give order to a message.
  4. Perception is influenced by expectation.
     Give instructions that call attention to elements, or directions for finding an answer in an illustration.
- ***Attention and preattention***—Attention is drawn to changes in how relevant ideas in a message are presented (by means of brightness, movement, novelty, asking questions, posing problems).
- ***Perceptual elements and processing***—Such char-

acteristics as brightness, color, texture, form, and size should be selected and arranged carefully because they have a positive influence on perceptions.

- ***Perceiving pictures and words***—Use the visual channel for presenting spatial (space) concepts and the auditory channel for presenting temporal (time) concepts.
- ***Perceptual capacity***
  1. For difficult material presented aurally, use short sentences, redundancy, and excellent technical quality.
  2. The most compatible modes that permit the highest information level are simultaneous auditory and visual presentation of a subject provided by slides and tape, sound film, and video recording.
- ***Perceptual distinguishing, grouping, and organizing***
  1. Use lines around, under, and between to cue groupings; accentuate and relate elements in a visual.
  2. Facilitate recognition of similarities and differences by presenting several related objects together.
  3. Make the organizational outline of a message apparent (subtitles, transitional statements).
- ***Perception and cognition***—The better an object or event is perceived (by means of applying the above-stated and other perception principles), the more feasible and reliable will be memory, concept formation, problem solving, creativity, and attitude change.

This is only a sampling of the perception principles important in the design of instructional media, as summarized by Fleming and Levie. For further explanations, examples, and illustrations, see the reference.

As you design instructional media, keep in mind the importance of carefully providing for desirable perceptual experiences in terms of the learner's experience background and of the present situation. Such production elements as methods of treating the topic (expository, dramatic, inquiry, or other), vocabulary level, kinds and number of examples, pacing of narration and visuals, and graphic techniques can each contribute to successful perception. In this way communication will be more effective and learning should be positive.

COMMUNICATION

Perception leads to communication. In all communication, however simple or complex, a sequence similar to this occurs:

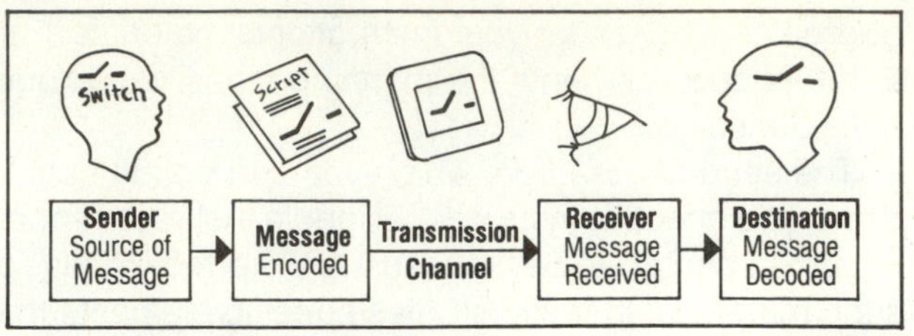

This model (originally developed by Shannon and Weaver) illustrates that a *message* (at the mental level), generally in the form of information, originated by a *source* or *sender* (the brain of an individual), is *encoded*—converted into transmittable form (a thought verbalized, as for conversation, by being turned into sound waves, or words written for a script). The message then passes through a *transmitter* (print, slides, film, videotape) via a suitable *channel* (air, wire, paper, light) to the *receiver* (a person's senses—eyes, ears, other sensory nerve endings), then to the *destination* (brain of the receiver) where the message is *decoded* (converted into mental symbols).

Effective communication is influenced by many human factors affecting *both* sender and receiver. Matters such as cultural background, experience with the subject of the message, and a personal attitude can influence the success of communication. These elements need consideration in message design.

Also, successful communication depends upon participation of the receiver. A person reacts by answering, questioning, or performing, mentally or physically. There is then a return, or response loop of this cycle, from receiver *to* sender. It is termed **feedback.** It happens through words, expressions, gestures, or other actions. This reverse communication advises the originator how satisfactorily the message was received. Feedback enables the originator to correct omissions and errors in the transmitted message, or to improve

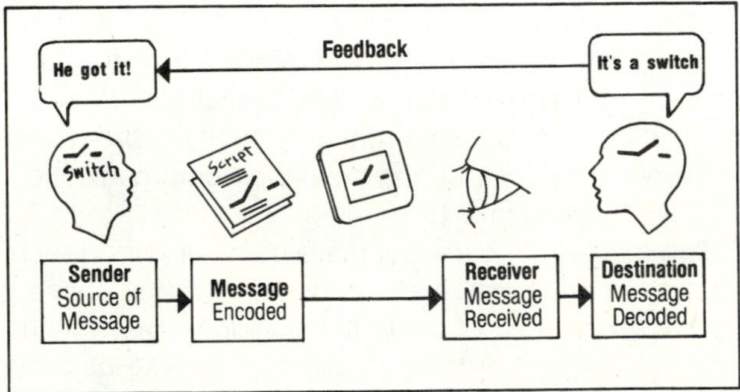

the encoding and transmission process, or even to assist the recipient in decoding the message.

One additional element must be added to this communication model:

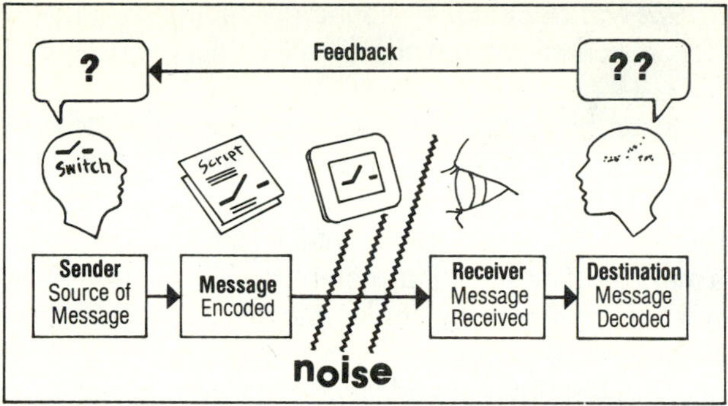

Noise is *any* disturbance that interferes with or distorts transmission of the message. The **noise** factor can have a serious impact on the success or failure of communication. Static on a radio broadcast is a simple example of noise. A flashing light can be a distracting "noise" when a person is reading a book. Ambiguous or misleading material in a film can be deemed noise. Noise can be created internally, within the receiver, to upset satisfactory communication—for example, a lack of attention. Even conflicting past experience can be an inhibiting noise source. Recall the importance of an individual's background experience in affecting perception. Noise clouds and masks information transmission to varying degrees and must be recognized as an obstacle to be overcome.

At times noise cannot be avoided, and in planning materials the factor of **redundancy** is often used to overcome the effect of evident or anticipated noise. Redundancy refers to the repeated transmission of a message, possibly in different channels, to overcome or bypass distracting noise. Examples of redundancy are showing and also explaining an activity, projecting a visual and distributing paper copies of the same material for study, and providing multiple applications of a principle in different contexts.

In working with instructional media you should understand where the materials, as channels of communication, fit within the framework and process of message movement between senders and receivers. Then, you should know how the various elements, along with factors of noise and redundancy, function to affect the success of your efforts to communicate effectively.

INSTRUCTIONAL AND LEARNING THEORIES

The process of learning is an individual experience for each person. Learning takes place whenever an individual's behavior is modified—when a person thinks or acts differently, when he or she has acquired new knowledge or a new skill.

Since a major purpose for preparing instructional materials is to affect behaviors that serve objectives, it is appropriate to turn to the psychology of instruction and learning for help in locating principles to guide the planning of effective instructional materials.

A number of major theories have influenced psychology and education. They have received much attention from practitioners since the mid-twentieth century. Brief overviews of twelve important theories are considered here.

Operant Conditioning

The theory of operant conditioning is built on Skinner's view that *learning is behavioral change* (Skinner, 1954). Behavior is the result of an individual's response to events taking place in one's environment. These are **stimuli** (messages), which elicit **responses** (learning) in the learner. A response produces a consequence, such as defining a word, solving a math problem, or writing a chemical formula. Thus, by continuing with this stimulus-response (S-R) pattern, the individual is conditioned to respond. Hence the term **operant conditioning** (or **behaviorism**).

Following successful responses, the learner has a feeling of accomplishment and satisfaction. Some type of "reward"—verbal approval, a prize, or a grade—may be received. This serves to reinforce the learning. **Reinforcement,** important in operant conditioning, may be any consequence that strengthens continued, desirable behavior.

Skinner's approach to learning has been applied in "programmed instruction," designed as programs in book format or through mechanical devices called "teaching machines." The emphasis is on presenting sequences of small amounts of subject content, requiring an appropriate response to each item, and then following with immediate knowledge of results (**feedback**). If the response is correct, the learning is reinforced.

Much of the attention being given to individualized learning follows this pattern. Operant conditioning is applied when the microcomputer is used to teach basic skills like identification, discrimination, and problem solving (see examples on page 277), often in drill and practice programs.

Domains of Learning

Starting in 1948, at the American Psychological Association meeting in Boston (Bloom, p. 4), an attempt was made to develop a system for classifying the goals of the educational process. Its purpose was to standardize the terminology used to appraise learning. Such goals, stated in behavioral terms, could represent most kinds of human behavior. The result has been the development of *taxonomies,* or classification systems, in three areas:

- ***Cognitive domain***—knowledge, information, other intellectual skills
- ***Affective domain***—attitudes, values, appreciations
- ***Psychomotor domain***—skeletal-muscle use and coordination

For each of these domains, progressive levels of higher-order behavior have been identified. The **cognitive domain** includes six levels of intellectual activity (Bloom et al., 1956):

1. ***Knowledge***—recalling information
2. ***Comprehension***—interpreting information
3. ***Application***—applying information
4. ***Analysis***—breaking information into parts
5. ***Synthesis***—bringing together elements of information to form a new whole
6. ***Evaluation***—making judgments against agreed criteria

The **affective domain** consists of five levels of attitudes, interests, and/or personal involvement (Krathwohl et al., 1964):

1. ***Receiving***—attracting the learner's attention
2. ***Responding***—learner willing to reply or take action
3. ***Valuing***—committing oneself to take an attitudinal position
4. ***Organization***—making adjustments or decisions from among several alternatives
5. ***Characterization of a value complex***—integrating one's beliefs, ideas, and attitudes into a total philosophy

Although a taxonomy of the **psychomotor domain** has been developed, which includes six major classes of behavior from reflex motions to skilled movements and nondiscursive communication, its usefulness is difficult to interpret (Harrow). Another scale of physical activities may be of more value (Kibler).

1. ***Gross body movements***—arms, shoulders, feet, and legs
2. ***Finely coordinated movements***—hand and fingers; hand and eye; hand and ear; hand, eye, and foot
3. ***Nonverbal communication***—facial expression, gestures, bodily movements
4. ***Speech behaviors***—sound production and projection, sound-gesture coordination

These three taxonomies can be appropriate references as instructional materials are planned and developed. The objectives to be served by any media form represent the organizing point for your planning. Since a majority of instructional materials are designed to provide information, they serve objectives in the cognitive domain. The lowest level, knowledge, represents rote learning through memorization and recall of facts. The five other levels require higher intellectual learning. These latter levels should receive greater attention when designing instructional materials.

Another practical matter to recognize is that these three domains are closely related in two ways. First, a single objective can involve learning in more than one domain. For example, when teaching a skill, often it is also necessary to define terms and show relationships. Second, attitudinal development, like motivation, may precede successful learning in the other domains.

Conditions of Learning

As Gagné examined the complex nature of human learning, he realized that learning is a cumulative process (Gagné, 1985). Basic information or simple skills that are learned contribute to the learning of more complex knowledge and skills. Gagné identified five categories of learning:

- ***Verbal information***—learning names, dates, definitions, and facts, which provide basic terminology relating to a topic
- ***Intellectual skills***—learning how to use verbal information through discriminations, grouping facts with common features under a generalized name (building concepts), developing higher level generalizations involving statements that show relationships among two or more concepts (learning rules and principles), and using facts, concepts, and principles in various situations (problem solving)
- ***Cognitive strategies***—developing one's own abilities to remember and think in an organized manner, using verbal information and intellectual skills to do this
- ***Motor skills***—performing physical skills, such as typing, swimming, or tool use
- ***Attitudes***—developing beliefs and behaviors toward persons, objects, and events

Further, Gagné (1985) identified nine phases of learning that must be executed in sequential order. They are grouped under three headings by Bell-Gredler:

Preparation for Learning

1. ***Attending***—gain learner's attention
2. ***Expectancy***—inform learner of objectives
3. ***Retrieval of relevant information and/or skills to working memory***—stimulate recall of prior learning

Acquisition and Performance

4. ***Selective perception of stimulus features***—present distinctive stimulus features
5. ***Semantic encoding***—provide learning guidance
6. ***Retrieval and responding***—elicit performance
7. ***Reinforcement***—provide informative feedback

Retrieval and Transfer

8. ***Cueing retrieval***—assess performance
9. ***Generalizing***—apply the theoretical framework comprising Gagné's conditions of learning as in the Gagné, Briggs, and Wager plan for instructional design (page 4)

Component Display Theory

The **component display theory** (Merrill) provides more details for designing specific instructional sequences than does Gagné's theory of conditions of learning. It classifies outcomes of learning in two dimensions: **content** (facts, concepts, procedures, and principles) and **performance** (remembering, using, and finding a generality).

Then, in the delivery of instruction, this theory gives attention to the following:

- ***Primary presentation forms***—expository presentation of both a generality (a rule) and an instance (an example), inquisitory generality (recall), and inquisitory instance (practice)
- ***Secondary presentation forms***—prerequisite material, attention-focusing help, mnemonics, and feedback

In practice, component display theory requires that each lesson segment identifies an objective, based on the content and performance elements. Then, instruction will consist of selections from the primary and secondary presentation forms. This procedure provides detailed guidelines for presenting stimuli, contributing to learner guidance, and promoting transfer of learning.

Elaboration Theory

An alternative to the cumulative approach to sequencing content advocated by Gagné is the **elaboration theory** model proposed by Reigeluth (1983), in which instruction is ordered in terms of increasing complexity. In teaching a procedure, the most simple and representative application is taught first. Subsequent lessons add further conditions and details to the original presentation until the degree of complexity required by the objective is attained. Furthermore, elaborations that relate to more than a single idea or concept of new knowledge are more effective in enhancing learning. Also, at each step in this elaboration process the learner is reminded of the procedure as a whole.

This review and synthesis enables the learner to see the reason for each step in the learning process, whereas in conventional cumulative learning, the learner is often advised that the relevance of a particular segment will become apparent at a later time in the instruction.

Instructional Transaction Theory

Instructional transaction theory (Merrill, Li, and Jones) is an extension of component display theory. It involves a knowledge representation system called an **elaborated frame network.** Knowledge is represented as **entity, activity,** and **process** structures called frames. These knowledge frames relate to specific components:

- **Parts** for entities
- **Steps** for activities
- **Events** for processes

Knowledge frames are also organized into class, superclass, and instance structures called **abstraction hierarchies.** Also, they can be linked together in **association networks** that enable learning by answering these questions: "What is it?" "How do I do it?" "How does it work?" This multidimensional representation provides a syntax that facilitates knowledge acquisition from subject matter experts and representation in electronic databases.

Instructional transaction theory also involves a library of **instructional transaction (Tx) shells.** These are collections of instructional rules, often implemented as expert systems. Different types of transaction shells have been identified for different kinds of knowledge and skill. Some of these are as follows:

- An **identify** Tx shell for learning parts of an entity and their location
- An **execute** Tx shell for learning steps of an activity and their sequence
- An **interpret** Tx shell for learning the events of a process and their consequences

- A **classification** Tx shell for learning to categorize instances
- A **decision** Tx shell for learning the selection of alternatives
- A **judge** Tx shell for learning the ordering of instances or classes on one or several dimensions
- A **transfer** Tx shell for enabling activities and processes learned in one situation to be applied in new situations

Most instruction involves several of these Tx shells working together as a **transaction family.**

An important advantage of instructional transaction theory is that it provides for the development of intelligent authoring tools. When implemented as expert systems, a knowledge acquisition system and instructional transaction shells enable subject matter experts to create interactive instructional materials, such as computer-based instruction or interactive video, much more effectively and efficiently. These tools can automate much of the instructional design and program development procedures.

Information-Processing Theory

The mental processes whereby human beings perceive, organize, and remember the great amount of information received daily have been the subject of **information-processing** research (Norman). A basic premise of this work is that the human brain is a complex, active organ for processing information. It follows that how an individual selects, encodes, and stores information, as influenced by any prior knowledge, relates to one's learning ability.

This theory recognizes two types of memory—**short-term** and **long-term.** Short-term memory holds information for immediate recall. There is evidence that short-term memory has the capacity to retain about "seven chunks" of information. If incoming information exceeds this load capacity, then some existing memory is lost. This has implications for considering the quantity of information to be included in a segment of instructional material.

When information has been retained in long-term memory, learning is said to have taken place. Evidence of this is the conscious retrieval of the information as it is needed. Therefore, the purposes of instruction are to guide the mind in the reception of new stimuli (the selection process) and the facilitation of encoding (transforming stimuli into a summary code for memory).

To accomplish these tasks, information-processing theorists suggest that attention be given to the following:

- Use of **advance organizers,** such as examples and analogies that relate information to be learned to already learned knowledge.
- Development of instruction-based aids, such as synonyms for difficult words, questions placed in a text, summaries, and review questions that can serve as cues.
- Use of learner-generated cues, such as key words, rhymes, acronyms, and images for encoding and building associations that are helpful for information recall and pattern recognition.

Each of these techniques should be considered at appropriate places when designing instructional materials. Furthermore, the relationship between information processing and aspects of computer technology indicates some of the potential, practical applications of these theories. Research into artificial intelligence and the design of complex problem-solving programs are pertinent examples.

Social Learning Theory

In **social learning** theory, attention is given to personality factors and the interactions among people (Bandura). This theory states that certain learning takes place through the ability of individuals to observe the behaviors of other persons (serving as models). This allows them to make choices among these behaviors, which they adapt for themselves (modeling) to emulate. Three assumptions support the principles of social learning theory:

- The learner's mental processes and decision-making abilities are important factors in learning.
- The three-way interaction among the environment, personal factors, and behavior models is reponsible for much learning.
- The outcomes of learning are individual visual and verbal cues of behavior.

Further, in addition to contacts with live models, other sources of information and experiences are important influences in social learning of both children and adults. The range of behaviors and attitudes exhibited through the mass media (primarily films and television) serve as models and contribute significantly to individual behavior and learning.

Thus, increased violence and aggression in society at large are explained, in part, by the observational learning described by social learning theory. Therefore, positive influences upon learning can be realized through carefully planned and produced instructional materials based on appropriate instructional objectives.

Attribution Theory

Attribution learning theory seeks to identify ways by which individuals seek understandings for events taking place in their world (Weiner). It is built on cognitive processes—meaningfulness, understanding, and organizational abilities—considered to be fundamental characteristics of human behavior. A person uses understandings to achieve personal fulfillment and self-actualization. There is a close relationship among achievement-related outcomes, causal beliefs, and the subsequent emotions and activities of an individual.

The term *attribution* refers to an inference made by a person about the causes of an event or of a particular outcome. The following are major attributions:

- ***Ability***—feelings of confidence or incompetence, or of pride or shame
- ***Effort***—feelings of pride for success
- ***Luck***—no change in success expectancy
- ***Task difficulty***—no enhancement of self-esteem for success outcome

An individual typically selects one of these causes to explain success or failure outcomes and the links between these outcomes and subsequent behavior.

The search for understanding is a primary source of motivation for human behavior. Thus, motivation plays an important role in this theory. Feedback from success or failure and actions following an outcome affect individual motivation and the determination to continue with learning activities.

Constructivism

An aspect of cognitive psychology receiving increased attention is **constructivism.** Its major premise is that knowledge, with resulting learning, is derived from one's experiences (Duffy and Jonassen). We use our individual experiences to construct a mental reality that leads to learning, and can transfer to real-world applications.

According to Bednar et al., constructivism is based on these assumptions:

- Knowledge is constructed from experience.
- Learning is an active process, with experience leading to meaning.
- Learning is a personal interpretation of one's own world.
- Learning should occur in realistic settings.
- Growth in understanding concepts comes from experiencing many perspectives relative to a situation, then adjusting beliefs in response to new perspectives.
- Testing should be integrated with the task, not treated as a separate activity.

The implications of constructivism for education will result in an emphasis on **problem/solution**-oriented learning. Faced with a realistic problem to solve, students would first decide what to do, why, and how to do it by engaging in realistic activities. The teacher serves as a guide, while providing meaningful environments in which learning can take place. While gathering data and analyzing sets of experiences, each learner would have a different set of experiences that lead to a personal interpretation of the world.

Adult Learning (Andragogy)

A growing segment of students in higher education consists of working or retired adults. The needs of this population, plus the extensive training needs of employees in business, industry, government, and health care, require that adults be treated as a distinct group, in contrast to conventional school and college learners. Through the efforts of Hiemstra, Knowles, Zemke, and others, a body of reliable knowledge about adult learning can be summarized as follows:

- Adults enter an educational or training program with a high level of motivation to learn. They appreciate a program that is structured systematically, with requirements (objectives) clearly specified.
- Adults want to know the benefits of the education they will receive. They expect the material to be relevant and they quickly grasp the practical use of the content.
- To adults, time is an important consideration. They expect class to start and finish on time, and they do not like to waste time.
- Adults respect an instructor who has a thorough knowledge of the subject and presents it effectively. Learners quickly detect an incompetent or unprepared teacher.
- Adults bring to class extensive experience from their personal and professional lives. These experiences can be used as major resources by helping learners relate to the subject being studied.
- Most mature adults are self-directed and independent. While some adults lack confidence and need reassurance, they would prefer that the instructor serve as facilitator to guide and assist, rather than as an authoritarian leader.
- Adults want to participate in decision-making. They want to cooperate with the instructor in mutual assessment of needs and goals, in the choice of activities, and in deciding on evidence for evaluation of learning.

- Adults may be less flexible than younger learners. Their habits and methods of operation have been developed into a routine. They do not like to be placed in embarrassing situations. Before they accept a new or different way for doing something, they want to know the advantage of doing so.
- Adults like to cooperate in groups and socialize together. Small group activities and an atmosphere for interaction during breaks are important.

These practices must be considered when education and training programs for adults are planned, instructional materials designed, and instructional activities carried out.

Motivation

Finally, as an aspect of learning theory, we consider the topic of motivation. An important factor that contributes to success in learning is the *degree of commitment* exhibited by an individual when starting and then continuing with a learning activity. This behavior relates to motivation. Motivation has both direction and magnitude components, and its level is evidenced by the intensity of performance toward completion of a learning task.

Keller (1983) has identified four conditions for successful motivation that require attention in instructional planning. He suggests a number of strategies for implementing the conditions. Here are the conditions and some strategies:

- ***Interest***—arousing and sustaining the learner's curiosity and attention
  Strategies: Use novel, surprising, incongruous, contradictory, unresolved, or uncertain events in instruction. Give people the opportunity to learn more about things they already know about or believe in, but also give them moderate doses of the unfamiliar and unexpected.
- ***Relevance***—relating the instruction to how a learner can satisfy personal needs or a highly desired goal
  Strategies: Use concrete language, and use examples and concepts that are related to the learner's experience and values. Provide opportunities to achieve standards of excellence under conditions of moderate risk.
- ***Expectancy (confidence)***—perceiving the likelihood of success in learning and the extent to which success is under learner control
  Strategies: Increase expectancy for success by increasing experience with success or by using attributional feedback and other devices to help learners connect success to personal effort and ability.
- ***Satisfaction***—combining extrinsic rewards and intrinsic motivation to influence the accomplishment of the instructional goal and provide further motivation to continue pursuing similar goals
  Strategies: Use task-endogenous rather than task-exogenous rewards. Use verbal praise and informative feedback rather than threats, surveillance, or external performance evaluation.

As with other learning theories, the conditions and strategies identified by Keller should be kept in mind and applied as instructional materials are developed.

Generalizations from Theories

There are areas of agreement and similar emphasis among the various learning theories from which generalizations can be made. The following psychological conditions and general principles are important factors to consider in the design and use of instructional media.

1. **Motivation.** There must be a need, an interest, or a desire to learn on the part of the learner before attention can be given to the task to be accomplished. Moreover, the experiences in which the learner will engage must be relevant and meaningful to him or her. Therefore, it may be necessary to create the interest by means of motivational treatment of the information presented in instructional materials.
2. **Individual differences.** Persons learn at various rates and in different ways. Such factors as intellectual ability, educational level, personality, and cognitive learning styles affect an individual's readiness and ability to engage in learning. The rate at which information is presented in instructional media should be considered in terms of the anticipated comprehension rates of learners.
3. **Learning objectives.** When learners are informed of what they can expect to learn through the use of instructional media, their chances for success are greater than when not so informed. Also, as we will see in Chapter 4, a statement of objectives to be accomplished with the materials is helpful to those who will plan the materials. The objectives indicate what content will receive attention in the learning materials.
4. **Organization of content.** Learning is easier when content and procedures or physical skills to be learned are organized into meaningful sequences. Learners will understand and remember material longer when it is logically structured and carefully sequenced. Also, the rate of information to be presented is established in terms of the complexity and difficulty of content. By em-

ploying these suggestions in the design of instructional materials, the learner can be helped to better synthesize and integrate the knowledge to be learned.

5. **Prelearning preparation.** Learners should have satisfactorily achieved the preparatory learning or have had the necessary experiences that may be prerequisite to their successful use of the instructional media to be studied. This means that, when planning materials, careful attention should be given to the nature and expected level of preparation of the group for which the materials are to be designed.
6. **Emotions.** Learning that involves the emotions and personal feelings, as well as the intellect, is influential and lasting. Instructional media are powerful means of generating emotional responses, such as fear, anxiety, empathy, love, and excitement. Therefore, careful attention should be given to instructional material design elements if emotional results are desired for learning or motivational purposes.
7. **Participation.** In order for learning to take place, a person must *internalize* the information; merely seeing or hearing it is not enough. Therefore, learning requires activity. Active participation by the learner is preferable to lengthy periods of passive listening and viewing. Participation means engaging in mental or physical activity interspersed during an instructional presentation. Through participation, there will be a greater probability that learners will understand and retain the information presented.
8. **Feedback.** Learning is increased when individuals are periodically informed of progress in their learning. Knowledge of successful results, a good performance, or the need for certain improvement will contribute to continued motivation for learning.
9. **Reinforcement.** When the individual is successful in learning, he or she is encouraged to continue learning. Learning motivated by success is rewarding; it builds confidence, and it will affect subsequent behavior in positive ways.
10. **Practice and repetition.** Rarely is anything new learned effectively with only one exposure. For knowledge, or a skill, to become a confirmed part of an individual's intellectual repertoire or competencies, provision should be made for frequent practice and repetition, often in different contexts. This can lead to long-term retention.
11. **Application.** A desired outcome of learning is to increase the individual's ability to apply or transfer the learning to new problems or situations. Unless a learner can do this, complete understanding has not taken place. First, the learner must have been helped to recognize or discover generalizations (concepts, principles, rules) relating to the topic or task. Then opportunities must be provided for the learner to apply the generalizations or procedures to a variety of new, realistic problems or tasks.

Each one of these conditions or principles of learning can be applied directly or indirectly in the design of the various instructional media. Many of these principles also relate to the manner in which the technologies of instruction are subsequently used in correlation with accompanying printed materials and learning activities. Therefore, the planning and production phases cannot be entirely separated from plans for utilization. When all factors are considered, the quality of the instructional materials and their resulting effectiveness for learning can be greatly enhanced.

SUMMARY

It has been shown that there are principles and practices from the fields of perception, communication, instruction, and learning theory that can contribute to the design and development of all instructional technologies. Fleming and Levie express the need to be cautious when using this information:

> Adherence to the procedures and principles offered will not automatically result in better learning and these ideas are not offered as substitutes for experience and creativity. It is hoped, however, that this information may guide the insightful designer to analyze problems from more than one point of view, and may suggest effective solutions that might otherwise have been overlooked.

Finally, a media psychologist (Witt) suggests some practical guidelines for designing materials to present factual information:

1. Design the production for your specific audience.
2. Tell your viewers what is coming, and what they should learn from the media presentation.
3. Associate new facts and ideas with ones the viewer already knows.
4. Rely on visuals and mental imagery (associating words with pictures) to help viewers remember.
5. Don't overload your production with information.
6. Give the viewer time to "let the information sink in."

7. Use repetition to hammer in critical facts.
8. Present a closing review of the major points in an organized pyramidal structure.

What You Have Learned About Perception, Communication, and Instruction/Learning Theories:

1. In your own words, what is "human perception"? How does perception relate to the design of instructional media?
2. If you wished to make an in-depth study of perception as background for designing instructional materials, to what reference might you refer?
3. On page 13, a number of major conclusions regarding perception are presented. To which heading does each of the following relate?
   a. When preparing to take pictures, place the tools on a background of contrasting color so they are easy to see.
   b. Include a person in the scene as size comparison for the equipment.
   c. Use a number of the recognized principles of perception when designing a slide/tape program.
   d. Ask this question: "In what way does this object differ from the one shown on the previous page?"
   e. An audio recording might be the best medium to use when time relationships are to be presented.
   f. As a procedure is shown, explain each action with a few words.
   g. For narration—"In frame 8 examine the two related diagrams."
   h. Introduce a new section of the program with a title and brief introductory statement.
4. Recall the seven elements of the communication process in the communication model presented in this chapter. Where do instructional media fit into the model?
5. To which learning theory, presented in this chapter, does each phrase or statement apply?
   a. Explains how a person selects, encodes, and stores information.
   b. Includes factors of reinforcement and feedback.
   c. Relates to the level of performance intensity exhibited by a person toward completing a learning activity.
   d. Modeling behavior can result from observing how persons are shown in television shows.
   e. Involves collections of transaction shells.
   f. Supports use of advance organizers, cues for associations, and summaries.
   g. Treats intellectual skills and cognitive strategies.
   h. Based on the pattern of stimulus-response.
   i. Learning results from a personal interpretation of one's experiences.
   j. Recognizes conditions of interest, relevance, expectancy, and satisfaction.
   k. The factors of environment, along with individual personality and behavior, affect learning.
   l. Explains the ways a person attempts to understand an event or an outcome.
   m. Groups phases of learning as preparation, acquisition, and retrieval.
   n. Includes consideration of the factors of ability, effort, and luck relative to causes for success or failure.
   o. Implemented as applications of expert systems.
   p. Sequences instruction in terms of increasing complexity of content.
   q. Relates to short-term and long-term memory.
   r. Classifies learning results in terms of content and performance, and gives attention to primary and secondary performance forms.
6. To which psychological condition or principle of learning does each statement refer?

a. Your decision to include a slide/tape presentation as part of a study unit.
b. Make a list of what students should be able to do after viewing the videotape recording and inform them of these anticipated outcomes in the introductory materials.
c. Show the trainee the accepted answer to a problem after his or her work is completed.
d. Interpose questions for students to answer as the transparencies are presented.
e. Design materials for each person to use individually, at his or her own pace of study.
f. Have each person demonstrate present skill with equipment before starting advanced training.
g. Provide a kit of materials so each person can carry out the procedures illustrated, after studying a technology-based presentation.
h. Present new situations in which the student must use the information learned from the media.
i. Answers to review questions, associated with the mediated presentation, reveal that students are consistently correct.
j. Divide the topic into small sections and relate them sequentially.
k. Show a brief mediated presentation, as an introduction to build interest in the subject to be studied.
l. Divide content for a topic into small sections with participation activity for each section before student starts next section.
m. Show a film to a class as introduction for a new topic.
n. Follow Gagné's structure of content for designing activities.

7. What are the *three* domains of learning? Which domain is the most difficult for instructional technologies to serve?

8. To which domain of learning does each activity relate?
a. Throw a football.
b. List six important practices when applying for a job interview.
c. Take blood pressure with a sphygmomanometer.
d. Agree to contribute time to a community agency.
e. Drill holes accurately in a sheet of metal.
f. Judge the quality level of units as they are assembled.
g. Be on time for all assignments.

9. The cognitive domain includes a low recall level (knowledge) and higher intellectual levels. Which of the following learning activities would be on a *low* level and which ones on a *higher* level?
a. Decide which tool to use for correcting a malfunction.
b. List the steps to follow in a procedure.
c. Repeat a name after hearing it.
d. Formulate a plan to solve a problem.
e. Describe an event in your own words.

10. Which statements are *true* relative to adult learners.
a. They do not like to waste time on unimportant matters.
b. They are flexible and can easily adjust to unexpected developments.
c. Learners can determine for themselves the relevance of content being presented.
d. Learners should be provided with learning objectives for a topic.
e. Adults prefer to be in regular size classes for most instruction.
f. Most instructors can cover themselves when unprepared for a class so learners cannot detect this.

See answers on page 375.

REFERENCES

PERCEPTION

Fleming, Malcolm, and Levie, W. Howard, eds. *Instructional Message Design: Principles from the Behavioral and Cognitive Sciences.* Englewood Cliffs, NJ: Educational Technology Publications, 1993.

COMMUNICATION

Hill, Harold. "Communication and Educational Technology." In *Educational Media Yearbook 1981.* James W. Brown and Shirley N. Brown, eds. Littleton, CO: Libraries Unlimited, 1981, pp. 40–49.

Marsh, Patrick O. *Messages That Work: A Guide to Communication Design.* Englewood Cliffs, NJ: Educational Technology Publications, 1983.

Randhawn, Bikkar, and Coffman, William E. *Visual Learning, Thinking, and Communication.* New York: Academic Press, 1978.

Shannon, Claude, and Weaver, W. *The Mathematical Theory of Communication.* Urbana, IL: University of Illinois Press, 1949.

Sless, David. *Learning and Visual Communication.* New York: Wiley, 1981.

INSTRUCTIONAL AND LEARNING THEORIES

Adult Education Quarterly. American Association for Adult and Continuing Education. 112 16th Street, NW, Washington, DC 20036.

Anderson, John R. *Cognitive Psychology and Its Implications.* San Francisco: W. H. Freeman, 1985.

Ausubel, David P. *Educational Psychology: A Cognitive View.* New York: Holt, Rinehart, and Winston, 1968.

Bandura, Albert. *The Social Foundations of Thought and Action: A Social Cognitive Theory.* Englewood Cliffs, NJ: Prentice-Hall, 1986.

Bednar, A. K. et al. "Theory into Practice: How Do We Link?" in *Instructional Technology: Past, Present and Future.* Gary J. Anglin, ed. Denver, CO: Libraries Unlimited, 1991.

Bell-Gredler, Margaret E. *Learning and Instruction.* New York: Macmillan, 1986.

Bloom, Benjamin S.; Englehart, Max D.; Furst, Edward J. *A Taxonomy of Educational Objectives. Handbook I: The Cognitive Domain.* New York: Longman, 1977.

Duffy, Thomas M. and Jonassen, David H. "Constructivism: New Implications for I.T.?" *Educational Technology* 31 (May 1991): 7–11.

Gagné, Robert M. *The Conditions of Learning.* New York: Holt, Rinehart, and Winston, 1985.

Gagné, Robert M.; Briggs, Leslie J.; and Wager, Walter W. *Principles of Instructional Design,* New York: Holt, Rinehart, and Winston, 1988.

Harrow, Anita J. *A Taxonomy of the Psychomotor Domain.* New York: Longman, 1979.

Hiemstra, Roger. "Moving from Pedagogy to Andragogy." *Instructional Development.* Syracuse, NY: Syracuse University School of Education. Fall 1990.

Joyce, Bruce and Weil, Marsha. *Models of Teaching.* Englewood Cliffs, NJ: Prentice-Hall, 1986.

Keller, John M. "Motivational Design of Instruction." In *Instructional-Design Theories and Models.* Charles M. Reigeluth, ed. Hillsdale, NJ: Lawrence Erlbaum, 1983.

Keller, John M., and Suzuki, Katsuaki. "Use of the ARCS Motivation Model in Courseware Design." In *Instructional Designs for Microcomputer Courseware.* D. H. Jonassen, ed. Hillsdale, NJ: Lawrence Erlbaum, 1988.

Kibler, Robert J. *Objectives for Instruction and Evaluation.* Boston: Allyn and Bacon, 1981.

Knowles, Malcolm. *The Adult Learner: A Neglected Species.* Houston, TX: Gulf Publishing, 1984.

Krathwohl, David R.; Bloom, Benjamin S.; and Masia, Bertram B. *A Taxonomy of Educational Objectives. Handbook II: The Affective Domain.* New York: David McKay, 1984.

Lachman, Roy; Lachman, Janet; and Butterfield, E. C. *Cognitive Psychology and Information Processing.* Hillsdale, NJ: Lawrence Erlbaum, 1979.

Merrill, M. David. "Component Display Theory." In *Instructional-Design Theories and Models.* Charles M. Reigeluth, ed. Hillsdale, NJ: Lawrence Erlbaum, 1983.

———. "A Lesson Based on Component Display Theory." In *Instructional-Design Theories in Action.* Charles M. Reigeluth, ed. Hillsdale, NJ: Lawrence Erlbaum, 1987.

Merrill, M. David et al. "Instructional Transaction Theory: An Introduction." *Educational Technology* 31 (June 1991): 7–12.

Norman, Donald A. *Memory and Attention: An Introduction to Human Information Processing.* New York: Wiley, 1976.

Reigeluth, Charles M. "Lesson Blueprints Based on the Elaboration Theory of Instruction." In *Instructional-Design Theories in Action.* Charles M. Reigeluth, ed. Hillsdale, NJ: Lawrence Erlbaum, 1987.

Reigeluth, Charles M., and Stein, Faith S. "The Elaboration Theory of Instruction." In *Instructional-Design*

Theories and Models. Charles M. Reigeluth, ed. Hillsdale, NJ: Lawrence Erlbaum, 1983.

Rosenthall, Ted, and Zimmerman, Barry. *Social Learning Theory and Cognition.* New York: Academic Press, 1978.

Skinner, B. F. "The Science of Learning and the Art of Teaching." *Harvard Educational Review* 24 (2): 86–97, 1954.

———. *The Technology of Teaching,* New York: Appleton-Century-Crofts, 1968.

Weiner, B. *Human Motivation.* New York: Holt, Rinehart, and Winston, 1980.

———. *Attribution Theory of Motivation and Emotion.* New York: Springer-Verlag, 1986.

Witt, Gary A. *Media Psychology for Trainers.* Dr. Gary Witt, 9th and Brazos, Suite 800, Austin, TX.

Zemke, Ron and Susan. "30 Things We Know for Sure About Adult Learning." *Training* 25 (July 1988): 57–61.

CHAPTER

3

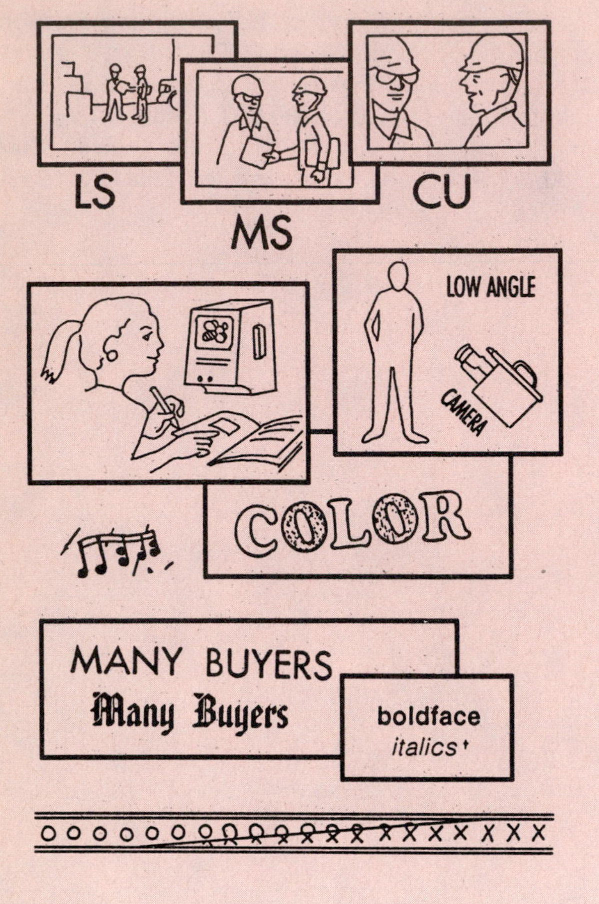

TREATMENT OF SUBJECT

INTELLECTUAL ABILITIES OF LEARNERS

PRESENTATION ELEMENTS

CAMERA ANGLES

COLOR

SPECIAL EFFECTS

DIRECTING ATTENTION

PICTURE-NARRATION RELATIONSHIP

NARRATION

MUSIC

PRINTED INSTRUCTIONAL MATERIALS

COMPUTER SCREEN DISPLAY

LEARNER PARTICIPATION AND KNOWLEDGE OF RESULTS

INTERACTIVE MEDIA DESIGN—EMPHASIS ON VIDEODISC

LEARNER CONTROL

USE OF MEDIA

USE OF MULTIMEDIA

Research in the Design, Production, and Use of Instructional Technologies

Chapter 2 summarized the available knowledge derived from perception, communication theory, and learning theories, which should be of value in the design of instructional materials. Now, we turn to the conclusions derived from research studies directly relating to the planning, production, and use of instructional technologies. It is important to be informed of this evidence so that materials to be prepared and used will have the maximum effectiveness in accomplishing the stated objectives.

A large part of the research on instructional technologies consists of comparison studies contrasting the use of specific technologies with the use of conventional teaching methods. In a small number of studies a particular aspect of a technology-based presentation has been controlled or varied in order to determine the effect on learning of that particular factor. Results of the latter group have relevance for the planning and subsequent production of instructional materials.

Many studies were carried out some years ago. The majority were concerned with variables relating to motion picture design and production factors. These included such topics as format, camera angles, use of color and special effects, narration, and music. Many of the results apply as well to video recordings, videodiscs, sound-slide, or to multi-image programs. In addition, there has been a sizable research effort concerning preparation aspects of printed materials. Only a few of the conclusions reached have been questioned or retested in recent years. The reports provide evidence that can serve as guidelines for most instructional material design situations.

As computer and interactive learning technologies receive increasing attention for instructional purposes, it is important to examine the available evidence that can assist in their program designs. Evidence relating to computer screen display, videodisc design, and learner control of instruction is reported.

Summaries of research findings have been prepared by a number of writers. From the earlier summaries and the more recent ones, the findings relating to the planning, production, and use aspects of instructional technologies have been abstracted and are presented in this chapter. Following each statement, the name in parentheses relates to the literature source listed as a reference at the end of the chapter. Readers who have access to the original reports should refer to them for more detailed information.

Applications of these findings should be considered in terms of a particular learning situation. Considering the nature of the learners, the content along with objectives to be served, chosen method of instruction, and other instructional design elements (page 4), can influence the suitability for using some findings.

A particularly useful summary of principles for instructional message design and use, derived from both the behavioral and cognitive sciences, has been edited by Fleming and Levie. Refer to their publication for in-depth treatment of research results.

The findings reported here are fairly numerous and probably cannot be remembered or applied easily. At the end of the chapter, to assist in your understanding and recall of these findings, applications are offered for appraisal in a review exercise. The number of each finding is referred to in the review exercise.

In addition to the conclusions stated in this chapter, principles and generalizations presented in other chapters also relate to the planning and production processes. Of particular importance are the following:

- Principles of perception and learning theories in Chapter 2
- Picture composition factors on page 97
- Design principles for graphic materials on page 116
- Legibility standards for projected and nonprojected materials on page 132

As you read through the following statements, in some instances you will find one generalization reemphasizing or extending another one. This indicates the value and strength of the conclusion. On the other hand, there are a few situations in which contradictory statements are included. Obviously, there will be variations in testing situations and learner responses may also differ over a period of time. Thus, writers summarizing the research might then have reached different conclusions.

TREATMENT OF SUBJECT

1. Present the relevant information in an introduction and tell the viewer what is expected to be learned. (Hoban and van Ormer)
2. Summarize the important points in a clear, concise manner. Summaries probably do not improve learning unless they are complete enough to serve as repetition and review. (Hoban and van Ormer)
3. Ideas and concepts should be presented at a rate appropriate to the comprehension ability of the audience. (Hoban and van Ormer)
4. Instructional content may be more completely learned if it is presented to the learner two or more times, in identical or varied forms. (Allen, 1973)
5. Organize the material so that important sequences or concepts are repeated. Repetition

is one of the most effective means for increasing learning. (Hoban and van Ormer)

6. The learning of performance skills from media will be increased if you show common errors and how to avoid them. (Hoban and van Ormer)
7. Learning may be enhanced by organizing instruction sequentially to permit establishing subordinate skills before teaching those of higher order. (Allen, 1973)
8. A demonstration should include only the basic elements of what is to be learned, but oversimplification can have a deleterious effect. (Travers)
9. When a presentation involving a media form can be reduced in complexity so that only the factors that directly contribute to accomplishing the task are included, learning will be more predictable and replicable. (Levie and Dickie)

INTELLECTUAL ABILITIES OF LEARNERS

Materials designed for learners of low mental ability should employ these design techniques (Allen, 1975):

10. Preparatory or motivational procedures that establish a readiness to learn the material, with attention to overviews, verbal directions, and questions to answer
11. Organizational outlines or internal structuring of the content
12. Attention-directing devices that point out, emphasize, or refer to relevant cues in the communication
13. Procedures that elicit active participation and response from the learner to the content of the communication
14. Provisions for correcting or confirming feedback to responses made by learners
15. A slow rate of development, or a slow pace of presentation of the content to be learned

Materials designed for learners of high mental ability should employ these design techniques (Allen, 1975):

16. High information density; high pictorial and conceptual complexity; and richness of images, ideas, and relationships
17. A format that places requirements on the learner to organize, hypothesize, abstract, and manipulate the stimuli mentally in order to extract meaning from it
18. Rapid rate of development of information and concepts being communicated

PRESENTATION ELEMENTS

19. Stimuli that are pleasing, interesting, and satisfying are positive reinforcers and will increase the probability that the learner will remember and can reproduce what was presented in the media. (May)
20. Simplified line drawings or pictures can be more effective as information transmitters than either shaded drawings or real life photographs; full realism pictures can flood the viewer with too much visual information. (Brown)
21. Motivators, such as color, dramatic presentations, humor and comic effects, and inserted printed questions cause the learner to pay close attention, to look or listen for relevant and crucial cues, to have a "set" or put forth effort to learn, and to respond or practice. (May)
22. Cue identifiers, such as color, arrows and pointers, animation, and "implosion" techniques (having assembled parts fall into place without being handled by the demonstrator), help the learner identify and recognize the relevant cues in a media presentation. (May)
23. Simplifiers, such as improving the readability of narration, eliminating irrelevant pictorial materials, repeating illustrations, or adding additional illustrations, are procedures for making presentations more effective. (May)
24. Incorporating dramatic sequences, such as comedy, singing commercials, or realistic settings to teach factual information, has not been shown to improve learning effectiveness. (Hoban and van Ormer)
25. Because color, optical effects, and dramatic effects have little to do with increasing learning, it is possible to eliminate them. (Hoban and van Ormer)
26. A crude presentation (pencil sketches of visuals) may be at least equal in effectiveness to a polished media presentation. (May and Lumsdaine)
27. The rate of development or pacing should be slow enough to permit the learners to grasp the material as it is shown. (Hoban and van Ormer)
28. If the audience is familiar with the setting being pictured, learning may be improved. (Hoban and van Ormer)

CAMERA ANGLES

29. Show a performance on the screen the way the learner would see it if actually doing the job (subjective camera position). (Hoban and van Ormer)
30. When taking a picture, avoid excessive detail by moving the camera closer or changing the viewpoint. (Saul)

COLOR

31. The fact that color adds to the attractiveness of a training device does not necessarily mean that it improves learning. Black-and-white is as effective as color for instructional purposes except when the learning involves an actual color discrimination. Learners prefer color versions despite the fact that the addition of color does not generally contribute to learning. (Travers)
32. There is an increasing amount of empirical evidence to support the use of color in visual illustrations as evidenced by improved achievement of specific educational objectives. (Dwyer)
33. Color is preferred in learning materials since it provides motivation and can focus attention. (Lamberski)
34. Color facilitates discrimination in perceptual situations in which complexity or quantity may preclude use of other cues. (Lamberski)
35. Color seems of more value in self-paced learning materials requiring active learning than in externally-paced (passive learning) materials as in conventional lecture situations with the emphasis on one-way communication. (Lamberski)

SPECIAL EFFECTS

36. Special effects used as attention-getting devices have no positive influence on learning. (Hoban and van Ormer)
37. A film or video recording in which straight cuts have replaced optical effects (such as fades, wipes, and dissolves) teaches just as effectively as instructional materials that use these effects. (Hoban and van Ormer)
38. The special effects (fades, dissolves) that are used to represent lapses in time and other events are not effective in conveying the intended meanings. Printed titles seem to be more effective. Special sound effects appear to provide much more challenge to the producer than aid to the learner. The same can be said of humor and of other special means intended to retain the interest of the learner. (Travers)

DIRECTING ATTENTION

39. Instructional materials that treat discrete factual material appear to be improved by the use of an organizational outline in titles and commentary. (Hoban and van Ormer)
40. Liberal use of titles, questions, and other printed words can improve teaching effectiveness. (May and Lumsdaine)
41. The meaning of a visual message is often ambiguous and subject to personal interpretation. The use of words to direct attention (to cue) is essential. (Thompson et al.)
42. It is useful to direct the learner's attention to particular elements of instructional messages through visual cueing and other attention-attracting devices. (Allen, 1973, Beck)

PICTURE-NARRATION RELATIONSHIP

43. The audio channel is much more capable of obtaining attention if it is used as an interjection on the pictorial channel rather than in a continuous parallel with it. (Hartman)
44. While concepts and principles can be acquired solely on the basis of visual presentations, to rely *only* on visual lessons is inefficient. Words serve an important cueing role and should be incorporated, for this secondary purpose, into a visual presentation. (Gropper)
45. Multi-channel communications that combine words with related or relevant illustrations will provide the greatest gain because of the summation of cues between channels. (Severin)
46. Multi-channel communications that contain unrelated cues in two channels will cause interference between channels and result in less information gain than if presented in only one channel. (Severin)
47. When information is received simultaneously from several sources, one source can degrade, accentuate, or bias other sources. There is an interaction among sources. (Fleming and Levie)
48. When an audiovisual presentation is too rapid,

the perceiver must choose between the two channels. The individual will recognize separate strings of auditory information from one channel or visual information from the other channel. Only at slow rates can the individual interrelate information from both channels. (Fleming and Levie)

49. In material designed to teach performance skills, the pictures should carry the main teaching burden. (Hoban and van Ormer)

NARRATION

50. The number of words in the commentary has a definite effect on learning. Care should be taken not to "pack" the sound track. (Hoban and van Ormer)
51. Use direct forms of address (imperative or second person) in narration. Avoid the passive voice. (Hoban and van Ormer)
52. Instructional materials that provide opportunity for the audience to identify with the narrator will be more successful than that not providing such an opportunity. (Hoban and van Ormer)
53. Except where the use of live dialogue can have marked superiority in meeting particular objectives, narration has great advantages. (May and Lumsdaine)
54. The audio channel is much more capable of obtaining attention if it is used as an interjection on the visual channel rather than being continuously parallel with the visual. (Thompson et al.)

MUSIC

55. There is little evidence to support the opinion that background or mood music facilitates learning from media productions. (Seidman)
56. Musical accompaniment enhances the emotional impact of a media production. (Seidman)
57. Music can provide continuity by tying together various scenes in a script. (Seidman)

PRINTED INSTRUCTIONAL MATERIALS

58. A wide variation in design seems permissible without greatly affecting efficiency in reading. (Wilson et al.)
59. Typographic styles with serifs and Roman type (page 132) are considered easier to read than line type with sans serif, except for small letter sizes. (Pettersson)
60. Words are identified most rapidly when composed of lowercase characters. (Hartley and Burnhill)
61. Spacing characters very close together does not aid legibility. (Hartley and Burnhill)
62. The brightness contrast between letter and background is one factor determining perceptibility of letters. (Wilson et al.)
63. Very short lines slow perception, while very long lines increase the number of regressions and cause inaccuracy in locating the beginning of each new line. (Wilson et al.)
64. There is little evidence to support the effectiveness of printing all lines in equal lengths (justified). (Wilson et al.)
65. The use of headings and underlining serves to accentuate selected elements in printed text with the expectation of improving learner acquisition and retention. (Wilson et al.)
66. Boldface or italics should not be used for continuous text. They may, however, be used for emphasis of small parts. (Pettersson)
67. Inclusion of pictures in printed material can substantially improve learning. (Levin)
68. There is reader preference for double-column format on a page. (Wilson et al.)
69. The generous use of open space in printed instructional materials is a necessity for aiding comprehension. (Wilson et al.)
70. For text printed in black, all paper surfaces are equally legible if they have a reflectance of at least 70%. The most legible combination is a black text on a light yellow background. (Pettersson)

COMPUTER SCREEN DISPLAY

71. While the screen permits 80 characters per line and 24 lines vertically, readers prefer a 62-character line and a depth of 19 lines. (Rubens and Krull)
72. When possible, text should be presented at a character density of 80 characters as opposed to 40 characters per line. (Hooper and Hannafin)
73. Text presented with more than 40 characters per line should always be double spaced. (Hooper and Hannafin)
74. Break lines at ends of words rather than hyphenating words. (Rubens and Krull)

75. Use uppercase and lowercase characters for best legibility on the display screen. (Rubens and Krull)
76. Since the screen provides fewer lines on which to place vertical columns of text, a single-column format is recommended. (Rubens and Krull)
77. Unjustified text (page 188) is more suitable for computer display screen use. (Hartley)
78. Left-justified text on the screen is read faster than either centered or right-justified text. (Rubens and Krull, Hooper and Hannafin)
79. Use predetermined and consistent units of line spacing to convey the structure of text from one screen to the next. (Hartley)
80. Scrolling or moving text is more difficult to read than is a static text. (Hartley)
81. Since the left half of a screen has a strong influence on user attention, use that area for "cueing" (headings and other placement information for the reader). (Rubens and Krull)
82. To assist the reader in locating specific items on the screen, it is desirable to box blocks of text. (Rubens and Krull)
83. Boldface, serif type increases legibility, does not decrease reading speed, and is useful for cueing. (Rubens and Krull)
84. Use color for quick identification and as a cueing device. (Rubens and Krull)

LEARNER PARTICIPATION AND KNOWLEDGE OF RESULTS

85. Learning will increase if the viewer practices a skill while it is presented, provided the explanation is slow enough or time is allowed for the learner to practice without missing new material. (Hoban and van Ormer)
86. Participation, relative to what is learned through media, does not have to be overt. Mental practice is also effective. (Travers)
87. When a student participates frequently by responding actively to some stimulus, learning of the material will be increased. (Allen, 1973)
88. Furnishing knowledge of results, as part of the participation process, also has positive effects upon learning. (Travers)
89. After studying a topic, encouraging a student to self-evaluate his or her own learning and performance can provide motivation for continued learning. (Keller in Fleming and Levie)

INTERACTIVE MEDIA DESIGN—EMPHASIS ON VIDEODISC

90. The fundamental elements of well-designed interactive instruction are comparable to procedures for a well-designed lesson in any medium. (Hannafin)
91. Any interactive instructional program should reflect the instructional needs of a wide variety of potential learners. (DeBloois)
92. Attention should be given to structuring an interactive lesson so as to serve *both* high ability students who can make decisions and move ahead on their own and low ability students who need external assistance. (Hannafin)
93. The level of difficulty of an interactive lesson should be perceived by learners as challenging and as requiring considerable effort. (Hannafin)
94. Video (or other audiovisual media) should provide the primary instruction; the computer should manage and control instructional sequence decisions. (Hannafin)
95. Interactive instructional material presented to learners in videodisc format must be of the highest quality. (DeBloois)
96. Numerous options in interactive functions, such as sequence and amount of instruction and content display time, allow individual learners to adapt a program to their unique needs and capabilities. (Hannafin)
97. Questions appearing periodically in an interactive lesson can either increase attention and subsequent learning or monitor comprehension. (Hannafin)
98. Questions for interactivity that involve high-level processing tasks (above factual recall) and require more mental effort will improve reading. (Hannafin)
99. Generally, when instructional tasks consist of complex content requiring extensive prerequisite knowledge, the program control should be greater than learner control in instructional decisions. (Hannafin)
100. Learner feedback should take both serious and humorous forms and be a constant design feature. (DeBloois)
101. Attempting to increase student achievement to reach a high mastery level may require more study time than is warranted. (Hannafin)
102. Interactive project planning and management is critical; project control can be gained through the use of appropriate planning tech-

niques and devices. (DeBloois)

103. The time and expense required for developing interactive videodisc systems warrant accountability and evaluation relative to the system's accessibility, quality, effectiveness, efficiency, and worth. (DeBloois)

LEARNER CONTROL

Interactive learning through computer-assisted instruction and computer/video is designed so that some degree of control of learning experiences may be given to the learner. It is believed that by giving learners greater control over various aspects of a program, they may tailor learning to their own style, thus enhancing efficiency of learning. Research indicates the following:

104. Too much control over their own instruction by learners may lead learners to acquire negative attitudes toward a lesson. (Gray)
105. Allowing all but the brightest and most knowledgeable learners free rein at controlling sequencing, pacing, amount of practice, and level of difficulty may result in disappointing performance. (Higginbotham-Wheat)
106. Learner control with advisement, including how to exercise control, when to use it, and amount of practice needed, can be beneficial in supporting positive attitudes and long-range retention of achievement. (Milheim and Azbell)

USE OF MEDIA

107. Motivated learners learn from any medium if it is competently used and adapted to their needs. Within its limitations, any medium can perform any educational task. Whether a learner learns more from one medium than from another is as likely to depend on *how* the medium is used as on *what* medium is used. (Schramm)
108. Learners react favorably to mediated instruction that is realistic, relevant to them, and technically stimulating. (Thompson)
109. Learners are positively affected when persuasive messages are presented in as credible a manner as possible. (Thompson)
110. Learners who are involved in the planning, production, or delivery of mediated instruction are likely to react favorably to the instructional activity, and to the message delivered. (Thompson)
111. Significantly greater learning often results when instructional materials are integrated into the traditional instructional program. (Moldstad)
112. When they are carefully selected and/or produced (taking into account both media attributes and learner characteristics) as well as systematically integrated into the instructional program, educational media have a significant impact on learner achievement and self-image. (Wilkinson)
113. Compared to conventional methods, equal amounts of learning are often accomplished in significantly less time when using instructional technology. (Moldstad)
114. Learners who participate in post-instructional discussions and critiques are likely to develop positive attitudes toward delivery methods and content. (Thompson)
115. Learners who experience a purposeful emotional involvement or arousal during instruction are likely to change their attitudes in the direction advocated in mediated messages. (Thompson)
116. Media are more effectively and efficiently used, and therefore have a greater impact on learners, when teachers have received specific training in their utilization. (Wilkinson)
117. Media are more effectively and efficiently used when the school provides an integrated media center based on the guidelines suggested by AECT and AASL. (Wilkinson)
118. When computers are used systematically as an integral part of instruction, it has been shown consistently that there is a marked decrease in time on task, no loss of performance in the face of significantly less lecture time, and a noticeable improvement in learner motivation and attitude toward learning. (Stennet)
119. A person who is somewhat knowledgeable about a particular subject can process information at a much faster rate and more strategically with text than with audio or visual media. On the other hand, an individual to whom the subject is new is likely to benefit from the ability to slow the rate of information processing, and move back and forth between text and visuals. (Kozma)

USE OF MULTIMEDIA

Benefits of multimedia, with particular effects on adult learning, have been summarized by Ragan and Smith.

120. Multimedia is at least equally effective as conventional forms of instructional delivery.
121. Frequently and significantly, multimedia instruction is more effective than conventional instruction.
122. Multimedia instruction is a more efficient means of delivery in terms of learning time (approximately 30 percent) than conventional forms of instruction.
123. Attitudes toward multimedia instruction are more positive than attitudes toward conventional instruction. Ragan and Smith also determined that certain instructional design features appear to enhance the quality of multimedia instruction.
124. Greater learning effects appear to result from:
    - Higher levels of interactivity
    - Program control or advised learner control, rather than total learner control
    - Multimedia integrated with other forms of delivery
    - Structured rather than totally exploratory learning

A person interested in planning, producing, and using instructional technologies should review and weigh all the evidence from the research findings and theory reported in this and the preceding chapters. These findings, rather than intuition, should be considered as you design and use your own materials for instruction. Start with these results and recommendations, realizing that some may have been derived from situations far afield of the applications you plan to make. (Yet they are starting points with positive evidence for improved learning at lower costs in terms of time, materials, and services.) Then adapt and change as you gain experience and test the results of your efforts.

REVIEW

What You Have Learned About Research Findings for the Design, Production, and Use of Instructional Technologies

Following are statements concerning instructional technologies that apply one or more of the findings described in this chapter. Some make recommended applications, while others apply elements in nonrecommended fashion. For each example indicate your *agreement* or *disagreement* with the proposed plan. Then check your answer, using the reference numbers at the right to locate the relevant numbered finding, or findings, used as a basis for each example.

	Agree or Disagree	Evidence
1. When demonstrating the proper method to use in casting with a fishing rod, show errors commonly made and ways to avoid them.	______	6
2. In demonstrating a skill, like fingering a musical instrument, color will add to the instructional value of the medium used.	______	25,31–35,80
3. In explaining the operation of a machine, use arrows to indicate each part as it is referred to.	______	22,41
4. Dramatic-type music can create a mood for an audience at the beginning of a slide/tape program.	______	55
5. To demonstrate how a person sews an intricate stitch by hand, film the action from over the shoulder.	______	29
6. In teaching a skill like welding, limit the amount of narration and depend on the visuals for the major instructional effect. In narration, use words in the present tense to direct attention ("hold the tool . . ."; "notice the color . . .").	______	42–48
7. A video recording that shows action in many locations is more effective if an optical effect like a dissolve is used between scenes to bridge distance rather than abrupt cuts from one scene to the next.	______	36,37,38

(continued)

8. To explain a sophisticated security system to new employees, present only the essential facts without repetition of any of the concepts. A brief, general summary should be included.	______	2–5
9. In describing an industrial process, quickly present only the essential information. The commentary should describe, at length, what cannot easily be visualized. If it is a lengthy subject, plan for the commentary to move along rapidly.	______	3,27, 45,50
10. Picture sketches from storyboard cards (page 65), converted to videotape, may be as effective as a high-quality polished treatment for illustrating a farming procedure.	______	20,23,26
11. In treating the subject of animal life in a mountain area, color should be used and important concepts presented through multiple examples.	______	31–35
12. Introduce the demonstration of a safety procedure with an explanation of the purpose of the demonstration and what the student is expected to learn from it. Include titles that indicate the sequence of steps in the procedure. Describe carefully and visualize new technical terms.	______	39–40
13. For learning to operate a piece of equipment, like a table saw, a short video recording that can be viewed any number of times may have advantages. Directions for the learner to stop the video, answer questions, and practice steps in the skill should be included. Correct answers to questions should be provided immediately after the questions are answered.	______	40,85–88
14. A self-learning package treating a topic for an electronics lab course includes a cassette recording on which the instructor outlines the facts basic to the topic and leads the student to laboratory applications.	______	1,7
15. When it is important that information be remembered for a media presentation, make the viewers feel uncomfortable and dissatisfied while watching the program.	______	19
16. The material designed for new trainees shown to have low intelligence should present ideas at the same pace as that designed to be used with other trainees.	______	10–15, 92,93,96
17. On a transparency and also on a computer screen, use capital letters for all words.	______	60,75
18. It may be preferable to have the instructor narrate the script rather than to use a professional narrator.	______	52
19. A media program is designed to start by having professional actors make fun of an important situation so the technicians attending would give their full attention to the message that followed.	______	21
20. Even though it is more costly to have a study guide printed with all text lines of the same length (justified), the use of this technique is preferred.	______	64
21. When setting up for an important step in a how-to-do-it picture, place the camera so that only the part being handled will be seen in the camera.	______	30
22. Underline key words for attention in an instructional manual.	______	65
23. Plentiful blank space is preferred on a printed page and also on the computer screen because it contributes to readability.	______	69,73,82
24. In a video recording you are careful to have only the essential behaviors role-played so as not to confuse the viewer with too many actions.	______	8,9
25. Questions in interactive programs should require high-level intellectual activities rather than only the recall of facts.	______	93,98

26. Dark lettering on a dark background is acceptable for good contrast on printed and projected materials. ______ 62
27. To have highly capable students benefit from an interactive media program you present a large amount of information developed rapidly and require students to generalize and solve complex problems. ______ 16–18, 92,93
28. Double columns are beneficial on a printed page, but not so on a computer screen. ______ 68,76
29. Lines that are of equal length, left and right, are easier to read. This is true for both printed material and the computer screen. ______ 64,77,78
30. Music used as background in a slide program may conflict with the narration. ______ 55
31. Easier reading results from letters placed very close together. ______ 61
32. The efforts to improve an interactive program in order to achieve the final few percentage points of high-level learning is justified. ______ 101
33. The realism of live voices is preferred to a narrator describing what is taking place in the pictures. ______ 53
34. Designing an interactive program requires planning procedures very different from those used in other media planning. ______ 89
35. Including diagrams and pictures in printed material interferes with understanding. ______ 67
36. Humor can be of real value in media materials. ______ 24,100
37. An important feature of interactive programs is that they should serve learners having different levels of preparation and abilities. ______ 91,92,96
38. Include only unfamiliar locations and subjects for best learning. ______ 28
39. Special techniques such as multiple exposures, animation, and flashing titles are very beneficial to learning from media. ______ 25,36,80
40. Between sequences in a media production, music can provide continuity. ______ 57
41. Trying new ideas when creating printed materials is not advisable, since the results may interfere with understanding. ______ 58
42. For emphasis, vary the spacing between lines of text within a series of computer screen images. ______ 79
43. If you incorporate well-designed instructional materials into your training presentations, the learning results should improve. ______ 111
44. If you have a very limited time frame for introducing new information to learners, you should consider using instructional media. ______ 113
45. Any person knowledgeable about a topic can successfully use media for instruction of the topic. ______ 114
46. If trainees are highly motivated to learn, the specific media selected are not as important as how well the media are used. ______ 107
47. Narration to accompany visuals should have some pauses rather than be continuous at a rapid pace. ______ 49,54
48. For printing text, sans serif type is preferable. ______ 59
49. All learners react positively to study with highly interactive programs. ______ 105
50. There is limited evidence to support the extensive use of computers in education. ______ 118
51. Use boldface text for emphasis, not as continuous text. ______ 66
52. The most legible print is in black on white paper. ______ 70
53. Viewing a media program that has an emotional impact can affect viewers' attitudes. ______ 115
54. Learners who plan and produce instructional materials find that such activities provide educational benefits. ______ 110

See answers on page 375.

REFERENCES

Allen, William H. "Intellectual Abilities and Instructional Media." *AV Communication Review* 23 (Summer 1975):139–170.

———. "Research in Educational Media." In *Educational Media Yearbook 1973.* James W. Brown, ed. New York: R. R. Bowker, 1973.

Beck, Charles R. "Strategies for Cueing Visual Information: Research Findings and Instructional Design Implications." *Educational Technology* 31 (March 1991):16–20.

Brown, James W. *Recent Manpower Studies: Some Implications for AECT. Media Manpower Supplement No. 2.* Washington, DC: Media Manpower, March 1971.

DeBloois, Michael L. "Principles for Designing Interactive Videodisc Instructional Materials." In *Videodisc/Microcomputer Courseware Design.* Michael L. DeBloois, ed. Englewood Cliffs, NJ: Educational Technology Publications, 1982, pp. 25–66.

Dwyer, Francis M. *Strategies for Improved Visual Learning.* State College, PA: Learning Services, Box 784, 1978.

Fleming, Malcolm, and Levie, W. Howard, editors. *Instructional Message Design: Principles from the Behavioral Sciences.* Englewood Cliffs, NJ: Educational Technology Publications, 1993.

Gray, S. H. "The Effect of Sequence Control on Computer-Assisted Learning." *Journal of Computer-Based Instruction* 14 (2) 1977:54–56.

Gropper, George L. "Learning from Visuals: Some Behavioral Considerations." *AV Communication Review* 14 (Spring 1966):37–70.

Hannafin, Michael J. "Keeping Interactive Video in Perspective." In *Educational Media and Technology Yearbook 1985.* Elwood Miller, ed. Littleton, CO: Libraries Unlimited, 1985, pp. 13–25.

Hartley, James. "Designing Electronic Text: The Role of Print-Based Research." *Educational Communication and Technology Journal* 35 (Spring 1987):1–17.

Hartley, James, and Burnhill, Peter. "Fifty Guidelines for Improving Instructional Text." *Programmed Learning and Instructional Technology* 4 (February 1977):65–73.

Hartman, Frank R. "Single and Multiple Channel Communication: A Review of Research and a Proposed Model." *AV Communication Review* 9 (November–December 1961): 235–262.

Higginbotham-Wheat, N. "Learner Control: When Does It Work?" *Proceedings of the Research and Theory Division of the 1990 Annual Meeting of the Association for Educational Communications and Technology.* Washington, DC: The Association, February 1990.

Hoban, Charles F., Jr., and van Ormer, Edward B. *Instructional Film Research 1918–1950.* Technical Report No. SDC 269-7-19. Port Washington, NY: U.S. Naval Special Devices Center, 1950.

Hooper, Simon, and Hannafin, Michael J. "Variables Affecting the Legibility of Computer Generated Text." *Journal of Instructional Development* 9 (4):22–28, 1986.

Kozma, Robert B. "Learning With Media." *Review of Educational Research* 61 (Summer 1991):179–211.

Lamberski, Richard J. *A Comprehensive and Critical Review of the Methodology and Findings in Color Investigations.* Syracuse, NY: ERIC (ED 194 063), April 1980.

Levie, W. Howard, and Dickie, Kenneth E. "The Analysis and Application of Media." In *Second Handbook of Research on Teaching.* Robert M. W. Travers, ed. Chicago: Rand McNally, 1973.

Levin, Joel R. "Pictorial Strategies for School Learning." In *Cognitive Strategy Research—Educational Applications.* M. Pressley and J. R. Levin, eds. New York: Springer-Verlag, 1983, pp. 203–237.

Lumsdaine, A. A. "Controlled Variations of Specific Factors in Design and Use of Instructional Media." In *Handbook of Research on Teaching.* N. L. Gage, ed. Chicago: Rand McNally, 1963.

May, Mark A. *Enhancements and Simplifications of Motivational and Stimulus Variables in Audiovisual Instructional Materials.* Washington, DC: U.S. Office of Education, contract No. OE-5-16-006, 1965.

May, Mark A., and Lumsdaine, A. A. *Learning from Films.* New Haven, CT: Yale University Press, 1958.

Milheim, W. D. and Azbell, J. W. "How Past Research on Learner Control Can Aid in the Design of Interactive Video Materials." reported in *Instructional Developments* 1 (3) Fall 1990: 16 Syracuse, NY: Syracuse University School of Education, Fall 1990.

Moldstad, John A. "Selective Review of Research Studies Showing Media Effectiveness: A Primer for Media Directors." *AV Communication Review,* 22 (Winter 1974):387–407.

Pettersson, Rune. *Visuals for Information: Research and Practice.* Englewood Cliffs, NJ: Educational Technology Publications, 1989.

Ragan, T. J. and Smith, P. L. *University of Oklahoma—Instructional Technology Effectiveness Study.* Atlanta, GA: Skill Dynamics, 1992.

Rubens, Phillip, and Krull, Robert. "Applications of Research on Document Design to Online Displays." *Technical Communication* 32 (Fourth quarter):29–34, 1985.

Saul, Ezra V., et al. *A Review of the Literature Pertinent to the Design and Use of Effective Graphic Training*

Aids. Technical Report SPECDEVCEN 494–08–1. Port Washington, NY: U.S. Naval Special Devices Center, 1954.

Schramm, Wilbur. *Big Media, Little Media: A Report to the Agency for International Development.* Stanford, CA: Institute for Communication Research, Stanford University, 1973.

Seidman, Steven A. "On the Contributions of Music to Media Productions." *Educational Communication and Technology Journal* 29 (Spring 1981):49–61.

Severin, William. "The Effectiveness of Relevant Pictures in Multiple-Channel Communications." *AV Communication Review* 15 (Winter 1967):386–401.

Stennet, R. G. *Computer-Assisted Instruction: A Review of the Reviews.* Ontario: London Board of Education, 1985 (ERIC No. ED 260 687).

Thompson, Ann D., Simonson, Michael R. and Hargrave, Constance P. *Educational Technology: A Review of the Research.* Washington, DC: Association for Educational Communications and Technology, 1992.

Travers, Robert M. W. *Research and Theory Related to AudioVisual Information Transmission.* Kalamazoo: Western Michigan University, 1967.

Wilkinson, Gene. *Media in Instruction: Sixty Years of Research.* Washington, DC: Association for Educational Communications and Technology, 1980.

Willows, Dale M. and Houghton, Harvey A. *The Psychology of Illustration, Volume I, Basic Research.* New York: Springer-Verlag, 1987.

Wilson, Thomas C.; Pfister, Fred C.; and Fleury, Bruce E. *The Design of Printed Instructional Materials: Research on Illustrations and Typography.* Syracuse, NY: ERIC Clearinghouse on Information Resources, Syracuse University, 1981.

Planning Instructional Media

PART 2

C H A P T E R

4

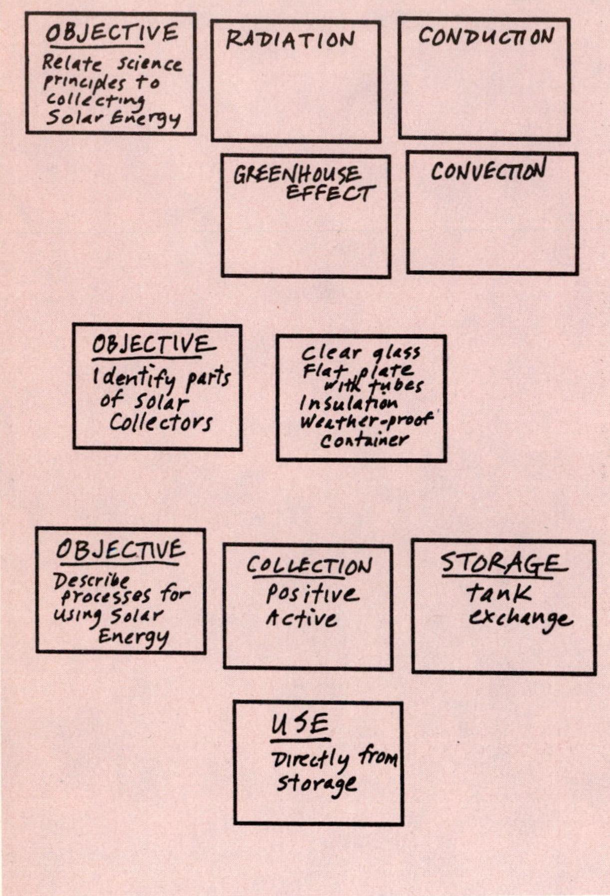

PLANNING AND CREATIVITY

START WITH A PURPOSE OR AN IDEA

CONSIDER THE AUDIENCE (THE LEARNER)

DEVELOP THE OBJECTIVES

USE A TEAM APPROACH

FIND RELATED MATERIALS

REVIEW WHAT YOU HAVE DONE

PREPARE THE CONTENT OUTLINE

DISPLAY CONTENT

VERIFY CONTENT

Preliminary Planning

All too often someone says, "Let's make a videotape to train our salespeople." Or, "How about shooting some slides to impress new staff members with their value to the organization?" Or, "We should have some transparencies to use with this report."

Unfortunately such statements are frequently the signal to start taking pictures prematurely and to produce instructional materials that often are disorganized and ineffective. These proposals are no more than bare ideas. To assure that the product will fulfill the need, they require further consideration, such as decisions about the objectives to be served, the specific content to be treated, and its organization into planned sequences of pictures.

Occasionally, it is necessary to make pictures without any prior planning. These situations arise either when an event happens unexpectedly or when activities take place over which you may have little, if any, control. Examples of this would be the need to document the visit of an official to an industrial plant or a ceremony at an institution. But most often, effective instructional media are carefully planned *before* production takes place.

PLANNING AND CREATIVITY

There are two related, although seemingly opposed, processes that should receive attention when developing instructional media. One is the structured planning procedure, which requires organization, attention to a logical sequence of components, and their integration into a unified message. The other is the unstructured free flow of ideas and expressions typified by creative thinking, leading to the solution of problems encountered during planning. The intermingling of both systematic planning and creative thinking is important if effective and interesting instructional products are to result.

During the planning process, many problems will be faced and numerous decisions must be made. Some are procedural—"Should we start on the storyboard now, or work on the script?" Or, "Can we consider using captions or depend entirely on narration?" Others are analytical—"Are the steps for the equipment operating procedure in the correct sequence? Has anything been left out?" As you proceed, ideas may come to mind that can influence the planning—"Let's include a dramatic sequence showing treatment with the drug before going to the research lab." Or, "You might show a diagram of the whole process followed by a detailed examination of each component."

Some of these decisions should be based on the principles relating to perception and learning theory presented in Chapter 2 and the research evidence summarized in Chapter 3. But many times ideas come to mind unexpectedly, or through brainstorming and other creative thinking efforts. These original thoughts can contribute significantly to the structure, appeal, and effectiveness of any instructional material.

An analysis of how the creative thinking process is successfully used reveals that most often six steps are followed:

1. ***Desire***—Have an initial motivation to want to solve a problem with which you are concerned.
2. ***Preparation***—Gather information relative to the problem as revealed by the planning stages of audience identification, objective specification, and content listing.
3. ***Manipulation***—Play with a number of ideas to devise one or more possible solutions, or to find a new pattern of treating the content that differs from that which has been familiar.
4. ***Incubation***—Takeover of the thought process by the subconscious mind, especially if a solution has not been attained.
5. ***Illumination***—Sudden revelation of a solution or a new pattern as the result of subconscious thought.
6. ***Verification***—Examine the solution to evaluate its feasibility, and then to accept it as being appropriate to the problem.

Each of us has the capacity to apply this creative thinking process, some persons to a greater degree than others. Both logical, sequential processing skills and random or creative thinking abilities are essential mental activities when developing instructional materials. Prepare yourself to handle both responsibilities as you move through the planning stages that follow.

In this chapter, and in the following ones in Part 2, we will examine each of the important elements that comprise the planning process. For some media forms—slide series, video recordings, multi-image presentations, and computer-based interactive instruction—attention should be given to all steps. For other media types—printed and display materials, overhead transparencies, and audiotape recordings—consideration need be given only to certain steps. The planning elements needing emphasis will be indicated for each medium at the beginning of its chapter in Part 4.

START WITH A PURPOSE OR AN IDEA

An idea, a problem situation, or a learning need identified within an instructional-design plan for a unit or a course should be the starting point for the development of your instructional materials. An idea may indicate an area of interest you have, but the more useful ideas are those conceived in terms of a need relating to a specific group—an audience's need for certain information or for a skill, or the need to establish a desired attitude.

So here is the first step: Express your idea or purpose concisely. For example:

1. Security has been an important issue within our company. We need to alert all employees to the need for maintaining a high level of security for company equipment, supplies, and new products under development.
2. As a financial advisor, you frequently are asked to meet with groups who are interested in making investments for future security. You would like to acquaint middle-aged people with advantages and limitations in alternative ways of investing money.
3. I conduct an adult education class on ecology and the environment. Each year I suggest topics of potential interest to the group for study. One that is frequently selected is the use of solar energy. Therefore, I want to develop a better understanding of how solar energy can be used in heating homes and for making hot water. (Note: The

example of using solar energy will serve as an illustration of the planning steps that follow.)

In the instructional-design procedure described in Chapter 1, (page 4) one element was to identify general purposes to be served by the topic. The purposes, as underlined in the examples above, are the beginning **ideas** referred to here. Take the time to state them clearly so that you, and other persons involved in planning, will understand the aim of the materials to be produced.

The expression **instructional media and technologies** represents the print, graphic, photographic, and electronic materials appropriate for communication in instruction and training. The procedures described here also are useful for satisfying such needs as intraorganizational communications and communications for external public relations.

To Motivate, to Inform, or to Instruct

Any one of three intentions may be served by instructional media when used with individuals, groups, or large audiences: (1) to **motivate** an interest or a degree of action; (2) to present **information;** or (3) to provide **instruction.** The difference among these three intentions should be recognized by the reader because the treatment of content will vary for each one.

For *motivational* purposes, dramatic or entertainment techniques may be employed. The desired result is to generate interest or stimulate members of an audience to take action (assume responsibility, volunteer service, or contribute money). This involves accomplishing objectives that affect personal attitudes, values, and emotions.

As discussed in Chapter 2, Keller (1983) identified four conditions that should receive attention for successful motivation—arouse curiosity and gain attention, show relevance to audience for the topic being presented, build confidence for success in understanding and learning, and provide a satisfactory experience with the media. As suggested by Keller, a number of strategies can be used to accomplish each condition.

When informational or instructional purposes are to be served, attention to motivational factors is important near the beginning of the production.

For *informational* purposes, the instructional material would most likely be used in a presentation made before an audience or class group. The content and form of the presentation would be general in nature, serving as an introduction, an overview, a report, or background knowledge. It also might employ entertainment, dramatic, or motivational techniques in order to attract and hold attention. When viewing and listening to informational-type materials, individuals are passive viewers and listeners. The anticipated response by people most likely would be limited to degrees of mental agreement or disagreement and to emotionally pleasant, neutral, or unpleasant feelings. However, do not expect that members of an audience, after seeing and hearing the material (a 10-minute slide/tape program or a 15-minute video recording, for example), will have immediately learned a great amount of the content. Materials that are designed for informational purposes can in turn lead a person to involvement with the idea or topic on an instructional level.

For *instructional* purposes, while the presentation of information is important, attention must also be given to involving the participants in mental or overt activities relating to the instructional media being used so that learning can take place. The materials themselves should be designed more systematically and be psychologically sound, in terms of learning principles, to provide effective instruction. At the same time they should be enjoyable and provide pleasant experiences. Making provisions for individuals to use the instructional media on their own can be desirable. In this way, each person will interact with the materials by answering questions, by engaging in performance as directed by the materials, by checking understanding, and by making use of information presented.

In the examples cited previously, the company's security awareness would be an illustration of a motivational purpose; the solar energy topic has an instructional purpose; and the financial advising situation represents an informational purpose.

Keep in mind the differences among instructional media to be used for motivation, for information, and those to be used for instruction. The planning and treatment for each type differ in certain aspects. Although major emphasis is given to planning materials for instructional purposes in the following chapters, reference will be made, when necessary, to items that affect motivational and informational materials.

CONSIDER THE AUDIENCE (THE LEARNER)

The characteristics of the learner or audience—those who will be seeing, using, and learning from your materials—cannot be separated from your statement of objectives. One influences the other. Such audience characteristics as age and educational level; knowledge of the subject, skills relating to it, attitude toward it, cultural context; and individual differences within the group all have bearing on your objectives and treatment of the topic. The audience is the determinant when you consider the complexity of ideas to be presented, the rate at which the topic is developed, the vocabulary level for captions and narration, the number of examples to use, and the kinds of involvement and degree of participation of the learner. These and similar matters will influence the complexity of the objectives and the way you should handle the topic.

At times more than one audience may fit your plans, but generally it is advisable to plan for **one major audience group.** Then consider other **secondary** ones that also might use your materials. Describe the major audience, explicitly.

For the example of solar energy indicated previously:

> The audience will be middle-class adults who have at least a high school education and likely some college experience. They are very inquisitive and particularly interested in environmental matters that affect their lives.

If you plan instructional media for use with a group of young children or with individuals from an ethnic minority culture, anticipate difficulty with understanding language and accepting situations based on experience or cultural factors that differ from their own.

Make sure that the subject and the activities selected are appropriate to their interests and their abilities. Your own enthusiasm for a topic may take you far beyond your audience's limits of interest. Also, give careful consideration to the complexity of the subject so that your group does not become burdened with too many details and lose interest as a result.

DEVELOP THE OBJECTIVES

Keeping the audience in mind, build upon the idea or generalized statement of purposes. Doing this means translating the general idea into a clear-cut and specific statement of one or more objectives for the planned learning within an instructional context. For a motivational or informational presentation, the objectives often are more broadly stated than for instructional purposes.

Much attention is given in the literature to the topic of **learning objectives;** these have a key role in instructional design as well as in choosing learning activities.

To plan successful instructional media and other learning experiences, it is necessary to know specifically what must be learned. The purpose of formulating objectives is to provide clear guidance that permits an orderly presentation of content leading to learning by the identified audience.

When learning takes place, a person changes in some way. This may be a mental growth as the individual acquires new knowledge (definitions of terms, steps in a procedure, criteria for making a decision). The learning can also become evident by the way the individual now performs a skill, spells a word, argues a position, or treats other persons. In each situation, as the result of the learning experience, the individual behaves differently.

In order to provide for the desired learning, objectives are written. They indicate what should be the outcome of the learning. Objectives are grouped into three major categories as described in Chapter 2—the **psychomotor** area, represented by performance skills involving the use of muscles as a task or job is being carried out; the **cognitive** area, which includes knowledge and information, represented by thinking and other intellectual skills; and the **affective** area of attitudes, appreciations, and values. This last category requires the most care when objectives are being specified.

The difficult problem is to spell out the objectives so that (1) learning experiences can be developed to satisfy each objective, and (2) tests or performance measurements can be designed to find out whether the learning has taken place.

The general, nonspecific words that are often used to describe instructional purposes—to *know,* to *understand,* to *become familiar with,* to *appreciate,* to *believe,* to *gain insight into,* to *accept,* to *enjoy,* and so forth—are unsatisfactory guide words for objectives. They do not permit verification through specific observable behavior and they are open to many interpretations of how their accomplishment may be measured. Such expressions may be acceptable only as indications of generalized objectives for motivational- and informational-type presentations.

Useful statements of objectives for instructional purposes are made up of two grammatical parts. First: a specific ACTION VERB, for example, to *identify,* to *name,* to *demonstrate,* to *show,* to *make* or *build,* to *order* or *arrange,* to *distinguish between,* to *compare,* or to *apply.* Second: CONTENT REFERENCE that follows the verb, for example, to name the *five steps in a process,* to assemble *all parts of a machine* properly, to write a 500-word *theme,* to apply a *rule,* to solve four of five *problems.*

Notice that in addition to the action verb and the content reference, we may add a STANDARD OF COMPETENCY *(five steps, all parts, 500 words, four of five problems).* The standard further provides for setting an attainment level that can be measured.

With this awareness of measurable learning objectives, how can we specifically indicate the objectives for the general idea example on solar energy?

It is *not* sufficiently specific to write:

To understand how solar energy can be used

It *is* specific to write:

1. To list at least two features of each of the three processes required in utilizing solar energy for heating
2. To describe the planning necessary for using solar energy
3. To assemble a solar collector with 100 percent accuracy when provided with four essential parts
4. To assume responsibility for engaging in a solar energy project

Statements 1 and 2 specify cognitive objectives (1 on a low level—recall of information; 2 higher intellectually—comprehension level). Statement 3 is a psychomotor objective, requiring physical performance by the learner. Statement 4 specifies an attitudinal behavior. It is much more difficult to indicate behaviors and measurements for attitudes and appreciations than to do so for either knowledge/intellectual skills or performance skills. To repeat, only when the objectives are stated in terms of an individual's mental learning or physical performance is there much guidance for the design of instruction. (For further explanation of and suggestions for developing objectives, see Chapter 7 in Kemp, and others.)

Remember that each topic for instruction (as in the solar energy topic) requires a number of objectives, each to be considered individually or as a related set, in designing learning experiences. Therefore, it takes time and careful thought to develop and state objectives. Also, as was indicated during the discussion of instructional design in Chapter 1 (page 4), it is natural to move gradually from general to specific objectives. Finally, realize that some objectives may become clearly evident only when content is being selected or even when specific instructional materials are in the planning stage. In such a case, return to this beginning point, the statement of objectives, and check how well the content and learning experiences fit the stated objective; you may want to revise the statement.

You might prepare media for many instructional purposes. Here are some major general purposes with specific examples. They are stated as objectives in terms of student or audience's behavioral changes, from the learner or audience viewpoint.

- ***To learn about a subject***—for example, "to determine how a worker should be selected for a job when there are several qualified applicants"
- ***To apply the steps in a process***—for example, "to measure a patient's blood pressure within ± 5mm Hg"
- ***To practice a certain attitude***—for example, "to form the habit of using safe procedures in operating shop equipment"
- ***To respond to a social need***—for example, "to offer your services in a youth recreation program"

In planning materials, limit yourself to no more than a few concisely stated achievable objectives. However much you feel it necessary *to cover the whole topic,* you will realize eventually that limitations should be set. If you do not set limits, your materials may become too complex and unmanageable. You can maintain limits by aiming at a series of related instructional media, each of which includes a single phase of a large topic.

For the solar energy topic a number of matters require attention—forms in which energy is used in the home, scientific principles applied in collecting solar energy, process of energy collection, storing the energy, and so forth. For the purpose of the planning stages that follow, *collecting solar energy* is selected as the topic. You have identified the audience. The objectives will be as follows:

1. To explain how four scientific principles are applied for creating heat in a solar collector
2. To identify four parts of a solar collector and the functions of each
3. To assemble a solar collector when provided with the four essential parts

Finally, objectives do not stand alone. It is obvious that they are dependent on the subject content that will be treated and are influenced by the needs and dispositions of the learner or intended audience.

USE A TEAM APPROACH

You may be capable of planning and preparing your instructional materials without the assistance of others. If you are, you have skills in three areas. First, you have a good knowledge of the subject. Second, you know how to plan instructional materials and how to interpret the subject visually. Third, you have the necessary technical skills in photography, graphic arts, and sound recording.

However, if you feel inadequate in any of the areas mentioned, you should obtain assistance or carefully use this book (in the second and third areas). Nevertheless, there is value in getting reactions and suggestions from other people, so plan to involve others during some phases of the planning and preparation processes.

Three individuals or three groups might make up the **production team.** The *subject matter expert* (**SME**) is the person or persons having broad knowledge of the content to be treated and most often is familiar with the potential audience. The *instructional developer* is the individual who knows how to handle design (treatment, script writing, camera angles, and related essential knowledge and skills) and knows the advantages, limitations, and uses of the various instructional media so that the resulting materials will achieve the anticipated purposes. (This person may also serve as the instructional designer during the planning described in Chapter 1. Such a function is essential when something as complex as an interactive videodisc is to be produced.) Finally, the *technical staff* comprises those responsible for the photography, the videotaping, the art work, the lighting, and the sound recording.

These separately described areas naturally overlap. The communications person may also take the pictures; or, as was mentioned, you may fill all three jobs. The important thing to recognize is that all three jobs exist. Keep them in mind as you consider the stages of planning and preparation that follow. For example:

> While planning learning materials on collecting solar energy, I will consult with a friend who is an engineer with a local heating and air conditioning company that sells and installs solar collectors. He and I in combination will fill the role of subject specialist. I will request assistance also from the adult education center's media coordinator, who will thus function as instructional developer. Since I have a good skill in photography, I will prepare the visual materials, but I will be assisted by a technical staff of three students, from the class, who have abilities in photography and art.

Find Related Materials

Before carrying the planning of your instructional materials to an advanced stage, locate and examine any materials already prepared on your general topic or on topics closely related to it. They may offer you some useful ideas, or you may find that all or part of such materials may fit one or more of your objectives, thus reducing the need to prepare materials.

Refer to Chapter 17 for suggestions on where to locate commercially produced instructional materials (page 305), for a list of source references (page 311), and for a procedure for evaluating materials (page 308) in terms of criteria you should consider important relative to your needs. The last offers a valuable way to judge the suitability of other resources for possible examination and use.

Review What You Have Done

The planning steps thus far examined are: (1) state an idea or a specific purpose; (2) from this statement develop your objectives, with due regard for the intended audience and its characteristics; (3) obtain assistance as necessary, from persons who have special knowledge and skills relative to the topic being developed or from already prepared materials.

Examine the examples in Table 4–1. Are the steps clearly stated and easy to follow? Are the objectives stated in behavioral terms? Which of them may not be so stated? The review questions at the end of the chapter help you to correct any improperly stated objectives.

Prepare the Content Outline

Now consider the subject matter that relates to the objectives. Consult with your subject matter expert (SME), or, if you are handling the content yourself, do any necessary research work. Facts about a subject and details of a task are often found through interviews, during visits to suitable facilities, and in the library. After this background work you can feel confident that your basic facts are correct and that you will include all pertinent information on your topic.

From the data you have gathered prepare a content outline. This outline becomes the framework for your instructional product. It consists of (1) basic topics that support your objectives and (2) factual information that explains each topic. If you are treating a specific task like assembling, operating, or troubleshooting equipment, then list the details or steps to be performed.

A word of caution: Keep in mind the people who will be your audience—their interests and their limitations. Decide what information must be included in detail and what can be treated lightly; what you can suggest for additional study and what should be left out or considered for other instructional materials.

In the sequence of the instructional design, the examination of content follows the objectives. At this stage you are not as yet concerned about specific materials. There is no gain in asking at this point whether a video recording, slides, a set of transparencies, an audio recording, printed materials, or an interactive program will best serve the objectives. You must find out what content is required to support the objectives. Then you can make decisions about specific format.

Display Content

While you can prepare an outline of the content with a word processing program on a computer, a good way of relating content to objectives is to connect the two

TABLE 4-1 EXAMPLES OF INITIAL PLANNING STEPS

IDEA	AUDIENCE	OBJECTIVE
(1) Learn about plants in the community	a. High school biology classes b. Nature clubs	To identify characteristics of 25 most common species of seed-bearing plants in our county
(2) Understand anatomy and physiology of fetal circulation	Junior level nursing students	a. To name the two blood vessels found in the umbilical cord b. To locate the two shunts that are normal in fetal circulation c. To label a diagram of fetal circulation
(3) Introduce new employees to the operation of our company	Employees of the ABC Insurance Company	To understand their role in the successful operation of our company
(4) Acquire the skills of soldering	Electronic technicians	To solder three types of conductor splices with 95% accuracy
(5) Persuade a potential customer to become interested in our XYZ equipment	Managers, electronic assembly departments	To request a demonstration of the XYZ equipment
(6) Take part in the youth program of our church	a. Children and teenagers of church members b. Church sponsors and adult members	a. To take part in youth group activities b. To know how youth activities help to develop sound character and religious understanding among our young people

visually. In Chapter 6 we will examine the method of preparing a **storyboard,** the term given to a series of sketches or pictures which help visualize the treatment of a topic for an instructional product. This same technique has value now.

Write each objective on a 3 × 5 inch card or slip of paper (3M Post-it note pads can be useful). Tack or tape the cards to a wall for display. Then, make a second set of cards listing the content—the factual information related to each objective—and display these cards under or beside each appropriate objective card. At this stage, list all the available content relating to the objectives, without considering what you may use and what will be discarded.

A planning board for displaying cards consists of plastic or cardboard strips stapled to a stiff backing board. As illustrated, a card is held firmly in a strip, but it can be slipped in and out easily. (For further details on making and using a planning board see Chapter 10 in Kemp and others.)

It is advisable to use cards of one color for objectives and of a second color for the content. Later you can add additional cards for specific materials that relate to single objectives and items of content, or to groups of either category.

You will find that displaying cards frees you to exper-

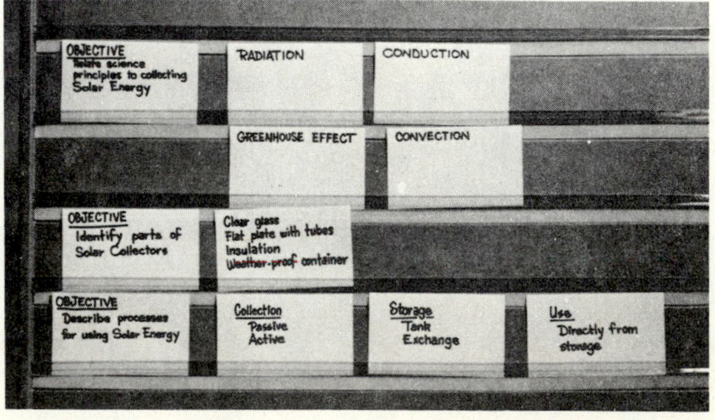

EXAMPLE: A Content Outline

Objective 1

To demonstrate how four scientific principles are applied for creating heat in a solar collector

A. Radiation
   1. Energy is generated within the sun
   2. Travels through space to the earth

B. Conduction
   1. Molecules become active at heating point
   2. Heated molecules vibrate
   3. Vibration causes increased motion of adjacent molecules

C. Greenhouse effect
   1. Container with transparent cover
   2. Heat is trapped inside

D. Convection
   1. Heated material becomes less dense and rises
   2. Replaced by cooler material that is heated in turn

Objective 2

To identify four parts of a solar collector and their functions

A. Clear glass or plastic cover
   1. Allows light and heat to enter
   2. Important in greenhouse effect to trap heat

B. Flat plate with tubes
   1. Metal or plastic
   2. Tubes filled with fluid
   3. Coated dark to absorb heat
   4. Circulation of fluid after heating

C. Insulation
   1. To prevent loss of heat
   2. Consists of plastic foam, fiber glass, or similar material

D. Wooden or metal weatherproof container

Objective 3

To assemble a solar collector when provided with the four essential parts

A. Construct wooden container
   1. Mark dimensions for frame and backing
   2. Cut 2 x 4 frame and 3/4-inch plywood backing
   3. Nail container together
   4. Notch upper edge for cover glass

B. Place insulation in container
   1. Cut 2″ styrofoam to size
   2. Set in container

C. Assemble flat plate
   1. Place flat plate on insulation
   2. Cut holes in frame for tubing
   3. Solder inlet and outlet tubes

D. Cover with clear glass
   1. Caulk edge of container
   2. Set glass in place
   3. Attach molding

iment with the order of the ideas until they are in a logical sequence. What you start with as the first point may later become the last one. Additional objectives that occur as you organize can also be added easily at this stage, while anything that apparently disrupts the sequence can also, just as easily, be eliminated or relocated. Later, during the actual storyboarding and scripting, you may find need for further changes, but now you have a simple, natural guideline to follow.

It should be reemphasized that at this stage you include as much as possible about the content—facts, examples, locations, and special reminders. It will be easier to eliminate some points later than to search for them if needed. While you are listing content, visual ideas may come to mind. Note them also on cards, or in computer memory.

VERIFY CONTENT

Once the content has been listed in relation to the objectives, you may consider this to be a **checkpoint.**

Although you may already have a team that includes subject consultants, it is a good idea to bring in one or more qualified persons to examine your work. This may be a colleague, a manager, or other individual who either initiated the project or has final approval for its acceptance. They may find that something important has been left out or may offer a comment that strikes a spark to give a direction you had not considered.

Also, there is real benefit in asking one or more members of the potential audience group to review your planning as you proceed. The perceptions that they may have for your topic and its organization may differ appreciably from yours. Involve them at this checkpoint and others that will be indicated. Their suggestions can be of real value.

Your content outline has been developed in the light of an idea, audience, and objectives. You are now ready to make decisions about the single medium or combination of media to carry the objectives and content. Before deciding on the media to use ask yourself such questions as these:

- Will the instructional product be for motivation, information, or instruction?
- Is sound (narration, lip synchronization) necessary, or can a silent medium (printed material or slides) with titles and directions be used?
- Is motion important or can still pictures convey the ideas and information?
- Is there to be study by individuals or is the emphasis to be on group use?
- Is color important or will black-and-white be satisfactory?
- Will there be any problems in keeping the materials up to date?
- Will I be able to overcome any technical problems in preparation, or do I know where to get help if necessary?
- Will there be problems of duplication, distribution, or storage of the completed materials?
- Will budget and time permit a good job?
- What problems may be encountered when using the materials (facilities, equipment, size of group, and any others)?

Now consider the various media available to you in terms of characteristics, advantages, disadvantages, and limitations. Then make choices to best serve your objectives.

REVIEW

What You Have Learned About Preliminary Planning:

1. This chapter introduces *four* steps in preliminary planning. What are they?
2. What type of thought is probably most important during the creative thinking process?
3. Relate the following elements of preliminary planning on the topic of *Dog Training* to the *four* steps above:
   a. to lead a dog when wearing a collar and leash
   b. stand at "heel" position; give command "sit"; pull on leash and press down on dog's hindquarters; release pressure and give praise
   c. acquire skill for teaching a dog proper behavior
   d. to direct a dog to "sit"
   e. teenagers who have received a young dog

4. What are the *three* broad purposes for which instructional media can be developed?
5. Relate the following items to each of the purposes in number 4:
   a. introducing a new topic to a class of students
   b. engaging a trainee in self-study activity
   c. designing a dramatic role-playing situation to raise interest
   d. providing background as orientation for new medical treatment
   e. requiring employees to review modified procedures periodically so they can function competently
   f. illustrating uses for equipment whose operation will be taught
6. What are *four* characteristics of a potential audience for which you might want information when starting your planning?
7. What are *three* parts of a properly stated objective?
8. Which verbs might you select when writing instructional objectives?
   _______ a. learn
   _______ b. assemble
   _______ c. explain
   _______ d. arrange
   _______ e. understand
   _______ f. become aware of
   _______ g. name
   _______ h. compare
   _______ i. predict
   _______ j. master
9. These questions relate to Table 4–1 on page 46.
   a. To which category of objectives does each example relate?
   b. Are any objectives not properly stated and how might they be reworded?
10. What are *three* roles that personnel should fill during the planning and production of instructional materials?
11. For what *two* reasons can it be useful to examine other materials that relate to a topic you are treating?
12. What suggestion is offered in the chapter as a flexible, visual way to organize the content information relating to the objectives?
13. Select a topic you would like to see developed into an instructional material and complete each of the following:
    a. Express an *idea* or *purpose* to be served.
    b. With what *audience* would you use the materials?
    c. Write the *objectives* you would want to serve.
    d. What are some of the *audience characteristics* you feel important to consider?
    e. With regard to the three *personnel roles* that must be filled, which role(s) would you fill? What are your qualifications?
    f. Would you ask for assistance in any of the three areas?
    g. How would you go about finding out whether any instructional materials have already been prepared on your topic?
    h. Develop a *content outline* for the topic.
    i. Relate the *content* to *objectives* on cards of different colors.

See answers on page 376.

REFERENCES

CREATIVITY

Bear, George G., and Callahan, Carolyn M. *On The Nose: Fostering Creativity, Problem Solving and Social Reasoning.* Mansfield Center, CT: Creative Learning Press, 1984.

Gardner, Howard. *Art, Mind, and Brain: A Cognitive Approach to Creativity.* New York: Basic Books, 1982.

Glassman, Edward. *Creativity Handbook: Shift Paradigms and Harvest Creative Thinking at Work.* Chapel Hill, NC: Leadership Consulting Services, 1991.

Olsen, Robert W. *The Art of Creative Thinking: A Practical Guide Including Exercises and Illustrations.* New York: Harper & Row, 1986.

Rawlinson, J. Geoffrey. *Creative Thinking and Brainstorming.* New York: Halsted Press, 1981.

Swansea, Charleen W. *Mindworks: How to Be a More Creative and Critical Thinker.* Spartanburg, SC: South Carolina ETV, 1990.

Von Oech, Roger. *A Whack on the Side of the Head: Creative Thinking.* New York: Warner Books, 1990.

OBJECTIVES

Bloom, Benjamin S.; Englehart, Max D.; Furst, Edward J. *A Taxonomy of Educational Objectives: Handbook I, the Cognitive Domain.* New York: Longman, 1977.

Gronlund, Norman. *How to Write Instructional Objectives.* New York: Macmillan, 1990.

Harrow, Anita J. *A Taxonomy of the Psychomotor Domain.* New York: Longman, 1979.

Kemp, Jerrold E., Morrison, Gary M. and Ross, Steven M. *Designing Effective Instruction and Learning.* Columbus, OH: Merrill, 1993.

Krathwohl, David R.; Bloom, Benjamin S.; and Masia, Bertram B. *A Taxonomy of Educational Objectives: Handbook II, the Affective Domain.* New York: Longman, 1984.

Mager, Robert F. *Preparing Instructional Objectives.* Belmont, CA: D. S. Lake, 1984.

———. *Goal Analysis.* Belmont, CA: D. S. Lake, 1984.

Martin, Barbara L., and Briggs, Leslie J. *The Affective and Cognitive Domains: Integration for Instruction and Research.* Englewood Cliffs, NJ: Educational Technology Publications, 1986.

C H A P T E R

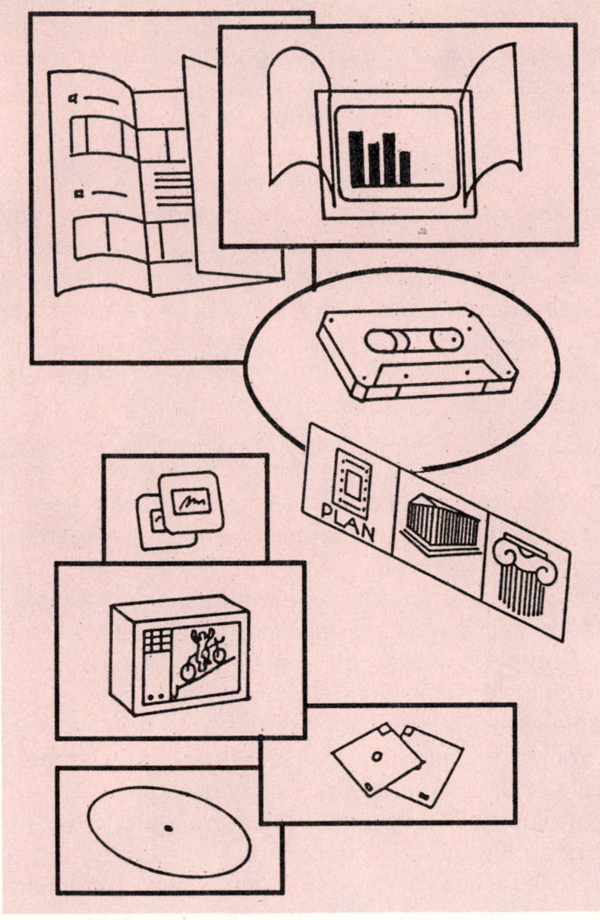

Printed Materials

Overhead Transparencies

Audio Recordings

Slide Series and Multi-Image Presentations

Video Recordings and Videodiscs

Reactive, Interactive, and Multimedia Learning Technologies

Summary

Selecting Media for Specific Needs

Notice the sequence that is being developed. First, consider your **audience** and establish **objectives;** then **organize the content** to fit your objectives. Now **select the specific instructional media** and other experiences to achieve your goals.

Why this sequence? Because instructional media are channels through which content stimuli are presented to the learner—stimuli to motivate, direct attention, inform, evoke a response, guide thinking, and instruct. Therefore, only after establishing **what it is that you wish to communicate** are you properly able to select the channel or medium through which the content will most likely elicit the proper response that serves the objective. Review the findings in Chapter 2 concerning the effects of media on learning.

If motion is inherent in the subject, consider a video recording; but if motion is not important, consider materials that demand simpler skills, less time, or less money, yet do the job equally well. To think further: A series of photographic prints with captions, which can easily be studied in detail at a work station, may be preferable to a slide/tape program and less difficult to make and use. Also, consider using combinations of

The Kinds of Instructional Media and Technologies

media to serve your purposes: A series of overhead transparencies that outline a process can be supplemented with a set of slides and the two used concurrently for effective instruction; or for motivational purposes, a dynamic three-screen multi-image presentation may be effective. If you recognize the benefits of having learners participate actively during learning, then some form of interactive learning media may be preferred.

On the other hand, for practice or perhaps because you have certain equipment available, you may wish to prepare a specific material, possibly a series of synchronized slides with tape, a video recording, or a computer-based interactive video program. If this is your starting point, select a subject and establish purposes that will use the medium to its best advantage.

Any one or more of a number of instructional media may be applicable to serve an objective and its content. The decision for selection may be based on your skills, equipment requirements, convenience, or cost. But each of the several types of instructional media makes certain unique contributions to improving communications and subsequent learning. All require careful planning before preparation—some more than others. When selecting the ones to serve your purposes, examine all of them and become aware of their special characteristics and specific contributions to communication and learning.

PRINTED MATERIALS

A number of materials, prepared on paper, may serve instructional or informational purposes. They are classified as printed media and consist of three groupings: (1) **learning aids,** (2) **training materials,** and (3) **informational materials.**

Learning aids comprise resources designed for use by individual learners or trainees, as a person follows precise directions for performing a task. A **guide sheet** or **job aid** may be a checklist of steps or procedures to follow when assembling, operating, or maintaining equipment. A more complete learning aid includes line drawings or photographs along with words for better explanation. These materials are often used at job sites or when the need for a handy reference arises after class instruction.

Training materials also relate directly to instruction. **Handout sheets** may be similar to guide sheets. They are usually more informational than procedural. A **study guide** is a set of pages that prepares and directs the learner through a unit or course of study. An **instructor's manual** provides guidance and assistance to the instructor when preparing for and delivering the instruction. It includes directions and information relating to each topic or unit to be taught.

The last group consists of items that serve informational and motivational purposes. **Brochures** are announcements about a program or service. **Newsletters** report on activities of an organization. They may range from a simple one-page typewritten sheet to a highly professional, multipage, full-color publication. An **annual report** can also be unpretentious or elaborate, with much attention being given to pictures, charts, and diagrams.

Printed materials can be designed and prepared easily and quickly using a personal computer with word-processing and graphics software programs. After page layouts are completed, a printer can reproduce the results. This system, called **desktop publishing,** is widely used for all forms of publications.

In addition to commonly used printed materials, like books and manuals, a **CD-ROM** (compact disk-read only memory) is a commercially prepared reference source for learning. A CD-ROM permits storage of a large amount of verbal and pictorial information on a small optical disk to be accessed directly with a reader, or controlled by a microcomputer.

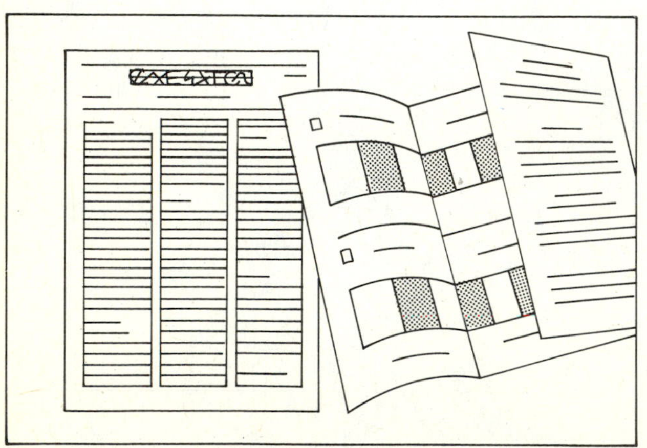

OVERHEAD TRANSPARENCIES

Transparencies are a popular form of instructional media. The use of large transparencies is supported by the development of small, lightweight, efficient **overhead projectors** combined with simple techniques for preparing transparencies and by the dramatic effectiveness of the medium.

The projector is used from near the front of the room, with the instructor standing or seated beside it, facing the group. The projection screen is at the front wall, and room light is at a moderate level. Transparencies are placed on the large stage of the projector, and the instructor may point to features and make marks on the film. The results appear immediately on the screen.

Progressive disclosure of areas on a transparency and adding **overlay** films to a base transparency are special features that make the use of this visual medium effective in many subject areas.

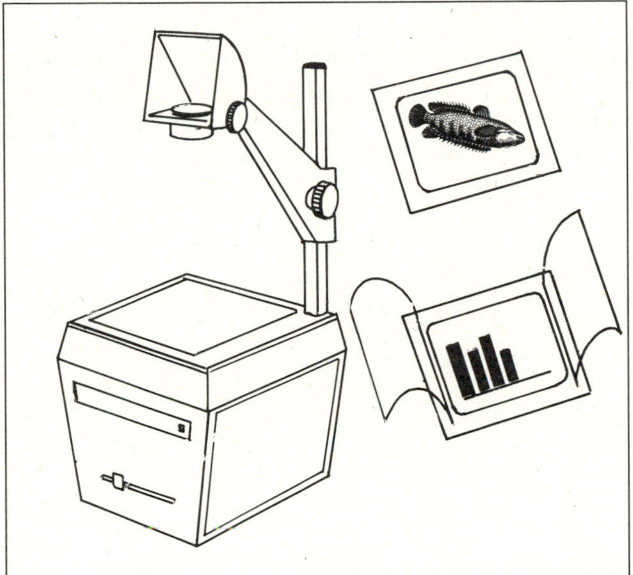

Overhead projectors are especially useful for instructing large groups on all levels. Investigate the range of techniques for preparing transparencies, and select the most appropriate ones for use. Some methods require no special equipment or training, while for others experience in photography and the graphic arts is necessary.

AUDIO RECORDINGS

Audio materials are an economical way to provide certain types of informational or instructional content. Recordings may be prepared for group or, more commonly now, for individual listening. Small, compact **audiocassette recorders** make the use of audio materials easy and convenient. Increasing attention is being given to recordings, either by themselves or in combination with printed materials.

Recordings can be used for many purposes. These include documenting or summarizing a speech, serving as a verbal record of interviews and meetings, recording role-playing situations for followup analysis, explaining procedures, and providing drill in various subjects.

For instructional purposes, recordings often are correlated with readings and worksheets in an **audio-notebook** format. When a recording is the central element of a complete instructional program that includes

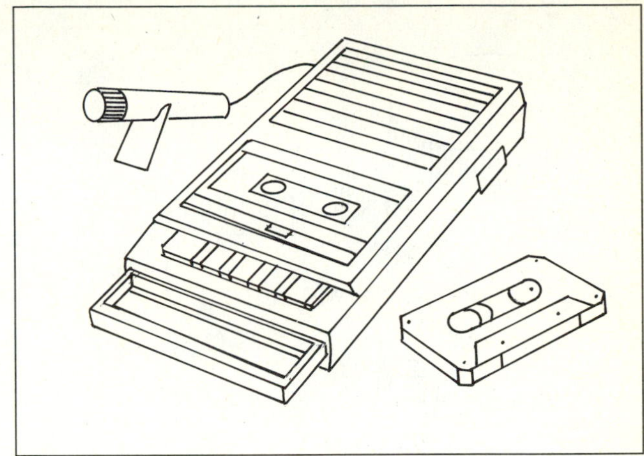

a variety of learning experiences, an **audio-tutorial** approach is being employed.

Care must be taken in preparing recordings so that they are of high quality and presented in an informal, conversational manner. Lengthy verbal lectures should be avoided. Equipment is available to speed up ordinary speech while maintaining its intelligibility. Tape duplicating equipment is necessary when multiple copies, often as cassettes, are required.

SLIDE SERIES AND MULTI-IMAGE PRESENTATIONS

Slides are a form of projected media that are easy to prepare; hence they frequently serve as the starting efforts in a media production program. Pictures are generally taken on reversal color film, which you can process and mount yourself or send to a film laboratory.

For many uses, any 35mm camera will make satisfactory slides. However, for filming some subjects and for close-up and copy work a 35mm single-lens reflex camera with an appropriate light-metering system and lens is recommended.

The standard slide dimensions are 2×2 inches. Since the slides are small, they are easily handled and stored. Their sequence can be changed, and slides can be selected from a series for special uses. Nevertheless, this flexibility entails some disadvantages. Slides can be placed out of order, be lost, and sometimes be accidentally projected upside down or backwards. Most of these disadvantages can be overcome by the use of trays that store the slides and hold them during use. Also, remotely controlled projectors permit a person making a presentation to change slides by pressing the control button. Tape recordings can be prepared to accompany slides and the latter can be shown automatically as the taped narration is heard. The availability of slide viewers also provides many op-

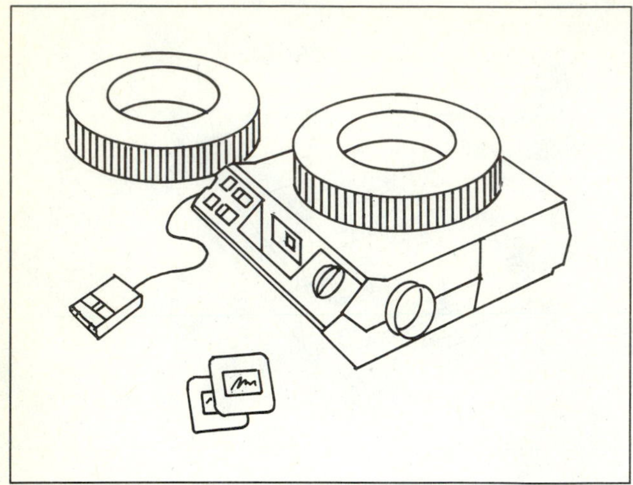

portunities for using slides for self-paced learning purposes.

Combinations of visual materials can be effective when used concurrently for specific purposes. If two or more pictures are projected **simultaneously** on one or more screens for group viewing, the term **multi-image** is used. The simplest form is to aim two slide projectors at the same screen and *dissolve* from the slide in one machine to one in the other projector, and so on.

Then there may be coordinated slide images on two or three screens with synchronized narration, music,

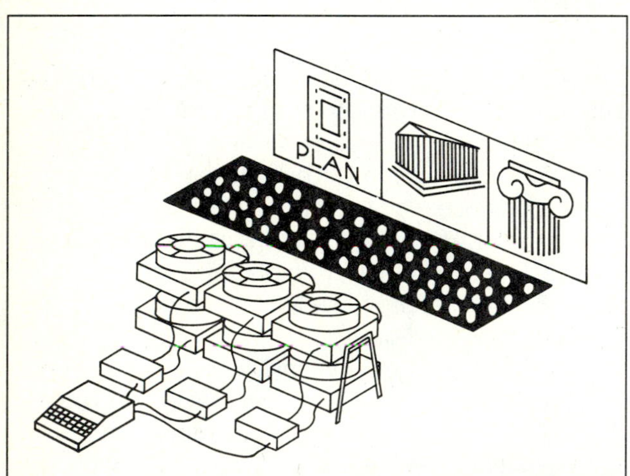

and even sound effects. Brief motion-picture sequences or overhead transparencies may be shown along with slides for special impact or to carry appropriate information. Side-by-side images permit comparisons, relationships, perspective views, or multiple examples.

Multi-image presentations often motivate by creating a high level of interest in a subject as well as by effectively communicating large amounts of information in a short time. They generally are reserved for very special events and should not be overused.

VIDEO RECORDINGS AND VIDEODISCS

Video should be considered for use whenever motion is inherent in a subject. Also, video can be more effective than other instructional media for relating one idea to another, for building a continuity of thought, and for creating a dramatic impact.

Video is a medium in which images are recorded electronically on magnetic tape along with sound. The essential equipment includes a video camera with microphone and a videocassette recorder. The immediacy of being able to see what has just been recorded is a key feature that differentiates video from the motion picture. Once recording is completed, the original tape can be used or edited electronically into final form.

Video cameras are compact and portable. Many products on the market consist of the camera and video recorder as a single, compact unit called a **camcorder.** With television monitors and large-screen video projectors, recordings can be shown to groups or used by individuals for self-pacing their own learning.

Because of the many advantages of video, it has replaced motion picture cameras and film in most nontheatrical uses. Therefore, almost no attention is given to the use of film for local media production.

A variety of media, including videotape recordings, slides, and audiotape recordings, can be transferred to a master **videodisc** from which copies can be prepared. Although the master disc is expensive to produce, depending on the number of copies needed for distribution, the disc unit cost is very reasonable. The videodisc can contain still pictures or motion sequences in any arrangement. Information at any location on the disc can quickly be located, and it is easy to move almost instantaneously from one spot to another. Videodiscs can be used with groups or by individuals.

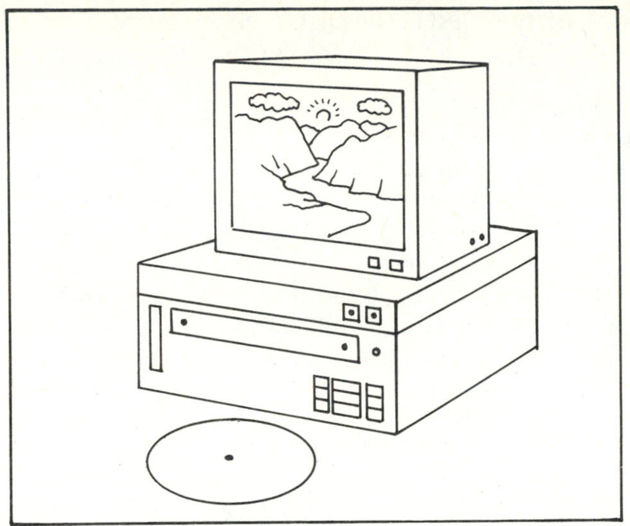

Because of the many significant features of videodiscs, they have become an increasingly important media format for instructional purposes.

REACTIVE, INTERACTIVE, AND MULTIMEDIA LEARNING TECHNOLOGIES

Instructional materials can be designed so that answering questions, selecting paths to follow, or other learner-directed activities are necessary as a person proceeds through a lesson using the materials. If a student moves through a program, responding periodically to questions and receiving feedback on answers, the materials would be classified as a **reactive medium** (see Cartier reference). Various forms of media can be designed or adapted for reactive uses. Print (the book!), an audio recording, or a slide/tape program, with an accompanying worksheet or a workbook, may incorporate reactive features.

When a computer becomes the instructional resource, then **interactive learning** may take place. Instead of a linear sequence, as takes place with reactive materials, through computer-based instruction information can be presented, then, based on the learner's response, the sequence that follows can be different for that individual.

Computer-based instructional materials are planned in much the same way as are other instructional materials. However, since CBI permits alternative instructional sequences, more sophisticated planning is required. The availability of powerful, low-cost microcomputers for CBI uses requires a basic understanding of computers and the available **software,** as computer programs are called. Special software packages, called **authoring systems** or **transaction shells,** can be used to guide the preparation of programs to serve particular needs.

Computers are also used to control other forms of instructional hardware. A videocassette player can be connected or **interfaced** with a computer. Then, based on an answer to a question or the selection of a video segment for viewing, the computer program directs the videocassette to play a specific section of the recording. Thus the student controls the pace and order of the instructional sequences.

When a computer and a videodisc, or other laser-based disks, are interfaced, the most sophisticated type of interactive learning can take place, as the laserdisk responds to computer commands almost instantaneously with random selection of text, data, graphics, sound, still or moving color images with synchronized sound, and animation. Such **multimedia** applications, along with features of **interactivity,** can utilize the strengths of individual resources in coordinated fashion to produce very dynamic learning. See the media selection procedure on the next page.

SUMMARY

The seven categories and types of instructional media and technologies—printed media, overhead transparencies, audio recordings, slide series, multi-image presentations, video, and reactive/interactive learning technologies—have various planning requirements and different degrees of complexity in their production and use. Some require close adherence to all steps in the planning process, while others can be developed with a less formal procedure. Refer to the appropriate sections in Part 4 of this book for guidance as you study the planning steps that follow in succeeding chapters.

SELECTING MEDIA FOR SPECIFIC NEEDS

In this chapter we have examined seven kinds of instructional media that can be produced locally. Table 5–1 compares the characteristics, advantages, and limitations of each type. These summaries may be enough to assist you in making decisions about appropriate media to serve your objectives and content.

However, many of us select media for use on the basis of what we are most comfortable with or what is conveniently available. The choice is a subjective one,

TABLE 5–1 SUMMARY OF CHARACTERISTICS OF INSTRUCTIONAL MEDIA AND TECHNOLOGIES

MEDIUM	ADVANTAGES	LIMITATIONS
Printed materials	1. Include common types of materials 2. Have wide variety of applications 3. Simple types are quick to prepare 4. Permit quality productions easily with desktop publishing	1. Sophisticated types are costly to prepare 2. Require suitable reading ability by user
Overhead transparencies	1. Can present information in systematic, developmental sequences 2. Use simple-to-operate projector with presentation rate controlled by instructor 3. Require only limited planning 4. Can be prepared by variety of simple, inexpensive methods 5. Particularly useful with large groups	1. Require special equipment, facilities, and skills for more advanced preparation methods 2. Are larger than slides used with other projectors
Audio recordings	1. Are easy to prepare with regular tape recorders 2. Can provide applications in most subject areas 3. Equipment for use is compact, portable, easy to operate 4. Can be used either as individual elements of instruction or in correlation with programed materials 5. Duplication is easy and economical	1. Have a tendency for overuse, as lecture or oral textbook reading 2. Rate of information flow is fixed 3. Used in small portable recorders with low fidelity
Slide series	1. Require only filming, with processing and mounting by film laboratory 2. Result in colorful, realistic reproductions of original subjects	1. Require some skill in photography 2. Require special equipment for close-up photography and copying

TABLE 5–1 (*CONTINUED*)

MEDIUM	ADVANTAGES	LIMITATIONS
	3. Can be prepared with any 35mm camera for most uses 4. Are easily revised and updated 5. Can be easily handled, stored, and rearranged for various uses 6. Have increased usefulness with tray storage and remote control by presenter 7. Can be combined with taped narration for greater effectiveness 8. May be adapted to group or to individual use	3. Can get out of sequence and be projected incorrectly if slides are handled individually
Multi-image presentations	1. Have excellent motivational capabilities by demanding attention and creating strong emotional impact on viewers 2. Can compress large amounts of information in short presentation time 3. Provide for more effective communications in certain situations than when only a single medium is used	1. Require additional equipment, complex setup, and careful coordination during planning, preparation, and use 2. Equipment and production costs are high for complex programs
Video recordings and videodisc	1. Are particularly useful in describing motion, showing relationships, and giving impact to topic 2. Allow instant replay of video recording 3. Videotape is reusable 4. Easy to record lip sync on videotape 5. May include special recording techniques (animation, time-lapse) 6. Can combine still and motion on videodisc 7. Allow instant access to individual frames on videodisc	1. Cost is high for studio production equipment 2. Resolution is limited for fine detail close-ups 3. Video format types are incompatible 4. Mastering costs are high for videodisc
Interactive and reactive learning technologies	1. Involve students actively in learning 2. Apply many principles of learning 3. Allow conventional media forms to be adapted for reactive uses 4. Serve needs of learner with multiple paths in sophisticated, interactive forms	1. Require detailed, careful planning 2. May require special interface equipment 3. Are commonly used by one or several persons at one time 4. Require special equipment and services for complex applications

often with little consideration to objective criteria for selection. Can more specific guidelines be established that could offer somewhat closer relationships between the various media and instructional requirements?

This question has been examined by various educational researchers. Their general conclusion is that most media can perform most informational and instructional functions, while no single medium is likely to have properties that make it best for all purposes.

We should not leave the matter of media selection to those who make casual choices, nor can we wait patiently for the results of future research. We need some basis for making logical, educated guesses that will lead to practical media decisions. Fortunately, there are some efforts in this direction.

Media Attributes

The most useful results are derived from a consideration of what Levie and Dickie term **media attributes,** also called **attributes of media.** These are the capabilities of a medium to exhibit such characteristics as motion and color, and include sound. The important media attributes are the following:

- pictorial representation—photographic or graphic
- factor of size—nonprojected or projected
- factor of color—black-and-white or full color
- factor of movement—still, motion, or a combination of the two
- factor of language—printed words or oral sound
- sound-picture relationship—silent picture or picture with sound
- factor of arrangement—visuals in linear order, or in variable order by user choice

In terms of the objectives and subject content of your topic, ask yourself questions such as these:

- Should enlarged photographs of real subjects be shown?
- Is motion important?
- Is the ability to randomly vary the order of visuals important as the learner studies the topic?

Decide for yourself which media attributes are necessary. This becomes the basis for media selection.

This approach to media selection has been attempted by some developers. Tosti and Ball identified six "dimensions of presentation" and broadly related media decisions to them; Reiser and Gagné use objectives, domains of learning, instructional setting, and reading ability of learners as the bases for selecting media. Flow diagrams with questions lead to media decisions. Bretz employs a similar technique as questions point the way through levels, terminating in a particular medium or group of related media. A more expansive version of this method has been designed by Reynolds and Anderson.

Selection Procedure

A similar practical approach to media selection can start with answers to three general questions:

1. Which teaching-learning pattern (page 6)—presentation, self-paced learning, or small-group interaction—is selected or is most appropriate for the objective and the nature of the learner group?
2. Which category of learning experiences—realistic experiences, verbal or printed word abstractions, or sensory media experience—is most suitable for the objective and instructional activity in terms of the selected teaching-learning pattern?
3. If sensory experience is indicated or selected, which attributes of media are necessary or desirable?

Upon answering the three questions, refer to the appropriate media selection diagram (Diagrams A, B, and C in Figure 5.1) on page 59. Each diagram is a sequence chart for a teaching-learning pattern. Questions that match media attributes to learning objective needs are answered at various levels and lead to media choices.

Sometimes the decision reaches a group of related media, such as motion pictures. Each motion-picture form—for example, videotape or videodisc—would provide equally effective instruction for an individual. The choice, then, is based on the most practical form to use, considering the relative merits of a number of empirical factors, such as those shown in Table 5–2 on page 60.

Use this table as a worksheet by rating each alternative medium on the appropriate criteria. Some media will rate high on one criterion, moderate on a second, and possibly low on a third. Thus, you will see how each medium rates in total. By following this procedure, you will have an objective basis on which to make the final media decision.

Finally, media decisions should be made not for a gross entity of learning as large as a *topic,* but rather for groups of objectives that collectively make up the topic. Within a given topic, carefully designed combinations of media, in which each performs a particular function based on its attributes and reinforces the learning effects of the others, may be required to achieve the kind of communication or instruction for a group or individual that is most effective.

As an example for media selection, let us recall the unit on solar energy from Chapter 4. The objectives on

MEDIA SELECTION DIAGRAMS

Based on instructional objectives and subject content, what attributes are required in the resources?

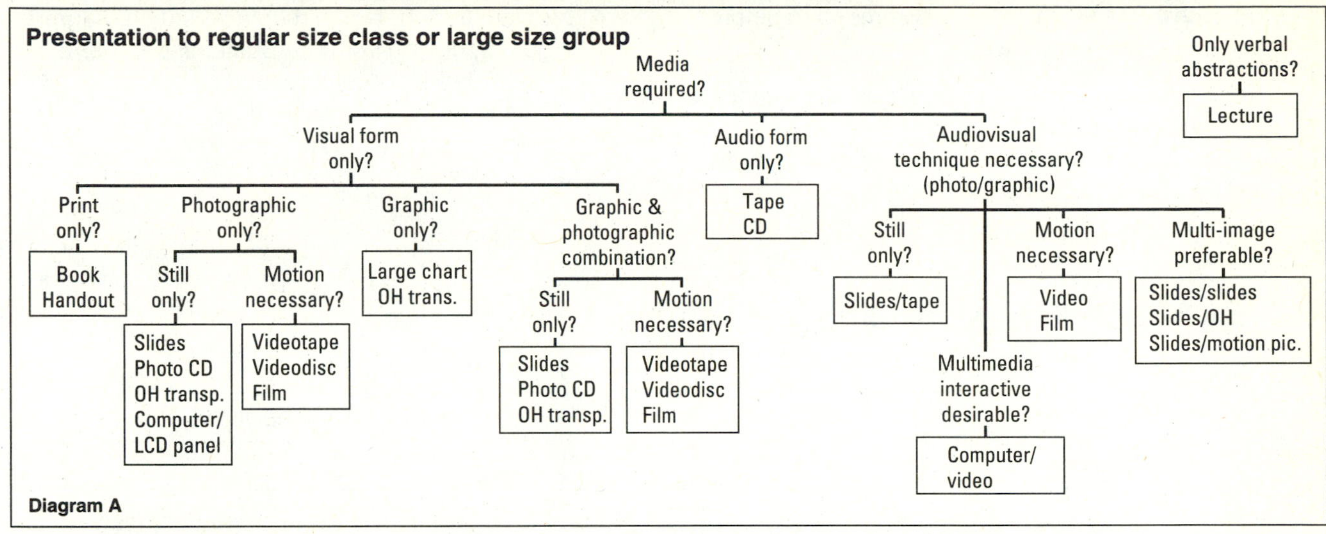

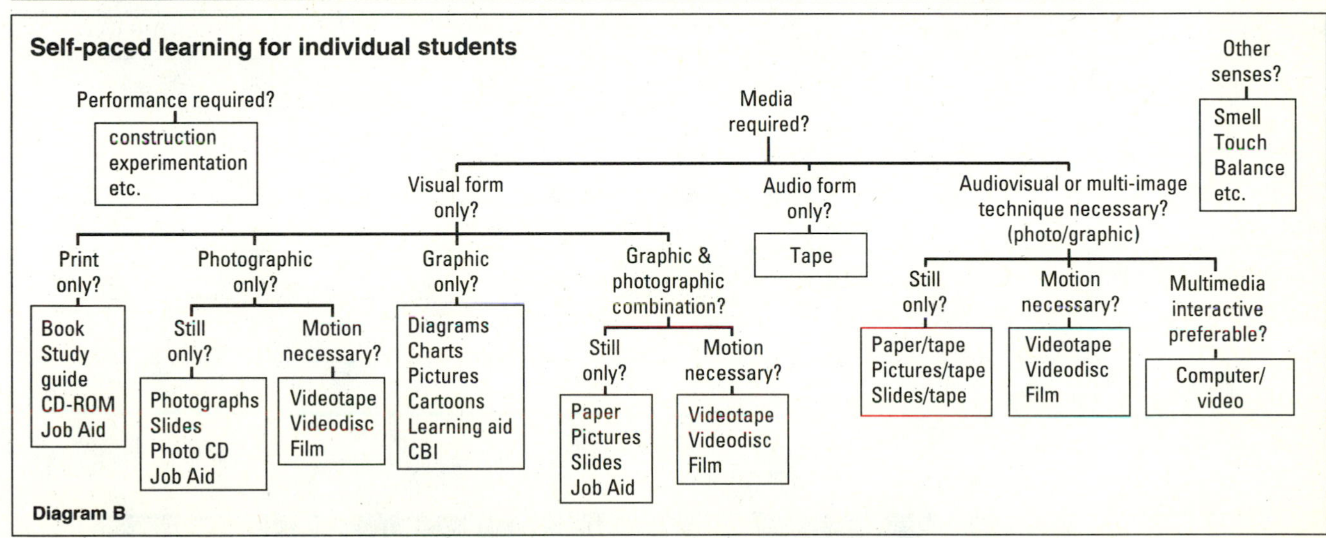

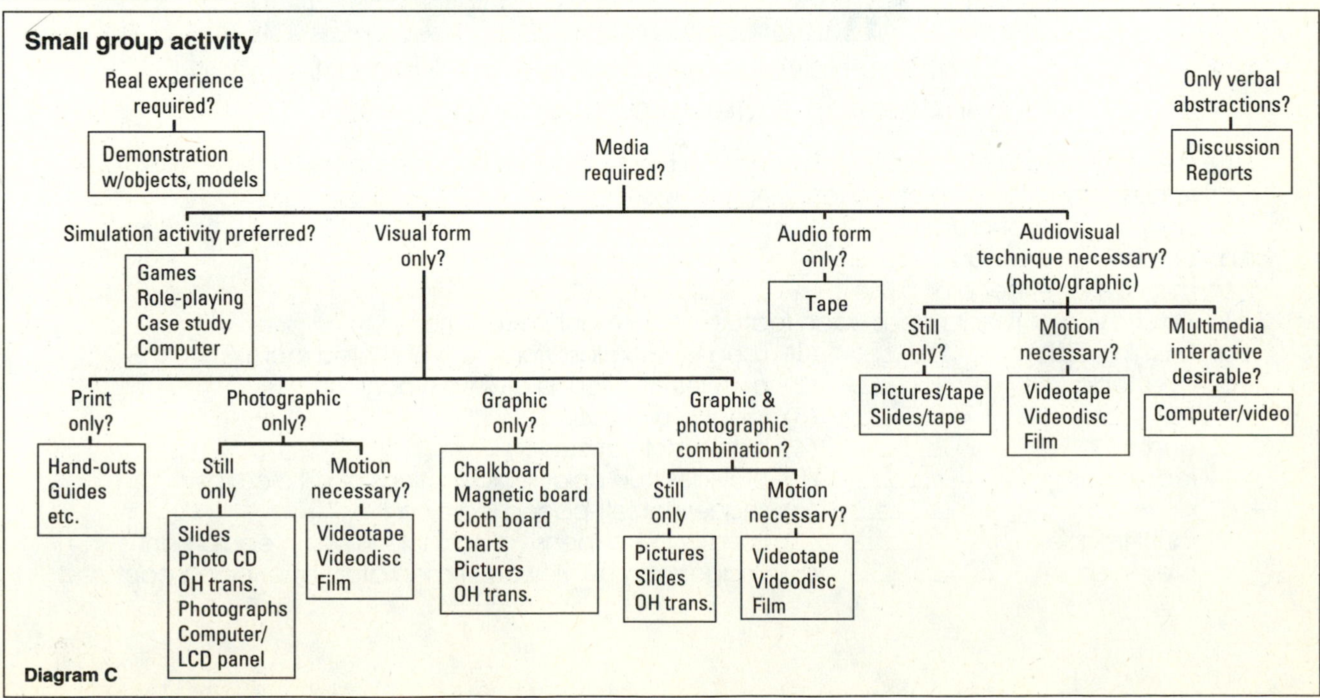

page 44 relate to collecting solar energy. The content in terms of the objectives is listed on page 47. Applying the approach to media selection recommended before, we reach a decision as follows:

1. Teaching-learning pattern—self-paced learning by learners (page 6)
2. Learning experiences—media required for visualizing complex concepts
3. Attributes of media—graphic and photographic still pictures in color with sound
4. Media category—from media selection diagram, Figure 2; choice from box containing paper/tape, pictures/tape, slides/tape, and so on
5. Final media choice—comparing costs and other factors for alternatives in Table 5–2; final choice is tape/slides

TABLE 5–2 FINAL MEDIA CHOICE WITHIN A CATEGORY

	ALTERNATE MATERIALS	
CRITERIA	VIDEOTAPE	VIDEODISC
Commercially Available		
Preparation Costs		
Reproduction Costs		
Time to Prepare		
Skills, Services Required		
Equipment Available		
Maintenance, Storage		
Student Preference		
Instructor Preference		

REVIEW

What You Have Learned About the Kinds of Instructional Media and Technologies:

1. Of the seven types of instructional media and technologies described in this chapter, which ones best apply to each of the following categories?
   a. primarily for group use
   b. primarily for individual use
   c. may be for either *a* or *b* use

2. To which type of media does each feature on the right *best* relate?

a. learning aid	______	(1) used with a class from front of lighted room
b. overhead	______	(2) pictures and sound always synchronized
transparencies	______	(3) prepared on paper
c. audio	______	(4) highly motivational
recordings	______	(5) provides true color reproductions of still pictures
d. slides	______	(6) sequential self-paced learning
e. multi-image	______	(7) used with inexpensive, portable listening equipment
presentation	______	(8) images can be viewed immediately after being captured

f. video recordings
g. videodisc
h. reactive learning media
i. interactive learning media

_______ (9) shows information sequentially on large sheets of film
_______ (10) quick reference for explaining procedures
_______ (11) provides variable paths for different learners
_______ (12) often combined with audio recording
_______ (13) easily correlated for use with printed material
_______ (14) prepared with a 35mm camera
_______ (15) most directly applies learning principles of participation, reinforcement, and feedback
_______ (16) used with subjects having movement
_______ (17) requires more equipment for use than other media
_______ (18) combines still and motion images that can be rapidly accessed.

3. Which of the following "attributes" of media are helpful in the selection process?
_______ a. black-and-white or color
_______ b. still or motion
_______ c. instructor or student preference
_______ d. photographic or graphic
_______ e. self-prepare or purchase
_______ f. silent or sound
_______ g. symbolic/verbal or real

4. Refer to the media selection diagrams (A, B, and C in Figure 5.1) on page 59. For each situation indicate (1) the questions you would ask in sequence, leading to a decision, and (2) your media choice.
a. presentation to a group—visual diagram of an industrial-flow process with segments shown sequentially
b. self-paced learning—still color pictures with narration of architectural styles for 2000 learners
c. self-paced learning—simulated classroom situations structured with decision points, alternative choices, and resulting actions to provide learner practice
d. small-group interaction—report on community recreational facilities, showing activities and interviewing individuals
e. presentation to a group—services of a major charity organization for motivating interest at large fund-raising meetings
f. self-paced learning—procedures for handling new-type savings accounts for bank employees (to be studied during free time or at home)

5. Which factors are useful for making a final media decision?
_______ a. purchase cost
_______ b. preparation time
_______ c. instructor preference
_______ d. length of material
_______ e. equipment maintenance requirements
_______ f. handling materials by students
_______ g. proven to be a better way of learning

6. In question 13 following Chapter 4 on page 49, you were asked to select a topic and start to plan the preparation of instructional media. Now, what media form would you choose? What are the objective reasons for this choice?

See answers on page 376.

REFERENCES

INSTRUCTIONAL MEDIA

Heinich, Robert; Molenda, Michael; and Russell, James D. *Instructional Media: The New Technologies of Instruction.* New York: Wiley, 1993.

Power On! New Tools for Teaching and Learning. Washington, DC: U.S. Congress, Office of Technology Assessment (U.S. Government Printing Office), 1988.

SELECTING MEDIA

Bretz, Rudy. *A Taxonomy of Communications Media.* Englewood Cliffs, NJ: Educational Technology Publications, 1971.

Cartier, Francis. "Words About Media Selection." *Performance and Instruction* 31, (January 1992):9–12.

Levie, W. Howard, and Dickie, Kenneth E. "The Analysis and Application of Media." In *Second Handbook of Research on Teaching.* Robert M. W. Travers, ed. Chicago: Rand McNally, 1973, pp. 858–882.

Reiser, Robert A., and Gagné, Robert M. *Selecting Media for Instruction.* Englewood Cliffs, NJ: Educational Technology Publications, 1983.

Reynolds, Angus and Anderson, Ronald H. *Selecting and Developing Media for Instruction.* Cincinnati: Van Nostrand Reinhold, 1992.

Tosti, Donald T., and Ball, John R. "A Behavioral Approach to Instructional Design and Media Selection." *AV Communications Review* 17 (Spring 1969):5–25.

C H A P T E R

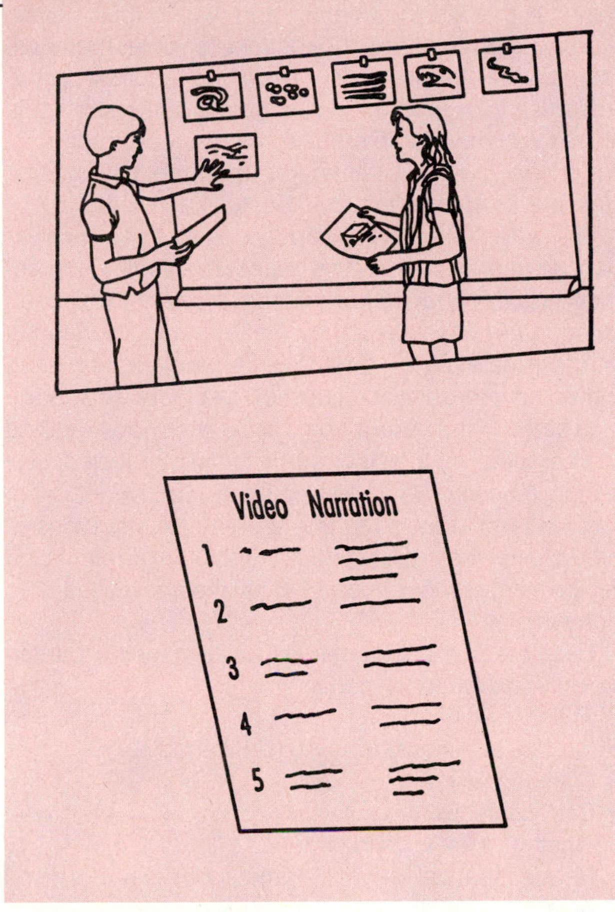

PLAN FOR PARTICIPATION

WRITE THE TREATMENT

MAKE A STORYBOARD

DEVELOP THE SCRIPT

CONSIDER THE LENGTH

PREPARE THE SPECIFICATIONS

You have your content organized in terms of the audience and objectives. You are aware of the kinds of instructional materials you may consider for preparation, their characteristics and particular contributions, advantages, and limitations. And you have some empirical procedures for materials selection. In putting all these together you must decide which materials can best communicate the content of specific objectives. Your plans may require that a single medium (video, slides, transparencies, or such) carry your message. Or, in the design approach, a number of media may be integrated, each serving one or more specific objectives and content.

Examine the cards you prepared listing objectives and content. Then decide on the medium or media to use. If more than a single medium is to be employed, make cards for each one and organize the objective and content cards with the appropriate medium cards. This plan will give you a visual reference to the flow and relationship of elements within the total topic. Now, start planning for production of your instructional materials.

There is no single best manner in which the details of the content outline can be transformed into meaningful and related pictures and words. Two approaches have been established through experience, but they are by

Designing Instructional Materials

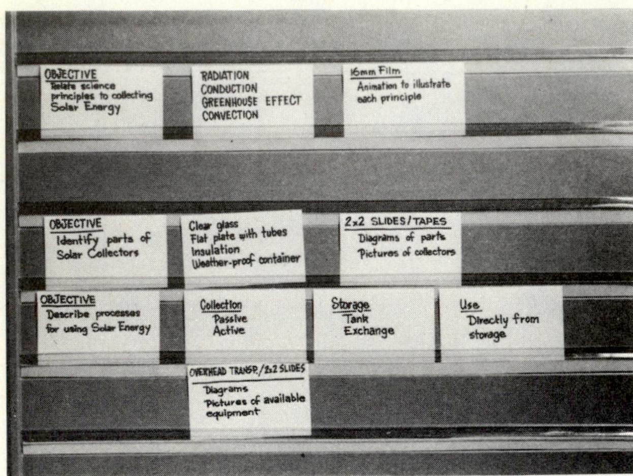

no means the only sound ones. First, many successful materials carry an audience from the known to the unknown; they start with things familiar to the audience (perhaps by reviewing the present level of understanding) and then lead to as many new facts and new relationships as the material is meant to achieve. Second, many materials are successfully built around three divisions—the introduction, which motivates and captures the attention of the audience; the developmental stage, which contains most of the content and in effect tells the story (or involves the viewers in active participation); and, finally, the ending, which may apply, summarize, or review the ideas presented and suggest further activity.

Recall from Chapter 3 that there is evidence from research to show that detailed introductions and summaries in films, and probably in other instructional media, do not add much to effectiveness. This finding may be particularly true of a series of integrated materials, each of which serves a specific objective or a related series of objectives. The brief video recording illustrating a process and the short audio recording containing explanatory information for a topic are examples of such integrated materials. A printed study guide or an instructional module can introduce, relate, summarize, and direct student participation. The material itself contains just the essential facts, explanations, demonstrations, and so on, without any embellishments.

PLAN FOR PARTICIPATION

A number of investigations of the effectiveness of instructional media designed for instruction have shown the value of having the learner participate in some way during, or immediately after, studying the material. These experiments, without reservation, have proven that *active participation definitely helps learning.* But most producers of commercial instructional media continue to ignore this principle. Video recordings, films, filmstrips, and sets of transparencies are designed primarily to present information and, within themselves, provide no opportunity or directions for other than passive activity—mentally or mechanically following the presentation. Hopefully, the treatment of the subject is so motivational that interest is maintained throughout. But often it is not. It is then left up to the instructor or presenter to plan for pre- and postuse activities.

The way to create participation is to make involvement an inherent part of the material itself. The expressions *reactive* and *interactive* learning were introduced on page 55. Essentially they mean that while working with the material, a student is frequently directed to make a choice, answer a question, or otherwise engage in an activity. The purpose is to ascertain understanding and competency to use or apply the information or skill being presented. The simpler form, reactive learning, can easily be applied to the design of many types of instructional materials. (See page 273 for participation design suggestions used with interactive learning technologies.)

Here are some suggestions for developing participation in instructional media:

- Include questions, requiring an immediate written or oral response.
- Direct other written activity (explain, summarize, give other examples, and so forth).
- Require that selection, judgment, or other decisions be made from among things shown or heard.
- Require performance related to the activity or skill shown or heard.

These participation techniques often require a break in the presentation—having the student stop the projector or recorder to do something, or promoting immediate activity after studying a section of the material.

In addition, be sure to plan for evaluation of the participation results and provide *feedback* to the student indicating the correct reply or a comparison of measurement for the level of accomplishment.

If materials are designed for motivation or information rather than for instruction (as described on page 42), you still want a response. Possibly, it is acceptance as expressed by applause, or an action to follow the viewing. Whatever the purpose, plan for the desired outcome at this time.

WRITE THE TREATMENT

Carefully examine the example of a content outline (page 47) and form an idea of how you might develop the generalizations visually. This is called a **treatment** or **vehicle.** It is a descriptive synopsis of how the content of the proposed instructional materials can be organized and presented. A treatment is similar to a verbal summary in which you describe to someone the story line of a book you have read. This provides a mental visual description of how the content is handled.

There are various formats a treatment might take. The most common is a straightforward informational presentation, known as **expository.** Then there may be an emotional form—**dramatic** or **personal involvement.** See the examples that follow on page 66.

Another treatment approach involves the use of a **vehicle** to carry the story line or message to the viewer. Some scriptwriters create an interesting character with the idea that the viewer would receive the message through the eyes of this fictitious character. Several different vehicles could be used to achieve the same results for a given topic, audience, and objectives.

Using the example of solar energy once more (page 44), one vehicle may be a cartoon character named "Solarwoman." Solarwoman becomes the vehicle that the scriptwriter uses to take the viewer through the experiences necessary to achieve the desired learning. Another writer might select a completely different vehicle, like a "consulting engineer" who visits a solar energy site. As the engineer describes an analysis, the viewer is informed about the subject. In this case, the cartoon approach might be a better treatment for a younger audience, while the consulting engineer is better suited for a more mature audience.

You might develop two or more treatments that handle the subject in different ways. Obtain reactions from other persons and make your own judgment of the value of one treatment approach over another.

Commercial television has a great impact on the "visual literacy" of most people. We have learned to accept fast pacing of commercials and dramatic programs. The sophistication that results from these experiences is an inevitable comparison of your material with other forms of visualized entertainment and advertising. People have been conditioned to expect a strong opening that captures their attention. This then requires that many instructional materials be planned to move briskly both in content treatment and visual techniques.

Writing the treatment is an important step, since it causes you to think through your presentation in terms of the project objectives and to put it in a sequential, organized form that you and others can follow easily. The treatment provides the framework for the planning elements that follow.

While deciding how to treat or approach the subject (or later, when the script is being written), the idea of including some already available sequences may come to mind. Historical and political subjects, wildlife scenes, space exploration, and underwater footage are some of the areas found in stock slide, film, or videotape collections. Stock visual materials can be purchased from many sources. See the list on page 73.

MAKE A STORYBOARD

As you develop your story, *try to visualize the situations you are describing.* Remember, you are preparing audiovisual material—with the emphasis on the word *visual.* Most people normally think in words, but now you may have to reorient yourself to learn to think in pictures—not in vague general pictures but in specific visual representations of real situations. Visualization can be aided by making simple sketches, printing graphic images generated with a computer (page 119), or by taking photographs that show the treatment of each element or sequence. (Polaroid film is ideal for this purpose.) These sketches or pictures, along with narration notes, become the **storyboard.**

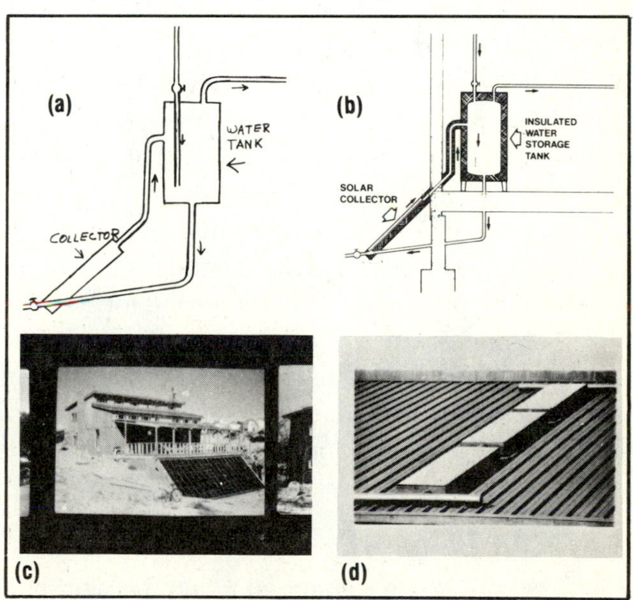

(a) Simple sketch, (b) Detailed sketch, (c) 35mm contact print (or 2 × 2 slide), (d) Self-processing film print

Put the storyboard sketches or pictures on cards, as was suggested for the objectives and content on page 45. Use 3 × 5 or 4 × 6 inch cards, or 8½ × 11 inch paper. These proportions approximate the format of most visual materials, the pictures being wider than they are high. Use a card with an area blocked off for the visual and space for narration notes or production comments. (See sample for storyboard cards inside the back cover of this book. Duplicate the page for use.)

Every sequence should be represented by one or more cards. Include separate cards for possible titles,

EXAMPLE: Treatment

Expository Treatment

About half of the heat and light generated by the sun reaches the earth and can be used if collected. A solar collector consists of a box covered with glass or plastic. Inside the box are tubes filled with fluid and attached to a dark-colored flat plate. Insulation prevents the loss of heat. Collectors can be placed on the roof of a new or older house, on a wall, or even on the ground. Solar collectors can be used efficiently for collecting heat in northern latitudes and at high elevations. Their size should be about 100 square feet for heating water and from 1/3 to 1/2 the floor area of the house for space heating. The collectors are most beneficial when facing south and tilted to an angle equal to the latitude of the location plus 15 degrees. In addition to house and indoor water heating, solar collectors are used to heat swimming pool water.

Personal Involvement Treatment

How much energy generated by the sun is available for use to meet the growing energy shortage? How would you go about capturing this energy? Two students decided to investigate this problem. They visited a local company that builds and installs solar collectors. They were shown what a collector looks like and its essential parts. On a tour to see how collectors were being used, they saw them on the roofs of new and older houses, on an apartment building wall, on the ground adjacent to a house; one was being used to heat water for a swimming pool. They learned these facts about installing collectors: (1) the collector should be placed facing south for gathering the most sunlight; (2) the collector should be tilted according to the degrees of latitude for the location plus 15 degrees; and (3) the collectors should cover 1/3 to 1/2 of the floor area of the house for space heating and should be about 100 square feet in size for heating water. From the literature they received they were able to design a solar collector of their own using the four main parts. The students next planned to build a collector to heat water.

Dramatic Treatment

What's going to happen when the world's oil supply runs out or when natural gas is no longer available? One source of energy that must get more attention is the sun. Forty-seven percent of the sun's energy reaches the earth and can be collected and used. Anyone can make use of it *now.* Solar collectors are placed on the roofs of new or even older buildings, on the ground near a house, or on the side wall of a building. Collectors covering 1/3 to 1/2 of the floor area of a house are necessary for space heating and about 100 square feet in size for heating water. The greatest amount of the sun's energy is gathered when the collector faces south and is tilted the number of degrees of latitude for the location plus 15 degrees. By applying this information, collectors can be efficient devices to gather heat in northern latitudes and at high elevations. When the four main parts of a solar collector are properly assembled and installed in sufficient numbers, each household has the potential, in part, for serving its own energy needs, which in turn helps to reduce the energy problem for the country.

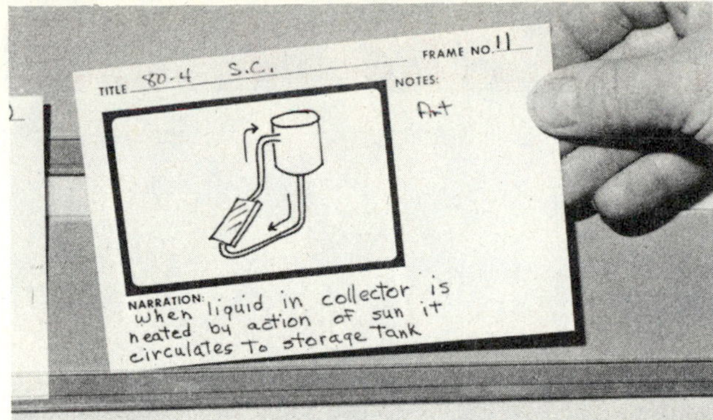

questions, and special directions (such as indications for learner participation). It may not be necessary to make a card for all anticipated scenes. The details, like an overall picture of a subject followed by a close-up of detail within the subject, will be handled in the script that follows.

Here is an example of a partial storyboard for *Collecting Solar Energy.*

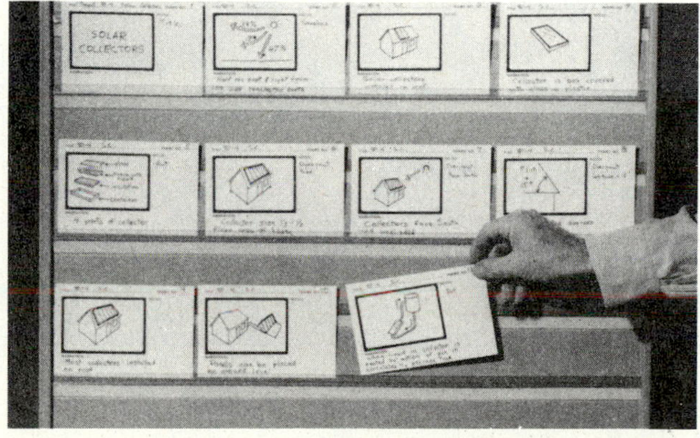

The storyboard is another important **checkpoint** stage in the design of your instructional material. The first was when the content outline (page 48) was completed. Display the storyboard; make it easy to examine. (For suggestions on preparing and using a **planning board** for displaying storyboard cards, see Chapter 11 in Kemp and others.)

Reactions and suggestions from those involved in the project or from other interested and qualified persons are valuable at this point. These people may offer assistance by evaluating the way you visualize your ideas and the continuity of your treatment. Often people studying the displayed storyboard point out things that have been missed or sequences that need reorganization. Rearranging pictures and adding new ones are easy tasks when the storyboard is prepared on cards.

Also, consider showing the storyboard to 2–3 members of the potential audience group for their reactions and suggestions.

DEVELOP THE SCRIPT

Once the treatment and the storyboard continuity are satisfactorily organized, you are ready to write your detailed blueprint, the **script.** This script becomes the map that gives definite directions for your picture taking, artwork, audio recording, or video recording and filming. The script is a picture-by-picture description with accompanying narration and audio effects. As was indicated for storyboarding, first plan what will be seen, then what will be said or otherwise heard.

One procedure is to prepare the script in **block format.** The visual description of a scene is written from margin to margin across the page, often typed in capital letters. The narration and indications for music and sound effects are shown in narrow columns centered below the visual. Some people prefer this format as the eye moves down the page, easily noting the continuous flow of action. (See the example on page 68.)

A more widely used format is the **two-column script** design. Camera positions and picture descriptions are placed on the left half of the page and narration on the right, opposite the appropriate scene description. (See the example on page 69.)

The placement of the camera for each picture, with respect to the subject, should be indicated. If the subject is to be at a distance from the camera the picture is a **long shot** (LS); if the camera covers the subject and nothing more, a **medium shot** (MS); while a **close-up** (CU) brings the camera in to concentrate on a feature of the subject. Whether the scene is to be photographed from a **high-angle** or a **low-angle,** or **subjective** position (from the subject's viewpoint, as over the shoulder) can also be specified. (For further information on camera positions, see page 97).

At this stage the **narration,** or verbal comments made to accompany the visuals, need not be stated in final, detailed form. It is sufficient to write narration ideas, or brief statements, that can be refined later. Only when an explanation requires that a videotaped scene be of a specific length must the narration be written carefully and in final form at this point.

Use script scene numbers for reference during picture-taking. The numbers help you to keep track when shooting out of sequence order.

Use Computer Software

Because a script must frequently be revised or completely restructured, a word processor can be a real time saver. If the two-column script is used, then the computer program must retain the spatial relationship between the visual and audio components of a scene. This means that when one part is modified, the two components adjust to match across the page.

The script is typed on the keyboard and appears on the display screen. At the same time, the script is held

EXAMPLE: A Block Format Script

Music up

FADE-IN

1. Title: RECONSTITUTING A DRY DRUG

DISSOLVE

2. Produced by Instructional Media Productions

DISSOLVE

3. Still Picture: SOLVENT BEING ADDED TO A VIAL
   Overprint: While viewing this tape have module #12 at hand

Music out

4. MS: NURSE REFERS TO ROUTE SHEET AND PICKS UP VIAL

Narration

Always compare route ordered in medication order form with route for which medication may be used on label of vial.

5. CU: LABEL OF VIAL
   While reading a label, check expiration date on the vial.
6. ECU: LABEL WITH INFORMATION ON RECONSTITUTING
   Amount and type of solvent to be used may be indicated on the label. If it is not . . .
7. MS: NURSE TAKES REFERENCE BOOK FROM SHELF
   Refer to the pharmaceutical literature for reconstituting information.
8. CU: SECTION OF PAGE WITH INFORMATION
9. MS: NURSE SELECTS BOTTLE OF SOLVENT FROM SHELF
   Locate the correct solvent (and so on . . .).

in the computer memory. A copy can be put on paper through an attached printer. The script should be stored on a disk and, when necessary, recalled to the screen for rewriting, making deletions, and repositioning sections. After these changes are made, a new copy can be printed. Much time spent on typing can be saved. See the references on page 73 for scriptwriting word-processing program sources.

Sometimes a group of persons works together on production planning, or a script is presented to a committee for review. In these cases, the computer can be connected to a video projector or to an LCD (liquid crystal display—see page 206) panel placed on an overhead projector. The script is projected onto a screen for all to see. (The previously developed content outline and treatment may be handled in this way also.) Changes can be quickly made, seen on the screen, and when agreement is reached, approved copies printed out. This use of technology can make planning sessions very productive and highly efficient.

Suggestions When Scripting

As you write the treatment and the script, keep in mind these suggestions:

- Open by capturing the attention of the audience with a dramatic sequence, by illustrating the importance of the topic to the viewer, by carefully using music and other sounds.
- Plan for variety in visuals (long shots, close-ups, low-angle shots) and a frequent change of pace as the narration proceeds.
- Realize that few words, or no narration or other sound, can satisfactorily carry meaning in some scenes.
- Use easily understood words and phrases.
- Introduce a technical term by showing it as an "overprint" on the screen, in context with a scene it represents.
- Do not belabor the message being presented; illustrate and concisely explain a concept, then move on.

EXAMPLE: A Two-Column Script

COLLECTING SOLAR ENERGY

Visuals	Narration Ideas
1. Title: Solar Collectors	Refer to objectives in workbook.
2. Art: Energy from sun; arrow with 34%	Light and heat energy from sun; 34% reflected back into space.
3. Art: Add arrow with 19%	19% remains in atmosphere.
4. Art: Add arrow with 47%	47% reaches the earth's surface and may be captured for use.
5. MS: Rooftop with solar collectors	Device used is a solar collector; can be placed on rooftop of new building
6. MS: Older building with collectors	or installed on older buildings.
7. LS: Collector on ground beside house	Collector panels can be on the ground
8. LS: Apartment building with collectors on wall	or attached to walls of a building.
9. LS: House with snow on rooftop collectors	Solar energy can be collected in northern latitudes and at high elevation.
10. CU: Worksheet, Part A Overprint: Stop the tape	Complete worksheet, Part A.
11. CU: Section of collector	A collector is like a box.
12. Art: Exploded view showing parts of collector with labels	It has four parts: clear glass or plastic top; tubes filled with fluid attached to a dark, coated plate; insulation; and a waterproof container.
13. LS: House with collectors on roof. Overprint: Face south	Collectors should face south and be unshaded.
14. MS: Another house with collectors. Overprint: 1/3 to 1/2 floor area; 100 square feet	For space heating, size of collector should be one-third to one-half of the floor area of house. About 100 square feet are needed for heating water.
15. MS: Another house with collectors. Overprint: Degrees latitude plus 15	For efficiency, collector tilted up according to degrees of latitude at location plus 15.
16. CU: Collector on roof for swimming pool	A major use of inexpensive collectors is
17. MS: House and swimming pool	to heat swimming pools.
18. CU: Worksheet, Part B	Complete worksheet, Part B.

- In visualizing a procedure, show common errors in action, but *always* end with the proper performance.
- Humor and unusual situations will create and maintain interest.
- Consider the value of music as a complement to narration (see page 158 for reasons to include music in a script).
- Explain the importance, to the viewer, of the information being presented.
- Recognize that there may be a limitation to the amount of detailed information that can be communicated through the media; consider accompanying materials to carry details.

Narration is important not only for the part it plays in explaining details as the *audio* of audiovisual; it also may call attention to relationships and indicate emphasis that should be given in some pictures (center of attention or camera position) when filming. A unity of words and pictures is required to communicate information effectively.

Be alert to problems that may arise with narration. If it is not related closely to the visual so as to reinforce the visual, the narration may interfere or inhibit learning. Review research evidence in Chapter 3 about the relation between visual and audio channels in instructional materials.

When developing computer-based materials or an interactive video program, either storyboarding or scripting procedures may require the use of **flow charts** (types include linear and branching techniques). These may precede the writing of scene or "frame" descriptions. See page 280 for further discussion of flowcharting methods.

If you must obtain approval of the script before picture taking starts (another possible **checkpoint**), either read the narration or put it on audiotape for the client to hear while viewing the storyboard pictures. A script is to be heard. Its effect is much different than when being read. Anyone (including you) reviewing the script should mentally examine the visual flow—the continuity, smoothness, and overall unity of the information being presented.

On page 69 is an example of a script for *Solar Collectors,* developed chiefly from the expository treatment, with some details adopted from the other treatments.

Consider the Length

The content to be treated in instructional materials affects the time needed to present it. An instructional presentation may require extensive explanation or sufficient time for the user to study details. On the other hand, a motivational or informational presentation must have dynamic movement and include a variety of scenes in order to maintain a high interest level.

Some people do not realize that carefully planned and produced instructional materials can effectively present a large amount of information in a short time. For example, a 10 to 12 minute presentation is a "long time" in media terms and can be a sufficient period of time to fully communicate the content for a topic's objectives.

There is only one rule for length. A scene or a group of scenes, forming a sequence, should be on the screen long enough to present the required information for satisfactory viewer understanding. This should not be so long that the audience will lose interest and the picture lose its effectiveness. Or, if images change too rapidly, their communications value may be lost and the viewer can become confused.

The length will be determined by the time needed to develop the subject visually in combination with the sound. You will learn from experience that, for example, a projected slide may remain on the screen for only a few seconds or that a complex image may hold attention for about 30 seconds. The average film or video scene runs for about seven seconds.

When you (and your team) appraise your script against the amount of time desirable or available, you may need to review it to see whether the needed time can be shortened, or the content divided into two or more outlines for a series of presentations.

Prepare the Specifications

You have prepared a map, the script. Now you face the questions: What specific things are to be done now, next, and thereafter until the instructional materials are ready to be used? What is to be made or purchased? What are the timelines for completing the production? The answers to these questions are the **specifications.**

The more complex the projected media, the more numerous the specifications. Naturally they need to be organized and classified. Some classes of specifications have no bearing on some kinds of materials, while on others (slide series, video recordings, interactive videodiscs, multi-images) all may be needed. Here are some examples of specifications, with detailed and specific points that must be considered and choices that must be made:

- ***Type of instructional media***—learning aid, training material, informational material, display media, slide series, audio recording, overhead transparencies, video recording, multi-image presentation, computer-based instruction, or interactive video unit.
- ***Material and size***—35mm Ektachrome 100 film, thermal transparency film, ½-inch VHS videotape, and so on.

EXAMPLE: Simple Specifications

Specifications

30 2 x 2 color slides
Five or six titles and overprint captions and four or five drawings for close-up photographic copy work
Synchronized tape-recorded narration of 5 to 6 minutes duration
Materials to be prepared during May for use in September
- May 2 preplanning completed
- May 8 script written
- May 8 to 18 photography
- May 10 to 18 audio recorded
- May 20 picture and sound sync completed
- May 21 final tryout
- May 22 to 25 revisions
- May 28 project completed

All facilities, equipment, and personnel available at no cost
Locations for picture-taking
- House with collectors on roof
- Older building with collectors
- Collector on ground beside building
- Apartment building with collectors
- House with snow on collector
- Collector near swimming pool
- Another house with collector on roof

Budget:

Two rolls 35 mm 36-exposure Ektachrome 100 film, with processing	@$12	$24.00
Two sets slide duplicates	@$15	30.00
Art supplies		10.00
One roll 300 feet x 1/4-inch magnetic recording tape		7.50
Two C30 audiocassettes	@$2.50	5.00
		$76.50

- ▸ ***Sound***—tape-recorded narration, synchronous sound, silent reading matter, titles, captions, and so on.
- ▸ ***Length***—approximate number of pages, photographs, slides, transparencies; running time for audio or video recording.
- ▸ ***Facilities and equipment***—locations for filming and recording, camera equipment, recorders, and accessories, graphic and photographic studio equipment, computer facility.
- ▸ ***Special assistance required***—for acting, filming, lighting, graphics, sound recording, film processing, editing, programming, printing, duplicating, secretarial.
- ▸ ***Timeline and completion date***—schedule for shooting at locations, completing artwork, recording sound, and other phases of production; date for completion or use.
- ▸ ***Budget estimate***—including film and other materials, equipment purchase or rental, film laboratory and other services, salaries (if applicable), and overhead charges.

What You Have Learned About Designing Instructional Materials:

1. What *three* elements of materials planning are introduced in this chapter? What is the meaning and value for giving attention to each one?
2. *Two* general methods for handling the content for instructional materials are described near the beginning of this chapter. What are they?
3. What do we mean when we say "participation" relative to using instructional media?
4. What is the value of having students participate while using or immediately after using the media materials?
5. What are *three* forms in which a treatment may be written?
6. In what *four* visual ways can a storyboard be prepared?
7. What *four* kinds of information may be put on a storyboard card?
8. Mark each statement as *True* or *False*.
   a. A script is always prepared in two columns.
   b. A two-column script has visual descriptions on one side and sound elements on the other side.
   c. The visual side of a script includes camera placement and scene description information.
   d. Carefully write narration in final, complete form whenever a script is prepared.
   e. Every scene requires some narration.
   f. It is preferable to record the narration and have other persons listen to it, for evaluation, than to have them read the script.
   g. A script can easily handle detailed explanations for any information on a topic.
   h. Two key concepts for a good script are *variety* and *change of pace*.
9. What is a good rule to follow in determining the proper length of a scene?
10. What is the purpose for setting *specifications* for instructional materials?
11. What *nine* categories for specifications are listed?
12. Show that there is more than one way of handling your topic's content. Prepare two brief treatments of the topic you selected on page 49, each having a different approach and giving a different emphasis to the topic. Keep in mind your audience and your purposes.
13. Consider the type of instructional material you would like to prepare. Does it fit the presentation of the content?
14. Sketch a few sequences of your storyboard on cards.
15. Prepare a script from the treatment and storyboard. Describe the scenes carefully, using letter abbreviations for camera positions. Write narration ideas if appropriate.
16. List the specifications necessary for your materials.

See answers on page 376.

REFERENCES

SCRIPTING

Carliner, Saul. "Audiovisual Words: The Scriptwriter's Tools." *Technical Communication* 34 (First Quarter 1987): 11–14.

Cohen, Fred. "Scriptwriting: Getting It Down on Paper." *Corporate Video Decisions* 2 (June 1989): 22–27.

Edmonds, Robert. *Script Writing for Audiovisual Media.* New York: Teachers College Press, 1984.

Floyd, Steve. "Visualization: The Key to Effective Scriptwriting." *Technical Communication* 34 (First Quarter 1987): 8–10.

Hagerman, William L. "Write and Wrong." *Audio-Visual Communications,* 20 (November 1986): 36–41.

———. "Write and Wrong II." *Audio-Visual Communications,* 20 (December 1986): 35–45.

Lehtinen, Rick. "Starting Out Write." Part 1. *Video Systems* 17 (January 1991): 66–68.

———. "Starting Out Write." Part 2. *Video Systems* 17 (February 1991): 62–68.

Matrazzo, Donna. *Corporate Scriptwriting Book.* Portland, OR: Communicom Publishing, 1985.

Swain, Dwight V. *Scripting for Video and Audiovisual Media.* New York: Focal Press, 1983.

Van Nostran, William. *The Scriptwriter's Handbook: New Techniques for Media Writers.* White Plains, NY, Knowledge Industries Publications, 1989.

DESIGNING THE MEDIA

Witt, Gary A. "How to Design a Production that Viewers Will Remember." *Instructional Innovator* 26 (October 1981): 37–43.

———. "How to Present Information That Viewers Will Remember." *Instructional Innovator* 26 (November 1981): 37–43.

COMPUTER SOFTWARE PROGRAMS FOR SCRIPTWRITING

AV Scripter. Tom Schroeppel, 4705 Bay View Ave., Tampa, FL 33611.

MovieMaster and *ScriptMaster.* Comprehensive Video Supply Corp., 148 Veterans Drive, Northvale, NJ 07647.

ScreenWright Professional. Paul D. Vadler Associates, 338 Prospect Place, #4C, Brooklyn, NY 11238.

ShowScape (for WordPerfect), Lake Compuframes, Inc. P.O. Box 890, Briarcliff Manor, NY 10510.

Split/Scripter. Ixion, Inc. 1335 No. Northlake Way, Suite 102, Seattle, WA 98103-8918.

SOURCES FOR STOCK FILM FOOTAGE

Archive Film Productions. 530 West 25th Street, New York, NY 10001.

Film Search. 21 West 46th Street, New York, NY 10036.

Lumbard, Paula A. "Footage Research: Stretching Your Stock Footage Dollars." *AV Video* 13 (March 1991): 28–30, 42.

Media Research Association, Inc. 1629 K Street, N.W., Washington, DC 20036.

National Archives and Records Service, Audiovisual Archives Division, Stock Film Library Branch. 1411 South Fern Street, Arlington, VA 22202.

National Geographic Society, Stock Shot Film Library. 1600 M Street, N.W., Washington, DC 20036.

"The Stock Report: A Selection of Libraries." *AV Video* 14 (March 1992): 24–27.

Stock Search. 44 Ralston Avenue, Mill Valley, CA 94941.

SOURCES FOR STOCK PHOTOGRAPHS

Four By Five. 485 Madison Avenue, New York, NY 10022.

Frederick Lewis, Inc. 134 West 29th Street, New York, NY 10001.

Historical Pictures Service. 921 West Van Buren, Chicago, IL 60607.

Fundamental Production Skills

Part 3

C H A P T E R

7

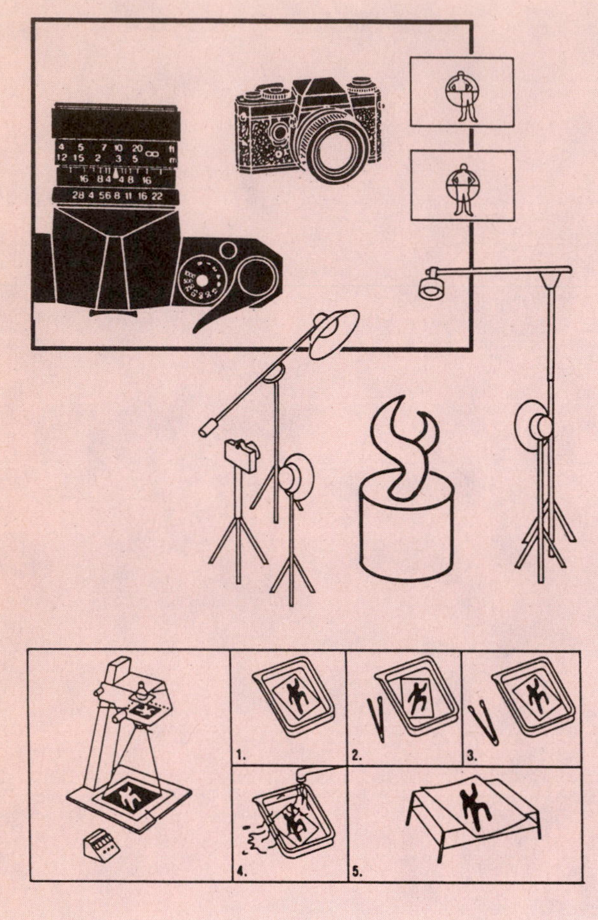

Photography

Advances in photographic equipment allow you to give more attention to the important job of taking pictures, rather than being concerned with routine matters of exposure, distance settings, and so on. Your emphasis now can be on composing the picture and catching the decisive instant of action.

While recognition is given in this chapter to many newer developments, such as electronic imaging, an understanding of the fundamental elements of photography will help you to make choices and decisions that can result in high-quality visual materials, prepared with a sense of pleasure and satisfaction.

YOUR CAMERA

Although cameras can be classified into groups according to film size or operating characteristics, all cameras, with the exception of digital electronic imaging cameras, are basically similar and include seven essential parts:

- ▶ **A.** Light-tight enclosure (camera body)
- ▶ **B.** Lens
- ▶ **C.** Lens diaphragm
- ▶ **D.** Shutter
- ▶ **E.** Viewfinder
- ▶ **F.** Film-support channel
- ▶ **G.** Film-advance and rewind knobs

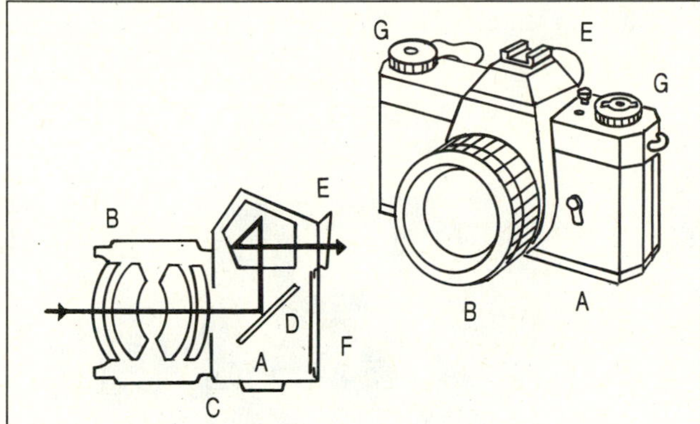

In addition, all cameras except the simplest have some means for changing the distance between the lens and the film plane in order to focus the image on the film. The more expensive kinds have features and attachments that offer greater versatility when filming. These include manual or automatic methods of changing lens-diaphragm openings, shutter speeds, and focus. Adjustable diaphragms and shutters are desirable because they can be adapted to changing light conditions and to different kinds of subjects. Lens quality differs over a wide range and has important bearing on the price of a camera.

Small-Format Cameras (35mm)

This is the most widely used type of camera for preparing visual materials, principally as slides for slide series or multi-image presentations. Color and black-and-white prints can also be made from appropriate 35mm film.

These cameras have either *window-type viewfinders* or a *prism and mirror system* that allows the subject to be framed and focused through the camera lens for more accurate viewing. The latter type of camera is called a **single-lens reflex** (SLR) and is especially convenient for close-ups and copy work. This is the type of camera generally used for preparing instructional media. Lenses and shutters of high-priced cameras can be adjusted over a wide range of settings, which broadens the possibilities for taking pictures under varying conditions.

Some models of 35mm cameras have automated features, controlled by a microchip, that permit fast and

precise exposure and focus settings. There are models of window-type viewfinder cameras with these features that are very compact, fitting easily into a coat pocket. They may be called "aim and shoot" cameras.

Another product in the small format camera category is the *disposable* camera. It consists of a roll of 35mm film within a cardboard or plastic box that has a lens and preset shutter. Usually exposure is set at *f*/11 for 1⁄100th second. Available models are capable of making daylight color prints, panoramic color prints, underwater photographs, or flash pictures. Resulting prints are standard sizes while panoramic prints are about 3½ × 10 inches.

Quick operation is a feature of 35mm cameras, and there is an economy with film in that many exposures can be made on a single roll before reloading. For more details on the characteristics of 35mm cameras, see page 222.

Medium-Format Cameras

These cameras use a film size (generally 120) larger than 35mm, thus providing 2¼ × 2¼ inch (6 × 6 cm) or 2¼ × 2¾ inch slides, color negatives, or black-and-white negatives. The larger size may be preferable when considerable enlargements and exceptionally sharp images are required. One disadvantage of this slide size is the higher cost and, often, the unavailability of projectors to view them.

There are two subcategories in this group. Both focus the image, when viewing, on a ground-glass surface. The most useful type has a **single lens,** with a mirror that reflects light to the ground glass. The mirror moves upward to clear the film plane just before the shutter opens as in a 35mm single-lens reflex camera. An advantage of most of these cameras is that the camera back, which functions as a film cartridge, can be easily removed and interchanged. This allows the use of different films (black-and-white, color reversal, or color negative) without unloading the roll presently in the camera.

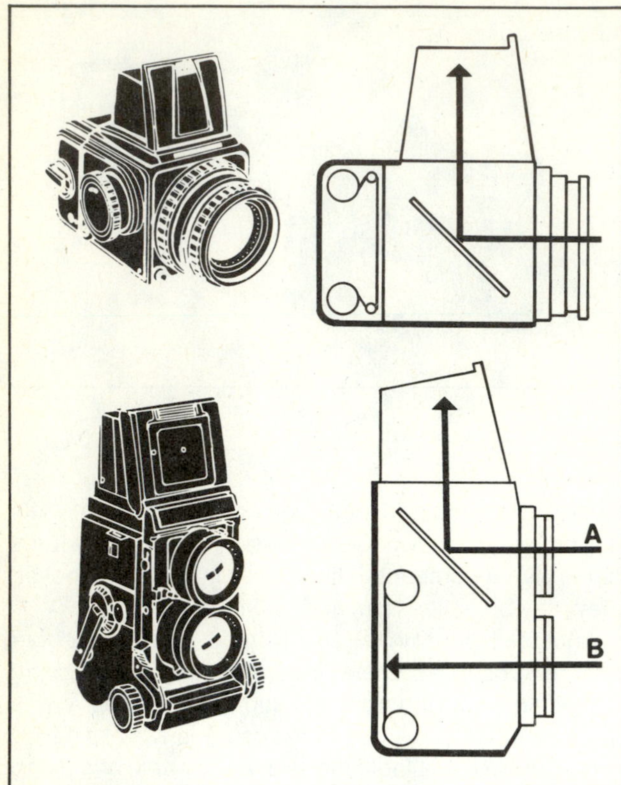

The other type of medium format is a **twin-lens** camera. Its lower lens (B) is for taking pictures, while the upper one (A) carries light rays to the ground glass. The **parallax** problem caused by the separation between the viewing and photographic lens positions (page 103) is a limitation of the twin-lens camera when used for close-ups.

On the other hand, with the twin lens the subject can be viewed as the shutter is released during exposure. Because of mirror movement in the single-lens camera, at the instant of exposure, viewing is eliminated momentarily.

The method of viewing the subject as it appears on the ground glass of these cameras can be another advantage because the image is generally the same size as it will appear on the film, although on certain cameras it may be reversed left to right. Image size may be especially important when accurate composition or careful positioning of a subject for a multi-image slide presentation is required.

Polaroid Film Cameras

The outstanding feature of this type of camera (manufactured by Polaroid Corporation) is that the film is developed automatically into a print in the camera, thus eliminating the need for darkroom work. The results of your picture taking are seen almost immediately. Prints and slides in both black-and-white and color can be produced in 1 minute.

The film consists of light-sensitive negative material and a nonsensitive positive stock (paper on film). To the latter are affixed sealed pods, one for each picture, that contain developing chemicals. After a picture is taken, a pull on the tab (or motorized movement) advances the film, then rollers squeeze the developer from a pod, allowing gelatinlike material to spread between the negative and positive stock. Development takes place quickly. The result is a print or slide ready for use.

A reversal color film (ISO 40), available from Polaroid, can be exposed in a regular 35mm camera and then immediately processed in an "autoprocess" unit. Thus slides can be shot and the results seen in a few minutes. Continuous-tone black-and-white and high-contrast 35mm films are also available in this process.

Electronic Still Cameras

Developments in video imaging and computer technology have created a new photographic medium—the hand-held, electronic still camera. It is also called a still-picture videocamera. In the camera, at the film location, a microchip (an image sensor), converts light energy received from subjects and scenes, to electrical charges that are recorded onto a magnetic two-inch floppy disk within the camera body. Twenty-five or more, high-resolution, electronic photos can be recorded. Then, either the recorded disk is inserted into a playback unit, or the camera is connected to a standard video monitor. Each image can be displayed; then with a videoprinter, full color paper copies can be made.

With the right configuration of editing hardware, the digitized images can be copied, rearranged, enhanced, and even enlarged. The images can be down-

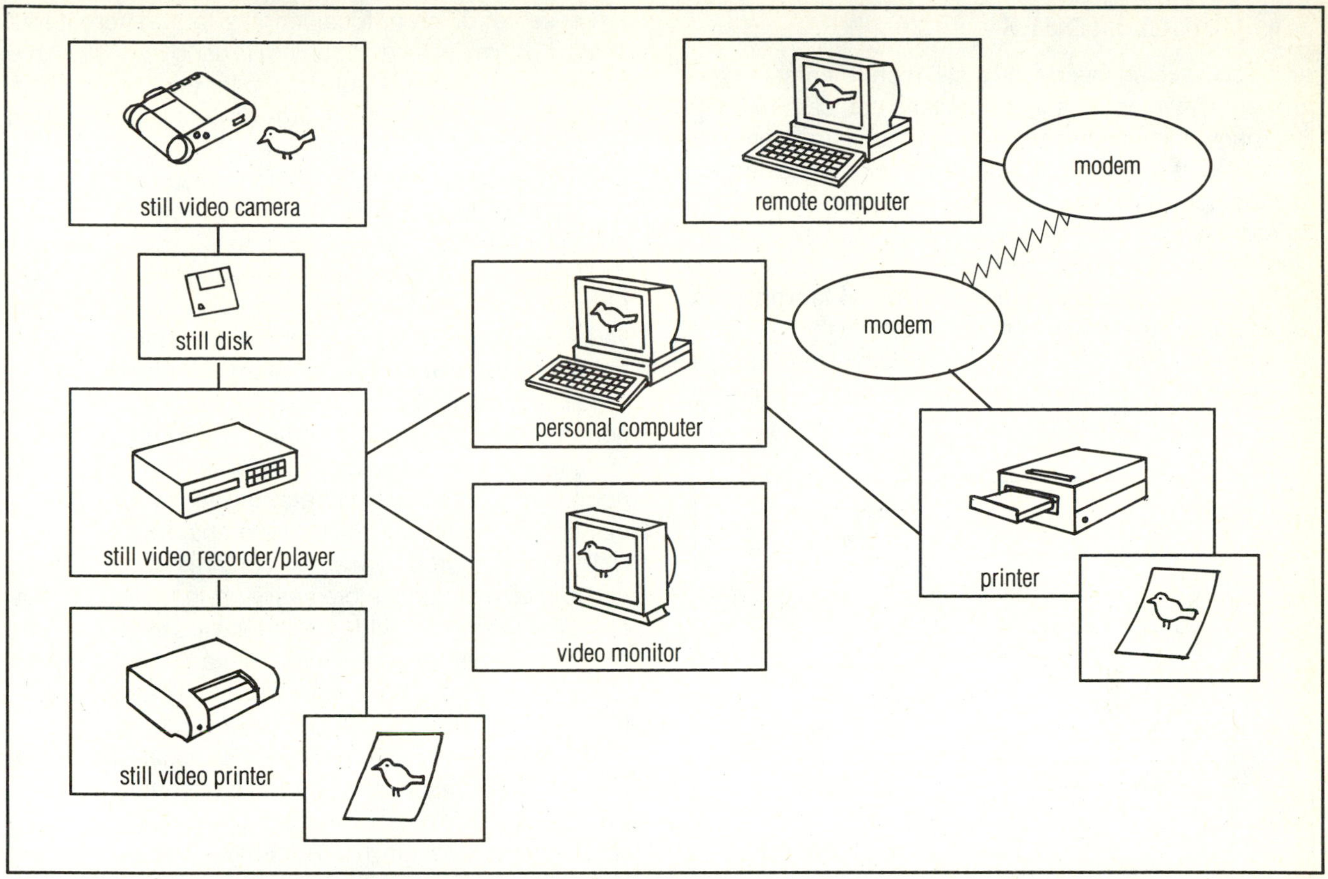

still video camera
remote computer
modem
still disk
modem
personal computer
still video recorder/player
printer
video monitor
still video printer

loaded to application software on a microcomputer for use in computer graphics programs, for transfer to videotape, or for printing and publishing. Also, by using a modem, the images can be transmitted over a telephone line to any location.

A related digital imaging system (called a Photo CD) uses a scanner (page 120) to capture images from film negatives and slides, storing them in a computer memory. These images can be combined with those from an electronic still camera and used in presentations or publications.

Videocameras

The features of videocameras and their operating principles are described on page 240.

What You Have Learned About Camera Types:

1. Examine your own camera. Locate the seven parts as shown on page 77.
2. If your camera is a 35mm-type, is it single-lens reflex or one with a window-type viewfinder?
3. What type of camera would best fit each situation?
   a. Used to prepare photographs quickly and easily immediately after the pictures are taken
   b. Used as a roll-film camera for accurately viewing a subject in same size and appearance as it will be filmed
   c. Used to produce a quantity of color slides
   d. Used to record an image and then immediately put it into computer memory for a graphics program

See answers on page 377.

CAMERA LENSES

If you have an inexpensive still-picture camera, you probably have only the standard lens that came with it. But many of the higher-priced cameras permit removal of the original lens and its replacement with other lenses for special purposes. There are advantages in using different lenses to film various subjects under certain conditions.

The major feature of a lens is its **focal length.** This term refers to the distance measured from the center of the camera lens to the film plane within the camera when a subject at a far distance (infinity) is in focus.

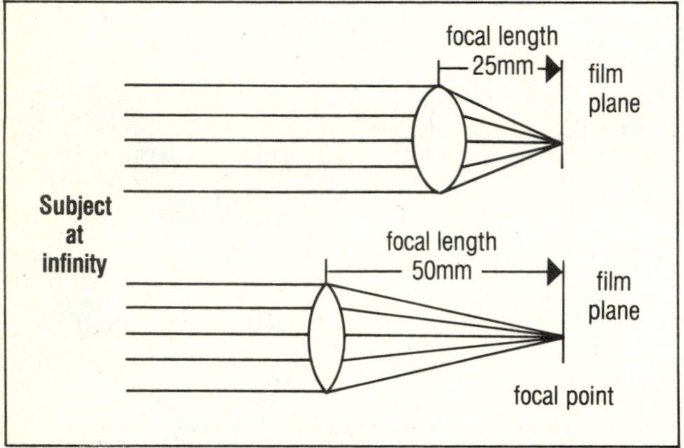

Lenses of different focal lengths form different-size images on film (when the camera is used from the same position). As you substitute a lens for another one having a *longer* focal length, a *larger* image is projected to the film. Thus, on the film you record only a portion of the image you had with the first lens. If you use a lens of *shorter* focal length, a *smaller* image reaches the film and you record a *greater* area of the subject.

The focal length of a lens is measured in millimeters (mm). A *normal* focal length has been established for various cameras. For the 35mm camera the normal focal length, or **normal lens,** is 50mm. A lens with a *larger* or *longer* focal-length number (135mm) than that of the normal lens is called a **telephoto lens.** A lens with a focal-length number *smaller* or *shorter* (28mm) than the normal lens is called a **wide-angle lens.** For a 35mm camera the relationship is illustrated below.

By selecting from lenses with different focal lengths, you can take pictures more easily under difficult conditions. For example, a wide-angle lens is useful when you cannot move far enough away from a subject to shoot with a normal lens. When you cannot get close to a subject or do not want to, a telephoto lens may be helpful.

However, recognize that some unusual optical impressions can be caused by both wide-angle and telephoto lenses. A person viewing a wide-angle picture will get the impression that the camera was farther away from the subject, an exaggerated feeling of depth. With

Field with Wide-angle Lens (28mm)

Field with Normal Lens (50mm)

Field with Telephoto Lens (135mm)

Wide-angle Lens

Normal Lens

Telephoto Lens

Varying Perspectives of a Subject with Different Focal Length Lenses

extreme wide-angle lenses, objects close to the camera will appear proportionately larger than they really are. Also, near the edge of a picture straight lines are bowed, resulting in a distorted picture.

A telephoto lens may give the impression of compressing the distance between objects in a scene so that the foreground and background elements appear very close together.

A **zoom lens,** which in effect is a series of lenses within one housing, allows you to rapidly change the focal length along a predetermined range. Such a lens may be marked 35–70mm, 75–200mm, and so forth.

In using this lens, you choose your subject by zooming in or out without moving the camera with respect to the subject. With this lens on a video camera, you can also continuously change the size of a subject by zooming while filming. Occasionally, a slow zoom—to center on the action or to show relationships between elements of a scene—can be effective as well as dramatic. However, there is a tendency to overuse the zooming feature, which can be distracting to the viewer.

When using a zoom lens, always focus your subject with the lens set at the *longest* focal length (close-up view of the subject) and with the lens aperture at its *smallest f/* number (largest opening). By following this instruction you will be sure to keep the subject in focus for all positions within the zoom operation.

In summary, as compared with a normal lens, a lens with a *longer* focal length has a *larger* millimeter number and is called a *telephoto* lens; while a lens with a *shorter* focal length has a *lower* millimeter number and is called a *wide-angle* lens. A *zoom* lens has focal lengths that can be varied over a certain range.

Special lenses, called **macro lenses,** provide great flexibility for the user. Many macro lenses can be adjusted for normal 50mm use or for close-up and copy work. They are designed to reproduce details more sharply than other lenses and yet speed up the process of going from a normal lens to extreme close-up use.

By setting a zoom lens at various focal lengths, you have access to different perspectives. The zoom lens will change both the **magnification** and **depth-of-field** (page 84) relationship between foreground and background objects in a scene.

What You Have Learned About Camera Lenses:

1. Make a sketch to illustrate the meaning of focal length for a lens. Label the parts.
2. What numerical measure is used to indicate focal length?
3. Into what three groups are lenses placed?
4. Which lens would you select for each situation?
   a. General picture taking of a group of children on a playground
   b. General scene in a factory showing as much of the equipment as possible
   c. As close a view as possible of a track start on the athletic field when filmed from the grandstand
   d. Two-by-two-inch slide of a bird in a nest, which is in a bush at some distance
5. Into what group(s) would you place the lens(es) you have with your camera?

See answers on page 377.

CAMERA SETTINGS

If you have an automatic-setting camera, you may feel you have little need to recognize and understand the purposes for the settings made on an adjustable camera. But your camera may allow you to override the automatic feature and, for special situations, make settings to ensure correct exposure. For example, when filming a *backlit* subject (sun or other light source *behind* the subject, with much of the subject in shadow), or when making close-ups of an object on a light-colored background, you face situations in which the general exposure determined by the camera may be incorrect.

There are three essential settings on adjustable cameras—lens diaphragm, shutter speed, and focus for subject distance.

The amount of light that enters a camera is controlled by the lens diaphragm and the shutter, working together. The *lens diaphragm* controls the *amount* of light that can reach the film; the *shutter* controls the *length of time* the light can reach the film.

Lens Diaphragm

Light enters a camera by passing through the lens. The intensity of light entering is controlled by a metal diaphragm, which is located either directly behind the lens or between two elements of the lens. The **lens diaphragm** acts somewhat like the iris of an eye. It is always open, but its size can be changed to control the intensity of light passing through the lens.

Lens-diaphragm settings are indicated by a series of numbers—4, 5.6, 8, 11, 16, . . .—called ***f/*numbers** or ***f/*stops.** *The larger the f/number the smaller the opening.* A lens setting of *f/*11 admits only *half the amount of light* passed by an *f/*8 setting.

Thus, adjacent numbers in the series admit light in the proportion of 2 to 1 (permitting the passage of *twice as much light* or *half as much light*).

An *f/*number expresses the relationship between the focal length (page 80) and the diameter of the lens's aperture. Thus, for *f/*11 the opening has a diameter one-eleventh that of the lens's focal length. In commonly used terminology, a lens with a low *f/*number (*f/*2 or *f/*1.4) is considered a "fast" lens. This means that the camera equipped with such a lens is capable of picture taking under low light conditions.

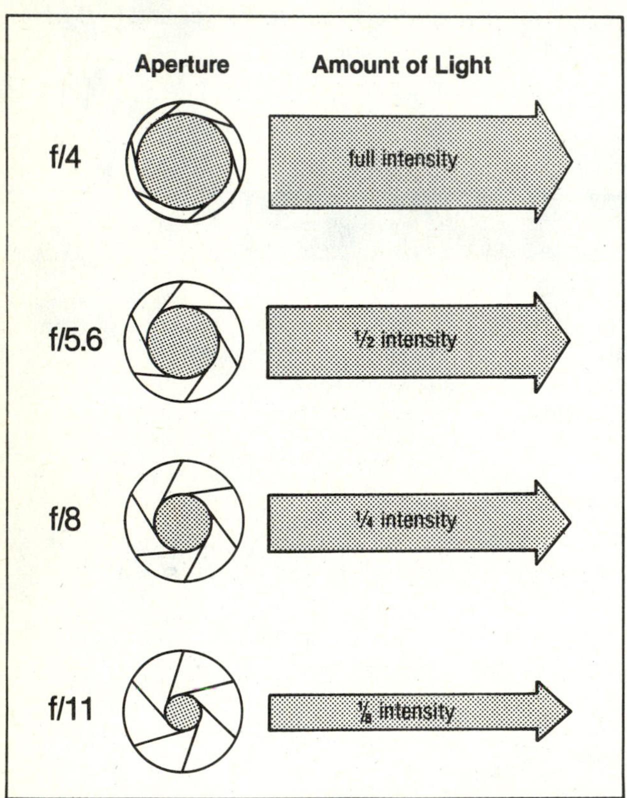

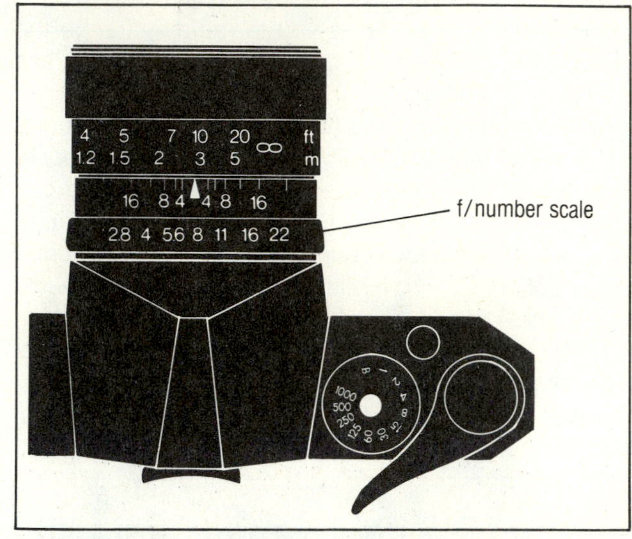

Shutter Speed

A second camera setting is the **shutter speed.** The camera shutter is similar to the eyelid as it closes and reopens rapidly. In the camera the shutter remains closed until opened to permit the lens to "see."

The most common type of shutter is placed between the elements of the lens and consists of thin pieces of metal that can be moved to allow light to pass for various lengths of time. (See between-the-lens shutter illustration.) The other method of permitting light to reach the film is with a cloth or metal curtain located just in front of the film plane. The curtain has a slit in it, and at the instant the picture is taken the curtain moves across the film at a selected speed to expose the film to light. (See focal-plane-shutter illustration on the next page.)

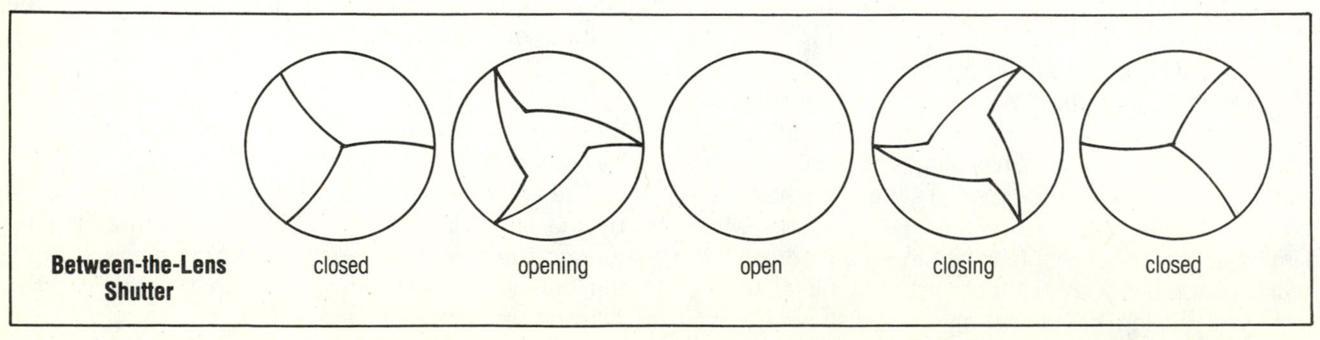

Between-the-Lens Shutter

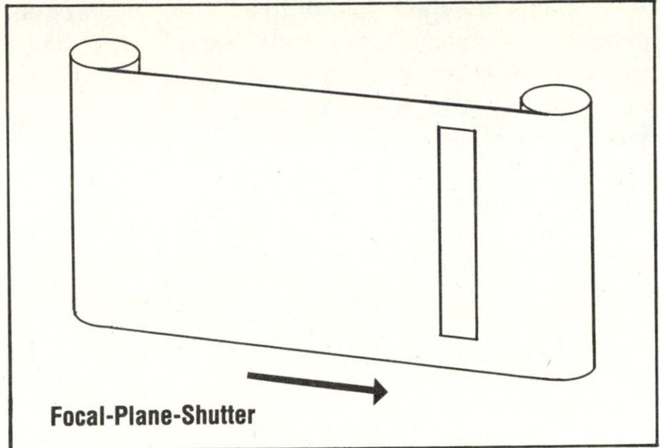

Generally, shutter speeds are measured in fractions of a second: 1/2, 1/4, 1/8, 1/15, 1/30, 1/60, 1/125, and so on. On the camera they are printed as whole numbers instead of fractions, the number shown being the denominator of the fraction. A shutter speed of 1/60 second is *slower* than a speed of 1/125 second, admitting light for *twice* as long a time.

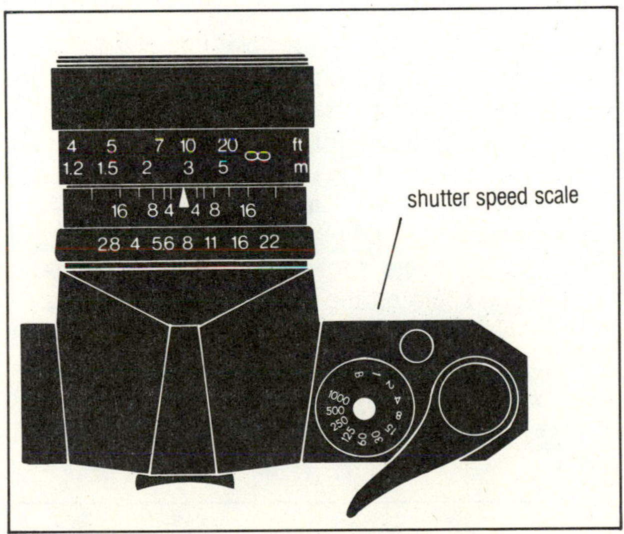

Thus, adjacent speeds are in the proportion of 2 to 1 (permitting the entrance of light for approximately *twice as much* or *half as much time*—1/60 is twice as much as 1/125; but 1/60 is half as much as 1/30).

On your camera you may have many speeds from which to select. For general scenes, a shutter speed of 1/60 or 1/125 is suggested. But when a moving subject is to be filmed, the choice of a shutter speed is dependent on the speed of movement, the distance from camera to subject, and the direction of movement relative to the camera.

Since both the adjacent lens-diaphragm settings and the adjacent shutter speeds are in the 2-to-1 proportion, they may be used in various combinations to

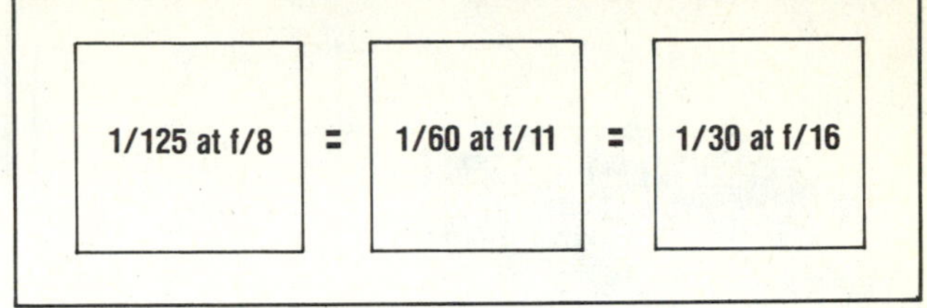

allow the same amount of light to reach the film. As you will see, the selection of such combinations is important to obtain specific effects.

Focus

The third setting on many cameras is for focus. With your camera you may be able to focus the image on the ground glass. Or your camera may include a built-in **rangefinder** coupled to the lens, which, upon proper adjustment, automatically sets the lens for the correct subject-to-camera distance.

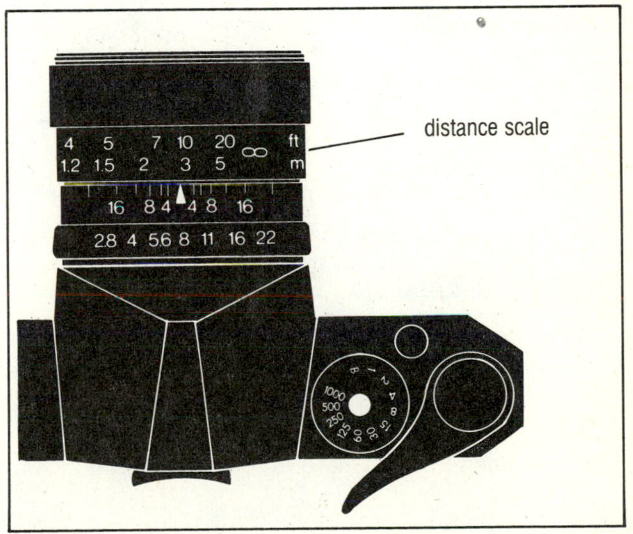

The rangefinder may be either of two kinds: **superimposed-image** or **split-field.** The former will show two images unless the focus is correct, at which point the two images are superimposed to make a single image. The split-field rangefinder will show two half images, one below the other, unless the focus is correct, at which point the two halves are matched together to make a complete image. See the illustration on page 84 for a visualized explanation.

Some cameras now include an *automatic* focusing feature. When the focus is adjusted, an electronic pulse, like a small sonar beam, is emitted from the camera. It strikes the subject toward which the camera is pointed. The time for the pulse to reach and then reflect from the subject is measured. This period of time is translated

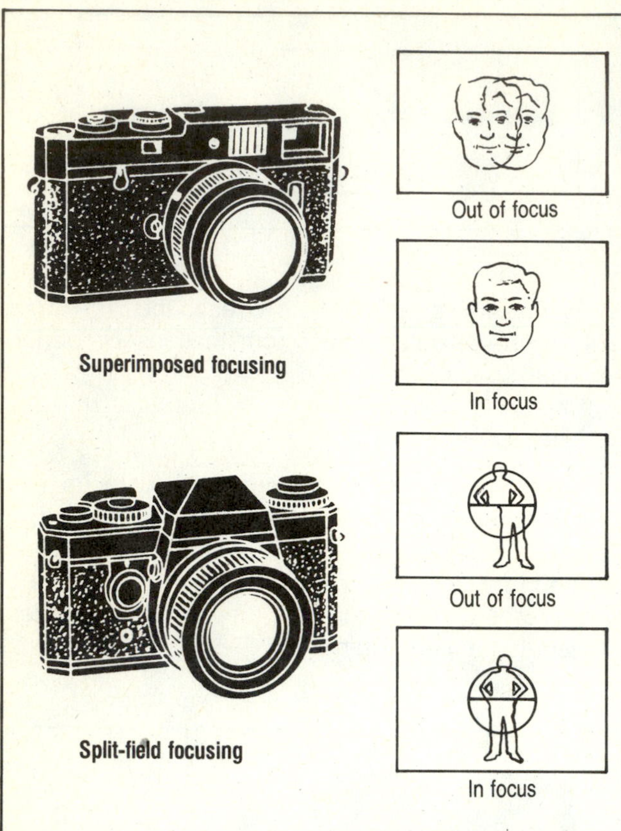

into a distance (feet or meters), and the camera lens is focused automatically.

Depth-of-Field

While lens-diaphragm openings and shutter speeds work together to admit various amounts of light into the camera, lens-diaphragm openings and distance settings can also be coordinated to get sharp pictures.

In this scene the camera is focused at 3 feet, but points both closer and farther than 3 feet also appear sharp. This distance from the closest sharply focused point to the farthest spot in focus is the *depth-of-field* of the lens at the *f*/number used. To get a sharp picture, a photographer must have the subject in this field.

Scene with Maximum Depth-of-Field (f/16)

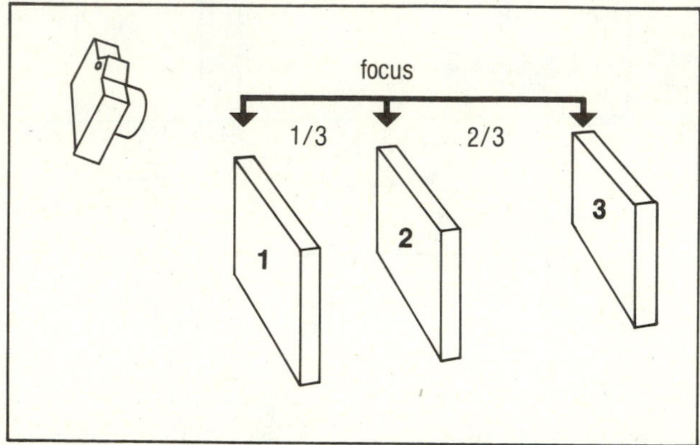

Of the total depth-of-field within a scene, about one-third is included ahead of the point of actual focus and about two-thirds beyond the point of focus. Therefore, to get the maximum value from the depth-of-field factor, focus your camera lens on a point that is about one-third of the way into a scene. If your camera gives you more exact information, use it.

Your camera may include a depth-of-field scale adjacent to the focusing ring. Refer to this scale to determine the depth-of-field for any combination of lens setting and distance to the plane of focus. The illustration shows how this scale is to be read in combination with the distance scale on the focusing ring. Note that its graduations are like those on the lens setting scale: 4, 8, 16, 22 (the 2.8, 5.6, and 11 points are omitted for legibility in the scale used in the illustration). It should be easy to observe the two important facts. First, what-

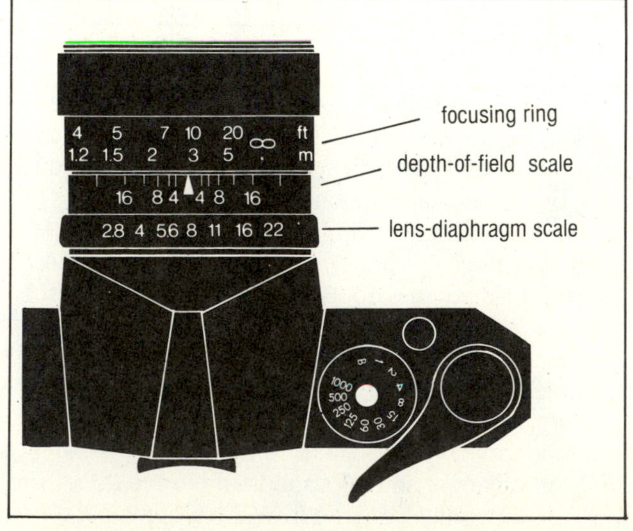

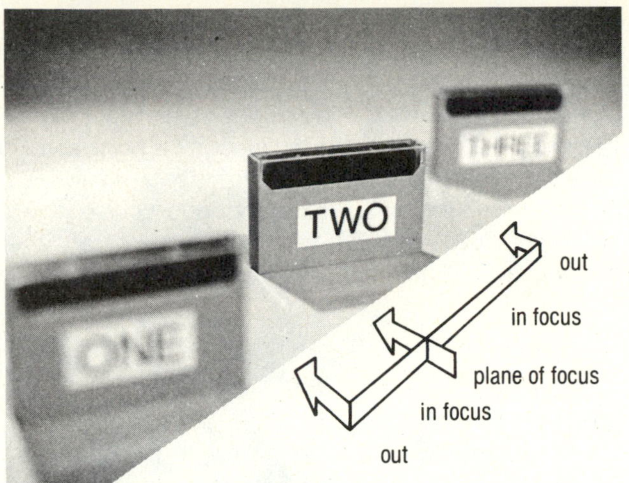

Scene with Limited Depth-of-Field (f/4)

ever the lens setting, it provides greater depth-of-field at far distances than at near distances. Second, whatever the distance, it provides greater depth-of-field at higher-numbered lens settings than at lower-numbered ones.

In summary: On adjustable cameras three settings must be made—lens-diaphragm opening (*f*/number), shutter speed, and distance. Study their relationships carefully and learn how to use them. Remember, to ensure sharp pictures:

- Try to select an *f*/number in the middle of the scale (11, 16) for maximum picture sharpness.
- Hold the camera steady.
- Use a sturdy tripod whenever shutter speeds slower than 1/30 second will be used.
- Focus on a point one-third into a scene.
- Squeeze, don't punch, the shutter release, or use a cable release.

What You Have Learned About Camera Settings:

1. If a lens setting of *f*/8 permits a certain amount of light to pass into a camera, then how much light does a setting of *f*/5.6 admit?
2. What shutter speed would you select to "stop" the action of (a) a person diving off a board, (b) a car driving past at 25 mph, or (c) a child walking by you?
3. If *f*/11 and 1/125 second are correct exposure settings, but you want to increase the depth-of-field by two *f*/stops, what camera setting would you now use?
4. What is the depth-of-field on the lens on page 84?
5. Does a lens setting of *f*/4.5 permit *greater* or *less* depth-of-field as compared to that of *f*/11?

See answers on page 377.

THE FILM

Selection of film is determined by a number of factors:

- Kinds of subjects, such as general scenes, action shots, or close-ups of fine details
- Lighting conditions, such as daylight, floodlights, flash, or low-level room light
- Use for materials, such as enlarged photographs, slides, overhead transparencies, or motion pictures

In addition, choices are based upon characteristics of different films, including:

- Degree of light sensitivity (film speed or exposure index, see explanation following)—*slow* films, such as Kodachrome 25 (ISO 25), Kodalith Ortho Type 3 (ISO 8); *moderate-speed* films, such as Kodachrome 200 (ISO 200) and Kodak TMAX TMX (ISO 100); *fast* films, such as Kodak TMAX TMZ (ISO 3200) and Kodacolor Gold (ISO 1600)

- Reproduction quality of colors in a subject
- Useful exposure range to reproduce a range of tones from highlights to shadows

The terms **film speed, exposure index,** and **ASA** (American Standards Association), or **ISO** (International Standards Organization) **rating,** refer to the degree of light sensitivity of a film or the degree of speed at which the film will create an image. These expressions are used interchangeably and are scaled by a number assigned to each film. The number is a relative one; the higher the ASA/ISO rating the less time and/or less light is required for proper exposure. A film with a speed of 200 requires less light for proper exposure than one with a speed of 100, and vice versa.

Information about a few types of black-and-white and color films is summarized in Table 7–1 below. The data are correct at the time of writing; however, changes and new developments are to be anticipated. Check carefully the data sheet packaged with your film for the latest assigned exposure index and other details.

Roll film is available in various lengths for 35mm cameras. Also, many types of film can be purchased in rolls of up to 100 feet in length. This permits you to spool off small amounts or full rolls and load your own film cassettes. To do this you will need a bulk film loader and reusable 35mm film cassettes. If you process film

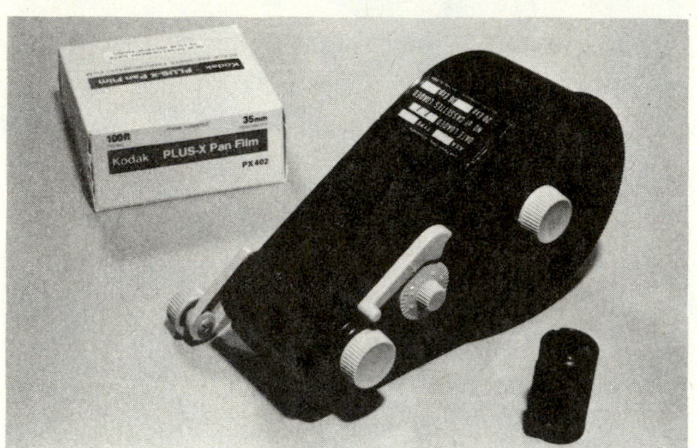

TABLE 7–1 CHARACTERISTICS OF SOME WIDELY USED FILMS

BLACK-AND-WHITE FILMS	EXPOSURE INDEX (ISO)	LIGHT SOURCE	SUGGESTED USE
Kodak Panchromatic		Daylight or Tungsten	
Technical Pan	25		• Variable contrast for high definition pictorial work, copy work, or extreme enlargements.
Plus-X	125		• Medium speed for general use. Fine grain, excellent sharpness.
Tri-X	400		• High speed for photographic action, for use with existing light, and extending flash distance range.
Kodak T-Max	100, 400, 3200	Daylight or Tungsten	• Extremely fine grain film, very high sharpness, expanded exposure latitude, high resolving power, and high degree enlargement. Uses new emulsion technology.
Fuji Neopan	400,1600	Daylight or Tungsten	• Professional high speed films with very fine grains with greater sensitivity. Excellent for push processing. Yields fine texture and sharpness.
(Professional films; local photo source can explain special handling)			
Ilford Plus		Daylight or Tungsten	• Fine grain films with wide latitude of exposure and great flexibility for push processing without loss of contrast, sharpness, and clarity. ISO can be determined by a variety of processing agents, which allows flexibility in exposure index.
Pan F	50		
FP4	125		
HP5	400		

Table 7–1 (*Continued*)

COLOR PRINT FILMS	EXPOSURE INDEX (ISO)	LIGHT SOURCE	SUGGESTED USE
Kodak Gold Plus	100, 200, 400, & 1600	Daylight	• Excellent general purpose color film.
Kodak Extar	25,100,1000	Daylight	• Micro-fine grain, high sharpness and excellent enlarging capabilities.
Kodak Vericolor	160, 400	Daylight	• Professional film that maintains excellent skin tones and good color reproduction. Moderate contrast, excellent for photographing people or products.
Fujicolor Super HG	100, 200, 400, & 1600	Daylight	• Uses sigma crystal technology to get fine grain at very high exposure indexes. Uses new emulsion technology to increase sharpness, skin tones, and color saturation. General use film for a variety of light conditions.

SPECIAL FILMS	EXPOSURE INDEX (ISO)	LIGHT SOURCE	SUGGESTED USE
Kodalith Ortho 6556, Type 3	8	Daylight or Tungsten	• High contrast film used for copying line art or text for titles. Wide latitude of exposure.
Kodak Ektagraphic HC slide film	8–25	Daylight or Tungsten	• Designed to be used for making black-and-white title slides and masking slides.
Ilford XP1	400	Daylight or Tungsten	• Very fine grain, fast film with the convenience of being processed in C-41 color chemistry, yielding high quality black-and-white photographs with high degree of enlargement and sharpness.
Fujichrome Reala	100	Daylight	• Color negative film with new emulsion technology that creates a full highlight to shadow gradation to improve color reproduction, sharpness, and grain quality.
Velvia	50		• Professional color slide film with an extra fine grain, excellent sharpness, and high resolution that provides real flesh tone and color renderings to ensure high quality reproduction.

through a commercial laboratory, contact them to be certain they will develop self-loaded film. Some labs will not do this.

Using bulk film has certain advantages: cost of film is reduced appreciably; waste is lower, because you can measure off only what will be needed for a job; and film consistency is assured, because you can use the same film emulsion lot for a project. If you do load your own film cassettes, be sure to label each one with the name of the film being used.

Black-and-White Film

Black-and-white films are inexpensive and simple to process and print. Their primary use is in making enlargements from negatives onto paper.

Black-and-white films are available in both high-contrast and continuous-tone emulsions having a wide range of film speeds. The former is used for photographing black line material on a white background, while the latter reproduces subjects in all tones of gray as well as in black and white.

Color Negative Film

Color negative film is versatile, since it may serve as negative for color prints, for black-and-white prints, and for positive color slides. On a color negative the colors of the subject are complementary to their normal appearance (yellow in place of blue, magenta for green, and cyan or blue-green for red). Kodak Gold 100, 200, 400, 1000, and 1600 are the principal color negative films available. Also, Fuji film is commonly available and offers a range of film speeds. The negative color films, available in sizes for most cameras, are more expensive than black-and-white, but they can be processed with prepared kits (C-41), thus reducing the cost when a large number of rolls is handled.

Color Reversal Film

After exposure and processing, color reversal films become positives—slides, filmstrips, or motion pictures. In processing, the image on the film is **reversed** to make a positive picture.

Color reversal films are supplied for 35mm and other standard-size roll-film cameras. They are available in a range of film speeds and in various types, each type designed for a specific light condition—daylight or artificial light (tungsten). The light supplied by these sources differs in "color temperature," a characteristic measured in degrees Kelvin (°K). Daylight contains more blue wavelength rays, while artificial light contains more rays from the red end of the spectrum. Therefore, each film type has an emulsion balanced for a specific color temperature, such as 6000°K for daylight film or 3400°K for Type B film (used under photoflood lights).

Correction filters are employed to permit use of a film under lighting conditions that differ from its Kelvin rating, or when duplicating a slide to correct the overall color of a scene. A filter will pass light of its own color and block out light of its complementary color. For example, if you use daylight color film indoors under artificial (tungsten) light, place an 80A filter (blue) over the camera lens to correct the excess red color of the artificial lighting by filtering out yellow.

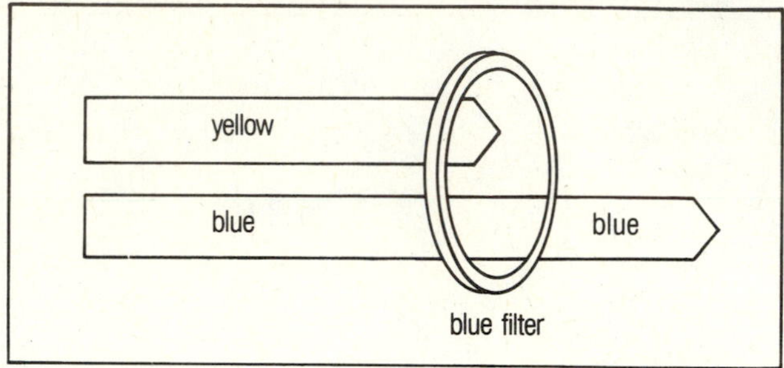

Because a correction filter reduces the overall light reaching the film, the exposure must be increased two *f*/stops if a meter, separate from the camera, is used. If the camera has an internal meter, set the ASA/ISO normally and the meter will compensate for the loss of light. Thus, it is better to use the film appropriate to the light conditions so as not to lose effective film speed.

Color prints can be prepared directly on color printing paper from color slides (page 111). It is not necessary to make a color negative from a slide before a color print can be made.

All film packages are stamped with an expiration date. For best results, use the film before this date, since film quality deteriorates with time. The changes are accelerated with high temperature and high humidity. Therefore, store unopened film to be kept for a long period of time under refrigeration (50°F or lower). To avoid damage from moisture that may condense on cold film, always allow the package to warm up to room temperature before being opened. This can vary from 2 to 8 hours. Then process exposed film as soon as possible after exposure to avoid deterioration of the latent image on the film.

REVIEW

What You Have Learned About Film:

1. Most reversal color films are available in two types. The selection of the type to use depends on what major factor?
2. If you wanted to have both color slides and enlarged color prints from the same subject, what film would you select to use?
3. What does the number in the ASA or ISO rating indicate?
4. What is the reason for selecting a film with an exposure index of 200 in preference to one with an index of 64?
5. On what principle of light does the selection of a filter depend?

See answers on page 377.

Black-and-White Negative

Enlarged Black-and-White Print

Black-and-White Slide

Color Reversal Slide

Color Print from Color Slide

Color Negative

Color Slide

Print in Black-and-White or Color

CORRECT EXPOSURE

How do you put together information about *f*/numbers, shutter speeds, and film characteristics to get correct exposure? The simplest method is to refer to the data sheet packaged with the film, on which a table gives you *general* guides to proper exposure.

KODAK EKTACHROME 100 HC Film (Daylight)

DAYLIGHT EXPOSURE: Cameras with automatic exposure controls – Set film speed at ISO 100. **Cameras with manual adjustments** – Determine exposure setting with exposure meter set for ISO 100 or use the table below. If camera has DX encoding, film speed setting is automatic.

Bright or Hazy Sun on Light Sand or Snow	1/250 sec	f/16
Bright or Hazy Sun (Distinct Shadows)	1/125 sec	f/16*
Weak, Hazy Sun (Soft Shadows)	1/125 sec	f/11
Cloudy Bright (No Shadows)	1/125 sec	f/8
Open Shade or Heavy Overcast	1/125 sec	f/5.6

*f/8 at 1/125 sec for backlighted close-ups.

For general pictures to be taken under bright sunlight, you can use the **f/16 rule.** Set the lens at *f*/16 and the shutter speed at (or close to) the ASA/ISO rating of the film. For example, using Ektachrome 200, the exposure would be *f*/16 at 1/250 second.

But what about situations involving particularly dark or unusually light-colored subjects or backgrounds? What corrections should you make when the sun is behind the subject rather than over your shoulder? How do you determine camera settings when doing copy work or when using floodlights? These are common problems, and their solutions may require more information than that provided by the data sheet tables or a simple rule.

Using a Light Meter

The most accurate method for determining exposure is with the use of a **photographic light meter.** Your camera may have a built-in meter that automatically sets the *f*/stop, or it may give you an indication of where to set the aperture. Also, you can use a separate, handheld light meter.

Light is measured by an exposure meter in either of two places: at the place where the subject is or at the place where the camera is. The **incident-light method** measures the light where the subject is, with an **incident-light meter** held at or near the subject's position and pointed toward the camera. The **reflected-light method** measures the light where the camera is, with a **reflected-light meter** held at or near the camera's position (or as part of the camera) and pointed toward the subject. Another way of describing the two methods is to say that the incident-light method measures the light that *falls on* the subject, whereas the reflected-light method measures the light that *reflects off* the subject.

Some meters measure light by only one of these methods; many have attachments or components that permit measurements to be taken in either way.

If your camera has a built-in meter it is used as a reflected-light meter. A photoelectric cell is located at a separate window or, as with a 35mm single-lens reflex camera, behind the lens. With the latter type, the amount of light that actually reaches the film is measured.

When you use light meters such as those described here, you obtain a general exposure provided by an

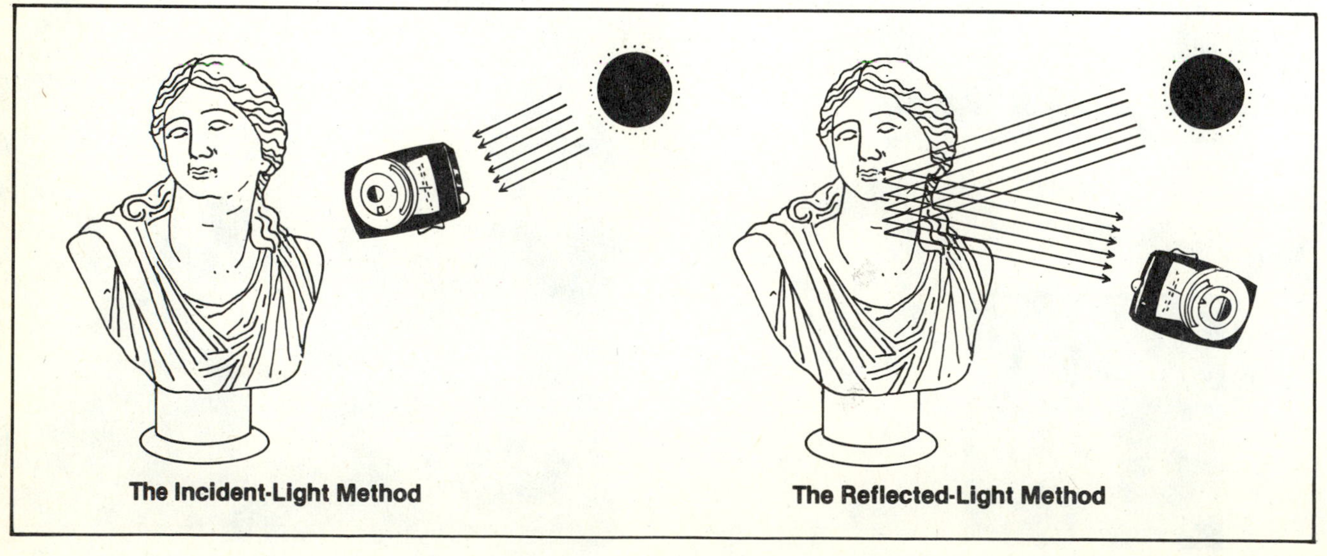

overall or average brightness measurement. Should you want to expose for a small, critical part of a scene that may be lighter or darker than the overall area, then a selective reading should be taken from it—for example, a piece of stainless steel equipment on a light-colored background, or the face of a person dressed in a white uniform. A reflected-light meter can be held close to the important part of the subject (avoid reading a shadow cast by the meter), or you can use a special reflected-type, a **spot meter.** This meter has an optical viewing system with a narrow angle of light acceptance (1 degree as compared with 30 degrees for a regular reflected-light meter). It can be used from the camera position to measure accurately the light from a small portion of a scene.

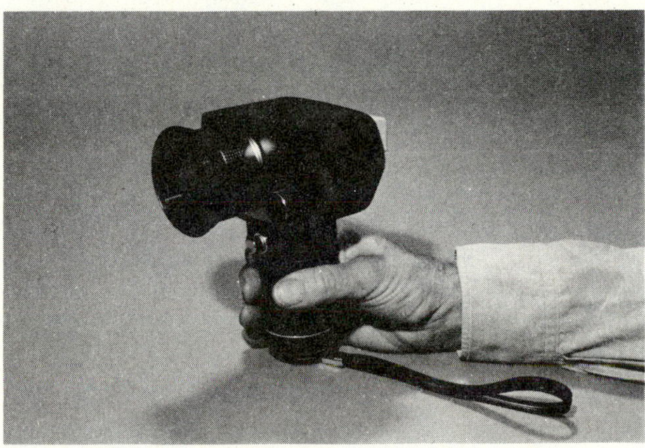

An exposure meter measures light through its photoelectric cell as shown by a needle on a light level scale or as digital numbers. With a hand meter, you then use this measurement to compute *f*/number and shutter speed on a dial scale or as digital readout. With a built-in meter, you directly set the lens or shutter speed to center the needle on the light level scale. Some cameras automatically set either the *f*/number or shutter speed that correlates with either an *f*/number or shutter speed you have selected already.

To use a hand-held light meter, follow these steps:

1. Note the exposure index (ISO) of the film you are using (as 160 for Ektachrome 160) and set the meter's exposure-index scale at this number.
2. Take your light level reading and note the light level indicated by the needle.
3. Adjust the movable scale until its pointer points to this light level.
4. You will now find lens openings and shutter speeds matched on two dials. Select the pair you will use.

The following illustration presents an example of the ap-

Three Kinds of Exposure Indications Appearing in Viewfinders of Single-lens Reflex Cameras, Including (at top) Liquid Crystal Display (LCD) for Shutter Speed and f-number

pearance of an exposure meter after it has been set as directed before.

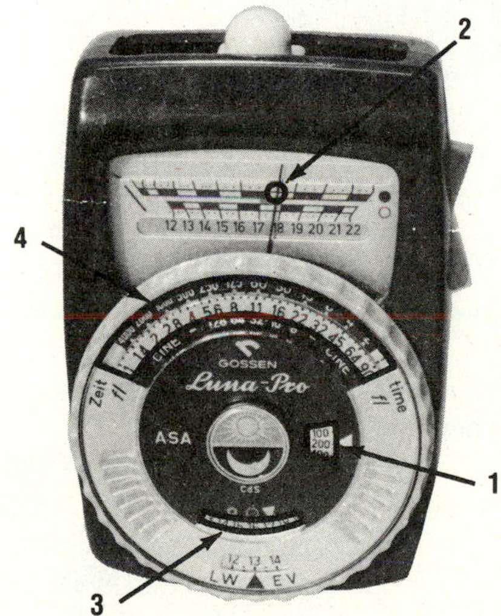

Because shutter speed and lens opening work together, as has been explained, to admit the proper amount of light to the film, correct exposure is shown by any paired values for *f*/number and shutter speed. Can you read the paired figures in the illustration? If you find *f*/16 paired with $1/30$, then other pairs will be *f*/11 at $1/60$, *f*/8 at $1/125$, *f*/5.6 at $1/250$, and so on.

Now which pair should you choose? Your selection is based upon answers to two questions:

1. How much movement is there in the scene? (Recall the examples of shutter-speed selection on page 83; the faster the motion, the higher the necessary speed.)
2. How much depth-of-field is desired? (Recall the

discussion of depth-of-field, page 84; for greater depth-of-field, use a setting with larger *f*/number.)

Now apply some of these relationships. Can you explain why the particular exposure settings were selected for the two following examples?

f/4 at 1/500 second

f/22 at 1/15 second

A good exposure meter is a worthwhile investment. Use it *carefully* for correct exposure determinations.

- When using an incident-light meter, hold it in the center of the scene and aim the white cone toward the camera.
- When using a reflected-light meter, aim it at the subject, especially for exterior scenes. Do not tip the meter and record too much light from the foreground or from the sky.
- Average the readings of a reflected-light meter taken from various objects in a scene; avoid taking readings with a reflected-light meter from very bright or very dark parts of the scene, unless you wish to expose especially for such a part.
- With an incident-light meter, when a subject is backlighted (that is, when the sun or other light source is behind the subject and parts of the subject facing the camera are in shadow), open the lens to one additional *f*/number beyond that indicated on the meter.
- Use an incident-light meter to determine the evenness of illumination in a scene when photoflood lighting is used.
- When filming under photoflood lights, follow the additional suggestions for using a meter that you will find on page 91.
- When doing close-up and copy work, make use of the exposure information on page 105.
- When using color reversal film, an underexposed scene will appear darker overall, while an overexposed scene will appear thin and washed out.
- Follow other suggestions found in the instruction manual accompanying your light meter.

Keep a careful record of light and subject conditions, choice of exposure, and the quality of resulting pictures. From this record you can judge how well your meter is serving you and establish the modifications you must make in using it.

A final word about automatic cameras. On such cameras an exposure meter is coupled directly to the lens diaphragm or shutter, and as light strikes this meter it automatically sets the lens (*f*/number) to correspond to a preselected shutter speed, or sets the shutter speed for a chosen lens setting. This diaphragm-shutter setting will be satisfactorily *provided two requirements are fulfilled:*

- The light must come over your shoulder as you take the picture.
- The meter must not be measuring any unusually bright or unusually dark large areas (such as a white shirt or a background) that are unimportant to the picture (these could cause underexposure or overexposure of the main subject).

Automatic cameras are almost foolproof—but your own experience should guide you to vary the camera setting under certain conditions.

REVIEW

What You Have Learned About Determining Exposure:

1. What three numbers, relating to exposure, can be determined from a film data sheet? Which two can be used directly to make camera settings and which one is for a setting on a light meter?

2. What camera setting would be made under the "*f*/16 rule" when film with an ISO of 100 is used to take pictures under bright sunlight?
3. What two settings are required on a light meter before determining exposure?
4. When these two settings are made on the meter, what pair of numbers results?
5. When may a camera with a built-in meter *not* give a reliable reading or automatic setting?
6. According to the setting illustrated on the incident-light meter on page 91, if a subject requires extreme depth-of-field what camera shutter speed would you use? (First, would you select *f*/2 or *f*/32?)
7. The type of light meter on which the measurement of light intensity is not affected by the color or other characteristics of the subject itself is the ———.

See answers on page 377.

ARTIFICIAL LIGHTING

The purposes of artificial lighting are to provide sufficient illumination for satisfactory exposure and to create either a natural or special appearance of the subject to the viewer. The latter may mean that there is an illusion of depth or a 3-dimensional impression created by shadows on a 2-dimensional surface.

Indoor Available Lighting

Offices, classrooms, laboratories, and many other areas are usually well illuminated by daylight entering through windows or by fluorescent lights. Frequently this available light is sufficient for many filming purposes, with high-speed color film or with moderate-speed black-and-white films. But there are limitations to overhead fluorescent lighting. It causes a very flat type of illumination with few shadows, and is uneven as you measure light levels from the ceiling to the floor. For these reasons, it is often necessary to add supplementary lighting to a scene that will be shot under fluorescent lighting.

Also, because color films respond differently to various light sources, fluorescence may cause unusual effects. Test your film to determine any variations in color rendition and film speed (for example, tests show that Ektachrome 200 daylight-type film, under certain classroom fluorescent lights, at an exposure index of 80 and using an FLD filter over the lens, gives highly acceptable results in terms of accurately reproducing flesh tones).

An alternative is to add artificial light to the scene with one or more photoflood lights equipped with *blue bulbs*. With this lighting, skin tones will appear natural.

Electronic Flash Lighting

Notice the difference in brilliancy and in shadow detail between otherwise identical photographs below, two taken with the natural available light and one with added flash light.

By using electronic flash units, you create your own light. Even in sunlight, flash lighting can be used to add light to shadow areas. A flash is most useful for lighting relatively small areas or for lighting larger ones that have light-colored backgrounds. The light falloff from flash is so great that the background, if it is too far behind the subject (over 10 feet or so), will appear undesirably dark. Conversely, if flash is used too close to a subject, the subject may appear too light or washed out. (See illustrations on the next page.)

The exposure for taking pictures with a manual-type electronic flash unit is determined by the following formula, using a **guide number** for the flash unit and the type of film in your camera.

Exposure for Subject

Exposure for Background

Exposure Balanced with Flash

Flash with Distant Background

Flash with Near Background

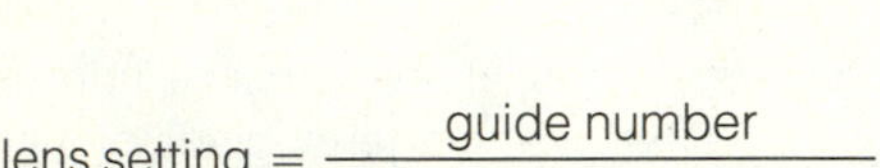

$$\text{lens setting} = \frac{\text{guide number}}{\text{flash-to-subject distance}}$$

Many electronic flash units have scales on the unit from which correct exposure can be determined directly. Note the following data with the sample picture below, and the use of these data in computing the *f*/number.

- Ektachrome film, ISO 64
- Guide number 45
- Shutter speed 1/60 second
- Distance 10 feet (flash to subject)

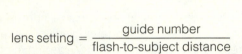

$$\text{lens setting} = \tfrac{45}{10} = 4.5$$

$$\text{lens setting} = f/4.5$$

(*Note: f*/4.5 would be set between the 4 and 5.6 "click stops" on your lens.)

An automatic flash unit contains a light-sensitive cell that reacts to the light being reflected by the subject and automatically controls the flash intensity to produce correct exposure. A predetermined *f*/stop is used for all settings. Some flash units can be adjusted to accommodate a number of *f*/stops to create different effects.

These units usually are quite accurate, but can be fooled under certain conditions. For example, a subject standing closely in front of a white wall will often be underexposed and appear dark. If the subject is in front of a very dark background, or if the background is far behind, the subject will often be overexposed. In order to work effectively with an automatic flash unit, you should learn to recognize these conditions and adjust your camera to correct for them.

Here are some other points to keep in mind when preparing to use flash lighting:

- Guide numbers are for determining exposure with average subjects under average conditions. Darker or lighter subjects or the color of walls can affect light reflections. Modify the guide number accordingly.
- Because the duration of an electronic flash is so short, the guide number is the same at any shutter speed. But use a slow speed, especially with a camera that has a focal plane shutter (1/60 second) for satisfactory synchronization of the flash with camera shutter opening.
- Aim the flash unit toward the ceiling to **bounce** the light before it reaches the subject. Soft, even lighting will result. (Be alert that a ceiling color will be picked up by the reflected light and will change the color tone of the scene.) For bounce lighting, open the lens setting at least two additional *f*/stops as compared to direct flash used at the same distance.
- When using an automatic flash unit to bounce light, make certain that the electric eye is pointed at the subject.
- Test your own equipment with the films you use to determine the best settings that give you proper exposure.

Photoflood Lighting

If controlled lighting is necessary, consider using photographic floodlamps. They may be essential for video recording. Even for still photography floodlights are often better than flash, since you see exactly what effect the lights are creating (reflections, heavy shadows, or uneven lighting) and can make corrections before taking pictures.

Two major types of photoflood lamps are available. The traditional incandescent-filament lamp, with wattages of 250, 500, or 1000 in a hemisphere-shaped reflector, may be used. Lamp technology has made available small tubular units consisting of a quartz envelope containing a tungsten filament and filled with a halogen gas, commonly iodine vapor. These quartz-iodine lamps provide a very bright, narrow ribbon of light and project an extremely even illumination. People appearing in scenes in which quartz iodine lamps are used should be warned not to look directly into the light, because the brightness of the source can cause eye discomfort.

When it is desirable to use available light, but a supplement is needed to raise the light level, "bounce" light is beneficial. From near the camera position, aim a floodlight at the ceiling or floor. It will "snap up" the scene without lights being reflected directly off the subject. (See illustration in next column.)

If floodlights or a flash are aimed directly at the subject, sharp, dense shadows are created somewhere in the scene. They must be controlled. Floodlamps placed close to the camera will light the subject only from the front. Such lighting results in a flat, shadowless subject with heavy background shadows, which is usually undesirable.

It is better to place one light about 45° to the side of the camera, somewhat closer to the subject, and 30° above the camera. This becomes the main source or

Available Light

Bounce Light Added

key light. It substitutes for the sun, which shines on an outdoor scene, or represents light from a window or a lamp. Therefore it should be the brightest light source (either by wattage or closeness to the subject).

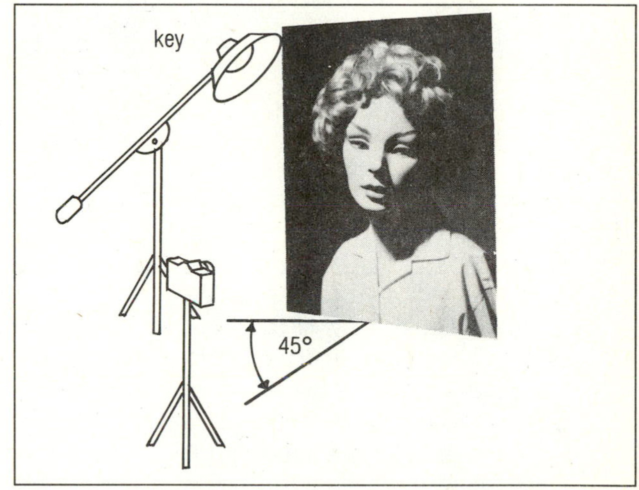

Place a second light (or two) beside the camera (on the side opposite the main light) and at camera height. This light serves to fill and soften shadows created by the key light, thus bringing out more detail in the subject. It is called the **fill light.**

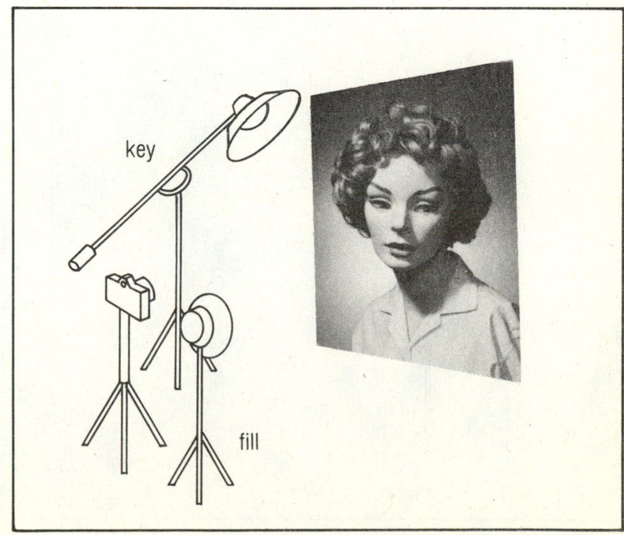

Some light from the key may fall on the background, but a third light (or two), aimed evenly at the background, will illuminate it, thus separating the subject from the background and giving the scene some depth. This is the **background light.** Always keep the subject at least 2 or 3 feet away from the background to minimize heavy shadows created by any lights.

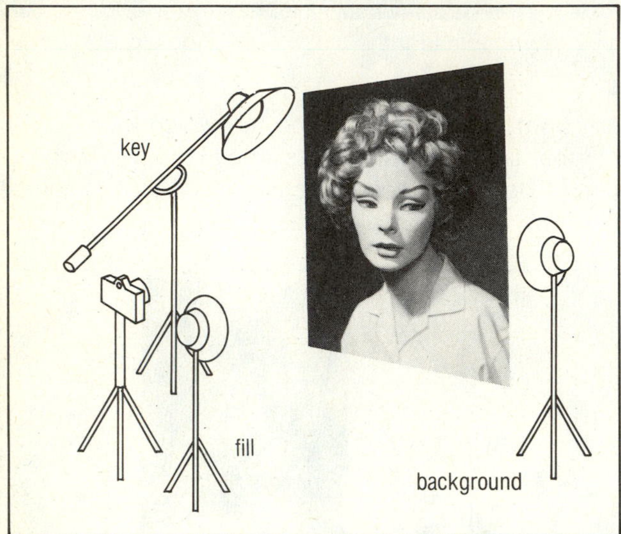

These three lights—key, fill, and background—form the basic lighting pattern for good indoor lighting. With color film, the key, as the brightest light, is placed so that it illuminates the subject with *twice* the intensity of the fill light. Intensity is measured by holding an incident light meter at the subject and aiming it at the light source. When the intensity of the key light is *twice* the intensity of the fill light (meter readings may be: key—100, fill—50) we say the "key to fill ratio" (**lighting ratio**) is 2 to 1. This will result in soft shadow areas being recorded on the film.

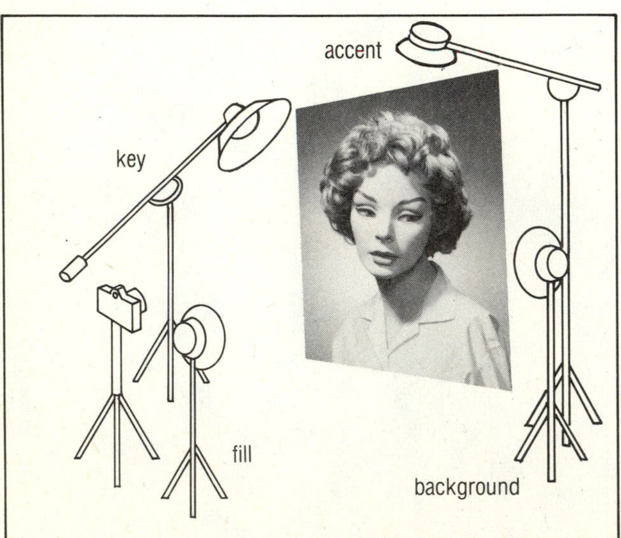

For close-up scenes, to reduce shadows, the intensity of the fill may be equal to that of the key light—key to fill ratio of 1 to 1. (Set a light for the intensity you want by moving it closer to or farther from the subject.) When black-and-white film is used, the key to fill ratio may be as high as 5 to 1.

One or more background lights may be set to illuminate the background evenly with a meter reading one-half to one stop lower than the general reading within the scene. Sometimes a spotlight (or photospot) is used as an **accent light** to highlight a person or an object in the scene. For most subjects, whether portrait, table top setups, or in a large area, this lighting pattern can be applied.

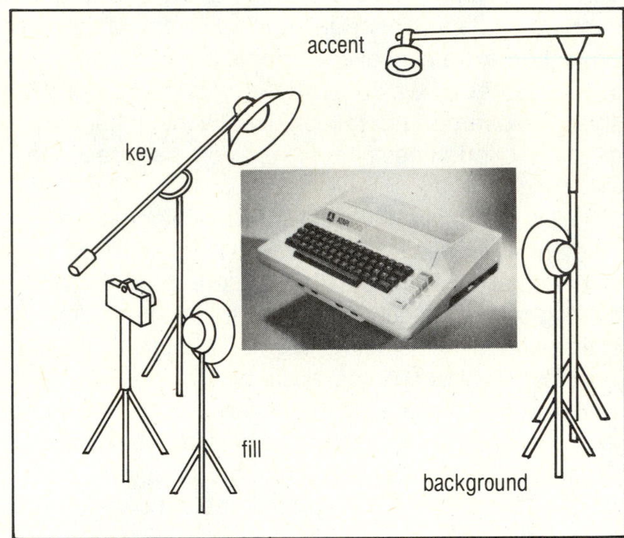

Lighting Metal and Glass Objects

When shiny metal surfaces or glassware are illuminated with the normal lighting pattern just described, the result usually is undesirable reflections and dark or light areas of the subject. See the first picture in each set on the next page.

Indirect or diffused lighting should be used with such subjects. Place objects with metal surfaces in an enclosure consisting of tracing paper or other translucent material sides. Aim lights through the sides to illuminate metal subjects. Light is softened as it passes through the translucent paper, thereby eliminating hot spots and uneven reflections.

To avoid reflections on glassware, place the objects to be photographed on a sheet of glass, raised above the table. Set a sheet of white cardboard on the table, under the objects. Aim a floodlight at the cardboard. Light will reflect from the cardboard through the glassware, providing even, nonreflecting illumination of the subject.

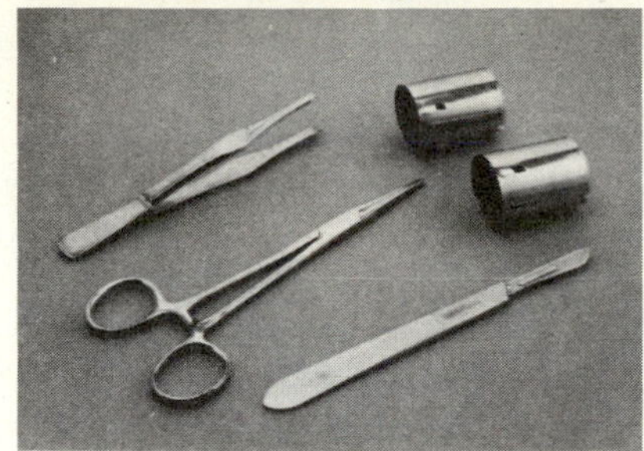
Result with Direct Lighting

Diffused Lighting Setup

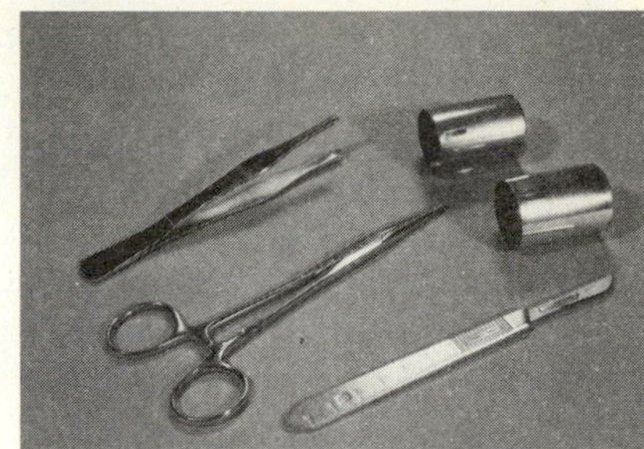
Result with Diffused Lighting

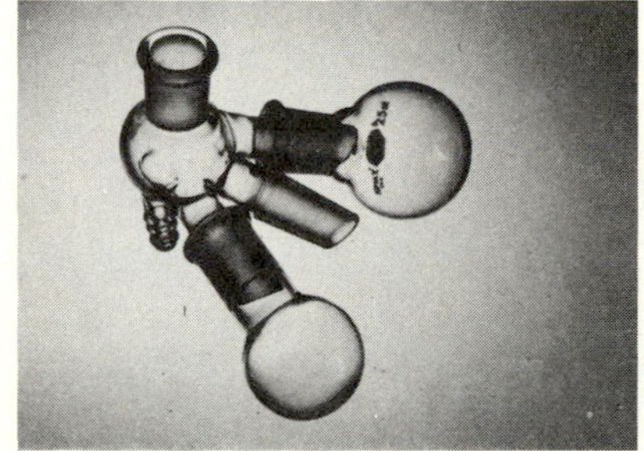
Result with Direct Lighting

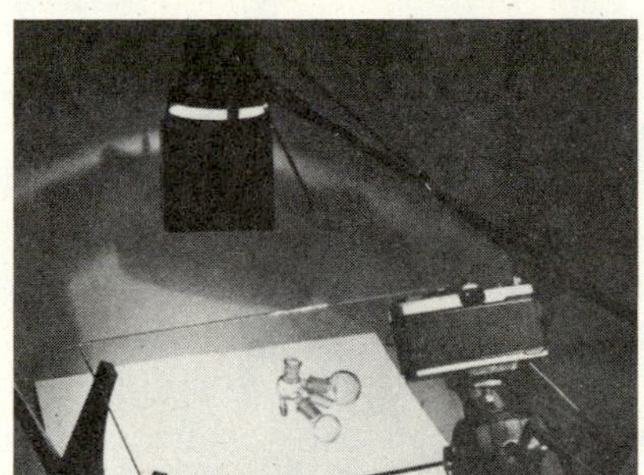
Reflected Lighting Setup

Result with Reflected Lighting

REVIEW

What You Have Learned About Lighting:

1. Is electronic flash effective for lighting *small* or *large* areas?
2. Apply the correct formula to determine *f*/ number: flash guide number for film is 100, distance of camera to subject is 6 feet.
3. In a scene including people and large objects, what are some disadvantages of using lights placed only right beside the camera?
4. What is meant by the expression, "Key to fill ratio is 4 to 1"? Is this an acceptable ratio to create pleasant shadows on color film?
5. What method would you use for determining exposure under floodlighting?
6. Explain the positioning and purpose served by each light—accent, background, key, and fill. In what order is each set for use?
7. Why is it necessary to give special attention, when lighting, to metal surfaces and glassware?

See answers on page 377.

CAMERA SHOTS AND PICTURE COMPOSITION

The effectiveness of instructional media is strengthened by giving attention to two aspects relating to picture composition—framing of the total image within the camera's viewfinder and arranging the necessary elements that comprise the image. These matters are important for all photographic visuals—still scenes in slides or motion scenes for video and motion pictures.

Framing the Picture

The composition of a scene should be carefully decided when viewed through the camera lens. Therefore, the camera must be placed in the best position for recording all necessary elements in a scene. In deciding where to place the camera, two questions should be asked:

▸ What is the best *viewpoint* from which the picture

should be taken (including action or movement)?

- How much *area* should be included in the scene?

The description of each scene (or "shot") in the script or on the storyboard provides information that helps you to answer these questions. In doing this, you give attention to the various kinds of camera shots as each question refers to the relation between the camera position and the subject.

Basic Shots

Three types of scenes are common in photography:

- The **long** or **wide shot (LS)**—a general view of the setting and the subject. It provides an orientation for the viewer, by establishing all elements in the scene, and if important, shows size proportions relating to the subject. This often becomes an **establishing shot** within a sequence of shots.
- The **medium shot (MS)**—a closer view of the subject, eliminating unnecessary background and other details.
- The **close-up (CU)**—a concentration on the subject, or on a part of it, excluding everything else from view.

When the subject is the same, three successive shots assume a relation to each other.

LS, MS, and CU do not mean any specific distances. A long shot of a building may be taken from a distance of hundreds of yards, whereas a long shot of equipment may be taken from a distance of only a few feet. You may be close-up to a building when you are across the street, but you may need to get within a foot or so of the equipment to take a close-up.

Although LS–MS–CU is a fundamental sequence, it is not to be rigidly followed in successive sequences, and there is no set rule for the use of these three basic shots. The visual effect desired should determine the sequence.

Sequences need variety; without variations, your media may become monotonous. A still-picture sequence can include a number of relatively similar successive shots, while a videotape recording or film requires more diversity so it does not lose its pacing or impact.

For straightforward explanation the LS–MS–CU sequence may be satisfactory. For a slower pace, gradually increasing interest, LS–MS–MCU–CU may be used. For suspense or drama, consider CU–CU–CU–LS.

Note the differences in the shots that comprise the two sequences on the following page.

Although the subject does limit the kinds of shots that are called for in the script, two photographers covering the same subject may film the three basic scenes differently, each imparting his or her own interpretation and emphasis. To say that one version is right and the other wrong would most likely depend on personal preference (see illustration on page 100).

At the two ends of the LS–MS–CU sequence you can introduce *extremes* if they are important to your story—

Long Shot

Medium Shot

Close-up

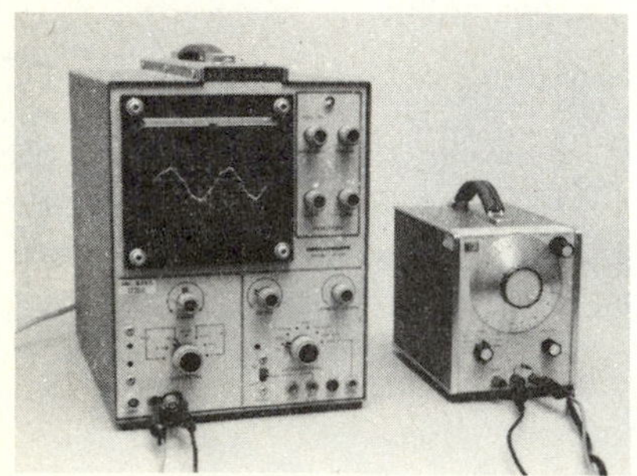

Long Shot

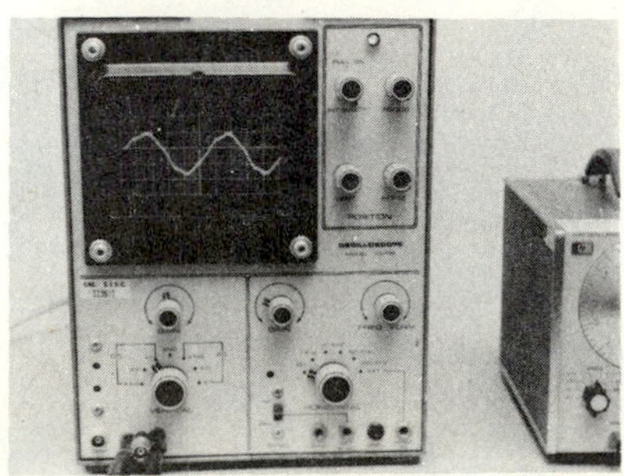

Medium Shot

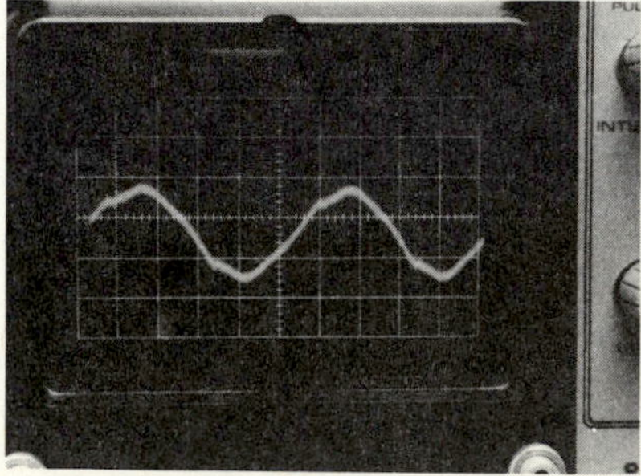

Close-up

Sequence 1

LS

MS

MCU

CU

Sequence 2

MS

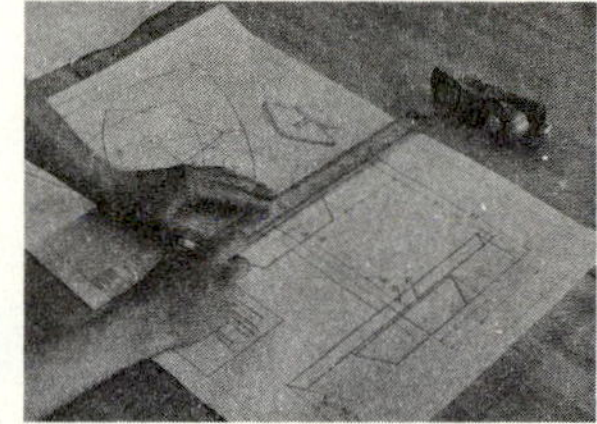
CU

LS

MS

extreme long or **wide shot (ELS)** and **extreme close-up (ECU).** Also, there are situations in which you may designate a scene between two basic shots—a **medium long shot (MLS)** or a **medium close-up (MCU).**

Angle and Position Shots

Variety, emphasis, and dramatic effect can be accomplished through the use of *camera angles*. The normal or neutral camera position is at about eye level for a person standing. A camera in a higher position, looking down on the subject, makes a **high-angle shot** that gives the illusion of placing the subject in an inferior position, reducing its size and slowing its motion. A camera in a lower than normal position, looking up at a subject, makes a **low-angle shot** that seems to give the subject a dominant position, exaggerating its height and speeding up movement. High- and low-angle shots can be used to eliminate undesirable background or foreground details.

The camera may be placed in the position of the eyes of the observer, that is, of an audience. This is an **objec-**

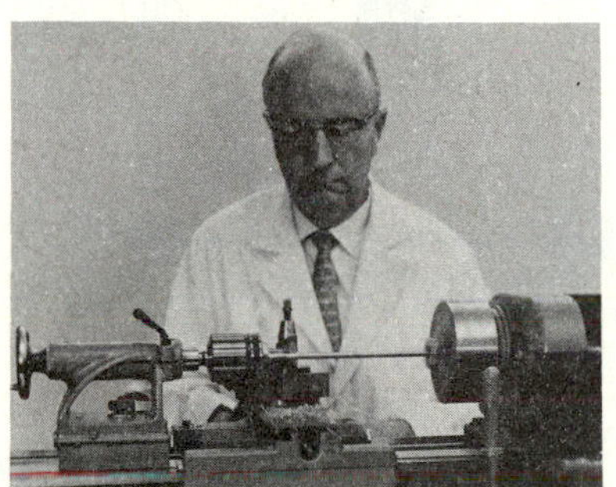
Objective Scene

Subjective Scene

High-angle Shot

Neutral Shot

Low-angle Shot

LS, Photographer A

LS, Photographer B

MS, Photographer A

MS, Photographer B

CU, Photographer A

CU, Photographer B

Extreme Long Shot (ELS)

Extreme Close-up (ECU)

tive scene. Or, the camera may be placed in the position of the subject's eyes (over the shoulder) to see the performance of an operation or the behavior of an object as the subject sees it. This is a **subjective scene.** In the latter, the photographer may shoot over the subject's shoulder, with the camera at a high angle.

In summary, there is a variety of filming shots at your disposal:

- Basic shots—long shot, medium shot, close-up
- Extremes—extreme long shot, extreme close-up
- High-angle and low-angle shots
- Objective and subjective camera positions

To these shots, when using a videocamera, *moving* camera shots such as *panning* and *tilting* can be added. These are treated in the video chapter on page 247.

Each scene requires placing the camera in the best position for viewing the setting and action. Thus, camera placement determines image size and angle. These factors contribute to the communication value of any photographic media, whether still or moving.

Arrangement of Elements

Studies of perception and artistic design have established a number of composition principles that will ensure that the content of a picture will be clearly recognizable, easily understood, and convey a certain feeling. Those principles appropriate to the design of graphic-type materials are considered on page 116. Refer to them since they also relate to photographic images. The following principles apply when photographing pictures:

- Most visual materials normally have a horizontal format. If possible, plan your content for this format. Try not to mix vertical photographs or slides with horizontal ones in a series if there is a possibility that they might be used in a video recording.

- Have only one major subject or center of interest in a scene. Do not clutter a picture or make it tell too much. Eliminate or subordinate all secondary elements and focus attention on the main one.

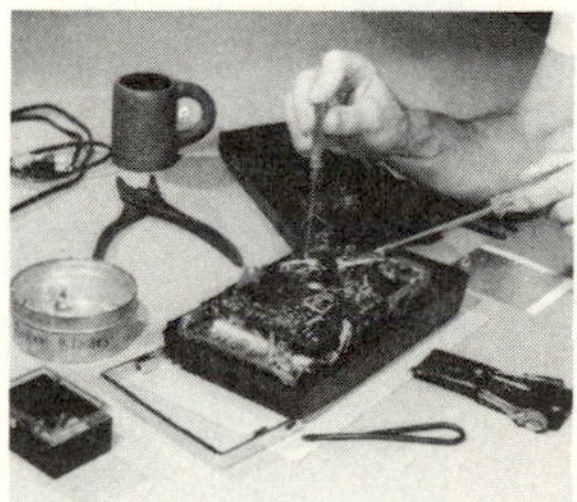
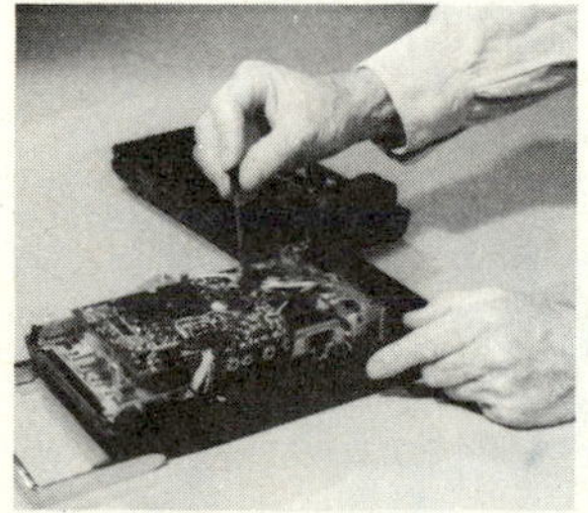

- Because viewers have no way of judging the size of unknown objects in pictures, it is important to include some familiar object for comparison.

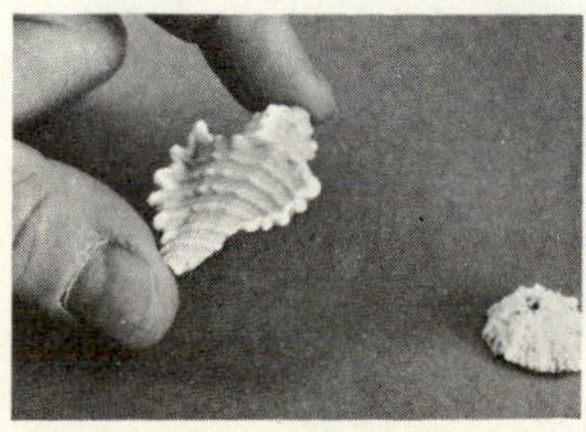

- Keep the background simple. Eliminate confusing background details by removing disturbing objects, by putting up a screen to hide the background, or by throwing the background out of focus (using a smaller *f*/number, thus controlling the depth of field).

- Place the center of interest near to but not directly in the physical center of the picture area. By making the picture slightly asymmetrical you create a dynamic and more interesting arrangement.

- Try not to be static from one scene to another by shooting from the same relative camera position or angle. Plan to vary camera positions. Changing angles creates a dynamic impression and gives variety to composition.

- If action or movement is implied in a picture allow more space or picture area in the direction of the action rather than away from it.

- Include some foreground detail to create an impression of depth (principally in long-shot exterior scenes). Foregrounds help to balance the picture and to make it interesting.

- Finally, use common sense in composition. Ask yourself, What am I trying to accomplish with this picture or scene? Then pick what appears to be the best angle and the best distance for the camera. If necessary, view the scene from two or three positions and make pictures from each one for future selection.

We have examined a number of suggestions and guidelines that should be helpful in creating good composition. Yet, there is personal choice when framing and arranging picture elements because there are no hard rules to follow mechanically. Each situation is different, requiring a unique decision. Use these principles for guidance, along with your own experience to ensure that the images will best serve the scripted purpose.

REVIEW

What You Have Learned About Camera Shots and Picture Composition:

1. Relate the shots—high-angle, low-angle, objective, subjective—to the following situations:
   a. Exaggerate subject height
   b. Slowing subject movement
   c. Over-the-shoulder filming
   d. Filming from an audience viewpoint
   e. Eliminating a disturbing background
2. Which type of basic shot is used to establish the subject location?
3. Label the types of camera shots illustrated by each scene in the sequence that follows. In what order would you arrange these scenes to make a meaningful sequence?

(a) (b) (c) (d)

(e) (f) (g) (h)

4. Following is a group of six pictures (scenes); each one composes the same subject differently. Which one do you prefer? Why?

(a) (b) (c) (d) (e) (f)

See answers on page 377.

CLOSE-UP AND COPY WORK

In photography it is often necessary to photograph subjects at a very close range, such as for titles, reproductions of charts and pictures, and for close-ups of subject details.

Your camera may be unsatisfactory for such close-up work unless you can make adjustments and allowances in two respects: *viewfinding* and *focusing.*

Viewfinding and Parallax

As discussed before, in some cameras the viewer and the taking lens do not see exactly the same area, which causes the phenomenon of *parallax.* The different areas that the taking lens and the viewfinder see are illustrated in two pictures on the next page.

Single-lens reflex and view cameras permit through-the-lens viewing. The subject is observed directly through the taking lens and focused on a ground glass. These cameras are preferred for close-up and copy photography. (See illustration on next page.)

If your camera does not have built-in features to deal with the parallax error, it is difficult to do close-up and copy work.

Focusing and Exposure

Cameras are adapted for close-up photography (picture taking close to the subject, often under 2 feet) by one of three devices:

- ► A lens specially made for close-up focusing, which maintains a flatness of field and does not distort lines in a subject (a *macro lens*).

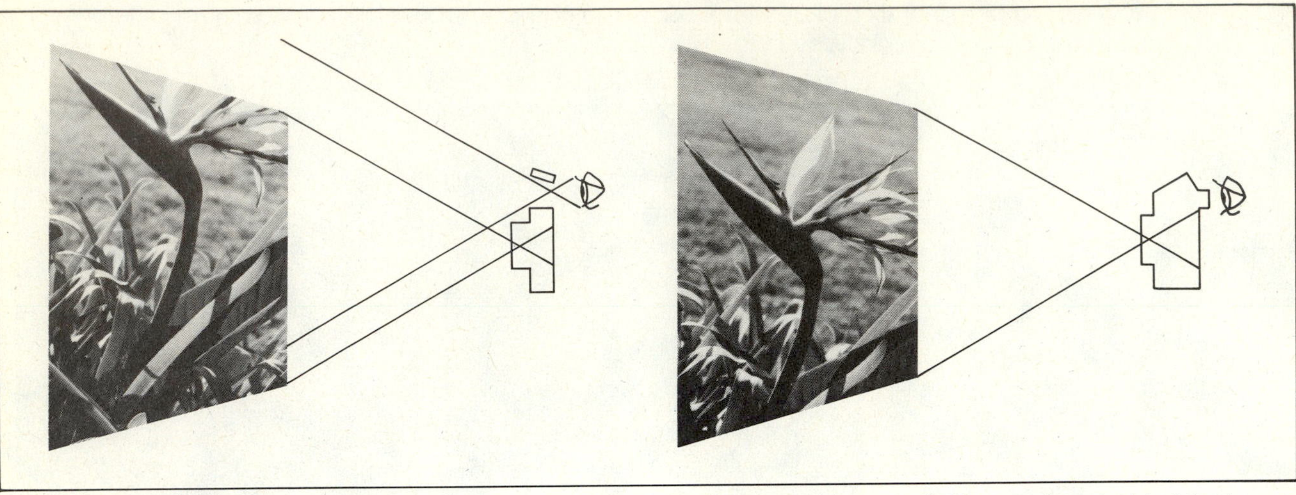

Camera with window-type viewfinder parallax results in cutting off a portion of the subject

Camera with ground-glass surface behind the lens: no parallax

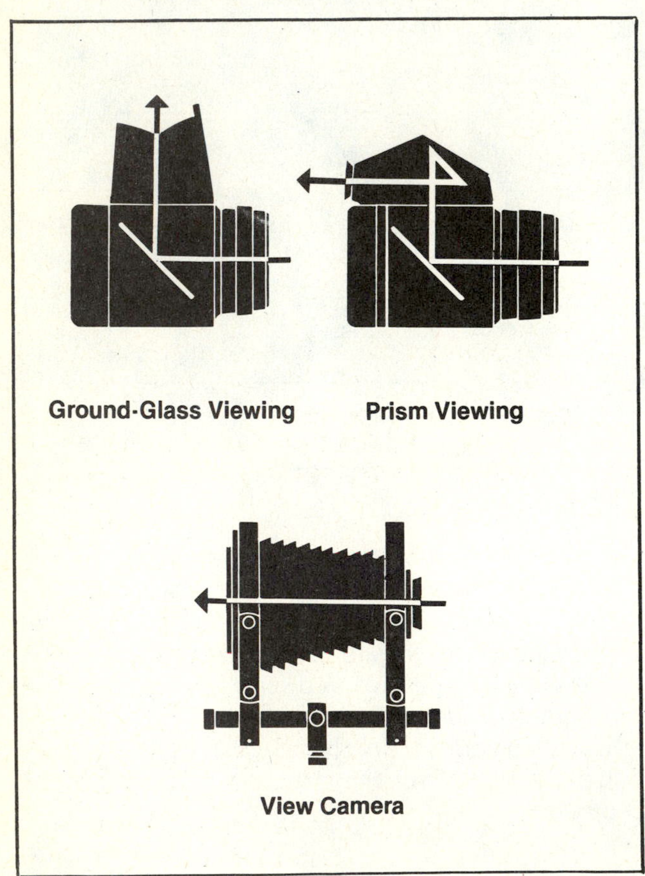

Macro Lens

Extension Tubes

Close-up Lens

- The camera permits the use of separate extension tubes or bellows, attached between the camera body and the lens, that lengthen the lens-to-film distance.
- A close-up attachment can be mounted on the lens to change the optical character of the lens system.

When you use extension tubes for close-ups, you are using the same lens that you would use to take pictures at normal distances. But exposure must be adjusted because of the increased distance between lens and film. A through-the-lens meter accommodates the exposure for any extension. When a separate meter is used, the exposure for close-ups under these conditions is found by the usual exposure-meter procedure plus an additional computation. The additional computation takes into account the focal length of the camera lens (which is printed or engraved on the lens housing) and the amount of extension of the tubes. A formula can be used for measurements either in inches or in metric units. It is:

$$\text{increased-exposure factor} = \frac{(\text{length of extension})^2}{(\text{focal length of lens})^2}$$

The application of this formula to a specific problem is illustrated:

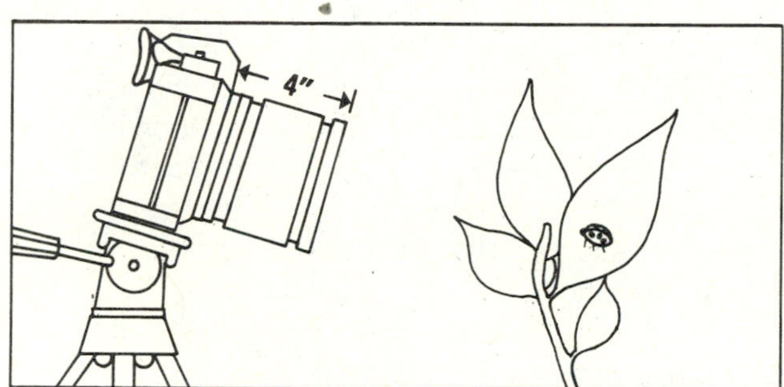

- Focal length of lens; 50mm or 2 inches
- Length of extension; 100mm or 4 inches
- Normal exposure; *f*/8 at 1/60

Using the formula with the distances in inches gives:

$$\text{increased-exposure factor} = \frac{4^2}{2^2} = \frac{16}{4} = 4$$

Therefore, exposure must be 4 times the normal exposure. This increase can be accomplished by opening up the diaphragm of the lens 2 *f*/stops (to give exposure of *f*/4 at 1/60 second) or by reducing the shutter speed one-fourth (to give exposure of *f*/8 at 1/15 second). To ensure best focus and maximum depth-of-field when working close, use a larger *f*/number, which means a smaller lens diaphragm opening.

Review the explanation of *f*/number-shutter speed relationships on page 83 and the selection of a lens setting to increase depth-of-field on page 84.

The majority of cameras can be adapted for close-up work with one or more supplementary lenses (close-up attachments) placed in a retaining ring and attached over the regular lens. With this method no compensation for exposure is required as with an extension tube when focusing close to objects.

Using a Copy Stand

A **copy stand,** which holds your camera at various positions, is useful to accommodate materials of different sizes. Vertical stands are more serviceable than horizontal ones because of the difficulty of securing books in a vertical position.

Commercial Copy Stand

Suggestions for Close-up and Copy Work

- Use a sturdy tripod stand to steady your camera.
- Use either photoflood lamps in reflectors or lamps with built-in reflectors. For copying set the lamps evenly at 45-degree angles to each side of the camera and at a sufficient distance to avoid uneven lighting, reflections, or "hot spots." Check for evenness of lighting with your meter.
- When copying from a book or other source that does not lie flat, hold the material in position with a sheet of nonreflecting glass (available from photo-supply, art-supply, or hardware stores).
- For close-ups of three-dimensional objects, avoid most shadow areas by using *flat lighting* (that is, use a key to fill light ratio of 1 to 1 as explained on page 96).

- Use a meter to determine exposure. An incident light meter gives a direct reading when placed in the position of the subject or material. If you use a reflected light meter, read either from a gray card (Eastman Kodak's neutral test card) or from a sheet of white bond paper held against the main portion of the subject. Because such paper reflects a large portion of the light, a reading from it will be *5 times too high.* To correct for this high reading, divide the exposure index of the film by 5 and set your meter at the closest value (example: Ektachrome 64, exposure index 64, set meter at 64 ÷ 5, that is, at 13).

- Select camera settings of *f*/11 or *f*/16, which utilize the sharpest focus characteristics of the lens, and which ensure adequate depth-of-field.

Remember: You must have the copyright holder's permission to reproduce copyrighted materials (page 169).

Filming Titles

Titles are handled as is other copy work.

If a mask was used to frame the original art work, align the camera on the copy stand to take in the open area of the mask (page 115). Remove the mask. Then proceed with routine copying of materials made to its size and format.

If a mask was not used to prepare the lettering, adjust picture size by raising or lowering the camera. Keep in mind that acceptable legibility requires lettering size to be a minimum of one-fiftieth the height of the projected area. (See page 132 for description of legibility standards.)

When a title is prepared on a sheet of film (as in making an overhead transparency by methods described in Chapter 12) and placed over a background picture or art work, cover the total area with a piece of nonreflecting glass. This should press the film to the background, eliminating shadows of the letters and reflections from the film. Since most 35mm single-lens reflex cameras photograph a larger field than is seen through the viewfinder, adjust the camera distance so the title almost fills the viewfinder. Generally this will provide large words and sufficient background bleed on the resulting slide.

Titles to appear over a special background as **white letter overprints** may require double exposure (see page 140 for preparation of art work). First film the background slightly dark (½ to 1 *f*/stop underexposed). Then, on the same negative without advancing the film, expose the lettering. Many cameras permit you to bypass the release button in order to make two exposures on a single frame of film. Check your camera before planning to carry out this technique.

REVIEW

What You Have Learned About Close-up and Copy Work:

1. Of the cameras described at the beginning of this chapter (page 76), with which ones would you expect to have a parallax problem in viewing?
2. If a close-up lens is used over the regular camera lens, need there be a calculation for change in exposure? Would this also be true with a bellows extension?
3. What is the name of a lens that may be directly used on the camera in place of the regular lens for close-up and copy work?
4. In close-up work is a higher or lower *f*/number desirable? Does this mean that a *slower* or *faster* shutter speed is used? Therefore, a tripod or stand *is* or *is not* essential?
5. Explain how a reflected-light meter can be used with a sheet of white paper to determine exposure for copying. In such a situation, what setting for exposure index (film speed) is made on the meter for Kodak Ektachrome 160T (Tungsten) film having a rated ISO of 160?

See answers on page 377.

PROCESSING FILM

You may choose to send exposed film to a commercial film processing laboratory for developing and even for printing. But in recent years the processing of both black-and-white and color film has been greatly simplified.

Facilities and Equipment

- Light-tight room for film loading (a daylight-loading tank eliminates this need)
- Sink with running water and countertop working area
- Clean, ventilated area for film drying
- Roll-film developing tank with one or more reels for

the film size being used or one or more tanks and film holders for cut film

- Prepared chemicals for processing film
- Graduated or other calibrated measuring container and a funnel
- Thermometer
- Timer or watch with second hand
- Three to six stoppered bottles, preferably of brown-tinted glass or plastic

Black-and-White Film

Practice loading an old roll of film onto the reel of your tank (see suggestions on the instruction sheet with the tank) until you can do it smoothly. Then, *in the dark,* load and thread the film to be processed. Each turn of the film on the reel must fit into a separate groove so film does not touch. Place the reel in the tank and cap it. From here on do all processing under normal room light.

The purpose served by each step in the process is:

- ***Developer***—acts upon the exposed silver chemicals in the film that have been affected by light during picture taking, depositing the silver as tiny grains to form the black silver image of the negative.
- ***Rinse***—removes excess developer from the film.
- ***Fixer***—sets the image by changing the remaining undeveloped silver chemical so that it may be removed.
- ***Washing***—removes all chemicals that may cause discoloration of the negative or deposits on its surface.
- ***Dry***—allows wash water to evaporate, film surface to harden, and film to curl to its natural shape.

Refer to the information sheet packaged with your film for recommended developer and for specific processing instructions. Follow all directions, especially those for time and temperature controls.

Examine your negative and judge its quality by these three points:

- A good negative will have a considerable amount of detail, even in its very darkest and lightest portions, unless these portions represent parts of the picture that were themselves entirely lacking in detail.
- A good negative will be transparent enough, even in its very blackest areas, so that you can read a newspaper through it.
- A good negative will have no part of the picture quite as clear as the borders of the film.

Color Negative Film

Kodak Gold 100, 200, 400, 1000, and 1600 films can be processed by a film laboratory or with a color processing kit (Process C-41). Processing time in a tank is under 30 minutes with careful timing and critical temperature control (the first step requires a constant temperature of 100°F ± ¼°F and the remaining six steps

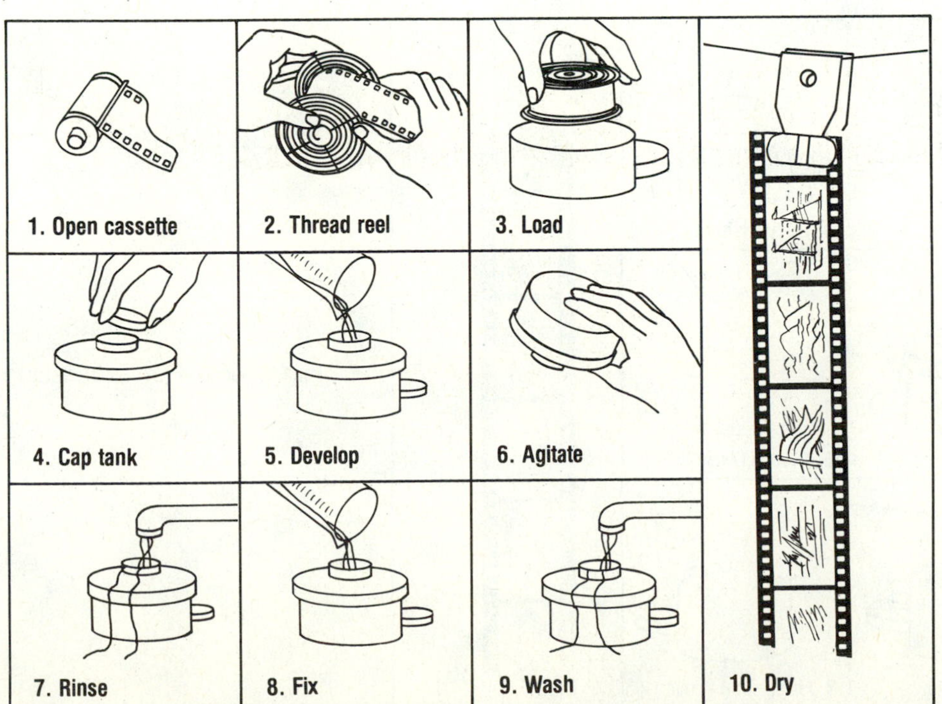

Black-and-White Film Processing

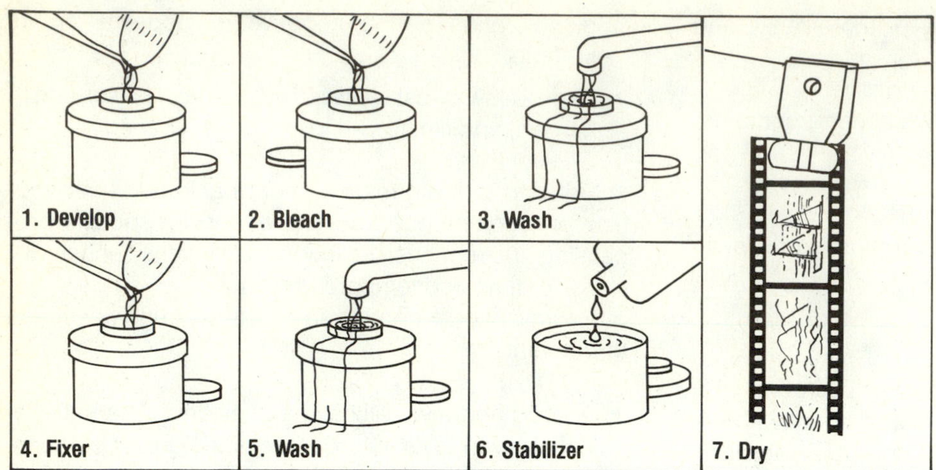

Color Negative Film Processing

should be within a range of 75° to 105°F). See the illustration above.

Mix the chemicals according to instructions with the processing kit. Store each solution in a tightly closed bottle. Write the date of preparation on each bottle. The useful life of the developer is six weeks and that of other solutions is eight weeks. Before use, place the bottles in a tray of running water maintained at the proper temperature.

Color Reversal Film

All color reversal films, except Kodachrome, can be "home" processed. Kodachrome is handled only by authorized processing laboratories. As with color negative films, processing kits allow handling of one or more rolls in normal room light with the film in a light-tight tank during the initial part of the process. Here again, temperature (100°F ± ¼°F for the first developer and 92° to 102°F thereafter) and timing must be carefully maintained. The procedure for Ektachrome roll film (process E-6) is illustrated below.

In some filming situations, the light level is too low for normal exposure. It is possible to increase the effective film speed (ASA/ISO rating) and then adjust the time of the first developer to obtain satisfactory color slides. For example, by increasing Ektachrome 160T (Tungsten) from an ASA/ISO of 160 to 320 you are in effect under-

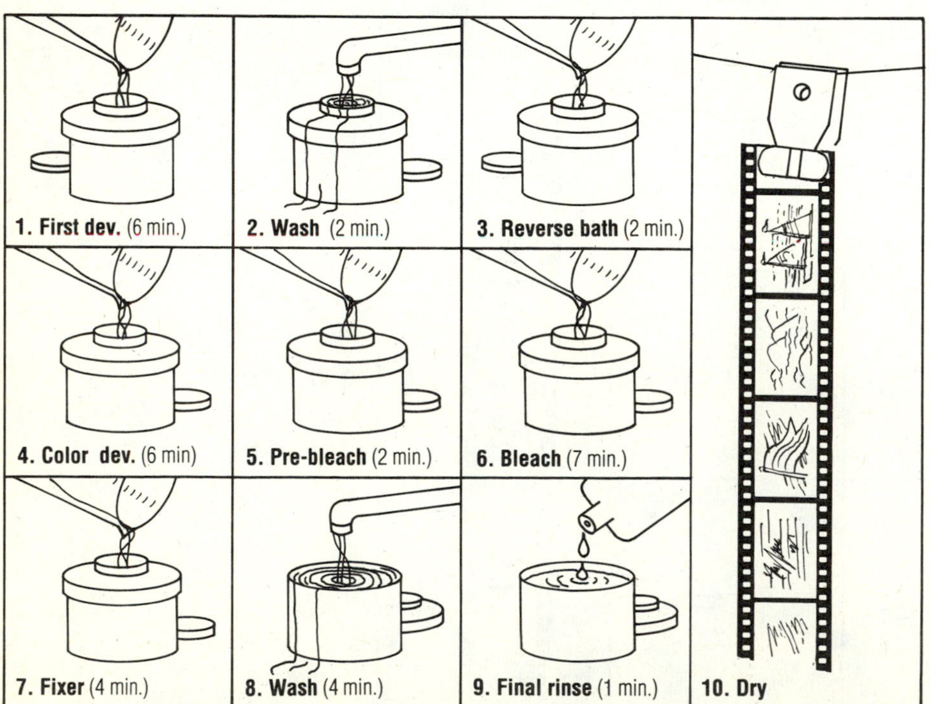

Color Reversal Film Processing

exposing by one f/stop. To compensate, increase the first developer by one-and-a-half times. Film speeds up to four times normal can be used with modified processing times.

If you will be processing many rolls of negative or reversal color film, or roll lengths longer than 36 exposures, consider using automated equipment. In such a machine, film moves continuously through separate tanks containing chemicals for each processing step. Development time is controlled by the length of time film remains in each tank.

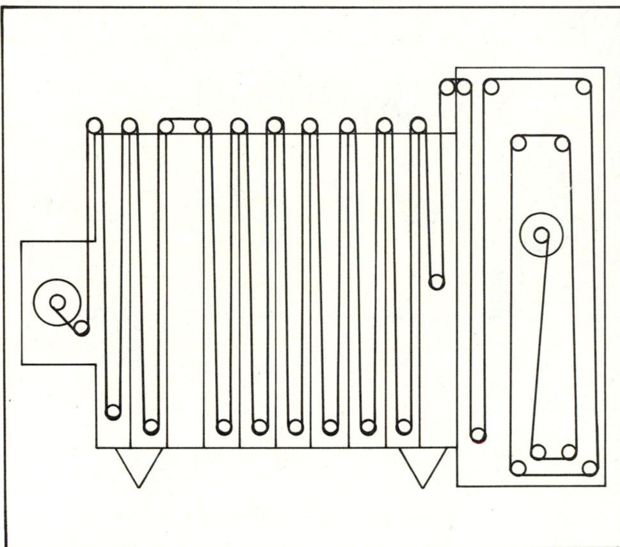

Negative

Contact Print Sheet

Enlarged Print

MAKING PRINTS

For successful contact printing and enlarging you need to know about:

- The selection of contact and enlarging papers (printing papers are classified by speed, weight, finish and surface texture, contrast, color or tone of image, contrast, color of image, and base material)
- Exposure—length of time for contact printing; lens diaphragm opening and length of time for enlarging
- The selection of chemicals—developer, stop bath, fixer
- Using filters for contrast control and color correction
- Processing time and procedure with each solution
- Washing, drying, and finishing

The negative is used to prepare a positive print on paper or film. *If the print is to be the same size as the negative,* the process is **contact printing,** but *if the print is to be larger than the negative,* the process is **enlarging.**

Facilities and Equipment

The standard equipment and materials for a darkroom consist of the following:

- A darkroom 6 × 8 feet or larger, equipped with running water (temperature controlled), countertop workspace, storage, and electrical outlets
- A contact printer or printing frame
- An enlarger with easel and timer
- A print washer or tray siphon
- A print dryer
- One or more sets of trays (three to a set) in various sizes (8 × 10 inches, 11 × 14 inches, and so on) or a processing machine
- Clock, tongs, and miscellaneous small items
- One or more safelights (with color filter based on printing paper to be used)
- Photographic contact and enlarging paper
- Prepared chemicals for developer (or activator), stop bath, and fixer

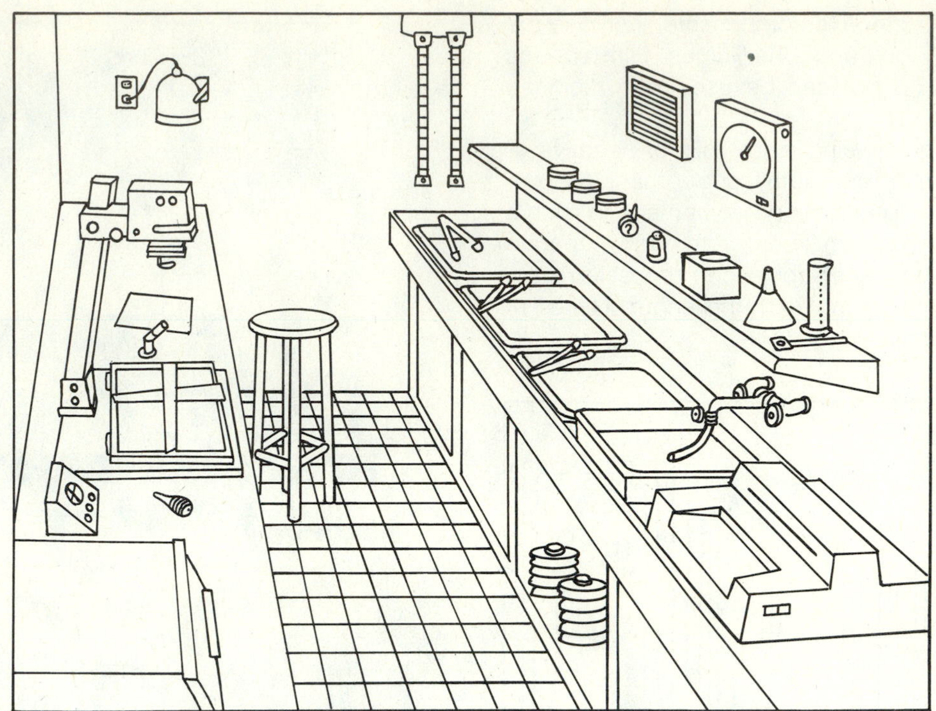

Contact Printing

This method is particularly useful for rapid preparation of **proof sheets** from negatives. A whole roll of negatives (12 to 36) can be printed at one time on a sheet of contact paper (8 × 10 inch). From these **contact prints,** negatives can be selected for enlargements.

Place the negative (emulsion, or *dull side,* down) on top of a sheet of photographic contact paper (emulsion, or *shiny side,* up); cover them with glass and expose the pack to light. Or use a contact printer with a pressure platen and a built-in lamp for exposing. Develop the paper as illustrated in the next section. The resulting print will contain positive images the same size as each negative.

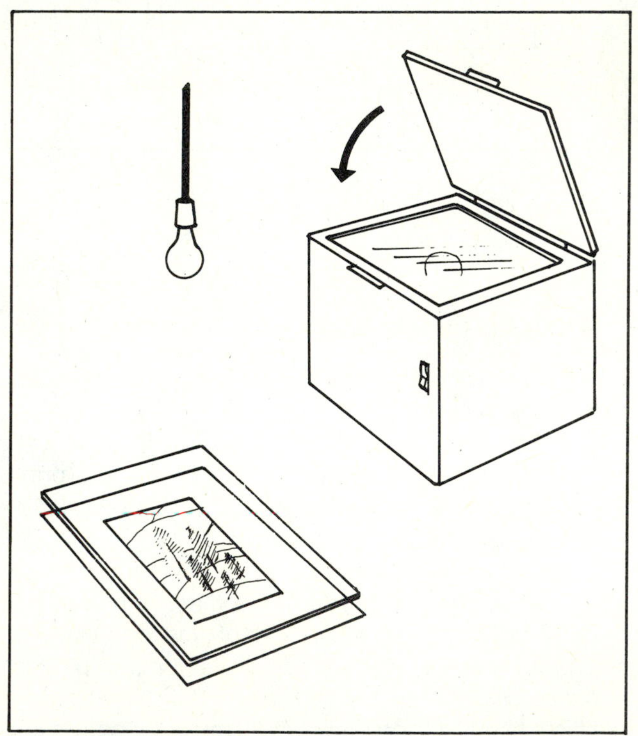

Enlarging from Black-and-White Negatives

Select printing paper (or a contrast filter) to match the contrast of the negative. For example, a contrasty negative requires number 1 paper or polycontrast filter 1.

Place the negative in the enlarger and project it through the lens onto a sheet of enlarging paper. Make tests on strips of paper to determine the correct combination of enlarger lens setting and exposure time before preparing the final prints.

After the black-and-white photographic paper is exposed to light, processing follows. Use the same general chemical treatment as for film—develop, stop, fix, and wash (for a paper print, a paper developer is used in place of the film developer).

Instead of manually processing the exposed paper in trays, a tabletop processor can be used, which makes darkroom routine operation simpler, more reliable, and efficient. In addition, this averts the need to continually immerse your hands in potentially hazardous chemicals. Some processors require manual operation, but others have temperature controls, automatic

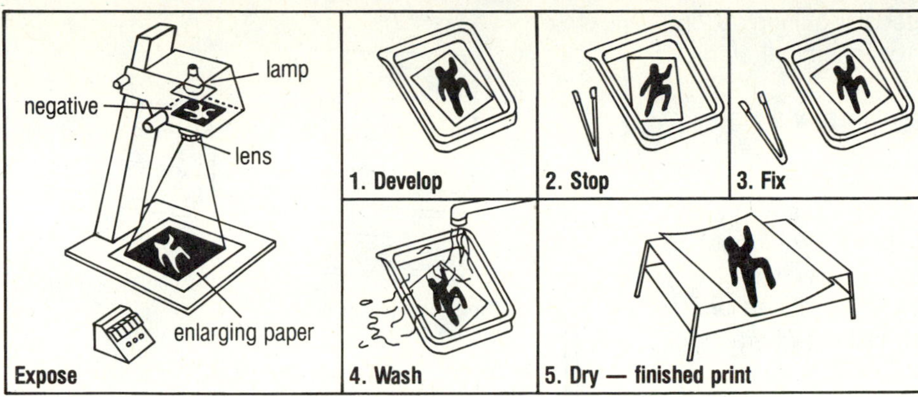

Enlarged Black-and-White Print from Negative

timing, and require little or no attention until the paper emerges dry, ready to use.

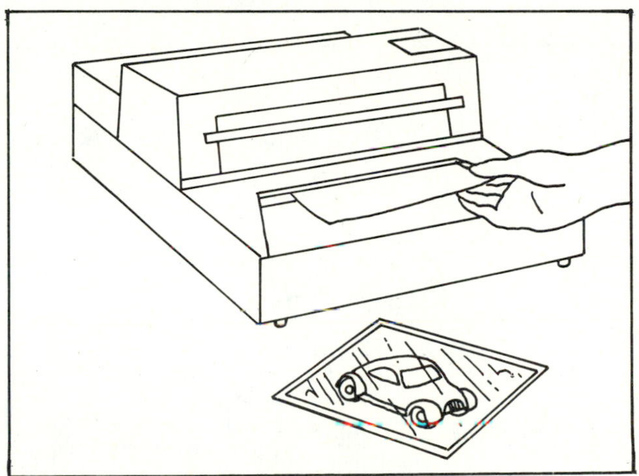

A two-step **rapid-processing method** for black-and-white paper is widely used. This method takes only a few seconds for developing and fixing exposed paper. It also eliminates the need for an extensive darkroom with a large sink and trays. It does require the enlarger and processing unit. In this method, known as **photostabilization,** the developing agents required are incorporated in the paper emulsion. The paper is carried automatically in timed sequence by a system of rollers, first through the **activator** and then through a **stabilizer** bath. The paper emerges damp, especially if RC (resin-coated) photographic paper is used. The stabilizer arrests development and stabilizes the image (the chemistry is similar to, but not exactly the same as, fixing with hypo). Thus, processing is automatically accomplished in a matter of seconds. Because the print will fade in time, it is recommended that for greater permanence, a print processed by this method be fixed in regular hypo and then thoroughly washed and dried. In addition to various kinds of photographic papers, high-contrast and continuous-tone sheet films are available for use in the photostabilization process.

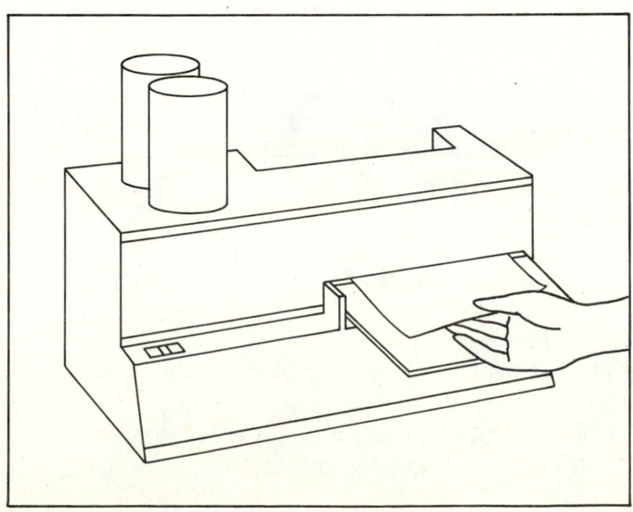

Enlarging from Color Negatives

In the past, the procedure for printing from color negatives was complex and time consuming. Now, rapid, simple processes are available that use automatic, darkroom-operating processors. The result can be high-quality color prints.

As an example, with Kodak Ektacolor RA chemicals, exposed color paper is developed in rotary-tube or drum processors. Processing involves six steps—prewet, develop, stop, wash, bleach-fix, wash, and then dry. The results can be high quality prints from color negatives.

Enlarging from Color Slides

Formerly it was necessary to make a color negative from a positive color slide and from it prepare a positive color print. Today materials are available to produce a positive color print directly from a color slide, such as these:

- Ilford Cibachrome color print material requiring a 12-minute processing period in three chemical steps with drum processing
- A Polaroid fully automatic Polaprinter preparing instant color prints

In the past, because of time requirements and expense, photographs for instructional purposes generally were prepared in black-and-white. Now, with the simplified processing available and the reduced unit costs, consideration should be given to the preparation of photographs in color.

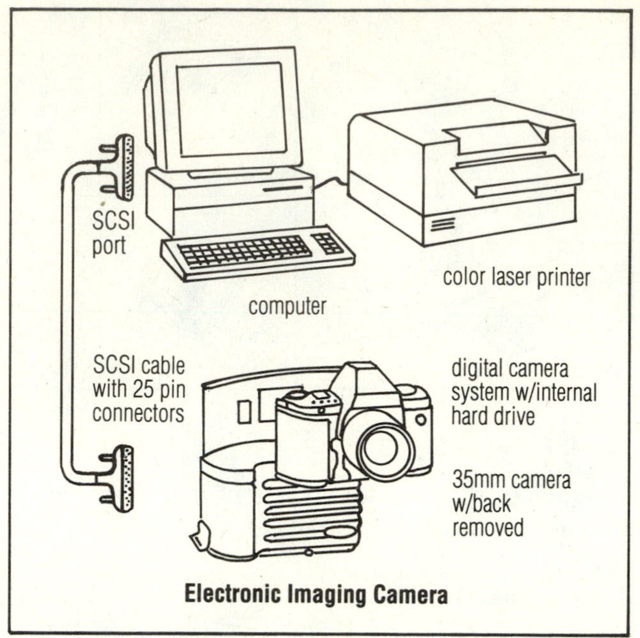

Electronic Imaging Camera

ELECTRONIC IMAGING

As presented in this chapter, conventional photography essentially is a three-step process: *exposure, development, printing.* Electronic imaging (also called digital photography) also employs a three-step process. Now the terms are *capture, enhancement,* and *display.*

Image capture can be through regular exposure on film, followed by the use of a scanner (see page 120) to convert the image to digital format. By using an electronic still camera, or a Photo CD unit, creation of the image in digital form can take place immediately.

Next, the captured image may be enhanced to achieve a desired result. This would be comparable to printing a negative in the darkroom. With the digital image on file in computer memory, processing software allows correcting, modifying, and merging of images.

Third, the resulting image is displayed. This can be on the computer screen, copied to videotape, as a print on paper or film through an ink jet or color laser printer (see page 120), or even integrated onto a printed page with a desktop printing program (see page 182). As the technology is refined, image quality approaches that of high resolution photographs or slides. Storage can be on a compact disc (CD) for filing, instructional uses, or further production purposes.

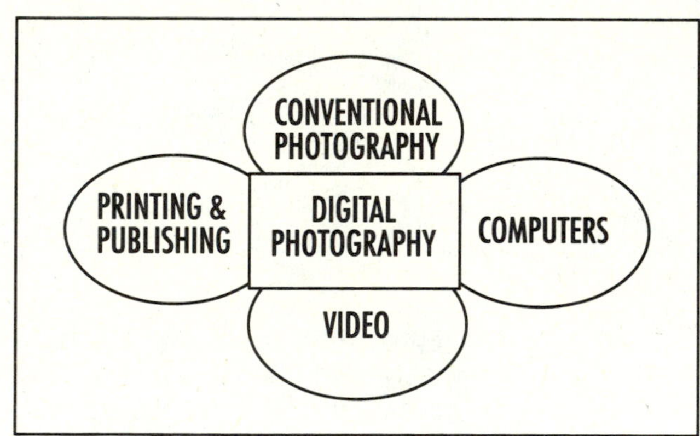

REVIEW

What You Have Learned About Processing Film and Making Prints:

1. What are the five steps necessary to develop black-and-white film and the purpose of each step?
2. What are some characteristics of a good black-and-white negative?
3. In what ways and with what materials do the four steps in tray processing of black-and-white paper differ from those in developing of black-and-white film?
4. What purpose is often served by making contact prints of a roll of black-and-white negatives?
5. What are two advantages of using the photostabilization process for processing paper over the regular tray process?

6. What is the major difference in film processing procedure between color negative and color reversal processes?
7. If you plan to prepare a series of color photographs to explain how to operate a piece of equipment, what procedure would you follow to make the photographs?
8. To which stage of electronic imaging does each operation apply?
   a. Changing colors
   b. Scanning a photograph
   c. Printing an image on paper
   d. Adding an image to a collection for storage on a CD
   e. Combining two images

See answers on page 377.

REFERENCES

(Many references in the following sections are available from Eastman Kodak Co., 343 State Street, Rochester, NY 14650, or from a local photographic supply dealer. Following each of these titles is the Eastman publication code number without any other source indication.)

PICTURE TAKING

Close-Up Photography. KW-22, 1989.
Electronic Flash. KW-12, 1989.
Existing Light Photography. KW-17, 1990.
Foss, Kurt. "The New Age of Digital Cameras." *Photo Electronic Imaging* 35 (January 1992): 34–39.
How to Take Good Pictures. AC-36, 1990.
Lenses for 35mm Cameras. KW-18, 1984.

FILMS

Guide to KODAK 35mm Films. AF-1, 1990.
KODAK Professional Black-and-White Films. F-5, 1990.

FILM PROCESSING AND PRINTING

Basic Developing and Printing in Black and White. AJ-2, a987.
Black-and-White Darkroom Techniques. KW-15, 1990.
Using KODAK Ektacolor RA Chemicals in Rotary-Tube and Drum Processors. J-39, 1990.

JOURNALS

Advanced Imaging. PTN Publishing Co. 445 Broad Hollow Road, Melville, NY 11747.
Industrial Photography. PTN Publishing Co. 445 Broad Hollow Road, Melville, NY 11747.
Photo Electronic Imaging. PPA Publications and Events, Inc. 1090 Executive Way, Des Plaines, IL 60018.
Photomethods. Box 490, Hicksville, NY 11802-0490.

ELECTRONIC STILL CAMERAS

Anderson, Paul. "Options in Electronic Still Color Hard Copy." *Advanced Imaging* 4 (April 89): 24–26, 76.
Foss, Kurt. "The New Age of Digital Cameras." *Photo Electronic Imaging* 35 (January 1992): 34–39.
Larish, John. "Digital Photography." *Photo Electronic Imaging* 35 (February 1992): 35–36.
———. "Electronic Photography—Already Diverting the Mainstream." *Advanced Imaging* 6 (August 1991): 40–42, 59.
———. *Understanding Electronic Photography.* Blue Ridge Summit, PA: Tab Books, 1990.
Staples, William J. "Putting Electronic Still Cameras in Context." *Industrial Photography* 40 (July 1991): 14–15, 52.

CHAPTER 8

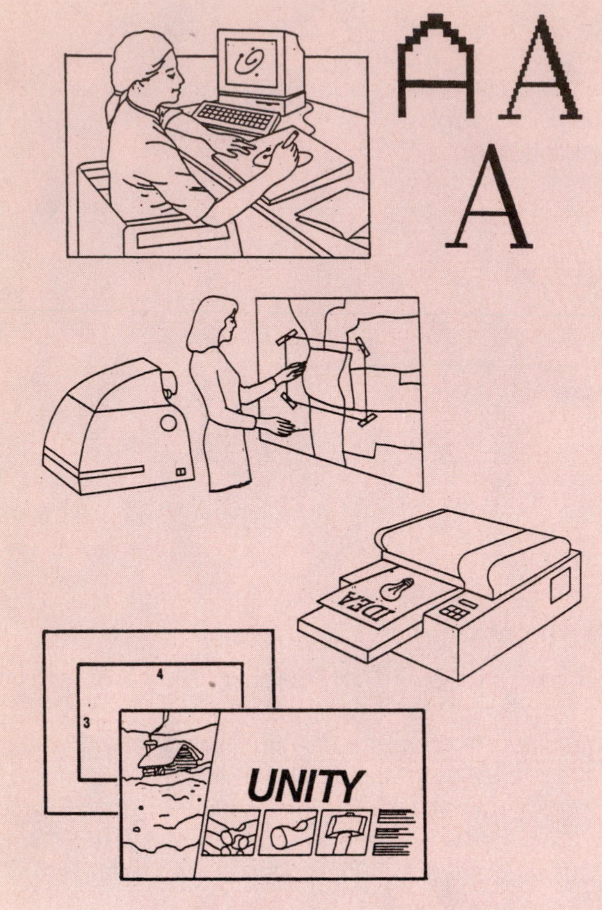

Planning Art Work
Using Computer Graphics Systems
Other Illustrating Techniques
Visualizing Statistical Data
Using Graphic Tools and Basic Materials
Coloring and Shading
Legibility Standards for Lettering
Lettering and Titling Techniques
Background for Titles
Mounting Flat Materials
Protecting the Surface (Laminating)
Making Paste-ups

Graphics

Visualization of instructional materials can take place in either one or a combination of three forms—photographic, electronic, or graphic. Photography and video (electronic) provides illustration through pictures that closely represent the reality of a subject or situation. Graphic materials (including computer-generated electronic images) are symbolic and artistic representations of a subject.

The success of many instructional media can be attributed in large measure to the quality and effectiveness of the art work and related graphic materials. These are achieved through organizing preliminary thoughts, careful planning, and applying the techniques outlined in this chapter.

Many persons who develop instructional materials have little or no professional art background. Their efforts, however, need not result in amateurish and poor-quality graphic materials. First, they can consider a number of common-sense practical suggestions and guiding principles, then apply them as the need arises. Second, there are a number of easy-to-use manipulative devices and computer-based techniques that, with little practice, will ensure results of a professional quality. The process is a skillful union of materials and techniques.

PLANNING ART WORK

Your art work must be planned with consideration for the size and dimensions of the working area, for the proportions of your visual materials, for design and layout features, for backgrounds, and for the resources, skills, techniques, materials, and facilities that you can employ.

Size of Working Area

Whether working on a computer screen, on cardboard, or on paper, decide on a size or format that can be handled easily. Give attention to these requirements when deciding on a working surface:

- Lettering and drawing can be done easily.
- Sufficient margin (*safe* or *bleed area*) should be allowed on all sides of the visual.
- Parallax and close-up difficulties in the camera, if there are any, can be easily overcome when copying (see page 103).
- The art work is easy to store.

The minimum dimension that is likely to meet these requirements is 10 × 12 inches; therefore use cardboard or a computer-image ratio of this size or larger. You can cut boards 11 × 14 inches without waste from standard-size 22 × 28 inch sheets, which are sold in 8-ply or 14-ply thickness. Commonly used working areas, on boards of either size, are 6 × 9 inches and 9 × 12 inches; minimum lettering sizes for these areas are suggested on page 134. Compose within the proper proportions (see next column) of your selected instructional media. Provide generous margins around the sides of all work so the camera does not inadvertently film beyond the background.

The end papers inside the front cover of this book contain recommended mask sizes for overhead transparencies and 35mm slides. The end paper inside the back cover has a diagram for the mask to use with the video format.

If many scenes require art work and lettering, standardize your size and prepare a mask with a cutout of the proper working area. The mask will serve as a margin and as a frame when you view the prepared art work and will also be useful as a guide for positioning art work and camera during copying.

If titles, labels, or diagrams must be placed one over the other or over a background, you need equipment to hold them in *alignment,* or *register.* If you need to make only a few such graphics, you may be able to work on an ordinary drawing board with masking tape. If you have any quantity of work, a commercial **register** or **pin board** will save time and allow accurate alignment. Use either prepunched paper and film, or obtain a punch that corresponds to the location of the pins on the register board. The register board can be used both during preparation of the materials and also when filming the final assembly.

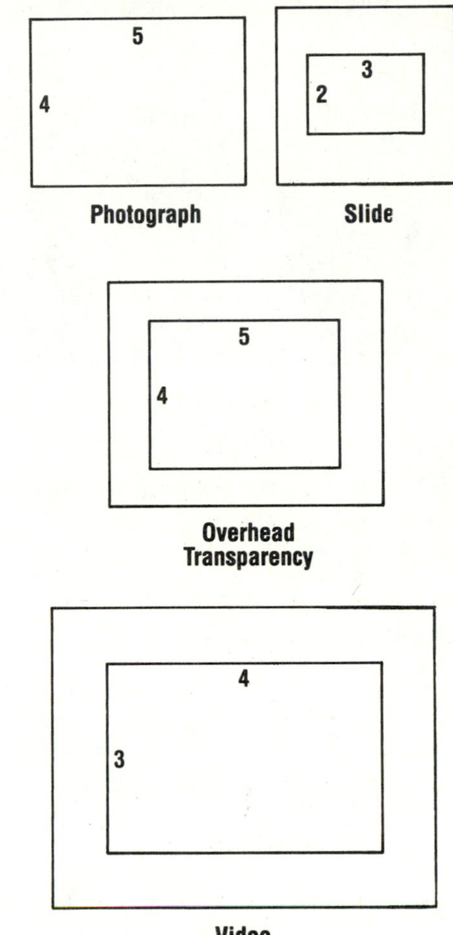

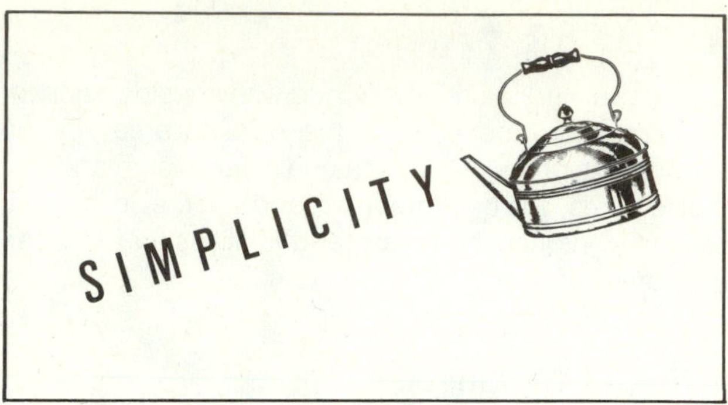

Proportions of Instructional Media

The proportion of each type of media, referred to as the **aspect ratio,** determines the shape of the area within which each visual should be composed.

Visual Design and Layout

Examine some of the graphic materials that are a common part of your everyday world—magazine advertisements, outdoor billboards, animated cartoons, television titles and commercials, and so on. You can find many ideas for designing your own materials by studying the arrangement of elements in such commercial displays.

The process of combining the various elements that comprise a visual (picture or art work, lettering, texture, color, and so forth), in order to create a pleasing entity, is known as **layout.** The layout must be understandable, legible, and aesthetically pleasing in terms of the purpose it is designed to serve.

You may be planning a title for a slide series, a diagram, a transparency, a cartoon for a video recording; or your plans may deal with art work for a chart, a diagram, a poster, or even an instructional bulletin board. In these and other planning situations you should be aware of certain design principles and visual design tools. Then be prepared to apply those that can help you.

Design principles to consider include *simplicity, unity, emphasis,* and *balance.*

Simplicity Charts, graphs, and diagrams suitable for page printing may not be suitable for projection. They may include large amounts of information and be acceptable in a printed report or for a manual, but these permit detailed, close-up study, which is not usually possible with projected materials. A cutting from a publication, used in a slide, might be so complex that it would be confusing. Therefore, evaluate the suitability of all items you consider for inclusion in your visual materials and try to limit your selection or design to the presentation of one idea at a time.

Generally speaking, the fewer elements into which a given space is divided, the more pleasing it is to the eye. Subdivide or redesign lengthy or complex data into a number of easy-to-read and easy-to-understand related materials. Limit the verbal content for projected visuals to 15 or 20 words.

Drawings should be bold, simple, and contain only key details. Picture symbols should be outlined with a heavy line. The necessary details can be added in thinner lines since they should appear less important. Many thin lines, particularly if they are not essential, may actually confuse the clarity of the image when viewed from a distance.

Finally, for simplicity use plain, easy-to-comprehend lettering styles and a minimum of different styles in the same visual or series of visuals.

Unity Unity is the relationship that exists among the elements of a visual when they are perceived as all functioning together. This is particularly appropriate in display materials and other items to be viewed with little or no direction or guidance. Unity can be achieved by

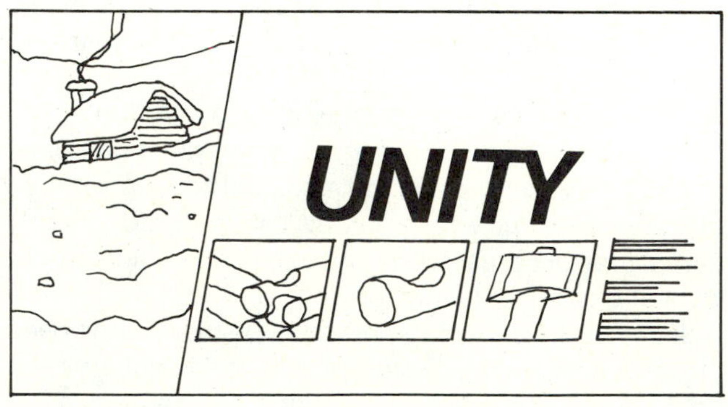

overlapping elements, by using pointing devices such as arrows, and by employing the visual tools (line, shape, color, texture, and space) described on the following page.

Emphasis Even though a visual treats a single idea, is simply developed, and has unity, there is often the need to give emphasis to a single element—to make it the center of interest and attention. Through the use of size, relationships, perspective, and such visual tools as color or space, emphasis can be given to the most important elements.

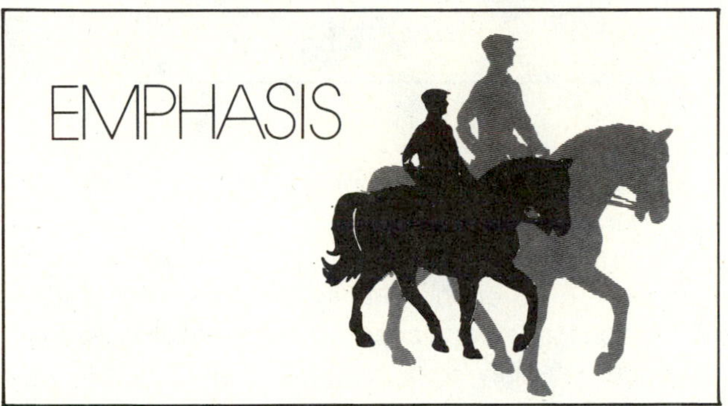

Balance There are two kinds of balance—formal and informal. Formal balance is identified by an imaginary axis running through the center of the visual dividing the design so that one-half will be the mirror reflection of the other half. Such a formal balance is static.

Informal balance is asymmetrical; the elements create an equilibrium without being static. It is a dynamic and more attention-getting arrangement. It requires more imagination and daring by the designer. The informal balance may have an asymmetrical or a diagonal layout.

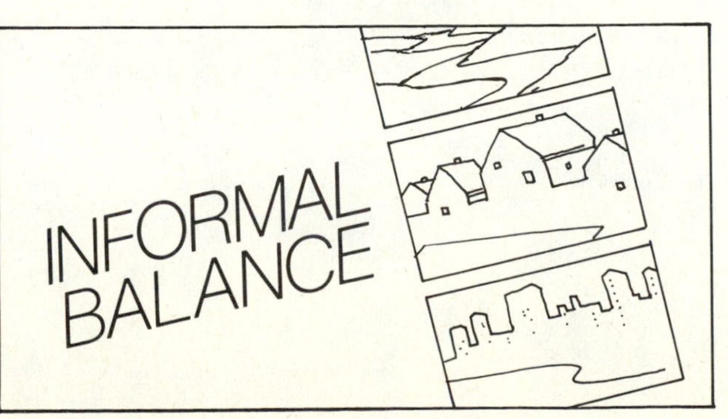

For titles, a symmetrical balance of lettering is formal in effect and is desired for many uses. It requires accurate positioning of letters and extra care when filming to ensure even margins (equal side margins, but a somewhat greater area at the bottom than at the top).

Informal arrangements, when appropriately combined with sketches or pictures, make attractive titles. Such arrangements eliminate the problem of centering but not the problem of accurate positioning.

Try various arrangements before doing the final lettering.

The **visual tools** that contribute to the successful use of the above design principles include *shape, space, line, texture,* and *color.* These tools can direct viewer attention and guide a person through the elements of a visual display.

Shape Objects and space within a display can be identified or symbolized by the use of shapes. An unusual shape can give special interest to a visual.

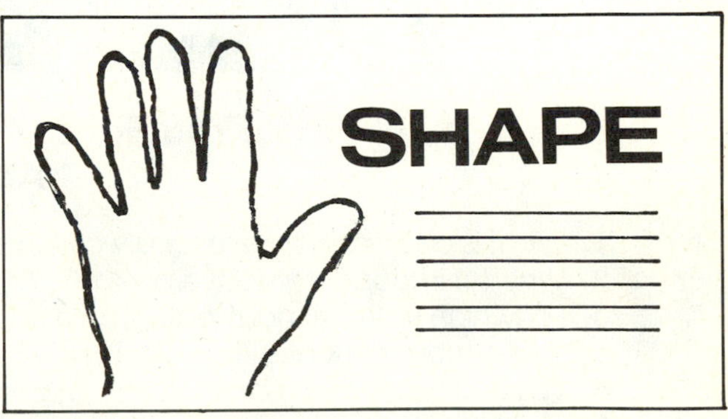

Space Open space around visual elements and words will prevent a crowded feeling. Only when space is used carefully can the elements of design become effective.

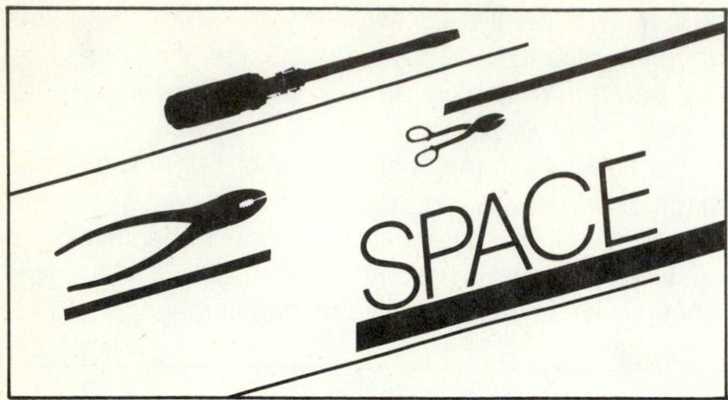

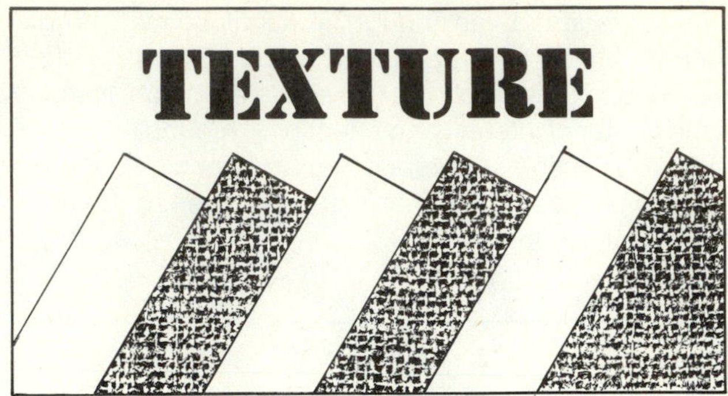

Line A line in a visual can connect elements together and will direct the viewer to study the visual in a specific sequence.

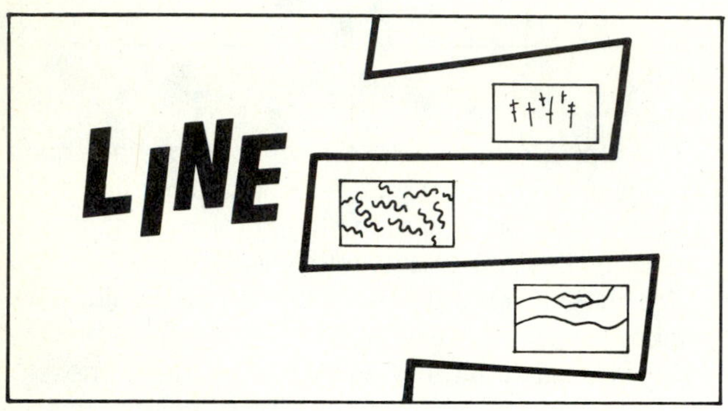

Texture Texture is a visual element that may serve as a replacement for the sense of touch and can be used in much the same way as color—to give emphasis or separation, or to enhance unity.

Color Color is an important adjunct to most visuals, but it should be used sparingly for best effects. Apply it to elements of a visual to give separation or emphasis, or to enhance unity. Select colors that are harmonious together, because colors that are dissonant (of equal intensity and complementary on the color wheel, like orange–blue and red–green) create annoyance in the audience and consequently interfere with a clear perception of the message.

Other emotional impacts of specific colors have been identified. Some common ones are *red*—danger or action; *orange*—warmth or energy; *blue*—aloofness or clarity; *green*—freshness or restfulness; *violet*—depression; and *yellow*—cheerfulness.

When selecting color for visual materials, attention should be given to three matters. First the *hue*, the choice of a specific color (red, blue, and so on). Second, the *value* of the color, meaning how light or dark the color should appear in the visual with relation to other visual elements. Third, the *intensity* or strength of the color for its impact or coordinated effect. See page 129 for further information on selecting colors.

What You Have Learned About Planning Art Work:

1. What is a satisfactory size for a working surface on which to prepare art work?
2. Why is it important to leave a wide margin around art work?
3. For which instructional media would these pictures or art work have satisfactory proportions (dimensions in inches): 8 × 10, 12 × 18, 9 × 12?
4. When is a register board used?
5. To which design principle or visual tool does each relate?
   a. Prevent a crowded appearance
   b. Careful alignment of all elements
   c. Uncluttered with few elements
   d. Hue—Value—Intensity
   e. Center of interest or attention elements
   f. All functioning together

6. Which *principles* of design and *visual tools* for design are applied in each illustration?

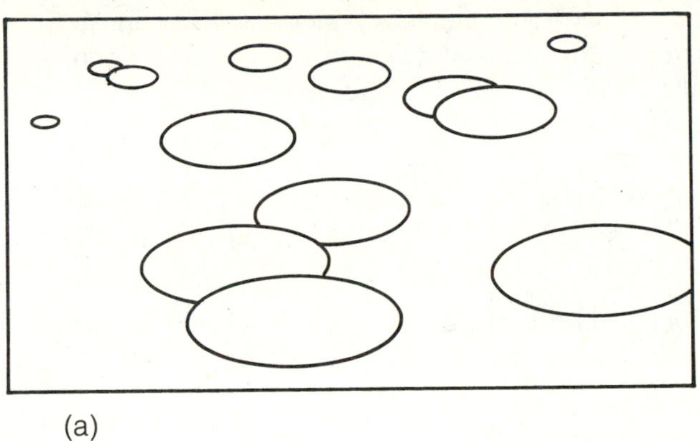

(a)

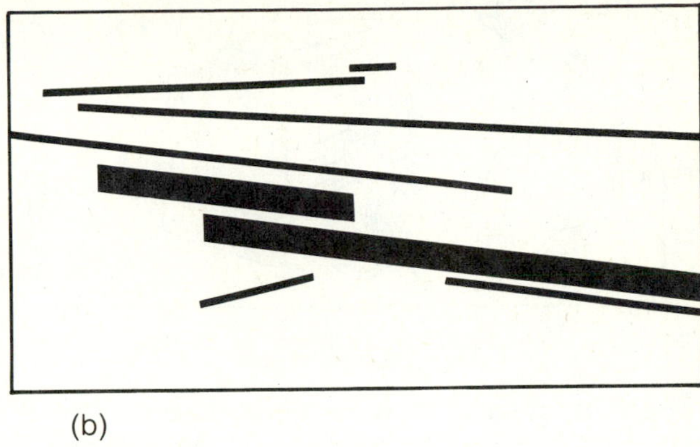

(b)

See answers on page 378.

USING COMPUTER GRAPHICS SYSTEMS

Computers are used to produce media such as art (charts, graphs, cartoons, and illustrations), 2 × 2 inch slides, overhead transparencies, video graphics, and animation. Computer graphics systems offer many advantages beyond conventional methods of production. These advantages include the following:

- ***Increased speed of production***—Generating a typical word slide (a few lines on a colored background) by conventional graphic techniques requires such intermediate steps as lettering, paste-up, high-contrast photography, and color photography. The entire process can take from 15 minutes to several hours, depending on the procedures used and the complexity of the slide. Producing a word or graphics slide with a word processing or computer graphics program eliminates almost all handwork other than entering information through a keyboard or other input devices—a process that typically takes just a few minutes.
- ***Ease of revision***—With conventional production methods, even a "minor" revision can result in many hours of work. But since the information used to construct a computer-generated visual is stored electronically, it takes only minutes to retrieve the stored information in the computer, use the keyboard, a mouse, or other input device to make revisions, and generate the revised visual.
- ***Increased emphasis on design***—Because the color, size, location, or style of the elements within a computer-generated visual can be altered rapidly, you are able to explore alternative layouts before selecting the final design.
- ***Greater sophistication of images***—Complex images can be created to appear in true perspective, as mirror images, and as three-dimensional images, all with an array of vivid colors. From one visual to the next in a series, text can be moved, overlays added, colors changed, and special effects used; all of which can have strong visual impact.
- ***Reduced storage space***—Hundreds of visuals can be stored electronically in the space normally occupied by a single piece of conventional art.

Components

While computer graphics systems vary somewhat in appearance and operation, they tend to have components with similar functions. The heart of any computer system is the *central processing unit* (CPU). Frequently a special *graphics add-on card* or board (like a VGA—video graphics array) must be installed in an expansion slot of the system unit for creating and displaying sophisticated graphics in conjunction with specific software programs.

Input Devices In addition to the keyboard and a mouse, the following peripherals are widely used for inputting graphics and other visual materials to computer memory:

- A **light pen** looks like a ballpoint pen, containing a light-sensitive tip. When touched to the screen, the photoelectric circuit is activated and drawing takes place on the screen. An image created can be saved in computer memory.

- An **electronic stylus** or a **puck** (a small, clear plastic window with a crosshair to peer through) is used on a **digitizing tablet.** The drawing surface has a network of wires within it. When the stylus or puck moves over the surface, to draw or trace a line, electronic impulses are recorded and images are created on the screen and recorded in memory.

- A **scanner** converts material on paper into an electronic image in the computer. A flatbed scanner works like a copy machine as the original sheet is placed on a platen and the scanning head moves across it. A handheld scanner is manually drawn over the page. Other units are available for scanning 35mm slides. Special software is required for controlling the scanning process within the computer. Scanners are available for black line, gray tones, and color subjects. Also, still video images can be scanned with a **video digitizer** into computer memory for use and manipulation when a special graphics board is installed in the system unit.

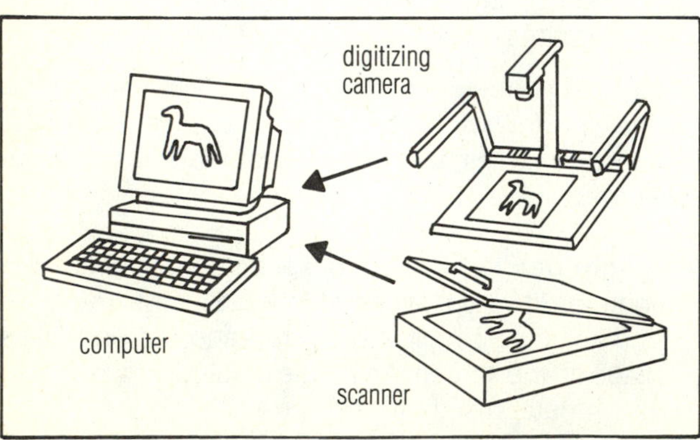

Storage Devices Both floppy disks and a hard disk can be used for external storage of graphic materials.

Output Devices In addition to the computer display screen, a film recorder and any of several printers can be used for recording graphic data created with a computer program.

- A **film recorder** is a light-proof box containing a camera (usually a 35mm camera loaded with slide-film) aimed at a tiny, high resolution cathode ray tube (CRT). The graphic image sent to the CRT is recorded on film. Most desktop film recorders provide 4000 lines of resolution and take about 15 minutes to fully expose an image.

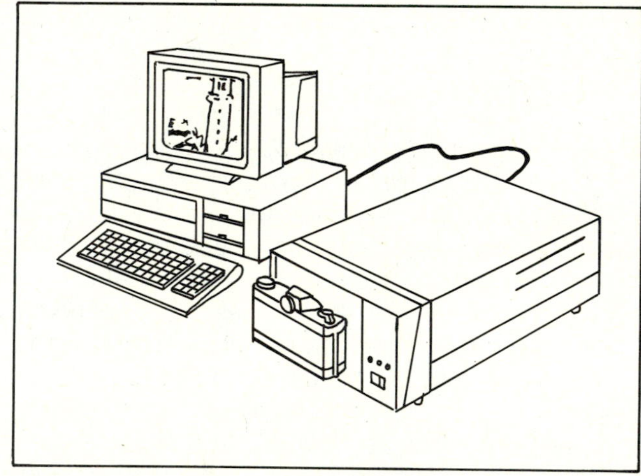

As explained on page 183, there is a variety of printers in the *impact* and *nonimpact* categories. The following are the most useful ones for outputting graphic images onto paper or film:

- **Ink jet printer** that provides relatively high resolution (about 200 dots per inch), black-and-white and color images, very quiet operation, and low cost.
- **Thermal transfer printer** that produces higher resolution (300 dots per inch), bright, and more saturated color images. Limitations are the special glossy-type paper required and the greater cost for equipment and paper.

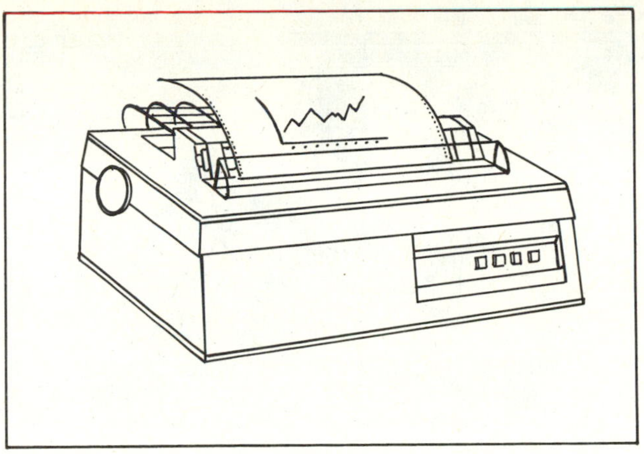

- **Laser printer** that produces the highest quality images in black, gray tones, and colors. The widely-used black-image printers are relatively low in cost and can print ten or more images per minute. The gray-tone printers produce black-and-white photo quality images at a six per minute rate. Color printers have resolution of 300–400 dots per inch, print five pages per minute, but are expensive.

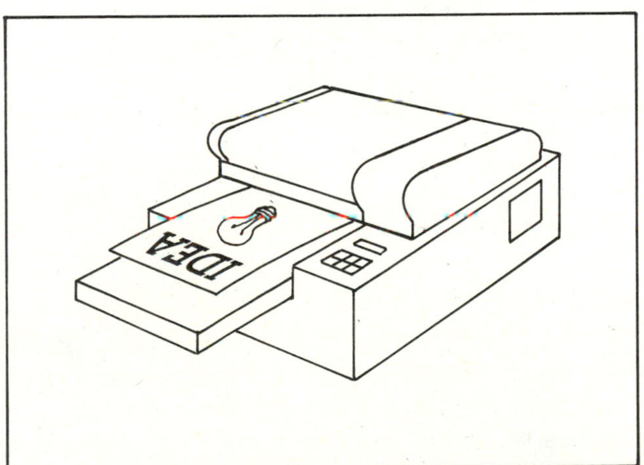

Software

Based on your needs, your computer experience, and available equipment, including a compatible graphics board and amount of computer storage memory (RAM), you must decide on the most appropriate software to use. The subject could be developed on paper, for slides, as overhead transparencies, or for direct projection with an LCD unit (page 206) or a video projector. Some products may incorporate computer-generated 3-dimensional forms, animation, or modified computer images for more dynamic and appealing visuals. The output of a word processing program, clipart, and scanned images can be imported into a graphics program.

Graphics software packages on the market are many and varied. They range from detailed "follow-the-instructions" programs for rapid preparation, designed especially for users with little, if any, training in art, to sophisticated programs allowing full freehand drawing and manipulation capabilities designed for experienced artists. Always check the **documentation** (instructions and reference material) that comes with a software program to match it correctly with the required computer equipment, memory capacity, and other factors.

Personal computer graphics software can be grouped into three categories.

- ***Preformatted drawing programs***—Using a series of menus consisting of content lists and options, the user chooses from among already-prepared standard **preformatted graphics.** These may include charts, graphs, tables, diagrams, organization charts, and word lists or text. All the elements of a visual—style, layout, lettering format and sizes, background, and color choices—are "formatted." These elements are specified or there are limited, fixed options from which you make a choice as you enter the data for the visual (usually words and num-

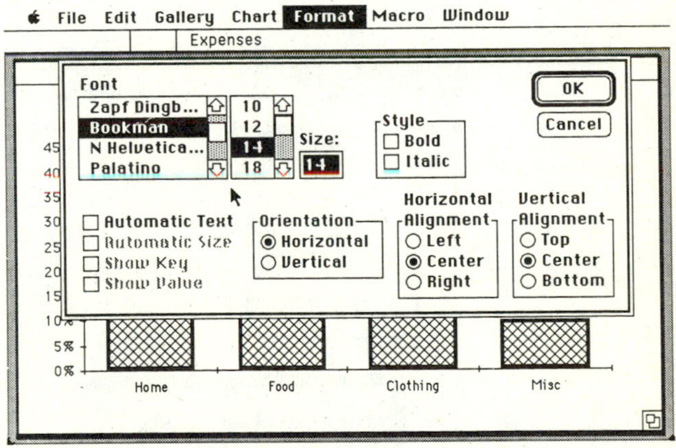

Instruction Format for Preformatted Drawing Program

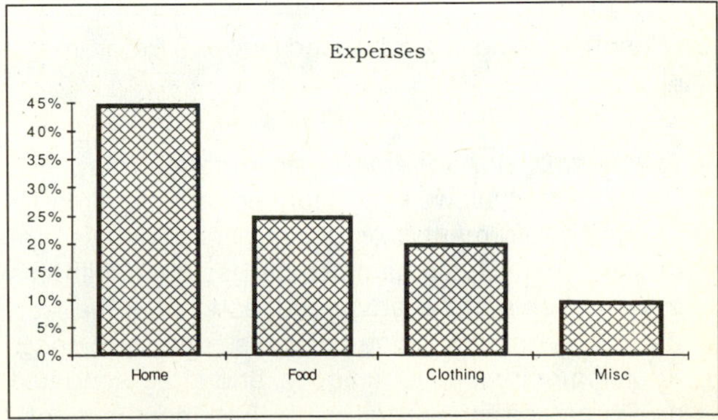

Result of Using Preformatted Drawing Program

bers). If you do not reply to a question for making a selection, the program "defaults" to preselected styles, lettering, sizes, color, or such.

- ***Object-based drawing programs***—This category allows the design of nonformatted visuals. Various building blocks are provided—lines, circles, rectangles, polygons, and so on. By adjusting and manipulating these basic shapes and adding lettering, coloring, and background, you can design a variety of images with a range of complexity. The basic graphic components are developed from instructions as in a preformatted program. Then the user manipulates and changes the image as viewed on the display screen.

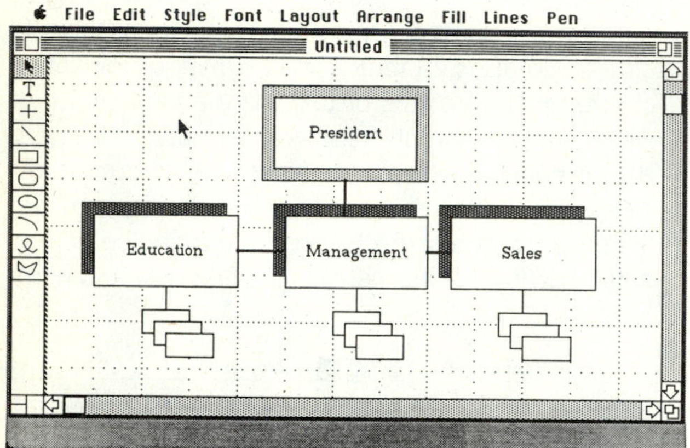

Instruction Format for Object-based Drawing Program

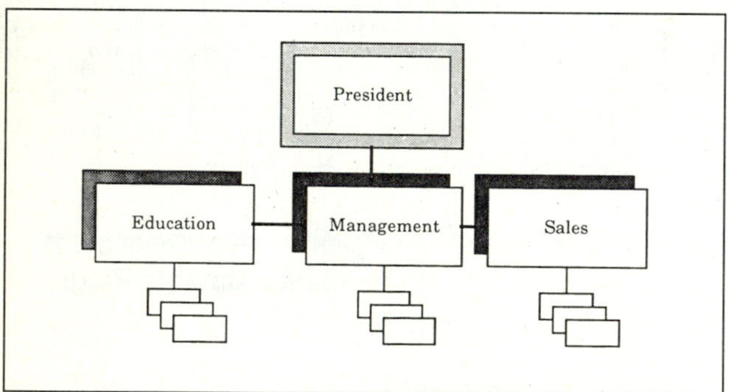

Result of Using Object-based Drawing Program

- ***Paint and enhancement programs***—This is a package that allows you to further improve already-created preformatted or object-based visuals. Totally original visuals can also be designed with this system. Some of the advanced techniques that can be applied include using paint systems for coloring, applying animation techniques, and integrating text and graphics in unusual ways. Enhancement software treats a wide range of applications and approaches for making visuals both more attractive and sophisticated.

Instruction Format for Paint and Enhancement Program

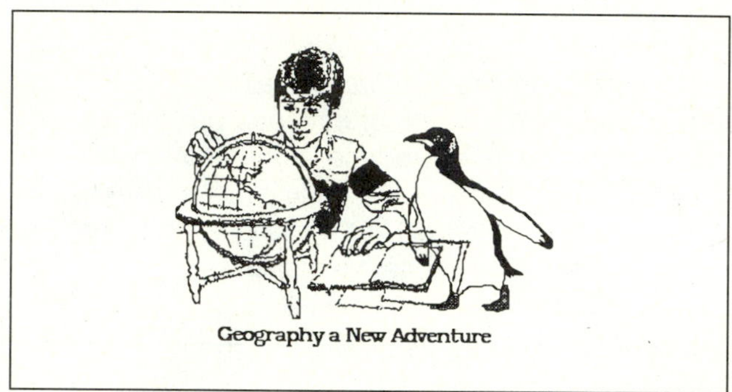

Results of Using Paint and Enhancement Program

Production Factors

As you plan computer-generated graphic visuals, the same attention should be given to design and preparation factors as that for other media forms. Although many parts of a graphic display may be preformatted, you should be alert to the best choices and decisions that are possible. The image on the display screen must communicate effectively whether the result remains as a frame in a computer program, becomes printed art work, or is converted to a slide or an overhead transparency.

Review the computer screen display conclusions summarized from research evidence on page 30.

As presented in this chapter, the following three production factors require careful attention:

- ***Screen design and layout***—Treat a single concept or a portion of a complex concept in each visual. Reword lengthy sentences to brief, clearly understood phrases. Separate and space parts of a visual for ease in viewing and reading. Consider and apply the screen image design suggestions on page 280 and the design principles and visual tools discussed on page 116.

- ***Colors***—Select and use colors purposefully. This may be to identify key parts of a visual (title, legend), to highlight specific information, to indicate relationships, or to increase the overall appeal of the visual. For best separation, contrast background color with foreground colors. See further discussion of color factors on page 129.

  The gray tones or colors that comprise a computer image are stored as "bits." The number of bits determine how many gray tones or colors can be displayed.

- ***Lettering***—Select lettering style and size for best readability. A sans serif style generally is preferable. Choose the largest size of lettering in keeping with the amount of information to be shown. Do not crowd lines of lettering or letters themselves close together. Use bullets or other symbols to set off or emphasize lines of text. See additional suggestions under Legibility Standards on page 132.

Image Resolution

A computer-generated image is created by a moving electron beam inside the picture tube that scans across the screen. This movement creates rows of tiny dots called **pixels** (short for *picture elements*). The sharpness or resolution of the image is directly proportional to the number of lines (rows of pixels) comprising that image.

Visuals created on systems containing relatively few lines (for example, 200) appear to be extremely coarse. Curved lines and angles drawn on such systems take on a sawtooth or ragged appearance. Visuals created on systems containing many lines (for example, 2000) have much higher resolution, and curved lines drawn on such systems will appear smooth. For comparison, a television image approximates the resolution of a computer graphics system with 500 lines.

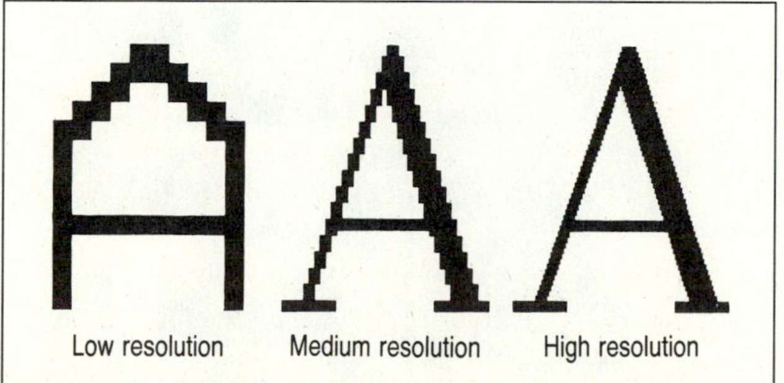

Image resolution is the factor that most affects the price of a computer graphics system. A working 200-line system can be assembled for less than a thousand dollars. However, the resolution of such a system limits the value of the material produced on it. A full-scale computer graphics system with 2000 to 4000 lines of resolution can cost much more. Such systems are capable of producing art work, slides, and transparencies that only a trained person can differentiate from art work prodcued by conventional means. Nevertheless, if your needs do not require high-resolution graphics, then a low-resolution system might be adequate.

Typical Approaches

There are several approaches to the use of computer graphics. The approach you take will depend upon your needs, your budget, the volume of work, and the availability of outside services.

- ***Complete systems***—Complete in-house computer graphics systems typically consist of a computer with a keyboard, a mouse, a graphics tablet, and other input devices, at least two disk drives, a computer display screen, and an output device such as a printer or a film recorder. The larger systems may provide multiple terminals so that more than one operator can work at a time. These systems produce 35mm slides, overhead transparencies, paper prints, and video images.

- ***Partial systems***—In an attempt to save money, organizations frequently invest in partial systems that do not include output devices such as a film recorder. The operator uses the computer system to design the visual and then transmits the information by telephone line from the computer, using a **modem,** to a remote site that has a film recorder where the visuals are produced. Production turnaround time is usually 1 to 3 days, and a service charge is paid for each slide produced. Systems such as these have reduced the start-up costs for computer graphics systems. By using a microcomputer as the graphics design station, and transmitting by a modem to a remote film recorder, high resolution art can be created for word slides, charts, and graphs.

- ***Computer graphics production services***—Computer slide services that will prepare slides on a per-item basis are available in many areas. You submit a job request to the service and a trained computer operator produces the slide to your specifications. Prices for such a service can vary from twenty to several hundred dollars per slide, depending upon the complexity of the visual. Average prices range from twenty-five to eighty dollars per slide or transparency.

What You Have Learned About Computer Graphics Systems:

1. In what final forms can computer-generated graphics be produced?
2. What are *three* advantages to using a computer to generate graphics over regular hand methods?
3. Categorize each of the following as an *input* device, *output* device, or *storage* device.
   a. light pen
   b. laser printer
   c. film recorder
   d. video digitizer
   e. keyboard
   f. magnetic disk
   g. computer display screen
   h. digitizing tablet
   i. mouse
   j. scanner
4. Which category of software program would be chosen for each situation?
   a. To combine two visuals already stored in computer memory so as to create a new visual.
   b. To input data you have collected to make a regular bar chart.
   c. To combine prepared geometric shapes to design a new, complex visual.
5. What three graphic production factors need particular attention when making computer-generated visuals?
6. Define these terms:
   a. pixel
   b. mouse
   c. formatted program
   d. modem
7. Which type of graphics printer produces the highest quality results?
8. When quality and price of a computer graphics system are important considerations, what matter should receive careful attention?
9. If your organization cannot afford a high-quality computer graphics system, what are the alternatives for obtaining computer-generated graphics products?

See answers on page 378.

OTHER ILLUSTRATING TECHNIQUES

A number of easy-to-apply methods can be used to adapt or copy available illustrations.

Using Ready-Made Pictures

There are many sources for pictures that may be used in instructional materials.

Tearsheets Pictures from magazines, from free or inexpensive booklets, or from similar sources can serve your needs for some illustrations. As you collect pictures, develop a file with folders under subject or topic headings. It becomes your tearsheet collection. This can be a useful resource that may save much time when searching for illustrations to be used in a presentation or called for in a script. With the availability of Video Presentation Stands (page 356), tearsheets have become increasingly important.

At times, part of a picture or combined sections of two or more pictures may serve a need. Mount pictures on cardboard (page 141) and add lettering if it is appropriate (page 136). However, always remember that such pictures may be copyrighted and to use them beyond face-to-face teaching you need the permission of the copyright holder (page 169).

Clipart Booklets For certain general uses **clipbook** pictures are ideal. Clipbooks on many subjects are available commercially (see the list on page 149 for sources). Each book contains a variety of black-and-white line drawings, on paper. These may be cut from the page or, more frequently, duplicated; pictures or copies are then combined with suitable lettering in paste-ups (page 147) to make titles or visuals. To use these, copy them on a high-quality copy machine (page 191).

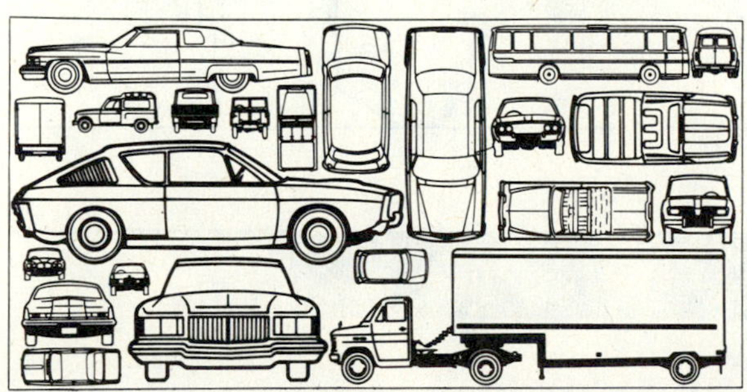

In addition to line drawings, printed sheets containing arrows, circles, stars, and other symbols in multiple sizes are available. They are used directly or can be reproduced.

Computer Clipart Clipart is also found in computer graphics software. Illustrations can be called up from memory, observed on the display screen, manipulated (size or appearance changed, and images combined), then reproduced on a laser printer for use.

Images of available diagrams, graphic art pieces, photographs, and even video frames can be captured and input to computer memory for use. This requires a *scanner* for handling original materials on paper and a *video digitizer* or *frame-grabber* for inputting from video. For details see page 120.

Enlarging and Reducing Pictures

The most common way to adjust the size of a small illustration is to use an office copy machine that permits enlargement or reduction to be made. But the best way to alter the size of a picture, while maintaining the best quality, is to photograph it.

Photo Modifier A device especially designed for enlarging and reducing art work is the **photo modifier.** It resembles a large camera with a ground-glass back against which tracing paper can be taped. The size of the original picture can be reduced or enlarged in accurate proportion by moving the device and then focusing the image by adjusting the bellows. Perspective can be changed and distortion created by tilting the ground-glass surface or the front lens.

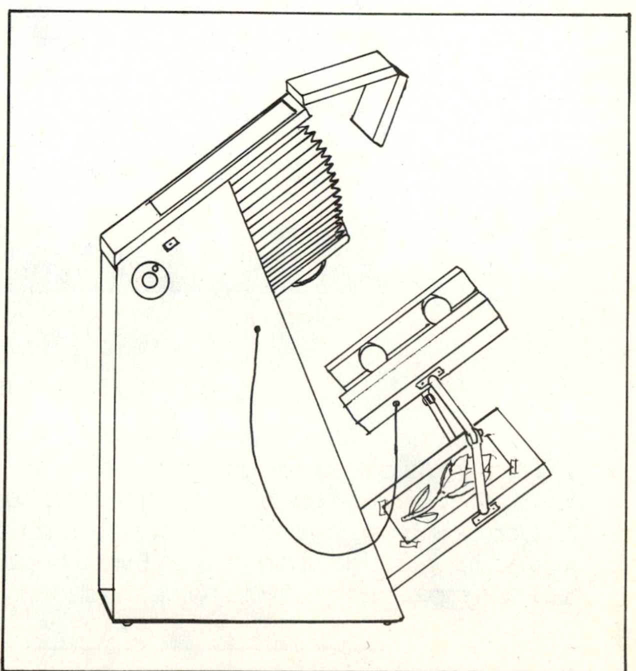

Opaque Projector A small picture on a single sheet or in a book can be enlarged by using an **opaque projector.** Place the paper or book on the holder of the projector and attach a piece of cardboard to a wall. Adjust the size of the projected picture to fit the required area on the cardboard: move the projector *closer* to the cardboard *to make it smaller* or *farther away* from the cardboard *to make it larger* and focus as necessary. Then trace the main lines of the projected picture with pencil. After completing the drawing, ink in the lines using pen and ink or a felt pen. This is one of the easiest and quickest ways to enlarge a picture.

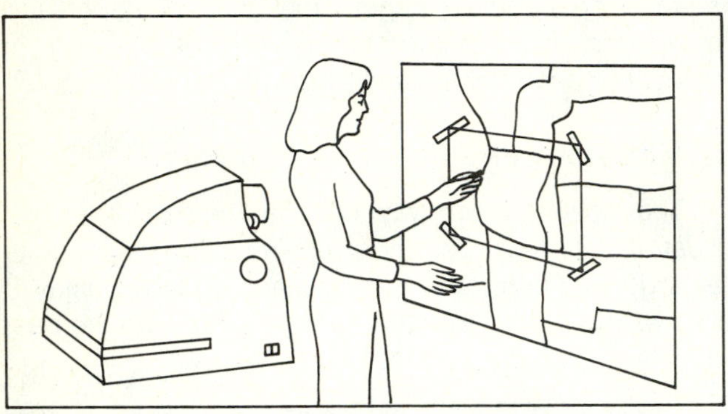

Projected Tracing If a transparency or a slide of the original diagram is available or can be made by one of the processes to be described later in this book, an overhead projector or a slide projector can be used to make a greatly enlarged copy onto cardboard.

Reverse Projection Tracing With the **overhead projector,** large pictures can be *reduced* to fit 8½ × 11 inch or other formats. This technique uses the overhead projector in reverse fashion as compared to its normal enlarging use. The original, large diagram is attached to a wall and a light (floodlight or a slide projector) is aimed at it. Sufficient light must be reflected from the diagram through the lens of the projector to be visible on a white sheet of paper placed on the projection stage. A cardboard light shield, placed on the edge of the projector stage, will block out stray light and make the image more visible on the paper.

Move the lens up and down to focus the image on the paper. Control the size by moving the whole projector closer to the wall or farther from it. Sketch the visual over the image on the sheet of paper.

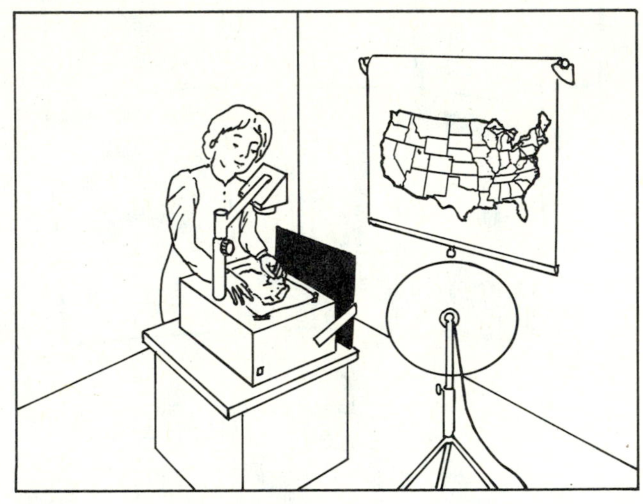

REVIEW

What You Have Learned About Illustrating Techniques:

Which method of illustrating would you use for each situation?

1. Enlarging a diagram of a map without the use of a camera
2. Locating pictures on a current topic for a bulletin board
3. Combining two pieces of art found in a software program
4. Reducing a large chart to fit on 8½ × 11 paper
5. Enlarging a small graph to twice the size

See answers on page 378.

VISUALIZING STATISTICAL DATA

Illustrating the numerical relationships among various factors and visualizing tabular information are important applications of graphic methods. These functions are accomplished by designing various types of graphs. There are three basic kinds of graphs—*line, bar,* and *circle.* A different purpose may be served by each one.

Line Graph

A line graph usually relates a factor of changing quantity to successive time periods. Points, representing quantities at each time period, are joined together as a line or a smooth curve.

If the space under a line graph is shaded, it becomes a *surface* chart and gives emphasis to the area under the curve. The effect will dramatize the data being presented.

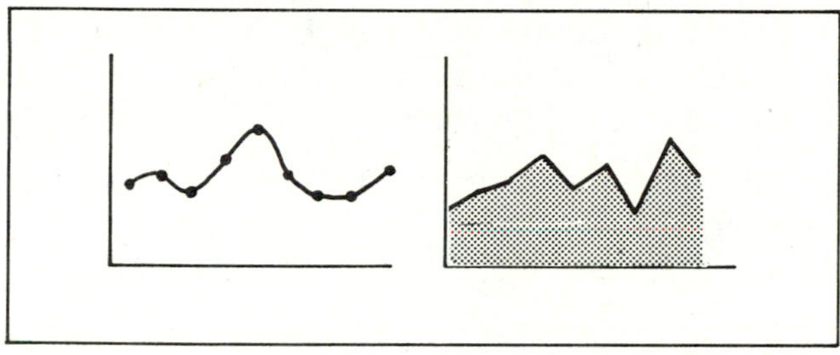

Bar Graph

A bar graph makes simple quantitative comparisons. The lengths of the bars represent amounts, and when drawn side by side, relationships and changes can be observed. When a bar chart is arranged vertically it becomes a *column* chart. Such a graph can make comparisons at various points in time.

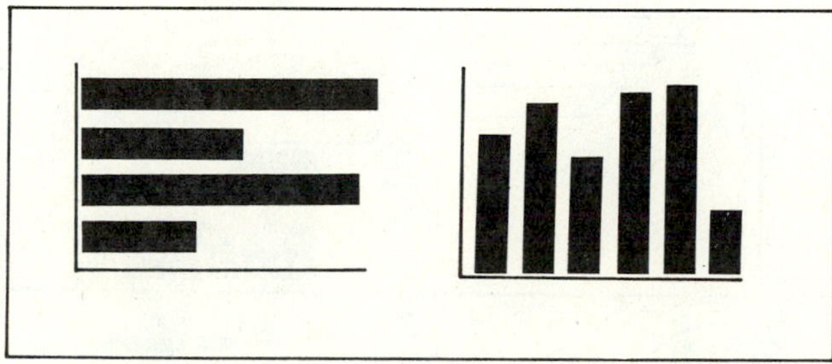

Circle or Pie Graph

A circle graph illustrates the proportion of the whole that each element of a subject represents. The elements are numerically shown as percentages. In total, they add to 100 percent.

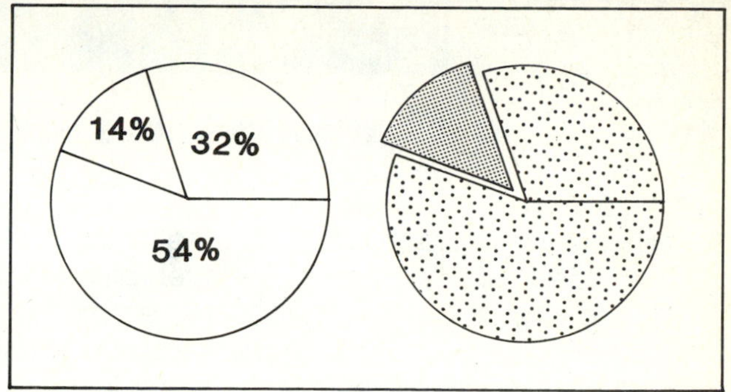

When preparing a graph, in addition to the actual graph lines, bars, or circle segments, give attention to these other elements that are necessary for proper communication of the visualized information:

- Title—briefly describes the topic treated in the graph; preferably placed at top of the visual.
- Scales—shown as vertical and horizontal axes and section lines for line and bar graphs; spacing between adjacent sections should permit a fair interpretation of data (not too compact or exaggerated); numerical values are written for each section.
- Axes captions—each scale (horizontal and vertical) requires a brief descriptive phrase or caption.
- Labels—as necessary for identification, label graph lines, bars, and circle segments; if parts are visually distinguishable (solid—as opposed to dashed, dotted, or hatched; different colors; and so forth), identify components in a boxed legend.

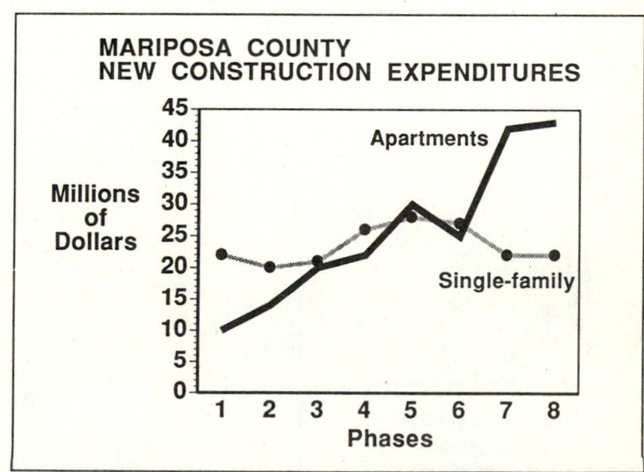

Appropriate computer programs allow you rapidly to convert statistical data into any of a number of graphic forms, thus eliminating much of the basic handwork described here.

What You Have Learned About Visualizing Statistical Data:

Which type of graph would you use for each situation?

1. Relating product sales to the three divisions of a company for a three-year period.
2. Showing proportionate uses of energy in the average home for heating and to run appliances.
3. Illustrating the consumption of gasoline in a state for a long series of months.
4. Comparing the amounts of calories found in ten different foods.
5. Indicating the extreme change in the population of an endangered species for the last ten years.

See answers on page 378.

USING GRAPHIC TOOLS AND BASIC MATERIALS

In order to obtain professional results when preparing graphic materials on paper or cardboard, it is necessary to become familiar with and to properly use the basic tools of the trade. Attention should be given to the items that follow.

- ***Working surface***—Use a smooth tabletop, a drawing board, or a drafting table that can be slightly tilted.
- ***T-square***—Rides along the edge of the working surface to provide an accurate horizontal axis when positioning artwork, drawing horizontal lines, or guiding triangles and other devices.
- ***Paper and cardboard***—Select a high-quality bond paper with a smooth finish, or use a translucent material such as tracing paper or good quality *vellum.* The cardboards suitable for media graphics range from inexpensive 6- to 8-ply (thickness) "railroad" board to 14-ply display or illustration boards, all of which are available in numerous colors.
- ***Triangles***—Used to draw vertical and diagonal lines when placed against a T-square.
- ***Compass***—Can hold either a lead pencil or drawing ink pen for making circles and arcs.
- ***Dividers***—Have sharp needle-like tips at both ends for measuring and transferring lines, or dividing a space into equal parts.
- ***Curved surface tools***—Include plastic templates containing circles, ellipses, or other shapes in various sizes.

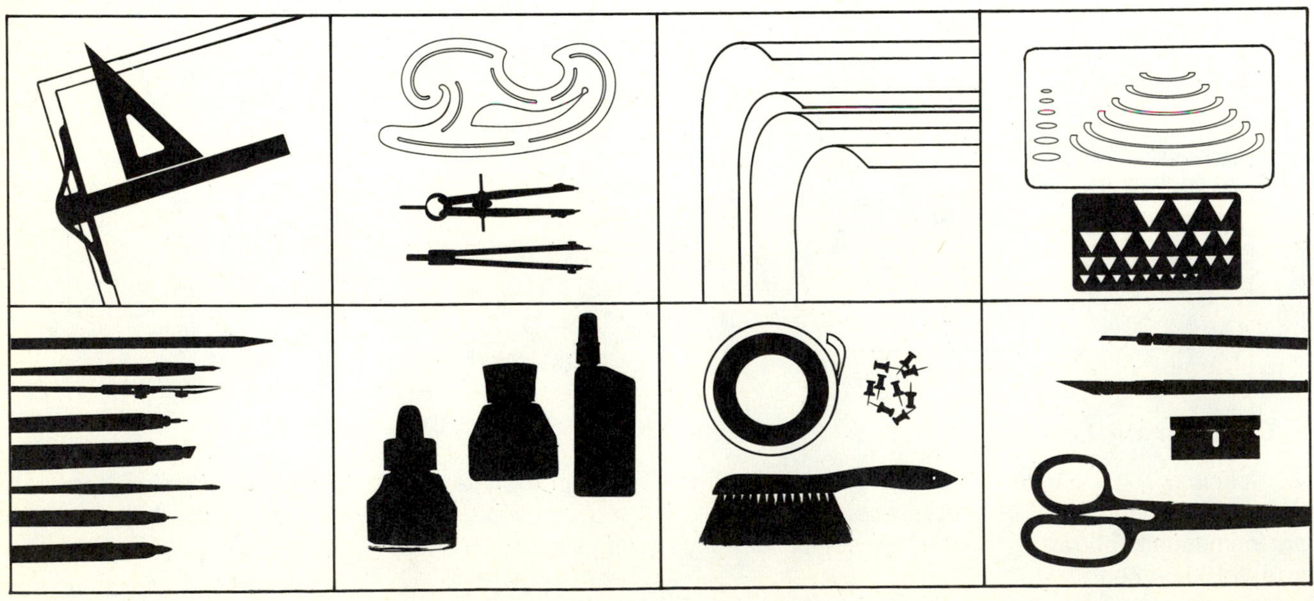

- ***Cutting tools***—Use scissors, single-edge razor blade, or a pointed blade in a handle (called an *X-acto knife*) for cutting paper or cardboard. A trimmer or mat knife is used with thick cardboard.
- ***Pencils***—Select a pencil for use according to its degree of hardness (soft: 6B–3B, medium: 2B–3H, hard: 4H–9H). Use softer pencils for sketching and harder ones for final layout over which ink lines will be drawn.
- ***Pens***—Choose from narrow-tipped or broad-tipped felt pens, ruling pens, or technical drawing pens. The latter, with a hollow tip fed from an ink reservoir, is preferred when crisp, even-edge lines are required.
- ***Erasers***—Remove pencil marks with a soft, white rubber eraser. An ink eraser is hard and abrasive to the surface.
- ***Material for securing art work***—Hold paper or cardboard in place with masking tape, push pens, or thumbtacks adhered to the corners.
- ***Drafting brush***—Keep the work surface and art work clean by sweeping them with a drafting brush. Its soft bristles prevent smearing and scratching.

REVIEW

What You Have Learned About Using Graphic Tools and Basic Materials:

Which type of graphic tool or material would you use for each situation?

1. A high-quality material as the surface for a display.
2. Drawing six lines, all of same length.
3. Locating and drawing horizontal lines across a sheet of paper.
4. Drawing numerous long, smooth lines with ink.
5. Drawing a number of circles, all having the same diameter.
6. Cutting an irregular shape out of paper.
7. Drawing lines to designate vertical columns.
8. Drawing lines on cardboard over which a felt pen will be used.
9. A material on which to draw when it is necessary to see a diagram under it.

See answers on page 378.

COLORING AND SHADING

Color is an important tool in visual design (page 118). While color makes visual materials more attractive, the choice of colors can make the communication process more effective. See references on page 148.

Guidelines for Using Colors

Using certain color combinations or coloring selected parts in a complex diagram will contribute emphasis, legibility, and even clarification. Here are some suggestions as you consider the selection of colors for use with computer-generated graphics or materials on paper or cardboard:

- Limit the number of colors in a visual to a maximum of five hues.
- Group related elements in a visual by placing them over a common background color.
- Use color brightness and intensity to attract attention, with yellow for items or parts of a visual that should be noticed first.
- Use warm colors (red, orange, yellow) to signify action, like the need for a response. Items in red will be remembered for a longer time than will items in other colors.
- Use cool colors (green, blue, violet) to indicate status quo or for background information.
- Use color change (such as increasing the intensity of a color) to indicate progressive change in value or a sequence of levels.

Selecting colors for text, lines, and areas in relation to backgrounds should be done carefully. This is of particular importance with the extensive choice of colors in computer-generated graphics. Table 8–1 on page 130 suggests the best and worst color combinations for elements of a visual in relation to background color.

Those who have art backgrounds may be able to use such techniques as wash drawing and airbrushing; even those with limited training may consider using several of the simple techniques discussed next.

TABLE 8–1 BEST AND WORST COLOR COMBINATIONS

BEST COLOR LINES, TEXT, DESIGN AREAS	BACKGROUND COLOR	WORST COLOR LINES, TEXT, DESIGN AREAS
yellow, white, black	red	magenta, cyan, blue, green
red, blue, black	orange	yellow, white
red, blue, black	yellow	white, cyan
black, blue, red	green	cyan, magenta, yellow
white, yellow, cyan	blue	green, black
blue, black, red	cyan	green, yellow, white
black, white, yellow, blue	magenta	green, red, cyan
white, yellow	black	blue, red, magenta
blue, black, red	white	yellow, cyan

Felt Pens

Colored lines of various thickness can be made with felt pens. Both permanent and water-based inks are available in a variety of colors. Felt pens are useful for coloring small areas. Since the colors are transparent, apply them carefully; each overlapping stroke deepens the tone and may produce uneven coloring in large areas.

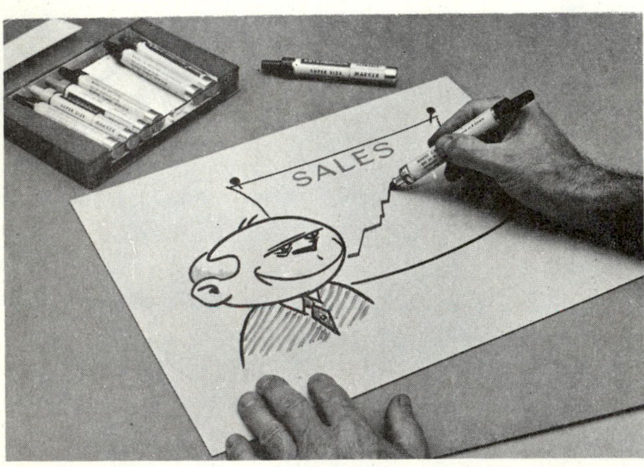

Spray-Can Paints and Airbrushing

Paint in pressurized cans can be used to apply color to areas on a visual. This technique is also used to color cardboard around three-dimensional letters, which are removed, after spraying, to reveal the unpainted image of the letters. By controlling the distance between the spray can and the surface to be sprayed, either a spatter effect or an even paint covering can be achieved. Protect parts of the visual not to be colored by covering with paper attached with masking tape.

Carefully controlled color spraying can be done with an **airbrush,** which is a pen-like spraying device attached to a compressed-air line or to a pressurized-air can. By adjusting the airbrush nozzle and depressing the control knob the spread of spray is controlled. As with the spray-can paints, it is necessary to cover parts of a visual around the area to be colored.

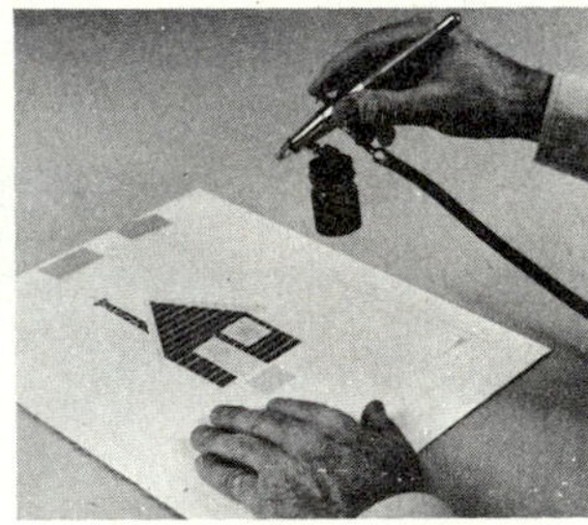

Color and Shading Sheets

Prepared **color** and **shading sheets** are excellent for use on areas of any size. They are available in a wide range of patterns and colors, both transparent and translucent. They will adhere to all surfaces.

Translucent color sheets have an adhesive wax backing, which makes them partially opaque. Such sheets should be used to color art work prepared on cardboard. Transparent color sheets are prepared with a clear adhesive backing so the color will project brilliantly when applied to an overhead transparency or to other visuals for projection.

The shading or color is printed on a thin plastic sheet, which has an adhesive backing. This in turn is

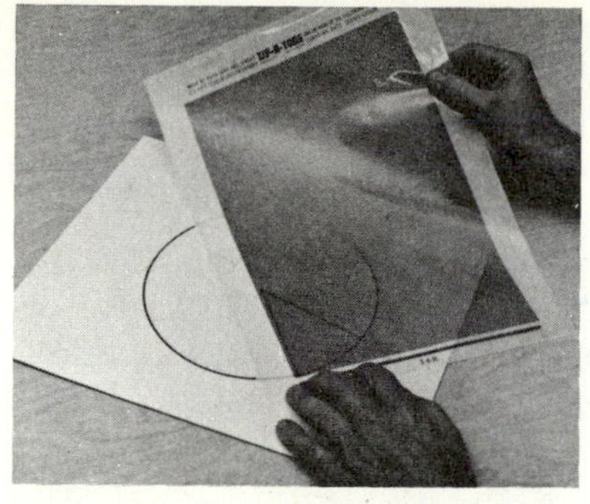
1

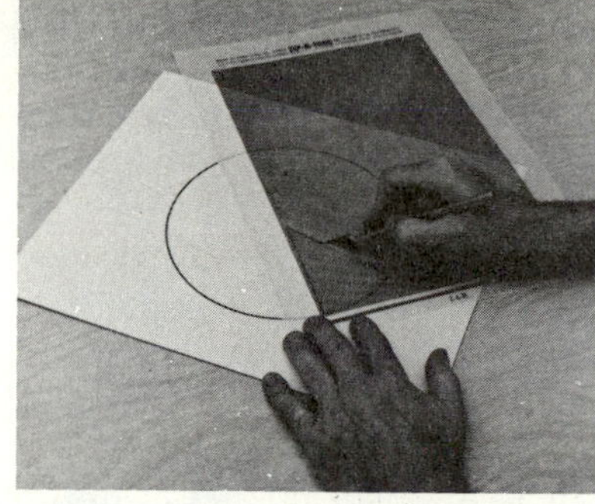
2

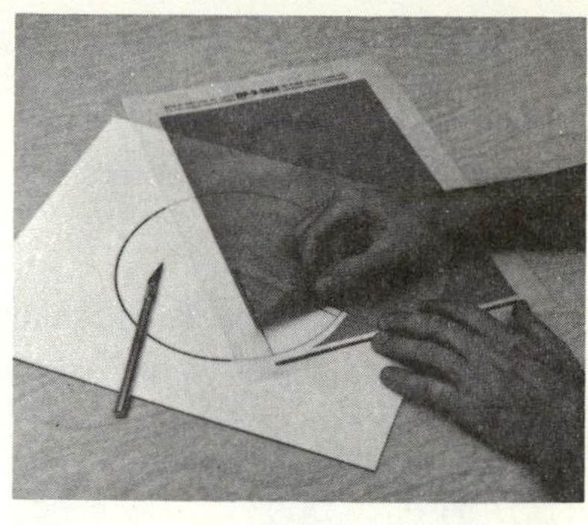
3

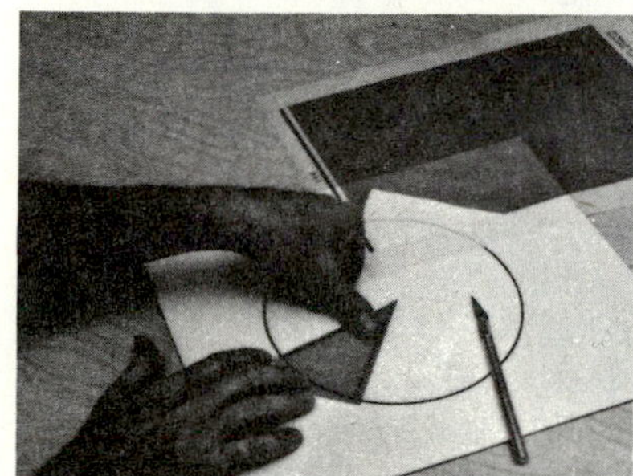
4

5

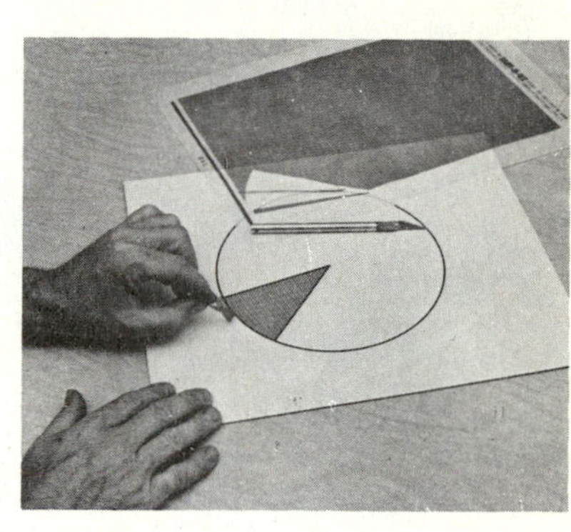
6

protected with a backing sheet. To work with these sheets, use a razor blade or a sharp X-acto knife and follow the procedure illustrated below.

1. Place a sheet of the selected material over the area to be shaded or colored.
2. Lightly cut a piece slightly larger than the area to be colored or shaded. (Try not to cut through the backing sheet.)
3. Peel the cut piece from the backing.
4. Place the cut piece of adhesive-backed material over the area and rub to adhere.
5. Cut to match the area, using lines in the diagram as guides.
6. Peel off the excess pieces of the coloring or shading material.

REVIEW

What You Have Learned About Coloring and Shading:

1. What three purposes can be served with color when designing visual materials?
2. What two aspects in a visual should be considered when colors are being selected?
3. How does the use of felt pens compare to the use of spray paints for coloring moderate-sized areas?
4. When using a color adhesive sheet, why is it *not* proper to cut through the color sheet *and* the backing sheet when first cutting the piece for use? Also, why should you *not* cut the piece to be used the exact size at first?
5. Of the coloring methods described, which one might be selected to carefully tint a large, irregular area?
6. Which color combinations are preferable when preparing titles on backgrounds?
a. gray background, orange title b. green background, magenta title

See answers on page 378.

LEGIBILITY STANDARDS FOR LETTERING

The **legibility** of the words, numerals, and other data that an audience is expected to read is frequently neglected during the planning and preparation of visual materials. This neglect is especially common since simple and quick methods have become available for duplicating and projecting computer-generated, typewritten and printed materials. An illustration with lettering copied from a book usually is not as easy to read when projected on a screen as it is on the printed page.

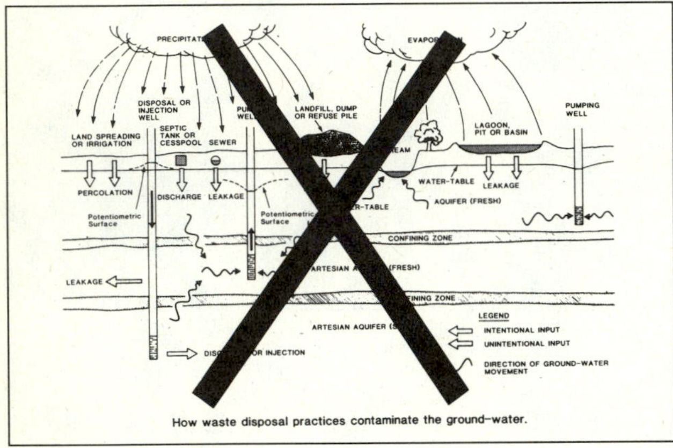

How waste disposal practices contaminate the ground-water.

Planners must give proper attention to legibility—hence to methods of lettering, sizes of letters, and styles of lettering. These matters physically control the amount of information that can be presented in one visual unit. Reciprocally, the established psychological limits on the amount of information a viewer can effectively receive also affect the choices in respect to lettering. Keep in mind, therefore, the methods for dividing lengthy or complex data into a sequence of visuals (page 201); see the discussion of layout and design earlier in this chapter.

The suitability of lettering is further complicated by a number of other factors—characteristics of the meeting room, such as its shape; the type of screen surface (rear-screen transmitted projection is not as brilliant as front-screen reflected projection and will require larger lettering for legibility); and the amount of ambient or outside light that cannot be controlled.

If your instructional materials are designed for use in a specific room, then take into account as many of these factors as possible in deciding on lettering sizes. But no one can predict or be prepared for all eventualities in viewing situations. Often visuals must be presented under less than ideal conditions; therefore, it is advisable that *minimum standards* be recognized. As a general guide, select minimum lettering size for *all* materials so that any member of an audience, seated at an anticipated maximum viewing distance, can easily read titles, captions, and labels. If you do not heed this advice, you are likely to find members of the audience losing interest in your presentation because they cannot read the lettered information.

Following are guidelines that apply equally to projected and nonprojected media types. They also deserve consideration when designing words, expressions, and sentences for the computer display screen.

Guidelines

To assist with good legibility, the following guidelines are recommended:

- Select a readable letter style, like a sans-serif or gothic type, which is composed of evenly drawn, medium-width strokes. Typefaces widely used for projected visual media include Helvetica medium, Futura bold, and Univers.
- Avoid script letter styles because the letters are difficult to distinguish, one from another.

MANY BUYERS
A Gothic Letter

MANY BUYERS
A Sans-Serif Letter

MANY BUYERS
A Condensed Sans-Serif Letter

MANY BUYERS
A Modern Letter with Serifs

Many Buyers
A Script Letter

Many Buyers
An Old English Letter

STRUCTURAL FEATURES OF PROTEINS

1 Amino acid (AA)

$NH_3 - C(H)(R) - C(=O) - OH$

Amino end — Acid end — Side chain

2 Peptide

AA_1 Peptide bond AA_2

$- C(=O) - N(H) -$

3 Polypeptide chain

$AA_1 — AA_2 \cdots\cdots AA_{200} — AA_{201}$

- For a visual, or series of related visuals consisting of verbal information, use no more than three different **typefaces** (two are preferred). The typefaces should harmonize with each other. They can be of various sizes. See examples on previous page.
- Use capital letters for short titles and labels, but for longer captions and phrases (six words or more) use lowercase letters with appropriate capitals, since the lowercase letters are more easily read.

A HISTORY
OF
OUR CHURCH

The Forty Most Common
Deciduous Trees and Shrubs
in Vernon County

- As stated previously, include no more than 15 to 20 words in a single projected visual. Also, leave extra blank space around the edge of the visual so it appears uncrowded. This tends to increase readability.
- Separate lines within a caption so that adequate white space is left for ease in reading—about 1½ times the height of the lowercase letter *m*, measured from an *m* on one line to an *m* (or comparable letter) on the next line.

Extensive testing has been made by companies in both photothermal and photovoltaic applications.

Too Close

Extensive testing has been made

by companies in both photothermal

and photovoltaic applications.

Too Far

Extensive testing has been made by companies in both photothermal and photovoltaic applications.

Good

- Space letters *optically.* Equal measured distances between all letters do not look equal. *Make spaces look equal,* regardless of measurement. This is known as *kerning* and can be handled automatically in a computer graphics program.

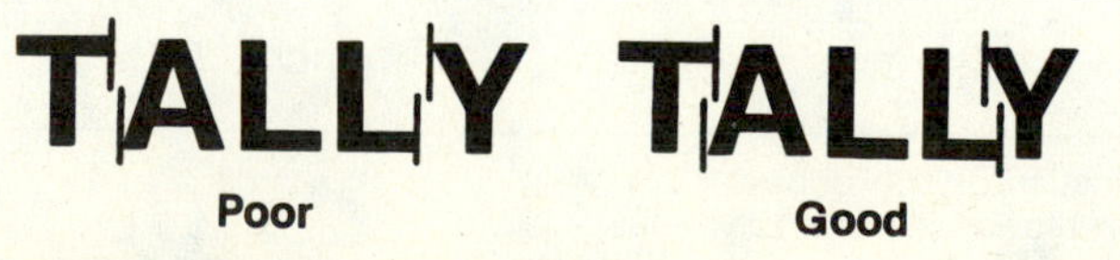

- Space letters so they do *not* appear to either blend together or lose their continuity for forming letters.

FLOOD	F L O O D	FLOOD
Too close	Too far	Good

- Allow 1½ letter widths for the space between words and 3 widths between sentences. Too much or too little space, again, makes reading difficult.

Holdlidfirmly. Raisearm.

Too close

Hold lid firmly. Raise arm.

Too far

Hold lid firmly. Raise arm.

Good

- Thickness of line is important to legibility. A thin line is difficult to see. A moderate, bold line is preferred because it increases the area of a letter that is visible to the viewer. Extremely bold lines reduce legibility because parts of letters that should be open appear somewhat filled in.

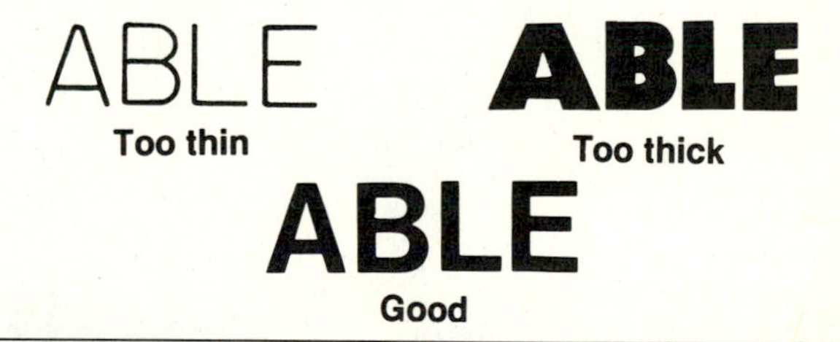

- Contrast the lettering in color or tone with the background so that separation contributes to good legibility.

Red Lettering on Yellow

Black Lettering on Blue

- Light letters against a dark background have greater visibility than dark letters against a light background.
- For satisfactory legibility, dark letters on a light-colored background require a wider width stroke than do light letters on a dark background.

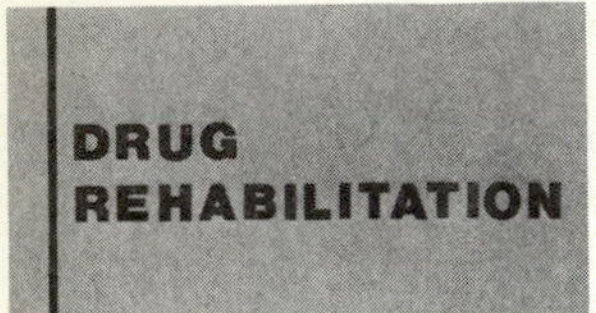

Nonprojected Materials

For displaying materials that will *not* be projected, follow these recommendations:

MAXIMUM ANTICIPATED VIEWING DISTANCE	MINIMUM LETTER HEIGHT (LOWERCASE LETTER *M*)
8 feet	¼ inch
16 feet	½ inch
32 feet	1 inch
64 feet	2 inches

Capital letters, alone or with lowercase letters, should be correspondingly larger than the recommendations above because they are less legible.

Special note: Size (height) of letters may be stated in various ways in addition to inches:

- As millimeters (25mm = 1 inch)
- As points (72 points = 1 inch)
- As picas (6 picas = 1 inch)

Projected Materials

For slides and transparencies, minimum letter size also is based on the maximum anticipated viewing distance. This maximum, as a standard, is accepted as being 8 times the *vertical dimension of the picture on the screen* (that is, 8H). Thus, for a screen 6 feet high, filled with a picture, the maximum viewing distance of 8H is 48 feet (Eastman Kodak).

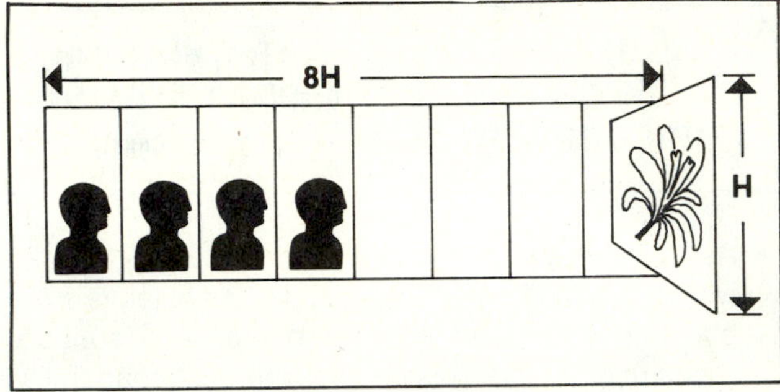

The recommendations of minimum letter size in Table 8–2 are supported by McVey. But in reviewing the research on legibility of projected information, Sharpe concluded that a suitable ratio for minimum letter size should be 1 to 30 rather than 1 to 50 and letter height should be ¼ inch minimum rather than ⅛ inch. From their experiences, the authors strongly support the Sharpe conclusion. Thus, you should recognize the value of using lettering that is larger than the minimum shown in Table 8–2 below.

Rear-screen projection does not permit as bright or as contrasty an image as does front projection. For suitable legibility, lettering half again as large as that for front projection is required for rear-screen projected materials.

TABLE 8–2 MINIMUM LETTER SIZES FOR VIEWING DISTANCES OF VARIOUS PROJECTED INSTRUCTIONAL MEDIA

MEDIUM	MAXIMUM VIEWING DISTANCE	MAXIMUM RATIO OF LETTER HEIGHT TO HEIGHT OF ART WORK AREA	MINIMUM LETTER HEIGHT (LOWERCASE LETTER *m*) FOR AREA 6 × 9 INCHES
Slides Transparencies	8H	1 to 50	⅛ inch (9 point)
Video	16H–24H	1 to 25	¼–⅜ inch (18–30 point)

Source: Information adapted from *Legibility—Artwork to Screen,* publication S-24 (Rochester, NY: Eastman Kodak Co., 1988). See the Legibility Calculator in this pamphlet for application to various distance situations.

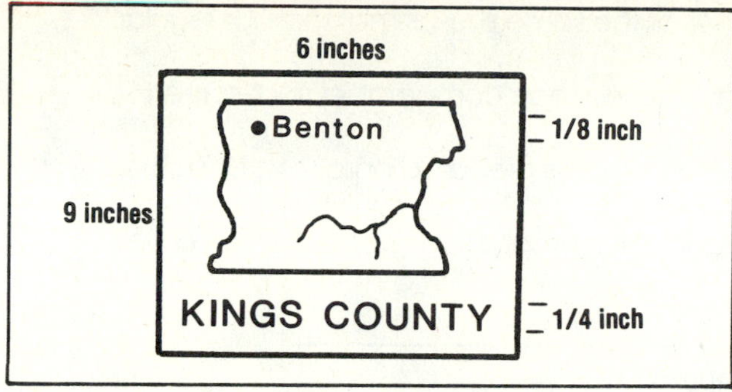

The maximum group viewing distance for video, in terms of the screen size, is greater—16H to 24H. As you might expect, minimum letter size for video is therefore greater.

You can make a rough test of the legibility of lettered materials for projection by first measuring the width of the art work in inches, then dividing this number by 2 and placing the material that many feet away from a test reader. If the person reads the lettering easily, then for normal conditions the material, when projected, will be legible. But don't trust yourself as a test reader if you prepared the lettering or know how it should read—your memory may help your vision too much.

The recommendations for ensuring legibility of visual materials are only for your guidance. Be alert to special conditions in any situations—seating arrangements, light level, image brightness, and so forth. These may require larger images or bolder lettering to ensure satisfactory legibility.

Computer-Generated Lettering Special care should be taken when creating titles and other lettering with a computer. The following are some things to consider:

- Limit to 10 lines per screen and 25 characters per line.
- Use bold, simple lettering styles (Helvetica, Tempo, Metro).
- Use a pastel color, such as yellow, for words over dark (blue preferably) background.
- Use dark edging or drop shadow around light-colored lettering to add depth and dimension.

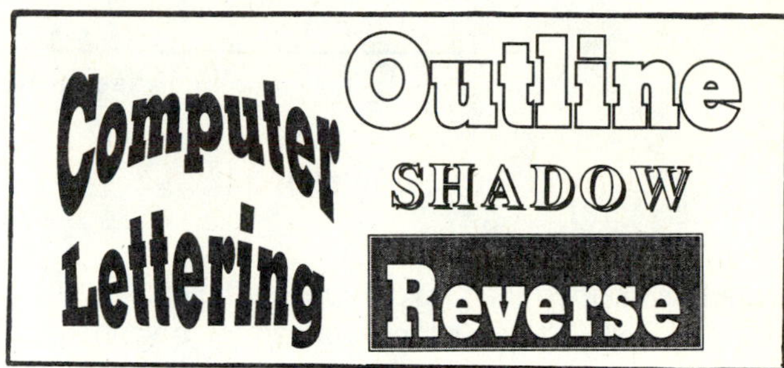

- Tone down the background to make lettering stand out.
- Defocus objects in background to make lettering stand out.
- Compose a picture or art work so clear space is left for lettering.

Extensive use is being made of liquid crystal display (LCD) electronic units, either built into a projector or as a window plate placed on an overhead projector stage (see page 206). With such a unit, computer-generated images can be projected directly from computer output. The resolution, contrast, and brightness of such displays are often less than those from standard media projection. Therefore, particular attention should be given to using *large, bold lettering for suitable legibility.* A better solution, if affordable, is to use a full color, video projector.

REVIEW

What You Have Learned About Legibility Standards for Lettering:

1. What is the single most important reason why legibility standards should be considered for projected materials?
2. How might you relate the degree of legibility to quantity of information possible in a visual?
3. What are five of the guidelines that will contribute to good legibility in lettering?
4. What is the minimum letter size for materials displayed at the front of an average-sized classroom (30 feet deep)?
5. What is the minimum size for lettering used in the direct preparation of a transparency (7½ inches vertical dimension)?

6. Should visuals for video use be lettered larger, smaller, or the same size as materials for regular classroom use?
7. Does rear-screen projection require larger or smaller lettering than comparable front-screen projection?
8. At what distance should legibility be checked when lettering is prepared on a 9 × 12 inch working area?
9. What matters need careful attention if computer-generated images with lettering are to be directly projected from computer memory?

See answers on page 378.

LETTERING AND TITLING TECHNIQUES

However good the photography and picture content of visual materials, their effectiveness can be enhanced by the appearance of the titles, captions, and labels. Neat lettering, simple designs, and attractive colors or background patterns all add a professional touch to your materials.

Titles generally require large, bold letters. Since there are relatively few major titles, their letters may be hand drawn, or set individually in place by hand. But such methods may be too slow for preparing captions that consist of many words; here other lettering techniques are appropriate, adequate, even better. You need to know and select techniques with regard to the results needed and the time available for preparation of your materials.

Some remarks follow concerning eight specific lettering techniques. No one technique is necessarily the best for any lettering job. You need to evaluate as many of them as you can for your own needs—in terms of their availability, cost, ease of use, time required for preparation, and resulting quality. At the end of this section (page 139) is a summary of lettering techniques.

Felt-Pen Lettering

The use of the felt pen for coloring has been described on page 130. These pens can also be used for lettering. For successful results:

- Hold the beveled-tip pen firmly in a "locked" or set position in the hand.
- Make no finger or wrist movement. *All* movements should consist of arm movements.

Sharp-tipped nylon pens make a thinner mark than the beveled-tip felt pens. They are easier to use and are good for quick lettering on all surfaces. The inks in some make permanent marks, but most have water-based inks.

Always replace the cap on a felt or nylon pen as soon as you are done using it. Since their inks dry quickly, uncapped pens will dry out, resulting in a hardened unserviceable tip. If this happens, soak the tip in lighter fluid (permanent-ink pen) or in water (water-based-ink pen).

Dry-Transfer Letters

These letters have sharp, clean edges, much like those printed from good type, and are easy to handle. They come in sheets of many sizes, styles, and colors. They are excellent for titles and labels—on many types of backgrounds. While suitable for short headings, their use for materials requiring many sentences would require a lengthy preparation time.

Dry-transfer letters are printed on the back of the sheet and each sheet is backed with a protective sheet of paper.

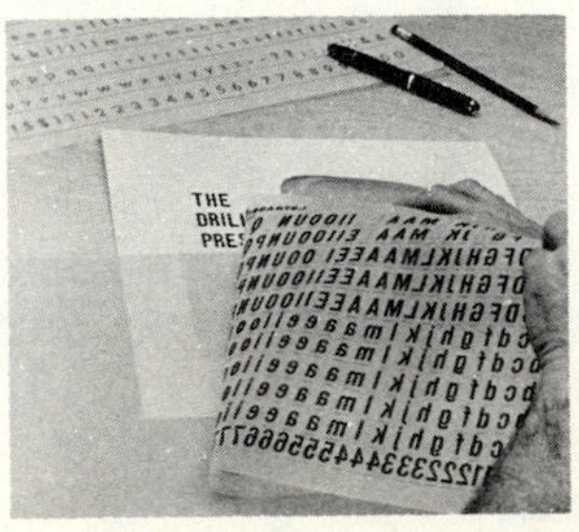

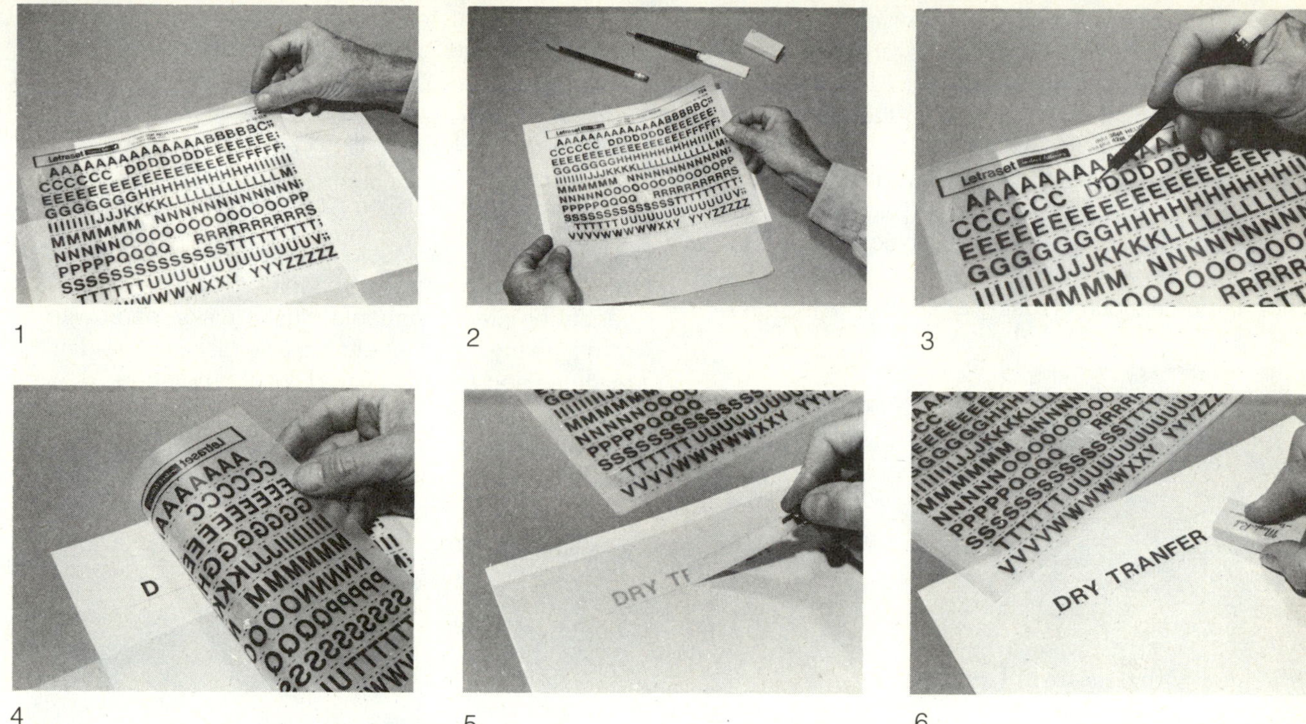

1 2 3 4 5 6

Follow this procedure in using dry-transfer letters, as illustrated above.

1. Slip the backing sheet below or above the row of letters that has the letter to be used.
2. Position the letter by aligning the printed line under the letters over the guideline drawn on the mounting surface.
3. Burnish (rub) the entire letter to the mounting surface with a commercial burnisher, the round part of a pen, or other blunt object on which you can exert pressure without tearing the paper. You will notice a slight change in color as the letter transfers.
4. Slowly pull the sheet of letters from the mounting surface. The letter will remain transferred.
5. To secure the letters to the surface, place the backing sheet over them and burnish firmly.
6. Replace the backing sheet behind the letter sheet. Then erase the guideline from the mounting surface.

Dry-transfer letters are also available in transparent colors for direct use on transparencies. When they are adhered to acetate, a clean transfer results with no adhesive residue appearing around the letter.

If a dry-transfer letter must be removed from paper or cardboard, this can be done by firmly sticking a piece of masking tape on the letter. Then carefully pull the tape up. A new letter can be adhered in the same place. Although letters are secured to the new surface, for protection, spray them evenly with light coats of clear plastic coating.

Cutout Letters

Inexpensive ready-to-use letters, cut out of construction paper or gummed-back paper in many styles, colors, and sizes, are easy to manipulate and are satisfactory for bold titles. They can be placed over any background. To align them neatly, use a T-square or lightly rule a guideline on the mounting material. Position the letters on guidelines. Attach construction paper letters with a small amount of rubber cement or other adhesive. Moisten the adhesive on the gummed-back letters with a sponge dipped in water. After the letters are in place, erase the guidelines.

Support System Functions

Cutout Letter Machine

Many schools have machines for teachers to use that die-cut letters from construction paper or colored cardboard. Besides several different sizes and styles of letters, there are also numerous decorative dies available. These include sets on holiday motifs, animals, geometric shapes, and music symbols.

Before punching out letters using the die-cut lettering machine, adhere dry-mount tissue to the back of the construction paper or cardboard in a dry-mount press, using silicon-treated release paper (page 144). Cut the construction paper or cardboard into squares. After the letters are die-cut, they are ready to be tacked into place and heat mounted using a press or hand iron.

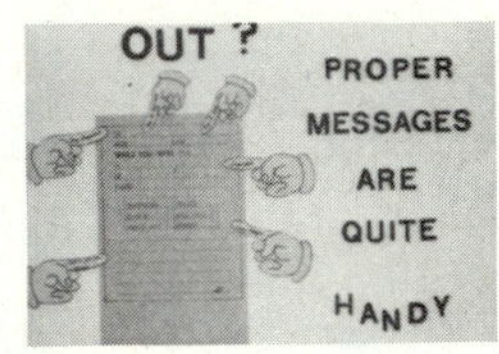

Three-Dimensional Letters

Three-dimensional letters are manufactured in cardboard, wood, cork, ceramics, and plastics, and are available in plain backs or pin backs. They are excellent for main titles, and when photographed with side lighting they give shadow effects and three-dimensional effects. Costs vary widely according to kind and size. Surfaces can be tinted with paint or watercolors. Position the letters against a T-square or on a guideline and adhere temporarily with rubber cement.

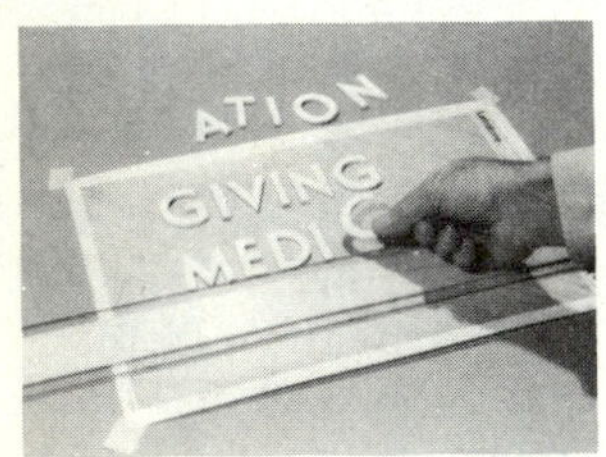

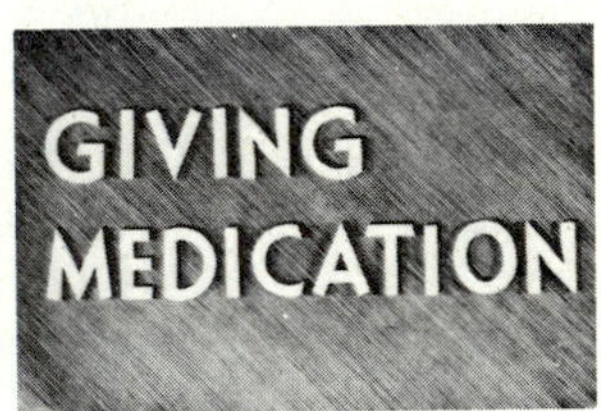

Stencil Lettering Guides (Wrico Signmaker)

Stencil lettering guides are useful for lettering large posters, banners, and other display items. They are offered in a variety of styles and sizes. The better ones can be used, after a little practice, to produce neat lettering, even in lengthy captions. These stencils are designed to be raised off the background and positioned against a metal guide. A special pen is used, which fits and follows the letter outline in the plastic stencil.

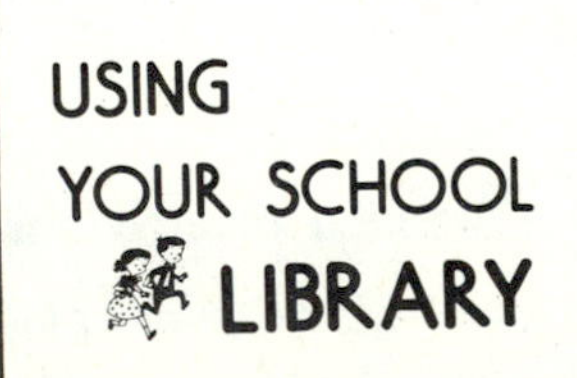

Pressure-Machine Lettering (Kroy/Merlin)

High-quality, professional lettering can be prepared with a tabletop lettering machine. The unit includes a variety of interchangeable plastic disks, each with its own type style and letter size. The disk is placed in the machine and the selection of letters, numbers, or symbols is controlled manually by dialing or pushing a button. Pressure is applied to a character, causing an impression on carbon paper to transfer to film having a paper backing. The film is peeled from its backing and pressed on paper or cardboard for use.

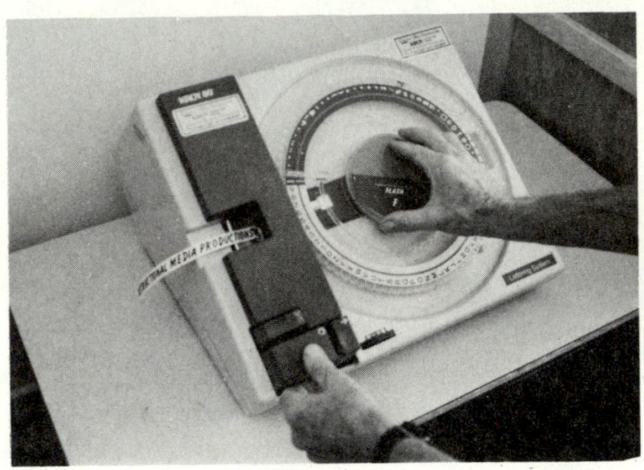

With an electronic keyboard version, as letters are selected, the words can be viewed on a screen and edited. Words, expressions, and sentences can be printed immediately or placed in memory for printing when the full input for a job is completed.

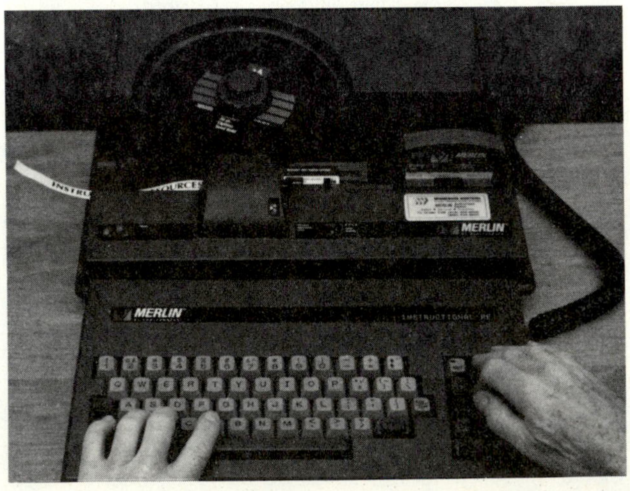

Microcomputer with Laser Printer

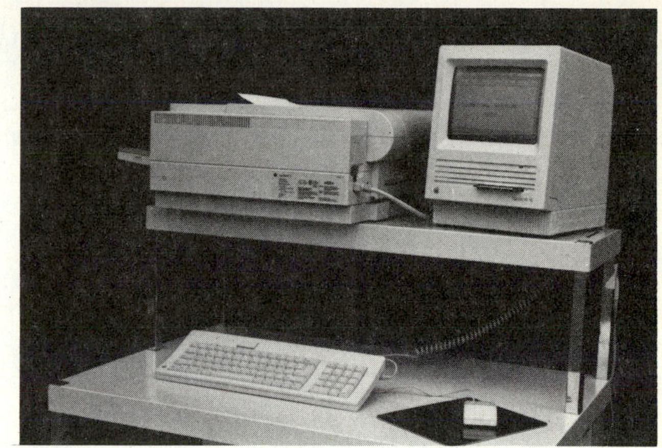

Quality lettering can be created rapidly with a computer graphics software program and then printed on paper with a laser printer. Also, masters for inexpensive photocopying and camera-ready masters for printing can be output. In addition, high-quality overhead transparencies can be made quickly with a laser printer.

Depending on the program and the model of printer used, various lettering fonts, styles, and sizes would be available for selection. For further explanation of this method of lettering, see information on computer graphics systems (page 119) and desktop publishing (page 182).

TABLE 8–3 SUMMARY COMPARISON OF LETTERING METHODS

TYPE	MAIN USE	QUALITY	RELATIVE EQUIPMENT COST	RELATIVE MATERIALS COST
Felt pen	Titles Labels	Good if lettering performed with care	None	Low
Dry-transfer	Titles Short headings	Excellent if handled carefully and surface protected	None	Moderate
Cutout letters	Titles	Good to superior if aligned carefully	Moderate	Low
3-D letters	Titles	Excellent with care in lighting when photographed	Low	Low
Stencil	Titles	Fair with careful use of pen	Low	None
Pressure machine	All uses	Excellent and fast to use	High	Moderate
Computer/laser printer	All uses	Excellent	High	Low

What You Have Learned About Lettering Methods:

1. What rules guide the holding and using of a beveled-tip felt pen?
2. How do you line up and space cutout letters?
3. What purpose is served by the backing sheet with dry-transfer letters?
4. What kind of tool can be used with dry-transfer letters?
5. What method of lettering might you select to prepare a caption of 12 words?
6. Which lettering method allows you to rapidly change typefaces and letter size, and see results, before deciding what to use?
7. What is the name of a machine that can be used to impress letters from a disk, through carbon, onto film?
8. The __________ felt pen is better for use on film for transparencies.

(continued)

9. Compare the lettering methods available to you in terms of best uses, time and skill to use, relative cost of equipment if required, and quality of results.

See answers on page 379.

BACKGROUNDS FOR TITLES

With a computer graphics program and the necessary graphics card in the computer, you can place titles over various backgrounds. In addition to creating patterns and textures, you can import special backgrounds, including scanned material and digitized images from video scenes (page 120), on which lettering can be overlayed. If such resources are not available, hand preparation methods can be used.

Select backgrounds that are appropriate to the treatment of the subject and that do not distract attention from the title. Such backgrounds will be inconspicuous in color and design, yet will contribute to the mood or central idea of the topic. Cool colors (blue, gray, green) are preferred for backgrounds, and warm colors (red, orange, magenta) for titles and visuals over the background. For backgrounds you may consider plain, colored, or textured papers; cardboards of various finishes and colors; wallpaper samples, or pictures and photographs.

For most uses, prepare simple titles directly on the background material. But for special purposes, you can make an **overlay** and place the title over the background before filming. Overlays are particularly useful when several titles or diagrams must appear over the same background. Each title is prepared as a separate overlay. Lettering for overlays can be black or in color.

If a title is to appear in white over a background or a scene, then an **overprint** is necessary. This requires making two exposures (double-exposure photography) on a single frame of film, as explained on page 106.

For applications of these techniques in preparing slides, see the section on titling for slides on page 106.

Illustrations of the following techniques are shown below.

▸ ***Black overlay titles***—Adhere individual letters directly to the background or prepare black-line thermal transparency (page 207) and place on background.

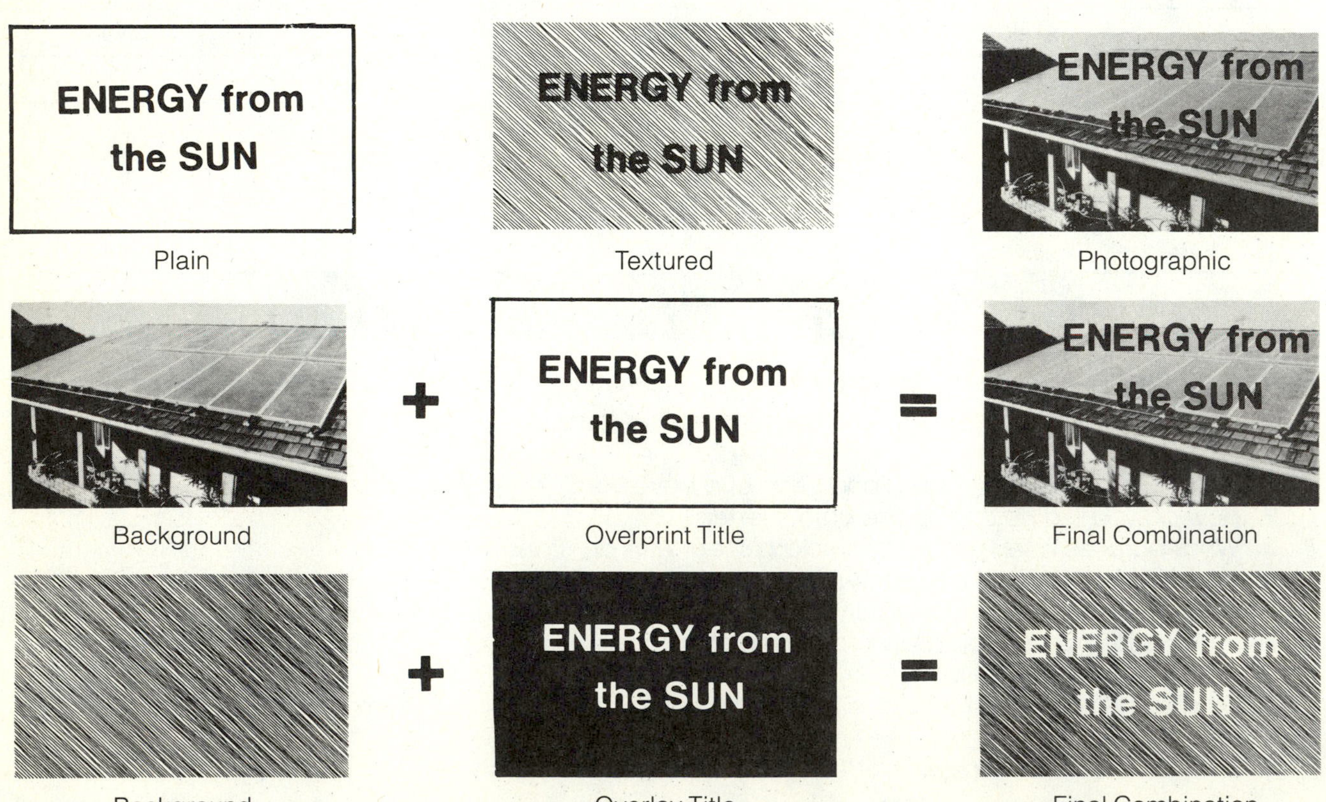

▸ ***White overprint titles***—Place white letters on black cardboard or film black letters on a white background to make a high-contrast film negative (page 275). Then prepare the final slide or other visual by double-exposing to record first the background and then the white-letter title.

▸ ***Color overlay titles***—Use colored dry-transfer letters directly on the background or on a sheet of clear acetate laid over the background. Color lettered thermal transparency can also be overlayed on the background.

What You Have Learned About Background for Titles:

Which titling method is appropriate for each situation?
1. Yellow letters over an outdoor scene
2. Black letters over an orange background
3. Clear letters on a blue background

See answers on page 379.

MOUNTING FLAT MATERIALS

A variety of techniques can be considered for mounting art work and for preserving finished visual materials and commercially available pictures, maps, charts, and so forth. These techniques have various characteristics: Final results are temporary, semipermanent, or permanent; special equipment may or may not be required; heat and or pressure may or may not be required; and sealing may be on cardboard, cloth, or other surfaces. Because of the variety of methods, you should study them carefully to evaluate them in terms of materials, and your needs.

The methods to be described on the following pages include:

▸ Rubber cement mounting
▸ Spray mounting
▸ Dry mounting on cardboard
▸ Dry mounting on cloth

Rubber Cement Methods

Mounting with rubber cement is a simple procedure that requires no special equipment. It will accomplish temporary or semipermanent mounting.

Temporary Mounting **Temporary mounting** is useful for making paste-ups (page 147) of line drawings and accompanying lettering that are to be photographed rather than used directly:

1. Trim the material to be mounted.
2. With rubber cement, coat the back of each piece to be mounted.
3. Place the coated pieces cement-side down on the cardboard, while the cement is wet. They can be moved as necessary for exact positioning and alignment, or picked up and repositioned.
4. Allow the cement to dry before using the paste-up. Rub away any visible cement.

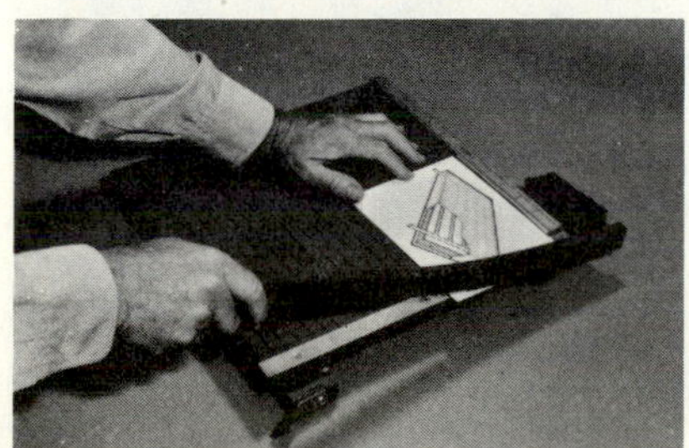
1

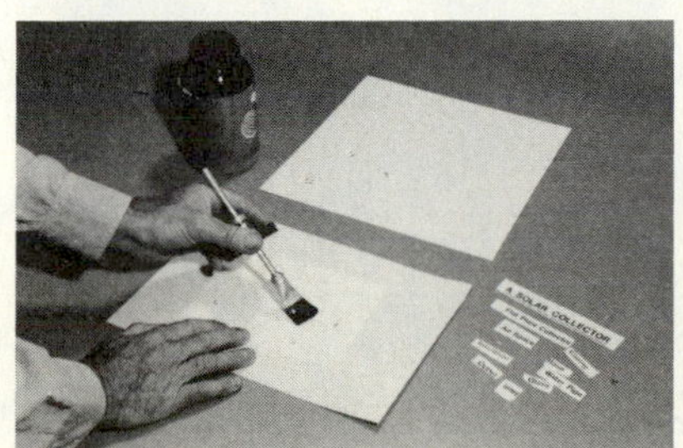
2

3

Semipermanent Mounting So-called **semipermanent mounting** is not truly permanent, but materials thus mounted with rubber cement will adhere for long periods. Rubber cement is spread on back of the picture *and* the cardboard surface. There are twelve steps:

1. Trim the picture or other piece to be mounted.
2. Place the picture on the cardboard backing; make guide marks for each corner.
3. Coat the back of the picture with rubber cement from the center out to avoid getting cement on front of the picture.
4. Coat the marked area on the cardboard with rubber cement.
5. Allow the cement to dry on both surfaces.
6. Overlap two waxed paper sheets on the cement covered cardboard after the cement is dry.
7. Align the picture on the guide marks as seen through the waxed paper.

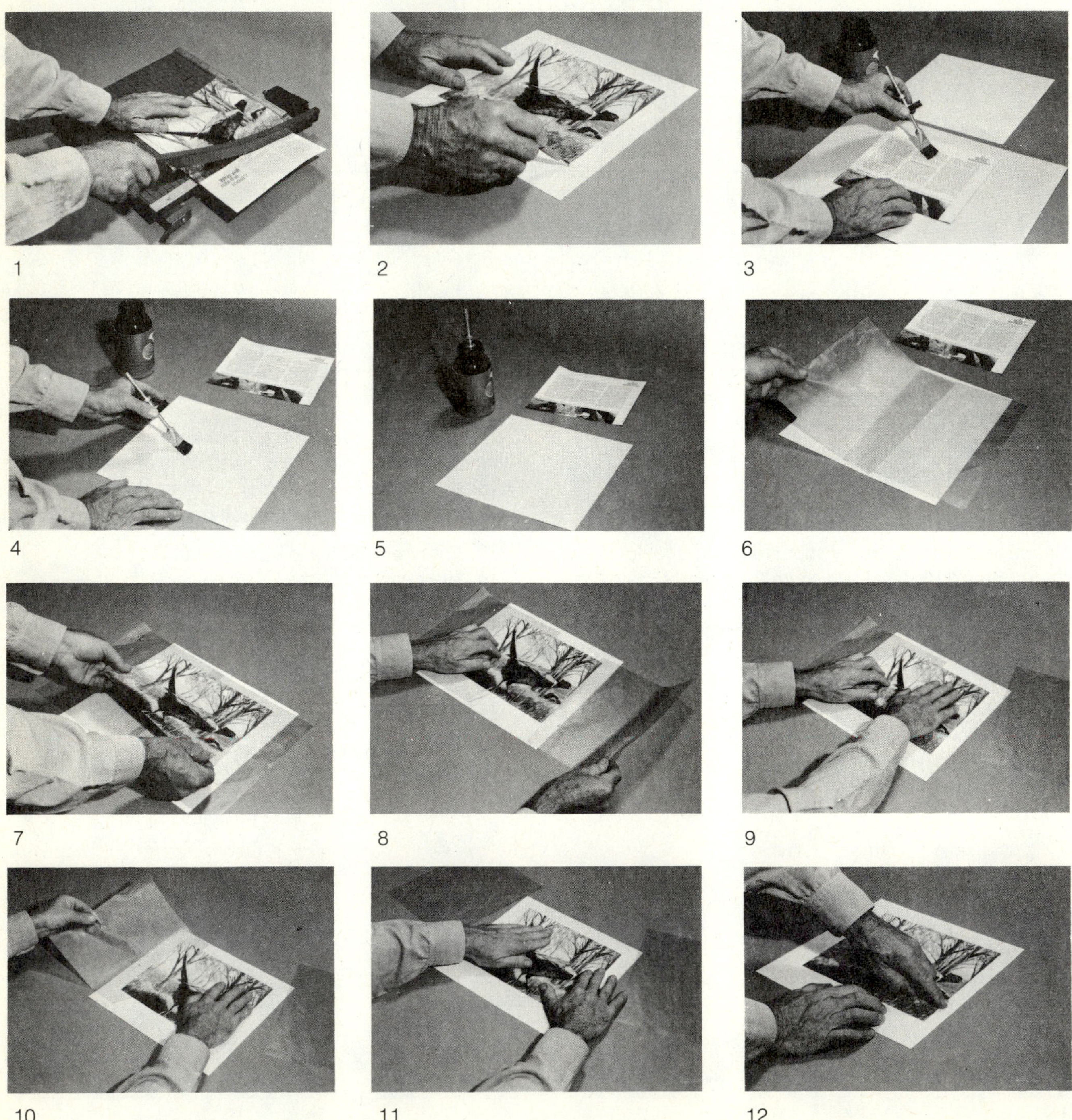

1 2 3 4 5 6 7 8 9 10 11 12

8. Slide out one sheet of waxed paper.
9. Smooth the picture to the cardboard on this exposed cement.
10. Remove the second waxed sheet.
11. Smooth the remainder of the picture to the cardboard.
12. Rub excess cement away from the edges of the picture.

Consider these additional details when using the rubber cement methods of mounting:

- Make guide marks in corners on mounting board lightly in pencil so they are not noticeable after the mounting is completed. Erase the obvious ones.
- Make sure the brush is adjusted in the lid of the cement jar so the bristles are below the cement level in the jar.
- Cement should flow smoothly from the brush. If it thickens it will collect on the brush and fall in lumps. Add a small amount of rubber cement thinner and shake the jar well.
- If colored cardboard is to be used, test the cement on a sample, as rubber cement may stain the surface.
- Apply cement with long sweeping strokes of the brush. Move moderately fast as cement dries quickly.
- Use rubber cement in a well-ventilated room and keep the lid on the dispenser jar tightly closed when not in actual use.
- In the semipermanent method, the cemented surfaces can be considered dry when they feel slightly tacky.
- The sulfur in rubber cement may react with the silver in a photograph to stain the face of the picture a yellowish-brown color.

Spray Mounting

Spray mounting is a fast and convenient method for mounting illustrations and lettering when preparing visual materials. Some spray adhesives are permanent and others are not. Semipermanent spray adhesive allows repositioning materials and is best used when making a pasteup. There are five steps:

1. Trim the illustration.
2. Make light guide marks for positioning on the cardboard.
3. Place the illustration face-down on newsprint or other disposable paper.
4. Spray an even coating of adhesive on the back of the illustration with a uniform motion.
5. Immediately place the illustration in its correct position on the cardboard. If you use semipermanent adhesive and a mistake in alignment is made, simply pull the item off and reposition it correctly. If you use a permanent spray, be sure to align the illustration carefully the first time.

Dry Mounting Method on Cardboard

Dry mounting is a fast method, resulting in permanent and neatly mounted materials. It is particularly useful when a number of photographs or other visual items are to be mounted. The procedure requires the use of a heat-sensitive adhesive and attention to three variables—temperature, pressure, and time—to ensure satisfactory **permanent mounting** of the picture to the backing surface. Temperature and pressure are controlled in a **dry-mount press,** and you select the time.

In the dry-mounting process, a tissuelike paper, coated on both sides with a heat-sensitive adhesive, is placed between the picture and the cardboard or other backing material. When heat and pressure are applied, the adhesive is activated. Upon cooling the adhesive forms a strong bond between the picture and the cardboard.

Thus the cooling phase of the process is particularly critical when preparing a successful dry mount. To ensure a satisfactory result, immediately after the heating and pressure phase, place the mount under a metal weight to allow cooling to take place undisturbed. The liquefied adhesive hardens to form a firm, even seal between the picture and its backing.

A shortcoming of the dry mounting method is the possibility that bubbles of steam may form under a picture when heat is applied if there is moisture in the paper or cardboard. Most bubbles can be eliminated by predrying the cardboard and picture. If bubbles do appear after mounting, puncture them with a pin and then reapply heat and pressure. Unfortunately, when bubbles do form, the paper may stretch, resulting in a wrinkle.

The dry mounting method requires seven steps:

1. Set the dry-mount press at the suggested temperature for the mounting product to be used. Preheat both the picture and cardboard for 30 seconds to remove moisture from them.
2. Adhere the dry-mount tissue to the back of the picture by touching the tacking iron directly to the tissue. Always protect the table top with paper.
3. Trim the picture and the tissue together on all sides.
4. Align the picture on the cardboard.
5. Tack the tissue to the cardboard in two corners.

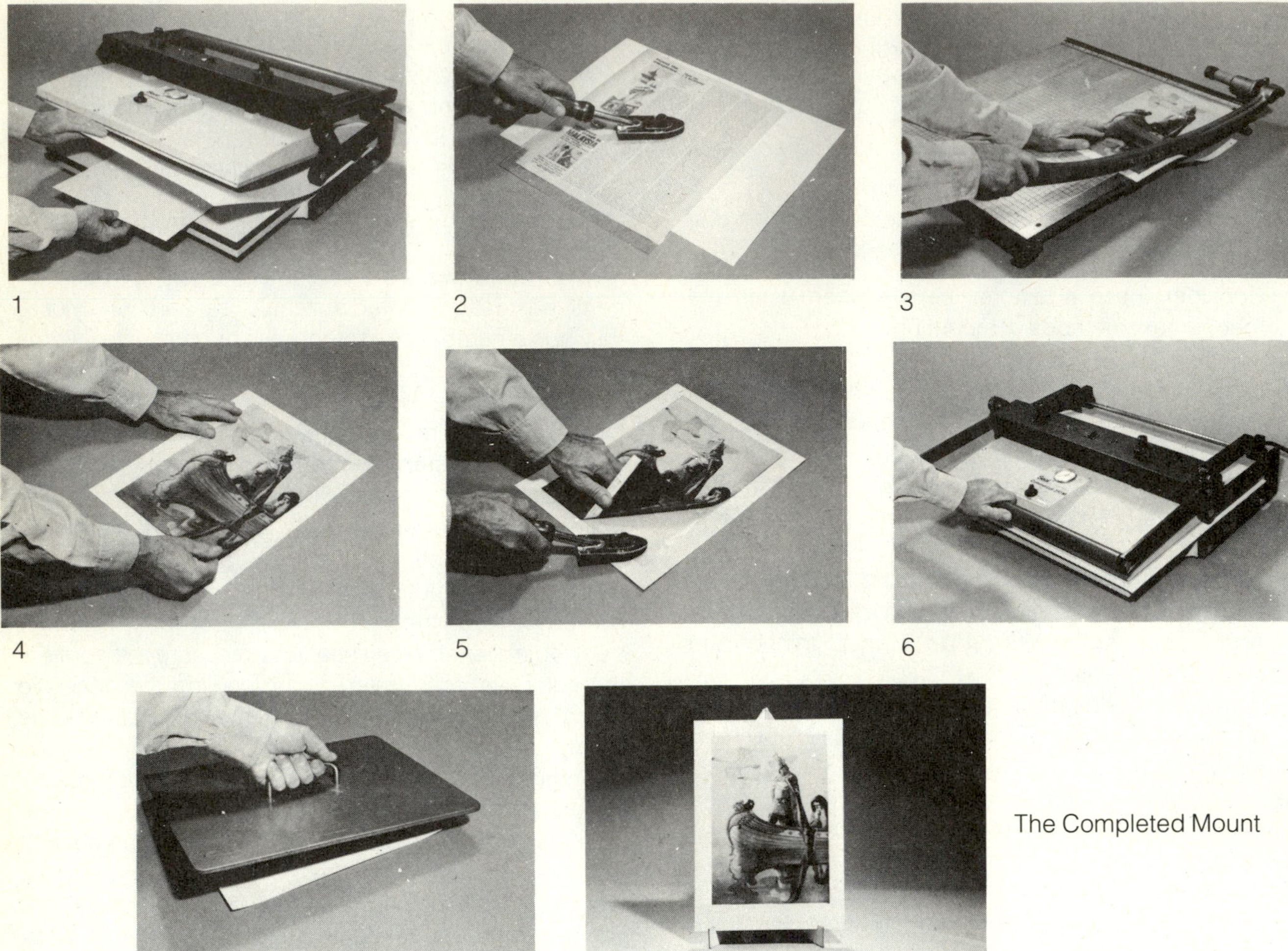

1 2 3 4 5 6 7

The Completed Mount

6. For protection, cover the picture with a sheet of silicon-treated **release paper** (Seal product). Seal the picture to the cardboard with heat and pressure for 30 seconds.
7. Cool the mounted picture under a metal weight for 1 minute or more.

Consider the additional details listed below when dry mounting:

- Every item placed in the dry-mount press should be covered with paper for protection, preferably with Seal Release paper. (Replace the carrier paper when it wrinkles.)
- In order to minimize any color change on color photographs, skip the preheat step when mounting color prints.
- If more than one sheet of tissue must be used, butt the edges together; do not overlap them.
- If a mounting is too large to be sealed in the dry-mount press at one time, seal it in sections. Make sure successive areas placed in the press are overlapped so none of the picture is missed.
- Be alert to temperature-sensitive materials such as resin-coated photo papers. Temperature of the press must stay below the melting temperature of the paper!
- When pressing is completed, *quickly* place the mount under a weight for cooling. This is when actual sealing takes place. A metal weight, which absorbs heat quickly, is preferred.

In addition to mounting complete rectangular pictures, cutouts around pictures can be made to eliminate unnecessary details. Be sure to tack tissue to the back of the picture before cutting it out. For added ease in cutting an irregularly shaped picture, first place the picture together with its tacked dry-mount tissue between two sheets of silicon-coated release paper. Put the total package into the dry-mount press for 5 to 8 seconds. This completely adheres the tissue to the picture's back, eliminating any shift of the tissue while cutting out the picture. After completing the cutout, tack the picture to posterboard by placing a protective piece of paper over the cutout and applying heat. Complete the dry mounting by following steps 4 to 7 listed before.

Various commercial products are available for use in dry mounting. Most are manufactured by Seal, Inc. Each one is designed for a special use:

- Colormount—designed for mounting photographic papers at a temperature of 205°F; with glossy resin-coated (RC) papers use Colormount Coversheet to preserve glossy finish of the print.
- Fusion 4000—low temperature adhesive (180°F) that can be pieced together, overlapped, and used on irregularly shaped items (as described previously), since it contains no tissue core; suitable for all low temperature uses; allows for removal of material mounted as with Fotoflat.
- MT5—general use, dry-mount tissue which bonds while it is heated in the press at standard 225°F.
- Fotoflat—low temperature (180°F), dry-mount tissue for mounting heat-sensitive materials; bonds as it cools, therefore can be used for temporary displays; picture can be removed from the backing by reheating in the press and then immediately peeling; electric hand iron (set at rayon or low) can be used with this material; start the iron from center of picture and move outward with slow movements and a moderate amount of pressure.

Dry Mounting Method on Cloth

Large materials, like charts and maps, or items that need to be pliable, can be backed with a dry-mount cloth (Chartex). This product will provide durability while maintaining flexibility.

The adhesive is a coating on one side of the cloth, which is ironed on the back of the materials or applied with a dry-mount press. Large materials can be mounted so as to be rolled or folded. Follow these steps:

1. Set the dry-mount press at 180°F and the tacking iron at *medium.*
2. Dry the chart in the press. Besides removing moisture from the paper, this treatment will flatten folds in the chart.
3. Cover the back of the chart with sufficient cloth. Place the adhesive coating (smooth side, on inside of roll) against the back of the chart.
4. Tack the chart to the cloth in one large spot.
5. Cut the cloth to match edges of chart or leave excess cloth all around for a cloth margin.

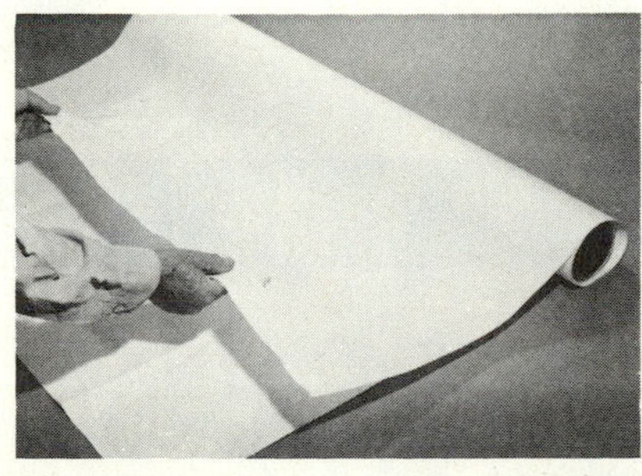

3

4

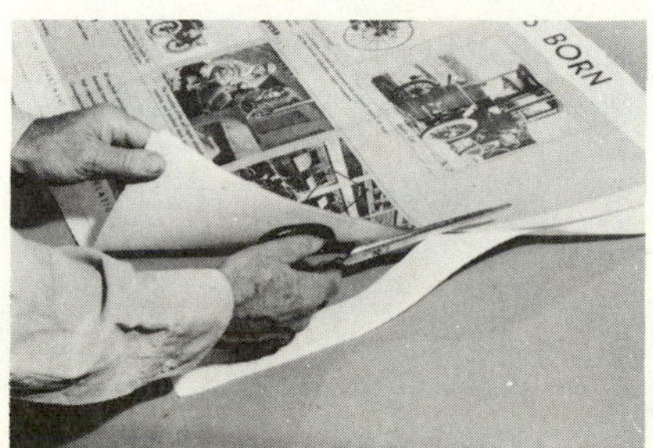

5

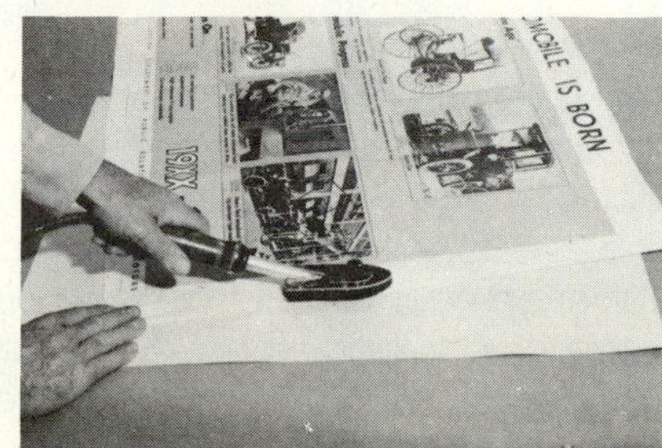

6

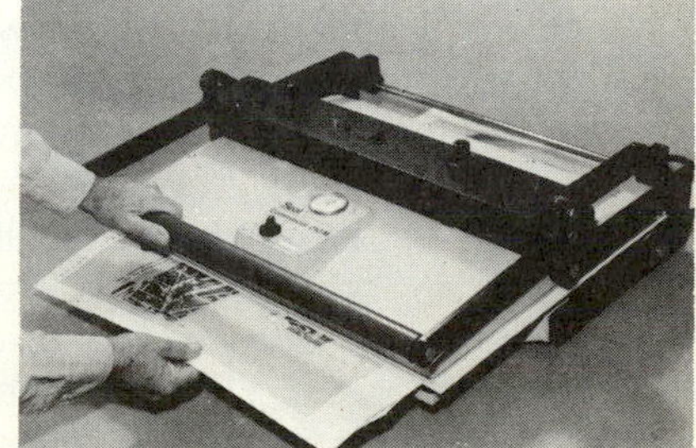

7

Completed Cloth-backed Mount (rolled)

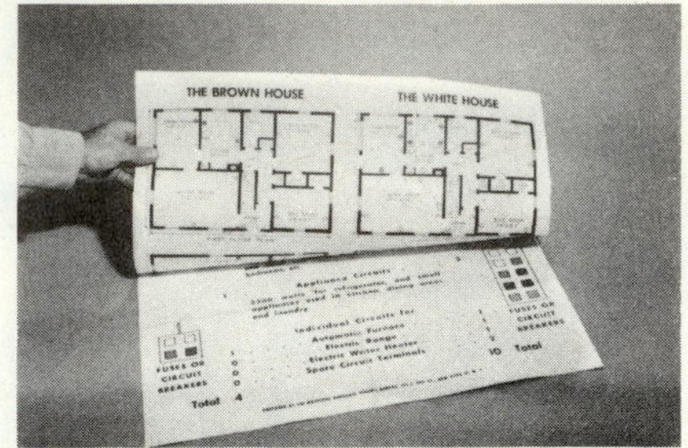

Completed Cloth-backed Mount (folded)

6. If you have left a margin, fold the cloth and tack it to the edge of the chart along the full length of each side.
7. Cover the chart with release paper and seal in the dry-mount press. Cool under a weight.
8. Check for bubbles or wrinkles. Reiron or repress as necessary.

A chart can also be cut into sections and mounted with a slight separation between adjacent sections. It can then be folded for easy storage.

Dry-mount cloth is available in rolls up to 42 inches wide and 100 feet long. For wide subjects, pieces of cloth can be spliced and overlapped.

Protecting the Surface (Laminating)

The face of a photograph or other mounted material to be handled a great deal needs protection. A clear plastic spray can be applied, but an even better and more permanent protection is achieved by **laminating,** or sealing a clear plastic film over the face of the picture. A dry mount press can be used. More consistent results are achieved with a laminator that applies heat as the material is fed through pressure-exerting rollers.

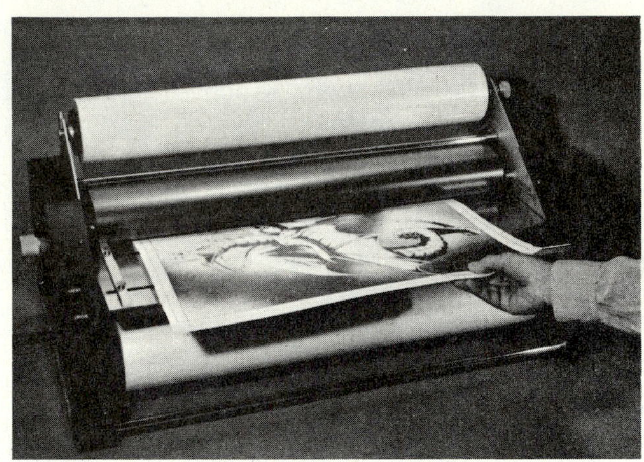
SeaLaminator (Seal, Inc.)

REVIEW

What You Have Learned About Mounting and Surface-Protection Methods:

1. What are two differences between *temporary* and *semipermanent* rubber cement mounting methods?
2. For what two reasons is wax paper used in the semipermanent rubber cement method?
3. What is an advantage for using spray mount over rubber cement for mounting pictures?
4. What is the principle of mounting with dry-mount tissue?
5. Why is tissue tacked to the back of the picture *before* the latter is trimmed to size?
6. What procedure is used if bubbles appear under a completed mount?
7. Compare three methods—rubber cement semipermanent, spray mount, and dry-mount press—in terms of speed of process, ease, equipment, cost, and quality of mount.
8. How can silicon-coated release paper help when making cutout mountings?
9. How do you decide whether to mount a map on cardboard, on cloth to be rolled, or on cloth to be folded into sections?

10. Why should cloth be trimmed flush with the chart?
11. How can you protect the surface of a mounted picture that will be handled a lot?

See answers on page 379.

Making Paste-ups

When a layout is to consist of a number of elements that have to be prepared or gathered separately, such as headings, texts, illustrations, symbols, captions, and labels, they must be assembled for reproduction. Arranging and adhering all these parts to paper or cardboard is a procedure called **paste-up.** For example, before printing, a paste-up was made for each page of this book.

Use either temporary rubber cement or semipermanent spray adhesive methods, as described previously, to adhere each item to paper or cardboard. Stick-glue and heated wax can also be used as a backing adhesive for paste-ups. The latter is applied with a hand-operated roller or a mechanical coating unit. The glue or wax backing permits ease of alignment and a tight seal between copy and paper. It also eliminates some of the cleanup problems that rubber cement presents.

The paste-up may be duplicated in single copies on an office copy machine (page 191). The result should be a clean copy, free of all paste-up marks. Paste-ups can also be used as masters for preparing overhead transparencies and other media materials.

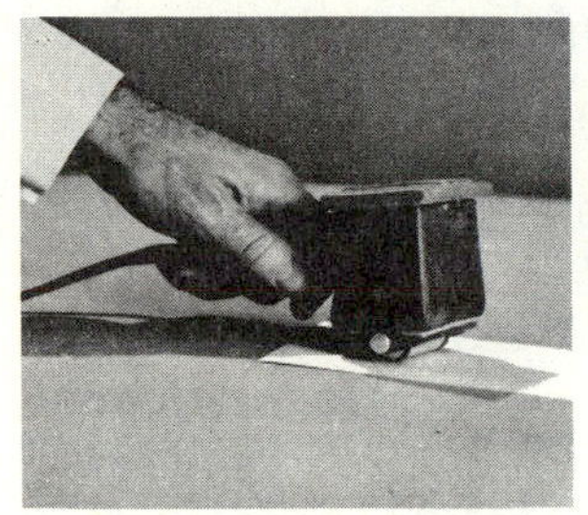

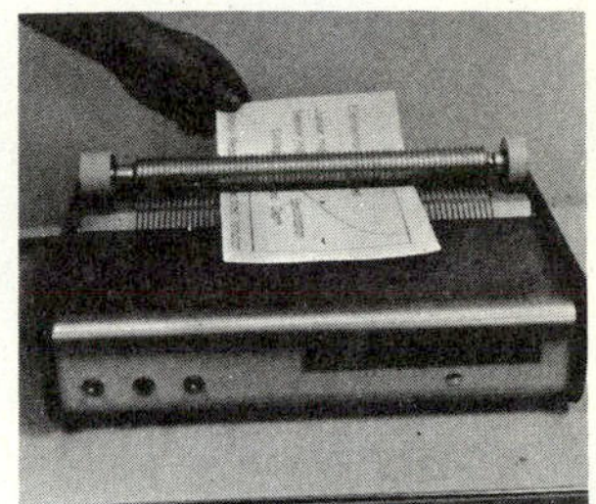

For many uses, the layout and preparation of pages can also be made with a computer and peripheral equipment. This eliminates the need to physically adhere elements of a page to paper. This is considered part of the *desktop publishing* procedure (see discussion on page 182).

What You Have Learned About Making Paste-ups:

1. How does a paste-up differ from preparing other materials?
2. What adhesive materials may be used?
3. How can a clean copy be made from a paste-up?
4. What procedure for preparing a page, consisting of a number of items, can be used other than paste-up?

See answers on page 379.

References

Design

Arnston, Amy E. *Graphic Design Basics.* New York: Holt, Rinehart and Winston, 1988.

Schmidt, Calvin F., and Schmidt, Stanton E. *Handbook of Graphic Presentation.* New York: Wiley, 1979.

Smith, Robert C. *Basic Graphic Design.* Englewood Cliffs, NJ: Prentice-Hall, 1985.

White, Jan V. *Using Charts and Graphs.* New York: R. R. Bowker, 1980.

Computer-Generated Graphics

Amiga Graphics Inside and Out. Grand Rapids, MI: Abacus, 1989.

Computer Pictures. Montage Publishing Co., 701 Westchester Ave., White Plains, NY 10604 (bimonthly journal).

Izatt, Joel and Lehtinen, Rick. "Designing Graphics that Get Results." *Video Systems* 17 (April 1991): 21–26, 30.

Kettelkamp, Larry. *Computer Graphics: How It Works, What It Does.* New York: Morrow, 1989.

McNeill, Dan. *Mastering Graphics on the Macintosh.* Greensboro, NC: Compute Publications, 1989.

Meilach, Dona Z. "Scanner Primer." *Photo Electronic Imaging* 35 (April 1992): 33–36.

Reis, Charles. "Your Range of Choices in Hard Copy Devices." *Advanced Imaging* 5 (September 1990): 54–59.

Rogers, D. F. and Ernshaw, R. A. *Computer Graphics Techniques: Theory and Practice.* New York: Springer-Verlag, 1990.

Sweet, Steven. "Clip Art—The Ultimate Time-Saver." *Computer Pictures* 10 (January/February 1991): 14–20.

Vince, John. *Computer Graphics for Graphic Designers.* White Plains, NY: Knowledge Industry, 1985.

Wershing, Stephen, and Singer, Paul. *Computer Graphics and Animation for Corporate Video.* White Plains, NY: Knowledge Industry, 1988.

Computer Screen Design

Aspillaga, Macareba. "Implications of Screen Design Upon Learning." *Journal of Educational Technology Systems* 20 (1), 1991–92; 53–58.

Galitz, Wilbert O. *Handbook of Screen Format Design.* Wellesley, MA: QED Information Sciences, 1989.

Garney, Kathleen H. "20 Rules for Arranging Text on a Screen." *CBT Directions* 111 (May 1990): 13–17.

Hooper, Simon, and Hannafin, Michael. "Variables Affecting the Legibility of Computer Generated Text." *Journal of Instructional Development* 9 (1986): 22–28.

Strauss, Roy. "Designing for the TV Screen." *AV Video* 14 (February 1992): 48–58.

Illustrating

Bostick, George. "Graphing Statistics." *Performance and Instruction Journal* 20 (March 1981): 11–13.

Brown, Mark G. "Improving Performance Using Graphs." *Performance and Instruction* 27 (November/December 1988): 28–32.

Coloring

Green, Ronald E. "AV Graphics: Communicating with Color." *Audio-Visual Communications* 12 (November 1978): 14–18.

Jones, Gerald E. "Color Use, Abuse in Presentations." *Computer Graphics World* 9 (May 1986): 119–120.

Lamberski, Richard J. *A Comprehensive and Critical Review of the Methodology and Findings in Color Investigations.* Syracuse, NY: ERIC Clearing House (ED 194 063), April 1980.

Murch, Gerald M. "Using Color Effectively: Designing to Human Specifications." *Technical Communication* 32 (Fourth Quarter 1986): 14–20.

Legibility Standards

Legibility—Artwork to Screen. Publication S-24. Rochester, NY: Eastman Kodak Co., 1988.

McVey, Gerald. "Legibility in Film-Based and Television Display Systems." *Technical Communication* 32 (Fourth Quarter 1986): 21–28.

Journals for Graphics Equipment and Materials Sources

AV Video
Montage Publishing Co., 701 Westchester Ave., White Plains, NY 10604.

CBT Directions
Weingarten Publications, Inc., 38 Chauncy St., Boston, MA 02111.

Computer Pictures
Montage Publications, Inc. (see above).

Modern Office Technology
A Penton Publication, 1100 Superior Ave., Cleveland, OH 44114.

New Media
Hypermedia Communications, Inc., 901 Mariner's Island Blvd., Suite 365.

Presentation Products
Pacific Magazine Group, Inc., 513 Wilshire Blvd., Santa Monica, CA 90401.

Sources for Equipment and Materials

Many of the common items needed for the graphic preparation of your instructional materials can be purchased from local art, stationery, photography, and engineering-supply stores. Other equipment and specialized materials are listed here. Although the headquarters or main-office address is given, you will find local offices or local dealers distributing most products. If you do not, write to the address given for further information.

COMPUTER-GENERATED GRAPHICS SYSTEMS

Apple Computers, Inc., 20525 Mariani Ave., Cupertino, CA 95014.

Chyron Corp., 265 Spagnoli Road, Melville, NY 11747.

Commodore Business Machines Inc., (Amiga) 1200 Wilson Drive, West Chester, PA 19380.

IBM, 1133 Westchester Ave., White Plains, NY 10604.

GENERAL ART SUPPLIES

Alvin and Co., P.O. Box 188, Windsor, CT 06095.

Dick Blick, P.O. Box 1267, Galesburg, IL 61401.

Arthur Brown and Bros., 5895 Maurice Ave., Maspeth, NY 11378.

Flax's Artist Materials, 1699 Market Street, San Francisco, CA 94108.

ILLUSTRATIONS

(Check computer graphics software for inclusion of clip art.)

Dynamic Graphics, Inc., P.O. Box 1901, Peoria, IL 61656-9941.

3-G Graphics, Inc., 114 Second Ave., South, Suite #104, Edmonds, WA 98020.

Valdez Associates, Inc., P.O. Box 362, Westbury, Long Island, NY 11590.

Volk Clip Art, P.O. Box 347, Washington, IL 61571.

COLORING AND SHADING MATERIALS

Peerless Color Laboratories, 11 Diamond Place, Rochester, NY 14609.

Thayer & Chandler, P.O. Box 711, Lake Bluff, IL 60044.

Zipatone Inc., 150 Fencil Lane, Hillside, IL 60162.

LETTERING EQUIPMENT AND MATERIALS

Ellison Educational Equipment, P.O. Box 8209, Newport Beach, CA 92660 (Die-cut letters and machine).

R. S. Beller Co., 3080 B McMillan Road, San Luis Obispo, CA 93401 (Die-cut and adhesive-backed letters).

Koh-i-noor Rapidograph, Inc., 4716 Austel Place, Long Island City, NY 11101 (Lettering pens).

Kroy Lettering Systems, 13900 E. Florida Ave. B, Aurora, CO 80012 (Pressure machine lettering).

Letraset, Inc., 33 New Bridge Road, Bergenfield, NJ 07621 (Dry-transfer letters).

Letterguide Co., 4247 O Street, Lincoln, NB 68510 (Lettering guides).

Varitronic Systems, 600 Highway 169 So. 300, Minneapolis, MN 55426 (Merlin—Pressure machine lettering).

MOUNTING AND LAMINATING EQUIPMENT AND MATERIALS

APOLLO, 60 Trade Zone Court, Ronkonkoma, NY 11779.

Seal Inc., 550 Spring Street, Naugatuck, CT 06770.

Tersch Products, Inc., 22401 Industrial Blvd., Rogers, MN 55374.

Wiko Ltd., 10490 West 164th Place, Orland Park, IL 60462.

CHAPTER

9

Recording Sound

The audio portion of instructional media should receive as much attention as the visual elements. Good sound quality will enhance the visuals and the effectiveness of a presentation; poor sound will detract and result in an ineffective program. For any type of material—whether projected or nonprojected, still or motion—the same procedures apply when preparing the accompanying recording.

Recording Equipment

Two basic pieces of equipment are required to make a recording. Narration can be recorded with a **microphone** and a **tape recorder.** If sounds from more than one source, such as from two microphones or a record player for music and a microphone, are to be combined, then a **mixer** and playback equipment are necessary.

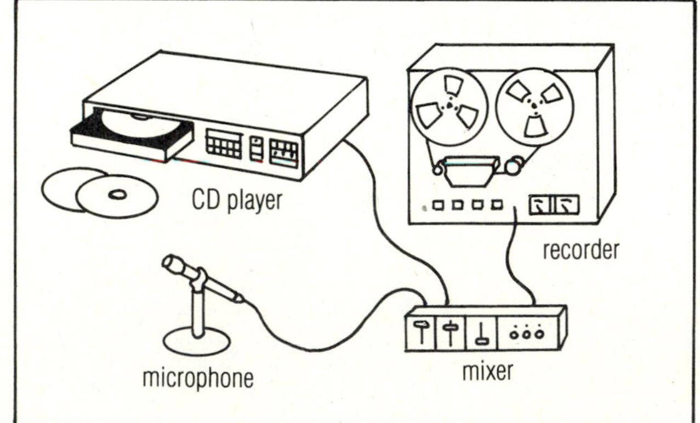

The Microphone

Small, portable cassette recorders include inexpensive built-in microphones that adjust automatically to the volume of the sound source. But this feature can be a drawback because recording volume is increased automatically as if adjusting to a low sound level. Therefore, extraneous sounds such as traffic noise or distant voices may be recorded.

The use of such a microphone results in a recording of poor to moderate quality. It should be used only to record a speech or a small-group discussion for documentary purposes. A separate microphone and manual volume control are necessary to produce a recording of acceptable fidelity without distracting noise.

The following are five common types of microphones used to produce instructional materials:

- ***Crystal*** or ***ceramic***—contains crystals or granules that produce electricity when pressure from a sound wave is applied; picks up a limited range of sounds; is not rugged; does not provide good fidelity; is included with many inexpensive cassette recorders.
- ***Dynamic***—has a diaphragm attached to a coil of wire placed within a magnetic field; produces electricity when the coil vibrates; picks up a wide range of sounds; is rugged; provides good fidelity.
- ***Condenser***—has a plate that vibrates according to sounds received, causing variations in current carried on an adjacent fixed plate; picks up an even wider range of sounds; is rugged; provides high quality sound; can be very small and unobtrusively clipped to clothing.
- ***Pressure zone***—contains a special electronic capsule that captures direct and reflected sound waves at the precise moment they reinforce each other, from any direction in a broad pickup pattern; low-level sounds up to 30 or more feet away are clearly reproduced.
- ***Wireless***—includes a small transmitter that clips to the user's belt or fits into a pocket with the signal sent through the air to a receiver.

In addition to the sound-generating feature of a microphone, each microphone has a sound pickup pattern. This refers to the way in which the microphone responds to sounds coming to it from different directions:

- ***Omnidirectional***—responds to sounds coming from all directions.
- ***Unidirectional*** or ***cardioid***—heart-shaped pattern that picks up sound with strength from one direction, some sound on the adjacent two sides, and almost none from the back side of the microphone.
- ***Bidirectional***—picks up sound only on two opposite sides.
- ***Shotgun***—accepts only a narrow angle of sound with good pickup, rejecting most other noises, when aimed at a distant subject.

To record a group of people, as for an interview or a discussion, use an omnidirectional or pressure microphone. Select a cardioid type for a single narrator or performer so that other sounds (audience and ambient noise) can be held to a minimum. A bidirectional type is desirable when two persons are to be recorded, as in an interview. When a speaker must be at a distance from the microphone, aim a shotgun microphone.

Use this information to select an appropriate microphone for each recording situation. A good microphone affects the quality of a recording just as a good lens on the camera relates to the quality of the resulting picture.

The Recorder

An audiotape recorder may be either a reel-to-reel (called **open reel recorder**) or a **cassette** type. An open reel recorder is preferred when recording music. It can be operated at a faster speed for higher fidelity sound (3¾, 7½, or 15 inches per second) as opposed to the speed of a cassette machine (1⅞ inches per second). The former is used when editing the tape because of the ease of manipulation. Although the principle of recording and playback of the two types is the same, the appearance and operating procedures are quite different.

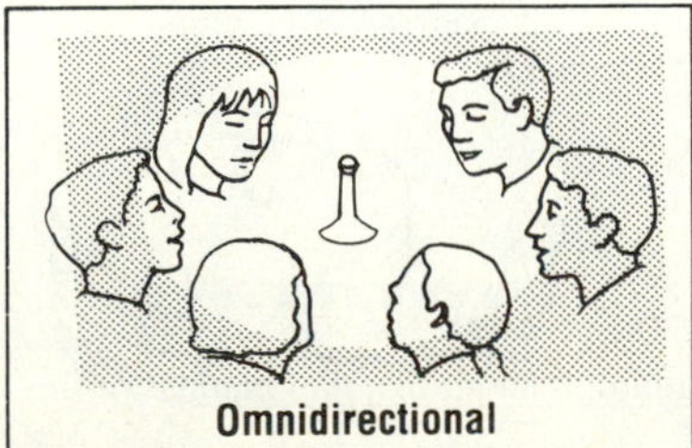
Omnidirectional

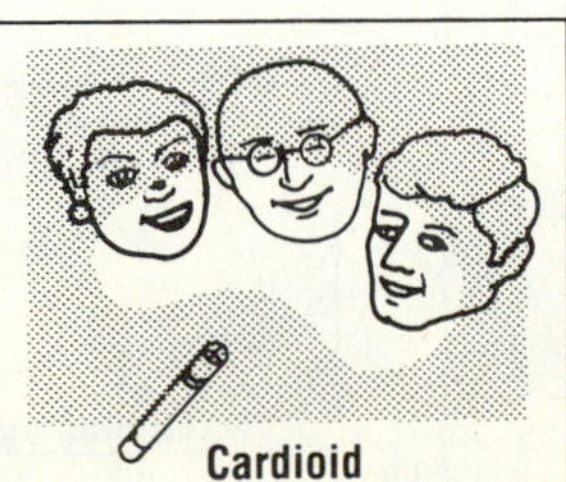
Cardioid

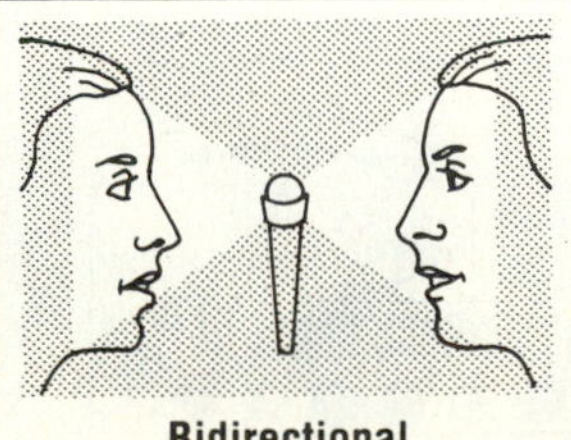
Bidirectional

Shotgun

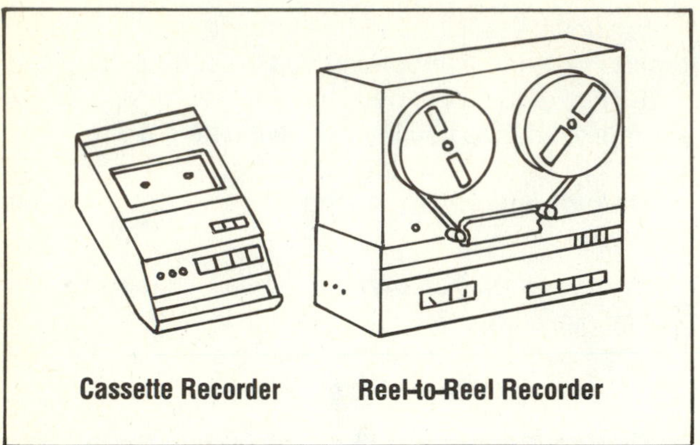

Electrical signals from the microphone or other sound source enter the tape recorder, where they are initially amplified to a satisfactory recording level. Then the current variations flow through the recording head, which is an electromagnet. As the recording tape passes the head, magnetic patterns are recorded according to the frequency of current variations and the intensity of the signals. The resulting patterns of the magnetic particles on the tape, when they are played back, create small electric currents through the playback head that vary in frequency and intensity. When these are amplified and fed into a loudspeaker, the recorded sound is heard. Prior to the recording operation, the erase head demagnetizes any existing pattern of signals on the tape.

Track Configuration on Open Reel Become familiar with the configuration of tracks (also called *channels*) on your recorder so that you will know its flexibility and limitations for combining sounds to create special audio effects, for adding synchronizing signals, and for permitting tape editing.

An open reel recorder may have any of these configurations and possible uses:

In **two-track monophonic** recording a single track is recorded on one half of the tape (Figure 1). When the tape is turned over, a second track is recorded on the other half of the tape (Figure 2). Each track is played back separately and is heard through a single speaker.

In **two-track stereophonic** recording, two separate tracks, each being one-half the width of the tape, are recorded simultaneously as the tape moves in one direction (Figure 3). On playback each track is heard at the same time through separate speakers. Although the main use of a recorder with this configuration is to record and play stereophonic music, it is possible to record a narration on one track and simultaneous music or an audible or inaudible control signal for changing visuals on the other track.

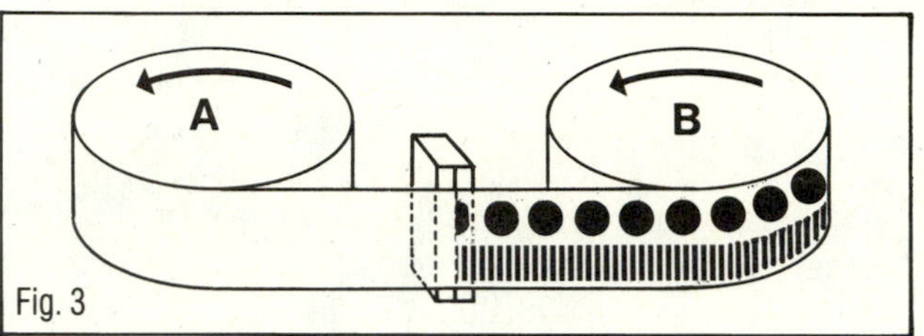

Fig. 3

In **four-track stereophonic** recording, two separate tracks (1, 3), each one-fourth the width of the tape but with room for another track between them, are recorded simultaneously as the tape moves in one direction (Figure 4). When the tape is turned over, the other tracks (2, 4) are recorded on the unused fourths of the tape (Figure 5). Thus four tracks or, more correctly, two sets of stereophonic tracks, are recorded and can be played back two at a time. This doubles the recording time on the tape from the previous two-track stereophonic configuration recorder. Most recorders of this type require that the recording be made on both tracks (1, 3 or 2, 4) at the same time. But some models permit separate track recording and erasing on each one. With the latter configuration, you can put narration on one track and add music, effects, or signals on the other one, in synchronization with the narration.

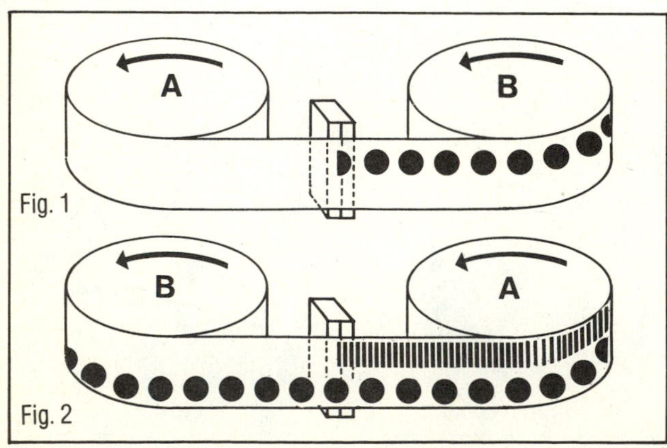

Fig. 1

Fig. 2

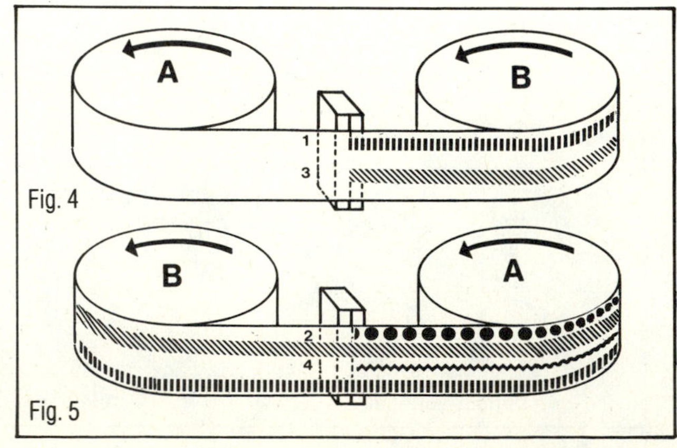

Fig. 4

Fig. 5

A professional recording is usually made on open reel, **multitrack recorders** with 4, 8, 16, or more tracks (Figure 6). Each track can be recorded separately with a different sound—narration, music, sound effects, or control signal. Each track can be played back separately, played together, or played in any combination. This configuration is the most flexible, because initial recordings and changes by rerecording on individual tracks can be made without affecting any other track. Then when a tape prepared on a machine with this configuration is dubbed to a cassette, any combination of tracks can be transferred together.

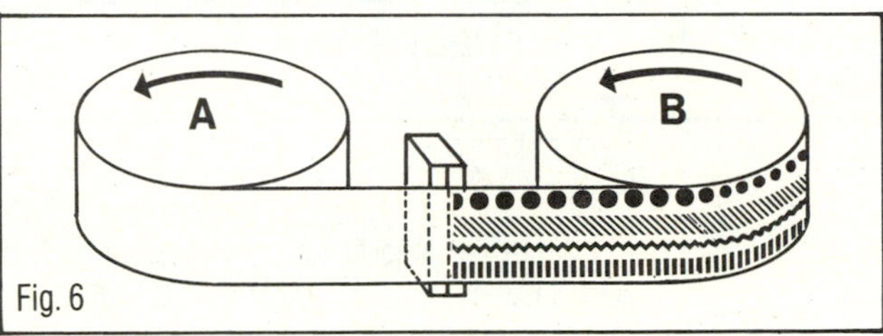

Fig. 6

Track Configuration on Cassette Audiocassette recorders can have either of two commonly used configurations.

The **monophonic** configuration is similar to that of the open reel two-track monophonic recorder. This is the format found on most commonly used audiocassette recorders. A single track is recorded on one-half of the tape (Figure 7). When the cassette is turned over, a second track is recorded on the other half of the tape (Figure 8). Each track is played back separately.

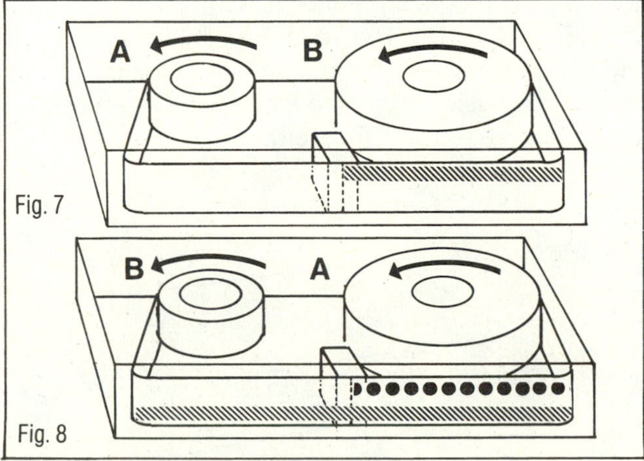

Fig. 7
Fig. 8

The **four-track stereophonic** configuration can be compared with the open reel four-track stereophonic recorder. The difference is in the location of the pairs of tracks. Two separate tracks are recorded simultaneously, side by side (1, 2), as the tape moves in one direction (Figure 9). When the cassette is turned over, two additional tracks (3, 4) are recorded at the same time on the other half of the tape (Figure 10). A stereo-recorded cassette can be played on a monophonic cassette player, because the side-by-side stereo tracks (1, 2 or 3, 4) are picked up by the same recording head. Thus narration and music or control signals, which had been recorded on separate tracks, are played simultaneously on the monophonic recorder.

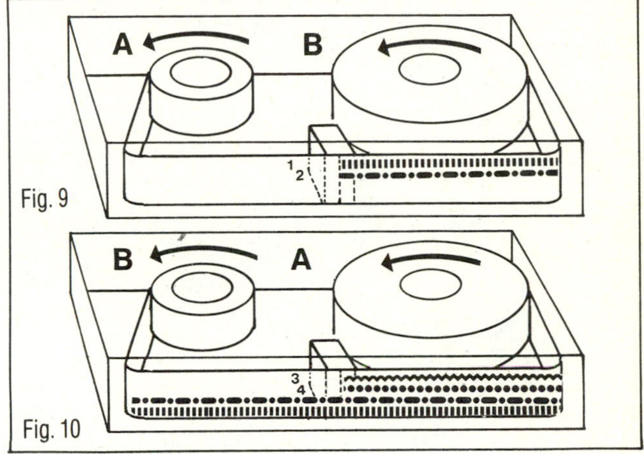

Fig. 9
Fig. 10

When more than a single track is recorded on an open-reel machine, editing tape by cutting and removing sections is not possible without damaging other recorded tracks on the tape. Editing tape in a cassette is difficult and not practical.

Maintenance After every 20 hours of use, or at least twice a year, two important maintenance operations on the recorder must be performed to avoid imperfections in recordings. First, remove specks of iron oxide that come off the tape as it passes over the heads, the capstan (the rotating cylinder that pulls tape across the heads at a constant speed), and associated rollers. Use a cotton swab wet with isopropyl alcohol or a recommended solvent to clean carefully all points that come in contact with tape. Turn the swab as you rub until no brown deposit is being collected. Thus all oxide is removed.

Remove accumulated magnetism from the heads by moving an electronic *demagnetizer* across each head (without touching the head). Cleaners and demagnetizers that are enclosed in cassettes can be used for maintenance of a cassette recorder.

The Mixer

Frequently sounds from more than a single source, such as persons speaking into separate microphones, must be blended and fed into a single track on the recorder. This blending takes place through a *mixer.* An operator balances volume levels, adjusts tones, and fades sounds in and out as they are received.

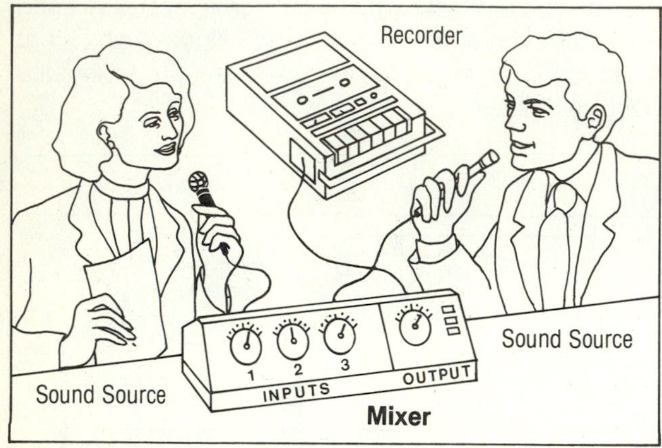

Other Audio Resources

Two other audio resources can have important implications when recording and using sound. One is the **compact disc (CD)** and the other is **digital audiotape (DAT) recording.** Both developments are based on **digital sound** rather than the **analog sound** techniques commonly used.

Analog sound is formed by waves consisting of alternating compression and expansion of air. These variations cause vibrations when striking a microphone diaphragm or an eardrum. From the microphone, voltage differences are created along a wire to the recorder. The changing voltages are recorded as wave patterns on magnetic tape, or as grooved tracks on a phonograph record.

Then the analog signals are reproduced by the movement of a needle in a phonograph record groove or by the varying magnetic fields created as magnetic tape moves across a sound head in the recorder. With good equipment and careful recording procedures, the quality of analog sound can be highly acceptable when initially recorded. However, as copies are made, the quality deteriorates. Distortion and noise levels naturally increase appreciably with every generation of reproductions. Also, variations in electrical power and temperature affect the shape of wave patterns and the accuracy of reproduction.

Digital sound uses the simplicity of the *binary code*—(*1*) Power ON and (*0*) Power OFF—as a series of "bits" to produce near-perfect sound quality. By a *sampling* and *quantization* process, the sound waves picked up by the microphone are first sampled, then measured with a decimal value, and translated into binary form. This procedure takes place thousands of

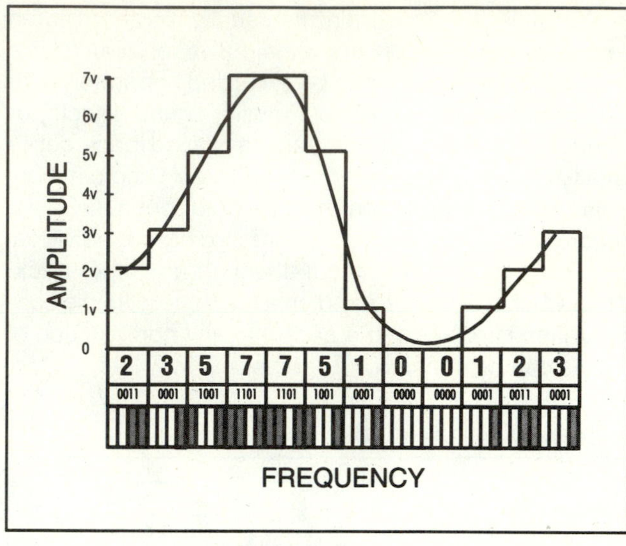

times a second. The series of pulses are transmitted to the rotating head in a DAT cassette recorder where they are digitally recorded on tape. The pulses can also guide the light beam of a laser to engrave the digital information on a record or disc.

During playback, the rapidly rotating tape head picks up the digital signals, while on a disc, the laser reads pits and spaces as digital data. The pulses are converted into analog patterns of sound. With the digital system, many generations of copies can be made without quality degradation.

Music and sound effects collections are available as **compact discs (CDs).** The sound has been recorded digitally with a laser beam. The beam focuses below the surface of the disc to the recording level. Therefore, during playback with the laser beam, nothing physically touches the recording. Potential scratching and other damage is minimal. The sound quality is consistently high and a small-sized disc can store a much greater amount of music (or printed information) than can be recorded on a regular LP record.

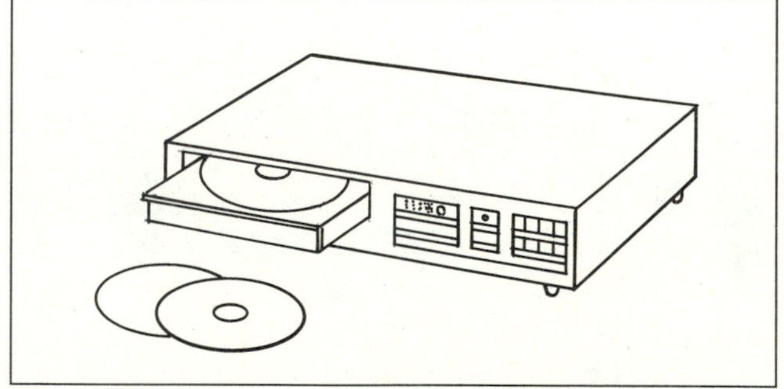

Digital audiotape (DAT), the second new development, can reproduce sound of comparable, or possibly better, quality to that of a CD. The tape is used with a portable cassette recorder containing a microprocessor chip. The equipment can serve for recording, editing, and mixing sounds.

Magnetic Recording Tape

Magnetic tape consists of a mylar base coated on one side with microscopic magnetic particles dispersed throughout a binding agent. These particles form the magnetic patterns that constitute the recording. The following are some basic characteristics of audiotape:

- *Base material*—Most commonly mylar or polyester.
- *Base thickness*—0.5, 1.0, 1.5 mil (a measurement in thousandths of an inch); the thinner the tape, the greater the amount that can be put on a reel and the longer the running time. But with thinner tape there is more chance of sound "print-through" from one layer to the next and more static cling of the tape.
- *Coating material*—particles of iron as ferrous oxide are most common, but a coating of chromium dioxide allows for higher quality recordings in terms of lower tape noise (hiss) level, a greater range of sound reproduction, and a higher sound output level. On many recorders a switch must be set according to the type of coating on the tape to be used. It adjusts circuits in the recorder so that the electronics will match the type of tape.

Your tape choice depends largely on how you plan to use your recording. The best guidepost is recording time per reel (at your chosen recording speed).

For a master recording, 1.5-mil tape offers the advantages of low cost, low print-through (signal transfer from layer to layer), and long life. It provides recordings of excellent quality.

For longer programs, a 1-mil tape is preferred. It provides 50 percent more recording time than the 1.5-mil tape on a reel of the same size.

The longest available playing time is provided by 0.5-mil polyester tape. Tape this thin usually is *tensilized,* a process that protects it from excess stretching during use. Some tape recorders will not handle this extra-thin tape; consult the instructions with your machine.

Table 9-1 below shows maximum recording time for two-track tape recorders *recording on both sides* at 7½ and 3¾ ips. Use half of the time shown for a recording made on only one side of the tape.

Audiocassettes are designated according to their recording and playback length of time. The number indicates the *total* time, of which one half applies to each side of the cassette.

- C-30—15 minutes per side
- C-45—22½ minutes per side
- C-60—30 minutes per side
- C-90—45 minutes per side
- C-120—1 hour per side

Exact tape lengths may vary in cassettes of the same size. Therefore it is advisable to record about 30 to 45 seconds less time on a side than the list indicates. Also allow 6 seconds at the start of the tape for the clear leader to pass. The C-120 size, because of its extremely thin base, jams many cassette machines and is not recommended for general use.

It may not be necessary to use an expensive tape solely for voice recording. Buy tape with a familiar brand name and avoid inexpensive tape; the latter not only produces lower quality sound, it also can foul a recorder with oxide or cause excessive head wear.

Write an identifying name or number on the reel or cassette before starting to record on it.

Table 9-1 Recording Times for Various Tape Lengths on Open Reel

Tape	Reel Size (Inches)	Tape Length (Feet)	Recording Time (Minutes)	
			At 7½ IPS	At 3¾ IPS
Standard, 1.5 mil	5	600	30	60
	7	1200	60	120
Long-play, 1 mil	5	900	45	90
	7	1800	60	180
Extra-long-play, 0.5 mil	5	1200	60	120
	7	2400	120	240

RECORDING FACILITIES

Good quality recordings are best made in an acoustically treated and soundproofed room. If possible, use a room having some wall drapes, carpeting, and an acoustically treated ceiling. Large foam pads that have an "egg carton" pattern can be adhered to walls for improving acoustics. Do not try to "deaden" the room entirely, as it would be difficult for the narration to sound vibrantly alive in such a room. When desirable facilities cannot be found, improvise a recording booth in a corner of a room with some drapes or blankets to reduce sound reflections. Or use a carrel or study booth by covering the sides with blankets. Then record after normal working hours to eliminate extraneous noises.

When selecting a room in which to record, keep in mind the fact that many microphones cannot distinguish between the sound coming from the narrator's voice and any ambient noise—machinery, a ventilating fan, or sounds you can hear from outside the room. Any of these extraneous sources can cause undesirable background noise on the recording. Furthermore, an annoying hum, caused by 60 cycle electrical interference, may be picked up by the microphone and recorded on tape. This is often caused by the close proximity of fluorescent lights or high voltage (220 volt) power lines.

What You Have Learned About Equipment, Tape, and Facilities for Recording Sound:

1. Which pattern of microphone pickup would you select in each situation?
   a. To record a narrator in a room while outside noise can be heard through a wall on the far side of the room
   b. To record comments by any of five people seated around a table
   c. To record interviews at a sporting event where the microphone will be handled a great deal
2. What two kinds of maintenance should be performed periodically on a tape recorder?
3. What type of recorder would allow each of the following?
   a. Using the full tape to record narration and music on separate tracks in synchronization
   b. Using the full tape to record, on separate tracks, narration, music, sound effect, and a picture-changing audible signal
   c. Using one half of the tape to record premixed voice and music
   d. Using a cassette to record two separate sounds at the same time
4. What four elements of sound control are handled through a mixer?
5. Explain, by words or diagram, the difference between analog and digital sound reproduction.
6. Which tape thickness and reel size would you select for recording voices and music in each situation?
   a. Average-quality tape for 46 minutes of recording
   b. Very durable and low print-through tape for a 35-minute recording that will be edited and spliced
7. Onto what size cassette would you copy a 25-minute recording?
8. Consider the recording facilities available to you. What arrangement would you make to ensure the best possible recording?

See answers on page 379.

The Narrator and the Script

Select a person who can read the script clearly and in a conversational tone. This means that he or she has the ability to raise or lower the voice for emphasis, to change the rate of speech according to the mood and intent of words, to provide pauses for variety, and to allow time for the listener to study the visuals. Evaluate a test recording before you decide on a narrator.

The narrator may be a friend or business associate having the necessary qualifications. Professional narrators are available in many communities. They may be listed in the yellow pages of the telephone book (one heading is "Recording Services"), or can be located through radio stations or media production companies. Even though there is a cost for the services of a professional, in addition to the quality of their work, there can be savings in recording and editing time.

Review the script with the narrator. Let him or her study it carefully and consider suggested changes in terms of the narrator's style and experience. The script should have markings to indicate points to be emphasized or to have special pacing. Verify the pronunciation of proper names and special terms, and indicate by writing them phonetically in the script. The script should have all cuing places plainly marked. See the sample narration script on page 176.

Preparation for Recording

The first step in preparing an audiotape recording is to record the narration. See page 326 on information for operating audio equipment. The quality of a recording depends primarily on proper microphone selection, its placement, and on regulating volume level. Follow these practices:

- If possible, attach the microphone to a stand or clip it to the narrator's clothing about 10 inches below the mouth so it cannot be handled or moved during recording.
- If a stand is not available, set the microphone on a table with a sound-absorbing towel or blanket under the microphone.
- Determine by test the best distance from the narrator's mouth at which to place the microphone for good speech intelligibility (about 10 or 12 inches) and have the narrator speak across the front of it rather than directly into it to avoid popping sounds.
- If only voice is to be recorded, a tape speed of 3¾ inches per second (ips) is satisfactory. Music, however, requires higher fidelity than voice; if it is to be included, the tape for narration and music should be run at 7½ ips. The faster speed also facilitates editing.
- Avoid use of the automatic volume level control if there is one on the recorder (marked as AGC, ALC, or AVL). See page 151 for reasons.
- Make a volume level check for each voice to be used. Select a moderately high volume setting, but one below the distortion level. This setting permits greater flexibility for controlling volume during playback and reduces background noise and tape hiss.
- Be sure to turn off fans and other apparatus that make noises which may be picked up by the microphone.
- Provide a comfortable yet alert working position for the narrator so that full energy can be put into reading the script. Allow him or her to stand or sit upright on a chair or stool. Standing is preferred as most people project their voices better when standing. Set the script, as separate sheets at eye level, on a music or other stand so the narrator will not have to handle the script too much or lower his or her head while talking. Change pages quietly to avoid possible paper rustle.
- Have a glass of water nearby for the narrator to "lubricate" the throat if necessary.
- Run a test recording of 2 to 3 minutes and listen to it to make sure all equipment is operating properly.

Recording Procedure

Three people may be necessary to make a recording: the narrator, a cue giver (you or someone familiar with the timing of the narration in relation to the pictures), and a person to operate the recorder. The roles of the cue giver and recorder/operator may be combined for a person who is familiar with the script and the equipment.

You may wish to develop a standard lead-in for identification at the beginning of the tape. Allow 6 to 10 seconds of silence for the leader to pass, although cassette tape is available without leader. Then identify the program by title, number, or both. Make certain that the volume and the tone levels are the same as those for the program content that follows.

Stand the person to give cues behind the narrator. This person will indicate when each section of the narration is to start by tapping the narrator on the shoulder. Some narrators like to make gestures and move their hands or body while reading, as in face-to-face communication. This normal behavior should be encouraged, because these actions can stimulate good voice delivery.

Watch the sound level meter (VU meter) on the recorder and make adjustments to maintain a consistent sound level.

Experience shows that the best recording takes

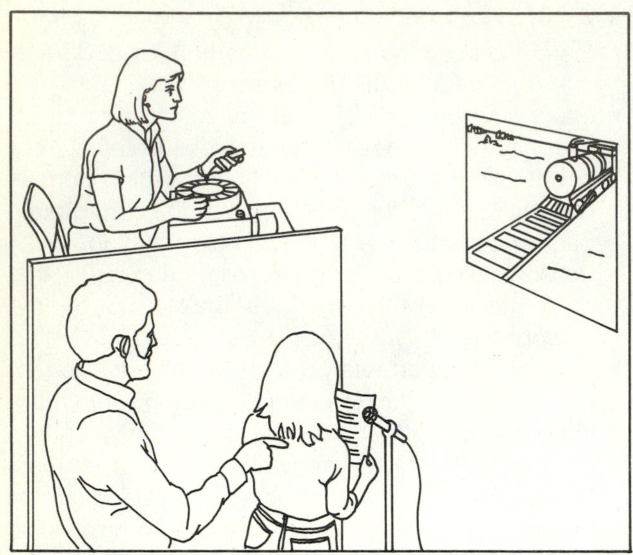

place in the first one or two tries. As the narrator repeats, there is a loss of spontaneity and errors can be made more frequently. Rehearse the presentation, and then make the recording. When the recording is complete, you and the narrator should listen to it together. Check it against the script to make sure that nothing has been left out, that no words are mispronounced, and that there are no extraneous noises. Your ear is the best judge of a successful recording.

Often when a tape is being edited, you will need to lengthen a pause to allow the listener time to study one or more accompanying visuals, to engage in an activity such as replying to a question on a worksheet, or to allow time for thinking about what has been presented. The length of tape that is added to provide the pause should have the same signal characteristics as the recorded tape, even though no sound is heard. Therefore, at the end of the recording session, ask the narrator to remain silently in position before the microphone. Record a few minutes of blank tape at the same volume setting as was used during the actual recording. Splice in lengths of this tape to adjust a pause period during editing.

Correcting Errors

It is unusual for a narrator to read through an entire script without making mistakes or mispronunciations. When a mistake is made catch it at that moment. It is easier to correct it immediately than to leave it until the end of the recording. At the end, the narrator might not match the intonations in context with the surrounding words and you must spend more time rearranging tape.

Two methods can be used to correct mistakes when they are made. First, stop the tape, rewind to the last correct sentence with a planned following pause in the script. This blank time allows you to start the recorder (in record position, which erases the unwanted material) and cue the narrator to reread the section. The narrator then proceeds normally on to the next part of the script. Second, make a correction by continuing to record. Call an identification such as "page 7, line 3, take 2." Then, after a short pause, repeat the material properly and proceed normally.

In the first method editing is unnecessary, because the correct recording is continuous. But with some standard recorders a click sound may be heard when the recorder is started at each correction. The second method requires that the unusuable takes be cut out and the correct ones spliced, with proper spacing, to the previous part of the narration.

Once the recording has been completed, sit quietly with the narrator and play back the entire recording. Listen to it carefully for any errors—mispronunciations, extraneous noise, machine sounds, or anything else that might have been missed during the recording session. It is best to catch imperfections and correct them now rather than to redo later.

MUSIC AND SOUND EFFECTS

Research evidence (page 30) indicates that background music is not essential to effective communications with instructional media. In some instances, indeed, it interferes with the message. But for other purposes it may help in creating a desirable mood and in setting the pace for the narration.

Music as background for titles will assist the projectionist or individual user to set the volume level for the narration that follows. Introduction music gets the attention of the audience, helping individuals to settle down for the presentation.

Here are some suggestions for selecting and using music:

- Always start music a few beats before the first image appears on the screen.
- When music is used under narration, maintain it at a low enough level so it does not interfere with the commentary or compete with the picture for the viewer's attention.
- Select music carefully. Avoid music with vocals unless the words are part of the message. Keep in mind the nature of the audience and the message to be communicated.
- A single musical selection may be suitable for the total production. Or, a number of brief musical cuts provide variety and support for the visuals. They must be carefully matched and mixed, in keeping with the nature and pace of the visuals and narration.
- The music chosen for the conclusion of the presentation should receive special attention, since it helps

to set the emotional attitude with which viewers leave the program.

Three potential sources for music are as follows:

- Selections from a commercial music library—can be purchased for unlimited use or for a "needledrop" fee (meaning that a payment is made each time a selection is played). See page 163 for a listing.
- Original music recorded from good local talent—from a single guitar or organ to a full orchestra.
- A professional music production company—can score original music for a fee.

Sometimes it seems easier to select music from popular, semiclassical, or other entertainment records. But remember that when a listener hears background music with which he or she is familiar, it can distract attention from the narration. If you do plan to use such selections, permission must be obtained from the copyright holder (page 169). Obtaining music rights is complex and time-consuming. Often a high fee is requested by such sources if your program will have wide use or commercial distribution. For details on acquiring clearance to use a popular musical selection, see Kichi reference.

Natural sounds, when carefully used, help a production to sound professional. **Sound effects,** which add a touch of realism, also are available commercially. If you do not want these commercial effects or cannot find them, you can record actual sounds on tape or create sound effects (see page 164 for a book on this subject). Sound effects on tape can later be transferred to the final audiotape or to videotape.

EDITING TAPE AND MIXING SOUNDS

After the narration recording is completed and other required sounds have been put on separate tapes, editing may be necessary to remove bad takes, to rearrange elements into a more cogent order, and to add tape for lengthening pauses. The resulting tape becomes the **master** recording.

Editing Tape

Audiotape may be edited by two methods. One is performed **electronically** and the other by **cutting and splicing** the tape physically. Electronic editing is a dubbing (duplicating) process in which a copy of the original recording is made, and the recorder on which the copy is being made is stopped while parts of the original recording are skipped or reordered. This requires the use of a high-quality recorder that can silently and easily pause, stop, and start again.

For physical editing, which requires cutting the tape, it is a good idea to make a quality dub and store the copy safely away. This will protect you if an incorrect cut is made while editing.

If the original recording is made on cassette equipment, it is necessary to make a copy on an open reel of tape. There is no practical way to cut and splice the thin, narrow tape in cassettes. Assuming that the recording is on a single track, follow these steps for successful tape editing:

1. Listen to the recorded tape, listing spots to be edited (use the index counter on the recorder to note locations on the tape).
2. Replay the tape and stop at the first spot.
3. Pinpoint the spot to be edited by moving the tape manually back and forth across the playback head.
4. Carefully mark cutting points on the base side of the tape. Use a fine-tipped felt pen or a china-marking (grease) pencil.
5. Listen to that part of the recording again to be certain that the mark is at the correct point.
6. Cut the tape; remove the felt-pen or grease-pencil marks; then splice the ends together or add tape as necessary.
7. Repeat the same procedure at the next editing spot.

Tape Splicing

Splicing is best and most conveniently done with a tape-splicing block. This is a piece of metal that holds a short length of recording tape in precise alignment while you use a single-edge razor blade to cut the tape at a 45-degree angle, following slots cut in the block to guide the razor and then apply the splicing tape. The 45-degree cut makes a strong splice and provides smooth movement between spliced pieces as they pass over the playback head of the recorder. Use a sharp blade to make straight, clean cuts. Follow this procedure when splicing:

1. Set one piece of tape, with shiny (base) side up, firmly in the splicing channel so it extends just beyond the cutting groove.
2. From the other side, do the same with the second piece.
3. Draw the razor blade across the 45-degree cutting groove to cut both pieces of tape at the same time. Remove the waste ends of both pieces of tape.
4. Cover the cut with a one-inch piece of splicing tape.
5. Rub splicing tape firmly with a fingernail or nonmetallic burnisher.

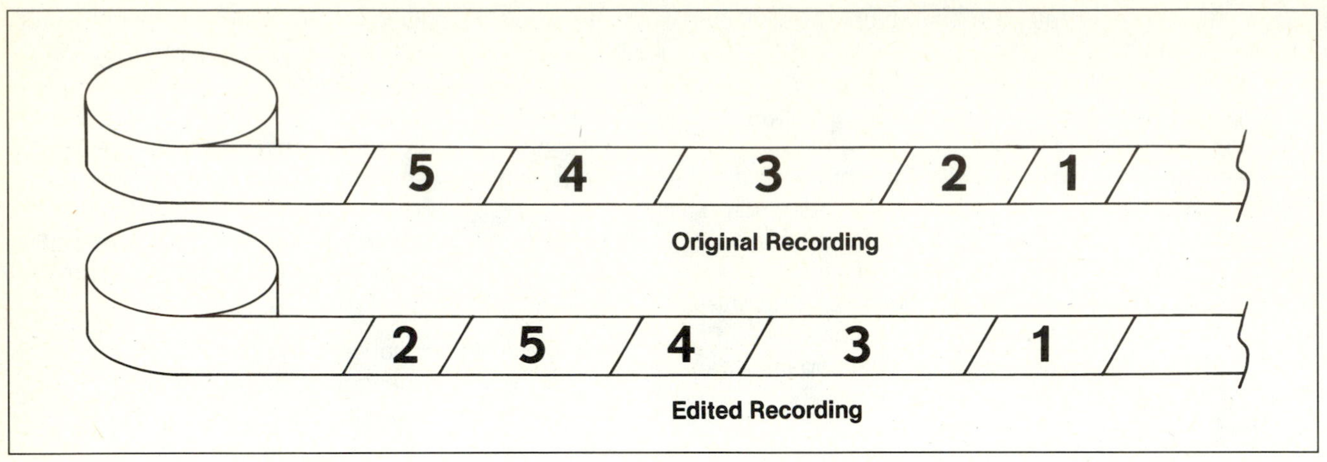

6. Draw the blade along both edges of the splicing channel to trim any excess splicing tape extending beyond the edges of the magnetic tape.
7. Examine the splice for strength.

Mixing Sounds

There are various methods for mixing sounds. It is best to do this electronically rather than with a microphone. By placing the microphone in front of a loudspeaker to pick up the sound from a recording as it is played, the quality will not be the best and extraneous room sounds may be recorded.

A preferable way to combine sounds from two recordings (narration and music), on a single track, is to use a **patch cord** (also called, **"Y" jumper cord**). Be alert to the types of connectors required on cables to connect equipment together. There are three major

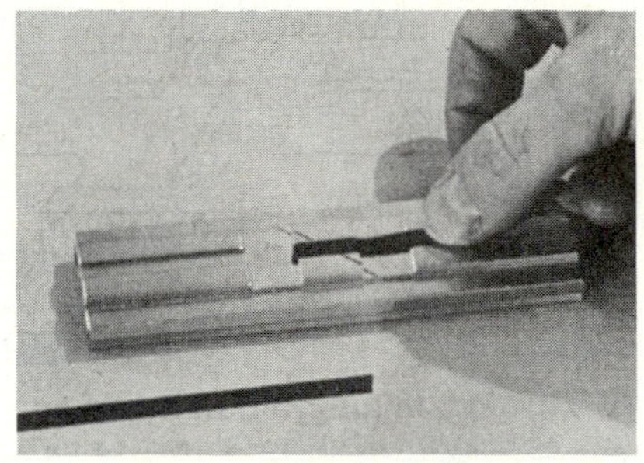
1

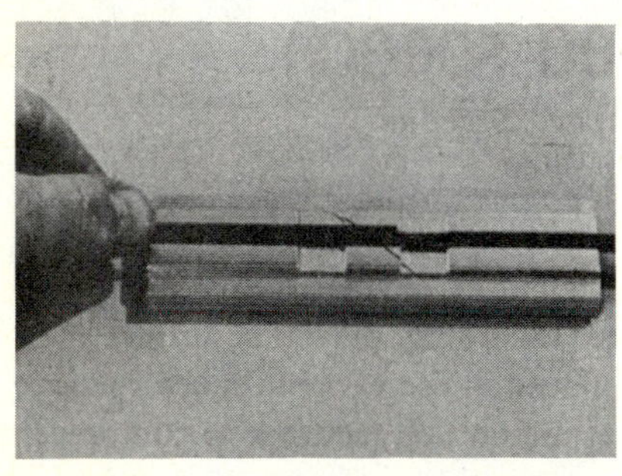
2

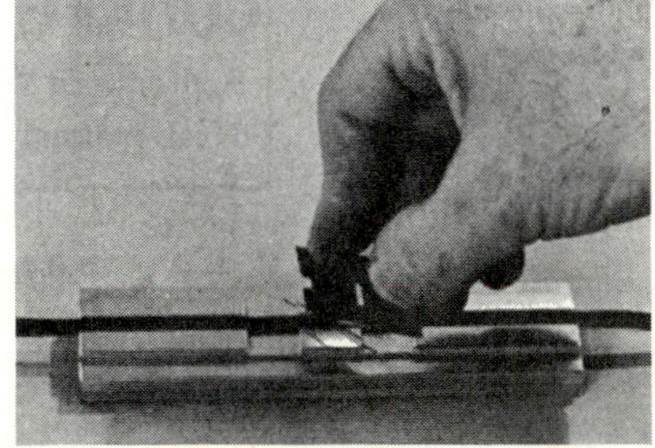
3

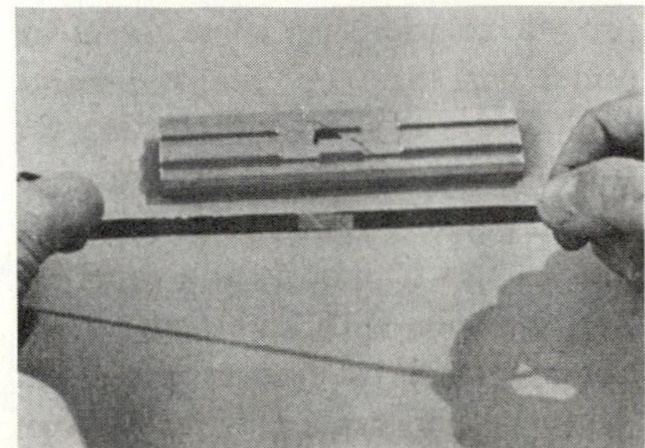
4

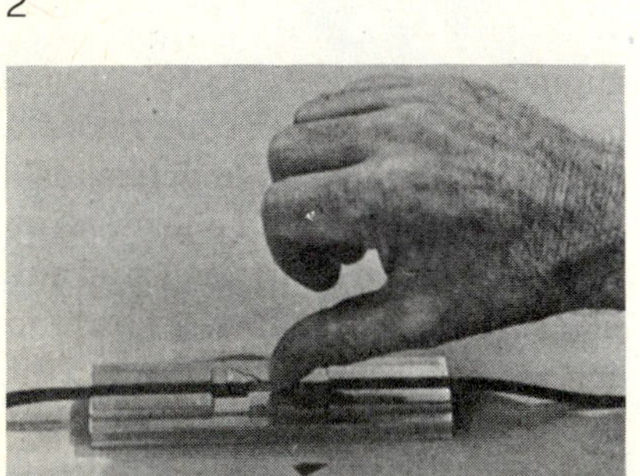
5

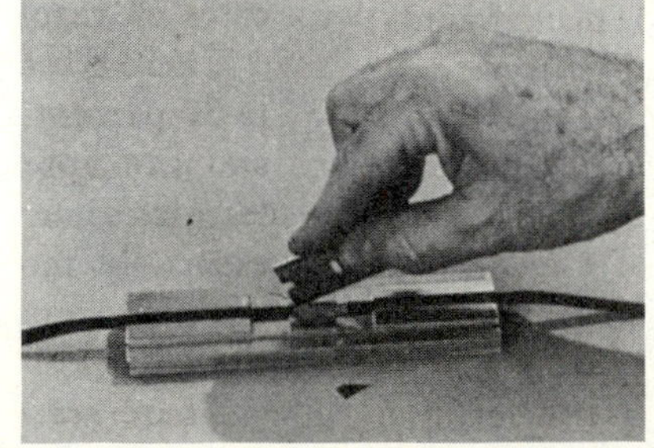
6

7

types of audio plugs—miniplug, RCA phono, and ¼-inch phone (see illustration on page 323). Connect an arm of the cord from the *output* of each source to the *line input* of the recorder for making the final master. After setting a volume level on the recorder, adjust levels for matching sounds at each source.

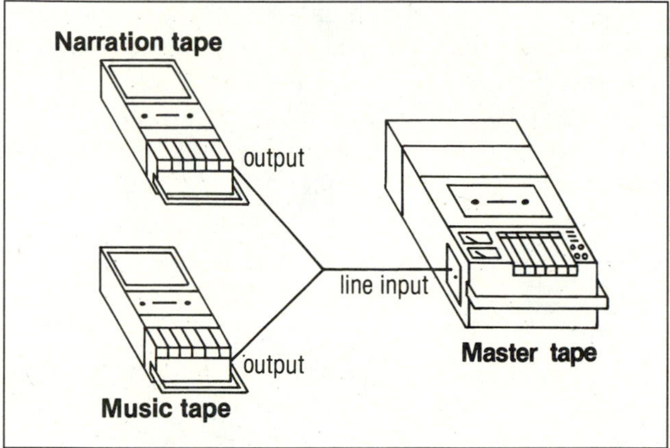

You may have used a **mixer** while making the original recording in order to combine voices or add music or sound effects to the recording. The same procedure can be used during editing as sounds from separate tapes are blended by controlling volumes and fading one in and the other out or under. Separate channels on the mixer are required for each sound component.

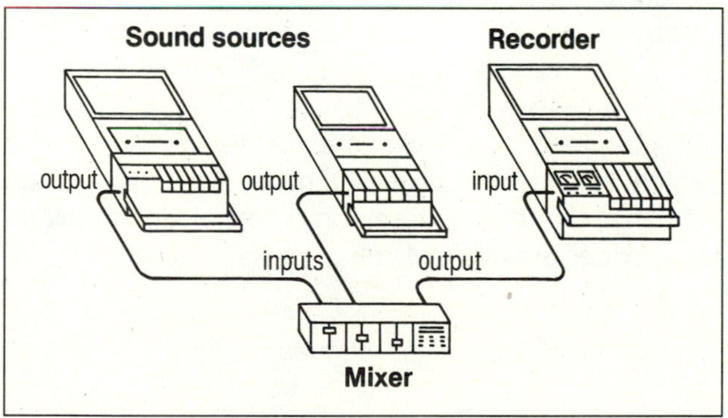

Through mixing, a number of tapes can be transferred onto a single track, or preferably different sounds can be dubbed to separate stereo or multitracks of a recorder. Copy the narration onto one track. Go back to the beginning, listen to the narration, and record music and sound effects on one or more other tracks in proper relationship to the narration. If mistakes are made, the music or effects can be redone without erasing the narration. Then the tracks can be played together or **dubbed** to another recorder as a single composite sound track.

When mixing sounds, be certain to make jumper cord connections properly (*outputs* from sound sources to *inputs* on mixer and from mixer *output* to recorder *input*). Balance playback levels carefully so sounds are heard in proper relationship (low level musical backgrounds under narration and realistic sound effect levels).

Consider passing a recording through an **equalizer,** which is a device with an arrangement of electronic filters. It permits you to selectively boost or subdue certain frequencies to modify the tonal quality of a recording. For example, with an equalizer, a 60 cycle background hum (caused by fluorescent lights) can be removed. Thus, by using an equalizer you can enhance the quality of a recording.

SYNCHRONIZING NARRATION WITH VISUALS

When sound is recorded on an audio track of a videotape, the picture and sound will be seen and heard in proper relationship. They are perfectly **synchronized** and always will remain so. But when pictures are separate from the recording, as with slide/tape or filmstrip/tape equipment, then another method must be used to synchronize the pictures and sound. This can be done in various ways. Explanations of four methods follow.

Marked Script

The simplest technique is to mark a copy of the script, indicating where each slide change should take place. Then use the marked script yourself, or give it to the projectionist, when presenting the program. This procedure requires that the operator stay alert so as not to miss a slide change.

Audible Signals

An **audible signal** informs the projectionist or the individual user when to change to the next picture. Such

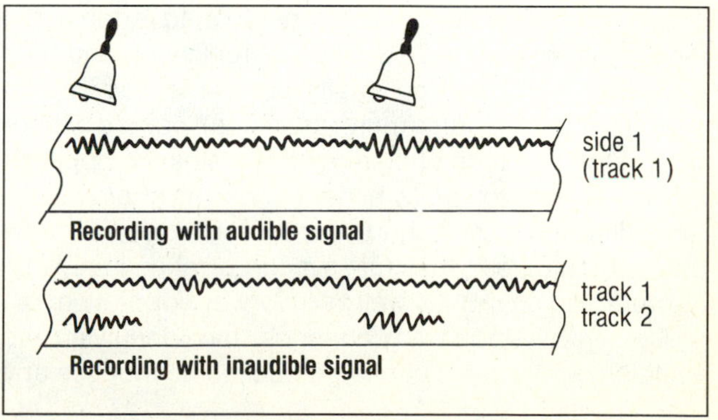

a signal could be made with a musical instrument, a door chime, a bell, a hand clicker, or even the click made by some ballpoint pens as the tip is exposed.

The best source for a controlled tone (preferably somewhere from 100 to 440 cycles per second—known as "hertz" or Hz) is an electronic audio "tone generator" keyed from a push button. The sound from any source should be of approximately one half-second duration. It is mixed with the master recording onto the same track or a stereo track of the recorder.

Inaudible Signals

Because audible signals are often distracting and may be annoying to the viewer, an **inaudible picture advance signal** can be used to control picture changes. Tape recorders with built-in inaudible signal generators are available. The recorder is connected to the slide or filmstrip projector. The signal, generally 1000 Hz, is recorded at picture change spots on the *second track* of a monophonic audiocassette as you listen to the recorded narration on the first track. See page 320 for information on operating audio synchronizing equipment. Upon playback each signal triggers a mechanism that activates the projector to change the picture in synchronization with the narration.

Some cassette recorders can also record an inaudible 150 Hz signal as a "stop" cue to pause the tape. This permits the user to reply to a question or do something else and then restart the tape.

Each signal on the tape requires sufficient time spacing from the previous signal to permit the projector to complete its projection cycle. Check the instructions with your equipment for the minimum time allowed (often 2 seconds) between signals.

Verbal Signals

If the resulting audio and visual materials are to be used by learners studying independently, consider indicating slide or frame changes verbally along with some identification of the forthcoming picture—like, "turn to frame 12" or "in the next slide of the city hall. . . ."

When audible or inaudible control signals are used, it becomes possible for the learner to inadvertently get the picture and sound out of synchronization and thus lose the meaning or continuity of the message being communicated. Furthermore, the signal method of controlling the advance of pictures eliminates the opportunity to go back to review either the narration or the picture, although some sound slide and filmstrip units, now on the market, can maintain synchronization in reverse (picture and sound) as well as in forward operation.

By verbally indicating changes and identifying the visuals, the learner is free to go back to hear or see any material again and then to easily move ahead with picture and sound synchronized.

DUPLICATING TAPE RECORDINGS

When your editing has been completed, with all sound and signals on a tape, this tape becomes the *master* recording. Label it as such. Make a copy of it onto an open reel or a cassette. Mark it as the *first-generation* copy. Punch out the "tabs" on the back edge of the cassette to prevent accidental erasure. File the master tape in a safe, cool, dry place. Use the copy for making the required number of duplicates.

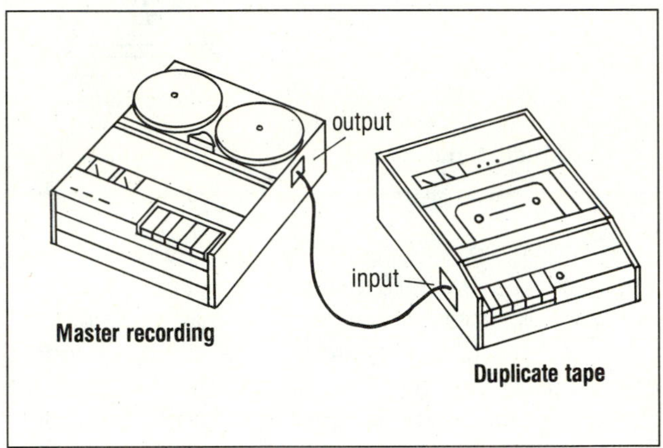

If the recording is made only on one side of the tape without a 1000 Hz synchronization signal on the second track, you can repeat the same recording on the second side so that the user need not rewind the tape after each use.

High-speed equipment is available in many media centers for producing one or a number of copies, most often in audiocassette form. Commercial tape duplicating services are available also.

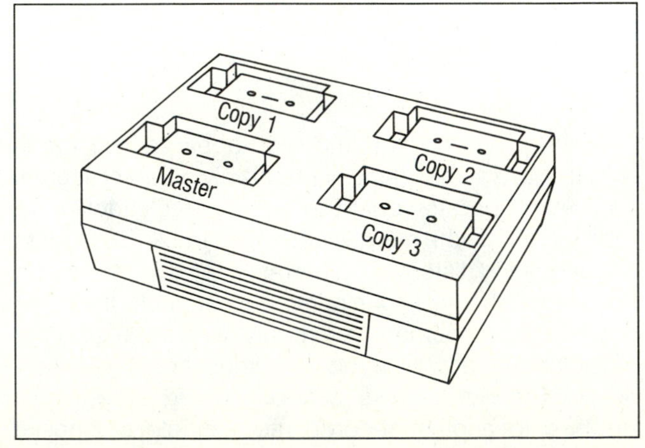

What You Have Learned About Sound Recording Procedures:

1. What factors are important in selecting a narrator?
2. What are five important practices when preparing for a recording?
3. How would you make a recording to include music from a disc along with the narrator's voice?
4. If you find it necessary to make a correction on tape while recording, what procedure would you use?
5. What are two advantages for including music along with a narration? What can be a major drawback?
6. What is the difference between physical and electronic tape editing?
7. What equipment, materials, and procedures would you use for splicing tape?
8. What are advantages in using a time-compressed speech recording?
9. What method might you select to add an audible signal to a tape recording for indicating slide changes?
10. For use with a slide series, in what form might the duplication be put on tape if the recording requires one side only?
11. Do you have available a tape recorder that allows the addition of inaudible signals to tape? If so, how would you proceed to add signals to a tape?
12. What method do you have available for duplicating tape?

See answers on page 379.

REFERENCES

RECORDING SOUND

Alkin, Glyn. *Sound Recording and Reproduction.* New York: Focal, 1991.

Alten, Stanley R. *Audio in Media.* Belmont, CA: Wadsworth, 1990.

Batzdorf, Nick. "DAT for AV Productions." *AV Video* 12 (October 1990): 62–70.

———. "A Guide to Micing and Mixing in the Field." *AV Video* 13 (May 1991): 44–47.

Behrend, Jack. "High Tech Sound." *Industrial Photography* 38 (September 1989): 18–19.

Nelson, Mico. *Basic Audio Production: Theory, Equipment, and Techniques.* White Plains, NY: Knowledge Industry Publications, 1992.

Nisbett, Alec. *Use of Microphones.* New York: Focal, 1989.

Pett, Dennis. "Design of the Audio Track for Instructional Slide Sets and Filmstrips." *Performance and Instruction* 28 (October 1989): 1–4.

Pohlmann, Ken C. *Principles of Digital Audio.* White Plains, NY: Knowledge Industry Publications, 1985.

Sound & Communications, 25 Willowdale Ave., Port Washington, NY 11050 (journal).

USING MUSIC

Kichi, John. "Music Rights and How to Obtain Them." *Educational and Industrial Television* 12 (December 1980): 40–42.

Seidman, Steven A. "What Instructional Media Producers Should Know About Using Music." *Performance and Instruction Journal* 20 (March 1981): 21–23.

Yungton, Al. "Scoring Shows with Music Libraries." *Audio Visual Directions* 5 (September 1983): 43–46.

———. "There Is No Perfect Music for the Job: What You Should Know About Copyright Laws and Music Libraries." *Audio Visual Directions* 3 (December 1981): 35–37.

MUSIC LIBRARIES

Capital Records Production Music, 1750 Vine St., Hollywood, CA 90028.

DeWolfe Music Library, 25 W. 45th St., New York, NY 10036.

Emil Ascher, 630 5th Ave., New York, NY 10111.

Folkways, 43 W. 61st St., New York, NY 10023.

Network Production Music, 11021 Via Frontera, San Diego, CA 92127.

Signature Music Library, P.O. Box 26-8554, Chicago, IL 60626.

Soper Sound, P.O. Box 498, Palo Alto, CA 94301.

27th Dimensions, Inc., P.O. Box 1149-74973, Okeechobee, FL 34973-1149.

Valentino, Inc., 151 W. 46th Street, New York, NY 10036.

Windham Hill Productions, Inc., P.O. Box 9388, Stanford, CA 94305.

Sound Effects Libraries and Reference

BBC Sound Effects Library, c/o Films for the Humanities, P.O. Box 2053, Princeton, NJ 08540.

Comprehensive Video Supply Corp., 148 Veterans Drive, Northvale, NJ 07647.

The International Sound Effects Library, Emil Ascher, 630 5th Ave., New York, NY 10111.

SFX Sound Effects, P.O. Box 401, Skokie, IL 60077.

Turnbill, Robert B. *Radio and Television Sound Effects.* New York: Holt, Rinehart and Winston, 1951.

Journals for Audio Equipment Sources

AV Video

Montage Publishing Co., 701 Westchester Ave., White Plains, NY 10604.

Presentation Products

Pacific Magazine Group, Inc., 513 Wilshire Blvd., Santa Monica, CA 90401.

Acoustical Material

Alpha Audio Acoustics/Acoustical Solutions, 711-N. Allison Street, Richmond, VA 23220.

Sonex Acoustical Division of Illbruck, Inc., 3800 Washington Avenue North, Minneapolis, MN 55412.

PART 4

Producing Instructional Materials

CHAPTER

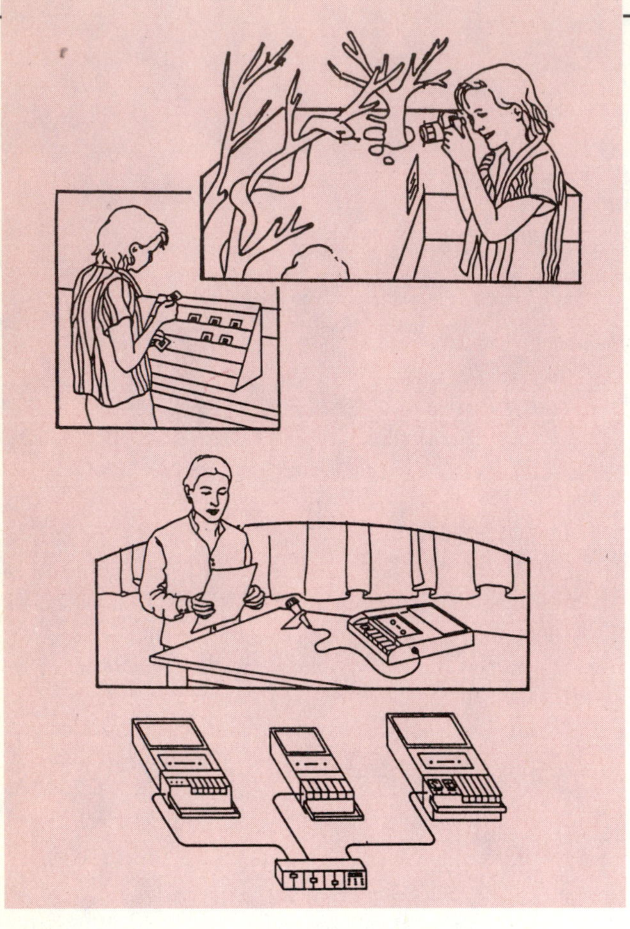

SCHEDULE THE PICTURE TAKING
TAKE THE PICTURES
WORK WITH ACTORS
KEEP A RECORD
OBTAIN PERMISSION FOR PICTURES
EDIT THE PICTURES
EDIT THE NARRATION AND CAPTIONS
PREPARE TITLES AND CAPTIONS
CONDUCT FORMATIVE EVALUATION
RECORD THE NARRATION
MIX SOUNDS
DUPLICATE MATERIALS
COPYRIGHT YOUR MATERIALS
EVALUATE RESULTS

The Production Process

Production is the point at which some people start their work on instructional media. Unfortunately, this is a mistake, but it is difficult to convince them that they need to do some thoughtful planning before preparing materials. They may feel they do not have the time to plan, or that they are too knowledgeable about their subject to have to plan. Or they may be so taken with the mechanical phases of production (camera use, audiotape or video recording, synchronizing slides with sound, and so forth) that they have an insatiable urge to do something and see results *right now!* If you deal with such persons, you probably will not be able to influence them differently. Let them go directly to production. Most often the results will show the fallacy of this approach and the added expense of unplanned production. Experience is sometimes the best teacher!

There is one situation in which unplanned picture taking may be necessary. It is when action over which you have no control is to be recorded. This is similar to the way an event is documented for the evening television news. See the discussion of *documentary* production that follows on page 168.

You will generally find, in contrast to what results from precipitous picture taking, that preliminary planning, storyboarding, and writing a script will enable you to visualize your ideas more clearly and that the final result will serve your purpose better because of its coherence and completeness. In the long run you will probably also save time and money by eliminating errors, reducing the need for retakes, and by not forgetting scenes when picture taking.

Fundamental production techniques were presented in Part Three, and the preparation of specific instructional media are treated in the chapters that follow in this Part. Considered here are the general procedures that relate to the production of most types of media, with the exception of printed media, overhead transparencies, audio recordings, and CBI.

Schedule the Picture Taking

From the script, make a list, grouping together all scenes to be made at the same location, those having related camera positions at a single location, or those with other similarities. Then schedule each group for filming or recording at the same time. Preparing and using this list will save you time. You will achieve further economies if you visit locations, check facilities, and gather items (props) for use prior to the time of filming. But remember—if you take pictures out of script order you must be especially careful to edit them back into their correct position and relationship with other scenes.

Example: A Filming Schedule

FILMING SCHEDULE—SOLAR COLLECTORS

10/12 (in driving order)

Scene 16—Williams house
17—Williams house
8—Village apartments
5—Quimby Road

10/15

Scene 6—James house
11—Community Center

To arrange

Scene 7—at beach house
9—at mountain house

Artwork

Scene 2
3
4
12

Titles

Scene 1
10
13
14
15
18

If you visited locations during preliminary planning you will be prepared to overcome obstacles that might delay picture taking. Also, by meeting persons in charge at these locations, you can better ensure their cooperation while filming.

Take the Pictures

In general, the script outline of scene content should be followed. Sometimes, however, as you prepare to take a picture, it becomes evident that a script change is needed. If a single picture, as planned, does not convey the intent of the script, two pictures may be necessary. Don't hesitate to take them. Or, if you are uncertain about exposure, make an extra take of the same scene with different camera settings. Also, if desirable, repeat a scene, shooting it from a second position or with a change in action. In such cases, the entry on the record sheet (see below) should indicate a **take** number, such as take 1, then take 2, and so forth, *all of the same scene.* Be flexible in your picture taking. You spend less time and energy making adjustments at this time than you would spend retaking pictures later if they are found to be unsatisfactory—and you have extra pictures from which to make choices during editing. This is one practice of a professional media producer!

When recording on videotape, rehearse each scene before shooting. Rehearsals permit a check on the action so that the cameraperson can "set" the shot and the actor can "feel" the action being performed. For still pictures, carefully set the scene and check the composition through the camera viewer before pressing the shutter release.

There may be times when a **documentary approach** to all or portions of materials production is necessary. In such cases, pictures are taken of events as they happen, without a detailed script. It is recommended that this approach be followed only for special cases (athletic events, meetings, ceremonies, production line work, and other uncontrolled situations). Sometimes two or more cameras are used and coordinated so as to capture all important action.

The documentary technique puts an extra burden on the photographers, and the editing stage becomes extremely important for making decisions that may affect the final treatment of the subject (see page 170 for suggestions concerning preparing a script *after* documenting an activity on tape or film). The producer of documentary media needs greater experience and must give more attention to technical details than does the producer of a planned and scripted material because in a documentary production there can seldom be any retakes. The cameraperson must think in sequences and not in individual shots. It is necessary to recall what went before and anticipate what will be happening and be ready to record it. Contrast to this the making of preplanned material in which all scenes are thought out in advance and action is controlled.

Work with Actors

The individual, whether a professional actor or amateur, who appears in front of a camera must portray normal behavior for the situation being recorded. Here are some suggestions for accomplishing this:

Example: A Log Sheet

LOG SHEET

Title: Solar Collectors
Film: Ektachrome 100
Camera: Olympus OM-1

Date: 10/12
Location: Community

SCENE	TAKE	f/STOP	SHUTTER	REMARKS
16	1	16	1/125	normal
	2	8	1/125	increase exposure
	3	22	1/125	less exposure
17	1	16	1/125	ok
	2	16	1/125	change position
8	1	11	1/125	possible reflections
	2	11	1/125	change angle
	3	8	1/125	change angle increase exposure

A Sample Release Form

Date:

I hereby give the unqualified right to (insert name of individual, group, or institution producing the instructional materials) to make pictures of me, of my minor child (insert name of child), or of materials owned by me and to put the finished pictures to any legitimate use without limitation or reservation.

Signature:
Name printed:
Address:
City: State/Zip:

Project:
Director:

- Treat the person with respect.
- If possible, allow the person to observe the recording of other scenes, which can help to put him or her at ease.
- Help the person to relax by maintaining a calm atmosphere at the location.
- Inform the actor of the purpose of the scene or sequence to be photographed or recorded.
- Invite suggestions relative to positions and how to carry out the action.
- Use prompting cards if necessary, but keep wording to a minimum, allowing the actor to speak naturally.
- Rehearse the scene until the actor feels comfortable.
- Allow for relaxation breaks if tension seems to build.

Keep a Record

Keep a careful record, a **log sheet,** of all pictures taken. It indicates the order in which scenes were photographed or recorded, and it includes data on exposure settings (unless a camera with automatic settings is used) and remarks about the suitability of the action. This record will be useful to you if pictures or scenes have to be reshot, and in evaluating picture quality and content when selecting scenes. These items are important:

- Scene number (according to the script)
- Take number (change each time the same scene is filmed)
- Light intensity (reading from light meter, if used)
- Camera settings (lens, shutter speed, and distance)
- Remarks (notes about the action, scene composition, reminders for editing, and any special concerns relating to other scenes)

Obtain Permission for Pictures

Almost everyone has the right to control the use of pictures of himself or herself, or of one's property. If you are producing instructional materials, you must respect this right. If you fail to do so, you may expose yourself to personal, professional, or financial embarrassment. Specifically, a person may either permit you or forbid you to show pictures of himself or herself, one's children, or one's property. It does not matter whether you show them free of charge or for compensation, to a large or a small audience, or whether you show them yourself or turn them over to someone else to be shown.

Most people readily agree to being filmed and to having the pictures used, but you should protect yourself and your associates by having them sign a **release form.** (A suitable release form is shown above.) The release authorizing the use of pictures of a minor child must be signed by the parent.

A special kind of property that must be covered by a signed release is the property in copyrighted materials—commonly, books, magazines, other printed matter, musical records, and footage from commercial products including films, video recordings, slides, and filmstrip frames. In this case you must get the clearance from the owner of the copyright, *not* the owner of the object. (You may own this book; but you do not own the copyright to it—see the back of the title page.) You will be wise if you assume that books and the like are copyrighted, and seek clearance before you use pictures of them or parts of them in your instructional media.

The provisions of the present copyright law are complex, and guidelines relating specifically to instructional media were not included, other than for off-air reproduction of television programs and copying phonorecordings. The most common interpretation for using copyrighted items is that an instructor can make, or have made, a *single* copy of *one* visual (photograph, chart, diagram, cartoon) from *one* book, periodical, or newspaper for purely noncommercial teaching use as long as the materials are for use *in the classroom.* This is the doctrine of "fair use" and applies to any instructional situation, whether in education or training.

The law does not permit the extension of this right of free reproduction to materials used by someone other than a teacher in *direct* classroom instruction. This means that copyrighted materials for use in slide series, audio recordings, video recordings, or on a laserdisc cannot be reproduced without permission. This applies to materials designed for individualized learning by learners, for use in audio listening centers, or those to be used by an instructor *other than the one preparing the material.*

To be on the safe side, if you wish to use copyrighted materials, write to the copyright owner and request permission to use the materials. Describe the use you will make of the material. In many instances you will receive permission to use the materials as long as you include an acknowledgment of the copyright. In other instances, a charge may be assessed. If your product will have widespread use, and especially if it will be marketed, you may be asked to pay a license fee for the inclusion of the copyrighted material.

There are sources of noncopyrighted materials or those for which permission to use is easily acquired. Clipbook art (page 125) can be reproduced. A directory of pictures for public use has been compiled (page 73). Certain collections of slides and stock motion picture footage are available for purchase and free use (page 73).

A particularly important area is the use of copyrighted music on sound tracks for instructional materials. Popular recordings you may have in your personal library fall into this grouping, and their use in media productions is often a violation of the copyright law. There are music libraries, which consist of many records containing all types of short selections, including sound effects. These can be purchased for unlimited use. See sources on page 163. Media production companies and video studios provide the use of music from recordings for a needledrop fee. Recall that needledrop refers to each use made of part or all of a musical selection in a media presentation.

The other side of copyright—how to protect your own product—is considered on page 175.

EDIT THE PICTURES

Once the pictures are prepared you are ready for the next major step in the production process. During filming or recording the pictures may have been taken out of script sequence, some scenes not indicated in the script may have been filmed, and more than one take may have been made of some subjects. During preparation of the script, the narration or captions were written in rough form or noted only as ideas. These changes and unfinished work give rise to the need for examination, careful appraisal, selection, then organization of all pictures, and the refinement of narration and captions. These activities become the all-important **editing** stage.

Using the script and the log sheets completed while filming or recording, put all pictures in proper order. Arrange slides on a viewbox (page 228). Prepare contact prints or proof copies of still pictures (page 109). Review video recordings.

Now choices must be made from among multiple takes of a scene. Examine all your work critically. You must be impersonal in your judgment and eliminate pictures that fail to make a suitable contribution to your specific purposes, and you must be firm in rejecting pictures or scenes that do not meet your standards.

Once you have made final choices of all pictures or scenes, ask yourself if the total visual flow is smooth. Is there a satisfactory *unity* and *continuity* among the images?

If you have made changes in the original script (page 67) by adding scenes or changing the sequence, rewrite the picture side to fit the edited picture version. Then complete the narration or caption side of the script as described next.

EDIT THE NARRATION AND CAPTIONS

Since your original script may have included only rough drafts or mere ideas for narration, there is need for further developing and rewriting the narration or captions in order to correlate words with the edited pictures or scenes.

As was indicated in explaining the storyboard on page 65, most of us think in words, and therefore we have a tendency to attempt to communicate with words more readily than with pictures. Even so, we comprehend things more effectively and retain information much longer when major ideas are presented visually in the form of pictures that are supplemented with written or spoken words. Thus, words have an important part to play in your materials but, generally, they should be secondary to the pictures. They can direct attention, explain details, raise questions, serve as transitions from one picture or idea to the next, and aid in preserving the continuity of the materials. If you find you have to use many words to explain what a picture shows, or to describe things not shown in a picture, perhaps the picture deserves another critical evaluation and possible replacement, or you may need to add a supplementary picture. *Let the pictures tell the greater part of your story.* If they do not, you will have a lecture with illustrations and you will fail to use the medium to its full potential.

Keep in mind your anticipated audience and its background as you refine the narration. The audience will have bearing on the vocabulary you use and on the complexity and pacing of the commentary. Lengthy narration and long captions are detrimental to the effects of visual materials. Distill concepts down to their essentials. As previously explained, the average narration should require viewing a slide for no more than 30 seconds; a caption or title frame should be no longer than 12 to 15 words. The average length of a video scene is 7 seconds; individual scenes, depending upon action and narration required, range from 2 seconds to possibly 30 seconds running time.

Here are some suggestions for refining narration:

- Write for the ear rather than the eye. Be conversational by writing the narration in simple, easy-to-understand phrases, and straightforward English—the way people talk.
- Avoid such expressions as "here we see," or "in the next slide. . . ." There is no need to tell the viewer what is being seen when it is obvious.
- Identify the picture subject being shown (especially if unusual) as quickly as possible with cue words or phrases. Identification that comes late in a written or spoken line may find the viewer lost in the attempt to understand what is being shown. (Example: "The rapid encoding of information on microfilm is being accomplished by *lasers*." Change to: "*Lasers* are accomplishing the rapid encoding of information on microfilm.")
- Carefully select the best word or phrase for quick understanding because hearing a narration is not like reading a book or newspaper. There is often little opportunity for the viewer to either go back and hear again what was said or to reflect on what was said.
- Be alert to where verbal transitions, sound effects, or musical bridges are needed to lead the user from one section of the presentation to the next.
- Although proper grammar and expressions are preferable, there may be times when sticking strictly to an accepted rule may make the sentence sound awkward or unnatural, and not appropriate to the particular audience.
- Keep sentences short (10 to 15 words) and avoid multiple clauses, tongue-twisting expressions, or awkward-sounding phrases. Place the subject and verb close together.
- Write enough to carry the picture as necessary—then stop writing. Do not assault the audience with a continuous string of facts.
- Have some pauses in narration, otherwise the audience will stop listening.
- Realize that one bit of narration can cover a number of pictures, and that narration can carry over from one scene to the next.
- Read the narration aloud to test expressions, the pacing, the emphasis, and to make sure there are no tongue-twisting expressions or awkward-sounding passages.
- Periodically plan to summarize and indicate relationships among the concepts and information presented.
- If music will be included on the sound track, refer to the suggestions on page 158.

Once the narration is refined, you will have a good idea of the final length of the material. This may change slightly according to the narrator's style and pacing.

See the sample revised script on pages 172–173. The resulting slides are shown for reference.

PREPARE TITLES AND CAPTIONS

Titles serve to introduce the viewer to the subject. The **main title** presents the subject. **Credit titles** acknowledge contributions of those who participated in or cooperated with the project. **Special titles** and **subtitles** introduce individual sequences and may serve to emphasize or to clarify particular pictures.

A little thought and some care in presentation and in filming will result in neat, professional-looking titles, captions, and labels. They should be simple, brief, easily understood, and large enough to be read when projected. Complex, vague, illegible titles confuse the audience rather than arouse its interest in an otherwise good production.

Other chapters of this book will assist you in the preparation and the filming of titles and graphic materials:

- Lettering for titles (page 136)
- Preparing artwork (page 124)
- Legibility standards for lettered materials (page 132)
- Photographic close-up and copy work (page 103)

Some materials, such as those to be less formally presented by integrated use within an instructional design, should not require extensive, formal titles. Keep these materials as simple as possible with an identifying number or brief title and incorporating captions, labels, questions, and directions as necessary. A formal end title may not be needed.

Part of a Revised Script, with Pictures for Reference

COLLECTING SOLAR ENERGY

Visual	Slide	Narration
Title: Solar Collectors		Before starting to view the slides, turn to page 4 in the workbook and read over the objectives for this presentation. When you are ready, restart the tape and change slides as the numbers are called. If you wish, you can go back to listen to any part or view any slide again.
2. Art: "Energy from sun"; add arrow with "34%"	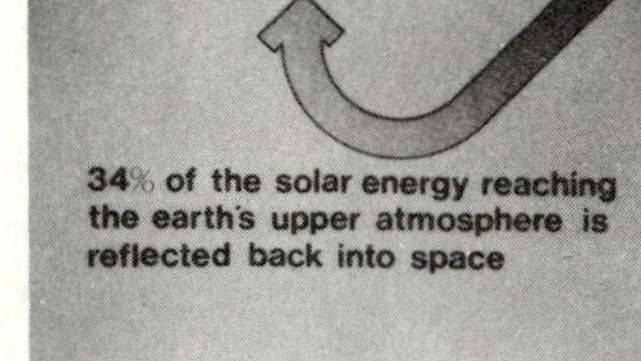	**Slide 2** Much of the energy from the sun is generated as light and heat. Thirty-four percent of this energy is reflected back into space.
3. Art: Add arrow with "19%"	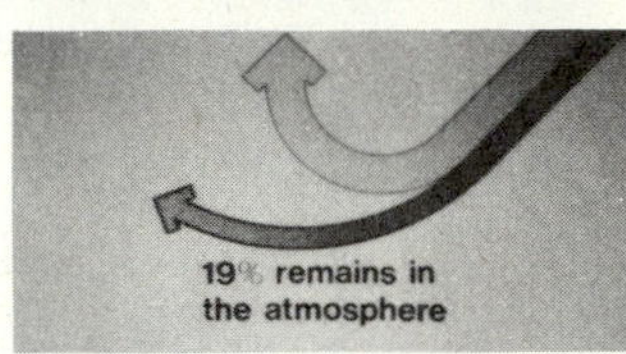	**Slide 3** Nineteen percent is absorbed by the atmosphere surrounding the earth.
4. Art: Add arrow with "47%"	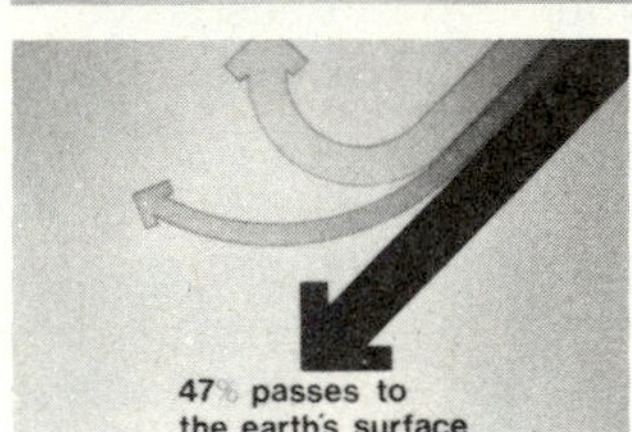	**Slide 4** And 47 percent of the sun's energy reaches the earth's surface. It may be captured for use.
5. MS. Rooftop of new house with solar collectors		**Slide 5** A solar collector can be placed on a roof to absorb the energy from the sun and convert it into heat.
6. MS. Older building with collectors on flat roof		**Slide 6** Collectors can be installed on older buildings as well as new ones, and a flat roof often facilitates installation.
7. LS. Collectors on ground level beside house		**Slide 7** Sometimes panels of collectors are constructed on ground level,

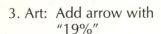

8. LS. Apartment building with collectors on side wall

Slide 8
or attached to walls of apartment buildings.

9. LS. House with snow on rooftop collectors

Slide 9
Even in northern latitudes and at high elevations, solar energy can be collected effectively.

10. CU. Worksheet, part A. Overprint: <u>Stop the tape</u>

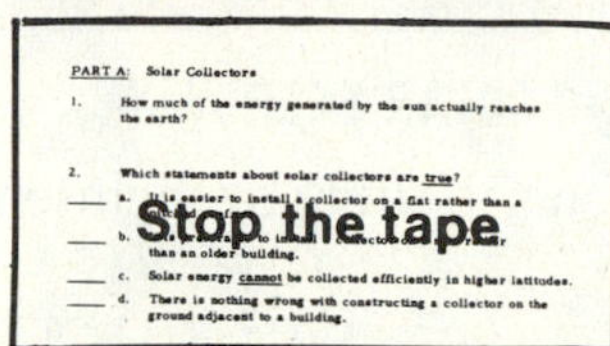

Slide 10
Now turn to the worksheet on page 4 and complete Part A. Stop the tape. After you have checked your answers, start again.

11. CU. Section of a collector

Slide 11
Solar collectors look like glass-covered boxes.

12. Art: Exploded view of collector showing parts with labels

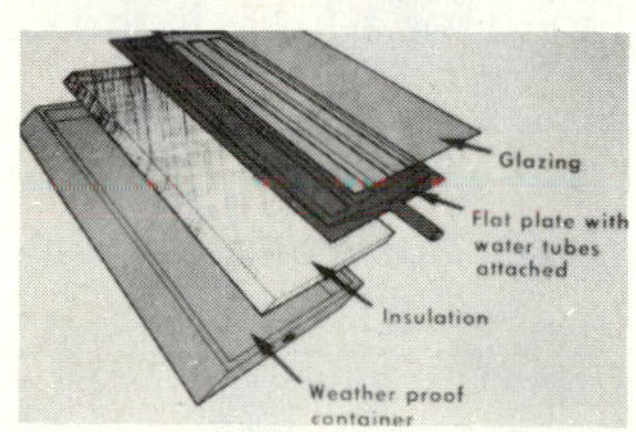

Slide 12
Each section consists of four basic parts—at the top, clear glass or plastic to trap the heat; next, tubes attached to a metal plate that conduct water or other liquid to be heated; behind the heat absorber, insulation to reduce the loss of heat; and around the whole device, a weatherproof container.

13. LS. House with collectors on roof. Overprint: <u>Face south</u>

Slide 13
Solar collectors are most effective when they are oriented south and are unshaded by trees or buildings.

14. MS. Another house with collectors. Overprint: <u>1/3–1/2 floor area for space heating</u>

Slide 14
To capture sufficient heat, the area of a collector should equal from one-third to one-half of the inside floor area of a house.

[and so on] . . .

CONDUCT FORMATIVE EVALUATION

As the production nears completion, judgments should be made as to how satisfactorily the materials do their intended job. Consider questions such as these:

- Does the material satisfactorily serve the original objectives?
- Is the content treated accurately?
- Is there a smooth flow from one picture or idea to the next?
- Does the narration aid in continuity and support the visuals?
- Is the material of suitable length, or is it too long overall, requiring deletions?
- Are there important points, not apparent before, that have been left out?
- Should some of the pictures be replaced or are additional ones needed for satisfactory communication?
- Is the material technically acceptable?

EXAMPLE: A Preview-Appraisal Questionnaire

COLLECTING SOLAR ENERGY

This set of slides is designed to allow students to study by themselves.

Objectives

1. To identify the four parts of a solar collector and their functions.
2. To describe the placement and size of collectors on various type buildings.

How well do you feel these objectives are accomplished?

____

Audience

1. These slides and the narration are designed for adults. Is the content appropriate?

   ____

2. Are the pacing of the narration and the vocabulary appropriate?

   ____

Content and technical quality

1. Has any important information been left out?

   ____

2. Are there any errors or inconsistencies in the presentation?

   ____

3. Would you suggest any reorganization? If so, specify.

   ____

4. Is the material technically acceptable? Would you replace any slides?

   ____

5. What is your rating of the slides and the narration in terms of the objectives to serve the indicated audience?

   ❑ Excellent ❑ Good ❑ Fair ❑ Poor

You may do better than quiz yourself. A good checkpoint for an evaluation of your materials, in terms of your objectives, can be provided by other subject and media specialists or even by a potential audience group. Show the edited visuals and read the narration or captions. A brief questionnaire for reactions and suggestions may be helpful. See the sample questionnaire on the previous page.

This **checkpoint** is often called the **formative evaluation** step. Feedback and reactions may reveal misconceptions that are conveyed, shortcomings, or other needs for improvement. At this time you can also observe how convenient the equipment is for use. You can still make changes before your materials are in final form and reproduced for actual use. The final product will be a better one for your having done a careful formative evaluation.

Record the Narration

Once the narration has been refined and, if possible, tested along with the visuals on a typical audience group, you are ready to record it on tape. Prepare the narration to be read by the narrator. Here are some suggestions:

- Type the narration on good quality paper. Use one side of the paper. Double-space lines.
- Do not carry a sentence from the bottom of one page to the top of the next.
- Spell phonetically any words you think will be unfamiliar to the narrator.
- Mark places that will require cueing, pauses, and special emphasis (see the example of a narration on page 176).

Then make the recording. See the suggestions in Chapter 9 for working with a narrator and for preparing the recording.

Mix Sounds

Along with the narration, the script may indicate music as an introduction and as background under the narration. The purpose of a musical introduction is to settle the audience down and prepare its members to be receptive to the ideas that will be presented. The musical introduction also allows the user or projectionist to set the volume level when the presentation starts. In addition, various sound effects (crowd noise, equipment sounds, animal sounds) may be required at certain points.

It is now necessary to assemble all these separate recordings onto a single tape as the final "master mix." Equipment for mixing sounds and the procedure to follow are explained on page 160. The final, edited version of the script becomes the guide sheet as you blend various sounds at appropriate times to create necessary moods. This process, like other phases of materials production, requires both creative and technical skills.

Duplicate Materials

You have spent much time and, no doubt, have gone to some expense to prepare your instructional materials. Protect the time, money, and work against loss by preparing at least one duplicate set of all materials, both audio and visual, and file all the originals in a safe place for any future need.

Copyright Your Materials

If you have developed instructional materials that you would like to protect, arrange to copyright the materials. It is a simple matter to let other persons know that this property is yours. Put a copyright notice on it. Use these three elements:

1. "Copyright" or the symbol ©
2. Name of the copyright owner or organization
3. Year of production or publication

A copyright notice should read:

- © Your name 1994

For a sound recording, use these elements:

1. The symbol p
2. The year of production or publication
3. The name of the copyright owner

The notice for a recording looks like this:

- p 1994 Your name

If a tape recording is part of a slide/tape, filmstrip/tape, or similar program, then the recording is copyrighted as part of the visual materials. The © symbol is used.

This notice should appear on the master material and all copies, generally on the title frame or first picture and also on the container label. If you plan to sell or otherwise distribute copies without this notice, you have no protection from anyone who duplicates the materials. (See the discussion about using copyrighted materials on page 169.)

Although this notice appearing on your materials is generally all that might be necessary to establish your

A Part of a Narration to Be Read for Recording

NARRATION—COLLECTING SOLAR ENERGY

// Point at which cue will be given to start reading.

_ Underlined words are to be emphasized.

... Brief pauses between phrases.

// Before starting to view the slides, turn to page 4 in the workbook and read over the objectives for this presentation. When you are ready, restart the tape and change slides as the numbers are called. If you wish, you can go back to listen to any part or view any slide again.

// Slide 2 ... Much of the energy from the sun is generated as light and heat. Thirty-four percent of this energy is reflected back into space.

// Slide 3 ... Nineteen percent is absorbed by the atmosphere surrounding the earth.

// Slide 4 ... And 47 percent of the sun's energy reaches the earth's surface. It may be captured for use.

// Slide 5 ... A solar collector can be placed on a roof to absorb the energy from the sun and convert it into heat.

// Slide 6 ... Collectors can be installed on older buildings as well as new ones, and a flat roof often facilitates installation.

// Slide 7 ... Sometimes panels of collectors are constructed on ground level...

// Slide 8 ... or attached to walls of apartment buildings.

// Slide 9 ... Even in northern latitudes and at high elevations, solar energy can be collected effectively.

// Slide 10 ... Now turn to the worksheet on page 4 and complete Part A. Stop the tape. After you have checked your answers, start again.

// Slide 11 ... Solar collectors look like glass-covered boxes.

// Slide 12 ... Each section consists of four basic parts—at the top, clear glass or plastic to trap the heat; next, tubes attached to a

[and so on] ...

rights, there are legal advantages to registering the copyright formally with the Copyright Office. This can be especially important if you anticipate selling or otherwise widely distributing your materials. You cannot file suit for infringement until your copyright is registered.

An application form for copyright protection is available from the Information and Publications Section, Copyright Office, Library of Congress, Washington, DC 20559. Request the form for the type of material that you wish to register. Two copies of the work and a fee of $20 are submitted. The term of copyright ownership is the life of the author plus 50 years.

EVALUATE RESULTS

Finally, plan to evaluate the effectiveness of your instructional materials. Recall that a suggested checkpoint during the *formative* evaluation stage of development was to gather reactions from colleagues and from a learner group for improving the materials at the time (page 175). When the material is used, encourage reactions. Determine changes in audience and individual learner behavior in terms of the objectives originally established. Accomplish this by observing specific actions of members of the audience and by administering performance or written tests to individuals. The results will allow you to answer the question, "How well have the materials done the job for which they were designed?"

Here are suggestions for items to include when evaluating the effectiveness of your instructional materials:

- How well do learners accomplish the objectives upon which the materials are based?
- Do reactions indicate the materials are appealing to the audience or to individual learners?
- If the materials do not meet the criteria of the objective(s), or lack appeal, what revisions can be made?
- Are the arrangements for use of the materials convenient for instructor and learners (applicable to individualized learning)?
- Was any difficulty encountered in using equipment?
- Were the facilities satisfactory?
- What were the development costs (professional and staff time, materials, services)?
- What are the operational use costs (staff time, materials, facilities use)?

Media Production Evaluation Form

MATERIALS EVALUATION

Title of Production: ____________________

(Place check mark for value along each line.)

	(LOW) 1 2 3 4 5 (HIGH)
MESSAGE	
Objectives realized	______
Satisfactory for audience	______
Stimulating/appealing	______
Length appropriate	______
TECHNICAL	
Pacing (number of slides related to audio)	______
Audio quality (clarity, mix of narration, voices, music)	______
Visuals (composition, exposure)	______
Overall rating	______
Revisions suggested:	

When seeking answers to these questions, it will be necessary to design appropriate evaluation instruments and gather data from members of the audience. The instruments may take any of a number of forms, depending on the purpose of the questions. Selection can be a checklist, a rating scale, or a questionnaire (consisting of either open-ended or alternative-response questions). Refer to the sample media production evaluation form on page 177. See the references under the headings of Formative Evaluation and Program Evaluation for assistance in developing such instruments.

On the basis of the results of the evaluation, revise the materials as necessary. Repeat the evaluation periodically to maintain a standard of effectiveness. Keep the materials up to date by adding or substituting new content when appropriate and eliminating the obsolete. Only by revision will your instructional materials be kept timely and maintained at your standards of quality and effectiveness.

REVIEW

What You Have Learned About Producing Materials:

1. Here is a list of the matters that should receive attention during the production of many types of instructional media. Write a number before each one to indicate the order in which each should be given attention.
   _______ a. edit pictures
   _______ b. keep a record of scenes filmed
   _______ c. try out materials with an audience group
   _______ d. prepare a schedule for making pictures
   _______ e. do the filming and sound recording
   _______ f. mix all sound
   _______ g. record narration
   _______ h. obtain permission to use copyrighted material
   _______ i. prepare and film titles
   _______ j. work with persons who will appear in scenes
   _______ k. prepare final copies of materials for use
   _______ l. have those appearing in scenes sign releases
   _______ m. edit sound portion of script

2. Answer *True* or *False* for each statement as relating to a phase of the production process.
   _______ a. It is frequently advisable to repeat scenes, shooting from different positions or for different action.
   _______ b. "Fair use," relative to copyright, gives the teacher permission to use single copies of visuals from printed sources before the class.
   _______ c. The reason for making a filming schedule is to be certain all scenes are shot in script order.
   _______ d. It is rarely necessary to make duplicate copies of instructional materials before use.
   _______ e. The expression "formative evaluation" is used when materials are tested or tried out before final completion.
   _______ f. Reasons for using titles include calling attention to or clarifying parts of a visual.
   _______ g. *All* published materials are copyrighted. You need permission to use any of them.
   _______ h. Explain to a person appearing in a scene the purpose of the action before doing the recording.
   _______ i. A *documentary* approach means to shoot pictures *precisely* as specified in the script.
   _______ j. According to the copyright law, you can duplicate any number of photographs in a book for instructional use.
   _______ k. Make your own clear decision about how to record a scene without any interference from an actor or other persons.

_______ l. When using a documentary approach to recording, the camera person should relate a scene being recorded to what was previously shot and try to anticipate what is coming next.

_______ m. The narrator reads the narration from the two-column printed script.

_______ n. A selection from your own music collection can be put on tape as background in a production without any restriction.

_______ o. Music is used at the beginning of a media presentation both to settle the audience and allow the sound level to be set properly.

_______ p. There are legal reasons for having a person sign a release when appearing in a media production.

_______ q. Editing means *both* to arrange scenes in order according to the script and to select the "best" *take* of a scene.

_______ r. Avoid introducing a scene with such an expression as "now you see. . . ."

3. Check the statements that apply *positively* to narration:

_______ a. be conversational

_______ b. identify the picture subject at the beginning of the scene

_______ c. avoid pauses in narration

_______ d. test the narration by reading it aloud

_______ e. limit the use of transitions from one section to another; they confuse the audience

_______ f. each scene should have its own complete narration

_______ g. choose words that communicate the intent of a message quickly to the audience

4. For what *five* reasons might you want to field test instructional materials as they near completion?

5. As you proceed with planning and production, *checkpoints* have been suggested:
  a. What purposes do such checks serve?
  b. List places at which checkpoints are recommended.

6. You are now ready for the production phase of the instructional materials you have been planning. Refer to the how-to-do-it sections in Parts Three and Four as you proceed.
  a. make a filming schedule
  b. select the persons who will appear in scenes
  c. do the filming and sound recording
  d. keep a log sheet
  e. obtain releases and copyright permission
  f. edit the pictures and narration or captions
  g. prepare titles
  h. if possible, conduct a formative evaluation of your materials—develop an evaluation form, conduct a tryout, examine results, and make any changes accordingly
  i. record narration
  j. mix sounds
  k. complete the project

7. For what matters would you like to gather information in evaluating the effectiveness of your materials?

8. What procedure would you follow to copyright instructional materials you produce?

See answers on page 379.

REFERENCES

WORKING WITH ACTORS

Carlberg, Scott. "Directing Nonprofessional Video Talent." *Photomethods* 24 (May 1981): 51–53.

SCRIPT REFINEMENT

Hagerman, William L. "Scriptwriting: Write and Wrong I." *Audio-Visual Communications* 20 (November 1986): 36–41.

———. "Scriptwriting: Write and Wrong II." *Audio-Visual Communications* 20 (December 1986): 35–45.

———. "Scriptwriting: Write and Wrong III." *Audio-Visual Communications* 21 (February 1987): 37–40.

COPYRIGHT

DuBoff, Leonard D. *High-Tech Law (In Plain English): An Entrepreneur's Guide.* Washington, DC: Association for Educational Communications & Technology, 1991.

Official Fair Use Guidelines. Washington, DC: Association for Educational Communications & Technology, 1989.

Sinofsky, Esther R. *A Copyright Primer for Educational & Industrial Media Producers.* Washington, DC: Association for Educational Communications & Technology, 1992.

FORMATIVE EVALUATION

"Developing Opinion, Interest, and Attitude Questionnaires." In *Instructing and Evaluating in Higher Education.* Ron. J. McBeath, ed. Englewood Cliffs, NJ: Educational Technology Publications, 1992, pp. 321–346.

Dick, Walter and Carey, Lou M. "Formative Evaluation." In *Instructional Design: Principles and Applications.* Leslie J. Briggs and others, eds. Englewood Cliffs, NJ: Educational Technology Publications, 1991, pp. 227–268.

PROGRAM EVALUATION

Bingham, Richard D. and Felbinger, Claire L. *Evaluation in Practice.* White Plains, NY: Longman, 1989.

Program Evaluation Kit. Newbury Park, CA: Sage, 1987.

CHAPTER

Printed Materials

An important category of media, useful for instructional, informational, or motivational purposes, is comprised of those types prepared on paper. These include the following:

- **Learning aids,** such as guide sheets, job aids, and picture series
- **Training materials,** such as handout sheets, study guides, and instructor's manuals
- **Informational materials,** such as brochures, newsletters, and annual reports

Each of these groups is unique, serving a special communication purpose. See the definitions and descriptions of each group on page 193. There are elements in planning and preparation that are common to all of them. These we will examine first, and then consider specific requirements for each group.

PLANNING CHECKLIST

When you have decided to consider developing some form of printed materials, start by giving attention to this checklist:

- Have you clearly expressed the **idea** to be served by the proposed materials (page 41)?
- Do you have a clear understanding of the nature of the intended **audience** or **learner group** who will read or learn from the proposed materials (page 42)?
- Have you stated the **objectives** that are to be accomplished by using the materials (page 43)?
- Have you determined whether the type of **printed material selected is suitable** to achieve the objectives?
- Are you aware of **when** the proposed materials will be needed, in what **number of copies,** and **how** they will be used?
- Have you gathered the necessary **information** or **subject content** for the topics to be communicated, or analyzed the **task** that needs to be learned in terms of the objectives (page 45)?
- Will **desktop publishing** techniques be used?
- What **production equipment** is available or will be needed?
- Have you considered whether there will be need for **assistants** and, if so, who might you ask to help or to provide professional or technical services?
- Do you know what **funds** will be available for producing and duplicating the printed materials?

Once these questions have been satisfactorily answered, and appropriate actions taken, you are ready to do the writing and to carry out the production. After an introduction to desktop publishing, the following sections of this chapter describe the important aspects of technical writing, page design, reproduction, and materials preparation appropriate for various kinds of printed materials.

ELECTRONIC DESKTOP PUBLISHING

A personal computer, with appropriate software and a printer, can be used to produce high-quality printed materials of many types. This is known as **electronic publishing.** The word *desktop* is used because the required equipment can fit on the top of a desk.

Software

Software programs provide the information and instructions that allow you to create printed materials. There are four levels of page-production software available for personal computers.

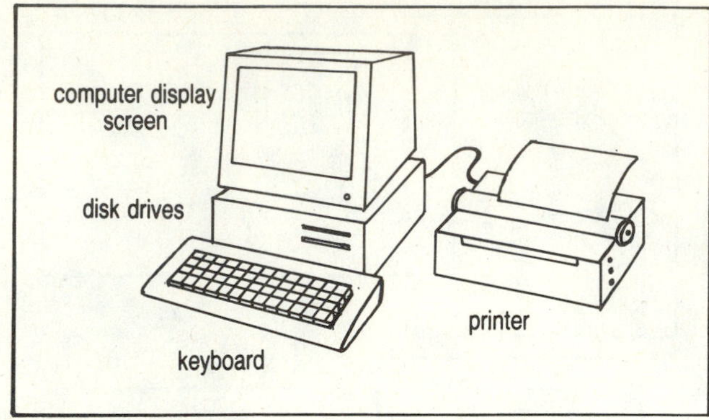

- **Text editors**—used for preparing textual material (stored in computer memory as a **text file**) that can be sent to a printer, using the font provided in the printer. Text editor programs cannot use graphics or other typefaces. Like a regular typewriter, they are mainly for creating text files.
- **Text-based word processors**—used for preparing and formatting text by using control codes. Such programs use the computer system to quickly display text, but as above, rely on fonts found in the printer to create printed text.
- **Graphics programs**—use their own fonts to create a page. In addition, lines, boxes, and shading can be added. Both draw-type and paint-type programs (page 121) can be used to create graphic illustrations, while from clipart collections (page 125), illustrations can be added. Also, with a scanner or video digitizer (page 120) available illustrations can be included in printed materials. The completed page is sent to the printer as a *graphics file,* ignoring the printer's fonts. The result is of better quality and offers more formatting and layout options.
- **Desktop publishing programs**—most widely used process that allows the intermix of text and graphics, without any preset structure, for preparing the final layouts. With such a program, text and graphics can be created or elements of a page imported from previously prepared graphics files, added to, supplemented with scanned materials, combined in various ways, and modified. Output is made through a printer as a graphic image.

Word processing and desktop publishing programs provide flexibility for selecting, adjusting, and manipulating the many factors that comprise the art of printing, called *typography.* These include the following:

- selecting fonts and letter style (normal, italics, bold . . .) from available typefaces
- choosing size of lettering from available point sizes
- adjusting character spacing (including kerning, page 133)
- removing or shifting parts of text within the document

- checking spelling throughout the entire document automatically
- creating columns
- justifying text (block left and/or right, or centering)
- composing or laying out pages, including placement of headings, text, columns, illustrations, or boxes

Design Procedures

The word processing and other desktop software programs can guide you through the preparation of the components that will comprise your printed material. Then it is necessary to organize these pieces into the final product. The same principles and many of the same practices that are important in designing any graphic materials and arranging the elements should be applied here. Much of the information in Chapter 8 on graphic techniques should be reviewed as you plan your desktop publication work.

Plan each page layout before working at the computer. Outline two facing pages on 8½ × 11 inch paper with the 11 inch side placed **vertically.** The useful page area is 7 × 10 inches, with margins of ½ inch on the sides and ¾ inch at the top and bottom. Establish the number of columns for each page. A full page, or single-column format, often used in reports, fills the 7 inch area. A two-column layout, used in newsletters and magazinelike publications, has 3⅓ inch (20 picas) columns with ⅓ inch (2 picas) space between them. Avoid too narrow a column, which wastes space between words, may require too many hyphenated words, or has a very ragged appearance, and makes reading difficult.

Within the selected page format, plan standardized spacing between various elements—headings and text, illustrations and captions or text. Consistent placement of elements, and spacing between them, will contribute to the overall attractiveness of the final material.

Once you have made sketches of pages, start to create them on the computer. Preview on the screen as you proceed. Where things do not fit the space planned, or do not match other parts as you expected, try different arrangements until you find satisfactory solutions. You can best judge the acceptability of a final page design by how it looks on paper. Is the page attractive, understandable, and clearly legible?

Print each page, or a set of pages, for examination and approval before the final run. Keep careful records of component sizes and space use for subsequent pages and future publications.

Desktop Publishing

The key to desktop publishing is the ability to mix high-quality text and sophisticated graphics in one document. The results can be publications, technical reports, instructional materials, proposals, and much more.

Too Narrow a Column

Desktop Publishing

The key to desktop publishing is the ability to mix high-quality text and sophisticated graphics in one document. The results can be publications, technical reports, instructional materials, proposals, and much more.

Preferred Column Width

Printers

Printers are the most common and widely used "hard copy" output devices for recording readable information from a computer. One category consists of **impact printers**. These printers form images when a key or character strikes a ribbon against paper as occurs with a typewriter.

- **Dot matrix** printers use small pins that are controlled by a set of magnets (solenoids) to print dots that form letters on paper with ink or heat. Most printers consist of 24-pin heads and are termed *near-letter-quality* printers.

```
     Asian grocery stores in th
California communities of San
Jose, Mountain View, and Berkele
were visited and lists were com
```

- **Daisy wheel** printers have a flat, circular print wheel with tabs extending from the center like petals of a daisy. Each tab has a letter or number at its end.

When a tab is in position, a small hammer strikes the wheel, pressing the letter against the ribbon. This printer is considered to be a *letter-quality* printer.

```
    Asian grocery stores in the
California communities of San
Jose, Mountain View, and Berkeley
were visited and lists were com
```

Another category of printers is the **nonimpact type** that forms an image with heat, ink spray, or laser.

- **Thermal transfer** printers use a heat process that melts waxy ink or dye onto special paper to produce images with strong colors. The printing element heats to a high temperature for a split second. Then heated pins, forming letters, numbers, and lines, contact a special ribbon (containing black and other colors), transferring ink or dye to paper.

> Asian grocery stores in the
> California communities of San Jose,
> Mountain View, and Berkeley were
> visited and lists were compiled of

- **Ink jet** printers have tiny nozzles that spray drops of cyan, magenta, yellow, and black ink from individual reservoirs to form characters directly on paper or film. This printer can prepare high quality images in one or several colors.
- **Laser** printers function like a photocopy machine (page 191) as the laser beam creates dots for an electrically charged image on a photosensitive drum. Then black toner, as used in a copier machine, is attracted to the charged dots and heat fixed to a sheet of paper or film. The popularity of laser printers is due to the quiet, rapid printing, the high quality of images created, and the ability to print more than one type lettering style and size on a page.

> **Asian grocery stores in the**
> **California communities of**
> **San Jose, Mountain View, and**
> **Berkeley were visited and lists**

With the availability of color versions of desktop publishing software, along with color graphics boards, color scanners, and color copiers, in-house publications, printed in color, are becoming more economical and feasible. There are also developments that allow the creation of printing plates with a laser printer. Such a "direct-to-plate" (D-to-P) procedure further simplifies the desktop publishing process with electronic printing technologies.

Study the manuals for the computer, peripheral equipment, and software you will use for desktop publishing. Identify the features and consider the applications that can be made. Then proceed to apply the following procedures for planning and preparing printed materials.

ORGANIZING AND WRITING

Whether you will be preparing printed materials in the form of a simple checklist of items as a guide sheet, or as a compilation of articles for a newsletter, your ability to communicate effectively in writing is essential. It is important that you employ both words and page design together to structure the final document. While you cannot be taught how to become a competent writer by reading these few pages, here are some suggestions that you should apply to better ensure that your materials will be effective:

- Use an introduction or overview at the beginning to alert the reader to what will be presented.
- Procedures, facts, events, ideas, or whatever content is to be treated should be organized so there is a logical flow of information, providing for a continuity of thought. The reader must be able to easily follow each idea in turn, making sense out of what is presented.
- The arrangement of information and instructions should parallel the logical order of understanding and action the reader will need to take.
- Keep the potential reader in mind as you write. This will affect your selection of vocabulary, the number of examples you use, and other practices, all of which contribute to suitable reading and comprehension.
- Use simple words that are readily understood, unless technical terms are required. Use them with moderation, after explaining and illustrating their meaning.
- Use proper grammar in sentence construction. In part, this refers to the placement and relationship of the elements of speech (subject, predicate, modifiers, and so forth) and the correct use of punctuation, especially commas and semicolons. (For ready reference, have at hand a good dictionary.)

- Set standards for consistency in capitalizing words and abbreviating expressions.
- Use short sentences rather than long, complex ones containing multiple clauses.
- Use short paragraphs because the appearance of lengthy ones on a page discourages careful reading. Each paragraph should treat one concept or aspect of a topic.
- Use headings and subheadings to identify and separate sections of the writing.
- As appropriate, periodically summarize the information presented. This repetition can increase the reader's understanding of the subject and also place the various elements of the topic in relative perspective.
- For a manual or a major publication, develop a table of contents with sufficient detail so that the reader can quickly find a needed section.
- Consider the inclusion of a glossary containing definitions of important terms and possibly an index if the publication will be an extensive one.

A test for effective writing has been to apply a **readability formula** to the document. This establishes a school grade level of reading difficulty. Such a procedure employs factors such as average number of syllables per 100 words and average number of sentences per 100 words. By comparing the averages of these two factors within an article or a guide, a grade level of reading difficulty can be ascertained. Fry, a recognized reading authority, has designated a Readability Graph using these variables of syllables and sentences.

Here are some examples from Fry's graph:

SYLLABLES PER 100 WORDS	SENTENCES PER 100 WORDS	GRADE LEVEL
124	7.5	4
138	5.0	7
148	4.3	9
154	4.3	11
162	4.0	12

The use of readability formulas (included in many word processing software programs) for measuring the difficulty of written material for adult readers has been questioned. By focusing a writer's attention on mechanical matters such as numbers of syllables, words, and sentences, and away from clear understanding and how people process information, you may be avoiding important considerations. The content, the organization, and the layout of pages should all be considered in determining the effectiveness of any document.

The best way to determine the usefulness of printed materials is to test the pages with a sample of potential users. Have them read the material, make use of the information presented, and judge the results.

CONSIDERING ILLUSTRATIONS

The inclusion of pictures and other illustrations along with printed text not only assists in the understanding of information and concepts, but also can produce positive effects on retention in a learner's memory. The functions that illustrations can serve include the following (from Willows and Houghton):

- **Decorative function.** Designed to make text more attractive, motivational, and engaging for the reader.
- **Representation function.** Used to reinforce information by conveying the same content as treated in the text. (For example, see photographs on Completing and Filing Transparencies on page 211.)
- **Organization function.** Selected to give greater coherence by illustrating distinctive features or how an operation or procedure is performed. (For example, see the rubber cement mounting methods illustrated on page 141.)
- **Interpretation function.** Included to clarify difficult-to-understand passages or technical terms in text by using drawings and other graphic illustrations. (For example, see diagram for Lens Diaphragm Settings on page 82.)
- **Transformation function.** Developed to assist the learner to construct visual images for ease of mental retrieval of complex or abstract concepts through the use of cartoons and other symbolic illustrations. (For example, see illustrations of transitional devices used in video recording on page 253.)

Carefully review the written material. Decide where photographs, diagrams, or other illustrations could be included to serve the functions described above.

EDITING THE TEXT AND PHOTOGRAPHS

You, or the person who does the original writing, will create the writing according to personal experience and knowledge. It is easy to make assumptions about what the reader may already know, and as a result one may fail to express oneself in ways that are clearly understandable. It is advisable that someone else review your writing and evaluate it in terms of organization, writing style, interest level, clarity, and probably the treatment of technical content. Editing involves making necessary changes in the writing so that it says, to the reader, exactly what you mean.

The person (or persons) who will be responsible for editing should be selected carefully. Possibly there should be one individual competent in the subject so as to check the content for accuracy and another individual responsible for grammatical structure and literary expression. It is desirable for the latter person to have an academic background in English composition and experience in writing. Thus, the qualifications for editing should include strengths in these two areas—subject content and English composition.

Editing or rewriting may also be necessary for reasons beyond the content and grammatical purposes. Articles and study materials may have to be adapted to fit available space (known as **"copyfitting"**). Headings and subheads might need to be added to separate and identify sections. Introductions may have to be written in order to relate a series of articles so there is a smooth transition from one section or article to the next one.

Another phase of editing takes place when photographs are selected for inclusion with the text. Usually more than one picture is taken of a scene or topic. Specific criteria must be used for choosing photographs—how well the subject is visualized, how well the picture is composed, how suitable is the technical quality, and so forth.

Picture editing may also include "cropping" photographs to improve composition. This requires putting marks at the edges of a print to indicate the visual area to be printed, thus eliminating unnecessary or distracting parts of the photograph.

PRODUCING THE MATERIALS

The production of printed material starts with editing. When adjusting the length of an article, there must be an awareness of space requirements and a plan for layout. To carry out production, a number of decisions and technical steps require attention.

Format and Layout

Some types of printed material require only a simple format; for example, a heading followed by a list of steps as for a procedure. Other types are more complex and may include a number of headings, printed text, artwork and/or photographs, captions, and special items such as masthead or a logo. The manner in which these elements are combined becomes the layout. This is the first thing a reader notices about any printed material. Each page of a publication may require a separate layout.

In designing a page, give attention to these matters:

- Placement of titles, headings, illustrations, and page numbers
- Number of columns
- Length of lines
- Width of margins
- Emphasis on specific content

The following sections of this chapter explain how many of these matters may be treated.

There can be three levels of layout preparation:

- ***thumbnail***—simple, quick sketch to try out ideas
- ***rough***—more detailed drawing to proper size, showing general placement of all elements
- ***comprehensive*** or final—showing each element to size, with color and accurate placement of all that will appear in final copy to ensure correct spacing

With a desktop publishing program various layout ideas and detailed plans can be developed, then modified, and printed out for examination.

In preparing a layout, many of the procedures described under the Visual Design and Layout section (page 116) of the graphics chapter should be considered. Questions such as the following may be important to consider:

- Does the design attract and hold attention?
- Should the layout be formal or informal?
- Is the continuity among all elements maintained so that the reader follows easily and understands?
- Are headings important to the design and understanding of the content?
- How many columns of text should be used on a page?
- Will this be a single color (generally black) product or will more than one color be used? What purposes will be served by a second color?
- Will the product be flat or folded, in a single sheet or multiple pages?

In seeking answers to these questions, the following facts will prove helpful:

- The unusual, or what is novel, attracts attention and arouses interest.
- When first looking at a page, the eye usually starts at the upper left corner and moves across the page and down to the right. This is true of most printed pages unless the page has a special layout, designed to attract attention differently.
- White space is important on a page to separate elements and to create a feeling of openness.
- For reading ease, a column should be neither very wide nor very narrow. See the examples that follow and also those on page 183.

Headings

The purpose of a heading is to orient the reader to the start of a topic in the text that follows. A **main heading** is the title for the overall subject, while **subheadings** introduce elements of the subject. Carefully decide on the need for subheadings so each one has a clear purpose and does not unnecessarily interrupt the flow of ideas. Then make sure they are consistent and parallel in structure.

Headings should be briefly worded, but explicit so they communicate quickly and effectively. By glancing at a set of sequential headings, the reader can gain a clear overview of the topic.

Taking the Initiative

The Governor's Remediation Initiative was developed with a commitment to three objectives. First, to create 100 to 150 reading and math remedial units throughout the high school system in South Carolina. Second, to create an administrative unit located at Winthrop College in Rock Hill, S.C. Third, to use some of the funds to develop curriculum and to review materials available commercially. Each objective had its own budget with separate funds allocated.

Special Recognition

In a report issued by the U.S. Department of Labor in March, the South Carolina Governor's Remediation Initiative was featured as one of eight examples of the application of technology to classroom learning.

The study, conducted by the National Commission on Employment Policy, includes a review of privately funded training programs. Since the study is not specific to the secondary school level, we feel quite

It All Started With Math

The math portion grew out of a program developed for the state technical training system. A developmental studies program for students entering the state college system was adapted to the needs of secondary schools.

Columns

Most typed or word processor-prepared materials are of full-page width. This arrangement may require slow reading as some people lose their place on a long line of text. Also, full-width lines do not make for attractive arrangements nor allow for page-design options.

A two-column format is often used for newsletters and magazines. Three columns on 8½ × 11 inch paper approach the appearance of a newspaper page.

Technology and Design

Technology has been equated with its products, or worse, with machines. But it is more appropriately associated with development, a process in which technique and knowledge have key roles. Technological tasks concern engineering inventions or things artificial; objects whose nature and existence depends on human goals. These objects range from automobiles to curricula, and even include things usually considered "natural." Today forests are managed and genes are modified. Economic, political, social, and many biological systems are artificial to some degree and can be engineered to some extent.

To function optimally, or even sub-optimally, the inner environments of artificial objects must be appropriate to the outer environments in which they operate. An airplane must have a structure that enables it to fly; a computer program must be devised to run on certain hardware. Accommodating internal and external environments is accomplished by design, and everyone designs who devises courses of action aimed at changing existing situations to preferred ones. Design involves problem solving, and successful problem solving depends on having relevant knowledge. Ironically, any design, when realized, will change the context affecting it. In addition, other factors alter this context so that, once designed, objects eventually have to be redesigned, fixed, or discarded. For example, instructional materials and devices wear out, the content taught becomes outdated, or existing instructional strategies are found wanting. These conditions generate needs for new materials, better strategies, and more sophisticated equipment.

Design links technology to the human mind and perhaps the heart and soul. As the world changes, we modify existing inventions and create new ones. The concept of design suggests technology is responsive to human goals and subject to human control. But what constitutes "control" is elusive, given a constantly changing milieu. Relevant knowledge is essential for successful design, but

during the training program. At the outset, participants were asked to critically examine two statements that were sent to them in the reading material. The first item, referred to as the statement of context, includes such expressions as:

- Adults are responsible for their own learning
- Learning requires active participation and reflection, and
- Each participant is responsible for creating value in the learning experience.

The second item, the course objectives, was also critically examined. Both items were thoroughly discussed and revised, as necessary, in order to make the training program work. Thus, the climate for "learning" was set on the first day, and the objectives were tailored to the needs of the participants.

Another important activity was the processing of the data generated from the pre-course instruments. Managers carefully reviewed their profiles from the Health/Stress Questionnaires and the MPI in the

After Training

At the end of the training, managers agreed to take their journals home to make revisions, type, and return them to the course coordinator within one month. The coordinator then mailed a complete set of one manager's weekly journal entries to all 24 participants for 24 consecutive weeks. Thus, for the six-month period following the course, each manager was able to relive the learning experience through the writings of a peer.

Managers also agreed to remain in contact with members of their support groups. The purpose of these groups was to strengthen individual change efforts and provide a structure for feedback and accountability. Accountability was achieved by appointing a team leader in each group to be responsible for keeping a record of each member's progress in meeting their change goals. The group's results were then sent to the course coordinator who summarized the results of all groups. These were post-training ratings. In analyzing the changes between pre- and post-training ratings, only those managers who provided post-training ratings were included. Analyses were made using SPSS, a packaged computer statistical analysis system.

The total number of managers who returned various MPI ratings were as follows:

- 250 returned at least one pre-training rating
- 126 returned both pre- and post-training self-ratings
- 116 returned both pre- and post-training boss-ratings
- 138 returned both pre- and post-training subordinate manager-ratings (at least one subordinate)

The fact that only about half of the follow-up questionnaires were returned was cause for concern. The reasons for not participating in the follow-up varied, but the majority involved reassignment of the manager. To determine if those managers who did not return the follow-up questionnaire differed statistically from those who did, the

The difference in line justification is shown in these examples. See following section.

Text

The most widely used method for preparing text is with a computer word processing program that is output with a high-quality printer (preferably laser) onto paper. For some purposes, an electric typewriter or typesetting by a printer could be considered. The decision of which method to use depends on these factors—desired level of professional appearance, money available, and preparation time available.

Consider these suggestions when preparing text:

- By automatically changing the spacing between letters and words, every line can be of the same length. This *justifies* the right-hand margin. Although right-side justified text looks pleasing on a page, it may make reading more difficult.

> The format is teams of three to four faculty who meet once a week to create the syllabus and calendar; to choose readings, films and guest speakers; to

Right Margin Justified

> The format is teams of three to four faculty who meet once a week to create the syllabus and calendar; to choose readings, films and guest speakers; to

Right Margin Ragged

- For printing on paper, either serif or sans serif lettering can be used. Adjacent letters in **sans serif** typeface appear less distinct from each other because they lack the small strokes added to the edge of **serif** letters. Therefore, serif type is easier to read. On the other hand, sans serif lettering is considered to have a more modern, cleaner look.

> Because electronic information is volatile and easily reproduced, respect for the work and personal expression of others is especially critical in computer environments.

Sans Serif Typeface

> volatile and easily reproduced, respect for the work and personal expression of others is especially critical in computer environments.

Serif Typeface

- Set type in upper- and lowercase letters for ease and speed in reading. Use uppercase words for emphasis and to attract attention.

> MODERN COMMUNICATION AND INFORMATION TECHNOLOGY ARE CAUSING PROFOUND CHANGES AROUND THE WORLD AND THIS PHENOMENON HAS IMPORTANT IMPLICATIONS FOR EDUCATION.

Uppercase Lettering

> MODERN COMMUNICATION and INFORMATION TECHNOLOGY are causing PROFOUND CHANGES around the world and this phenomenon has important IMPLICATIONS FOR EDUCATION.

Upper- and Lowercase Lettering

> Modern communication and information technology are causing profound changes around the world and this phenomenon has important implications for education.

All Lowercase Lettering

- Type characters are measured in **points.** Textual lines commonly are printed in 9 to 12 point type. For appearance and ease in reading, 2 to 4 points of "leading" or clear space between lines may be added. Thus, "10 point on 12" means 10 point lettering with two points of blank space between lines. Space between words is one-third the character point (4 points space for 12 point lettering).

> One possible source of power was heat. The English had been clearing the forest land for centuries. First, they burned the wood directly, then what was left had been nearly completely cleared by charcoal production.

10 point on 10

> One possible source of power was heat. The English had been clearing the forest land for centuries. First, they burned the wood directly, then what was left had been nearly completely cleared by charcoal production.

10 point on 12

- The length of a line is measured in **picas.** There are six picas per inch and 12 points equal one pica (thus, 72 points per inch).

- As you look at a page in this book, you will see that the typeface is Helvetica, chapter titles are printed in 30 point Caslon, main section headings are printed in 13 point Caslon, and text is printed as 9.5 point on 12.

If a number of items is to be listed, assist the reader to identify and study them by:

- Starting the first line of an item at the left margin, then indenting the first word of each following line
- Providing space between items for visual separation
- Numbering each item if the list is sequential
- Preceding the first word of an item with a large dot (called a "bullet") or other attention-getting symbol

To give special emphasis to a word, phrase, or sentence, consider these techniques:

- Enclose the expression in "quotation" marks.
- Underline the expression.
- Print words in CAPITAL LETTERS.
- Use a **boldface** type style for words.
- Use an *italics* type style for words.
- Draw a box around the phrase.

Headings and subheadings are bold and larger than the text. They are designed to attract attention and serve as the lead-in to what follows. There should be consistency in letter style between headings and text that follows. Headings can be prepared by typesetting, computer fonts, dry-transfer letters (page 136), or pressure-machine lettering (page 138) with excellent results. Give attention to the suggestions on page 132 when preparing lettering.

Proofreading

Once the text is computer-generated, typed, or set, and headings are prepared, all writing should be proofread. As previously pointed out, word processing programs include a "spell check" feature for ease of finding spelling errors. A printer supplies **galley proofs** for proofreading before printing. Photocopies of printed originals should be made for proofing. Check the galleys or copies carefully against the original manuscript.

Errors in printing or typing should be marked and corrected. When correcting copy, refer to a large dictionary or proofreading reference for the basic symbols that are used to communicate to the printer. At this stage, changes made by the author on typeset material may prove to be costly.

1. A *thrombus* forms, in ablood vessel, when intact and ruptured platlets adhere together on a vessel, wall. Factors which contribute to thrombus formation are:
   A) decreased smoothness of vessel lining
   B) decreased rate of blood flow
   C) increased blood coagbility

2. An *aneurysm* is a weakening or thin spot in an artery wall that may balloon out and finally rupture.

3. an infarction results there when is complete blockage of the blood dupply in cerebral or coronary arteries. Prolonged blockage deprives tissue of nourishment this causing cell death and permanent tissue damage

Proofread Galley Proof

1. A *thrombus* forms in a blood vessel when intact and ruptured platelets adhere together on a vessel wall. Factors which contribute to thrombus formation are:
   a) decreased smoothness of vessel lining
   b) decreased rate of blood flow
   c) increased blood coagulability

2. An *aneurysm* is a weakening or thin spot in an artery wall that may balloon out and finally rupture.

3. An *infarction* results when there is complete blockage of the blood supply in cerebral or coronary arteries. Prolonged blockage deprives tissue of nourishment, thus causing cell death and permanent tissue damage.

Repro Copy

The galleys or printed copy will accurately indicate space to be used. Therefore, the final layout can be prepared at this time.

From the proofread materials, final copy for reproduction, with all corrections, is prepared. This is called the **repro copy.**

Artwork and Photographs

Illustrations, in the form of diagrams, photographs, cartoons, charts, or graphs, when prepared for printed materials, can serve various purposes:

- Decorative, designed to attract attention to the page and even to enhance the pleasure derived from reading
- Illustrate and clarify what is written, thus contributing to understanding
- May provide information beyond what can be stated
- Contribute significantly to the retention of information

Line illustrations are prepared as black-and-white drawings (page 124). Toning and texture patterns, consisting of closely spaced dots or lines, can be added to artwork to create the impression of shades of gray. Artwork should be prepared either of a size to fit the area indicated on the layout, or of a larger proportionate size which can be reduced. See suggestions for doing artwork and sources for ready-made art (clipart) on page 149.

Graphs, tables, and other diagrams should be included when much statistical data are to be presented. It is easier for a reader to understand complex information when shown visually than when prepared as written text. See the discussion of graph types on page 127. With any graphics, reinforce or supplement the visual with supporting text. Be sure the graphics item and the text are placed on a page in close proximity.

Artwork also may be required for special parts of a publication—main title, logo (an identifying symbol that may be used in future issues), and as a cover page.

Photographs will be made as black-and-white prints

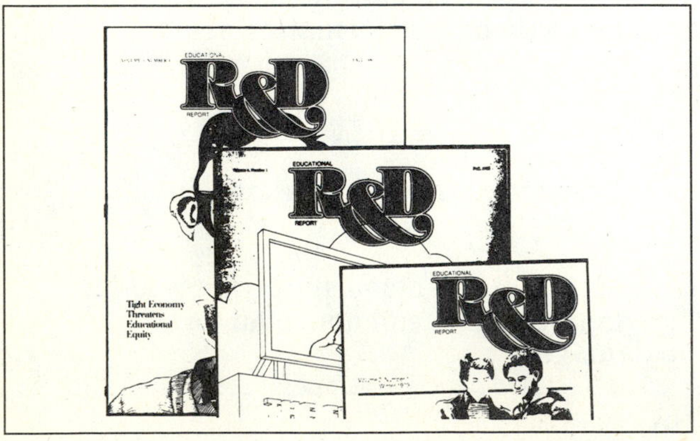

The operating budget has increased substantially over the last five years, although there was an appreciable decrease during the second year. Numerically, the initial budget was $15,000. For the first year there was a 9% increase to $16,350. Then, due to the need for reducing all allocations, the second year had an 11% decrease to $14,552. Starting with the third year, there has been a continual increase – 28% that year as the largest single-year growth to $18,625. During the fourth year the operating budget was $22,350. This represented a 20% growth. The fifth year was limited to a 9% growth to $24,360. We anticipate a moderate, continued increase for the next few years.

Printed Text

The following graph shows operating budget variations over a five year period. The reduction during the second year was due to cutbacks in all allocations. We anticipate a moderate, continued increase for the next few years.

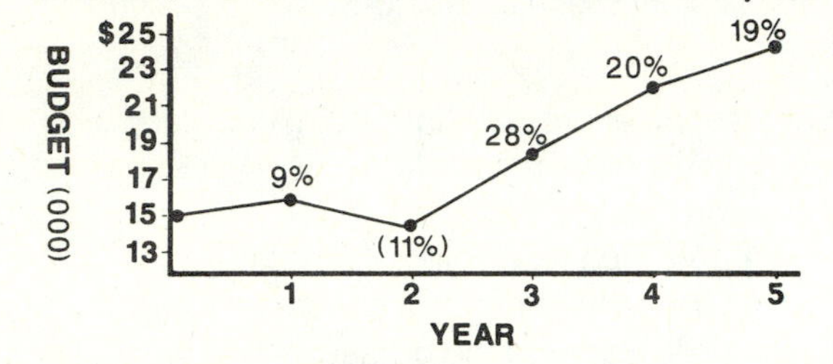

Text with Visual Information

unless four-color reproduction is possible or necessary. Black-and-white pictures should be printed to final size, or can be scaled to the available space for reduction by the printer. For the latter, prints on 5 × 7 inch paper are suitable. Photographs should be printed on single-weight, glossy finish paper. Full-color reproduction can best be made from a color slide. A size larger than 35mm (2¼″ × 2¼″ or 4″ × 5″) is preferred for quality reproduction. Review the photography chapter for detailed information on taking pictures and making prints.

Pasteup

Once repro copy, artwork, and photographs are in final form, everything needs to be assembled. This is the pasteup step (page 147). Gather all elements that will comprise each page and "paste" all parts on paper or cardboard, in accordance with the layout. With desktop publishing, the "pasteup" is performed electronically rather than using adhesive to attach all page elements to paper.

If a number of pages will have a similar format, use preprinted sheets (containing nonreproducible blue lines) showing columns for text areas and other elements to appear on each page. With these sheets, the pasteup process is simplified. When the pasteup is finished, the page is ready for duplication or reproduction.

See the explanation of the pasteup procedure on page 147. Use the temporary rubber cement mounting process (page 141), spray adhesive (page 143), or a waxing unit (page 147). Note how both black-and-white line copy and continuous-tone photographs are handled. Also, if the final material requires more than a single color, see how separate, registered parts of a page should be prepared.

Color

For printed materials, the use of color, other than black, may be important to separate elements or call attention to something of particular importance on a page. On the other hand, color may be used just as an attractive feature.

The two ways to obtain color are to print on *colored paper* or to use *colored inks*. Whenever a second ink color is to be used, costs go up substantially because a separate press run is required for each color. A careful choice of paper (weight, color, finish) can contribute appreciably to the appearance of any printed materials.

If an original colored illustration is to be included with printed materials, it can be reproduced with a color copy machine. Such equipment also will convert color slides to color prints. Color copy machines are available at commercial copy centers and may be found in reproduction operations at various institutions.

Reproducing Printed Materials

Once original printed materials are prepared, it is necessary to make the required number of copies. When a few copies (fewer than ten) are made, we use the term **duplication.** If a larger number of copies is run, we refer to this as **reproduction.**

A number of duplication and reproduction processes can be utilized. Each one serves one or more particular needs and has certain requirements, advantages, and limitations. We will examine three of the most commonly used methods. They range from inexpensive duplication to more complex, costly reproduction procedures. Since this is a rapidly changing area in the graphic arts, further simplified and automated developments can be anticipated.

Spirit Duplication

In public school offices, spirit duplicators are still in use for inexpensive reproduction, although many schools are employing other processes shown in this section.

For spirit duplication a master is prepared with colored carbon sheets placed in contact with the back side of the master paper. Impressions are made on the front side of the master by writing, typing, or drawing. At the same time a carbon impression is deposited on the back of the master sheet. Up to five carbon colors may be used to prepare one-color or multi-color copies.

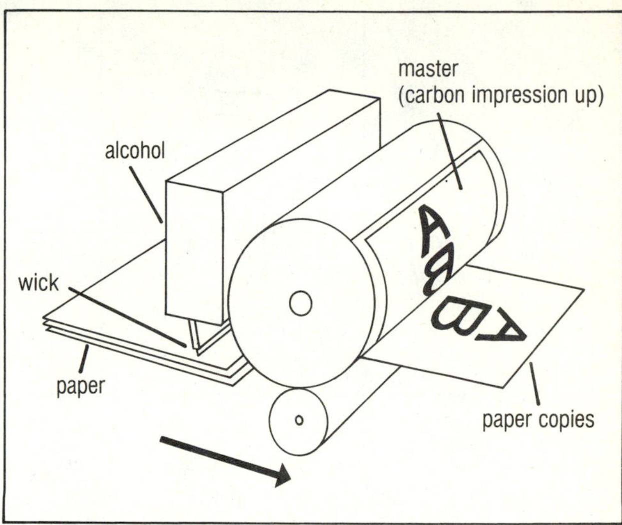

The carbon transferred to the back of the master is an aniline dye, soluble in methyl alcohol. In the spirit duplicator, alcohol is spread over the duplicator paper. When the master comes in contact with paper, some of the dye is deposited on the paper, producing a printed copy.

This is an inexpensive process resulting in fair quality copies. Printed sheets have a short life because the colored dyes that form the words and diagrams fade when exposed to light for a length of time.

Electrostatic Process

The electrostatic process is known as **xerography** and the copy machine used is a "plain paper" copier. The procedure requires a selenium-coated plate or drum, which is photoelectrically sensitive, to receive an electrical charge. The original to be duplicated is exposed to light, with the white area (and gray portions of

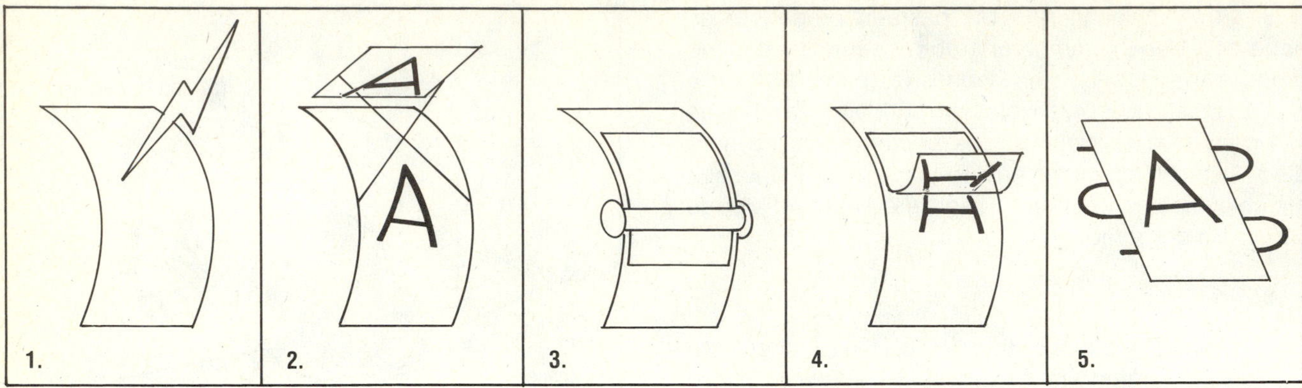

photographs) reflecting light to the charged plate. The light that reaches the selenium-coated surface dissipates the electric charge, leaving a charge only in the image area. The copy paper (any ordinary bond paper) is charged as it is fed into the machine, and a **toner** (a fine black powder) is transferred to it from the selenium surface and appears wherever there was an image on the plate or drum. Finally, the copy paper is heated to fix the powder permanently to the image area and it exits from the machine. To summarize:

1. Positive electric charge is placed on selenium-coated plate or drum.
2. Image of original is projected onto plate to form latent image.
3. Negatively charged powder *toner* is dusted onto selenium plate.
4. Sheet of paper is placed over plate and receives positive charge.
5. Final copy is heated to fix image on the paper.

There is a wide range of copiers that utilize the xerography process. They range from single-sheet, table-top models to large floor units that reproduce original material rapidly in quantity on both sides of a sheet, that permit enlargement or reduction, and that collate final pages. In addition, *full-color* originals can be duplicated or reproduced in full color with certain models of xerographic equipment.

Laser Printing

A laser printer is a computer output device (page 121). It is widely used to duplicate graphic material and to print pages in desktop publishing (page 182). Models range in capacity from a low output of 8 pages to a high volume of 100 pages per minute.

The laser printer operates in much the same manner as does the electrostatic printer described before. A laser beam reflects off the original sheet to a photosensitive drum, producing electrically charged dots corresponding to the image being reproduced. Copy paper

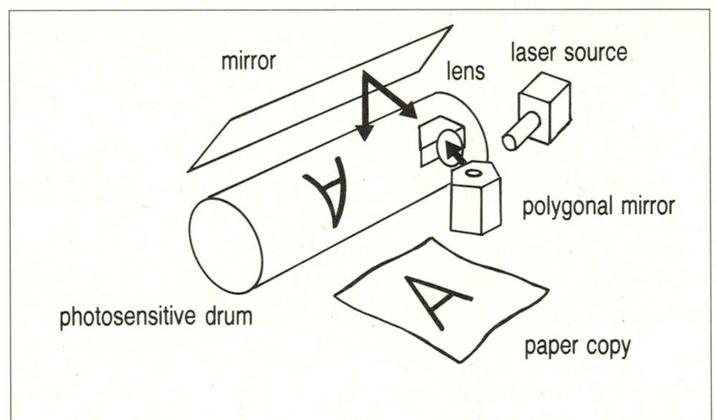

that is precharged picks up the toner, which is fused to the paper by heat. The result is a high-quality copy of the original.

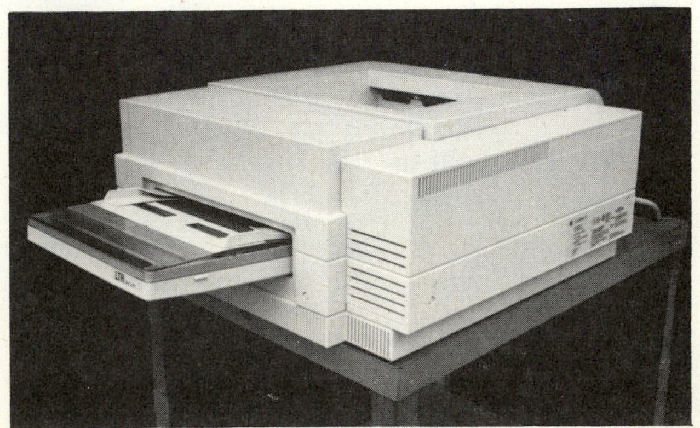

Laser printers are available for printing black line, halftone, and full color originals. The quality is satisfactory for many reproduction needs. Typically, long-run, high-quality printing is done by offset printing. This requires expensive equipment and trained personnel.

Binding

Once duplication or reproduction is completed, then single pages must be assembled and packaged. Binding can be accomplished in various ways:

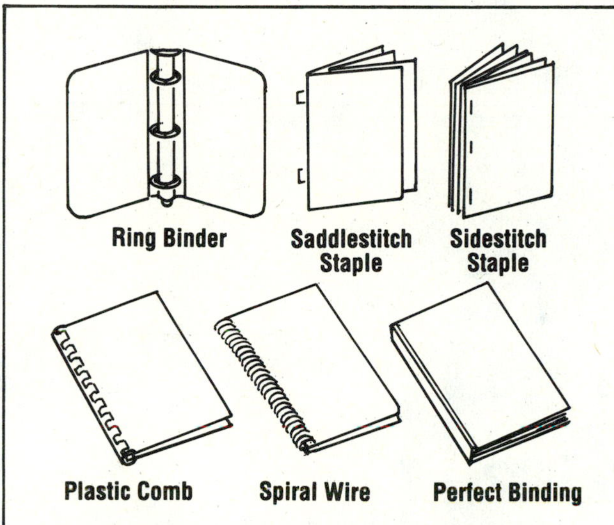

- Stapling the upper left corner or along the left edge to secure all sheets.
- Punching holes and putting all sheets in a two- or three-ring binder.
- Punching holes and securing sheets with metal or plastic spirals.
- Stitching and/or glueing all sheets (termed "perfect binding").

Select the binding to use by answering these questions about the materials:

- Must binding be inexpensive?
- Will frequent revision be necessary?
- Are there few or many pages?
- Is durable protection necessary?
- Must the material lie flat when used?

APPLICATIONS TO PRINTED MATERIALS GROUPS

The planning, writing, editing, and production stages for making printed materials have been described in terms of general procedures. Specific matters relative to each of the three printed media groups need special attention.

Learning Aids

Three forms of printed materials—guide sheets, job aids, and picture series—are designed to provide step-by-step instructions for performing a task. The purpose may be to assemble and then operate equipment, troubleshoot for repair or maintenance, or to apply the steps of a procedure. The information and directions provided must be specific, simple, and clear because most often the learner, new employee, technician, or whoever uses the material, does so individually, without receiving any assistance.

Depending on the information or task to be learned, the material may consist entirely of words (**guide sheet**), some illustrations (**job aid**), or many pictures (**picture series**).

Folding Sheets of Metal
on the Bar Folder

Making a Single Hem

1. The steps that should be followed for making a single hem on the bar folder:
   a. Loosen the locking screw.
   b. Place the sheet against the fingers and move the gauge until the line marked on the sheet is slightly outside the folding blade.
   c. Tighten the locking screw.
   d. Insert the edge of the metal to be folded between the folding blade and the jaw.
   e. Hold the metal firmly agginst the gauge fingers with the left hand and place the right hand on the operating handle.
   f. To fold the edge, pull the operating handle with the right hand as far as it will go. Keep the left hand on the sheet until the sheet is held in place by the wing.
   g. Return the operating handle.
   h. Remove the sheet and place it with the fold facing upward on the beveled part of the blade as close as possible to the wing.
   i. Pull the operating handle with a swift motion to flatten the hem.
2. The hem can be flattened by placing the sheet with the fold facing upward on the beveled part of the blade as close as possible to the wing, and then pulling the operating handle with a swift motion.

Guide Sheet

When planning, writing, and producing these forms of printed materials, give attention to the following:

- Analyze in detail the information, task, or skill to be taught and identify the arrangement of parts or the order of steps and sequences.
- If the task is complex, "storyboard" the various elements of a sequence (page 65) so you will be certain there is a logical, smooth flow of information and instruction.

THE PLANER

The planer, or surfacer, is used to bring material to uniform dimensions after any warp has been removed on the jointer. It is also used to smooth rough-sawn surfaces.

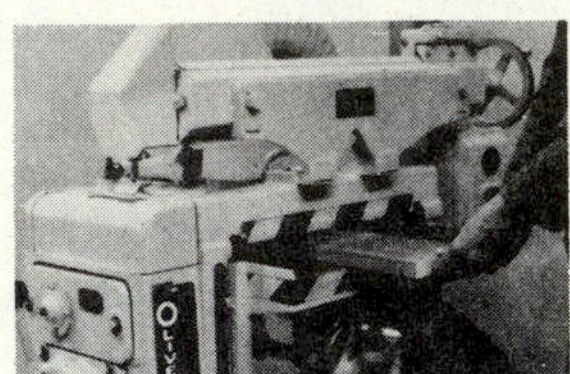

1. Measure each piece of faced stock to find greatest thickness.
2. Set depth-of-cut gauge to 1/16 inch less than thickest piece of stock.
3. Check direction of grain with hand. Know direction of rotation of cutter head.
4. Plane (surface) all pieces from which 1/16 inch will be removed at this depth-of-cut setting.

   Note: Stock normally remains straighter and warps less if an equal amount is removed from each side of the piece when planing.
5. Remove each piece as it emerges from the planer.
6. If necessary, reset depth of cut for thinner pieces.
7. Set depth-of-cut gauge to plane all pieces to final predetermined thickness.

Job Aid

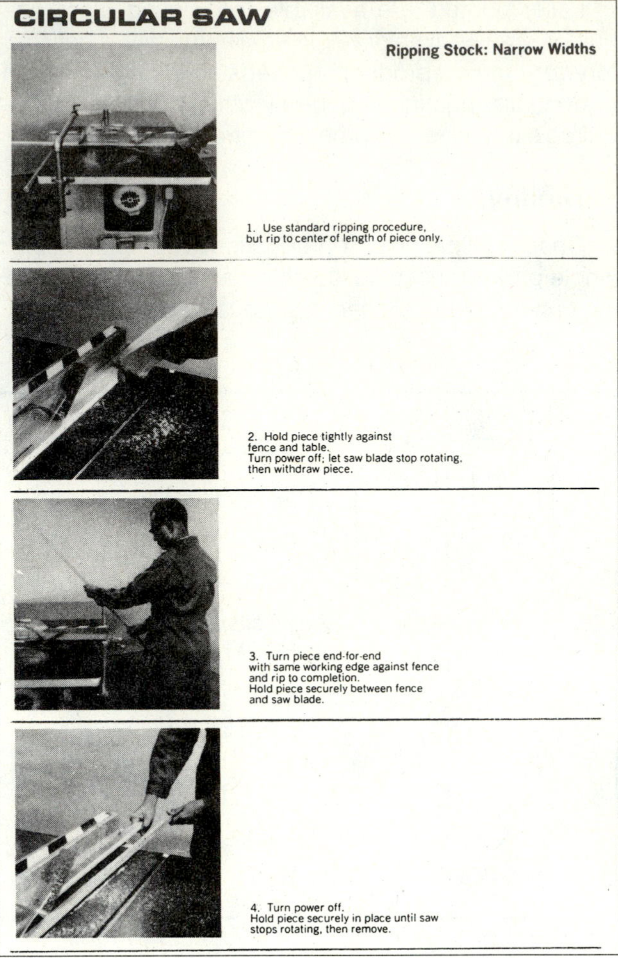

CIRCULAR SAW
Ripping Stock: Narrow Widths
1. Use standard ripping procedure, but rip to center of length of piece only.
2. Hold piece tightly against fence and table. Turn power off; let saw blade stop rotating, then withdraw piece.
3. Turn piece end-for-end with same working edge against fence and rip to completion. Hold piece securely between fence and saw blade.
4. Turn power off. Hold piece securely in place until saw stops rotating, then remove.

Picture Series

- Design the layout so the materials look appealing and are easy to follow. Use headings to guide the reader through the content.
- When writing directions, use simple English and explain or illustrate technical terms when each one is first introduced.
- Decide whether, and if so at what points, line drawings and/or photographs are needed to carry or clarify details. Remember that photographs are more expensive to prepare for printing than are line drawings.
- For special attention, highlight safety practices or other critical elements on the layout.
- If appropriate, provide a summary list of procedures and add questions for review to help the user relate and remember what was presented. For example: "Did you do ______ before doing ______?" "What tool do you use to ______?" "What should you do if ______ happens?"
- If photographs of a person performing a procedure are to be made, place the camera in a subjective position (page 99) and show the action in the scene with a close-up shot.
- Check diagrams and artwork at a preliminary production stage to be certain of accuracy in depicting events and details.
- Have contact prints (page 109) of pictures made and select those for use before enlargements for printing are made.
- Early in planning, decide on the final form material will take—single copy for use at a workstation, few copies for handing out to students on request, inexpensive multiple duplicates, or quantity reproduction for wide distribution.
- Another technique for analyzing a complex task is to develop a "flow chart" as used in computer-based instruction (page 280). The flow chart includes sequences of procedural steps and decision points for the learner or trainee.

Training Materials

Training materials—handout sheets, study guides, and instructor manuals—are forms of printed materials that provide directions, information, and activities for various instructional purposes. Whereas a handout briefly treats a limited portion of a topic, a study guide contains more details. They are both designed for learner or trainee use. They must clearly communicate what is to be learned and how it should be studied. On the other hand, instructor manuals are to guide and assist those who conduct the instruction.

Although the content and its treatment will be different for materials to be used by learners and those to be used by instructors, similar attention needs to be given to layout and graphic production techniques. **Handout sheets** and **study guides** should be carefully organized and simply written. Use outlines, lists, and brief statements. Employ logical page design, careful use of legible headings, typewritten or typeset text, and illustrations that motivate interest and communicate understanding. Depending on how extensive the development of a handout or a study guide, these matters of content should be considered:

- ***Title***—a descriptive statement for topic, unit, session, or course
- ***Rationale*** or ***purpose***—reasons why the study to be undertaken is important, explaining where the topic fits into the overall program
- ***Prerequisites***—units, courses, or experiences the learner should have successfully completed before starting
- ***Objectives***—list of learning objectives to be accomplished (see page 43), informing learner what is required and criteria against which learning and performance will be evaluated
- ***Schedule***—calendar of activities and required deadlines for completing phases of program

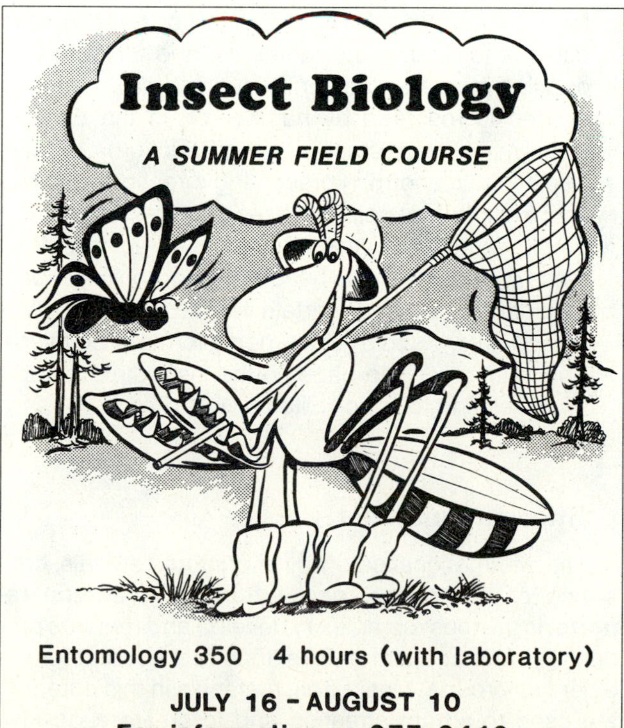

Insect Biology
A SUMMER FIELD COURSE
Entomology 350 4 hours (with laboratory)
JULY 16 - AUGUST 10
For information -- 277-3413

Handout Sheet

Name ______________ IS Time ______________ Date ______________

Read Smart, "Physical Characteristics and Skills," pp. 345-378 and "Physical Growth, Health and Coordination," pp. 493-527.

Objective: To test for motor coordination differences among two different groups.

ACTIVITY 18: Motor Coordination and Growth (2 hours)

Choose a child in the middle years to closely observe and put the sex and age here______________. Ask the child to do the following things for you and observe the ease with which they are accomplished. Supply a general description in Column 2.

(1) Task	(2) General Description
1. Stand on one foot.	
2. Touch nose.	
3. Close eyes and touch nose.	
4. Stand heel to toe.	
5. Catch a ball or other object.	
6. Throw.	
7. Wind a thread or yarn.	
8. Cut a circle.	
9. Jump, touch heels.	
10. Balance a rod vertically.	
11. Do a sit-up (with help)	
12. Do a sit-up (without help)	
13. Walk a straight line.	
14. Draw a circle.	
15. Dribble a ball.	

Find out as much as you can about the child's favorite active games and include in your description anything you think may have a bearing on the child's capabilities.

Now ask a teenager or adult to do the same tasks. Write the sex and age here ______________. Summarize a general description below, following all instructions for the middle years child.

Study Guide Sheet

- ***Resources***—books, supplies, equipment, and other items that learner should have or which will be available for specific uses
- ***Information***—content material in the form of outlines, descriptions, reproduced diagrams or articles (duplicated with permission)
- ***Activities***—learning experiences in which the learner may participate (during class period, for self-paced learning, or for group work)
- ***Exercises*** or ***worksheets***—questions to be answered during or following activities (be sure to provide sufficient space for writing answers)
- ***Problems***—application situations, case studies, or similar practical activities that require learners to make use of information, principles, or procedures that have been learned
- ***Answers***—acceptable answers to exercises, worksheet questions, and other participating activities
- ***Projects***—followup of major activities that require learner to apply further what has been learned
- ***References***—lists of other resources (books, journal articles, media, persons, or places) that may be assigned for use or might be of future value
- ***Tests***—written exercises to measure learning; may be self-administered by learner as self-check on learning, or as preparation for instructor's test

- ***Evaluation forms***—rating scales, checklists, and other instruments to evaluate results of projects, participation in class or group activities, and so on, making the learner aware of how learning will be evaluated
- ***Grading criteria***—description of how grading will be made, indicating the percentage or point basis value of each activity, project, or other requirement

This list of possible items to include in a study guide is extensive. Your own situation should indicate which of them are relevant for use. Because outlining, writing directions, and providing information in specific detail comprise the major portions of these materials, careful editing and proofreading are essential.

When planning an **instructor's manual,** although it is obvious, realize that the individuals who will use the manual probably have not been involved in planning the instructional program. While they may be highly qualified in the subject or skill area, the instructors have no familiarity with the manner in which the content is organized and treated. Furthermore, many newly appointed business and industrial trainers have limited, if any, teaching experience on which to base their classroom activities. Therefore, the manual must carefully lead instructors through the teaching requirements and provide sufficient information about resources and other necessary course logistics.

An instructor's manual may be divided into these parts:

- An **introduction** that explains the goal for the instructional program and specifies the major outcomes to be accomplished (often expressed a "terminal objectives"); may include information on how the manual is organized and should be used.
- Individual **units** or **topics** that comprise the course, each one treated as a separate section in the manual.
- A **supplement** or **appendix** containing test questions and/or answer keys, printed scripts for media, performance checklists, and other evaluation forms.

In developing each unit, or **lesson plan,** in the manual, consider the following:

- Specify objectives and requirements for learners so the instructor will clearly understand what needs to be taught in the unit.
- Design pages in a split-page format, as for a two-column script.
- Along the right side, present directions, information, questions (possibly with suggested answers), group and individual activities for instructor and learners, lists of references and resources, and so forth.
- Use the left side of the page to indicate suggestions for timing of lesson components, for handling the content, for learner assignments, and for obtaining or using media and other resources (may reference a specific resource by number or, in the case of visual materials, a small-size reproduction).
- Use an outline form in presenting directions and describing information to save reading time.
- Employ cues or "visual signals" to direct attention; these may be boldface headings or graphic symbols that mark locations of certain items (questions, summary points, video or other media forms to be used).
- Space items on the page so the instructor can add notes relating to specific items.

Topic: Immobilization due to Fractures

Objective: To apply splints to five parts of the body

Time	Contents	Activities/Resources	Notes
8-10 min	Fractures upper arm forearm ankle knee back	Introduce topic Show film clip #12A Discuss cause of fractures at various parts of the body	
10 min	Upper arm 8 steps	Show film clip #12B Demonstrate procedure Assign Workbook U-5	
15 min		Individual and team practice Checklist #5	See supply list #4
10 min	Forearm 7 steps	Show film clip #12C Demonstrate procedure Assign Workbook U-6	
15 min		Individual and team practice Checklist #6	Supply list #5
6 min 6 min		Discussion In what 3 places should you prevent movement to immobilize a fracture of the forearm?	Answer: broken bone end wrist elbow
	---	Break	---
10 min	Ankle 5 steps	Show film clip #12D Demonstrate procedure Assign Workbook U-7	
15 min		Practice Checklist #7	Supply list #6
12 min	Back 6 steps	Show film clip #12E Demonstrate procedure Assign Workbook U-8	
20 min		Practice Checklist #8	Supply list #7
		Discussion If a person must be turned and you suspect a back fracture, what should you do?	Answer: Turn entire body as unit

Instructor's Manual Page: Lesson Plan

Informational Materials

The informational category of printed materials, consisting of **brochures, newsletters,** and **annual reports,** is the most complex to develop and requires production skills at a higher level than that needed for the other two groups. Most often, materials in this category are used to attract attention and to create a positive impression about an activity or an organization.

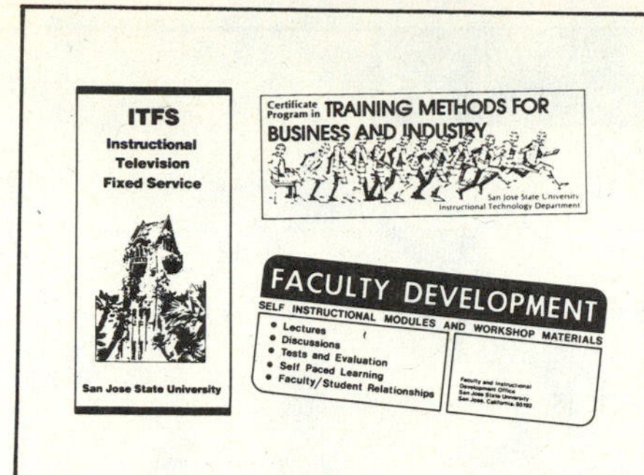

Brochures

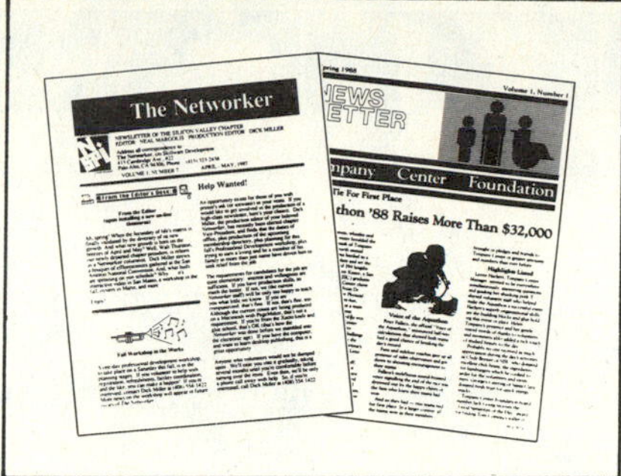

Newsletters

Annual Reports

These attitudinal objectives require special attention during the planning phase and when applying the production techniques described earlier in this chapter. Let us review these matters as they relate to this category of printed materials.

At the start of planning, consider the series of questions listed at the very beginning of the chapter. Of these, establishing clear objectives, recognizing the nature and interests of the potential readers, and being aware of financial constraints are probably most important. By responding to these questions, you can initiate planning that will likely lead to the successful development of your materials.

As you gather information for the publication, realize that in order to attract the reader you must create some excitement about the topic. This may mean attempting first to choose content that will arouse interest by being important to the reader, and then to treat the content in an unusual way—provocative, controversial, amusing—aimed at involving or otherwise stimulating the reader. Make certain the writing is simple, clear, to the point, and accurate in content.

Decide on an overall design in keeping with your treatment. Many of the usual rules of layout are sometimes violated as new ideas are explored; however, this may result in lively new arrangements of images and space that make a strong visual impact.

The visual structure of a page is enhanced by the careful grouping of items; recognize the need for sufficient white space and establish a practical column width for the text or articles. Also, limiting the length of paragraphs will contribute to the readability of printed materials.

As you move to the production phase, here are some suggestions:

- Use a simple art style for preparing illustrations or select from available high-quality clipbook art (page 125).
- Choose easy-to-read typeface styles.
- Use lines, tones, and texture patterns to emphasize certain parts of the layout or to create special effects.
- Select colors that arouse interest and create some enthusiasm for the subject.
- Develop tables and graphs in a form that makes their meaning explicit as well as interesting (page 127).
- Design an attractive, timely cover or first page, in good taste, and with eye appeal. You want it to cause the reader to pick up the publication and start reading!

As stated previously, much of the information presented under the writing, editing, and production sections relates directly to this category of printed materials. The above suggestions serve to reinforce some points already made.

Preparing to Use Printed Materials

Now the printed materials are ready for distribution and use. Distribution may be accomplished by mailing, bulk delivery to departments within an organization, by personally handing the printed materials to individuals, or by having it available for pickup at a meeting or in an office.

Attempt to gather reactions from those using or reading printed materials in order to evaluate their effectiveness. Consider giving attention to these factors:

- General appearance and appeal
- Organization of content
- Clarity and readability of content
- Value of illustrations
- Usefulness of content
- Response from users in the form of action relating to objective initially established

What You Have Learned About Printed Materials

1. What are the three categories of printed materials treated in this chapter and the forms each category can take?
2. To which category of computer software, relative to printed materials, does each situation relate?
   a. Creates page with various text fonts and can include illustrations with boxes and shading
   b. Uses special control signals in a program to prepare and format text with some alternatives to a single font
   c. Combines both text and graphics from various files as well as adding new text and graphic images
   d. Operates like a typewriter to prepare text limited to a single typeface
3. Which are features of word processing and desktop publishing programs?
   a. Adjusting letter spacing
   b. Checking spelling
   c. Evaluating how ideas are treated
   d. Aligning text left and right margins
   e. Selecting letter size
   f. Using a color monitor is important
   g. Selecting from various lettering fonts
   h. Shifting portions of text within document
4. To which category of computer-output printer *and* to which kind of printer does each relate?
   a. Heat melts waxy ink to produce colors
   b. Small pins controlled by magnets to form letters
   c. Nozzles spray ink to form letters
   d. Creates electrically charged image on photosensitive drum
   e. Tabs containing letters press against a ribbon
5. What *two* relationships are used to determine the readability level of written material?
6. What is the approximate readability level of this book as based on page 000 of this chapter?
7. For what reasons may readability formulas *not* be useful?
8. What are the three levels of layout preparation?
9. Which statements are *true*?
   a. Line justification at both left and right margins is desirable when preparing paragraphs of printed material.
   b. Serif style lettering includes extra strokes at letter ends.
   c. Uppercase lettering is easier to read than is lowercase.
   d. Full-page width lines are preferred to two-column format.
   e. Line length of printed material can be measured in picas.
10. What are three ways that special attention can be called to a word or a phrase on the printed page?
11. To which type of reproduction process does each refer?
   a. Electrically charged areas are transferred from a selenium-coated surface to paper, thus allowing for retention of toner powder to form image.
   b. Can print full color and halftone originals as well as black-line originals.
   c. Master is made on carbon sheet, and image is transferred with alcohol to paper.
12. What type of printed material might be selected for each purpose?
   a. To quickly review how to perform an operation that was learned some time ago.
   b. To give learners a complete self-study package on a topic.
   c. To announce a new program to be available for members of an association.

d. To provide a simple outline for all members of an audience attending a meeting.
e. To keep members of an organization informed of events.
f. To follow a sequence of steps in assembling a complex product.
g. To help a new engineer who will teach a course in his specialty.

See answers on page 380.

REFERENCES

PRINTED MATERIALS—GENERAL

Carlisle, Kenneth E. and Coulter, Philip D. "The performance Technology of Job Aids." *Educational Technology* 30 (May 1990): 26–31.

Faulkner, Linda, and Hinds, Mary. "Planning and Perception: Principles for Designing the Printed Page." *Performance and Instruction Journal* 20 (March 1981): 26–28.

Fry, Edward. "A Readability Formula That Saves Time." *Journal of Reading* 11 (April 1968): 513–516, 575–578.

Hartley, James. *Designing Instructional Text.* New York: Nichols, 1978.

Hartley, James, and Burnhill, Peter. "Fifty Guidelines for Improving Instructional Text." *Programmed Learning and Instructional Technology* 4 (February 1977): 65–73.

Jonassen, David H. *The Technology of Text.* Englewood Cliffs, NJ: Educational Technology Publications, 1985.

Levie, W. Howard, and Lentz, Richard. "Effects of Text Illustrations: A Review of Research." *Educational Communications and Technology Journal* 30 (Winter 1982): 195–232.

Redish, Janice C., and Selzer, Jack. "The Place of Readability Formulas in Technical Communication." *Technical Communication* 32 (Fourth Quarter 1985): 46–51.

Willows, Dale M. and Houghton, Harvey A., editors. *The Psychology of Illustration.* New York: Springer-Verlag, 1987.

Wilson, Thomas C.; Pfister, Fred C.; and Fleury, Bruce E. *The Design of Printed Instructional Materials: Research on Illustrations and Typography.* Syracuse, NY: ERIC Clearinghouse on Information Resources, Syracuse University, 1981.

COLOR PRINTERS

"Color Printers." *Computer Pictures* 10 (January/February 1992): 14–20.

Reis, Charles. "Your Range of Choices in Color Hard Copy Devices." *Advanced Imaging* 5 (September 1990): 54–59.

Pearson, LaTresa. "Color Copiers: Making a Big Splash in Presentations." *Presentation Products Magazine* 6 (April 1992): 34–44.

DESKTOP PUBLISHING

Lichty, Tom. *Design Principles for Desktop Publishing.* Glenview, IL: ScottForesman, 1989.

Miles, John. *Design for Desktop Publishing.* San Francisco, CA: Chronicle Books, 1987.

Misanchuk, Earl R. *Preparing Instructional Text: Document Design Using Desktop Publishing.* Englewood Cliffs, NJ: Educational Technology Publications, 1992.

Shushan, Ronnie. *Desktop Publishing by Design.* Redmont, WA: Microsoft Press, 1989.

White, Jan V. "Color: The Newest Tool for Technical Communications." *Technical Communications* 38 (Third Quarter 1991): 346–351.

BROCHURES, MANUALS AND NEWSLETTERS

Anema, Durlynn C. *Designing Effective Brochures and Newsletters.* Dubuque, IA: Kendall/Hunt, 1987.

Davis, Frederic E. and others. *Newsletter Publishing with PageMaker: Macintosh and IBM Editions.* Homewood, IL: Business/Irwin Publishers, 1988.

Mirel, Barbara, Feinberg, Susan, and Allmendeiger, Leif. "Designing Manuals for Active Learning Styles." *Technical Communication* 38 (First Quarter 1991): 75–87.

CHAPTER

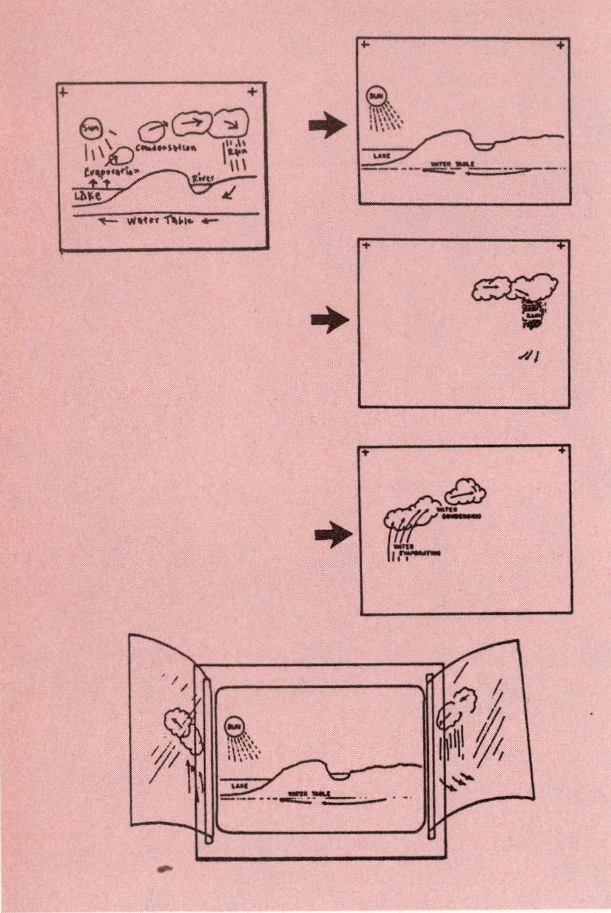

Dimensions of the Working Area

Design Considerations

Preparing Transparencies (five methods)

Completing and Filing Transparencies

Transparencies are large slides for use with an overhead projector by a presenter positioned at the front of a lighted room. They project a large, brilliant picture.

Transparencies can visually present concepts, processes, facts, statistics, outlines, and summaries to small groups, to average-size classes, and to large groups. For some uses they can substitute for writing on a chalkboard. In addition to using prepared transparencies, computer-output from spread sheet, word processing, and graphics programs can be directly projected with an overhead projector. This is an effective, time-saving way to present information. See page 348 in Chapter 19 for detailed procedures on using the overhead projector for instruction.

A series of transparencies is like any other instructional media in that it requires systematic planning and preparation. Before you actually set about making your transparencies, therefore, always consider this planning checklist:

Overhead Projection Materials

- What factors are important to consider about the **audience** that will see the transparencies (page 42)?
- What **objectives** will your transparencies serve (page 43)?
- Have you prepared an **outline of the content** to be included (page 45)?
- Are **transparencies an appropriate medium** to accomplish your purposes and to convey the content (page 58)? Might they be combined with other media for even greater effectiveness (page 59)?
- Have you **organized the content** and made **sketches** to show what is to be included in each transparency (page 65)?

DIMENSIONS OF THE WORKING AREA

The area of the stage (the horizontal glass surface) of most overhead projectors is 10½ × 10½ inches. The entire square can be used for the transparency, but it is better to avoid the extreme edges. Also, since a square is less attractive for most purposes than a rectangle, it is well to work within a rectangle having a height-to-width ratio of about 4 to 5. Thus a convenient transparency size, made on 8½ × 11 inch film, has a 7½ × 9½ inch opening (other formats are 8 × 10 and 7½ × 10 inches). This is normally projected with the 9½ inch dimension in horizontal position because the eyes have a greater field of vision horizontally.

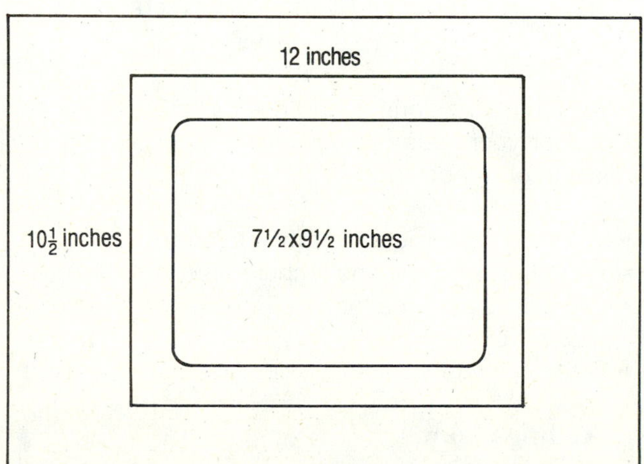

It is difficult to view some parts of vertically oriented transparencies in rooms with low ceilings or with suspended lighting fixtures. Avoid mixing horizontal and vertical transparencies in a presentation because this can be annoying to an audience and bothersome of the presenter.

You can buy cardboard or plastic frames with the opening cut in them, or you can make your own from 6- to 10-ply cardboard (10½ × 12 inches outside dimensions). An outline of the open area of a frame is printed inside the front cover of this book.

Whatever the size of the frame opening you plan to use, prepare all artwork, pictures, and lettering to fit within this opening. An alternative is to use this proportion if size changes are to be made by photographic or other enlargement or reduction methods.

DESIGN CONSIDERATIONS

The production of transparencies requires knowledge and skills in many graphics areas described in Chapter 8. Also see suggestions for design of computer screens on page 280 and lettering for computer-generated images on page 135.

Principles from learning theory, as described in Chapter 2, and evidence from research studies reported in Chapter 3 indicate the importance of learner participation during learning. Within a unit of study, develop some transparencies that involve the learner by requiring the completion of diagrams, replies to questions, or solutions to problems. Another way is to provide students with paper copies of the content of transparencies and instructions for activities relating to your presentation. These techniques contribute to learners' mental involvement, resulting in higher levels of interest and actual learning. Refer to other suggestions in Chapter 19 for using the overhead projector in instruction.

Design and Artwork

Limit the content of a transparency to the presentation of a single concept or a limited topic. Do not try to cover too many points in a single transparency. A complex transparency may be confusing and unreadable to the viewer and thus ineffective. Design a series of transparencies rather than a crowded single transparency.

If you select diagrams and printed materials from books or magazines to convert to transparency form, be alert to certain limitations.

- The format may be vertical rather than horizontal as recommended above.
- The quantity of information included in printed materials may be more than can properly be presented in a single transparency.
- Materials printed in a book, to be read and studied closely at the reader's own pace, may be too dense and thus not suitable for projection, which permits viewing for only a limited time.
- Finally, realize that copyright may impose limitations and it may be necessary to request permission for certain uses (page 169).

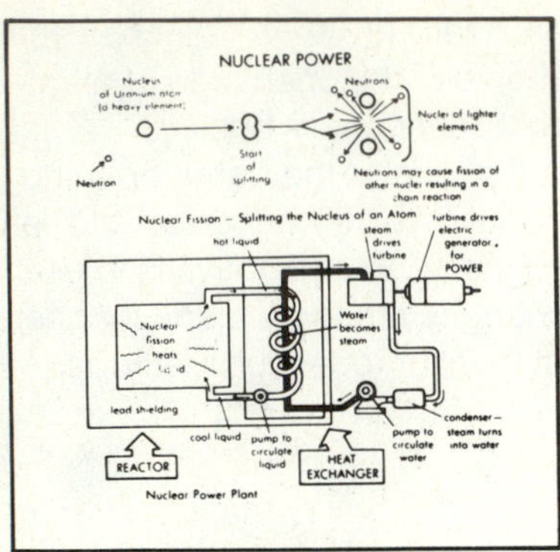

Original Subject

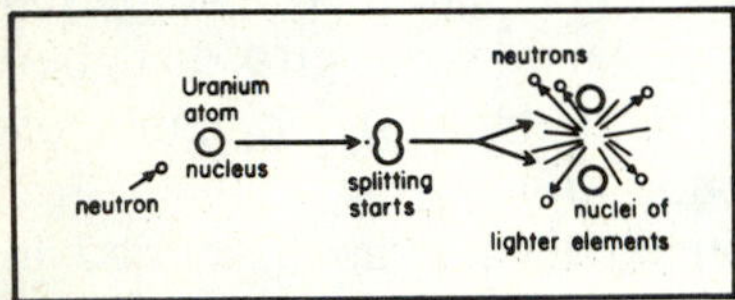

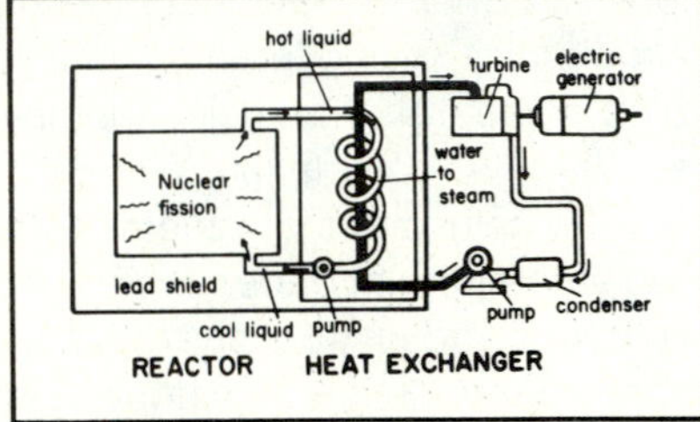

Subject Divided into Parts for Series of Transparencies

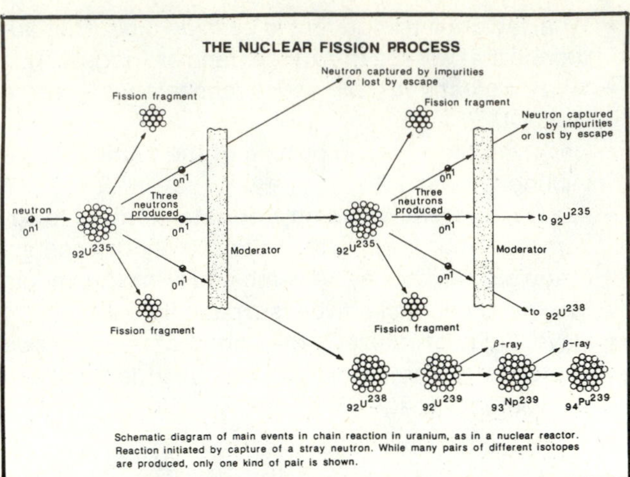

Original Subject

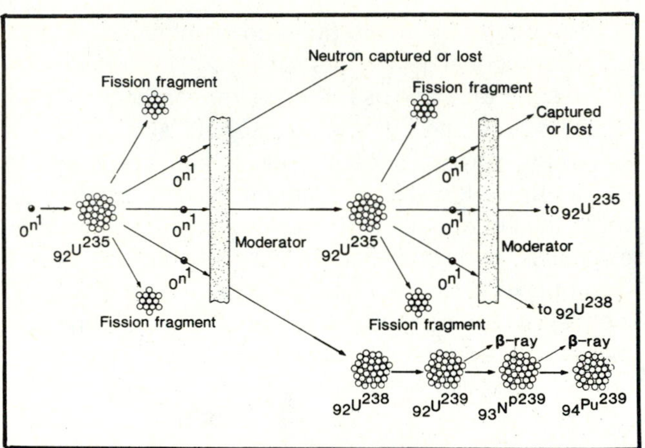

Unnecessary Details Eliminated and Lettering Replaced

Therefore at first glance some printed materials may look suitable for use, but may in actuality be too small, too detailed, and even illegible as transparencies. It may be necessary to modify an illustration by:

- Eliminating unnecessary details such as page numbers, printed text, and unwanted labels or subtitles. (Provide more complete information on paper for distribution to the audience.)
- Modifying visual elements and replacing necessary lettering with larger size type.
- Simplifying a complex diagram by dividing it into segments for separate transparencies or by applying masking and overlay techniques to be described subsequently.
- Avoid preparing a transparency directly from paragraphs of printed material. Select key points or concepts to summarize the information and elaborate on them verbally.
- If detailed information *must* be shown, provide paper copies of the transparency for the audience. The instructor simply uses this type of transparency to orient the audience. The audience must study the paper copy for details.

As you plan diagrams and outlines or captions and labels for your materials, consider the applications of these graphic techniques:

- Planning the design and artwork (page 116)
- Illustrating and coloring techniques (page 124)
- Legibility standards for lettering projected materials (page 132)
- Lettering materials and aids (page 136)

Adding Color

The addition of color to parts or areas of a black-line transparency can be used to separate details, to give emphasis to key elements, and to improve the appearance of the subject when projected.

Color must be transparent and can be applied in various ways:

- Use sharp-tipped felt pens directly on a transparency to write and draw lines (see page 136).
- Use broad-tipped felt pens to color areas on a trans-

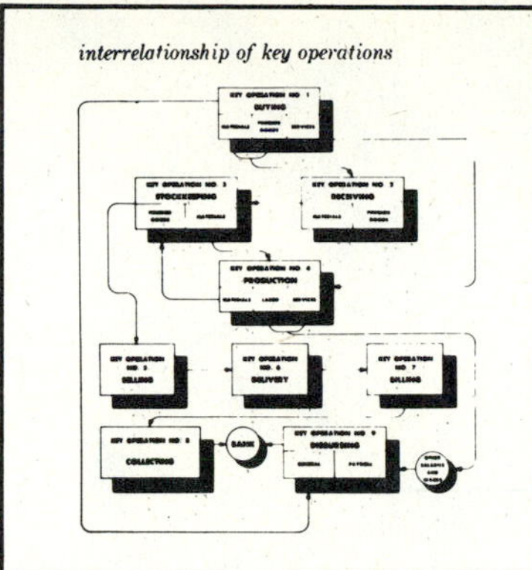

Original Subject

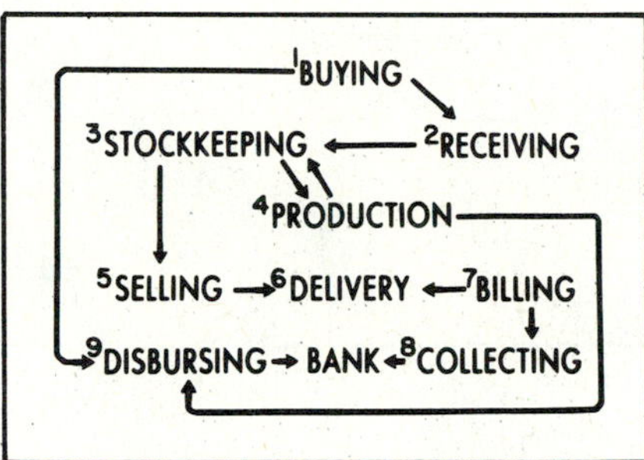

Redesigned for Transparency

parency. Color may be applied as a solid area, although overlapping strokes build up layers of color and these irregularities become visible. Felt pens can also be used to color by applying parallel lines, as in hatching, or by making dots, as in stippling.

- ▸ Use thermal film (page 207), which is available in a number of colors.
- ▸ Prepare computer-generated transparencies (page 206) on film, and then reproduce with a thermal transfer, ink jet, or other printer producing colors.

Progressive Disclosure

By covering areas of a transparency, you can disclose information in a sequential fashion. Select a covering material that is thick enough to block the image, but translucent enough to allow the presenter to see what is coming next. This technique maintains viewer interest and concentrates attention on each point or aspect of a diagram as you are ready to discuss it.

There are two masking techniques for disclosing information. The first, and simpler one, is to cover the transparency with a sheet of paper or cardboard and slide it down to uncover lines as you discuss each point. In the second, areas on a transparency can be overlayed with thin cardboard pieces (taped to the mounting frame) and progressively removed as the presentation proceeds. See the illustrations of masking techniques on page 212.

TREASURY SECURITIES

Treasury bills. It takes $10,000 to buy a Treasury bill, a type of government security that matures in either 90 days, 180 days or one year. The recent annualized yields on those maturities were 5.74%, 6.11% and 6.77%.

Treasury notes. If you won't need your money back for more than a year, consider Treasury notes, which have maturities as long as 10 years. Two-year and three-year notes sell in $5,000 denominations, four- to 10-year notes in $1,000 units.

U.S. Savings Bonds. The darling of payroll savings plans, Series EE savings bonds currently yield 7.17%. Not only is the interest tax-free at the state and local level, but it is also tax deferred at the federal level unless you *choose* to pay the tax every year.

The EE bond blossomed in 1982 when the Treasury spruced it up with competitive yields. Sold for as little as $25, it must be

Original Information

TREASURY SECURITIES

A. Treasury Bills
1. $10,000 minimum
2. 90, 180, 360 day maturity
3. Lower interest rates

B. Treasury Notes
1. 2 or 3 year maturity $5,000
2. 4 or 10 year maturity $1,000
3. Higher interest rates

C. U.S. Savings Bonds
1. $25 minimum
2. Hold 5 years
3. Variable interest above 6%

Key Points on Transparency

Making Overlays

One of the most effective features of overhead projection is the **overlay technique.** As indicated on page 202, problems, processes, and other forms of information can be divided into logical elements, prepared sep-

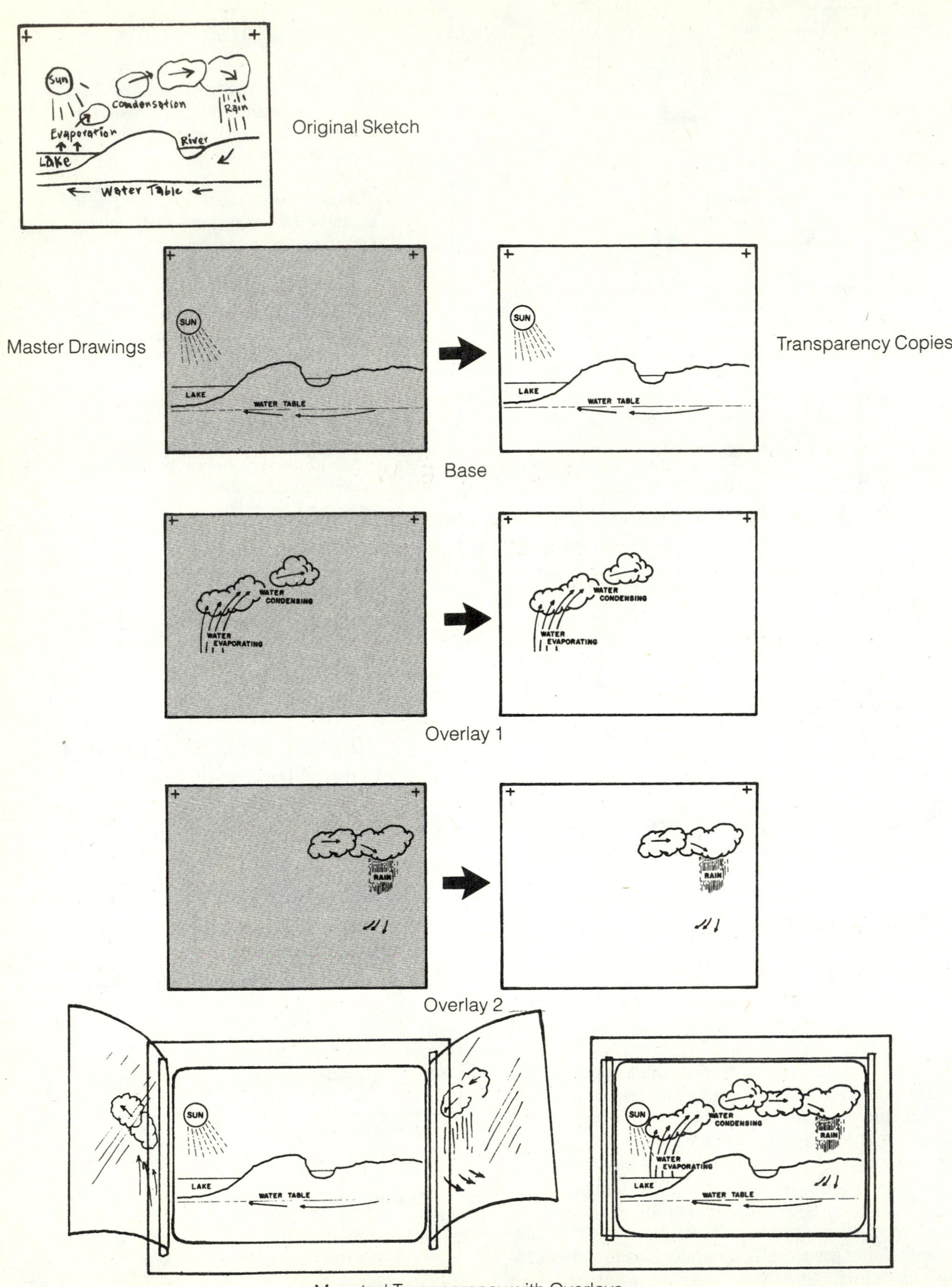

Mounted Transparency with Overlays

arately as transparency sheets, and then shown progressively for effective communication.

In preparing a transparency in overlay form, first make a sketch of the total content. Decide which elements should be the **base** (*projected* first) and which elements, from the original sketch, will comprise each **overlay.** Make separate **masters** for the base and each overlay. Then prepare a transparency from each master, using one or more of the techniques described in the following pages.

When mounting the final transparent sheets, attach the base to the underside of the cardboard frame and the overlays to its face on the appropriate sides (see page 211 for details in mounting).

To ensure proper alignment of all layers of the final transparency, carefully **register** the master drawings to the original sketch and also each piece of film to its master when printing. Do this by placing a guide mark (+) in each of two corners (outside the projected area) on the master exactly over the marks on the original sketch; or, preferably, use punched paper and film aligned on a register board (page 115).

See the previous page for an example of how an overhead transparency, consisting of a base and two overlays, is prepared. Notice the registration marks placed in corners of the original sketch and then on the master drawing, with them appearing on the transparent overlay sheets. Also see the arrangement for mounting the overlays on the cardboard frame.

What You Have Learned About Designing Transparencies:

1. Should you plan transparencies to be viewed horizontally or vertically, or does it matter? Reasons?
2. What are the inside dimensions of a standard transparency mount?
3. How might you plan for student participation when developing a series of transparencies?
4. For what reasons might it *not* be advisable to use available printed pages as transparencies?
5. What things can you do to modify a printed illustration for use as a transparency?
6. For what reasons might you use coloring on a transparency?
7. What should be the minimum letter size used on transparencies?
8. What lettering aids might you use in preparing transparencies?
9. To ensure proper alignment when preparing to make overlays, what procedure is followed?

See answers on page 380.

PREPARING TRANSPARENCIES

Many processes have been developed for preparing transparencies. They range from very simple hand lettering or drawing to methods requiring special equipment and particular skills. Of these, only the most practical and proven techniques are considered here. They are as follows:

1. Computer-generated process
2. Thermal film
3. Electrostatic (xerography) film
4. Clear acetate
5. Photographic processes on film

Which method or methods to use? First, consider those most appropriate to your purposes, the subject matter, and the planned use for the transparencies. Your final decision should be based upon accessibility of equipment and materials, on your skills and available time, costs, and, certainly not of least importance, on your standards for quality. Refer to Table 12–1, Summary of Methods for Preparing Transparencies, page 210.

Finally, consider these questions as you start your preparations:

- Is the layout of the subject simple and clear?
- Have you checked the accuracy of content details?
- Will this be a single-sheet transparency or should you consider using overlays to separate elements of the subject—or might progressive disclosure by masking and uncovering of parts be effective?
- Will you plan to write some information on the finished transparency in addition to what is presented?

(It is often more effective to add details to an outline or diagram as the transparency is used, or to involve the audience with activities relating to the transparency during use.)

- Is color important to the subject and treatment? If so, how should it be prepared?
- Is it satisfactory to do the lettering freehand, or should you consider using a lettering aid, like a computer word processing or graphics program, dry-transfer letters, or a pressure-lettering machine (page 138)? Remember to make lettering large enough for easy viewing—¼ inch (18 point) minimum size (Adams).
- Will duplicates of the transparency be needed for other users?
- Will paper copies of the content of the transparency, or related information, be needed for distribution to the audience?

Computer-generated Process

Transparencies, in black-and-white or full color, can be created by applying graphics methods with a computer. Starting on page 119, advantages for using computer graphics systems and the required equipment are described, followed by explanations of the procedures for preparing graphic materials. Many kinds of visual information can be designed with a microcomputer having sufficient memory (RAM), a color graphics board, and a suitable graphics program.

Transparencies can be designed by three methods:

- Using common transparency formats with design and details already in the program. You need only to select a format and enter heading, text, numbers, or other data to create a transparency. This is called a *preformatted drawing system* (page 121).
- Modifying the standard format as the text or other data are entered. This includes lettering style and size, arrangement of content elements, use of symbols lines, boxes, circles, and choice of colors for elements and background. Such a procedure uses an *object-based drawing system* (page 122).
- Creating your own design with full flexibility for selection and arrangement of elements, graphics factors, lettering, and colors. This requires a *paint and enhancement system* on page 122.

A separate technique, using a scanner (page 120), allows the direct transfer of prepared artwork, available pictures, and other graphic and photographic visuals to the computer memory. Once in memory, the materials can be used directly, modified, or combined with other newly created graphics.

When designing transparencies with a computer,

give attention to legibility matters presented on page 135. Be especially alert to the following:

- Design transparencies in a *horizontal* format—usually termed *landscape orientation* in a page requestor.
- Do not crowd too much information onto a single transparency.
- Make characters (words and numbers) of a suitable size (minimum ¼ inch or 18 points in height).
- Be aware of the possible limitations of your equipment to produce high-resolution images (page 123).
- Provide satisfactory space between lines of text.
- Make lines thick enough and of suitable resolution for satisfactory reading.
- For both characters and areas, select colors and their intensity so that strong contrasting images will be projected.

After previewing an image on the display screen, it can be transferred to paper or film by using a printer. Depending on the printer, this can be done in black-and-white or in multiple colors.

Overhead transparencies and 2 × 2 inch slides can be computer-generated by applying similar procedures. For further details, see the information under computer-generated slides on page 226.

Electronic Data Projection Computer-generated transparencies also can be directly projected with an overhead projector from data stored on a computer disk. This requires the use of an electronic unit called a **liquid crystal display** (LCD). This display panel, which looks like a glass window the size of an overhead transparency, is plugged into the microcomputer monitor output and placed on the glass stage of the projector. When an image is called up from the data file on the disk, it appears on the window and is immediately projected onto the screen, either in monochrome or full color projection, depending on the LCD model. Also,

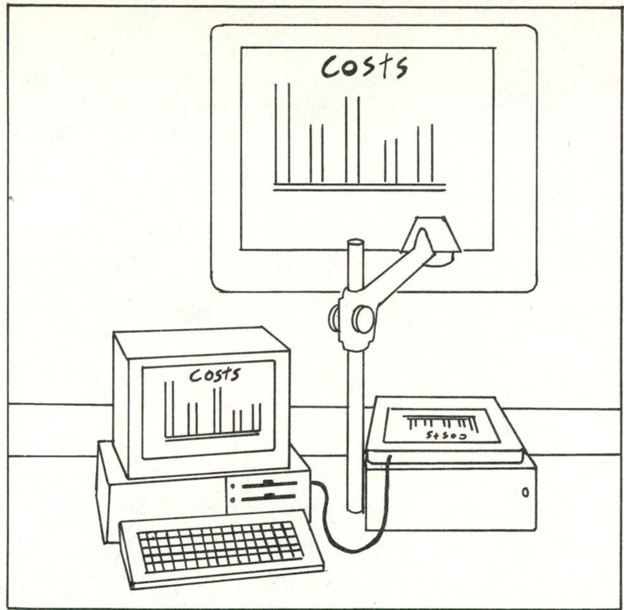

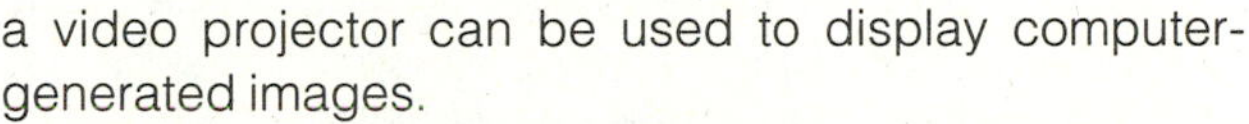

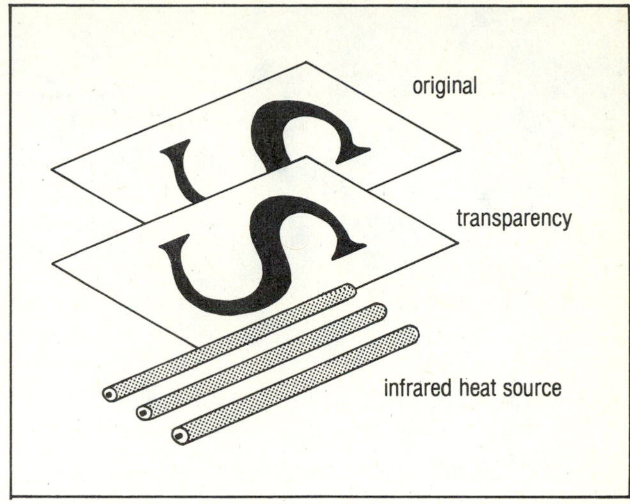

a video projector can be used to display computer-generated images.

By using the computer keyboard, or other input device, the image can be modified while it is being viewed. Be alert to the potential problems relating to the quality of LCD images. Review the suggestions on page 206. Plan and develop computer-based visuals so as to overcome the recognized limitations of LCD projection quality.

Thermal Film

Rapid process is a thermal film feature. It is completely dry, and transparencies are ready for immediate use. Heat from an **infrared light source** passes through the film to the original. The words and lines on the original must be prepared with "heat absorbing material," such as carbon-base ink or a soft lead pencil. These markings absorb heat, and the resulting increase in temperature affects the film, forming an image on it within a few seconds.

No special paper is required for the preparation of original printing or master diagrams. White bond paper is preferable and graph paper with light blue lines can be used as the lines do not reproduce. **Thermal film** also can be used to prepare transparencies from black line printed illustrations and those from electrostatic-process paper copies (page 208). The latter may be black-and-white copies of color originals, or paste-ups containing various items attached to paper.

The film to make thermal transparencies is of two types (check specific instructions with the product you use):

- Single sheet film
- Film with a disposal transfer sheet

A few brands of thermal copy machines are available. In each, the principle of thermal reproduction is the same. Most carry the original and film on a belt or between rollers around the infrared light source. The basic steps in the use of these machines are as follows:

1. Set the control dial as directed (usually at the eight or nine o'clock position). Turn on the machine if necessary.
2. Place the thermal film (with the notch in the upper

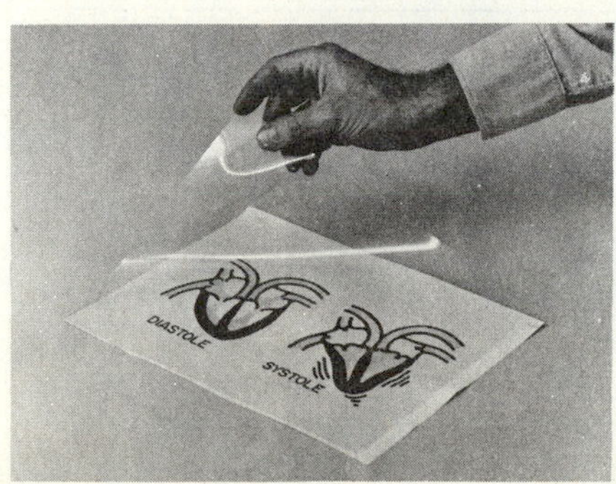

2

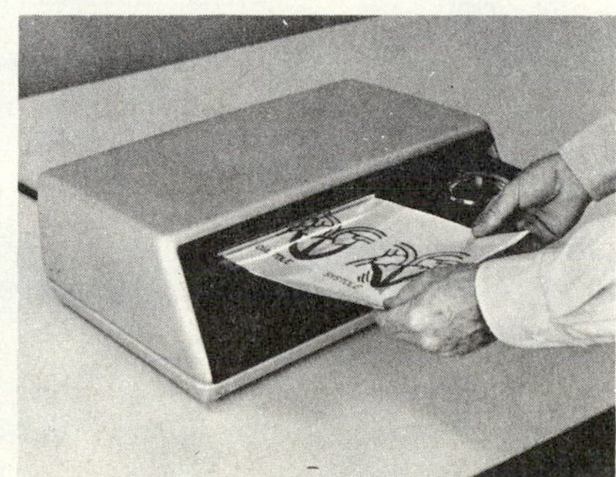

3

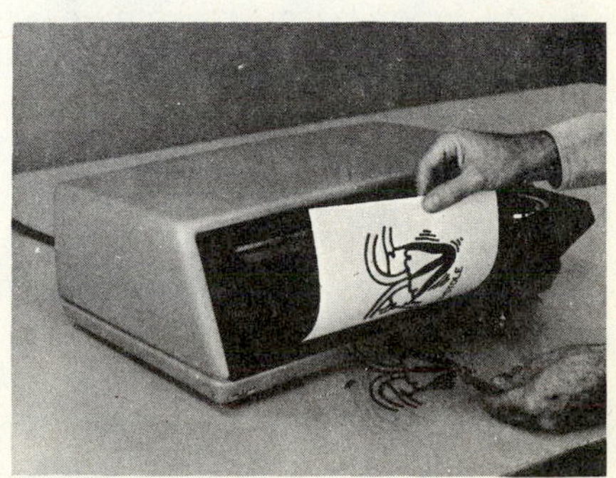

4

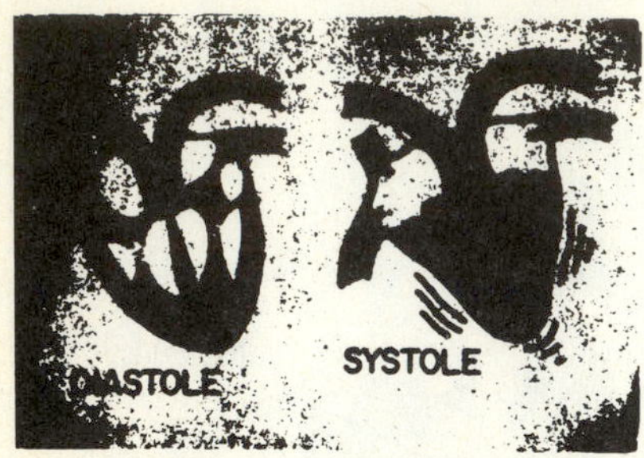

Overexposed

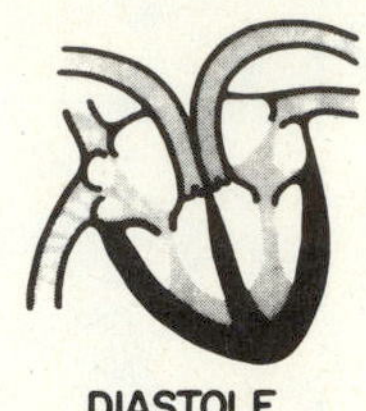

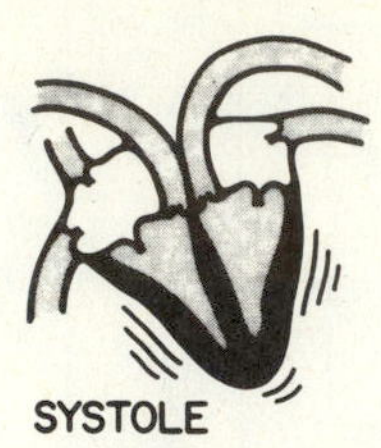

Correctly Exposed

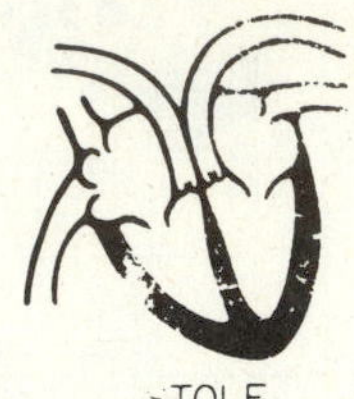

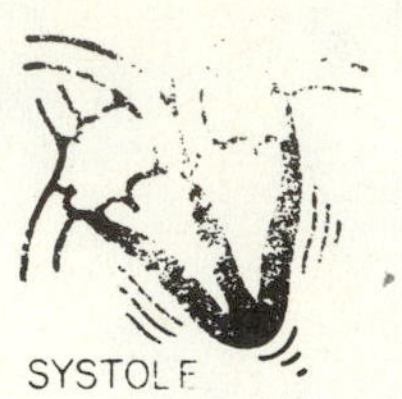

Underexposed

right corner when the film is held vertically) on the original material.

3. With the film on top, feed the two into the machine.
4. When the two emerge, separate the film from the original. Discard the transfer sheet if necessary.

The transparency image may be *too light,* or *too faint,* for satisfactory projection; if so, print it again with a fresh sheet of film, *increasing* the exposure time (that is, with the machine running at *slower* speed). A faint thermal transparency has been *underexposed.*

If, on the contrary, the transparency is *too dense,* or if there is *unwanted background tone,* print the transparency again with a fresh sheet of film, shortening the exposure time (that is, with the machine running at *faster* speed). A thermal transparency that is too dense has been *overexposed.*

Clean the belt or glass surface of the machine frequently to ensure transparencies without dirt spots.

The thermal process requires attention to a number of details and permits the use of a number of effective techniques:

- Original materials for thermal reproduction should be prepared with black drawing ink, soft lead pencil, or as a computer-generated paper copy from a laser printer. Also, electrostatic paper copies have carbon-based images and make excellent originals for thermal reproduction. Black printing inks are satisfactory, but inks of other colors, regular ball-point pens, and some felt-tipped pens are not suitable for thermal reproduction. However, with anything that is non-carbon-based, make an electrostatic copy and use it as a master in thermal reproduction.
- If using drawing ink, make sure the ink is completely dry before the master is run in the copy machine.
- If you are uncertain about correct exposure or about the reproduction quality of a diagram, use test strips of the thermal film before exposing a whole sheet. Cut six vertical strips, being sure to clip a corner of each for proper placement of the diagram.
- In addition to black-image film, various colored-image, tinted (color background for black image), and negative films (black background with clear or colored image) are available. While some presenters believe tinted-background film reduces eye fatigue, there is evidence that better visual acuity is achieved with clear-background transparencies (Snowberg).
- Add color to areas on a transparency with felt pens that are of the type that will project.

Electrostatic Film

With the appropriate electrostatic film for the brand of plain paper copier to be used, transparencies can be prepared from most printed or drawn illustrations. See page 191 for a visual description of the electrostatic process. An important feature of this process is that many electrostatic machines can reduce and enlarge illustrations to a suitable size to fit properly within the mounting frame.

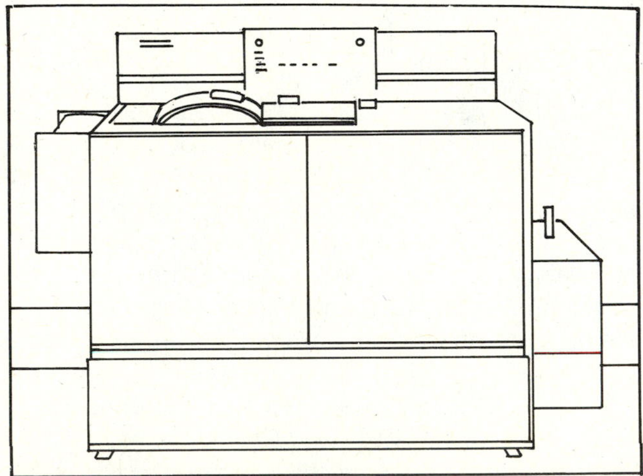

Black line electrostatic film is available with either a clear or colored background. In addition, color electrostatic copy machines can reproduce multicolor originals in overhead transparency format.

Here are some suggestions to consider when planning to make electrostatic transparencies:

- Any original, either drawn, printed, or computer-generated, can be used to prepare a transparency.
- Many machines will enlarge or reduce an original to fit the transparency format size.

- A transparency of uniform density and maximum clarity will be made from an original having a good black line image on white paper.
- By covering sections of an original, separate transparency masters can be made when overlays are to be prepared. Light lines that result at the edge of a mask can be erased.
- Colors and gray areas result in a transparency with varying degrees of density and clarity.
- Place only a single sheet of film on the paper feed tray and run through the machine. Repeat this procedure with each master for transparency preparation.
- Add color to areas on a thermal transparency with appropriate felt pens (page 130).

Clear Acetate

With the clear acetate technique transparencies are prepared easily and quickly. They are not durable. For repeated use, neater and more permanent methods are advisable. But use this technique for trying out your visuals; then, if necessary, make revisions before redoing them in permanent form.

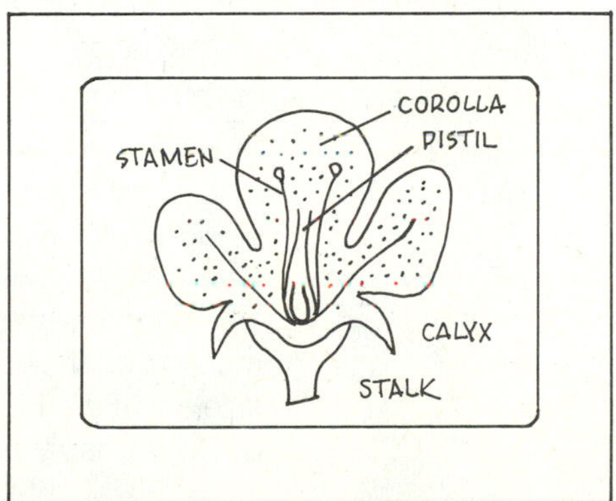

On paper, outline the boundaries of the opening in the mount that you will use. Still on paper, make a sketch or position an illustration for tracing. Then, using the appropriate tools, put your drawing or tracing on **acetate.** Complete the transparency as directed later in this chapter. As indicated on page 130 under Adding Color, the fine-tipped felt pens are designed for drawing lines and writing, while the broad-tipped ones are useful for coloring areas. Select felt pens that are suitable for use on acetate. They produce transparent colors that can be either *permanent* or *washable.* The permanent-type inks require a plastic cleaner or other solvent (such as lighter fluid) for removal. Marks made with water-base felt pens can be removed with a damp cloth.

To protect the surface of a transparency made with washable inks, cover it with a clear sheet of acetate.

Some inks tend to run slightly; therefore use pens lightly. Also, colors may not take to the acetate evenly; therefore consider using a stippling method (small dots of ink) to color large areas.

Photographic Processes on Film

Situations do arise in which the only way to create an overhead transparency is to produce it using photographic methods. An example may be when you have an existing photographic negative of a scene or an object that is of historical significance and you want to incorporate it into a presentation along with other transparencies. The best solution is to take the negative to a commercial photo shop and request an 8 × 10 enlargement on appropriate photographic film.

- Enlarge line drawings and print-based, black-line materials onto a lithographic or high contrast film.
- Enlarge black-and-white continuous tone negatives onto a fine-grain positive, continuous tone film.
- Enlarge color negatives onto an appropriate color positive film.

The costs for producing overhead transparencies by photographic methods can be considerably more than for the other methods discussed in this chapter.

Although not directly a photographic process, 35mm color slides and color prints or color pictures can be converted into overhead transparencies with some full-color electrostatic-type copy machines. Many copy centers provide this service.

What You Have Learned About Preparing Transparencies:

1. Which software system would you use to prepare computer-generated transparencies according to each of the following?
   a. Design transparencies according to preset factors but change arrangement of elements to

(continued)

TABLE 12–1 SUMMARY OF METHODS FOR PREPARING TRANSPARENCIES

METHOD	EQUIPMENT	COST OF MATERIALS (APPROXIMATE)	TIME FOR PREPARATION	EVALUATION
Computer-generated process (page 206)	Computer, program, and printer	\$2.00–\$20.00	Short	Design ideas can be tried out and best selected; complex graphics easily prepared in black-and-white or full color with suitable equipment
Thermal film (page 207)	Thermal copier	\$0.40–\$0.75	Very brief	Good method for rapid preparation of one-color transparencies from single sheets
Electrostatic film (page 208)	Electrostatic copy machine	\$0.50–\$1.00	Brief	Requires an expensive, but readily available, machine and a special film
Clear acetate (page 209)	None	\$0.20–\$0.30	Moderate	Suitable for quick preparation and temporary use; lacks professional appearance
Photographic processes—high-contrast film (high-contrast or continuous-tone copy) (page 209)	Camera and darkroom or commercial service	\$1.50–\$20.00	Up to 1 day	Most complex process in terms of skills, equipment, facilities, and time; but useful when original materials must be changed in size; results in high-quality transparencies

better communicate the information.

b. Arrange details for a transparency entirely as you would prefer to have them, including designing your own artwork.

c. Requestors on screen lead you to input data that create each transparency.

2. What are six factors to consider when using a computer program to design a transparency?
3. How do you finally get the transparency for use after generating it with a computer?
4. What equipment is required to project data directly from computer memory to the projection screen?
5. What single-step reproduction method can be used to make a transparency consisting of any writing material on any kind of paper?
6. What is the main thing to check when preparing or selecting a diagram to be made into a thermal transparency?
7. Is the kind of paper for the master important in the thermal process?
8. If lines on a thermal transparency are very weak and thin, is the firm *over-* or *underexposed?* The next time, must you *slow down* or *speed up* the machine?
9. How might small areas be colored on a thermal transparency?
10. Which process might be used to reproduce a printed diagram consisting of three colors?

11. Are all felt pens suitable for use on acetate?
12. How can you remove the markings of a permanent felt pen?
13. Do felt pens cover areas evenly?
14. How would you protect from smearing a transparency that has been made with water-base felt pens?
15. By what two methods can a small-size black drawing be reproduced as a transparency?
16. How can a slide be reproduced as a full-size transparency?

See answers on page 380.

COMPLETING AND FILING TRANSPARENCIES

Mounting

Mounting adds durability and ease to the handling of a transparency, but it is not always necessary to mount transparencies in cardboard frames. Those prepared on polyester film will lie flat. Transparencies to be used only once can be left unmounted since the cost of frames and the time to attach them may not be justified. It may be preferable to enclose transparencies in individual plastic folders that are punched for 3–ring binders (see 3M product in Sources listing).

The standard-size cardboard or plastic frame easily fits into letter-size filing cabinets. If overlays are to be used, mounting is essential. Another advantage for mounting transparencies is to block out light around the edge of the visual when placed on the projection surface glass.

Tape a single-sheet transparency to the *underside* of the frame. Use masking or plastic tape rather than cellophane tape for binding.

If the transparency consists of a base and overlays, tape the base to the underside of the mount as usual, and the overlays to the face. Be sure the overlays register with the base and with each other (page 204). Then, fasten each overlay with a tape or plastic hinge along one edge of the cardboard frame.

Overlays for successive or cumulative use can be mounted on the left or right sides of the cardboard frame, also if necessary on the bottom and top (the top edge should be the last one used). Trim any excess acetate from the edges of overlays so opposite or adjacent ones fit easily into place.

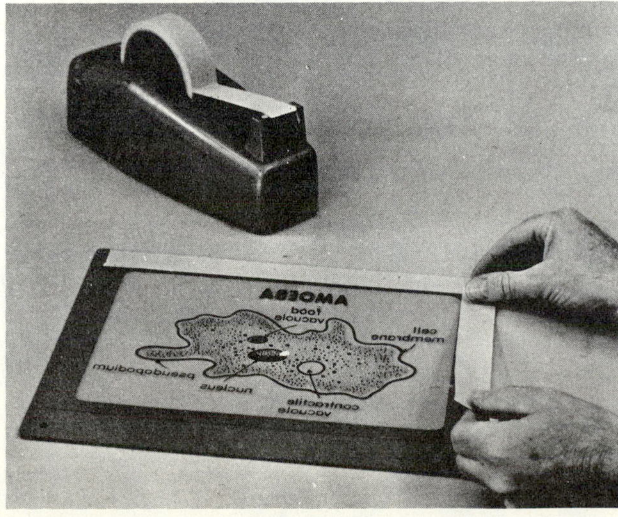

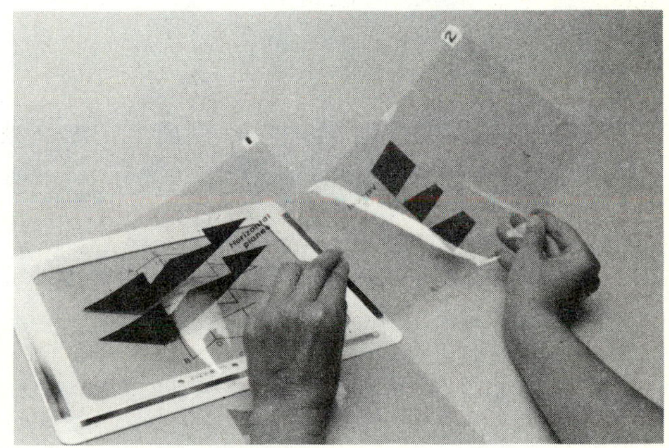

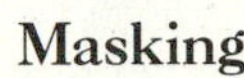

After mounting overlays, fold and attach small tabs of masking tape or adhesive-back labels on the loose upper corner of each overlay. Number them to indicate the order of use. These tabs are easy to grasp when overlays are to be set in place over the base transparency.

Masking

To control a presentation and focus attention on specific elements of a transparency, use a paper or cardboard mask, as was mentioned on page 203. The mask may be a separate unit, mounted to move vertically or horizontally, to expose portions of a transparency. Pieces of hinged cardboard can cover sections of content. Attach each one to an edge of the transparency frame and flip it back to reveal information in a sequential order.

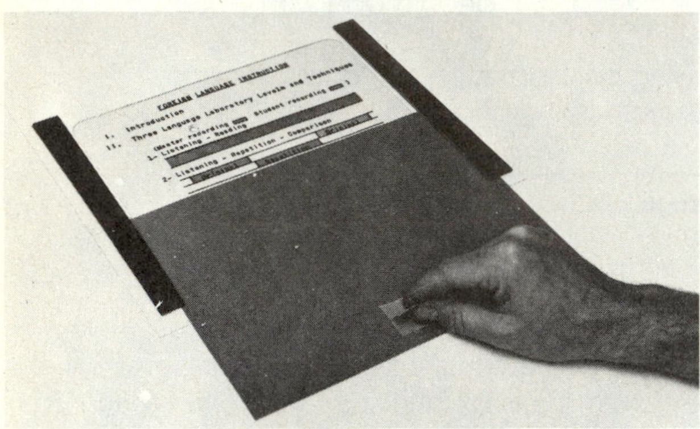

Adding Notes

Write brief notes along the margin of the cardboard mount for reference during projection.

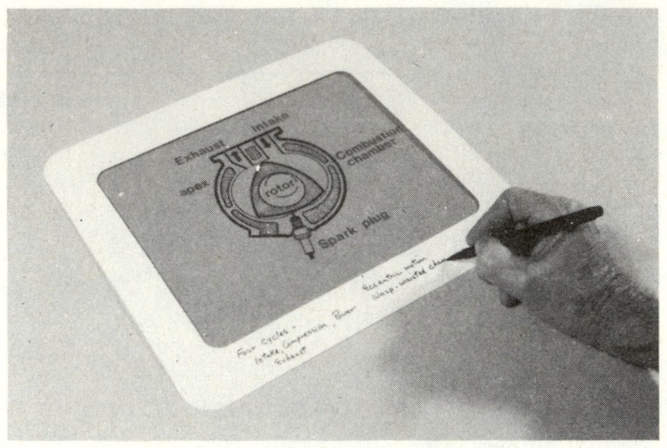

Filing

If your transparencies are in mounts 10 × 12 inches or smaller, they will fit in the drawer of a standard filing cabinet. File them under appropriate subject, unit, or topic headings.

What You Have Learned About Completing and Filing Transparencies:

1. Do you correctly mount a single-sheet transparency on the underside or the face of the cardboard frame?
2. How is a transparency with overlays mounted?
3. What are two ways of masking transparencies?
4. What filing system for transparencies might you use?

See answers on page 380.

REFERENCES

JOURNALS FOR SOURCES

AV Video
Montage Publishing Co., 701 Westchester Ave., White Plains, NY 10604.

AVC Presentations for the Visual Communicator
PTN Publishing Co., 445 Board Hollow Rd., Melville, NY 11747.

Presentation Products
Pacific Magazine Group, Inc., 513 Wilshire Blvd., Santa Monica, CA 90401.

Adams, Sarah; Rosemier, Robert; and Sleeman, Philip. "Readable Letter Size and Visibility for Overhead Projection Transparencies." *AV Communication Review* 13 (Winter 1965): 412–417.

Clark, Bill, and Creager, Agatha. "Communicating with Computer-Generated Transparencies." *Audio Visual Directions* 3 (October/November 1981): 69–73.

Green, Lee, and Dengerink, Don. *501 Ways to Use the*

Overhead Projector. Littleton, CO: Libraries Unlimited, 1982.

"LCD Panels." *Electronic Learning* 10 (March 1991): 46–49.

Moyer, Jim. "Using a Data Projection Panel as a Teaching Tool." *T.H.E. Journal* 17 (March 1990): 75–77.

Rauen, Christopher. "LCD Panels Bring Presentations Down to Size." *AV Video* 13 (May 1991): 50–57.

Snowberg, R. L. "Bases for the Selection of Background Colors for Transparencies." *AV Communication Review* 21 (Summer 1973): 191–207.

SOURCES FOR EQUIPMENT AND MATERIALS

Arkwright Corp., 538 Main St., Fiskeville, RI 02823.

Avcom Systems Inc., P.O. Box 977, 250 Cox Lane, Cutchogue, NY 11935.

Avery Commercial Products Division, 818 Oak Park Road, Covina, CA 91724.

Elmo Manufacturing Corp., 70 New Hyde Park Road, New Hyde Park, NY 11040.

Folex Film Systems, 6 Haniel Road East, Fairfield, NJ 07004.

Labelon Corp., 10 Chapin Street, Canandaigua, NY 14424.

Tersch Products, Inc., P.O. Box 118, 22401 Industrial Blvd., Rogers, MN 55374.

3M Company, Visual Systems Division, Bldg. A1–45–5N–01, P.O. Box 2963, Austin, TX 78769.

CHAPTER

13

Audio Recordings

Besides being used to play music, audio recordings can provide motivation, convey information, provide drill and practice, or teach a skill. With worksheets and other materials, audio recordings can serve as the study guide and information source for various instructional and training needs. Recordings also can be used in conjunction with projected visual materials. The latter use is described with specific instructional media in other chapters of this book. This chapter considers audio recordings by themselves or as the study guide along with other materials, for instructional purposes. In Chapter 19, on page 343, further attention is given to integrating audio materials with instruction.

RECORDINGS TO MOTIVATE OR INFORM

If the objective of your recording is primarily to provide an introduction, an orientation, or general information about a topic, then the preparation of the recording may require any of a number of techniques, from simply documenting a speech on tape to a sophisticated dramatic presentation or other multiple voice and sound combination.

Planning

Give attention to the following:

- Consider the **audience** that will use the recording so that you will be assured of meeting their interests and needs (page 42).
- Identify the broad **purpose** or specific **objectives** that will be served by the recording (page 43).
- Prepare an **outline of the content** to be treated, if appropriate (page 45).
- Develop a **script** in sequential, narrative, or dramatic form (page 67). This will indicate the role for each voice and the use of music or other effects.
- Detailed **notes** of the content may be all that is required for an informational narration.

Techniques

Because an audio recording is designed to appeal to only the sense of hearing, it is necessary to make an extra effort to hold a listener's attention. To do this, pace the message briskly and deliver it in a succinct, clear, personal, and informal manner. Then carefully edit the recording to eliminate lengthy pauses, distractions or repetitions, and any unimportant or inappropriate sections. The result can be a product that is superior to and more useful than the original recording.

As the listener interprets the verbal message, mental impressions are formed. To make these impressions as effective and memorable as possible, various techniques may be employed:

- Keep the recording short. While the complete recording may be 30 minutes in length, subtopics should be limited to only 5 to 8 minutes.
- Voice tone should be conversational, friendly, and direct.
- Condense speeches and other unscripted verbal presentations by eliminating extraneous material. Avoid long, complex sentences. Use a narrator's voice to make logical bridges from one section to the next, and to reinforce or summarize key points of content.
- Include music. It can provide a break between sections and continuity throughout the presentation.
- A recording that is dynamic and helps to maintain a high interest level may include a variety of features—two or more voices, music, sound effects, indications of being at different locations, and a summary of what has been presented.

The most common use of a tape recorder is to document a speech or other verbal event. In addition, for motivation and information purposes, a recording might be prepared to do the following:

- Report on highlights of a meeting
- Serve as a magazine or journal containing a report on new developments, programs, or personalities in a subject area or an organization
- Interview notable persons
- Provide for a group discussion or a question-and-answer presentation of a topic
- Introduce new personnel to a program, to a facility,

EXAMPLE: Script of Audiotape Recording to Inform

Our purpose is to explore some of the more promising alternative energy sources in view of the critical energy crisis period we are now entering. The causes for this crisis are threefold:

First, costs for fossil fuels are increasing. Second, the reserve of fossil fuels is limited and rapidly diminishing. And third, pollution of the atmosphere is an unfortunate result of both coal and oil uses.

What options are available to us for moving away from these fossil fuels and providing suitable amounts of clean, dependable energy at suitable prices within our technological know-how for our *own* personal or family uses and on a national level?

Most exploratory work and actual development of alternative energy production are related to nuclear, solar, geothermal, and wind sources. These represent the major hopes for both the short and the long term when supplies of oil and natural gas become too expensive to use and reach depletion. Let's examine each one in detail.

[and so on] . . .

to a procedure, or to the requirements for a task

- Document role-playing situations, as performed by members of a group, for following analysis
- Present or explain problem situations for groups or individuals to solve
- Serve as a major source of information and entertainment for blind persons

Producing the Recording

Preparing the tape will require attention to the various matters considered in Chapter 9. Follow those steps that are important in your situation in order to ensure a quality recording. If you plan to use more than a single voice, such as a speaker as well as someone to introduce, interpret, or summarize parts of the presentation, then you may be required to mix voices and edit the tape.

Packaging for Use

After the master recording has been completed and duplicate cassettes have been prepared, package the program for use. This should include attention to:

- Using an "indexing" method for locating sections of the recording, as described later in this chapter.
- Considering the advisability of copyrighting the recording (page 175).
- Making and applying labels to identify the program.
- Preparing printed information that outlines the content and suggests uses for the tape as related to listener job responsibilities in an organization. This material may be placed on the inside of the container cover or separately on paper.
- Obtaining containers for individual cassettes or albums for sets of cassettes.
- Providing for availability of cassette recorders to be used with cassettes.
- Planning distribution through a media service, an organization's office, or by mail.

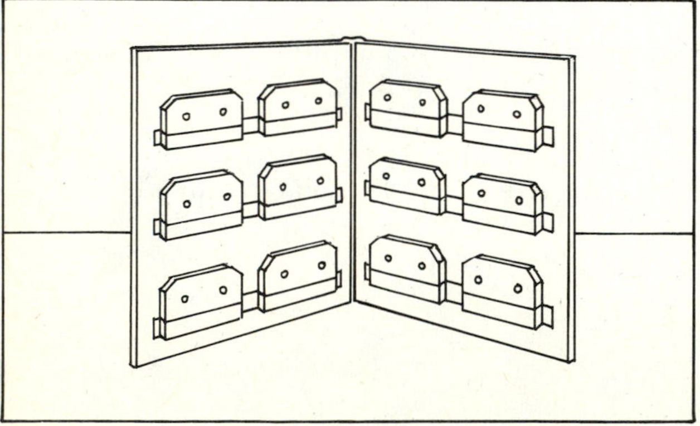

RECORDINGS TO INSTRUCT

Although instructional recordings might be used with a group as all members listen and participate in the learning activities, it is more common to provide them for individual self-paced learning. Differences in learning rates, the desire to replay a section of a recording, and the need for time to think about something just presented all indicate that for effective learning to take place each person should be allowed to use a recording at his or her own pace.

A key feature of successful instruction with audio recordings is the opportunity for an individual to react to the material being presented. This requires answering questions, solving problems, using the information, or applying the concepts and principles presented. The individual then receives feedback on answers, either on tape or on accompanying paper. See the introduction to *reactive* learning on page 296.

Tape recordings have essential roles in two instructional formats. One is the **audio-notebook** and the other is the **audio-tutorial** system (AT).

An audio-notebook consists of a study guide and workbook combination or separate worksheets that accompany the tape recording (Langdon). The tape may introduce the topic, explain or describe content, and periodically direct the user to activities in the workbook. The workbook may include questions, exercises, and problems that are to be completed. Answers and followup discussions are provided on the tape or provided on other pages. The study guide may contain supplementary reading materials, direct the learner to other references, and provide self-check tests for the learner.

In the audio-tutorial system a tape recording serves as the central part of a study unit (Postlethwait, Russell). The tape may provide information and also direct the learner to various learning activities—reading pages in a textbook, examining materials, making observations, performing experiments, completing worksheets, and so on. Feedback is provided on the tape as answers or topics offered for discussion. A major difference between the audio-notebook and the AT system is that with the latter, the resources and activities correlated with the audio recording generally go beyond what is immediately on paper for the learner to use.

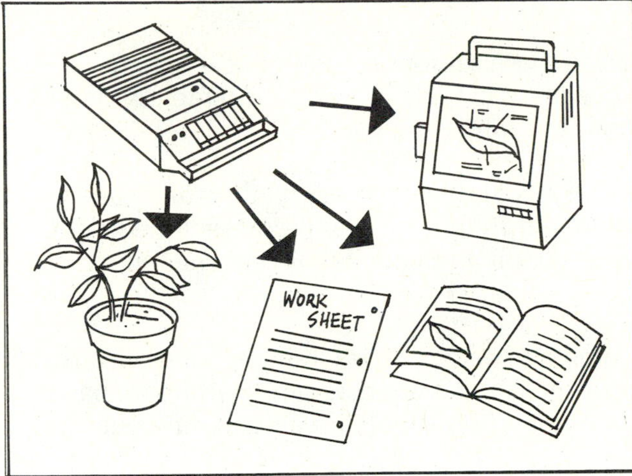

Another application of audio recording can be to provide a more efficient method of grading term papers and other written assignments. The instructor requires each learner in the class or training session to hand in a blank audiocassette with an assignment. As the instructor reviews the paper, comments are made on the tape, placed in a recorder. For example, the instructor may say, "On page three of your paper, the second paragraph has three spelling errors . . . see if you can find and correct them. Also, the first sentence would be better worded if you substitute the word *imperil* for *endanger.*" The instructor hands back the graded paper along with the audio recording to the learner. The recording is listened to as the paper is reviewed.

Planning

With either the audio-notebook or audio-tutorial method the following planning steps should receive attention:

- Consider the **group** or **individuals** who will use the materials (page 42).
- List **objectives** for the topic to be treated (page 43).
- Develop an **outline of the content** that relates to the objectives (page 45).
- Decide on the **activities** and **resources** relating to the content that will be used.
- Decide on **where** the recording will be used since this may affect how reference is made to obtaining and using support materials.
- Prepare the **script** or detailed notes for the recording (page 67).
- Write accompanying **worksheets, guides, activity sheets,** and so forth (page 194).

The recording portions of the lesson should be structured to contain the following:

- A motivational portion that introduces the lesson, lists the objectives, and indicates any special preparation required (unless these elements are provided in the worksheet)
- Explicit instructions for participation work
- Indications of the correct responses for immediate feedback
- Summary and/or instructions leading to other materials or activities
- Pauses of sufficient length (or instructions to turn off the recorder, or four to five seconds of music) to allow for completion of responses or performance of activities

Instead of initially preparing the script on paper, consider ad-libbing the necessary information as a recording on tape, then type out the material, edit the script, and rerecord in final form.

Producing the Recording

A special feature of this type of instructional material is that the recording should convey a warm, personal feeling to the learner using it. This means that your voice should be conversational and informal as if you were talking directly to a learner. If you speak too slowly, the pace will drag and learners will become disinterested. Many of the suggestions offered under the Techniques section in this chapter should be applied here.

When learners are first introduced to this method, they should be encouraged to stop the tape at any point and relisten to any portion. Remember that you are providing timely information, definitions, parenthetical explanations, and elaborations on other materials with which the learner is directed to study or work. The tone of your voice places emphasis on important points and expresses authority not served through the written word.

The recording for instruction should not be a straight-through lecture. Listening to only a voice for 5 to 6 minutes may be acceptable, but at approximately 10 minutes of continual listening, learner interest drops. A procedure such as this may be used: (1) information briefly presented on tape; (2) learner participation through an activity or through replying to questions about the information; (3) a review of the results of the activity or the correct answers; (4) on to further explanation or new information.

EXAMPLE: Script of Audiotape Recording to Instruct

The subject of this program is an examination of alternative energy sources. Please look over the objectives you are to satisfy on page 1 of the study guide. Then read the brief article by C. P. Nelson starting on page 2. It establishes a good base for the energy crisis that we now face. Identify the three main reasons for the crisis. Turn off the tape. Start again with me when you are ready. (Pause)

By reading the Nelson article, you should have identified these reasons for the critical energy crisis: (1) costs of fossil fuels are increasing; (2) the reserve of fossil fuels is limited and rapidly diminishing; (3) pollution of the atmosphere is a result of both coal and oil uses.

Now let's turn to the options. Most exploratory work and actual development of alternative energy production are related to nuclear, solar, geothermal, and wind sources. These represent the major hopes for both the short and the long term when supplies of oil and natural gas become too expensive to use or become depleted.

We'll examine each one—first, nuclear power. The potential energy locked in the nucleus of an atom can be released by two processes—*fission* and *fusion.* Look at the diagrams starting on page 5 of your guide as I discuss these two forms of nuclear energy. You should be able to differentiate between the two forms.

[and so on] ...

Plan for variety in pacing by including various kinds of activities requiring differing lengths of time. All these techniques can contribute to maintaining learner interest and alertness.

When you are ready to make the recording, refer to the preparation and recording procedures in Chapter 9.

Indexing the Tape

Instead of requiring that a person listen to the complete recording from start to finish, you may wish to provide flexibility for the learner to select parts of a recording for listening and omit other sections. This may relate to material for certain objectives that a learner needs, or chooses, to work with while electing to bypass other material. As a result of an answer to a question or problem, you may wish to "branch" the learner to the review or the advanced material. Additionally, the learner may wish to repeat only certain sections of a recording.

Normally, in order to satisfy each of these needs, the learner haphazardly moves ahead in the tape by using the fast forward control on the recorder, hoping to stop about where the listening should start. With the **Zimdex** method, index numbers are placed on the *second* track of a monophonic cassette tape that the learner will use in order to locate accurately any section of the recording (Rahmlow et al.).

The method works in the following manner:

1. On side 1 record the scripted information.
2. On side 2, starting at the beginning, record a series of numbers—1, 2, 3, 4, 5 . . .—for the full length of the tape. Leave a 5-second pause after each number.
3. Return to side 1 and listen to the material recorded. Prepare a list of the sections of content that you wish to index for location.

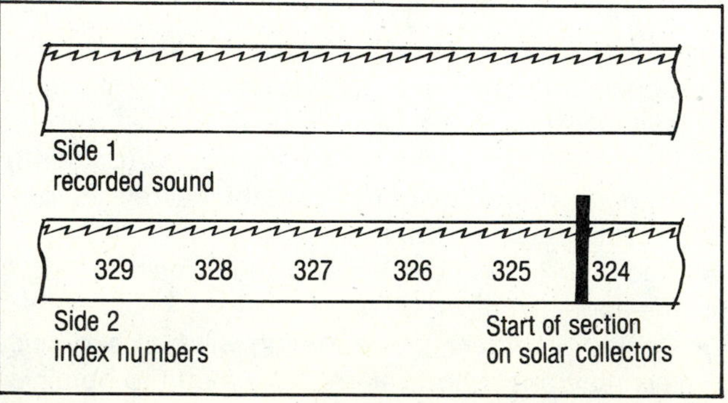

4. Play side 1 again. Just before the beginning of each section, turn the tape over and listen for the number that corresponds to the starting point for that section. Note the index number. An example of an index is shown in the next column.

A person wishing to locate a section of the recording starts on side 2 of the tape, moving the tape fast forward. Periodically the tape is stopped and played as the user listens for an index number. Right after the appropriate number is heard, the cassette should be turned to side 1.

Provide the user with a topic list along with index numbers like the following:

SUBJECT	INDEX NUMBER
Advantages of solar energy	385
Collection process	354
Solar collectors	324
Scientific principles used	281
Storing energy for space heating	259
Heating water	231

The beginning of the desired material is ready to be heard. If you have an extensive music collection on audiocassettes, the index numbers can help you to locate selections.

Preparing the Recording and Accompanying Materials for Use

When the master recording is completed, it will be necessary to:

- Make duplicate cassette copies of the tape (page 102).
- Prepare accompanying printed materials in final form and duplicate (page 193). It is often desirable to provide learners with a printed copy of an instructor's narration. Some learners prefer to read the words as they are spoken or use the script for review.
- Collect other materials that may be required as part of the unit.
- Consider the advisability of copyrighting the recording and/or complete package (page 175).
- Label individual items so that each is properly marked for easy identification.
- Package each unit or set of materials for use.
- Plan for distribution and use.

What You Have Learned About Making Audio Recordings:

1. How does a recording that is designed to inform differ from one designed to instruct?
2. What are *five* uses for which an informational audiotape might be prepared?
3. What are some techniques that may be used when preparing a motivational or informational recording?
4. What two formats might instructional tape recordings take? What is the difference?
5. What planning steps should be followed in preparing an instructional tape?
6. What are examples of the activities that can be correlated with the use of recordings for instruction?
7. What type of mood should the tape for an AT unit have?
8. What might be the limit of time for required listening to a section of an instructional tape having no other activity?
9. Of the procedures described in Chapter 9, which ones will you refer to for help in making your recording?
10. Describe how you might prepare an index for locating sections on a recording.

See answers on page 381.

REFERENCES

Hall, William. "Audio." *AV Video* (monthly column).

Langdon, Danny G. *The Audio-Workbook.* The Instructional Design Library, vol. 3. Englewood Cliffs, NJ: Educational Technology Publications, 1978.

Postlethwait, S. N.; Novak, J.; and Murray, H. *The Audio-Tutorial Approach to Learning.* Minneapolis: Burgess, 1972.

Rahmlow, Harold F.; Langdon, Danny G.; and Lewis, William C. "Audio Indexing for Individualization." *Audiovisual Instruction* 18 (April 1973): 14–15.

Russell, James D. *The Audio-Tutorial System.* The Instructional Design Library, vol. 3. Englewood Cliffs, NJ: Educational Technology Press, 1978.

Sunier, John. *Slide/Sound and Filmstrip Production.* New York, NY: Focal Press, 1981.

JOURNALS FOR SOURCES OF EQUIPMENT AND MATERIALS

AV Video
Montage Publishing Co., 701 Westchester Ave., White Plains, NY 10604.

AVC Presentation for the Visual Communicator
PTN Publishing Co., 445 Broad Hollow Rd., Melville, NY 11747.

Directory of Video, Computer, and Audio-Visual Products
International Communications Industries Association, 3150 Spring Street, Fairfax, VA 22031.

Presentation Products
Pacific Magazine Group, Inc., 513 Wilshire Blvd., Santa Monica, CA 90401.

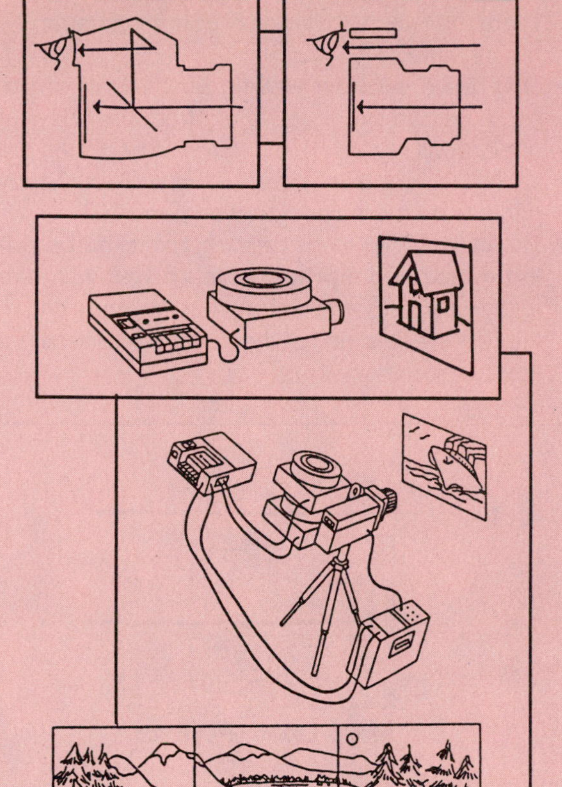

CHAPTER 14

There are both similarities and differences between a slide series and a multi-image presentation. While their structure is based on the projection of slides synchronized with sound, the multi-image presentation not only uses multiple images on one or more screens, but may also include other media, such as film footage or a video recording. Therefore the planning of a multi-image presentation is more complex, involving more elements.

PLANNING SLIDE AND MULTI-IMAGE PROGRAMS

Before making slides or a multi-image presentation, always consider this planning checklist:

- Have you clearly expressed **your idea** and limited the topic (page 41)?
- Will your program be for **motivational, informational,** or **instructional purposes** (page 42)?
- Have you considered the **audience** that will use the materials and its characteristics (page 42)?
- Have you stated the **objectives** your slide series should serve (page 43)?

Slide Series and Multi-Image Presentations

- Have you prepared a **content outline** (page 45)?
- Have you written a **treatment** to help organize the content and then sketched a **storyboard** to assist in your visualization of the content (page 65)?
- Have you decided that a **slide series or a multi-image presentation is an appropriate medium** for accomplishing the purposes (page 58)?
- Have you prepared a **scene-by-scene script** as a guide for your picture taking and sound recording (page 67)?
- Have you considered the **specifications** necessary for your materials (page 70)?
- Have you, if necessary, **selected other people to assist** you with the preparation of visual and audio materials (page 44)?

The production of a slide series or multi-image presentation involves nine major activities: (1) taking pictures, (2) preparing art work and title slides, (3) processing film, (4) mounting slides, (5) editing slides, (6) duplicating slides, (7) recording and synchronizing sound, (8) filing slides, and (9) preparing to use the program.

The information in Part Three, Chapters 7, 8, and 9, on photography, graphic techniques, and sound recording is basic to the successful preparation of a slide series or a multi-image presentation. As necessary, refer to the page references indicated with the following topics.

PREPARING AND TAKING PICTURES

Your Camera

Although other format cameras can be used, the majority of slides are made with 35mm cameras. Those cameras with adjustable lens settings (*f*/numbers), shutter speeds, and attachments for focusing are especially useful since their flexibility enables you to record various subjects under almost any light and action conditions.

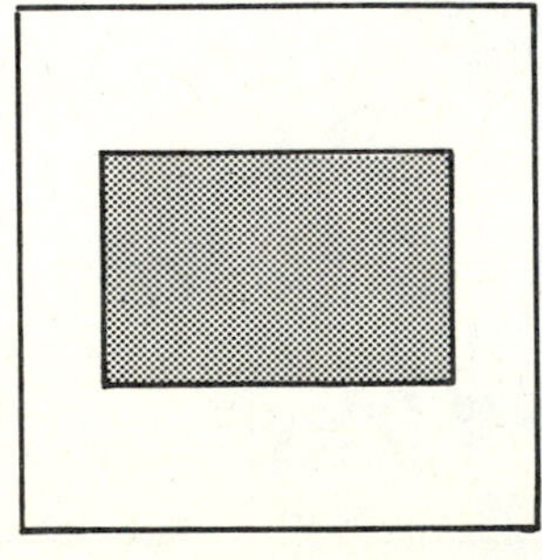

2 × 2 (35mm film)

There are two major types of 35mm cameras:

- One has a **window viewfinder** through which you see a picture slightly different from the one that the camera will record. This difference becomes greater as the camera gets closer to the subject. (Study the parallax problem described on page 103).
- The other (single-lens reflex camera) has a **reflecting mirror** and a **prism,** which permit you to accurately view the same picture that the lens transmits to the film—regardless of the distance from camera to subject.

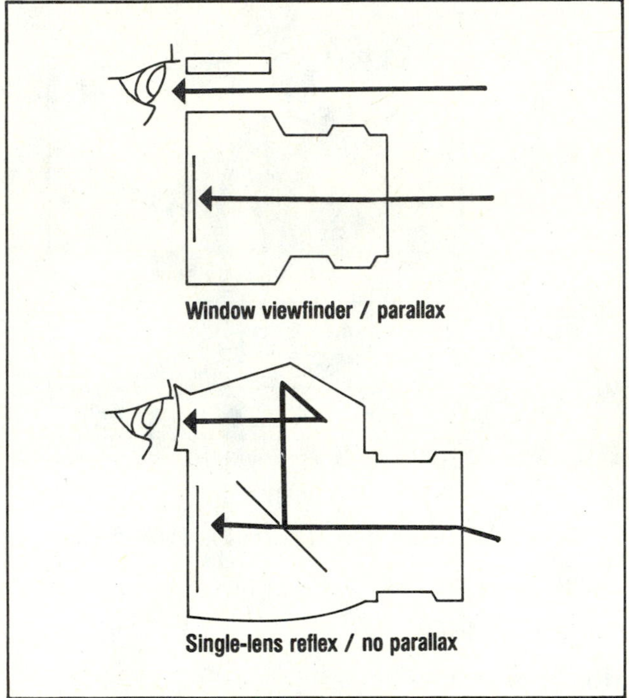

The single-lens reflex camera is preferable for picture taking in which framing is critical, as in close-up and copy work. On the other hand, the window viewfinder camera has the advantage of small size and compactness.

Carefully study the three settings that are made on adjustable cameras—lens diaphragm, shutter speed, and focus. Understand the purposes of each, the relationship of one to another, and to depth-of-field, and determine how each setting is made on your camera. These matters have been discussed and explained starting on page 81.

Accessories

You may find need for:

- A photographic light meter to determine exposure accurately (page 90)

- A tripod to steady the camera (When filming at shutter speeds slower than 1/30 second *always* use a tripod.)
- An electronic flash unit or photoflood lights for indoor scenes (page 93)
- A close-up attachment to photograph subjects at close range and to do copy work (page 103)
- A cable release to eliminate any possibility of jarring the camera during long exposures

Film

Select a reversal film to prepare slides when only one or a few copies will be needed. If many copies will be required, use a color negative film and have inexpensive positive slides made by contact printing the negative. If you wish to see the slides you shoot in less than 5 minutes, consider using Polaroid's *35mm Instant Slide System* (with Polapan film). It consists of color films for use with any 35mm camera. The film is developed in a manually operated processor for immediate viewing.

In addition to considering the factors about film explained on page 85, select film on the basis of the following:

- The main light source that will strike the subject (daylight, flash, or photoflood—3200°K; see the note about fluorescent lights on page 93)
- The anticipated light level (low, moderate, high)
- The desired reproduction of colors
- The expected number of pictures to be taken (based on 35mm 24- or 36-exposure cassettes or rolls)
- The manner of film processing (by film laboratory or by yourself)

The data about selected films given in Table 14–1 are correct as of the time of writing, but changes and new

TABLE 14–1 COMMONLY USED 35MM COLOR FILMS

FILMS (DAYLIGHT)	EXPOSURE INDEX (ISO)	LIGHT SOURCE	SUGGESTED USE
Kodak Ektachrome**	50, 64*, 100, 200, 400, 800/1600	Daylight	General purpose film with high color saturation, highlight detail, and sharpness.
Kodak Kodachrome**	25, 64, 200	Daylight	Extremely high sharpness under relatively high light conditions and good color saturation.
Fujichrome**	50, 100, 400, 1600*	Daylight	Versatile film for a variety of lighting conditions. Full gradation for brilliant highlights, vivid color reproduction, and sharpness.

FILMS (ARTIFICIAL LIGHT)	EXPOSURE INDEX (ISO)	LIGHT SOURCE	SUGGESTED USE
Kodak Ektachrome	64T*, 160T	Tungsten 3200K	High resolving power, fine grain, and sharpness. Excellent for copywork, or interior events.
Kodak Kodachrome (Type A)	40	Photolamp 3400K	Designed for studio work, making title slides, and copy work. Excellent definition.
Fujichrome	64T*, 160L*, 160S*	Tungsten 3200K	Professional tungsten films that give the variety of long and short exposure for optimum reproduction. High clarity, excellent for push processing and broad exposure latitude.

* These are professional films; your local photographic source can explain special handling.

** These film types have professional films available that have the same or similar film indexes.

TABLE 14–1 (*CONTINUED*)

DUPLICATING FILMS	FILM TYPE	SUGGESTED USE
Kodak Ektachrome Dup.	5071	Designed to duplicate Ektachrome Slides.
Kodak Ektachrome Dup.	Type K/8071	Designed to duplicate Kodachrome Slides.
Fujichrome Dup.	CDU	Universal duplicating film designed to be used with tungsten light sources. Wide exposure latitude.

developments can be anticipated. Carefully check the data sheet packaged with your film for the latest assigned exposure index and other details.

Exposure

Correct exposure is based on proper camera settings for the film used and for the light conditions under which pictures are to be taken. Your camera may have a built-in exposure meter and semi- or completely automatic features for determining exposure.

Film information sheets provide general exposure data for average conditions (page 90). For proper exposure, reversal color films permit only a narrow range of camera settings, limited to from ½ to 1 *f*/stop on either side of the correct setting.

Lighting

As indicated in Table 14–1, color films are designed for use with specific light sources. Select your film accordingly, although with a proper light-balancing filter a film can be used under other than the recommended light conditions. When such a filter is used, the exposure index of the film is reduced (example: Ektachrome 100 with exposure index 100 when used with photofloods requires a No. 80A filter and the exposure index is reduced to 32). Refer to the film information sheet packaged with each roll for detailed information about light-balancing filters.

The conditions under which a subject is to be filmed may require the use of artificial lighting. To boost the light level, flashcubes or electronic flash units can be used. *They are handy and easy to operate, especially when small areas must be illuminated.* Make sure that your camera is synchronized (at the recommended shutter speed) with the flash. Then apply the information and formula on page 94.

For more carefully controlled lighting use photoflood lamps. They are available in various sizes and are used with separate metal reflectors or have reflectors built into them. In place of regular photoflood lamps, consider using highly efficient **sealed quartz halogen lamps** of approximately 1000 watts. *Avoid flat lighting created by placing lights beside the camera only.* Instead, establish a lighting pattern involving a key light, fill lights, and supplementary background and accent lights. Study the purposes and placement of these lights and methods for determining exposure with them as described on page 95.

Composition

Composition must take place in the viewfinder of your camera when you film each scene; therefore, study the general suggestions for good composition on page 101. As you select subjects, keep in mind the proportions of the slides you are preparing.

If you can, prepare all slides with a uniform format—preferably horizontal.

Using Masks

Masks can block out unwanted areas of film, change proportions of a slide, create unusual outlines of projected images, or allow more than a single image to be put on one slide. A wide variety of paper, cardboard, or plastic masks is available or can be designed to be combined with slides when mounted.

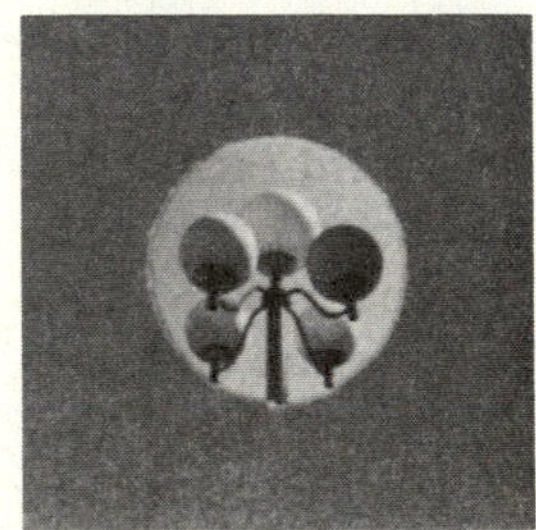

Also, black-and-white high contrast (litho) film (page 209) can be used to make masks. Prepare the mask from black paper with the area to be blocked from light *as clear.* Remember, the exposed and developed film will become a negative. It is mounted in a frame with the filmed subject.

Close-up and Copy Work

Close-up and copy techniques are often very useful when preparing color slides. Your script may call for close-ups of objects, for details in a process, or for copies of titles, maps, pictures, and diagrams. For these purposes, as has been mentioned, the single-lens reflex camera is necessary by reason of its accuracy in viewing. Refer to page 103 for guidelines; these deal with viewfinding, parallax, focusing, lens diaphragm openings, exposure timing, and equipment or attachments that you may need for this special kind of photography. Also refer to suggested procedures for copying flat materials.

Be alert to legibility limitations of printed materials. When printed matter is copied into slide format, lettering may not be readable. See the discussion of legibility standards for graphic materials on page 132. Also, give attention to the recommendations for preparing overhead transparencies from printed materials (page 201) to ensure viewer's ease in reading and understanding. The same suggestions are important when making slides.

A reminder—always remember to obtain a release when preparing to use copyrighted materials.

Illustrations

For preparing illustrations and diagrams:

1. Plan the art work in terms of the slide proportions (page 115). An outline of the open area of a 35mm frame is printed inside the front cover of this book.
2. Select suitable backgrounds (page 140).
3. Use appropriate illustrating, drawing, and coloring techniques (page 124).
4. Use suitable copy techniques to photograph each illustration as a slide (page 103).

Titles

Titles should serve the purposes noted on page 171. Be sure to take account of the legibility standards for projected materials (page 132) as you select lettering sizes for titles, captions, and labels. Then:

1. Word each title so it is brief *and* communicative.
2. Select materials or aids for appropriate lettering (page 136).
3. Prepare the lettering and art work (page 124), keeping in mind the correct proportions of your slides (page 115 and inside front cover), using simple yet effective design features (page 106), and selecting appropriate backgrounds (page 140).
4. Use close-up copy techniques to photograph each completed title on color film (page 103).

An alternative to hand methods for preparing title slides is to create them with a computer. See the information on page 226 and review the explanation for computer-generated graphics on page 119.

Also, high-contrast photography can be used to make a variety of title slides. Each method starts with a high-contrast, black-and-white negative prepared on Kodalith Ortho Type 3 film. This film is used mainly in graphic arts printing.

Here are title slides that can be prepared, starting with a 35mm Kodalith negative:

1. **Clear letters on black background.** Use the negative directly as a slide.
2. **Colored letters on black background.** Color the clear lettering by dipping the negative in transparent watercolor dye (or food coloring), by rubbing the emulsion (dull) side of the negative with a colored felt pen, or by mounting a piece of colored theatrical gel with the negative.
3. **Black letters on clear background.** Contact print the negative onto another piece of Kodalith film to make a positive (page 110).
4. **Black letters on colored background.** Prepare as in 3 above, and then dip the film in concentrated watercolor dye or use colored theatrical gel mounted with the film.
5. **Black letters over subject.** Prepare as in 3 above, and then seal the positive film and the 35mm subject scene together in the same frame. Because the two pieces of film will absorb heat, possibly separate and lose focus when projected, copy the slide onto a single frame of color film.

Other methods for combining lettering with background scenes for titles are described on page 140.

A variation of the **progressive disclosure** technique, used with overhead transparencies (page 203), can be applied to slides. Use this method if a series of titles or a list is to be shown, one item at a time, but in cumulative order.

Prepare the total list on white paper, then use the *negative slide* method (1) for preparation as described previously. Frame the entire list in the camera, then cover all items but the first one with a sheet of white paper. Film the first item. For the second picture, un-

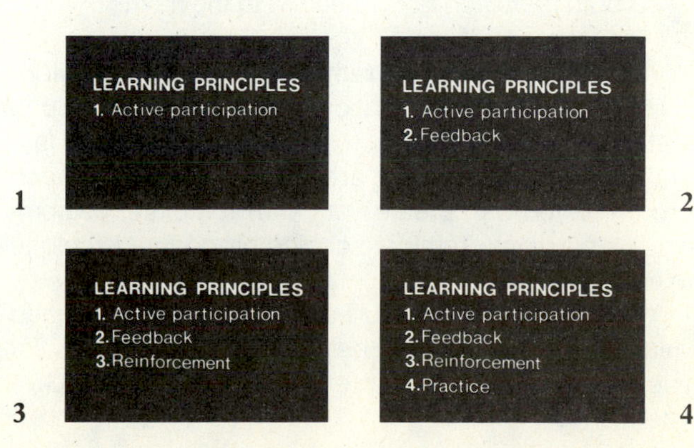

cover the second item and film the two that are exposed. Repeat with three items uncovered, and so forth. The result will be a series of slides, each one revealing an additional title or item on the list.

A variation of the above procedure is to shoot the required number of negatives, each one showing the total list of items. Then block out the unwanted items on each negative by brushing on opaque material used with high-contrast film.

After the slides are completed, use felt pen, food coloring, or theatrical gel to color the words comprising the list. Use a different color for each new item introduced on a slide. In this way the new item will stand out and be separated from the prior items on the list.

Using the Computer

Computer software programs allow for the creation of very professional and creative visual materials. The range of full-color materials that can become slides, in addition to titles, include charts, graphs, diagrams, and numerous art forms. Many presentation graphics programs guide the preparation of both slides and overhead transparencies. Commonly used programs include: *Lotus Freelance, Microsoft PowerPoint,* Aldus *Persuasion, Harvard Graphics, CorelDraw, and Presentation Express II.*

Each program consists of three components:

- An *outline* to structure the content of each slide. The content can be imported from a word processing program and from available visuals by scanning a picture or artwork.
- A *slide viewer* that allows you to create the visual format by drawing an object with available drawing tools, adding clip art, a logo, and symbols like bullets before a list of items.
- A *slide sorter* that shows all slides you create in reduced size on a single screen. By viewing all slides, as on a light box (page 228), you can check slides against the script. This may necessitate rearranging slide order, checking continuity, and verifying a smooth transition from one idea to the next.

All programs include **templates** which are guidelines for consistent application of various features. Such matters as color schemes, font styles and size, and layout treatment for content are predesigned. With each program, you can create your own template, customized as you wish. Template choice procedure is unique to each program.

While the program you use will guide you in good visualization techniques, be alert to the practices for effective communication presented in Chapter 8. Give attention to:

- Visual design and layout (page 116)
- Visualizing statistical data (page 127)
- Guidelines for using colors (page 129)
- Legibility standards for lettering (page 132)
- Computer-generated lettering (page 123)
- Suggestions for designing overhead transparencies that can apply to slides (page 206)

Once the image is created, it can be output to a film recorder and onto 35mm film (page 120). Also, black-and-white and color titles, outlines, or other graphics, prepared with a computer, can be printed onto paper with a laser printer (in black-and-white or color). The result can be photographed as a slide with a 35mm SLR camera on a copystand.

Computer-generated slides can be produced if your organization has all necessary equipment. An alternative is to have the terminal equipment and transmit electronic images of slides via modem and telephone to a company that has the film recorder. There are also production companies that will handle the complete job, preparing slides according to your requirements.

The choice of which service to use will depend on these factors:

- The number of slides needed over a period of time
- How quickly slides will be needed
- The level of slide quality (resolution, color selection) that would be acceptable
- Any confidential nature of slide content
- Financial considerations relating to equipment purchase or lease

Scheduling and Record Keeping

As you plan the slides, make a list of scenes that can conveniently be filmed together. Then schedule each group. Organizing the work thus will save time and facilitate your picture making. See the example on page 167.

Then, as you prepare to make slides, consider the suggestions on page 168. Keep a record of the scenes filmed, the number of times each is taken, the camera settings used, and any special observations. Develop a form similar to the sample log sheet on page 168.

Remember to obtain a release from the persons appearing in your pictures. See the sample release form on page 169.

For some purposes you may use a **documentary** approach for preparing a slide series. This means that you shoot slides treating a topic or event *without* knowing the specific content of scenes. Upon examining the resulting slides you *then* develop your script from them. See further discussion of the documentary method on page 168.

PROCESSING FILM

One advantage and convenience in using reversal color film is that after exposure, a roll can be sent to a film-processing laboratory (through your local photo dealer). The slides are returned mounted in cardboard or plastic frames ready for projection. But, if desired, many color films (Ektachrome, and color negative film) can be processed with kits of prepared chemicals. Time can thus be saved between filming and seeing the completed slides; moreover, money can also be saved if a number of rolls is ready at about the same time. The requirements and some of the cautions that must be observed when processing both reversal color films (E-6 process) and color negative films (C-41 process) are outlined on page 107. Maintaining the required temperature with little variation is most important.

There is a variety of equipment available for processing color reversal film (E-6 process). The simplest way is that of hand processing film on a reel in a tank as illustrated on page 108. This procedure is suitable for handling a few rolls of film (generally no longer than 36 exposures per roll) during a processing period. It requires constant attention to maintaining proper temperature and controlling other variables.

If large quantities of film will be processed frequently, then continuous processing equipment should be used (see page 109). Film, when fed into such a machine, passes through a series of deep tanks containing the required chemicals. Temperature and strength of the solutions are automatically maintained. With a continuous processor, consistent slide quality will be better assured than when hand processing. On the other hand, initial equipment expense is high, continual maintenance is necessary, and greater technical knowledge is required for successful operation of the equipment.

MOUNTING SLIDES

Slides can be mounted in commercial cardboard frames, in plastic mounts, or between glass plates. Each type has certain advantages and also disadvantages. Make your choice of the type to use based on the following:

- ***Cardboard***—least expensive, frame easy to mark with felt pen; slide held firmly if properly sealed; requires heat to seal; bends and frays easily, leading to possible jamming in the projector (use rounded-corner type); film may buckle during prolonged projection and lose focus in some projectors.
- ***Plastic***—rigid; edges do not fray; film mounting is easy and quick; somewhat more expensive than cardboard; more difficult to mark frame; film may shift position and buckle in less expensive types; better quality plastic mounts include pins that engage the film sprocket holes, locking the film in place (known as **pin registration**) for precise placement of an image on the screen during projection.
- ***Glass***—offers maximum protection for film; avoids buckle and loss of focus; heavy; most expensive; may include pin registration; requires more time to mount film; may not fit 140-slide tray; may break if dropped.

Slides may not need the protection of glass. In modern projectors they are removed from trays and returned to them mechanically during projection, and are touched by the hands only when being filed or rearranged in the tray. Also, some projectors automatically adjust focus as film heats and curls.

Mounting in Cardboard Frames

Use these tools and materials: cotton gloves, hand iron, cardboard mounts, gummed-back thumbspots, scissors—and the film to be mounted.

1. Cut the film along the frame line between the pictures.
2. Align the film in the mount.
3. Using an electric iron (set at "low"), seal all four sides.

If a large number of slides is to be mounted in card-

1

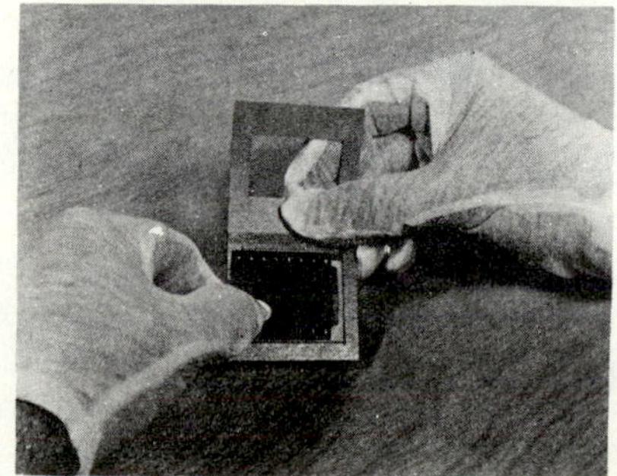

2

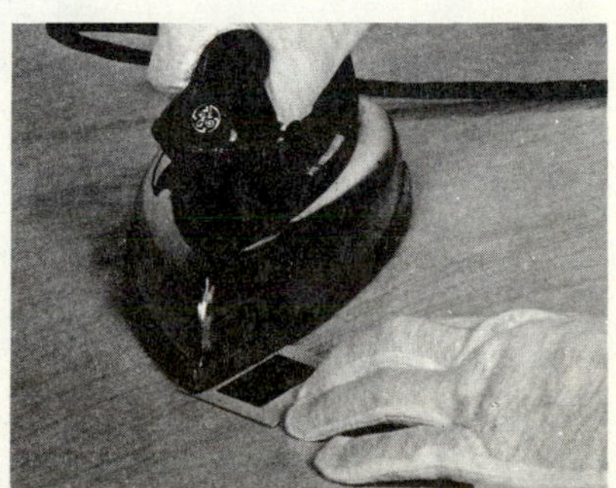

3

board, a faster method than using the hand iron may be preferred. A relatively inexpensive slide-mounting press consists of 2 × 2 inch heated pressure plates. The folded mount, holding a 35mm film frame, is placed between the pressure plates, which are then tightly closed. After a few seconds the plates are opened and the sealed slide drops out. Semi- and fully automatic slide mounting units also are available commercially.

A Hand-Operated Slide-Mounting Press

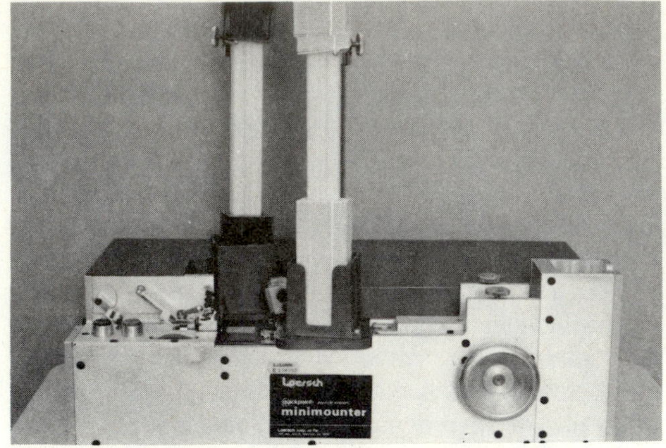

A Semiautomatic Plastic-Slide Mounting Machine

Plastic Frames with Glass Windows

Mounting in Plastic Frames

A variety of plastic slide frames is available for mounting slides. With one-piece frames, the film is either placed in one section, the other part folded over and secured or the two halves are gently pried apart and the film slipped between. Other types consist of separate parts that are snapped in place to hold the film.

Fold-over Frame   Snap-together Frame

Plastic Mounts

Mounting in Glass

With the availability of plastic frames in which the film and glass slip easily, mounting slides in glass can be accomplished quickly and with little effort.

Once slides are mounted, each one should be marked to indicate correct position for viewing—subject left to right and correct side up. Do this by placing a dot with a felt pen (permanent type on plastic or glass) in the *lower left* corner of the frame when the slide is viewed correctly. When placed in a tray for projection, the mark will be in the upper right corner. See illustrations on page 351.

EDITING SLIDES

Selections must be made from among all the slides—some are in addition to those called for in the script or are substitutes; others are multiple takes of the same scene but differ in exposure and composition.

Place all slides on a light box or other illuminated area for ease of inspection. Discard those so indicated on the log sheet prepared while filming. Examine the slides; eliminate the poorer ones until the remaining selection is limited to those of highest quality that fit or supplement the prepared script. Now revise the script as necessary and, if spoken or recorded commentary is to accompany the slides, refine it. Refer to the suggestions on page 170.

With the editing finished, your slide series is nearing completion. It may be advisable at this time to show the

series and to read the narration to other interested and qualified persons. Suggestions for developing a questionnaire to gather reactions that may help you to improve your slide series are on page 174.

DUPLICATING SLIDES

If the number of duplicate slides that will be needed is known before photographing begins, then all duplicates can be made as high-quality originals when the original subjects or materials are photographed. Should additional sets be required after photography has been completed, a film-processing laboratory can make duplicates of the original slides. There are also methods you can use to prepare your own duplicate slides.

The two major problems that should be recognized when duplicating slides are an increase in contrast (loss of detail in highlights and in shadows) and a shift in colors from those in the original slide (or the need to improve or correct colors in an original slide). To control contrast, use Ektachrome Slide Duplicating film 5071 (balanced for 3200°K) or Ektachrome Slide Duplicating film SO-366 (balanced for electronic flash). With either of these films, the resulting duplicate would show only a minimum gain in contrast.

In order to balance colors as close to those in the original, or to correct colors (such as replacing a blue cast with a warmer orange tone), place one or more special filters (CC filters for *color correction*) between the slide and the light source (or over the projector lens for the first method described below). It takes testing and experience to choose filters that will properly correct colors and result in duplicates that best reproduce original or desired colors in subjects.

Projector-Screen Method

Project the slide onto a matte-surface screen. Make certain that the projector is placed at a right angle to the screen in order to eliminate distortion of the image. A

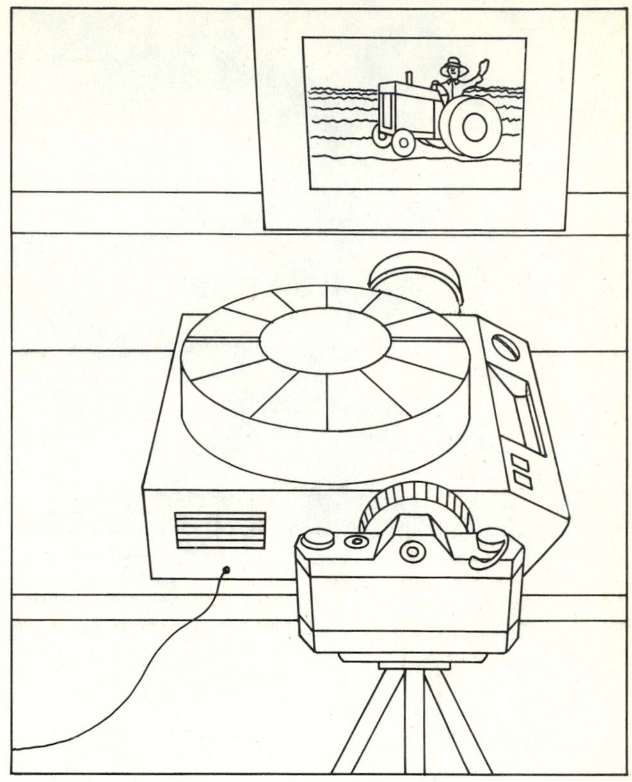

three-foot-size picture is suitable. Set the camera on a tripod as close to the projector as possible in order to avoid distortion when filming and to ensure that an even amount of reflected light is received from all parts of the screen. Adjust the image size or camera position until the image fills the viewfinder. It may be necessary to use a telephoto lens on the camera.

Use a film balanced for artificial light. Determine exposure with the meter built into the camera or use a reflected light meter. Bracket your exposure (take additional pictures at *f*/stops on both sides of the recommended exposure). With this method, it is difficult to avoid making a duplicate slide that will have more undesirable contrast than the original slide, and some loss of original color.

Slide-Duplicator Method

The most successful method of copying slides is with specially designed slide duplication equipment. It has a base with a translucent glass plate that holds the original slide to be copied. Beneath the glass plate is an electronic flash unit. A vertical bar holds the camera and the extension bellows. Some units include a camera; with others you attach your own 35mm single-lens reflex camera. A built-in light meter allows for accurate exposure determinations. Use a low contrast film such as Ektachrome Slide Duplicating film 5071.

Professional slide-duplicating equipment, available in table-top and floor-stand models, includes cameras

35mm SLR Camera Above Slide-holding Unit

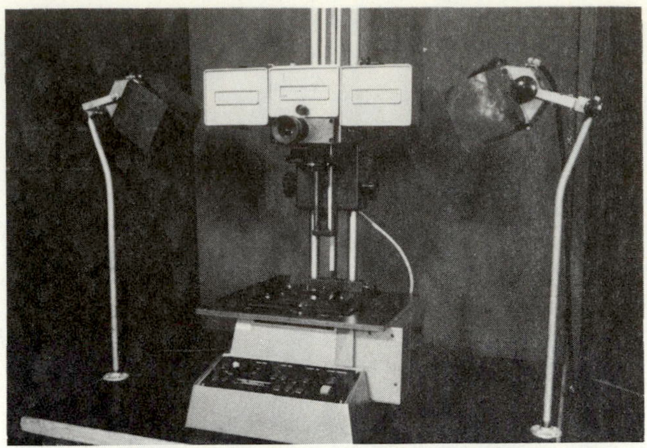

Professional Slide Duplicating Equipment

with accurate viewfinders that allow you to record *exactly* what you see on film (regular 35mm cameras usually record more subject area than you see through the viewfinder). The precision camera also includes film registration pins so the film moves to *precisely* the same position at the aperture with each advance (or reverse movement) of the film. Other features of this equipment may include bulk film magazines (100 and 400 feet), motorized camera movement, multiple exposure on the same frame, masking portions of a frame, and other special effects.

Many precision-camera systems are microprocessor controlled. The microprocessor controls camera functions and stores sequences and commands for future reference. These camera systems are used, not only for making duplicates and adding reference numbers in the corner of slides, but also to prepare title slides, special effect slides for multi-image productions, and filmstrips.

Videotape Method

For some uses, it may be desirable to transfer the slides, along with the sound track, to videotape. This provides a convenient way for showing slide/tape programs because the synchronization of picture and sound is automatic and only a videocassette player and television receiver are necessary for viewing.

Aim the videocamera onto a matte projection screen or a plain white wall. Use a three-foot image. Frame the image in the camera viewfinder with some clear or "bleed" space (video safe area) around the image to allow for possible loss of picture area on some television receivers. Connect the audio output from the audio playback unit to an audio input on the video recorder. Project the slides as the tape is played and record both the images and the sound track simultaneously on videotape.

With this method, be alert to two potential problems. First, if at any time a clear white image is projected to the screen because there is no slide in the projection position, damage can result to the video tube. Second, because of the automatic exposure feature of many videocameras, it is difficult to create a black screen or a fade-out when a dissolve control unit is used with slide projectors. (The lens diaphragm setting of the videocamera lens is automatically changed to overcome what seems to be an apparent underexposure situation.)

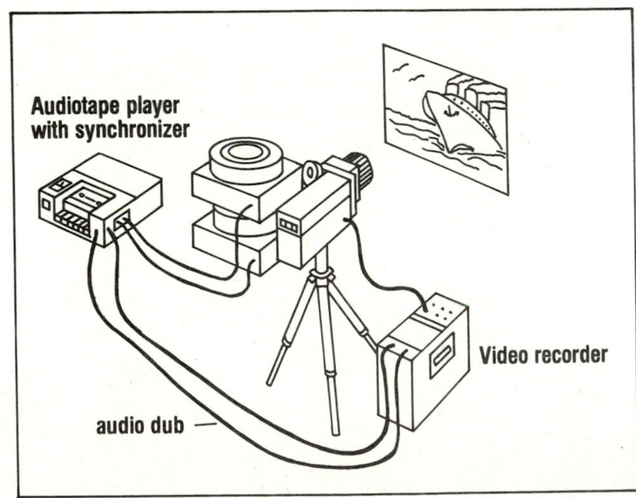

RECORDING AND SYNCHRONIZING NARRATION AND OTHER SOUNDS

Narration can be used with a slide series in the following ways:

- As informal comments while slides are projected

- As formal reading of narration as slides are projected
- As recorded narration and other sounds with an audible signal to indicate slide changes
- As recorded narration and other sounds with an inaudible signal that electronically controls slide changes

If an audio-recorded narration is to be prepared, refer to earlier suggestions concerning the selection and duties of personnel, recording facilities and equipment, recording procedures, sound mixing procedures, and audiotape editing (Chapter 9).

Synchronizing slides with tape requires the use of a **programer,** a unit either connected between the audio recorder and the slide projector or built into the audio recorder, which is directly connected to the projector. A signal generated by the programer (usually 1000 Hz) is recorded on tape. This signal, when the tape is played back, closes a relay that advances the next slide into projection position. See page 161 for further information about recording signals and page 235 for using programers.

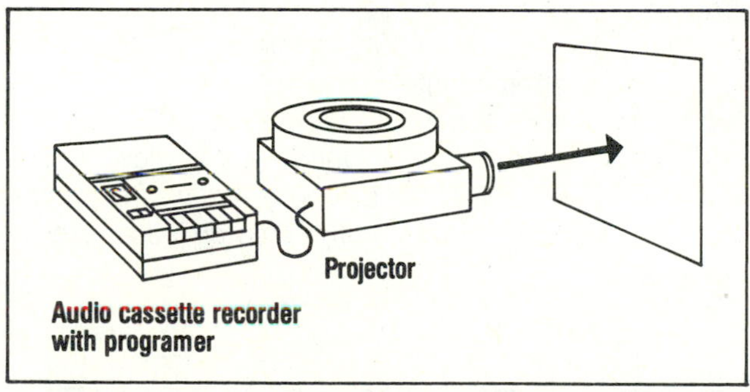

Some audio recorders include control devices that on a programed signal (150 Hz) will cause the tape to stop, allowing an observation to be made or a question to be answered. When ready, the user presses a button to restart the tape for the program to continue.

Another unit that can be useful for making a smooth, professional presentation is a **dissolve unit,** which is a compact box of electronics that increases or decreases electrical resistance in the lamp circuits of two projectors. It thus increases the intensity of light in one projector while it decreases it in the other. The two projectors are carefully aimed at the same screen so their images coincide. With a dissolve unit, the lamp switches on the projectors are set in the "fan" position. The images superimpose and change on command from the programer, with one image fading out and the next one on the screen fading in, thus creating an effective impression of gradual change and transformation as images blend one from another.

When dissolves are used, the screen is always illu-

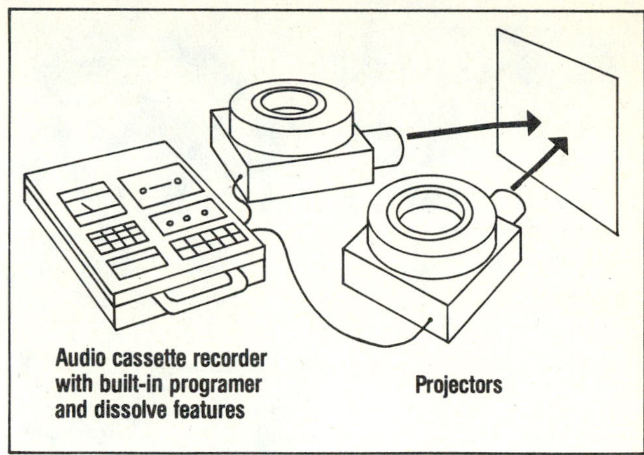

minated during slide changes, which helps to hold audience attention. Employing this technique of dissolving from one slide to the next creates a smooth visual flow as compared with the usual single projector slide change procedure that causes a sudden black screen between adjacent slides.

The simplest dissolve units have one or a few fixed dissolve rates for controlling two projectors. Other units allow for many precise rates of light control. Some sophisticated units can be programed to create numerous screen effects by controlling the on-off rates of projectors' lamps, of slide-change mechanisms, and even of shutters placed over projector lenses. Such controls can cause flashing, superimpositions, pop-ons, pop-offs, slide changes (forward, reverse, or hold), and simulated animation effects, all from static slides.

Programers and dissolve units are widely used in multi-image slide programs. See page 235 for further details.

FILING SLIDES

Initially most slides can be stored in the small 20- and 36-exposure boxes in which they are received from the processing laboratory. As quantities of slides are accumulated, some type of filing system becomes advisable so that individual slides can be located easily. Develop a numerical or color-coded filing system and consider the illustrated filing methods on page 232.

Indexing Methods

For visual reference purposes, numbered groups of slides can be placed on a light box, photographed on black-and-white film, and the negative printed to 8 × 10 inches. This sheet, with its numbered slide pictures, can be referred to when slides are being selected for a presentation or other use. Then, using the numbers, the slides are located in the storage file. Each topic in a file can be treated in this way and the slide

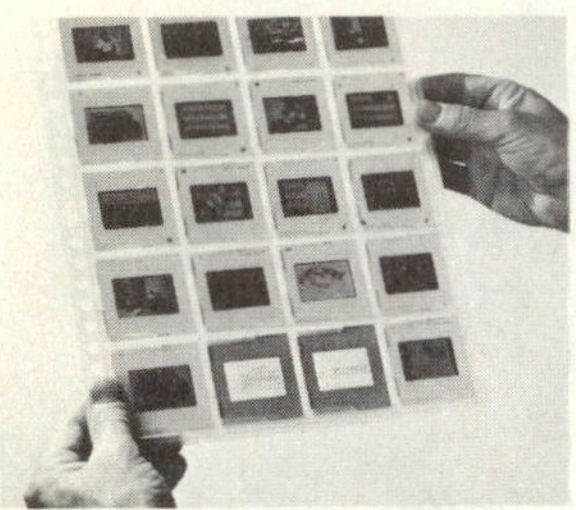
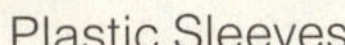
Plastic Sleeves

Projector Tray

Slide Box

Storage Display Cabinet

Slides on Light Box

Photosheets of Slides

picture sheets filed for reference in a notebook. This method is preferable to having to take each slide from a file and look at it when deciding on a selection.

Another way to locate specific slides that have been filed in a numerical system is by using a computer program. Most microcomputer systems have one or more inexpensive and easy-to-use filing (database) systems that can maintain information on a slide file. Depending on how you set up the software system, it can allow rapid retrieval of slides to fit specific requirements by any variable or combination of factors you desire (subject, location, photographer, film type, where used, and so forth). Many can also be used to generate listings of slides, or small printed labels that can be adhered to sets of slides or to individual slides.

If many thousands of slides have been accumulated, it may be worthwhile to copy them into videotape and transfer to a videodisc or compact disc. Become familiar with videodisc technology on page 267. The slides should be organized into categories (called *chapters*). For best quality, the copying procedure onto videotape and transfer to disc can be done by a service specializing in this work. From the disc, prepare a slide catalog including frame numbers on the disc and descriptions for locating slides.

REVIEW

What You Have Learned About Preparing Slide Series:

1. Is your camera a window-viewfinder or a single-lens reflex type? What are its advantages or limitations?
2. What film or films would you select for use? How did you arrive at your choice(s)?
3. What purposes can be served by masking a slide?
4. What method of making slide titles would you use in each situation?
   a. A general main title having black lettering on a colored background
   b. Colored letters on a black background
   c. A series of three titles to be shown progressively as negative slides with colored words
5. What equipment is required to prepare a high-quality color slide when a diagram is created by a computer?
6. How does the production of a *documentary* slide program differ from the nondocumentary method?
7. What is the designation for the reversal color film processing procedure you can carry out yourself?
8. What factors do you consider in making choices during editing of slides?
9. What are the three types of slide mounts and advantages of each kind?
10. How would you proceed to prepare duplicates of some original slides?

11. When preparing to duplicate slides, what two problems often occur? How do you handle each one?
12. What equipment is available for your use in synchronizing slides and a tape recording?
13. Why can a dissolve unit be used to present a smooth, uninterrupted slide presentation?
14. What method of filing your slides might you use?

See answers on page 381.

PRODUCING A MULTI-IMAGE PROGRAM

A multi-image presentation refers to the **simultaneous projection** of two or more pictures, on one or more screens, that may, among other applications, include:

- Sweeping panoramas

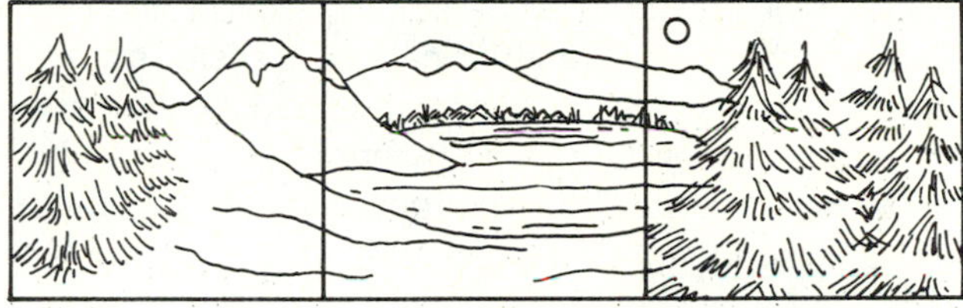

- Comparing or contrasting objects and events

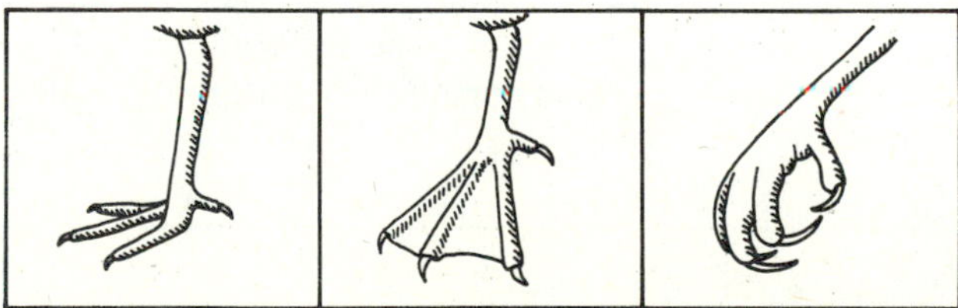

- Illustrating verbal information with supporting visuals

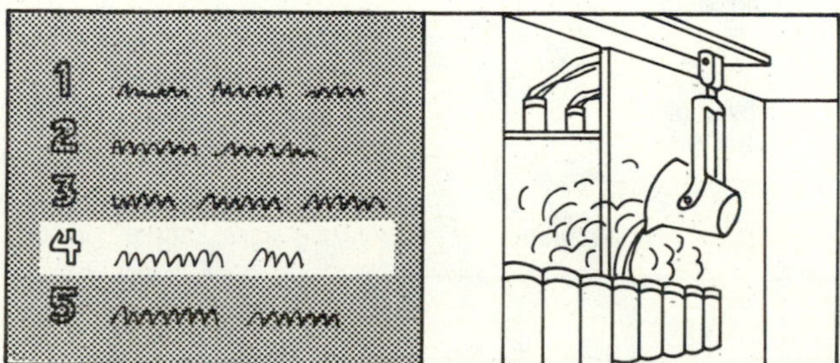

Most often the images are slides, but video, motion pictures, and overhead transparencies may also be used in conjunction with slides.

In all conventionally projected visual forms—slide series, motion pictures, or video recordings—the images are single and presented sequentially. The only exceptions are when split-screen or some other special technique is applied in order to present a simultaneous comparison or relationship. The sequential continuity of separate images conveys meanings to the viewer in a linear manner. When two or more images are viewed simultaneously, their immediate interaction can be more dynamic for the viewer, capturing and holding attention. The nonlinear nature of a multi-image presentation makes it a powerful instrument of communication.

There is research evidence to indicate that the use of multiple images is an effective media form. In a study of multi-image projection, Perrin concluded that "the immediacy of this kind of communication allows the viewer to process larger amounts of information in a very short time. Thus information density is effectively increased and certain kinds of information are more efficiently learned."

Besides being a motivating, exciting experience for the viewer, this efficiency of communication can be a major reason for using the multi-image presentation technique. The variety inherent in such presentations can be designed for audiences of any size.

Planning the Program

The use of two or more screens and possibly multitrack sound requires that special attention be given to preparing the storyboard or script. A form can be used that has separate columns for describing the images that will appear on the screen, columns for each sound element—narration, music, sound effects—and a column in which to specify the effect (slow dissolve, cut, flash, etc.) for bringing the visual to the screen and the length of time for each component to be seen or heard. This form can also serve as a programing or cue sheet when readying the presentation for use. See the example on page 234.

Preparing the Visual Component

When three images are used, the center area normally carries the major message and side areas show related pictures. Use this rule flexibly by purposefully changing the center of attention from one area to another as the subject development may dictate, or for reasons of variation.

Here are other suggestions for the visual component:

MULTI-IMAGE SCRIPT/CUE SHEET

VISUALS NUMBER/DESCRIPTION				SOUND		
Left	Center	Right	Effect/Time (min/sec)	Narration	Music	Sound Effects

- ▸ Treat ideas and concepts one at a time. More than one message, either visual or verbal, divides the viewer's attention, and both messages may lose effectiveness. But do realize that a continuity of meaning must be created as the presentation proceeds.
- ▸ Use the screen purposefully to communicate your message by not projecting images on all areas at all times unless pertinent to the message. By limiting the number of images at any one time, you can give emphasis and draw attention to particularly important visuals.
- ▸ Establish a rhythm, but also plan to vary the pace of image changes, which can contribute to interest and hold the viewer's attention.
- ▸ Select slides that are of good quality; consider composition and technical factors such as exposure and focus.
- ▸ Face people and objects on side areas inward toward the center if possible, unless a direction to simulate movement is necessary.

Preparing the Audio Component

When planning the audio for a multi-image presentation, consider these suggestions:

- ▸ Do not overnarrate; let the visuals carry much of the information or message.
- ▸ For some purposes, through the use of more than one voice the presentation can become more dynamic.
- ▸ Select music to set a mood and a rhythm for the presentation but do not allow it to interfere with or override the narration.
- ▸ Visuals may indicate the type of music needed; on the other hand, a piece of music selected as consistent with the topic being treated may provide the framework for the choice of visuals.
- ▸ Use of authentic sound effects gives realism to the presentation.

Two stereo or multitrack tape recorders often are used for mixing sounds. These stereo recorders must be of a type that allows recording to be made separately on each of the two tracks. Record or dub the narration on the first track of one stereo recorder; then music and other sound effects can be transferred from their original recordings, in proper relation to the narration, on the second track. If any errors are made while recording on either track, the recording can be erased and a rerecording made without damage to the other track.

Then the two tracks are mixed onto the first track of the other stereo recorder by connecting the output of the playback stereo recorder to the input of the first track of the second recorder. The second track of the resulting tape remains blank for program cueing signals.

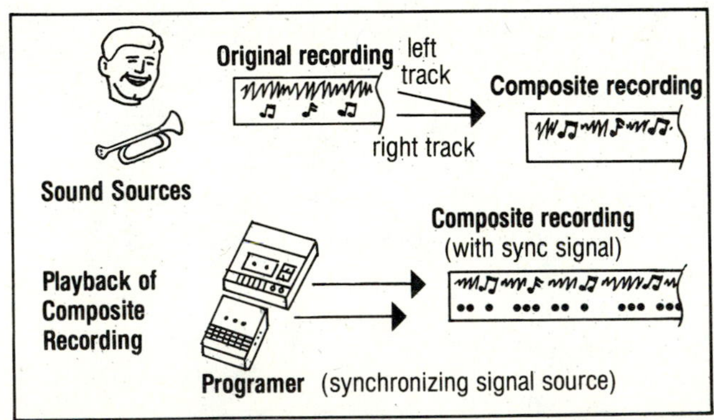

Programing the Presentation

In a slide presentation, verbal comments and audible or inaudible cue signals are used to pace the pictures correctly with the narration. Review the information on synchronizing slide/tape programs and using dissolve units on page 231. Careful programing all the elements is of even greater importance in the complexities of a multi-image presentation.

The starting point for synchronizing pictures and sound is the storyboard or script sheet. Once it is finalized, it becomes the cue sheet for programing the presentation.

A programer is used to synchronize the visual and audio portions of a multi-image presentation. In principle, the equipment is similar to that needed for synchronizing a single-projector slide/tape program or a two-projector program with dissolve. But now the programer should be able to handle many more functions. Essentially, it must turn projector lamps on and off at any rate—slow or fast—while advancing or backing up a slide tray, or holding a slide in projection position.

The effects that can be created include the following:

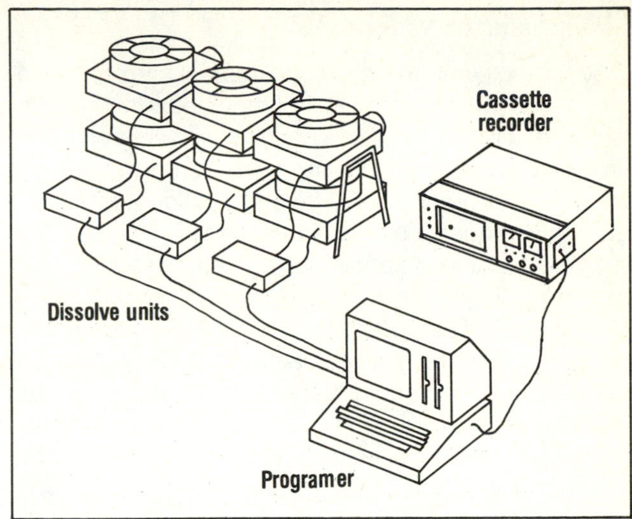

- ▶ ***Fade-in/fade-out***—lamp on one projector gradually going off **(fade-out)** or coming on **(fade-in)** to either have an image appear on a dark screen or to disappear, leaving the screen blank.
- ▶ ***Dissolve***—lamp gradually going off on one projector while the lamp comes up on a second projector; thus one image gradually fades out as a second, superimposed one fades in.
- ▶ ***Cut***—instantaneous reduction (or **cut**) of light from one projector while the light comes fully on from a second one; thus there is an immediate change in images on the screen.
- ▶ ***Flash***—repeated ON-OFF changes of a lamp while a slide remains in the projection position; the **flash** technique is effective for calling attention to the image.
- ▶ ***Freeze***—projecting two images together on the same screen as in overprinting or superimposing is called a **freeze.**
- ▶ ***Wipe***—removal or addition of one or more images or placement of images across two or more screens by fading or dissolving is termed a **wipe,** because it gives the impression of "wiping off" or "wiping on" the image or images across the screens.
- ▶ ***Animation***—flashing a series of images in sequential order, and possibly recycling them, creates **animation,** or the illusion of motion.

By combining a number of these techniques a range of creative effects can be accomplished with a programer. With a **tone-control programer** from six to ten different tones could be placed on an audiotape, in synchronization with the program sound track. Each tone would control a projector or dissolve function. By pairing tones you could cause a slow (using one tone) or a fast (using another tone) dissolve to take place. Programing is done in **real time**—the actual clock time required to run the program (12 minutes, 18 minutes, or whatever time).

A multi-image **microprocessor programer** can encode and then direct projectors and other devices during playback to carry out countless operations. Commands are stored in the microprocessor's memory as digital "bits." Errors are easily corrected by erasing a signal and replacing it with a new one. You can program various combinations of visual effects, see them on the screens, and then select the best one for transferring to the synchronization track of the audiotape containing all sounds.

Programing can take place in real time, as described with the previous tone-control units, or in **leisure time.** The latter means that you can press the keys for an order and the necessary speed factor (for example—a *dissolve* taking place for *5 seconds*), sit back and think about it or even try it with the slides. Then when you are ready, work on the next command or sequence of commands. The memory of the microprocessor will take this information and properly store it in relation to the prior cues. Then, on playback, the visual effect will take place accurately. It follows the previous cue in real time (for example—the 5-second dissolve and then the next command in proper time relation). This way of being able to program at your own leisure pace reduces much of the pressure that is inherent in real-time programing. You will find that it takes about 1 hour to program 1 minute of screen time using the leisure-time method.

Complex programers control more projectors and create a wide range of effects. Some microprocessor units can be connected to a videoscreen for visual display of the programed cues or to printers for obtaining a paper copy of the commands. With this visual facility, any errors in a program can be located easily and immediately corrected.

Transfer to Videotape

Most multi-image programs are designed for a single, major showing or are used repeatedly in one location. The setup of a multiple projector show is costly and time consuming, thus making the production available for use at a number of different locations difficult. If there are requests and advantages for using the program with many audiences, it may be advisable to convert it to a single, synchronized medium—videotape.

The disadvantages of doing this are the reduced image size and lower image quality. The 3 to 4 ratio of the television screen is so different from the three-screen format that there will be white or black space at the top and bottom of the frame. Follow a procedure similar to that for copying a slide/tape program onto videotape as described on page 230. Record color bars and an audio tone (page 257) on the videotape to set standards for playback.

Run and record the program. Check the resulting videotape recording for acceptability. Two potential problems when transferring the slide images to videotape may have to be faced. One relates to potential damage of the videotube (if a tube camera is used) if a bright white light is projected to a screen instead of a slide. A second problem is the difficulty in recording a fade-out because the camera's automatic exposure feature attempts to correct what is considered to be an underexposure.

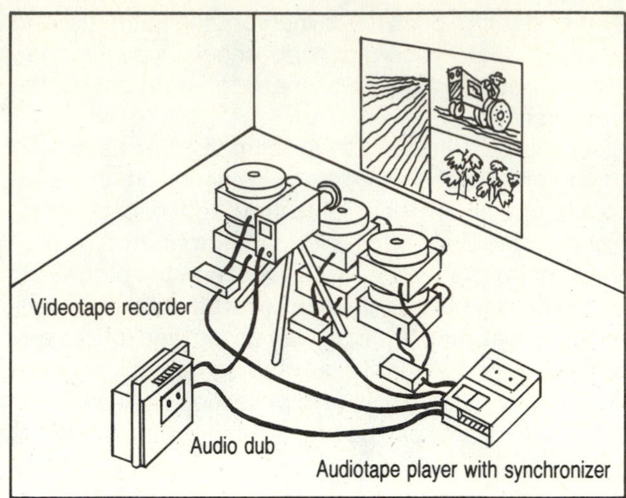

This method for transferring a multi-image program to videotape may result in a satisfactory recording. If a higher quality product is desired, there are professional services that offer "aerial image" transfer systems. Such a system consists of a combination of mirrors and prisms against and through which the images from the projectors pass while being aimed into either a video or film camera.

REVIEW

What You Have Learned About Producing a Multi-Image Program:

1. What are two general reasons why a multi-image presentation might be selected for use with a group?
2. List three instructional purposes that such a presentation can serve.
3. Which of these statements concerning the preparation of the visual and audio components of a multi-image presentation are TRUE?
   a. Project images on each one of three screen areas continuously during a presentation.
   b. Each separate area can be used to treat its own idea or concept.
   c. In composition, generally face people on side screens toward the center one.
   d. Major messages most often should be on the center screen.
   e. For a special effect, music can be used to dominate the narration.
   f. Sound effects and two voices are useful audio techniques in a multi-image presentation.
4. If you have a stereo recorder available, what simple method could you use to synchronize a two-screen presentation?
5. Do you have a programer available? If so, what type is it?
6. What unit accepts signals from a programer and controls the illumination changes on a projector?
7. What is the difference between real-time and leisure-time programing?
8. What is the name of a special effect associated with each description?
   a. Turning the projector lamp on and off rapidly while showing the same image.

b. Projecting two slides on the same screen for a period of time.
c. Allowing the screen to go black as light intensity in a projector is slowly reduced.
d. Showing an image move across the screens by dissolving a series of slides.

See answers on page 381.

PREPARING TO USE YOUR SLIDE SERIES AND MULTI-IMAGE PROGRAM

When your slides and recording have been completed, give attention to a number of final details as you prepare for their use.

The program may have been designed for motivational, informational, or instructional purposes (page 42). You may now need printed materials—information or summary sheets, guide sheets, or worksheets. Prepare and duplicate them in sufficient copies for the audience or for individual users.

Arrange for duplication of the master tape recording, (page 162). Labeling and packaging the slides and tape recording may be necessary. Refer to page 352 in Chapter 19 for information on using slides and slide/tape programs.

With a multi-image presentation the likelihood of problems arising is greatly increased due to the complexity of the electronic equipment and number of projectors required. Refer to page 352 in Chapter 19 for information on using a multi-image program.

REFERENCES

SLIDE PRODUCTION

Brandt, James B. "Slide to Tape Transfer." *Media and Methods* 27 (May/June 1991): 16, 38.

Effective Lecture Slides. Publication S-22. Rochester, NY: Eastman Kodak Co., 1988.

Green, Lee. *Creative Slide/Tape Programs.* Englewood, CO: Libraries Unlimited, 1986.

Hershenson, Martin. "Viewing Slides on Your VCR." *Industrial Photography* 40 (February 1991): 20, 54.

Meechan, Joseph. "Creating Text and Line Copy Slides: What Are the Options?" *Industrial Photography* 41 (April 1992): 32–34.

Slides—Planning and Producing Slide Programs. Publication S-30. Rochester, NY: Eastman Kodak Co., 1989.

Sunier, John. *Slide/Sound and Filmstrip Production.* New York: Focal Press, 1981.

MULTI-IMAGE PRODUCTION

Bullough, Robert V. *The Instructional Media Library: Multi-image Media.* Englewood Cliffs, NJ: Educational Technology Publications, 1981.

Gordon, Roger L. *The Art of Multi-Image.* Washington, DC: Association for Educational Communications and Technology, 1978.

Fradkin, Bernard. *A Review of Multiple Image Presentation Research.* Stanford, CA: ERIC Clearinghouse on Informational Resources, 1976.

Goldstein, E. Bruce. "The Perception of Multiple Images." *AV Communication Review* 23 (Spring 1975): 34–68.

Images, Images, Images—The Book of Programmed Multi-Image Production. Publication S-12. Rochester, NY: Eastman Kodak Co., 1981.

Lewell, John. *Multivision: The Planning, Preparation and Projection of Audio-Visual Presentations.* New York: Focal/Hastings House, 1980.

Perrin, Donald G. "A Theory of Multi-Image Communication." *AV Communication Review* 17 (Winter 1969): 368–382.

Slawson, Ron. *Multi-image Slide/Tape Programs.* Littleton, CO: Libraries Unlimited, 1988.

SOURCES FOR EQUIPMENT, MATERIALS, AND SERVICES

COMPUTER SOFTWARE FOR FILING SLIDES

Caption Power/Label Power, Power Software, 10 Post Office Road B-3, Silver Springs, MD 20910.

Photo SBM, Micro Software Solutions, P.O. Box 851504, Richardson, TX 75085.

Phototrack, Colorado Nature Photographic Studio, 6392 South Yellowstone Way, Aurora, CO 80016.

Professional Photo Catalog System, Bill Tucker, 26058 Blossom Lane, Grosse Ile, MI 48138.

JOURNALS FOR SOURCES

AV Video
Montage Publishing Co., 701 Westchester Ave., White Plains, NY 10604

AVC Presentation For the Visual Communicator
PTN Publishing Co., 445 Broad Hollow Rd., Melville, NY 11747

Directory of Video, Computer, and Audio-Visual Products
International Communications Industries Association, 3150 Spring Street, Fairfax, VA 22031

Presentation Products
Pacific Magazine Group, Inc., 513 Wilshire Blvd., Santa Monica, CA 90401

SLIDE MOUNTS AND MOUNTING EQUIPMENT

Byers Photo Equipment, 6955 West Sandburg Street, Portland, OR 97223.

HP Marketing, 16 Chapin Road, Pine Brook, NJ 07058.

Kaiser Corporation, 3555 North Prospect Street, Colorado Springs, CO 80907.

Pakon, Inc., 106 Baker Technology Plaza, 6121 Baker Road, Minnetonka, MN 55345.

Pic-Mount Corp., 2300 Arrowhead Drive, Carson City, NV 89706.

Wess Plastics, Inc., 70 Commerce Drive, Hauppauge, NY 11788.

SLIDE DUPLICATING EQUIPMENT

Charles Beseler Co., 1600 Lower Road, Linden, NJ 07036.

Kinex Corp., 34 Elton, Rochester, NY 14607.

Byers Photo Equipment, 6955 West Sandburg Street, Portland, OR 97223.

Maron, Inc., 2640 West 10th Place, Tempe, AZ 85281.

Oxberry—Division of Cybernetics Products, Inc. 180 Broad Street, Carlstadt, NJ 07072.

Radmar, Inc., 1263-B Rand Road, Des Plaines, IL 60016.

SLIDE DISSOLVE CONTROLLERS

AMX Corp., 12056 Forestgate Drive, Dallas, TX 75243.

Arion Corp., 701 South Seventh Street, Delano, MN 55328.

AVL-Audio Visual Laboratories, Inc., 123 White Oak Lane, Old Bridge, NJ 08857.

Commercial Electronics, Ltd., 1335 Burrard Street, Vancouver, B.C. V6Z 1Z7.

Eastman Kodak Company, 343 State Street, Rochester, NY 14650-0406.

Multivision System Inc., 1814 Algaroba Street, Honolulu, HI 96826.

RMF Products, P.O. Box 520, Batavia, IL 60510.

MULTI-IMAGE PROGRAMERS

Arion Corp., 701 South Seventh Street, Delano, MN 55328.

AVL-Audio Visual Laboratories, Inc., 123 White Oak Lane, Old Bridge, NJ 08857.

Commercial Electronics, Ltd., 1225 Burrard Street, Vancouver, B.C. V6Z 1Z7.

Multivision Systems, Inc., 1814 Algaroba Street, Honolulu, HI 96826.

RMF Products, P.O. Box 520, Batavia, IL 60510.

CHAPTER 15

- Advantages of Video Technology
- Video Production Equipment
- Selecting and Handling Videotape
- Planning a Video Recording
- Recording the Picture
- Types of Camera Shots
- Providing Continuity
- Special Video Production Techniques
- Other Production Factors
- Recording the Sound
- Editing Videotape
- Desktop Video
- Duplicating a Video Recording
- Producing a Videodisc
- Preparing to Use Your Video Recording and Videodisc

Video Recordings and Videodiscs

Video recording and motion picture films share a close relationship in that each one can portray a subject in motion, along with natural or appropriate sounds. Motion and sounds together give the medium its interest, its pacing, and its strongest feature—its sense of continuity or logical progression. In addition, both video recordings and films can present information, describe a process, clarify complex concepts, teach a skill, condense and expand time, and affect an attitude.

ADVANTAGES OF VIDEO TECHNOLOGY

Videotape has replaced film for almost all nontheatrical uses. Some of the reasons why video is now the preferred equipment for production are as follows:

- Unlike film, videotape is not sensitive to light, thus loading and unloading tape in the recorder as a cassette is easy and quick.
- Videotape does not have to be developed, while film must be sent to a film laboratory for processing. Therefore, videotape may be viewed right after recording, allowing for immediate evaluation of results.
- Videotape is lower in cost than film and can be reused many times.
- Sound and picture are more easily recorded together (in synchronization) on videotape than on motion picture film.
- Video equipment has become less expensive, and has improved in quality and ease of operation.
- Special effects, such as animation through computer graphics techniques, are available with video equipment for easier production than that on film.
- Editing procedures are simplified through the use of sophisticated electronics.
- When editing is completed, a video program, including all pictures and sound, may be ready for immediate use or duplication.
- Duplicate copies of a video recording are easy to make and lower in cost than film copies.
- Convenience of packaging and handling for use are distinct advantages.
- Videotape is the medium for the premaster necessary in preparing a videodisc and other laser-based materials.

As technology continues to improve the electronics of the video medium, and as greater standardization is realized, it is evident that video will increasingly become the major vehicle for most media production. Because of its many features and advantages, video is a key vehicle for interactive multimedia communications as treated in Chapter 16.

VIDEO PRODUCTION EQUIPMENT

It is common to have video equipment that combines the camera, microphone, and recorder in a single, compact unit called a **camcorder.** While this equipment records both video and audio on videotape, it can also be used to play back a recording, which is seen in the viewfinder or on a TV monitor. This unit is a very convenient and useful production tool.

Since the camcorder is widely used, the following discussion of equipment will emphasize features on the camcorder. Most descriptions apply equally to separate camera, microphone, and recorder units.

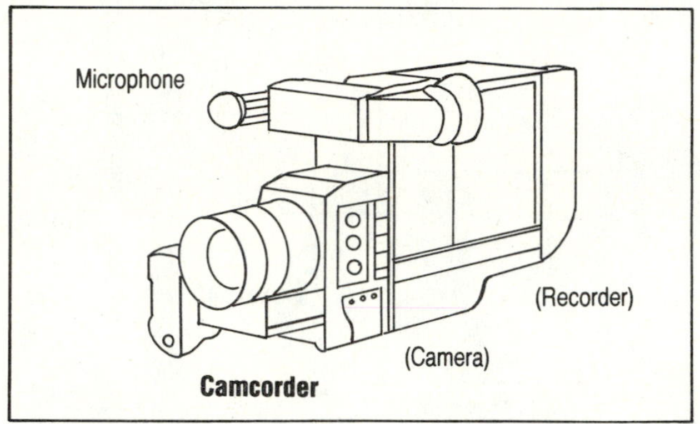

Camcorder

The Camcorder

All camcorders transmit images in color. Light from the subject passes through the lens of the camera. The image is focused on a light-sensitive surface within the camera. This surface consists of a microchip called a **charged-coupled device (CCD).** It contains tens of thousands of sensors to create the **pixels** (tiny dots in colors) that compose a video picture. The CCD is more sensitive, compact, and reliable than the light-sensitive pickup tubes used in other cameras. The result is a small, lightweight, and highly portable camcorder.

The following features are common to camcorders:

Optical

- ***Zoom lens***—(page 81) is standard. Extreme closeups can be obtained with "macro" setting on some zoom lenses or with closeup attachments (page 104).

- ***Viewfinder***—for observing the image through the lens. Most viewfinders are black-and-white although very small color monitors can be attached to a bracket on the camera for monitoring color when shooting. Besides normal viewing, many viewfinders can be turned to a number of positions for ease in viewing when the camera is held other than straight ahead.

- ***Exposure meter***—automatically monitors light level entering the camera; then it adjusts the diaphragm behind the lens (page 82) to allow an optimum amount of light to reach the CCD.
- ***Picture focus***—is controlled automatically.
- ***Override features***—for both exposure and focus so you can make adjustments under special conditions.

Electronics

- ***White balance***—setting must be made to adjust camera circuits to light conditions within a scene (either indoor or outdoor). Most models do this automatically (including indoor/outdoor filter choice) when a button is pushed. There may be an override control for use in special situations. Check color balance by observing a scene on a video monitor.
- ***Low light control***—can be used to boost video signal under low light conditions. Although this would increase the brightness of the image, the result is a more grainy picture.
- ***Fade control***—is used to end a shot with gradual fade to black or white (page 254).
- ***Camcorder functions***—are monitored by a number of lights or symbols appearing in the viewfinder. These include battery level, white balance status, tape speed indicator, recording standby or in progress, tape counter, and so on.

Tape Movement These are the buttons that control tape movement within the VCR component—Play, Stop, Record, Rewind. Additional controls may include the following:

- ***Record-Review***—allows a quick check of a scene by replaying the last few seconds recorded.
- ***Logic control***—allows fast-forwarding a tape to a predetermined point, then immediately playing a scene without using the Stop and Play buttons.

As previously noted, in addition to serving as the recorder, a camcorder can be the playback unit (termed the **Source**) for viewing and editing a recording.

Power A camcorder requires relatively little electrical power for its operations. Although with an adapter regular AC power can be used, usually electricity is supplied from rechargeable nickel cadmium (NiCad) batteries. When the low power level warning light is observed in the viewfinder, recharging is necessary. This takes about 1 hour.

Consider these suggestions when using batteries:

- Remove batteries from camcorder when equipment will not be used for a period of time.
- Store batteries in a cool, dry place.
- Generally discharge batteries fully before recharging. This will extend battery life.
- Charge batteries at normal room temperature.
- Avoid exposing batteries to sunlight and high temperature.
- Do not drop batteries or subject them to extreme vibrations.

Special Built-in Features

- ***Enhanced autofocus***—to overcome misleading signals from special subjects such as water or glass surfaces.
- ***High speed shutter***—beyond the normal 1/30 second for reducing image blur when recording fast action. Speeds of 1/250 to 1/1000 second may be selected.
- ***Controller***—for creating time lapse and similar effects (page 255).
- ***Editing features***—such as (1) **flying erase head** to provide a *glitch-free* transition (no disturbance or rolling of picture) from one scene to the next; (2) fade in and fade out of images; and (3) audio dub for adding additional sound (sound effects, narration, music) to a tape.
- ***Character generator*** or ***video title***—for lettering of titles over a scene or separately with a plain background. This titling feature may be an alternative to methods described with computer graphics on page 123.

Input and Outputs

- ***DC connection***—allows power input from a car battery or AC supply through an adaptor.
- ***Audio and video input***—connections for recording sound and images from other sources.
- ***Audio and video outputs***—for attaching a headset or earplug to monitor sound as it is recorded and then to allow the video signal to be shown on a TV monitor or fed to a separate videocassette recorder or player.

The Microphone

With video equipment, sound may be recorded on the videotape at the same time as the picture is being taped. This is known as **synchronized** sound. A camcorder includes a built-in microphone that is *omnidirectional* (page 151). Thus it will pick up extraneous sound from outside the picture area, like air conditioner and traffic noise. Therefore, it is strongly recommended that a separate microphone be used when possible. Refer

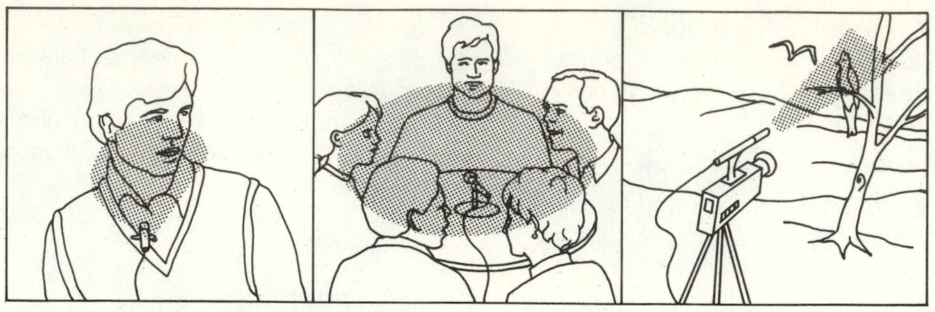

to the discussion of microphones for audio production on page 151.

Three microphone types are commonly used in video production. A **lavalier microphone,** designed to be hung around a speaker's neck or clipped to clothing, is unidirectional with a cardioid pattern, and picks up little sound other than the speaker's voice. A **fixed microphone,** attached to a stand that is placed on a table or suspended on a boom above the scene, is nondirectional to record remarks from a number of persons grouped around it. A third type is a unidirectional **shotgun microphone,** which is positioned away from the scene and is aimed at the speaker. It is highly directional and its main use is in documentary-type recordings that wish to capture sound in a natural, realistic way.

In addition to these types of microphones, a **wireless** or **radio microphone** may be used when wide or long shots are to be taken or the subject will be moving across a large area and the microphone itself, or its connecting cord, would be visible. This microphone acts as a radio transmitter, broadcasting the audio signal to a receiver placed out of the scene which is attached to an input on the videocassette recorder. A wireless microphone requires careful handling to ensure that a proper signal is being consistently recorded.

It is advisable to use an earplug or headphones to monitor sound as it is recorded. Then check the sound through a speaker when the recording is played back.

The Videocassette Recorder

The recorder section of a camcorder and separate video recorders operate on the same principles. Picture and sound signals, generated at the camera and microphone, are received by the videotape recorder through its recording heads. The electrical impulses are converted into precise magnetic patterns, representing picture and sound, on the tape surface.

The recorder requires videotape of a certain width. The common sizes used in education and training are ½ inch and 8mm. The ½ inch size consists of VHS, Betacam, and MII formats. All of these types are used on reels placed in a sealed cassette. Thus the designation **videocassette recorder (VCR).**

A tape can *only* be used with a recorder or playback machine that accepts that particular format tape. But different formats are electronically compatible since a recording on any tape can be duplicated to another tape of any size.

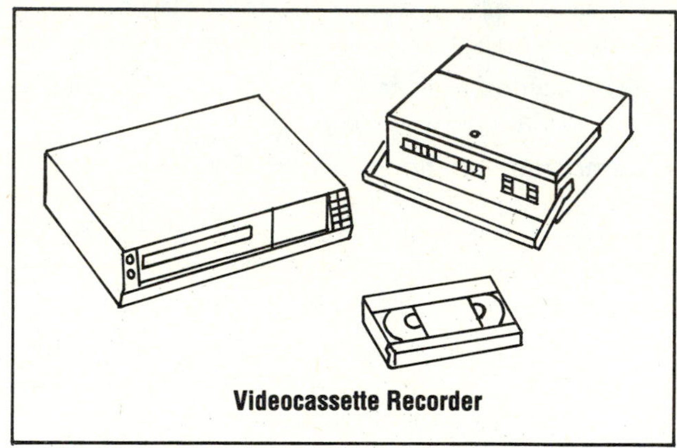

Videocassette Recorder

The video picture is recorded as a series of diagonal stripes across the tape, called "slant tracks." In a cassette up to four **audio tracks** are recorded along the upper edge of the tape after it leaves the drum. Thus, lip synchronous sound, narration, music, or sound effects can be recorded. Later during playback, the video playback heads in the drum, acting on the passing tape, convert the magnetic patterns for picture into electrical impulses, sending them through a cable to the television monitor. At the same time, the audio heads convert the magnetic patterns along the upper edge of the tape into electrical signals for sound to the monitor. Another recording head places very precise signals at regular intervals along the lower edge of the tape. This becomes the **control track** to regulate tape speed on playback.

Be alert to the fact that electronic standards established for video equipment used in the United States differ from the standards for equipment used in other countries. Electrical power requirements, number of scan lines on a frame, frames per second projected to

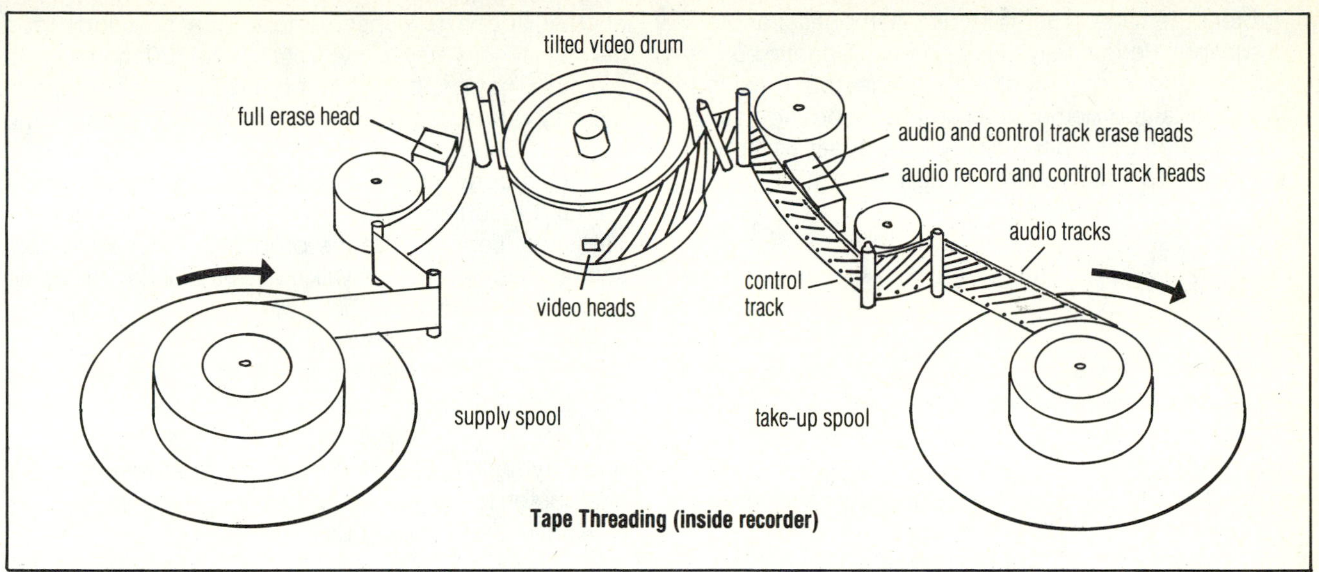

Tape Threading (inside recorder)

the screen, and method of encoding color are some of the variations that exist.

In the United States, Japan, and most of South America, video standards have been established by a *National Television Systems Committee* and are known as **NTSC** standards. They include 60 cycles of electricity, 525 scan lines per frame, and 30 frames per second. In England and parts of Europe, the *phase alternate by line* **(PAL)** standards are 50 cycles of electricity, 625 scan lines, and 25 frames per second. A third system, *sequential with memory* **(SECAM)** is used in other parts of Europe, including France and Russia. While SECAM has the same 50 cycles, 625 lines, and 25 frames per second as PAL, it differs in the way color is encoded on the video signal. A videotape recording produced with equipment of one standard must be converted for use on equipment of another standard.

Supplementary Production Equipment

Certain items are of value to supplement the basic production equipment:

- ***Video monitor*** or ***television receiver***—Because of the lack of color and size limitation of the camcorder viewfinder, it may be better to use a color video monitor or television receiver for viewing scenes after they are shot. Of the two, a **monitor** is electronically simpler and offers a superior picture. The video and audio outputs of the camcorder are wired directly into the audio and video inputs of the monitor. A **television receiver,** which is used in a home, receives television signals through an antenna or cable connection. The electronic signals are converted into video and audio impulses through a process called "demodulation" and then proceed through the circuits of the receiver to become the visible picture with sound.
- ***Tripod*** or ***shoulder-brace***—Because the camcorder is so small and lightweight, it may be difficult to hold it steady when recording. Therefore a tripod (or a one-legged device called a *monopod*) or a shoulder-brace can provide increased support for steadiness.
- ***Lights***—Floodlights should be available to illuminate indoor scenes. The lights may be used to supplement available light or to provide the main illumination following the key-fill-back-accent lighting pattern. A small light can be purchased as an accessory for a camcorder. The light slides into a bracket on top of the camera. It provides a small amount of supplementary light when recording subject detail closeups. The light operates from the camera battery pack. See page 93 for details about lights and lighting procedures.

Equipment Maintenance

In order to ensure satisfactory performance from your video equipment, careful handling is necessary.

- Do not aim a camera containing a videotube at the sun or other bright light. (Such light does not affect a CCD camera.)
- Keep a clear filter over the lens for protection.
- Turn the camera OFF when it will not be used for a period of time.
- Cap the lens when the camera is not in use.
- Keep the lens clean by dusting with a soft camel's hair brush.
- When not in use for a period of time, remove the battery from the camcorder.

Protect the camcorder from dirt, dampness, and direct sunlight. Periodically cleaning the magnetic heads is recommended as described on page 153. Cleaning internal parts and demagnetizing the recording heads should only be done periodically by a qualified technician, or when a malfunction is observed.

SELECTING AND HANDLING VIDEOTAPE

VHS and 8mm are the two commonly used tape formats. VHS is available in three types:

- Standard VHS
- VHS-C in a smaller (compact) cassette, used with an adapter in standard VHS recorders
- S-VHS (Super-VHS), an upgraded tape used in a modified recording and playback VCR for improved image quality

8mm is available as 8mm Standard or Hi8, which records a quality signal similar to S-VHS.

While a videocamera will record at only one speed (called Standard Play), most VCRs can operate at several speeds:

- SP—Standard Play provides best picture quality, but shortest recording time
- LP—Long Play
- EP—Extended Play at slowest speed setting

While a camera-recorded tape must be played at the SP setting, when a VCR is used to record a lengthy program from a TV receiver while being broadcast then another speed to conserve tape can be used. Tape playing times may vary from about 30 minutes to 8 hours. They are based on both the amount of tape in the cassette and the speed of tape movement in the recorder. See Table 15–1.

If the program to be recorded will be a long one, have on hand a sufficient number of videocassettes so you can shoot segments of the program on separate cassettes. This procedure will make it quicker to locate scenes when editing.

The technical quality of a recording depends to some degree on the characteristics of the videotape that is used. Poor-quality or worn tape may produce a distorted picture. Wrinkled tape can damage recording and playback heads in the recorder. To ensure that tape contributes to a satisfactory recording, keep these facts in mind in choosing and using videotape:

- Select a well-known brand of tape for use. Other brands may be a manufacturer's seconds or tapes that were improperly stored.
- Videotape consists of a magnetic oxide coating on a polyester base. Iron oxide had been the standard material for many years. Now chromium dioxide and other substances, including a high concentration of metal (8mm tape), are used as the coating for high-quality tape. They offer better picture and sound quality and improved image sharpness.
- If small black or white horizontal flashes are visible on the monitor when tape is played back, there has been momentary loss of head-to-tape contact. Such imperfections are called **dropouts** and can be caused by dust or dirt on the tape, flaking of magnetic oxide because of tape wear, a tape manufacturing defect, or dirty or worn heads in the recorder.

TABLE 15–1 VIDEOCASSETTE FORMATS AND RECORDING TIMES

FORMAT	TYPE (AMOUNT OF TAPE)	VIDEOCASSETTE RECORDING TIMES (MINUTES)		
		RECORDING SPEED SETTING		
		SP	LP	EP
VHS and S-VHS	T-30	30	60	90
	T-60	60	120	180
	T-90	90	180	270
	T-120	120	240	360
	T-160	160	320	480
VHS-C		20		60
8mm		15		30
		30		60
		60		120
		90		180
		120		240

- Before using a new videocassette, fast forward the tape to the end, and fully rewind it without stopping. This adjusts tape tension to the recorder and reduces any tendency for one layer of tape to stick to an adjacent layer.
- Tape, in its container, stores best when placed in a vertical position. This keeps pressure on the edges of the tape to a minimum and prevents stretching, creasing, and curling that can distort both picture and sound.
- Do not expose tape to dust, high humidity (40 to 60% preferred), or temperature extremes (60° to 70°F preferred).
- Store tapes away from TV receivers or other equipment that could generate a magnetic field. This can cause erasure of recorded signals on a videotape.
- Consider the effect of carrying video recordings (also audio recordings and undeveloped film) through an X-ray inspection station at an airport. A single passage may not be harmful, but repeated exposure to the X-ray can disturb electronically-created images. Either request hand inspection or place the cassette in a special leadfoil container.
- After recording on a VHS cassette, remove the cutout tab from the back so the recording cannot be erased accidentally. With an 8mm cassette, slide the tab into place as a lock against further recording.

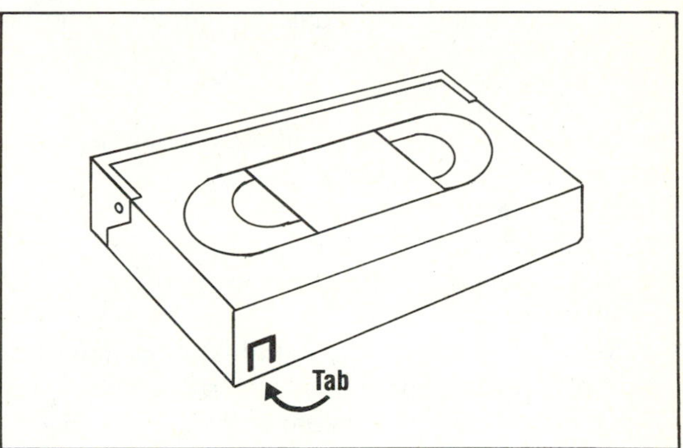

What You Have Learned About Video Equipment and Videotape:

1. Video has replaced film for most media production uses. What *three* major reasons justify this statement?
2. What are the *three* components of a camcorder?
3. What *two* settings relative to lighting should be made on a videocamera in preparation for using it to record a specific scene?
4. Why is the nondirectional microphone built into the camera not the best one to use?
5. Which videotape sizes are commonly used in education and training programs?
6. What statements are TRUE?
   a. The camera in a camcorder can record at various tape speeds.
   b. For best off-the-air recording, the SP setting should be used on a VCR.
   c. Avoid the possibility of erasing a recorded tape by giving attention to the tab on the cassette.
   d. Store tape cassettes flat on a shelf or table.
   e. Before using a new videocassette, run the tape through the VCR at regular speed.
7. Which set of video standards is used in the United States—PAL, NTSC, SECAM?
8. Define these terms:
   a. Videocassette
   b. Control track
   c. Glitch
   d. Dropouts

See answers on page 381.

PLANNING A VIDEO RECORDING

Because making a video recording seems to be so easy, there may be a tendency to choose a topic, pick up the camcorder, and start shooting. This procedure will rarely result in a satisfactory product. Before recording, planning is necessary—whether for treating a limited topic or an extensive subject. Organize the content and plan the method of visualizing the subject to be recorded or filmed. Consider this planning checklist:

- Have you considered the **audience** that will use the material and its characteristics (page 42)?
- Have you expressed your **ideas** clearly and limited the topic (page 41)?
- Have you stated the **objectives** to be served by your production (page 43)?
- Will your materials be for **motivational, informational,** or **instructional** purposes (page 42)?
- Have you prepared a **content outline** (page 45)?
- Have you considered whether a **videotape recording is an appropriate medium** for accomplishing the objectives and handling the content (page 58)?
- What video recording equipment is available (page 240)?
- What video editing equipment is available (page 260)?
- Have you written a **treatment** to help organize the handling of the content (page 64)?
- Have you sketched a **storyboard** to assist with your visualization of the content (page 65)?
- Have you prepared a scene-by-scene **script** as a guide for your recording (page 67)?
- Have you, if necessary, **selected other people** and related services to assist with the production (page 44)?
- Have you considered the **specifications** necessary for your production (page 70)?

Following careful planning, the preparation of a videotape recording requires attention to a number of production steps:

1. Recording scenes on videotape so they can be edited satisfactorily
2. Preparing titles, captions, and art work
3. Recording titles, captions, and art work on videotape
4. Recording narration, music, and sound effects on audiotape
5. Editing and mixing all elements above to a composite master video recording
6. Making duplicate copies from the master recording
7. Developing any correlated printed and visual materials for use with the video recording

The information in Part Three, Chapters 7, 8, and 9, on photography, graphic techniques, and sound recording is basic to the successful preparation of a video recording. As necessary, refer to the page references indicated with the following topics. In addition, give attention to the perception and learning theory principles discussed in Chapter 2, and the research on production factors summarized in Chapter 3.

RECORDING THE PICTURE

While planning a video recording is similar to planning other instructional materials, there is another factor to consider. It relates to the word *motion.*

The mere fact that someone or something moves in a scene is not enough to supply this motion. The *ideas* of the recording must move along their planned development. The audience must be given the sense of this kind of motion, even when seeing such stationary things as a mountain or a building on the screen.

Motion can be accomplished in various ways:

- Subject movement within the scene being recorded
- Physical movement of the camera as when panning (page 247)
- Psychological movement created during editing by the arrangement of scenes or by the length of adjacent scenes

In addition to the concept of motion, you should keep in mind the element of *time,* which is related closely to motion. A photographic print can be studied as long as the viewer wishes to "read" from it the information desired. Slides can also be held for any length of time for prolonged examination. But a scene on videotape is displayed only as long as it takes for it to pass the playback head (or hold a still frame).

Therefore, you must control the period of time the viewer will see a scene. You do this by the length of time the scene is recorded and then projected. You must develop a *feel* for how much screen time is required for the viewer to (1) *recognize* the subject being visualized, and (2) *comprehend* the message or the impression desired.

To shoot and then edit scenes to a proper length—not too long or too short—requires experience and practice. These can be gained to some extent by viewing and studying educational and entertainment films and video recordings. Also watch documentary-type television programs for subject treatment and scene length.

In handling this matter of time, the video medium is unique because it permits you to condense real time by eliminating unnecessary actions or extraneous details while the topic being treated remains logical and understandable to the viewer. A subsequent section on transitions explains how this can be done.

Today most people are visually sophisticated. They have been extensively exposed to the dynamics of television and theatrical films. Their visual orientation has been shaped in great measure by the rapid action of commercials and dramatic shows. The intent of these commercial or entertainment programs differs from the informational and instructional purposes served by instructional media.

If you want to express your ideas imaginatively with a camera, you are encouraged to use it creatively; but be cautioned that too many unusual effects, like a continually moving camera, out-of-focus shots, very quick cuts, and the like, can result in a distracting and boring film. Steady, unobtrusive camera work is often the best policy.

Shots, Scenes, Takes, and Sequences

A video recording is made up of many scenes, shot from different camera angles and put together into sequences to carry the message of the recording. While the terms *shot* and *scene* are often used interchangeably, a **scene** indicates the location of the subject ("technician in lab," "boat dock at the river"). A **shot** is the action being recorded ("technician picks up a scalpel," "sunrise over the water"). Each time you start tape moving past the recording head and then stop it, you have recorded a shot. You can shoot a scene from the script two or more times, calling each one a separate *take* of the particular scene. A **sequence** is a series of related shots depicting one idea. It corresponds to a paragraph in writing.

For easy shot identification, "slate" each one before recording starts. On a sheet of 8½ × 11 inch paper, held on a clipboard (or a small chalkboard), boldly write the scene number according to the script and the take number. Record 1 second of the slate on tape. Then start shooting for 7 to 10 seconds before the action begins (the proper directions are, "Camera start" . . . "Action start") and keep shooting for 7 to 10 seconds after the action ends unless you are filming to edit in the camera (page 255). In this way you not only make sure of getting the complete action, but have some additional tape needed for "roll time" when editing.

Also, because of the "time" factor it may be better to have a shot that is too long than one that is too short and may have to be reshot. Remember that it may take the viewer somewhat longer to identify and comprehend the subject than it does you, because you are very familiar with the subject.

A shot may run from 2 seconds to as long as 30 or more seconds; average shot length is 7 seconds. There is no set rule on shot length; the required action and necessary dialogue or narration must determine effective length. A scene with much detail and activity may require a longer viewing time than a static scene of only general interest. So keep shots long enough to convey your ideas and present the necessary information, but not so long that they drag and become monotonous.

The manner in which you visually treat the action within scenes, and then relate the shots, will determine the coherence and effective reality of your videotape recording.

TYPES OF CAMERA SHOTS

The appearance of a scene can be judged only when viewed through the viewfinder. How the camera sees the subject is important, not how the scene appears to the director, to a person in the scene, or to others.

Camera shots are defined according to the way the subject is framed in the viewfinder. This can be done in five ways:

- ***Distance***—long, medium, close-up
- ***Angle***—high, low
- ***Point-of-view***—objective, subjective
- ***Camera physical movement***—pan, tilt, dolly, truck
- ***Camera apparent movement***—zoom by changing focal length of camera lens

In the section Camera Shots and Picture Composition, in Chapter 7, the first three of these shot groups are explained and illustrated (page 97). Study them carefully. The camera physical movement category is used when a subject moves and you follow the action. Also, when a subject is too large to be included in a single, set shot, or when you want to visually relate two separate subjects, a moving camera shot is acceptable. The last category creates motion as the camera seems to move closer to or farther from the subject. These latter two categories include the following:

- ***Panning***—a left and right movement of the camera
- ***Tilting***—an up and down movement of the camera
- ***Dollying***—a movement of the camera away from or toward the subject
- ***Trucking***—a movement parallel to the subject
- ***Zooming***—a continuous change in focal length of the camera lens during a shot; simulates the effect of

apparent camera movement toward or away from the subject (page 81)

These techniques are generally overused. They are often unnecessary, and are frequently poorly done. If a subject in a scene moves, the camera might logically follow the action. This is a good use of camera movement. If a scene is too broad to be caught by the motionless camera, a pan (panorama) may show its size and scope. Also, you may pan or tilt if it is important to connect two subjects by relating them visually. However, generally do not pan across nonmoving subjects; this can be handled satisfactorily by a longer still shot or by two separate scenes.

Closely related to pans and tilts is the use of a zoom lens—zooming. Here the same cautions apply about overuse. A series of straight cuts (MS to CU) is often more effective. Save the zoom shot until you feel a real need and one that makes an important contribution to the continuity of your film.

The dolly and truck shots are the most difficult of the moving camera shots to perform smoothly and effectively. A scene shot as the camera is held in a moving car is one example of a dolly shot. Or the camera, on a tripod, can be attached to some device with wheels—a wagon, an office chair, a grocery cart, or a motorized factory truck—and slowly pushed or pulled in relation to the subject.

When panning, tilting, dollying, trucking, or zooming, apply these practices:

- Attach your camera to a tripod, make sure it is level, and adjust the head for smooth movement (a long handle on the head is desirable for good control).
- Always start a moving shot with the camera held still for a few seconds and end the shot in the same way.
- When shooting a moving subject, try to "lead" the subject in the frame slightly (page 251).
- Always rehearse the shot a few times before starting to record.

In summary, there is a variety of recording shots at your disposal:

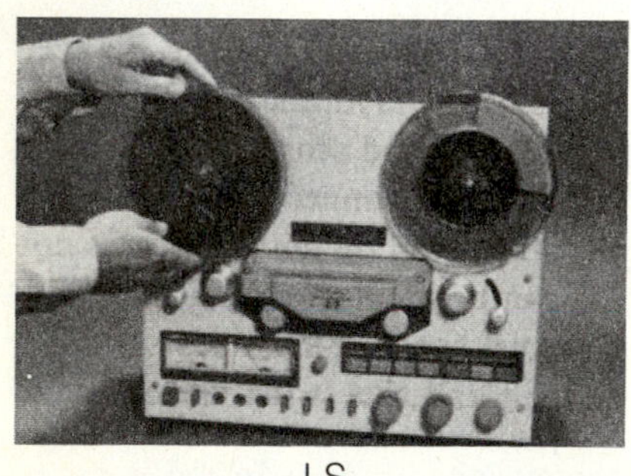
LS

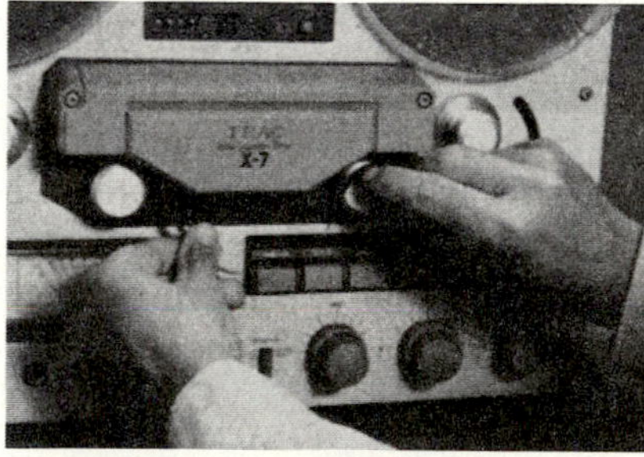
MS

CU

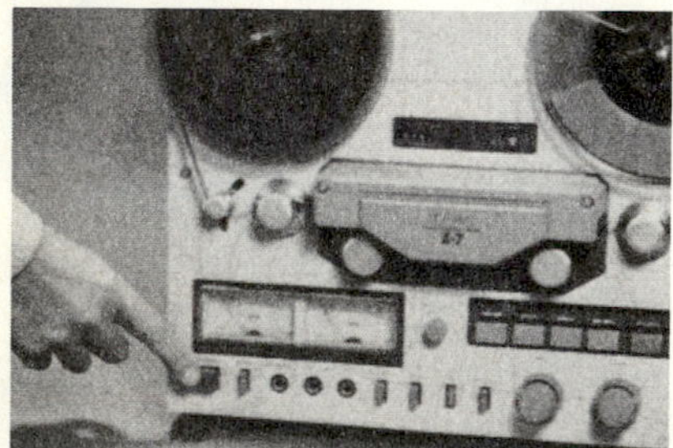
MS

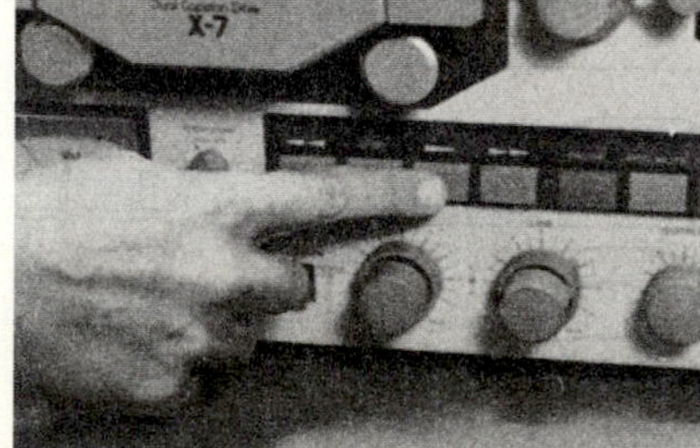
CU

LS

- ***Basic shots***—long or wide shot, medium shot, close-up
- ***Extremes***—extreme long or wide shot, extreme close-up
- ***High-angle*** and ***low-angle*** shots—looking down or looking up at subject
- ***Objective*** camera position—recording a scene from the audience point of view
- ***Subjective*** camera position—recording a scene from over the shoulder of the subject
- ***Pan, tilt, dolly, truck,*** and ***zoom*** shots—moving camera shots

Suggestions as You Plan Your Shots

When there are many scenes in a sequence that include a number of close-ups, *reestablish* the general subject for the viewer with an LS or MS so orientation to the subject is not lost. An establishing shot (LS or MS) is also important when moving to a new activity before close-up detail is shown. See example of the six scene sequence on the previous page.

If the viewer has to try and determine where the camera has suddenly shifted or why an unexplained change has occurred in the action, then you have done something wrong. Always plan your scenes to keep the viewer oriented.

Determine the *viewpoint* and the *area* to be covered for each scene, camera angle, and selected basic shot (LS, MS, or CU). Thus, as you choose camera position and lens you must answer two questions: What is the best viewpoint for effectively showing the action? How much area should be included in the scene?

To help in visualizing the content of key scenes and the placement of the camera in relation to the subject, consider making simple sketches to show the subject position and the area to be covered by the camera. Two examples are shown. These sketches will aid other people (including members of the production crew) to understand what you have in mind. These sketches do not serve the same purposes as the general pictures made from the storyboard during planning (page 65); they apply more specifically to the actual scene being shot.

Scene 10 MS Child Reading

Scene 22 CU (High Angle) Inserting Drill

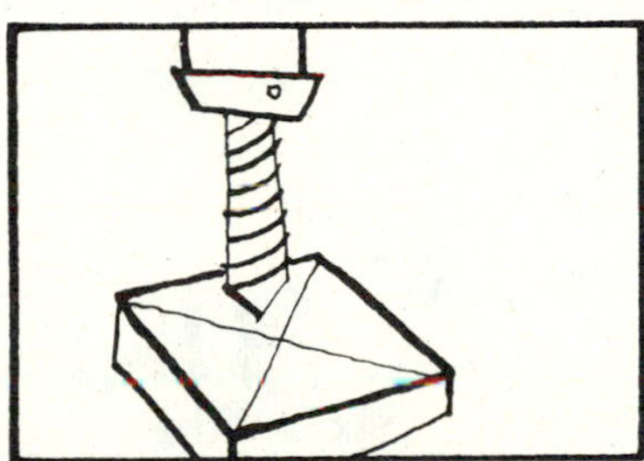

Visualization Sketches in a Shooting Script

R E V I E W

What You Have Learned About Recording the Picture:

1. What are the two concepts that differentiate a video recording from most other instructional materials?
2. Differentiate the terms *scene, shot, take, sequence.*
3. Relate the use of these techniques—pan, tilt, dolly, truck, zoom—to the following situations:
   a. Follow a person climbing stairs
   b. Smooth change from an MS to a CU
   c. Relate an object on a table to other nearby objects
   d. Taping a spread-out farm scene
   e. Recording as the camera passes by a number of buildings
4. When preparing to record a scene, how do you best determine whether the shot is set up as an MS or CU?
5. What is a *reestablishing* scene?

(continued)

6. Label the types of camera shots illustrated by each scene in the sequence that follows.

(a)

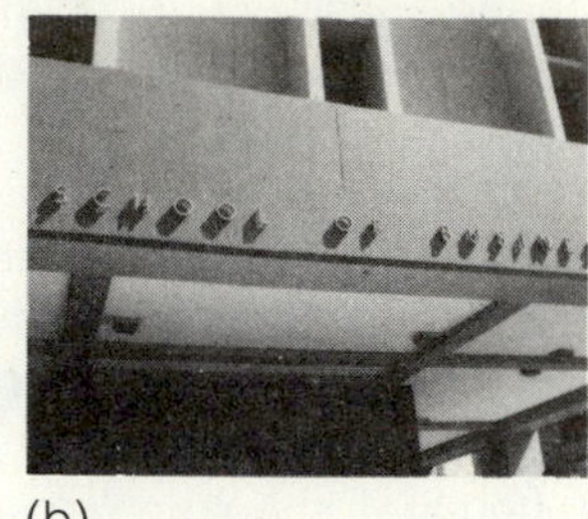

(b)

(c)

(d)

See answers on page 381.

PROVIDING CONTINUITY

Selecting the best camera positions, the proper lens, and the correct exposure under the best light conditions may result in good scenes, but these do not guarantee a good video recording. Only when one scene leads logically and easily to the next one do you have the binding ingredient of smooth **continuity.** Continuity is based on thorough planning and an awareness of a number of factors that must be taken care of during recording.

MS

CU

Matching Action

As you record scenes within the sequence, the subject normally moves. Shoot adjacent and related scenes in such a way that a continuation of the movement is evident from one scene to the next. Such continuation *matches the action* between scenes.

In order to ensure a smooth flow from the MS to the CU, match the action at the end of the first scene to the beginning of the second one. Accomplish this matching by having some of the action at the end of the MS repeated at the beginning of the CU.

Then, when editing, from this overlap of action select appropriate points at which the two scenes should be joined. This transition is most easily accepted by the viewer if the scenes are joined at a point of change—when something is picked up or shifted or similarly changed—and consistently follow the direction of movement. This is preferable to joining scenes in the middle of a smooth movement where the natural flow of action may be disturbed.

In this way "action is matched" and a smooth flow results. As you plan matching shots remember to:

- Change the angle slightly between adjacent shots to avoid a "jump" in screen action.
- Match the tempo of movement from an MS to a CU.

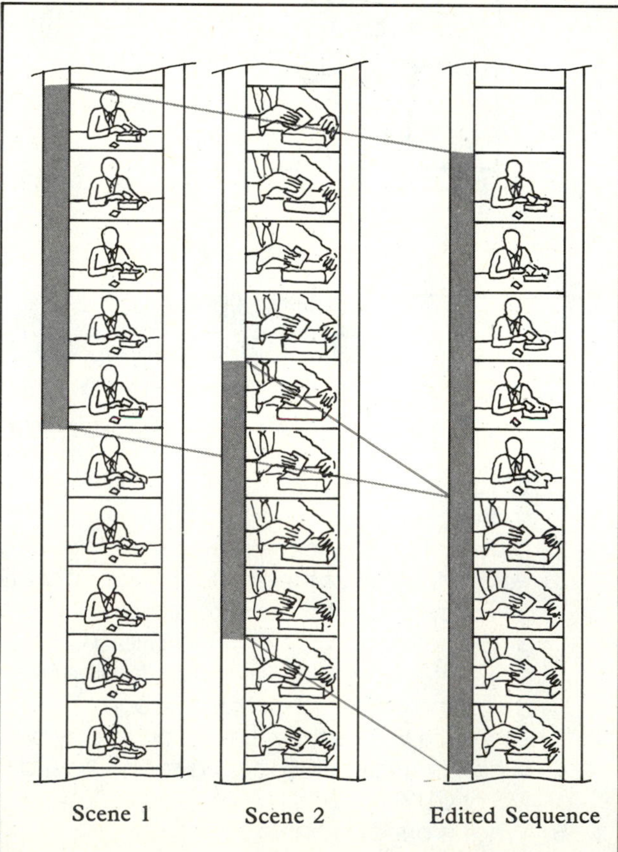

Because the action in a CU should be somewhat slower than normal or it will appear highly accelerated and disturbing to the viewer, the movement in the previous MS should be slowed down.

- Notice where parts of the subject or objects within the first scene are placed, which hand is used and its position, or how the action moves. Be sure they are the same for all closely following scenes. Be particularly observant if scenes are recorded out of script order.

It can be helpful to record a complex shot on Polaroid film as a record of details within the scene for future reference.

It is not always essential to match action unless details in adjacent scenes are easily recognizable to the viewer. An LS of general activity (for example, a sports activity scene) does not have to match an MS of a team in action, but when the camera turns from this group to an individual the action should be matched.

For some purposes, action can best be matched by using two or more cameras—one taking close-ups and the other long shots—both shooting scenes simultaneously while the action is continuous.

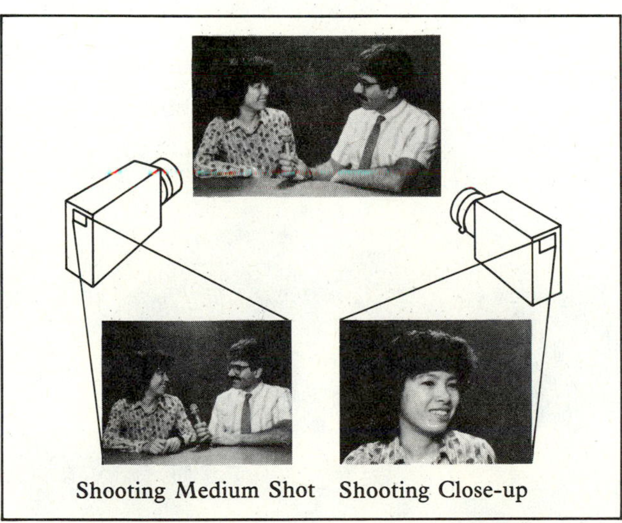

This **multicamera technique** speeds up recording and ensures accurate matching of action, even though it may require the use of more tape than when shooting with only one camera. Waste can be minimized by starting the second camera on signal just before the first one stops in order to provide the overlap. Multicamera shooting is particularly useful when documenting events such as athletic meets, meetings, teleconferences, demonstrations, and news events. Assign camera teams to work together and coordinate their filming to cover related activities at the same time from positions that will edit smoothly together. Keep a careful record of scenes shot.

Screen Direction

Another kind of matching action is required when a subject moves across the frame. If a person or object moves from left to right, make sure the action is the same in the next scene.

When action leaves the frame on one side, it must enter the next scene from the *opposite* side of the frame for proper continuity.

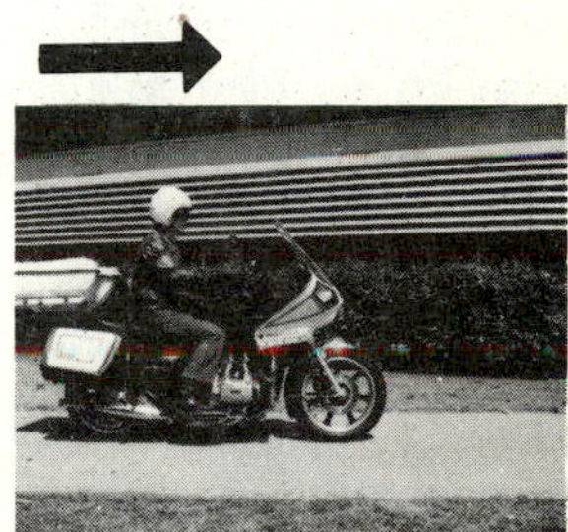

If directions must change between two scenes, try to show the change in the first scene by having the subject make a turn. If a turn is not possible, include a brief in-between scene of the action coming straight toward the camera. Then a new direction in the following scene seems plausible to the viewer. See example overleaf.

Be careful when recording parades, races, and similar activities with more than one camera unless someone is assigned to show the action changing direction (going around turns, or moving directly toward or away from the camera). If you do not do this and cameras are located on opposite sides of the activity one will show action from left to right and another from right to left. The audience will be confused and receive the impression that the moving subject has turned around and is returning to the starting point—and no one will ever get to the finish line!

If screen direction is to be reversed intentionally, include one or more scenes inserted between the two directions that show how the action reversed.

Protection Shots

Careful though you may be, there are times when things go wrong with your planning or recording. Possibly you did not quite match the action between scenes; the left hand instead of the right one was used in the CU, the screen direction between two scenes changes, or you create a *jump* by momentarily stopping the tape during a scene and then starting it again while the action is continuing. Often such situations are not discovered until the editing, and then you may be in trouble. Therefore, protect yourself from possible embarrassment and poor practice by shooting **cut-in** and **cut-away shots,** even though these shots are not indicated in the script. A cut-in is a CU (or ECU of some part of the scene being shot). It also is called an **insert.** Examples of common cut-ins are faces, hands, feet, parts of objects, and other items known to be in the scene.

A cut-away is opposite to a cut-in in that it is a shot of another subject or separate action taking place at the same time as the main action. This other subject or action is not in the scene (hence *away*) but is related in some way to the main action. Examples of cut-aways are people or objects that complement the main action; faces of people watching, or reacting to the main action.

Both cut-ins and cut-aways serve to distract the viewer's attention momentarily and thus permit acceptance of the next scene even though the action may not match the preceding one accurately. By using cut-ins and cut-aways in this way, two scenes can be given continuity even though they would be illogical in direct succession.

Keep these points in mind as you shoot cut-ins and cut-aways:

Cut-in Shot

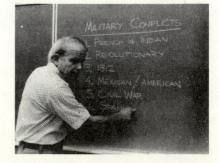

Cut-away Shot (reaction shot)

- Always shoot a number of them, as you may not know until editing whether you will need one or more.
- Make them long enough (a minimum of 10 to 15 seconds, although you may only use 2 or 3 seconds).
- Make them logical, in keeping with the appropriate sequences (watch expressions and backgrounds so they will be consistent with the main action).
- Make them technically consistent with related scenes (lighting, color, exposure).

Transitions

One of the strengths of a video recording is that it allows the use of techniques to take viewers from one place to another or to show action taking place at different times—all this presented in adjacent scenes within a very short period of actual screen time, and accepted quite realistically by the audience. How is this acceptance accomplished? It is achieved through the use of **transitional devices,** which bridge space and time.

The simplest method for achieving smooth pictorial transitions is by use of printed titles or directions placed between scenes.

Cut-ins and cut-aways can give the impression of time passing and may reduce a long scene to its essentials without the audience realizing that time has been compressed. An example of this may be showing the start of an activity, then a cut-in, then the completion of activity, with the inserted scene 2 to 3 seconds in length.

Exiting from a scene and subsequent entrance at another location creates an acceptable transition in

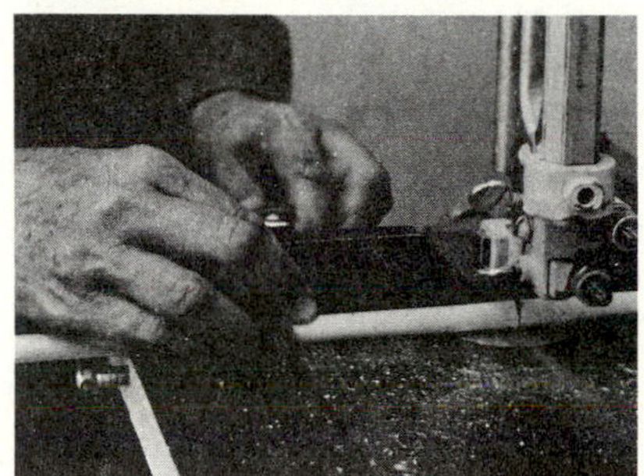

Cut all pieces
to size

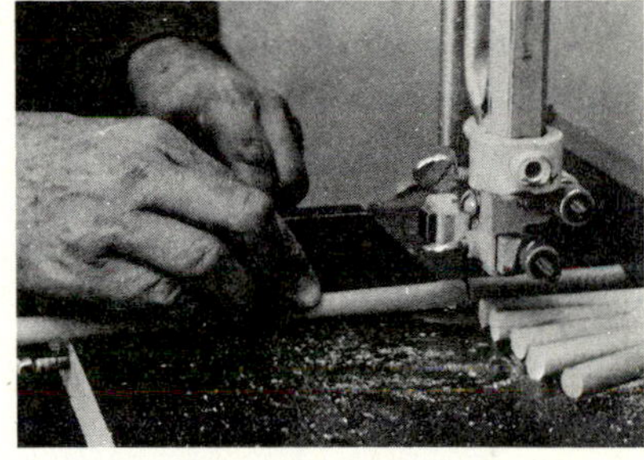

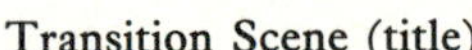

Transition Scene (title)

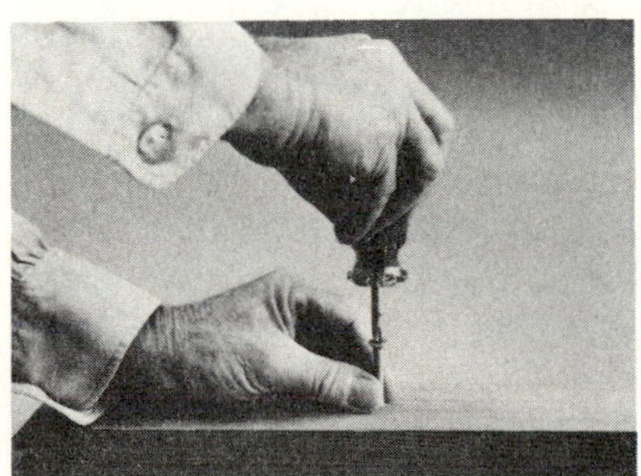

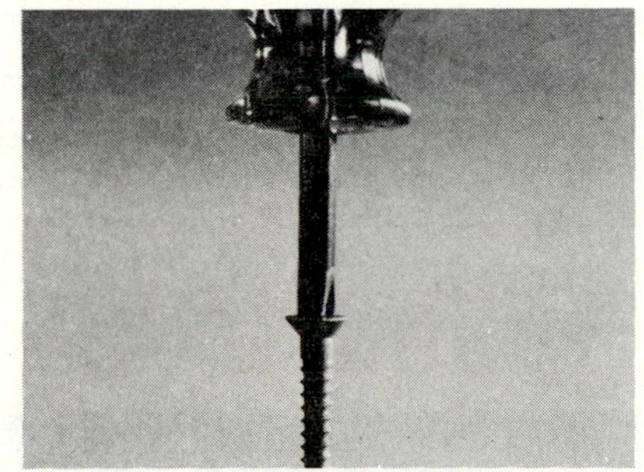

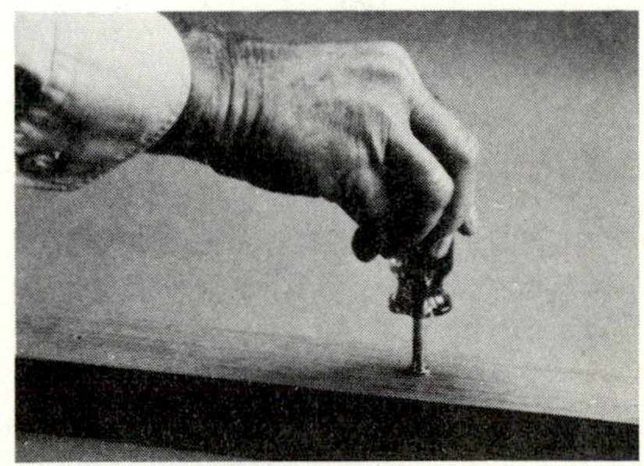

Transition Scene (cut-in)

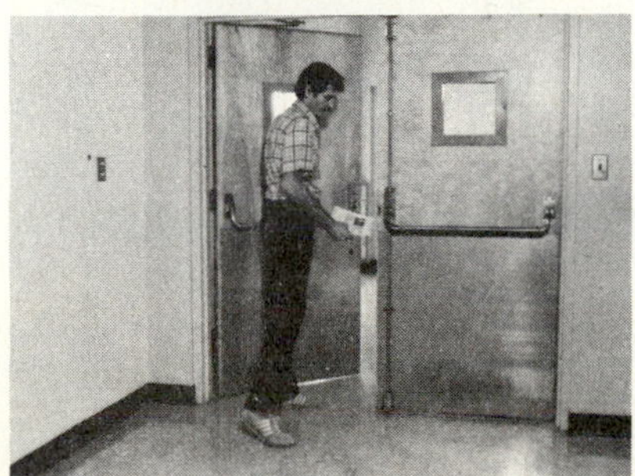

Transition Scene (exit/entrance)

time as well as in space. (Always record the scene for a few seconds after the subject has left the scene to insure an acceptable period of time for the subject to appear in the next scene at a different location.)

A **montage** is a series of short scenes connected by cuts, dissolves, or possibly wipes, used to quickly condense time or distance or to show a series of related activities and places. The audience accepts this rapid series of scenes as if the complete operation or various places had been seen in their entirety.

Visual transitions are other ways of expressing time and space changes. The most commonly used visual transition technique is the **fade-out/fade-in.** A fade-out and fade-in serve to separate major sequences in a recording. As mentioned before, they consist of the gradual darkening of a scene to a solid color like black (fade-out) followed by the gradual appearance (fade-in) of the first scene of the next sequence. Fades sometimes are used at the beginning of a recording (fade-in) and at the end (fade-out). Most videocameras contain a control lever or button that allows you to create fades. Use them sparingly, as overuse of fades may produce a disturbing effect that disrupts the flow of the visual presentation.

Other commonly used visual transitions are the **dissolve** and the **wipe.** In order to create them, a **special effects generator (SEG)** must be used when editing to relate scenes. Also see reference to the Video Toaster (commercial product) on page 264 that can produce various video effects.

A dissolve on videotape commonly indicates a lapse in time or a change in location between adjacent scenes. It blends one scene into another by showing the fade-out of the first scene and the *superimposed* fade-in of the next scene. This requires two videocameras connected to the special effects generator (SEG). When editing, a dissolve is sometimes used to soften the change from one scene to another. Some scene changes otherwise would be abrupt or jarring, due possibly to poor planning or incorrect selection of camera angles in adjacent scenes.

A wipe on videotape is a visual effect in which a new scene seems to push the previous scene off the screen. It is like a window shade that is pulled down to cover a window with a solid color or another scene. The wiping motion may be vertical, horizontal, or angular. This effect is infrequently used but may be important for situations that are closely related; the start of an experiment followed immediately by the result is an example. A group of scenes connected by wipes may give the impression of looking across a row or a series of objects.

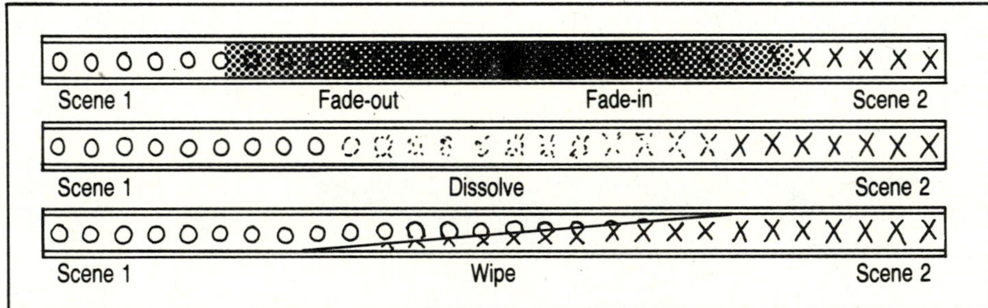

What You Have Learned About Providing Continuity:

1. What is meant by "matching action"?
2. Why should a constant screen direction be maintained in a sequence?
3. How can you provide for acceptable direction change?
4. What protection shot might you use in recording a sequence showing a person sewing a lengthy seam?
5. What transition device would you use in each of these situations:
   a. A board being painted and then used after it has dried
   b. A person leaving home and arriving at the office
   c. A scoreboard showing the score after the first inning and then at the end of the game

6. What purposes are served by visual effects?
7. What are the *three* common visual effects?

See answers on page 381.

SPECIAL VIDEO PRODUCTION TECHNIQUES

There are situations in which you must record a program *without* previously preparing a script, or you need to tape scenes in specific script order *without* any editing. In such instances special methods may be used.

Documentary Recording

As explained on page 168, there may be times when a topic is to be recorded in documentary style, without first writing a detailed script. Your understanding and application of all the aforementioned production techniques relating to camera shots and continuity are essential in documentary recording.

To end up with scenes that can be edited together and result in a coherent product, you must keep in mind what you have shot and try to anticipate what may be next. Because you cannot anticipate all the action, you may miss something of importance, or what you expect may not happen. Therefore, always record a number of cut-aways and cut-ins to be used as protection shots for insertion between scenes that may not go together naturally.

The editing stage for a documentary recording becomes especially important. Depending on the footage you have, editing may be a straightforward task or require careful decisions that can lead to alternative treatment or interpretation of the subject. See page 170 for suggestions on how to proceed with the editing of a documentary recording.

Editing-in-the-Camera Technique

You may want to prepare your recording without having to remove or rearrange any of the scenes shot. When you shoot one scene after another in sequence, from the first title through the end, the recording is edited in the camera. As opposed to the documentary approach, this **editing-in-the-camera technique** requires careful planning and following the script scene by scene. Obviously, when scene locations require shifts from one place to another and back again, taping in sequence can be very costly in time and travel.

A beginner in video production may believe that, like in motion picture filming, one scene can be recorded, the videocamera and videotape stopped, the next scene set up and shot, and so forth through the scenes of the script. The expected result is an edited-in-the-camera tape immediately ready for showing to an audience. When this procedure is used in video, the result may be unacceptable. Although adjacent scenes may have proper visual relationship and be of proper length, the electronic signal becomes discontinuous, and each scene change is evidenced by a rolling of the picture and other disturbance (called a *glitch*).

To overcome a glitch between scenes, many VCRs contain a **flying erase head** to insure clean breaks from one scene to the next. An alternative technique with older recorders is to place the control in PAUSE position instead of in STOP. The continued contact of the recording head with the tape will hold the picture and eliminate the image breakup. But the PAUSE control should not be used for more than one minute. It causes wear on the tape and on the video heads; also, it uses up battery time.

In using the editing-in-the-camera technique, each of the following is important:

- ▶ You are certain of the sequence of scenes.
- ▶ You can control all action to be recorded and know how long each scene will be. Rehearsals are important.
- ▶ Titles and illustrations are prepared and ready for recording. You must have the titles set up so you can turn the camera to them for recording in proper order and then go back to the next action scene.
- ▶ Light balance and camera movement will be correct for each scene.

Time-Lapse and Single-Frame Recording

Action that takes place *too slowly* to see the incremental changes can be speeded up for ease of viewing and study. By recording the action for a brief time at repeated intervals, and then playing back the tape at normal speed, action is visually compressed or speeded up. This recording procedure is called **time-lapse.** Also, the expression **single-frame** recording is used when one frame at a time is recorded.

With a camcorder or regular videocamera you will record about eight frames each time you push and release the control button to achieve a single-frame effect. Accessory units can be attached to a camera to more accurately control this short recording time. However, it is essential that the camera be equipped with a flying erase head to avoid glitches between shots.

This technique lets you record subjects having very

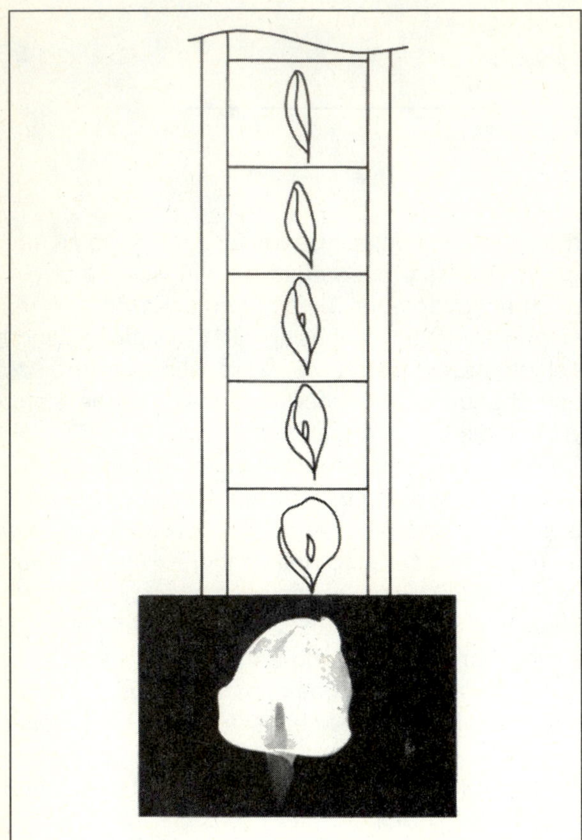

slow movement, like the opening of a flower bud, the formation and movement of clouds, and color changes or growths in laboratory experiments. Individual shots are taken at a predetermined rate, for instance 1 per minute or 1 per hour. Find out how long the action to be recorded normally takes. Then decide how much tape time you want to use and determine how often a picture should be shot. Here is a problem:

Purpose: To record a color reaction change in a test tube
Normal time for reaction to take place: 8 hours (480 minutes)
Recording time to be used: 10 seconds

$$\frac{\text{480 minutes}}{\text{10 seconds}} = \text{48 minutes of change for each second of recording time}$$

This means that for a period of 8 hours, at the end of each 48 minutes, a recording of 1 second duration should be made. (But first run about 3 seconds of recording time to familiarize the viewer with the subject before the time-lapse action starts. Then end with 5–10 seconds of the final image.)

Result: Eight-hour change is shown in 10 seconds.

Also, motion can be simulated by moving or zooming the camera into a preprinted still picture to record a close-up of part of the subject, or by moving out from a detail to a broader view. The picture can also be moved across the lens to create the effect of panning or tilting. In either situation, changes in camera position, lens focal-length setting, or picture placement should be only slight with each shot. When this sequence of separate movements is projected continuously, the illusion of motion—inward, backward, or across—results.

For success when using this technique, give attention to the following:

- Use a large still picture (at least 8 × 10 inches) for ease of moving across its surface
- Light the still picture adequately so as to set a larger lens *f*/number (smaller diaphragm opening—page 82) to ensure greater depth-of-field with satisfactory focus.

One tendency in making a recording this way is to shoot the still pictures for too short a length of time—sometimes 1 to 2 seconds per shot. This may be too brief a time for the viewer to grasp the meaning of the picture. You may have to experiment with recording times. Play back the recorded picture to see if you are accomplishing both the understanding and the effect you want to create.

Animation

As indicated under Desktop Video, animation software (page 264) can be used to create and record still images to make them appear as if they are moving on the screen. Images in motion attract attention, help to convey complex ideas, and explain technical processes. This procedure resembles time-lapse in that single-framing is used to record sequences and the method to determine movement per frame is similar. Computer software with animation features may have:

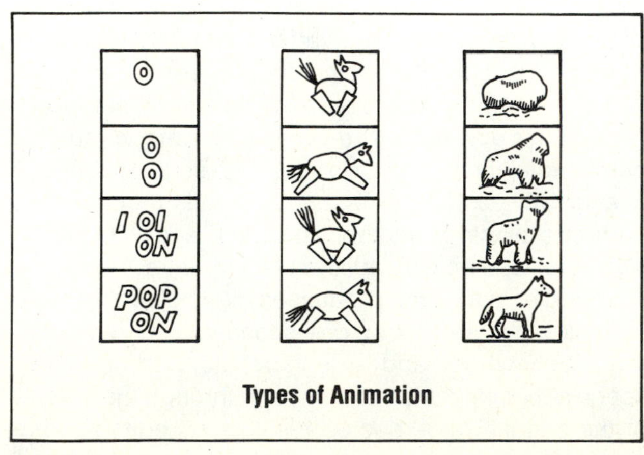

Types of Animation

- Animation as the main function
- Animation effects created by graphics paint programs
- Animation as part of 3D modeling programs
- Animation resulting from use of an authoring system that allows the combination of various media into an integrated presentation

What You Have Learned About Special Video Production Techniques:

1. To what matters should you give particular attention when preparing a documentary recording?
2. Why can you *not* successfully record a scene, stop the recorder, then record the next scene, and so on? What should you do to effectively record all scenes in sequence?
3. What is a "glitch?" How is it overcome in a VCR?
4. If you want to record a sequence of action without having to follow by editing the tape, to what matters would you give careful attention?
5. What does the *time-lapse* technique do? How is it used in video recording?
6. How often would a single-frame exposure be made if you wished to show the changes in clouds across the sky from 10:00 A.M. to 4:00 P.M. and covering 20 seconds of recording time?

See answers on page 382.

OTHER PRODUCTION FACTORS

The following are important matters for preparing successful video recordings. Give attention to each one at the appropriate time during production.

Video Reference Marks

In order to set a standard for the color quality of the video image professional producers record at least 30 seconds of **color bars** on the beginning of the first videotape for a production. This may be done with a setting on the camera. All scenes then appear in color relationship to these color bars. During editing and subsequent use of the videotape, the color bars serve as reference for adjusting players and television receivers for optimum color reproduction as created by the program director or camera operator.

In addition to the color bars, an audio tone is recorded on the tape, also for reference purposes. This can be done with a simple tone generator (usually 400 cycles) connected to the microphone input on the videotape recorder. It is recorded along with the color bars. The tone permits the proper setting of the audio levels during playback.

If color bars cannot be created in your camera, shoot a color chart, a commercial television station's color-bar-test pattern from the receiver, or a well-lighted scene that contains some flesh tones and a range of colors. Be certain the color temperature and white balance in the scene are all properly adjusted. Record the sound in the scene as the standard to set audio playback level.

Cinematic/Composition

Although composition is a matter of personal aesthetics, there are accepted practices to follow. Note the general suggestions for good composition on page 101.

The proportions of the video frame should always be kept in mind when selecting subjects and composing scenes. Since the frame has a 3 to 4 ratio (page 115), preference should be given to subjects with horizontal rather than vertical configurations.

Special care must be taken in composing scenes involving motion. Always lead a moving subject with more area in the direction of motion, and carefully rehearse anticipated movement so that proper framing or camera motion can be planned.

When a person handles an object or performs an operation, the camera should be situated for the best view (like from a subjective position as shown on page 99), although it may appear unnatural from the subject's viewpoint. Exaggeration and simplification are acceptable in informational recordings, or in recordings displaying a skill in order to convey a correct understanding or impression.

Lighting Scenes

The light levels necessary for color videocameras have been reduced to the point that much recording can take place under available room light. When necessary, a general boost in lighting can be obtained by aiming one or more floodlights at a light-colored ceiling. See information on using a camera light (page 95).

If an indoor location must be lighted, follow the information on using key, fill, and back lights (page 95). A close-up scene containing one or more faces requires particular care when being lighted. Also, to give a sense of depth to the subject, carefully control shadow areas (page 93).

Titles and Illustrations

Although titles and graphics can be prepared separately after live action is recorded, with proper equipment they can be added during editing. This will help ensure that they will be properly placed and effectively worded.

Similar techniques described for preparing titles and illustrations for slides on page 225 can be used now. Review these procedures:

- Word each title so it is brief but communicative.
- Keep materials simple, bold, and free from unnecessary details.
- Use suitable, clear-cut lettering.
- Limit outlines and other lists to 10 lines, each containing no more than 25 characters.
- Adhere to recognized legibility standards for ease of reading—minimum letter size is one-twenty-fifth the height of the frame area for video.
- Keep in mind the correct 3 to 4 ratio proportions of the video image area, use simple design features (page 116), and select appropriate backgrounds (page 140).
- Then, attach each prepared title and illustration to a wall or easel and record it with your camera on a tripod (page 105), or use a copy or titling stand.
- Record each title or other printed information for at least twice as long as it takes you to read the material completely.

Carefully consider the placement of content within the video format size. Provide for loss of one-sixth the marginal area on each side of the screen. Thus, keep important parts of a visual within the middle two-thirds portion of the screen. This restriction is necessary because of variations in the adjustments of television receivers. For planning titles and art work, an outline of the open area of the video frame is printed inside the back cover of this book.

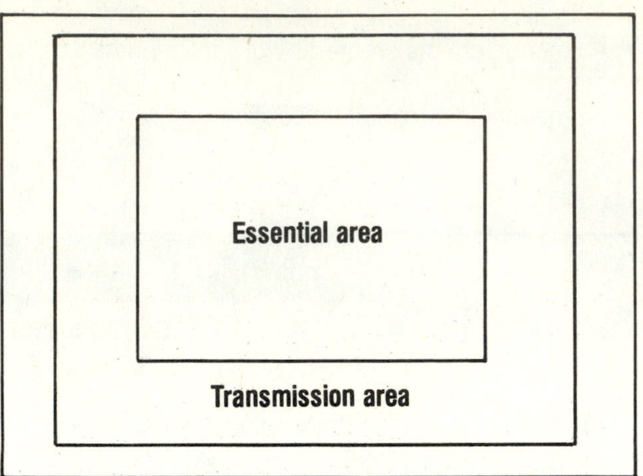

In addition to preparing titles with conventional lettering aids (page 136) and art work using illustration procedures (page 124), desktop video techniques can be applied (page 264). Word processing (page 182) and graphics programs (page 121) can be used to generate titles and to create illustrations. A character generator (page 241) will also serve for titling. If available illustrations are to be used, they can be scanned or digitized into computer memory, and then transferred to videotape.

Scheduling and Record Keeping

Follow the suggestions on page 167 for preparing a recording schedule, making arrangements for recording, checking facilities, and keeping a record (a log sheet) of all scenes as shot. To facilitate editing, identify each shot (scene number, take number, footage counter at start and end) and make notes about the suitability of each "take." When viewing the original recording, the scenes and takes can be identified and selected for final editing.

Be mindful of the need for obtaining permission from those appearing in scenes or from owners of copyrighted materials being used. For a sample release form, see page 169.

RECORDING THE SOUND

As part of a video recording, sound can take various forms:

- Synchronous voice or voices of persons appearing in a scene being recorded on the videotape at the same time as the picture is recorded
- Sounds integral to the subject (for example, animal, street, or machinery sounds) recorded on videotape at the same time the picture was recorded

- Sounds integral to or typical of the subject but recorded on audiotape separate from the picture (may also be obtained from a *sound effects* record)
- Narration that may be recorded by one or more off-camera voices either at the same time the picture is recorded, or, preferably, on audiotape and added to the picture after the latter has been edited
- Music as an introduction, as background, or between segments of the program, recorded on audiotape and then transferred to the videotape after editing
- Computer-generated music that can be designed specifically to fit the mood or style of your video recording

Any of these sound sources, alone or in combination, may be essential to your video recording. The realism and immediacy so important to the effect of a video program can be attributable to the way the sounds are handled, as well as to the pictures. The basic information in Chapter 9 about recording and mixing sounds applies when creating and handling sound for video. Multitrack audio recorders and a mixer are necessary for preparing off-camera recordings before they are transferred to the videotape and combined properly with the pictures.

Here are suggestions when recording sound for a video recording:

- Preferably use a microphone separate from the one built into the videocamera. Place it close to the subject for best quality—not over 3 feet away from a person speaking.
- Consider using a shotgun or wireless microphone (page 242) if it is difficult to keep the regular microphone, or its cord, out of the scene.
- If more than one microphone will be used in a scene, attach each one to an input on the audio mixer (page 150), which in turn is connected to the line input on the VCR. Adjust volume levels before recording starts.
- Start recording at least 15 seconds before the sound and action are to start and continue recording for at least 15 seconds after the sound and action are ended. The blank lead-in and lead-out will be necessary during editing.

When complex actions or detailed how-to-do-it sequences are to be recorded and explained, it may be desirable to record the narration or accompanying explanations as scripted on audiotape *before* each scene or sequence is shot. Then play back the sound as each scene is recorded so actions can be performed at appropriate times and at suitable length corresponding to the required narration. This can ensure sufficient action to cover necessary narration and reduce work during editing.

What You Have Learned About Other Production Factors and Recording Sound:

1. For what reason are "color bars" put on a videotape at the beginning of a recording period?
2. When preparing titles for a video recording, what *five* procedures should receive attention?
3. Besides copying titles during recording, how else can they be added to the videotape?
4. What are *four* kinds of sound that may be used on a video recording?
5. Why is it necessary to have blank lead-in tape before the actual recorded signal and blank lead-out tape after it?

See answers on page 382.

EDITING VIDEOTAPE

The selection of visuals and sound elements for the script, the choice of camera positions when shooting, the recording of sound, and finally the editing procedure for pictures and sounds make up the main creative aspects of a video production. If your program has been shot in sequence, using the "editing-in-the-camera" technique (page 255), then there is little need for editing. Since this is infrequently the case, you must be prepared to do some picture and sound editing.

Editing is the process of selecting, arranging, and shortening scenes by selectively copying them. Also, inserting scenes and adding sound may be important so that the final result satisfies the objectives you originally established. In order to accomplish this, a person must have a feeling for how to manage the video medium. A creative talent is required as well as patience and intuition so that suitable decisions will be made as editing proceeds.

With a staged studio production, editing takes place as the director selects shots and controls their sequential placement on the videotape by means of a switcher. The resulting recording, at the completion of shooting, is the final **master videotape** with all scenes, titles, and special effects in correct position, and of proper quality, ready for use.

Videotape recordings made with a single camera at various locations, or with two cameras recording independently, are a standard practice. The subject can be anything from a simple how-to-do-it technique at a machine to a complex documentary or drama requiring sophisticated shooting at many locations. Editing the variety of scenes then follows. This is done by electronically copying the desired scenes onto another tape to form the final master. The editing procedure has little effect on the original tape. It is not cut or spliced.

Preparation for Editing

Editing consists of two tasks. First, decisions concerning content, pace or flow, and continuity must be made. This requires ordering scenes; selecting takes; determining scene length or the usable portion of a scene; mixing narration, lip synchronization, and other sound elements; and reviewing the need for and placement of titles, captions, and special inserts.

The second task is technical, essentially a copying function. Each scene from the original tape, along with sound elements, is accurately transferred, in proper order, to the final master videotape.

Start by viewing the tape or the set of tapes that were shot in order to familiarize yourself with the material. Review the script that was used to guide the shooting, and the log sheets of shots and takes that were prepared during recording. Note changes that should be made in the script (unscripted scenes that were recorded, reordering of scenes, scenes that were combined or eliminated). If you documented an activity without having a script, now is the time to prepare a listing or plan from the recorded tape you view. Sometimes it is necessary to reshoot or add a new scene to complete a sequence.

Mark on the script the cassette number and the approximate footage location of each scene and which take to use. Also check where narration may replace synchronous sound, or where sound effects might be added. If the editing equipment you have permits the inclusion of titles or special effects (fades, dissolves, wipes, superimpositions, split frames), indicate places on the script where such titles and effects are to be placed. With these changes and additions, the previous shooting script now becomes your *editing* script.

Editing Procedures

There are various levels of videotape editing. Each one requires certain equipment and an exacting procedure. Reference will be made to two commonly used methods on different levels of complexity.

Manual Assemble-Mode Editing This is the simplest method of editing. It is similar to editing audiotape as you copy from one recorder to another. It employs two VCRs—one to play back the original videotape, called the *source* (it may be the camcorder), and the other to record scenes into a final program (known as the **edit/record VCR**). The editing VCR must give exact control of frames during forward and reverse operation.

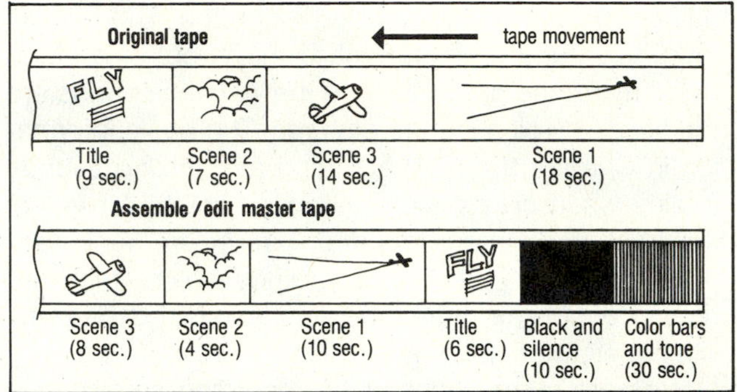

Here is the **manual assemble-mode** procedure:

1. Set up a VCR *source player* (with monitor) and a VCR *recorder* (with monitor). If the VCR recorder has a flying erase head then the discontinuity, or *glitch,* that often results when stopping or pausing the tape between two adjacent scenes can be avoided. Attach video and audio *outputs* on the player to video and audio *inputs* on the recorder.

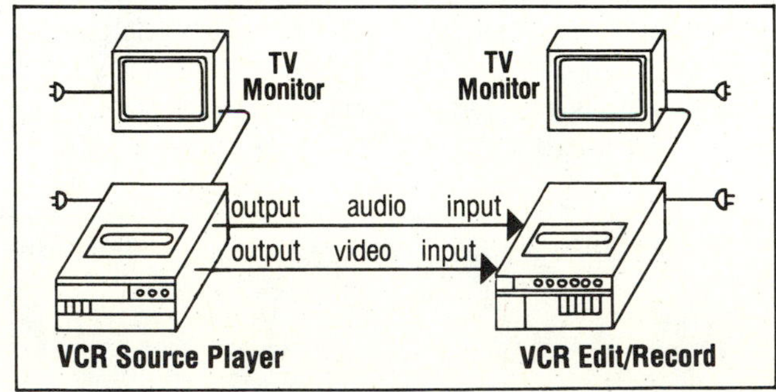

2. Preset the counters on both units to zero (although the counters are not accurate, they will closely indicate location of specific scenes).
3. Put a fresh videocassette, prerecorded with 30 seconds of color bars, in the edit/record VCR.
4. Review the original tape on the source VCR, se-

lecting scenes needed and note counter numbers for start and end points of each scene.

5. Dub first scene to recorder VCR. Exactly at the end of the scene put the recorder VCR into PAUSE. Do *not* STOP the recorder.
6. Find the start of the next scene on the source VCR.
7. Rewind the original tape for 10 seconds of playing time ahead of the scene's starting point.
8. Start the playback. At the end of the 10 seconds (or just before the image at the beginning of the scene appears on the monitor) release the PAUSE button on the recorder. Return to PAUSE at the end of the scene.
9. Locate the next scene to be copied and repeat the process.

This manual assemble-mode method is limited as to accuracy in assembling scenes at proper beginning and ending points. If the equipment is operated carefully, there should be little, if any, breakup of the image between shots. The PAUSE control will stay engaged for about 5 minutes, although after about one minute the tape can be damaged. This would be due to the continual rotation of the recording head drum, rubbing against the tape.

The availability of more sophisticated equipment would allow more accuracy and speed in editing, and more flexibility for inserting additional audio and visual elements.

Automatic Assemble-Mode Editing This method adds an **edit controller** between the source and edit/record units. The editor controller is a programing device that accepts editing location instructions for selected scenes (edit-in and edit-out points) as numbers on the counter, which are placed in the memory of the controller. The edit controller then automatically has the two VCRs backspace, stop, play, and record to ensure frame-accurate edits.

Although available models of edit controllers may have somewhat different operating procedures and control button labels, the procedure for **automatic assemble-mode** editing is:

1. From the source VCR connect audio and video outputs to audio and video inputs on the edit/record VCR. Connect each VCR to a monitor. Connect from the remote control on the VCR player to the player plug on the controller, and from the remote control on the edit/record VCR to the recorder plug on the controller.
2. Use a fresh videocassette with color bars and audio tone (or copy of a scene from a television program or commercial as explained on page 257) already in place as on the master tape in the edit/record VCR. It is important to record on tape this initial segment, which automatically includes the control track, the importance of which will be pointed out shortly. Once this initial piece is recorded, then the editing procedure for adding, or "tagging on," each following scene follows.
3. Using the *player* controls on the edit controller, locate the start of scene 1 on the player VCR. Press the PAUSE/STILL button on the controller to freeze the picture on the first frame of the scene. On the numerical keyboard of the controller, enter the counter number for this frame.
4. Using the *edit/record* controls on the editor controller, locate the point on the master videotape at which scene 1 should be entered. Press the PAUSE/STILL button on the controller to freeze the picture at this point. Enter the counter number into the controller's memory.
5. If you wish, preview the edit on the edit/record VCR monitor to be certain it appears at the proper spot. If it is wrong, reprogram the edit points.
6. Press the EDIT/RECORD button on the controller to effect the edit. The controller will automatically backspace both tapes on both VCR units the *same* distance, start forward, and at the proper point start the transfer of scene 1 to the master videotape. Stop the two machines after the scene ends.
7. Prepare to transfer scene 2 by starting with step 3 above and repeating the procedure.

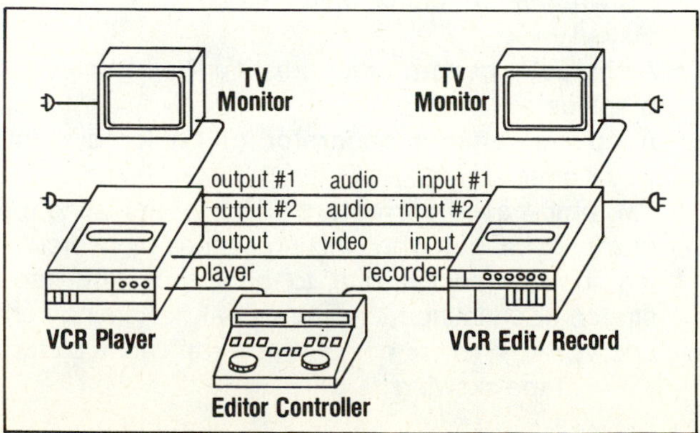

During the automatic assemble-mode editing procedure, the controller senses the position and movement of each tape according to pulses that were recorded on the *control tracks.* By counting these pulses, which are like sprocket holes on motion-picture film, the controller can back up a tape for about 10 seconds. This allows each VCR to start forward and stabilize to run at proper speed before the edit/record VCR starts to RECORD.

The controller starts both tapes playing forward at the same time. The controller will initiate the record function on the recorder VCR when the last of the pulses is reached. The transfer will continue either for the number of pulses (frames) that were programed into the controller's memory or until the edit/record VCR is manually stopped. Such an edit is accurate to within 1 to 3 frames of where you want it to take place.

If, at a later time, it is decided to change a scene within the program or re-edit in some way, then *everything from that point to the end of the program must be re-recorded.* By using the following insert-mode editing procedure, this deficiency can be avoided.

Insert-Mode Editing In addition to assembling scenes in order, there will be times when you want to insert (or substitute) a brief close-up or a cut-away (page 253) to replace part of a scene already on the master tape, or to add narration or other sound in place of synchronous sound. In such instances, you perform an **insert edit** onto the already-recorded master videotape. You may transfer a complete scene or either new picture or new sound, *leaving* the other component unchanged. The process requires that the new material be fitted into a certain space on the master tape. In this procedure it is necessary to locate *both edit-in* and *edit-out* points on the master videotape. Recall that in assemble editing *only* the edit-in point was necessary. Now you want to be certain not to erase any of the master tape beyond that portion in which the new material will be placed.

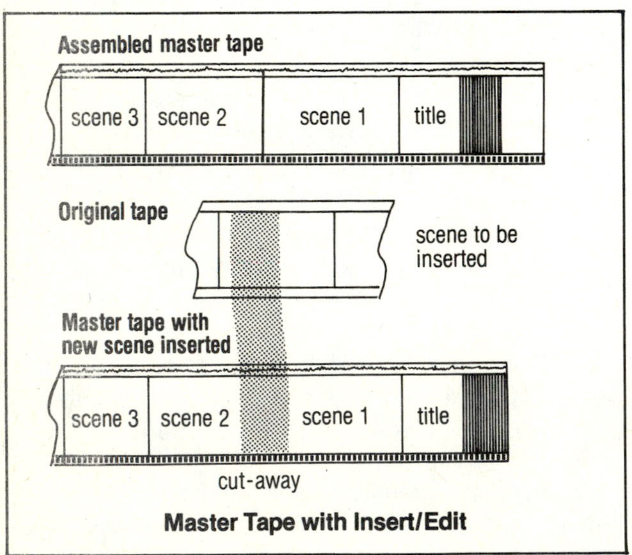

Master Tape with Insert/Edit

An essential part of this editing procedure is reference to the **control track** that is recorded along the lower edge of the videotape whenever recording takes place. If insert-mode editing is to be used (it may be advantageous to do *all* editing in the insert-mode), the control track is recorded on what will be the master tape *before* editing takes place. An unused tape cassette is placed in the camcorder (or edit/record VCR), the lens covered, and the camcorder set to RECORD. In this way, the complete control track is laid down the full length of the tape. Then, once you have located the editing points on the videotapes of both the source and the edit/record units, follow the above procedure. Use the appropriate control (RECORD PICTURE or RECORD AUDIO) to transfer the new segment as replacement of what is now on the master videotape. The insert-mode editing function does *not* disturb the control track, and therefore does not affect any scene following the insert as does happen with assemble editing.

For even more accurate editing use a **time code** system that accurately identifies each video frame. An eight-digit code number (hour, minute, second, and frame number) is recorded on an audio track of the videotape, or specially encoded in the video signal. It identifies each frame of the tape (page 285). This is done when the original tape is being shot or can be added to the tape prior to editing. A **time-code generator** is used for this purpose. During editing, each VCR relays the code to the edit controller. You select frame numbers for editing and program the controller with them. As described above, the controller backs up both tapes and then carries through the editing operation accurately.

Editing for Special Effects

Many of the techniques described under Desktop Video allow for superimposing a title or a symbol over a scene or for creating a visual effect such as a dissolve or a wipe. Without the necessary microcomputer, it is possible to edit tapes containing elements of the effects to create a composite, master recording. To record such effects you will need this equipment:

- Two **VCR players** with monitors
- A **switcher** to control which scene or scenes are played
- A **character generator** for creating titles and simple graphics
- A **special effects generator** (SEG) for creating visual effects
- Two **time-based correctors** (TBC) for adjusting the quality of images when mixing scenes by overcoming inconsistencies due to heat, humidity, tape stretch or shrinkage, or operational deviations from one VCR to another, any of which can cause picture jitter or tape skewing

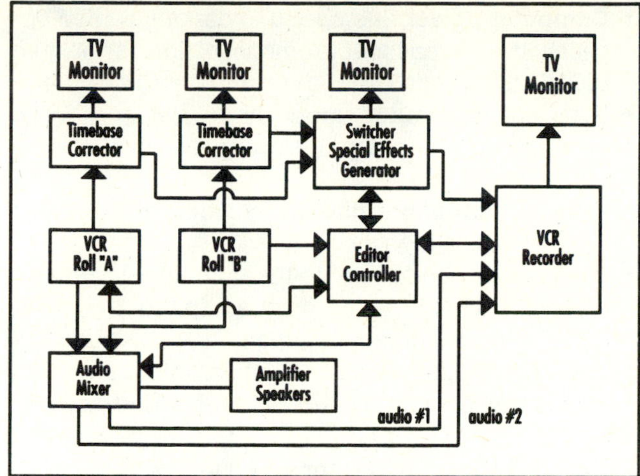

- An **edit/record VCR** unit with monitor
- An **edit controller** capable of handling all equipment

The two original videotapes containing the scenes to be combined are designated as **roll A** and **roll B.** As before, the VCR players are connected to the edit/record VCR. Any special equipment is in circuit with the edit controller.

The procedure for A and B roll editing is similar to the programed method using the edit controller described previously. The two VCR players and the edit/record VCR must all be programed to move together according to time codes. Each edit should be rehearsed and accepted before it is actually made.

In the above editing methods, only generalized procedures have been presented. Check the operational manual with your equipment for specific details and precautions needed when making assemble, insert, and special-effects edits.

Suggestions When Editing

- Avoid interruptions; try to complete a whole sequence during one work period.
- Keep your audience in mind, anticipating its lack of familiarity with the subject and the need for continuity of action, which you might overlook as a consequence of your own knowledge of the subject.
- Be alert to all motion media techniques—LS–MS–CU relationships, establishing scenes, the use of cut-ins and cut-aways, screen direction, matching action, and transitions.
- Use music and sound effects purposefully to create moods and to add a sense of realism to your production.

What You Have Learned About Editing Videotape:

1. What is the purpose for editing videotape?
2. When scenes are put together in script order, this is known as ______ editing.
3. What equipment is required for each of *two* editing methods discussed in this section?
   a. manual assemble-mode edit
   b. automatic assemble-mode edit
4. Which one of the above editing methods will result in the more accurate editing points?
5. What is meant by *insert* editing? When would the procedure be used?
6. What is the use and meaning of each of the following?
   a. control track
   b. edit-in point
   c. A and B rolls
   d. time code
7. What purpose is served by each of the following items of equipment?
   a. time-base corrector
   b. character generator
   c. special effects generator
   d. time code generator

See answers on page 382.

DESKTOP VIDEO

The expression **desktop video** refers to the use of relatively inexpensive and compact equipment to perform many functions that can result in a high quality video recording. Live video can be combined and edited with pictures, graphics, animation, and sound to create sophisticated presentations.

The central component of a desktop video system is a microcomputer. In addition to preparing program components, it can control a number of other equipment items, bringing together the audio and visual forms as an integrated product for presenting information. This is one application of **multimedia** technology.

While some software only allows for assembling various already-prepared media forms onto videotape, other programs serve as authoring systems (page 293) for creating various media elements and then combining them on videotape with prepared video sequences.

Equipment Requirements and Options

Depending on the variety and complexity of techniques to be applied, the following hardware and peripherals may be required:

- One or more **special boards** placed in an expansion slot of the computer's system unit. Such a board may be a **graphics processor,** a **single-frame animation controller,** a **math co-processor** (for animation calculations), a video output, or a single board that combines and controls a number of functions
- **Computer power** and **speed** to carry out video applications in a reasonable amount of time (at least an 80386 microprocessor in the computer CPU)
- Sufficient **computer memory** for storing large amounts of data (a hard disk with at least 50 megabytes of memory)
- Usual **computer peripherals** including a mouse and high resolution monitor
- **Genlock** device to enable the computer to receive and transmit NTSC video signals (page 243), synchronizing and combining them with computer image output, adding audio signals, and eliminating glitches when editing two or more video sources together.
- **Special effects generator** (SEG) to create overlays, super imposition of images, and transitions such as fades, dissolves, and wipes
- **Video titler** or **character generator** for creating lettering and moving text on the screen
- **Music synthesizer** and **audio mixer** to handle sound elements
- **Musical Instrument Digital Interface** (MIDI) for recording sound in digital form from electronic instruments on a computer
- **Edit controller** (page 262) for frame-accurate assembling of video scenes and recorded images onto a master videotape
- **Media equipment** like a CD or laserdisc player, or a VCR with audio dub feature that allows originally recorded sound to be erased and substituted without affecting the video image

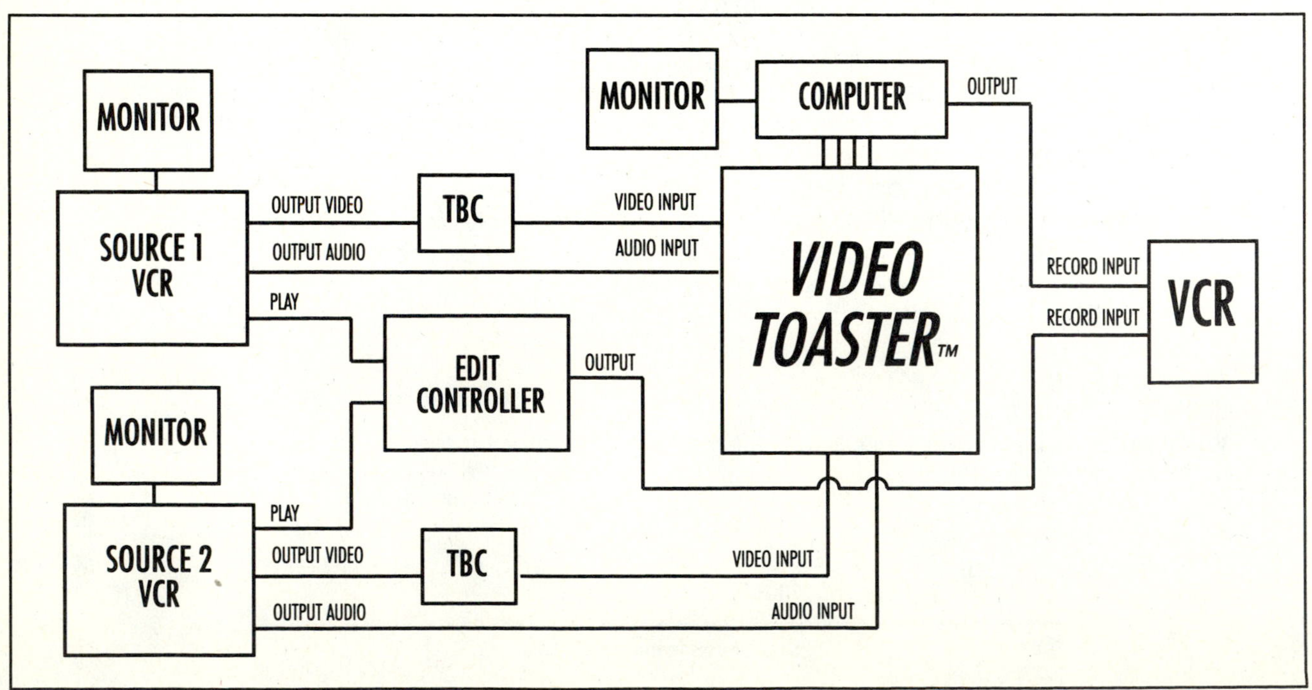

Software

All computer programs used for word processing and generating titles (page 182), creating graphics (page 119), composing music (page 158), and other desktop computer applications can be used in developing desktop video projects. Review the referenced pages.

Authoring systems that direct and control many of the multimedia functions may be required. Such software packages, like the following, are available for the major types of microcomputers, using a mouse and icon interface:

- MS-DOS—Microsoft Multimedia Extension of Windows
- Macintosh—QuickTime
- Amiga—AmigaVision

Carefully review the information and instructions with the software you will use for equipment requirements and operational procedures.

Animation

An important desktop video function may be to simulate movement of inanimate subjects. Animation can be created with a computer in a number of ways. Software programs can guide you to create the following:

- Produce animated effects by rapidly changing the colors of picture parts in cycling patterns. The color cycling makes parts of the picture, such as wheels or fluid, appear to move.
- Design or input an available image into computer memory and then specify its movement against a background. Do this in terms of the number of steps preferred between beginning and end points. The computer calculates the animated changes within the scene's time scale. The software generates all in-between points, creating a smooth movement.
- Construct or input individual frames with images superimposed on layers or cells. Effect movement by changing the content of particular cells (position of arm or facial expression around lips). The computer can produce intervening frames for the simulated movements.

These are just three potential animation techniques. Check software sources for specific animation programs and how they execute routines. Because the creation of animation is very time consuming, carefully consider whether an animated effect is appropriate for your production. Ask yourself how much value it can add, or if the message can be communicated satisfactorily by another method.

Music

Music and sound effects are available from many sources, as described on page 159. Music for opening and closing, background, or for special effects can be added to a video recording during editing. Remember permission is required to use copyrighted music (page 159).

You can prepare your own music or modify a free-use selection with music software. Consider the following:

- Change elements of a song to fit your needs. This could be the tempo, volume, or even the instruments being played.
- Edit the song's composition to vary the music being played.
- Develop "voice-like" effects by generating notes and combining instruments in a song.
- Create your own song by arranging notes on a composing screen and hearing the results.

Production Procedure

Apply regular video planning steps for desktop video production (page 246). Storyboarding (page 65) and scripting (page 67) are particularly important if a number of elements will be included. As described in this book, production techniques and standards relating to video, audio, and graphics should be followed. Once you create the components of a program on the computer screen, store them on a disk. Then output the images and information to videotape. During editing, you combine all components into a final video recording.

Because of the variety of possible components that can be created and then combined in desktop video, carefully plan the sequence of actions to take. If you are trying to combine live video, titles, animation, digitized still images, and music, each additional factor could be added in turn. The final product would be a *sixth* generation reproduction of the original video recording, thus not of very acceptable quality. Therefore, prepare and combine as many factors *at the same time* (for example, animation and titles together) as computer memory would permit.

For combining many video editing and sophisticated graphics techniques, the *Video Toaster* (or comparable commercial product) can extend the operational capacity of desktop video technology. It consists of an expansion board and a software program package for use with any personal computer. The following are some of the numerous features of the Video Toaster:

- Serves as a switcher by accepting up to five live video inputs, edits them to generate one composite output

- Modifies images, adds color effects, animates, and combines images
- Digitizes and manipulates images from a video frame in numerous ways
- Creates titles and text, and moves them in many ways
- Creates numerous special effects such as fades, dissolves, and wipes

What You Have Learned About Desktop Video:

1. What can a desktop video system do that just using a camcorder cannot do?
2. What are five equipment requirements and possible peripherals that you might use for desktop video?
3. For your computer system, what authoring system might you use in desktop video?
4. Which statements are TRUE concerning computer-generated animation?
   a. Create a motion effect by rapid color changes.
   b. Create smooth in-between movements when beginning and end points of an action are specified.
   c. Use time-lapse technique to record progressive changes in action.
   d. Show layers containing components of an action and change only layer positions as required by action.
5. What three techniques can be used to create or modify music with a computer?
6. What can be an undesirable result when creating and transferring five to six audio and visual components to videotape one at a time as opposed to creating and transferring a number of them at the same time?

See answers on page 382.

DUPLICATING A VIDEO RECORDING

Once the master recording is completed, copies may be needed for distribution purposes or because the playback machine to be used requires a tape format different from that of the master (8mm to ½ VHS). In either case, duplicate copies must be prepared.

Duplicating, like editing, requires two VCRs—one to play the master tape and the other to record the duplicate tape. If a format change is required the recording unit should match the appropriate format. The units are connected (from the *output* of the unit with the master videotape, set in the playback mode, to an *input* on the duplicate-tape unit, set in the recording mode). If proper care is given to audio and video level settings and machine alignment (**tracking control**), a good-quality recording can result.

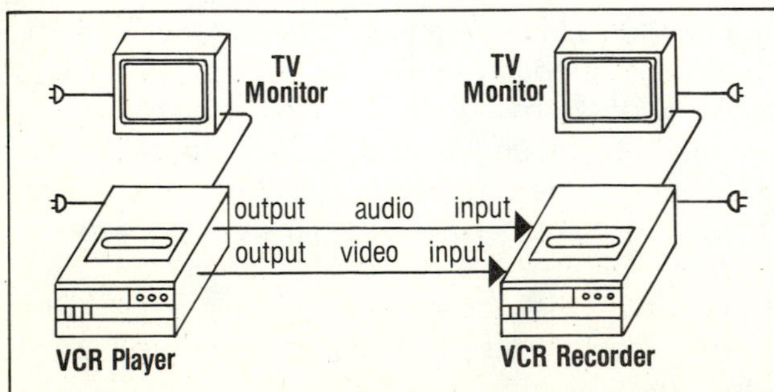

The original camera recording is termed the **first generation** tape. The edited master recording, made from the original camera tape, becomes the **second generation** copy. From the master, one or more **third generation** copies may be made. These latter ones usually will be the tapes to be used with audiences. If the master is to be protected and not played, and if a large number of final copies must be made, then a third generation copy will serve as the tape from which distribution copies (fourth generation) would be prepared. Be sure to label each videocassette copy for future reference.

With each successive generation, there could be a slight reduction in image quality. This degradation can be reduced by using the dub mode switch on the input unit if it is available. Also, with high quality formats such as S-VHS and Hi8 copies should be acceptable through at least three generations.

PRODUCING A VIDEODISC

An optical videodisc is composed of acrylate plastic with a shiny coating designed to reflect light from a laser beam. The audio and visual elements stored on the disc as tiny pits are arranged in spiral tracks in the shiny coating. As a disc is played, the laser beam strikes the pits and is reflected by a mirror to a decoder that converts the signal back into audio sound and visual images for display on a TV receiver.

Information in visual form that has been recorded on videotape can be transferred to a master videodisc for inexpensive multiple-copy preparation. The advantages for producing a videodisc are as follows:

- Large amounts of information, in any media form, can be put on a videodisc. Depending on the format, between 30 minutes and 1 hour of moving pictures with two sound tracks or 54,000 individuals frames of still pictures, text, or combinations of motion and still images can be stored on one side of a 12-inch videodisc.
- Pictures and sound are of high quality and do not degenerate with time or use. Sharp, crisp images with excellent color can be shown on a large screen, along with high fidelity sound.
- Information can be easily and quickly located. It is easy to move almost instantaneously from one spot on a videodisc to another for locating a segment or individual frame by using functions like: still frame, step frames through a sequence, slow and fast motion, scanning, and search.

The preparation of a videodisc requires application of **optical disc** technology. This refers to the use of a laser beam to transfer images and sound from a videotape recording to a master videodisc (also called a **laser disc**), from which duplicate copies are made. A similar procedure is used to make audio compact discs (CD), as described on page 154.

Disc Formats

There are two videodisc formats: **constant angular velocity (CAV)** and **constant linear velocity (CVL).**

In the CAV format, each videotape frame occupies one track or one revolution of the videodisc. This allows for 54,000 still-picture frames, 30 minutes of motion, or any combination of the two per side. Still-picture images will be steady when projected. Changing from one frame to another, or advancing in slow motion, can be performed smoothly.

In the CLV format, each frame occupies one-half track or half a revolution of the videodisc. This format is preferred for a continual running program, like showing a 20-minute instructional film, or a series of separate motion sequences. Titles, graphics, a table of contents, or other individual frames of information will require sufficient running time for the viewer to read or study the content. For this format, the program time can be up to 1 hour in length on one disc side. Up to 79 *search locations* (called **chapters**) can be programed onto a disc. This feature allows the viewer to choose particular segments for viewing in any order.

Production Factors

The most widely used method for producing a videodisc is to start with a video recording and from it have a qualified laboratory produce a master videodisc and then duplicate discs.

In order to ensure high-quality results, the videotape recording (called the **premaster**) should be prepared with broadcast quality equipment such as ½-inch Betacam or on 1-inch videotape. All original program materials from videotape, film, slides, and audio recordings are copied onto a single tape to make the premaster video recording. There must be careful control over the sequencing of visuals, framing of images, and balancing of colors. Each laboratory that offers this service has detailed specifications that must be applied. Contact the company that will produce your master disc for their requirements and their advice before preparing the premaster. See the illustration on the next page.

From the premaster videotape recording, the **master videodisc** is produced. The electronic images and sound from the videotape are etched with a laser beam into a disc. This is an exacting procedure. Costs for producing a master videodisc range from $1500 to $3000, depending on the quality and condition of the videotape premaster material source. Before duplicate discs are made from the master, a **check disc** can be ordered for about $500. It allows you to verify the quality and accuracy of all elements appearing on the disc. Then duplicates, at under $20 each, are made by a stamping or an injection-molding process.

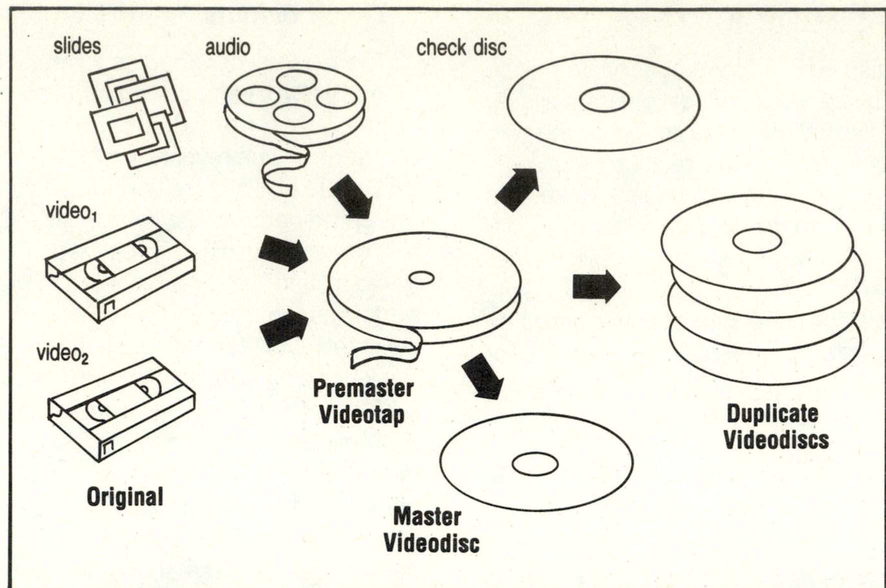

Once the master videodisc is prepared, changes or further revisions require the preparation of a new master videodisc. Because of the expense and careful attention to details that are required, producing a videodisc is feasible only when a relatively large number of discs will be needed.

An important application of optical videodisc technology is to provide for various levels of *interactive learning.* This requires numerical coding of images on the disc and either a microcomputer built into the videodisc player or an interconnection between the player and a computer for control and image-selection purposes. Chapter 16 contains further information on the more complex videodisc production requirements when coordination with a computer and interactive use are planned.

Equipment, although expensive, is available for local production of WORM (Write Once Read Many) videodiscs. Present uses are primarily for storing data in support of business applications.

In addition to the CAV and CLV disc formats, other specialized, commercially-prepared optical-based technologies are available. They include Digital Video Interactive (DVI), Compact Disc-Interactive (CD-I), and Compact Disc Read Only Memory (CD-ROM). See page 293 for further information on these products.

What You Have Learned About Duplicating Video Recordings and Producing a Videodisc:

1. For what reasons should a copy of a videotape be used from a generation that is closest to the master recording?
2. If it were necessary to prepare 200 copies of a videotape for distribution and use within an organization, what form might be the best for making the duplicates? What is one requirement for the videotape from which the copies would be made?
3. On what principle do videodiscs operate?
4. What are the three major reasons why videodiscs are becoming so popular for instructional uses?
5. What are the two videodisc formats? Which one is preferred for instructional purposes?
6. What is the production sequence for making a videodisc through a laboratory?

See answers on page 382.

Preparing to Use Your Video Recording and Videodisc

As with any type of media, the care you give to the preparation for using the materials is important to their ultimate success. You must provide and set up the equipment (videocassette/videodisc player and a sufficient number of monitors or video projector) for viewing the program satisfactorily, whether by individuals or for groups of various sizes. Arrangements for groups include placement on monitors in stands, seating distance with respect to the videoscreens, room light control, and sound level. Then consider how to introduce the program and integrate it with other, related activities, before and after viewing the videorecording. General suggestions for using media are presented in Chapter 21. Special considerations for using video materials start on page 354.

References

Video Production

Browne, Steve. *Videotape Editing: A Postproduction Primer.*

Cheshire, David. *The Book of Video Photography.* New York: Knopf, 1990.

Hunter, Peggi. E. "A Designer's Guide to Scriptwriting: Video Capabilities and Limitations." *Performance and Instruction* 29 (March 1990): 18–22.

Millerson, Gerald. *Technique of Television Production.* Stoneham, MA: Focal Press, 1989.

Rice, John. "Hello Mr. Chips, Goodbye Mr. Tubes." *AV Video* 13 (June 1991): 38–45.

Schihl, Robert J. *Single Camera Video: From Concept to Edited Master.*

Taylor, Margaret H. *Planning for Video: A Guide to Making Effective Training Videos.* New York: Nichols, 1989.

Utz, Peter. "Pseudo A/B Roll Editing." *AV Video* 14 (February 1992): 24–28.

———. *Today's Video Equipment, Set Up, and Production.* White Plains, NY: Knowledge Industry Publications, 1987.

———. *Video User's Handbook.* White Plains, NY: Knowledge Industry Publications, 1989.

Zettl, Herbert. *Television Production Handbook.* White Plains, NY: Knowledge Industry Publications, 1991.

Desktop Video

Speed, Austin H. III. *Desktop Video: A Guide to Personal and Small Business Video Production.* Orlando, FL: Harcourt Brace Jananovich, 1988.

Wells, Michael. *Desktop Video.* White Plains, NY: Knowledge Industry Publications, 1990.

Video Journals (including Sources for Equipment)

AV Video
Montage Publishing Co., 701 Westchester Ave., White Plains, NY 10604

AVC Presentation for the Visual Communicator
PTN Publishing Co., 445 Broad Hollow Rd., Melville, NY 11747

Corporate Video Decisions
Act III Publishing Technical Group
401 Park Ave., New York, NY 10016

Directory of Video, Computer, and Audio-Visual Products
International Communications Industries Association, 3250 Spring Street, Fairfax, VA 22031

Presentation Products
Pacific Magazine Group, Inc.,
513 Wilshire Blvd., Santa Monica, CA 90401

Videography
P.S.N. Publications,
2 Park Avenue, Suite 1820,
New York, NY 10016

Video Systems
Intertec Publishing Corp.,
9221 Quivira Rd.,
Overland Park, KS 66215

Videodisc

Capell, Peter S. "Planning Videodisc Production for an Intelligent Tutoring System." *Tech Trends* 36 (2) 1991: 26–37.

Sayre, Scott and Montgomery Rae. *The Feasibility of Low-Cost Videodisc Repurposing.* TDC Research Report No. 9. St. Paul, MN: Telecommunications Development Center, University of Minnesota, 1990.

Wood, R. Kent and Stoddard, Chuck. "Repurposing Videodisc for Local Production: Implications of Copyright Laws." *Educational Technology* 30 (July 1990): 44–45.

Utz, Peter. "Videodisc Basics: Building a Foundation." *AV Video* 13 (July 1991): 42–47.

———. "Videodisc Part II: How to Premaster Videodisc." *AV Video* 13 (September 1991): 32–38.

CHAPTER

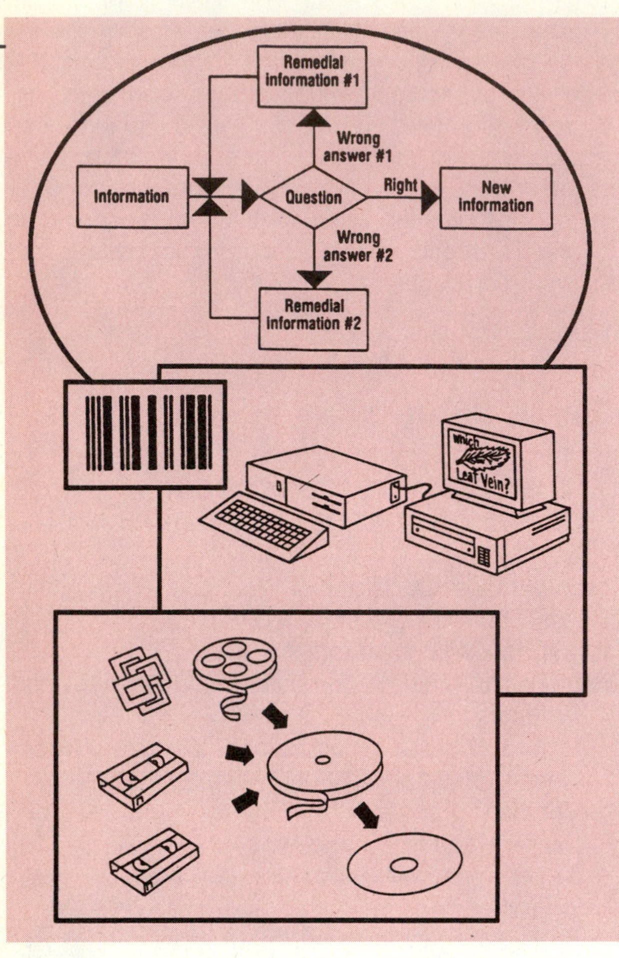

- FACTORS CONTRIBUTING TO INTERACTIVE AND REACTIVE LEARNING
- STEPS IN PLANNING FOR INTERACTIVE AND REACTIVE LEARNING
- LINEAR AND BRANCHING FORMATS
- COMPUTER-BASED INSTRUCTION (CBI)
- COMPUTER/VIDEOTAPE
- COMPUTER/VIDEODISC
- INTERACTIVE MULTIMEDIA
- MEDIA ADAPTABLE FOR REACTIVE LEARNING

Interactive and Reactive Learning Technologies

Most instructional media are designed so the audience or individual users are passive recipients of the information being communicated. They sit back, observe, and listen to the transmitted message. When it has concluded, they are expected to have learned the content or be prepared to act on the information presented. Rarely do people become competent after being only receivers of information.

We know from learning theory that the best learning takes place when individuals are actively involved in the process of learning (page 21). This may require replying to questions, choosing a visual sequence to observe, or making other decisions as a person proceeds through a lesson with media. Such activities can be important in group situations and especially for individuals working by themselves.

The term **interactive learning** is used to describe the interplay between a person and any media. It involves active learner participation in the learning process with the individual having a high degree of control over the *pace* and often the *sequence* of the instruction. When a learner moves through a sequential, linear program, responding periodically to questions and receiving feedback on answers, the materials provide for **reactive learning.** Continual involvement in the learning process motivates the learner and promotes interest in the subject. With success being more likely, both interactive and reactive methods of learning are profitable ways to learn.

Certain types of instructional media can be directly designed for interactive learning, while other, more conventional, forms could be adapted for reactive learning. Computer-based instruction would be a direct application, while by modifying an available slide/tape program a reactive lesson can result.

In this chapter, after considering the factors that contribute to interactive and reactive learning, and the steps in planning for interaction, we will first examine ways that computer-based instruction, computer/videotape recording, computer/videodisc, and combinations of media (multimedia) can be developed for interactive learning. Then we describe how four forms of other media—print, CD-ROM with a study guide or worksheets, audio recording with workbook, and slide/tape with workbook—can be adapted for relatively simple reactive procedures.

FACTORS CONTRIBUTING TO INTERACTIVE AND REACTIVE LEARNING

Before proceeding, review the learning conditions and principles described on page 20. They are among the key matters that require understanding and attention when planning for interactive instruction. Following is an elaboration of the procedures that should be considered when interactive learning techniques are to be applied:

1. **Specify objectives to be accomplished.** With regard to a topic or skill, enumerate what is to be learned or what is to be performed.
2. **Structure the content.** Subdivide the content or skill procedure into naturally grouped or sequenced segments. These will become the framework for all learning and interaction activities.
3. **Provide for learner control.** Permit learners to control how rapidly they wish to move through the instructional program. As practical, allow for flexibility, skips, alternatives, and choices.
4. **Provide frequent interaction or reaction opportunities.** Limit the length of presentation time or the amount of content presented so the learner must often respond or provide input in some way.
5. **Provide feedback on answers and actions.** Immediately inform the learner, through words and pictures, the results of answering questions, choosing solutions, solving problems, making decisions, or completing other actions.
6. **Provide for higher levels of learning.** Instead of limiting the learning activity only to memorization or recall of factual information, plan to have the learner manipulate and analyze information, observe results of actions, extrapolate data, apply rules, derive generalizations, infer conclusions, and engage in other types of thoughtful learning.
7. **Develop a pretest.** Allow learners to find out how well they are prepared for studying the topic. Ask the question, "Does the individual have satisfactory background knowledge or skill on the topic?" A pretest based on prerequisite objectives and related content can provide an answer. Also, since flexibility is an important aspect of interactive learning, the study of each unit or sections of the topic can be preceded by a pretest. This can allow individuals who show competence with some aspects of the program to skip those parts and move ahead more rapidly.
8. **Give specific directions and instructions.** Learners may have to be informed about operating media equipment, obtaining resources to be used for study, and possibly other matters. Procedural directions may be given separately on paper or as an introductory part of a program.

Each person should clearly understand how to proceed with his or her study. Usually, directions cannot be written until all components of the program have been developed.

9. **Develop student self-check review.** It is important for students to be able to check their own learning. An exercise or a brief test, with answers, allows them to determine how well they can accomplish the objectives for the topic. With success, each person can proceed to the instructor's posttest. If not ready, an individual can review and be better prepared for the evaluation of learning.
10. **Develop the posttest.** The final component in designing for interactive learning is to measure the degree to which learners have acquired the knowledge or can perform the skill specified by the objectives. For measuring knowledge, depending on requirements of the objectives, this could be an objective-type (multiple choice or true/false) test or written-answer (short answer or essay) test. A performance test will measure how a process is carried out and the quality of the resulting product. Also, testing could be based on visuals or episodes shown in the interactive or reactive format with required responses to questions or choices.

The above procedures are elements of good instructional planning. They receive attention in the **instructional design plan** (page 4). As you prepare to design interactive media, it is essential that you become proficient with instructional design principles and practices. See the bibliography on page 11 for useful references.

Learner Control

By providing learners with control over how they will proceed in their learning, each person can tailor a program to his or her own needs, interests, and learning style. These aspects of a program can be controlled by the individual:

1. Selecting a learning sequence
2. Reviewing material and repeating sequences
3. Observing a variety of examples, illustrations, or situations
4. Deciding when to be tested on knowledge and understanding
5. Selecting followup actions (or accepting remediation learning) after receiving confirmation of test results
6. Being retested as necessary

There is evidence that many learners may not be mature enough or sufficiently knowledgeable to use the above control elements effectively. Allowing some learners too much freedom could result in frustration and lead to unsatisfactory learning. Although control and choice should be key factors for interactive learning, here are some guidelines for determining when to use learner control (from Cooper):

1. Give learners control only when you believe there is a legitimate reason for using it. If a sequence has a required order, there may be no choice.
2. Know the learners—their maturity, motivation levels, preparation. These can help you to decide the degree of control to allow.
3. Provide enough information so learners can use their control wisely. Then they will know the reason for skipping or taking a certain path.
4. Help learners with their control. At important points, provide the option of making a choice or following a recommendation.
5. Keep control of "what" learners must learn, but let them control "how" they may learn. You establish the parameters of the content, while learners may be more aware of their own preferred style of learning.

STEPS IN PLANNING FOR INTERACTIVE AND REACTIVE LEARNING

Regardless of whether you develop computer-based technologies or adapt available conventional media, attention should be given to the following planning elements:

1. **Select the topic.** Topic may be related to a chapter in a textbook, a unit within a course, or even derived from a separate and new subject.
2. **State the learning objectives.** After examining the subject content of the chapter or other resource materials on the topic, derive the objectives learners are to accomplish. See page 43 for help with writing objectives.
3. **Develop an outline of content.** As related to the objectives and subject content references, list information, concepts, and principles in outline form. Refer to the content outline described on page 45. For further assistance in organizing content, refer to Gagné's conditions for learning on page 16 and the related references.
4. **Decide on the media form for use.** Each type of media receiving attention for interactive or reactive learning has certain advantages or limitations in terms of objectives and content to be served. There are also technical features that

need consideration when making selections. Chapter 5 presents a selection procedure and following sections of this chapter indicate features of applicable technology forms. All available information should be considered when selecting the medium to be developed for either interactive or reactive learning.

5. **Divide content into sequences.** Since learners will study the content in incremental sections, divide it into natural parts. This should be based on the complexity of the content and the known or anticipated ability levels of learners. If a textbook serves as the basis for instruction, then the content is readily available for subdividing. When preparing your own program, content may be written from the outline or sections excerpted from source materials.
6. **Plan exercises, provide answers,** and **consider alternative paths.** As learners complete their study of each content segment, they should check their recall of the information presented, their understanding of it, and have opportunities to use or apply the information. This can be done with one or more appropriate exercises—statements with fill-in blanks for word completion, short answer essay questions, multiple-choice or true-false questions, problems to solve, things to manipulate or construct, and so on. Based on results of one or more exercises, a learner might be directed to remedial work or allowed to skip ahead to an advanced part of the program. Thus a learner might follow a branching path for a portion of the program.
7. **Plan followup activities.** After completing the study, you may require that the learner further use the content by completing a special project. Such activities may require supplementary reading, and participating in group discussions, games, or simulation experiences.
8. **Develop a posttest.** Determine how well the learner has mastered the content and can use the information and procedures presented. Some form of evaluation—a test consisting of questions relating to the learning objectives, problems to solve, situations to resolve, or a project to complete—should be developed.
9. **Write a pretest.** With the content, objectives, exercises, and final test available, prepare another set of questions relating to:
   a. learner background preparation that should be prerequisite to study of the topic, and
   b. content of each major objective to be studied.

   Results of the pretest would indicate what an individual needs to review and what might be skipped while studying the topic.
10. **Write a student self-check review.** Refer to the posttest and ask yourself—"With what essential matters can students test themselves to determine their competence with the topic?" Develop the review and provide answers.
11. **Design the program, prepare and/or gather media and materials.** Apply programing procedures (flow charting, storyboard, script), produce video and other audiovisual media, develop computer software, and prepare accompanying written materials (study guide, worksheets, readings).
12. **Prepare directions.** Write necessary instructions so the learner will know how to proceed with his or her study. This includes where to start, sequence to follow, choices to make, reading materials and other media to use, when to complete participation exercises, where to find answers, how to obtain assistance if needed, and so on.
13. **Assemble the package.** Steps 1 through 11 comprise the work that is necessary to develop media for interactive learning. They are listed in this order because it is a logical sequence for development. For learner use, the actual materials might be organized as follows:
    a. Topic title
    b. Pretest (with answers)
    c. Directions
    d. Objectives for each segment
    e. Assignments for studying each segment, including readings, media use, exercises, alternatives, and answers
    f. Followup activities
    g. Final evaluation

    With all support materials completed and then duplicated, they should be packaged for learner use, along with copies of the interactive or reactive media.

LINEAR AND BRANCHING FORMATS

A key feature in designing an interactive or reactive program is how the learner is directed to progress through the information to be learned. This may follow a **linear** or **branching** format, or a combination of the two.

Linear Format

In a **linear program** (common in *reactive* programs), each increment of information is presented in a set or-

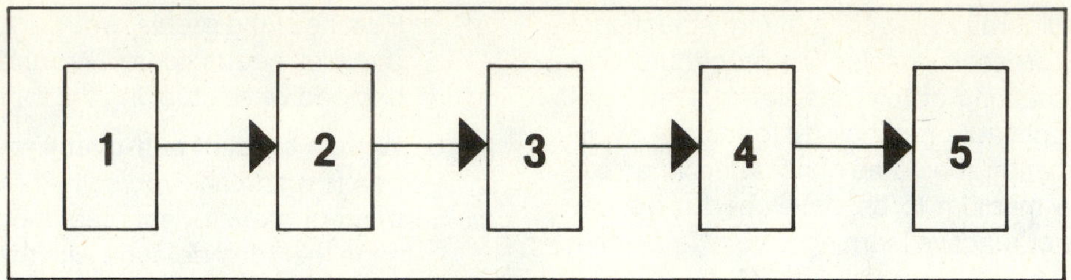

Linear Program

der for learner use. Interaction involves periodic questions or other participatory activities that are the same for each individual. Thus, each person progresses through the program, engaging in the same learning components. The only variable would be the pace of study exhibited by different individuals.

Branching Formats

A **branching program** makes it possible to provide optional, or **branching,** paths for the learner. For example, a person might be able to choose at what point or level in a program he or she wants to start. A pretest can indicate whether the individual is prepared to proceed from that point. Thus, different learners could start at different places in a program and move ahead accordingly. See illustration below.

Branching offers a greater adaptability to serving individual differences and also permits a knowledgeable learner to move through a program more quickly by following a more direct path. Five types of branching patterns are common:

- ***Linear format with repetition***—This is very similar to standard linear programming, except that questions are inserted as steps in the program between segments of information. If a learner answers a question correctly, he or she proceeds to the next segment. If not, the computer has the learner review the previous segment and asks the same question again, having the learner repeat the activity.

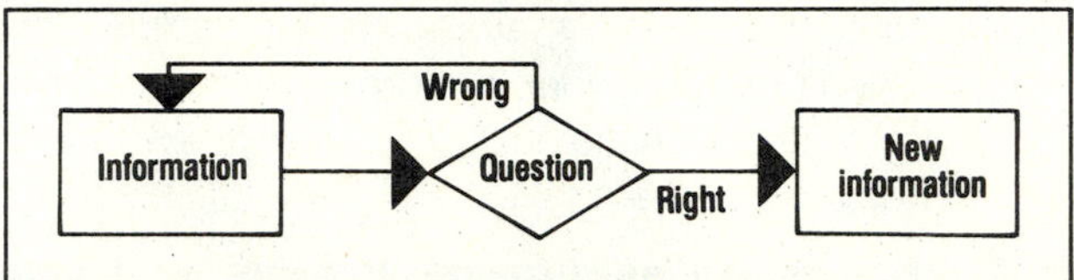

- ***Pretest and skip format***—In this case the learner is given a pretest prior to any instruction. The program then skips over any instructional segments which the learner has previously mastered. As a result the instruction becomes much more efficient for the individual.

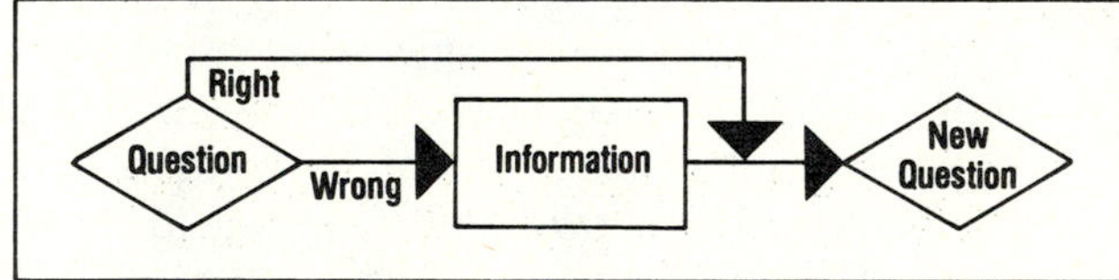

- ***Single remedial branch***—In this case the learner is provided with some information and then asked a question. If the answer is correct, positive feedback is received and the learner advances to the next segment. All incorrect answers receive the same remedial instruction.

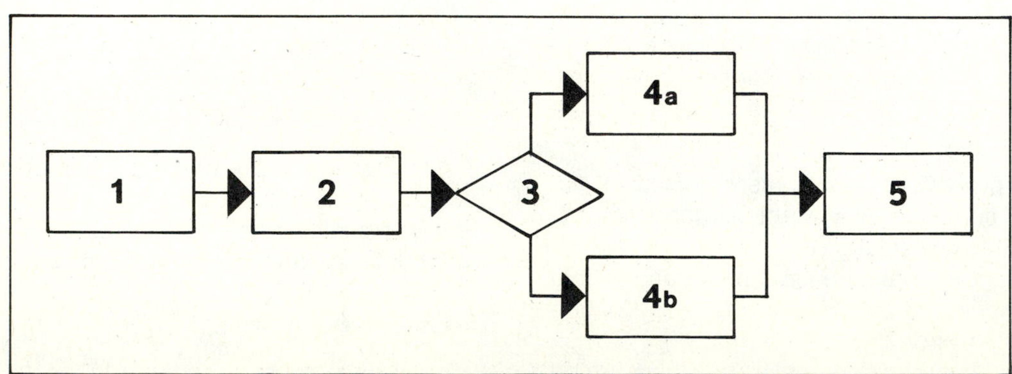

Branching Program

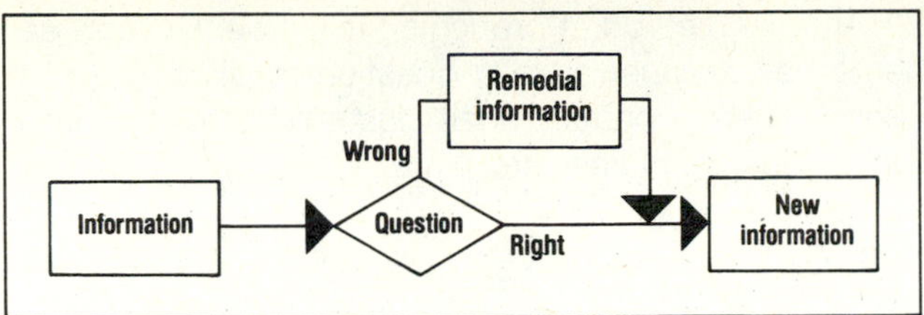

▸ ***Multiple remedial branches***—This is similar to the previous type except that each incorrect response results in a different type of remedial instruction. In this situation the learner is often allowed to continue selecting solutions until the correct answer is obtained. In some programs a predetermined number of incorrect responses, with remedial feedback, is allowed before the correct answer is revealed by the computer, and the instruction moves to new information.

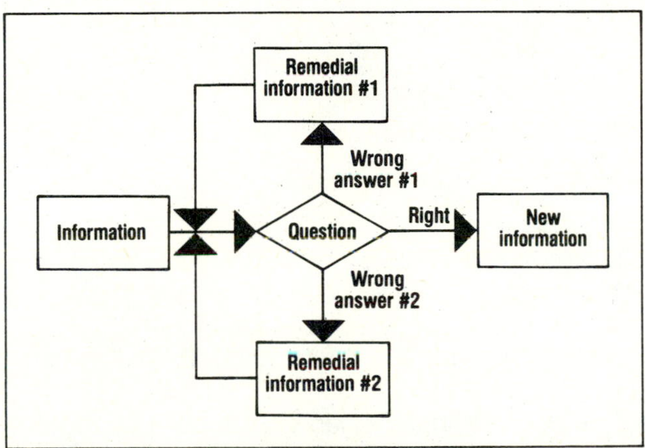

▸ ***Compound branches***—Patterns of this type are commonly used in diagnostic or problem-solving situations in which the questions can be answered with a simple yes or no. Each branch leads to a new question until a final solution is reached. Such programs can have very different results depending upon the answer to a question at a branching point.

Each of these five patterns might be used separately and repeated with progressive content sequences, examples, questions, and answers to form a complete instructional unit. Or a variety of patterns can be combined into a single unit as required to meet the specific instructional objectives of that unit. A visual technique that can help you to sequence elements within a branching pattern is to develop a series of **flow charts.** See page 280 for a discussion of this technique.

Questions

As previously described, the branching capability is a teaching tool that can permit learners to tailor the instruction to their own specific needs. A well-designed instructional activity will provide options that let the instructor or individual learner determine the level of difficulty and the sequence of instruction. Furthermore, the learner's responses can be used to continually shape the instruction so that the unmastered content is stressed, rather than treating all content as equal.

However, these capabilities are only available when they are designed into the program. As the designer, you must determine where branches should occur. Since most branches result from questions, those questions should be carefully selected to ensure that they clearly reflect the learning objectives.

Questions can be stated in a variety of forms. However, some forms of questions are much easier for a computer to score. Multiple choice questions are the easiest to judge since the learner must select one of a few predetermined answers.

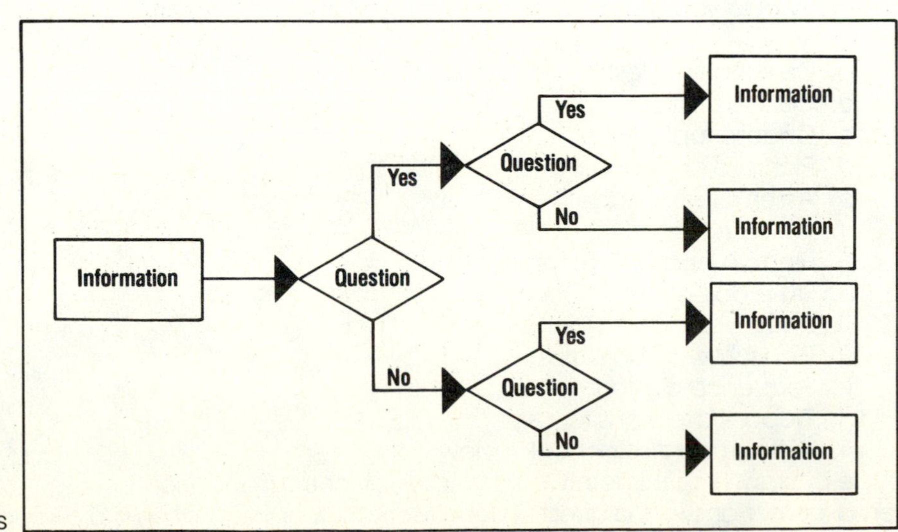

Compound Branches

On the other hand, fill-in-the-blank questions are much more difficult to score since the correct answer can often be stated in a variety of equally acceptable ways. The developer who designs questions of this type must specify *all* acceptable answers in advance. This is complicated by the fact that a learner might know the right answer, but be incapable of spelling it correctly.

Only the more sophisticated computer-based instructional systems are capable of correctly judging misspelled responses to open-ended questions.

Whatever form is used, your questions should be clearly stated and simple in structure so they will be understood by the learner. In addition they should indicate the type of response required (true-false, short-answer, or whatever).

Another method of branching is to use the reply selected as an answer to a question to direct learners along different paths. As an illustration, this might be one sequence of answers:

Reply 1: Correct answer . . . proceed to next program step.

Reply 2: Incorrect answer . . . try to answer question again.

Reply 3: Incorrect answer . . . receive further explanation; then answer same or a new question.

Reply 4: Incorrect answer . . . be directed to lower level or remediational information; be tested successfully before returning to this question or to a similar one.

REVIEW

What You Have Learned About the Factors Contributing to Interactive and Reactive Learning, Planning, and Linear and Branching Formats:

1. What is the difference between *interactive* and *reactive* learning?
2. To which factor, relating to the contributions for interactive learning, does each situation apply?
   a. You outline the information to be learned under four major headings.
   b. You carefully explain how a learner is to start studying and using the equipment.
   c. Each learner finds out where in the program he or she can start, as determined by individual learner's background.
   d. You devise activities for the program that require problem solving and judgments about case situations.
   e. You develop an answer key to questions.
3. What are five techniques that may allow a learner to control the pace of instruction?
4. What are three ways to ensure that learners can satisfactorily use control within an interactive program?
5. In what order would you plan and develop a program that gives attention to the following elements:

   _______ a. Develop final test
   _______ b. Outline content
   _______ c. Choose topic
   _______ d. Plan exercises and paths
   _______ e. Assemble package
   _______ f. Write pretest
   _______ g. Prepare and gather materials
   _______ h. State objectives
   _______ i. Decide on media form
   _______ j. Plan followup activities
   _______ k. Sequence content
   _______ l. Prepare directions for use
   _______ m. Write student self-check review
6. What type of branching pattern would you select for each situation?
   a. When a learner answers a question incorrectly, further information is provided, then the ques-

tion is repeated.

b. Based on the results of a test taken before studying the program, the learner is directed to those parts of the program with which she is not already knowledgeable.
c. Questions are interposed periodically as the learner goes through the program, but they do not affect the sequence of instruction.
d. When the learner answers a question incorrectly, as based on the answer selected, appropriate review is given and the question is repeated.
e. Each learner is led through the program along an individual path based on answers given at decision points.

See answers on page 383.

COMPUTER-BASED INSTRUCTION (CBI)

The computer, with its software programs, can be an effective resource for many forms of interactive learning. Then, when the computer is connected to control and direct other equipment, particularly a videocassette, CD, or a videodisc player, as described in following sections of this chapter, a further dimension of interactivity is added. There are many references, workshops, and courses available from which you can acquire understanding and fundamental skills relating to computer principles, operations, and their instructional uses.

Applications

As an individual uses a computer for learning, information is presented on the computer screen. Periodically, the person must make a choice or respond to a question. The computer can facilitate instruction in these categories (see examples on following page):

- ***Drill and practice***—The easiest and most common CBI task is to provide practice for reinforcement of a concept or skill. The computer is programed to provide the learner with a series of questions or exercises typical of those found in a workbook. The practice exercises might include working simple mathematical problems, estimating the size of an angle in degrees, or identifying geometric shapes. In this sequence a problem is posed, a response is solicited, the response is judged, and feedback is given before the next problem is posed. More elaborate programs will begin with questions or a pretest to assess the entry level of the learner and then use that information to provide practice at the most appropriate level of complexity.

  Some programs maintain a record of learner responses which are reported to the learner or instructor at the end of the exercise. The record of performance serves as a basis for prescribing additional instruction.
- ***Tutorials***—Tutorials attempt to emulate a human tutor. Instruction is provided via text or graphics on the screen. At appropriate points a question or problem is posed. If the learner's response is correct, the program moves on to the next block of instruction. If the response is incorrect the computer may recycle to the previous instruction or move to one of several sets of remedial instruction, depending upon the nature of the error.
- ***Problem solving***—In any subject area, problem-solving abilities are important for a person. A situation is presented on the screen. The learner requests additional information or pertinent data. The computer performs calculations, shows relationships, presents results, and allows the user to make evaluations for solving the problem. In the training of health professionals for example, individuals need to decide on the likelihood of a disease reaching epidemic proportions. The learner requests and examines specific data and builds inferences that lead to a decision.
- ***Expert systems***—An important application of computer technology that relates to *both tutorials* and *problem solving* categories is the use of expert systems. In an expert system, information from highly knowledgeable "experts" in a given subject is imbedded into computer-based software. The program is designed to allow the learner to query the experts and receive necessary information to perform the required task and become competent in the subject being studied. See example on page 279.

  Expert systems, a branch of the broader field of **Artificial Intelligence,** have many applications, making education and training more efficient and effective. As an example, medical applications have proven useful in helping doctors stay current in their practice. The doctor "interacts with the experts" via the computer, providing observations and data; the

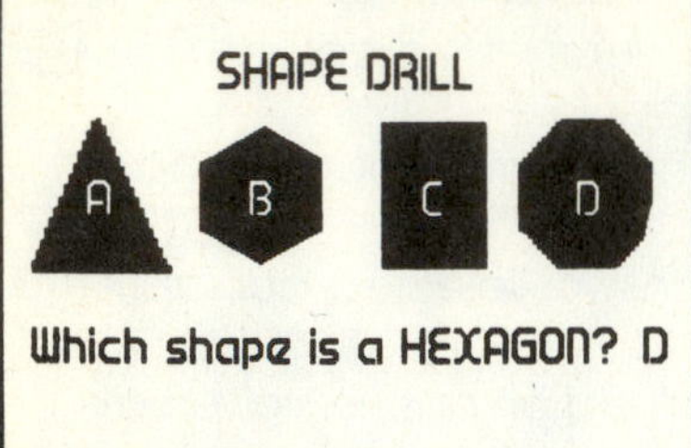

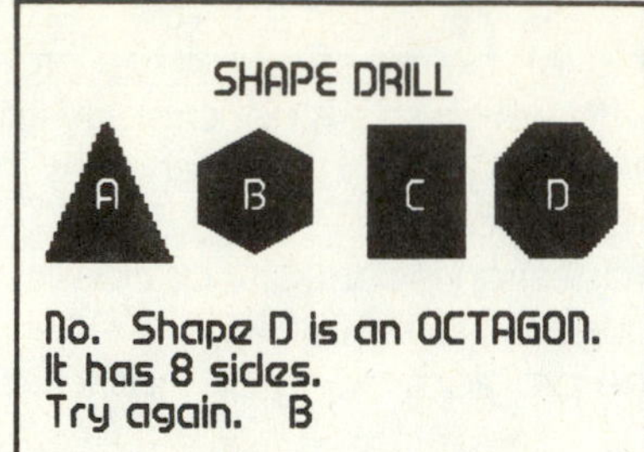

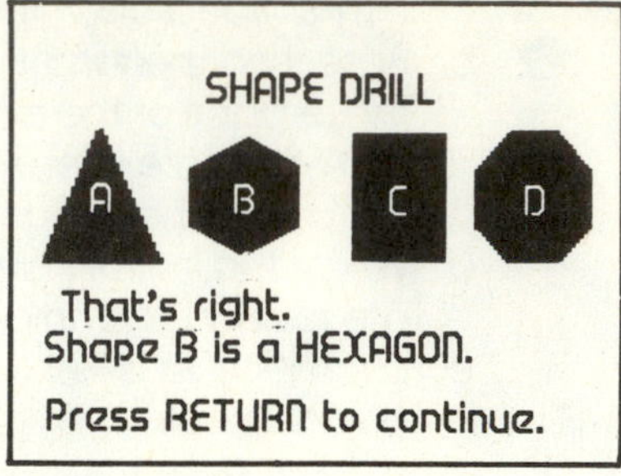

SHAPE DRILL

Which shape is a HEXAGON? D

SHAPE DRILL

No. Shape D is an OCTAGON.
It has 8 sides.
Try again. B

SHAPE DRILL

That's right.
Shape B is a HEXAGON.
Press RETURN to continue.

Drill and Practice

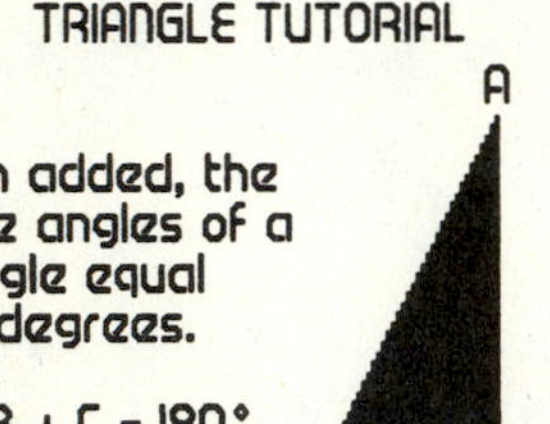

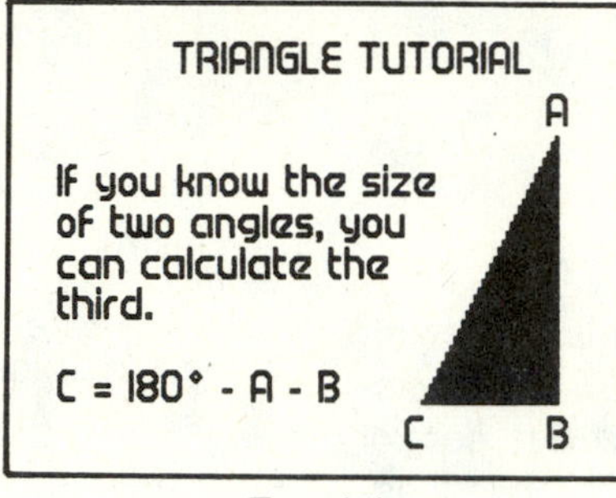

TRIANGLE TUTORIAL
When added, the
three angles of a
triangle equal
180 degrees.
How many degrees
are there in angle C?
A
If you know the size
of two angles, you
can calculate the
third.
C = 180° - A - B
C B

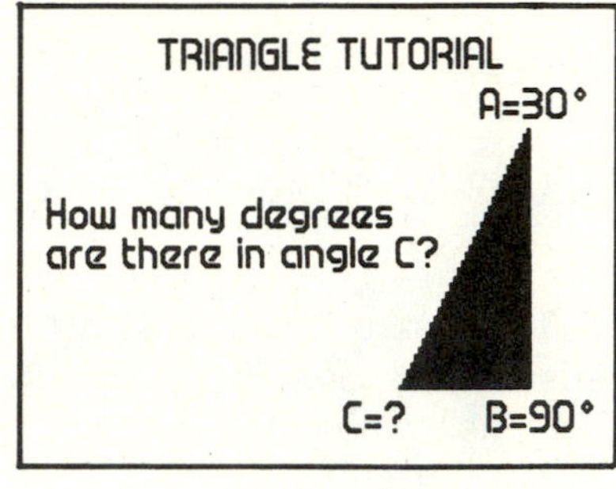

Tutorial

DEVELOP A STORY CHARACTER

You have been introduced to details within these three categories relating to the nature of a person in a story:

1. Personal characteristics
2. Personal behaviors
3. Impressions of the individual by other persons

Select a person. Type up to eight lines that describe the individual. Print your description. Evaluate in terms of:

1. What mental image is created of the person?
2. Is the image logical and realistic in terms of the role portrayed?
3. What important details differentiate this person from others in the story?

Use the information to describe one of the following persons:

A. An airline copilot in a first assignment on a a weather-delayed flight.
B. A professional athlete in the final game before retirement.
C. A judge pronouncing a mild sentence on a child molester against much public sentiment.

Problem Solving

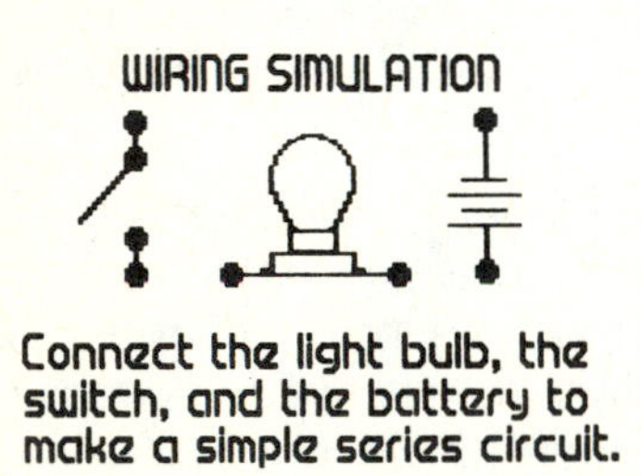

WIRING SIMULATION
Connect the light bulb, the
switch, and the battery to
make a simple series circuit.

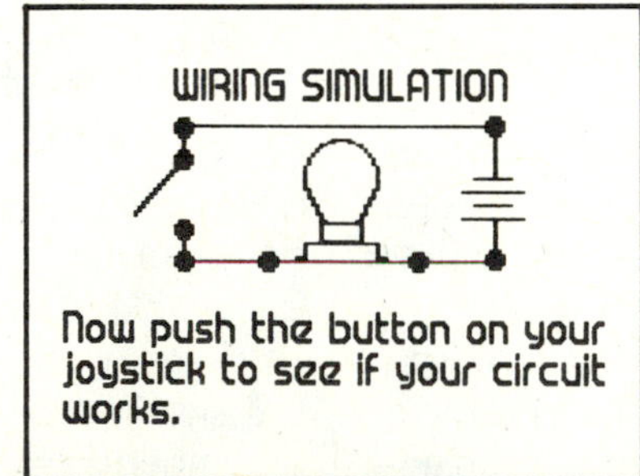

WIRING SIMULATION
Now push the button on your
joystick to see if your circuit
works.

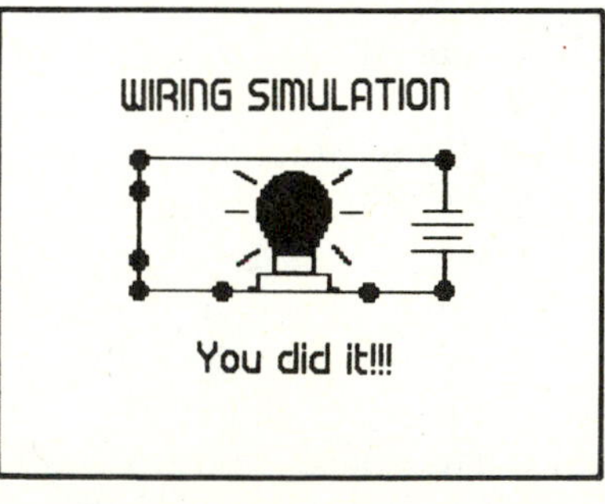

You did it!!!

Simulation

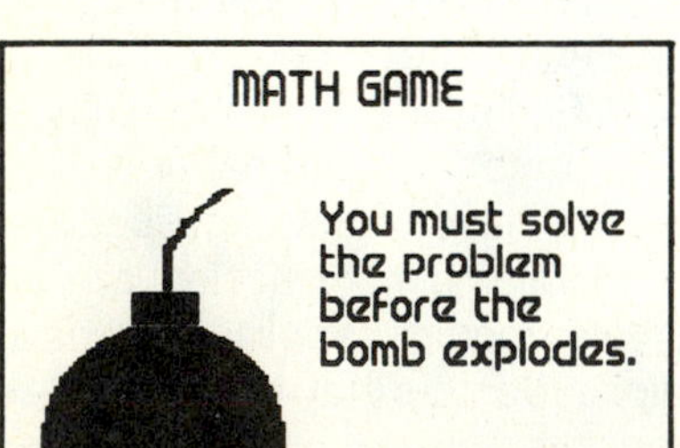

MATH GAME
You must solve
the problem
before the
bomb explodes.

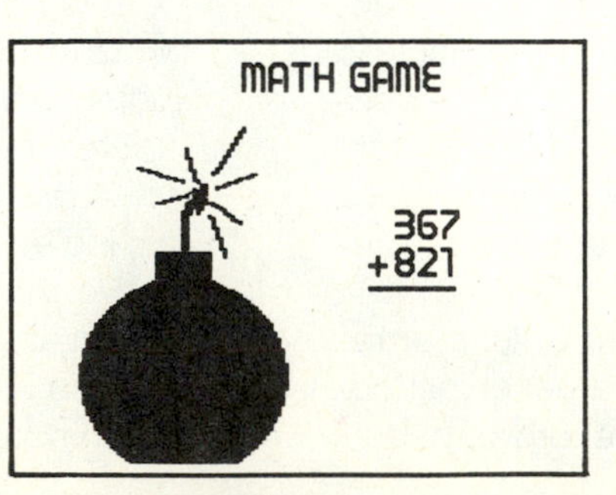

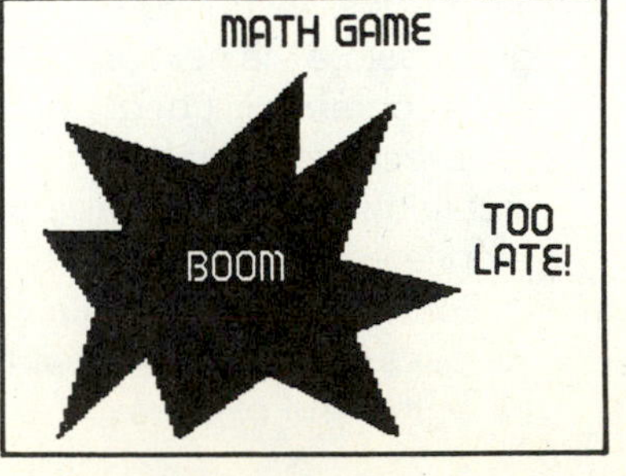

Game

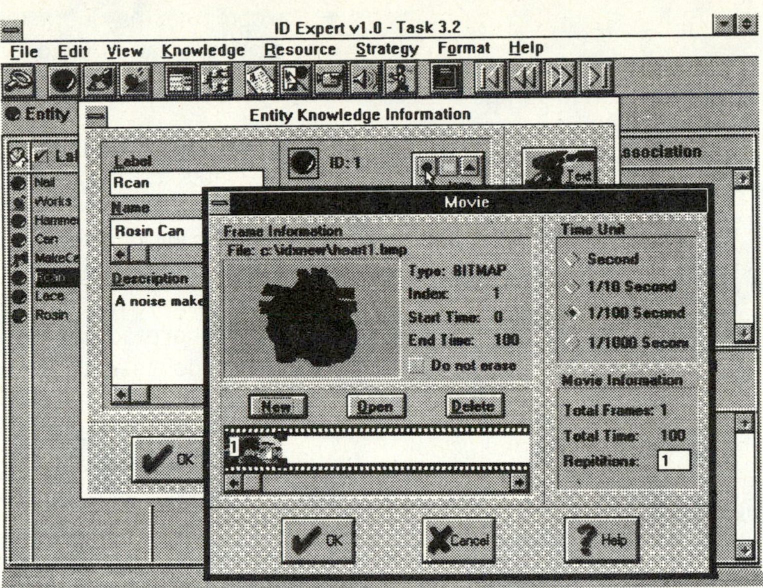

Source: ID$_2$ Research Group, Utah State University

computer in turn provides needed information and conclusions.

- ***Simulations***—Programs that attempt to emulate dynamic processes are called simulations. In some of the common examples, learners use microcomputers to simulate flying an airplane, running a small business, or manipulating the controls of a nuclear power generator to prevent a meltdown. Such programs offer the opportunity to experience "real world" problems without the associated risks such as a fatal crash, a bankruptcy, or a nuclear disaster. In addition, a well designed simulation can radically reduce the costs of instruction, while expanding or compressing the timeline to one more appropriate for learning.

  Simulations are one of the most powerful instructional applications of computers, but they are also the most difficult to achieve. To be effective teaching tools, they must accurately reflect the processes they model.

- ***Instructional games***—If properly designed, computer games can use the learner's competitive nature to motivate and to increase learning. One of the more successful educational games combines video arcade action with typing exercises to improve typing skills. The user must rapidly and correctly type the words that appear in the corners of the screen in order to keep from being zapped by the ever-menacing alien ships.

  As with simulations, good instructional games are difficult to design and designers must ensure that the integrity of the learning objectives is not lost in the attempt to provide a gaming atmosphere. Also, activities may require excess time for the learning that will result.

The above categories indicate the variety of activities and the kinds of learning that can be served through CBI. It is important to recognize that experiences can be provided that require active user participation at an intellectual level higher than that needed for solely memorizing facts. Similar applications can be made, with even greater impact, when visual images and sound are combined with computer technology as will be considered in the following sections of this chapter.

Preliminary Planning

The procedure for developing a topic into a CBI lesson applies the planning procedure outlined on page 272. Consider this preliminary checklist:

- Have you chosen a **topic** and established an **instructional purpose** that can be accomplished by CBI (page 41)?
- Have you considered the **learner group** that will use the program and its characteristics (page 42)?
- Have you stated the **objectives** to be served (page 43)?
- Have you divided the **content into sequences** for study (page 45)?

With this preliminary planning, you are prepared to design the details for presenting content and providing for interactions.

Flow Charting

To show how aspects of an instructional sequence would be treated, construct a flow chart. It can illustrate how the program presents information, provides decision points, raises questions to be answered, and shows resulting paths as alternatives.

Ask yourself these questions to guide flow charting:

- What information should appear on the computer screen?
- Can points be identified at which choices or decisions need to be made, or at which a question should be asked?
- What options should be available to the learner at these decision points?
- What form should a question take?
- Need there be provision for review or remediation?
- Should there be paper-based material accompanying the program?

Fairly complex flow charts can be constructed with a few symbols. Arrows indicate the direction of movement through the flow chart. The arrows should point down or to the right, but may point in other directions when other options are needed or the required branching is back to an earlier part of the program.

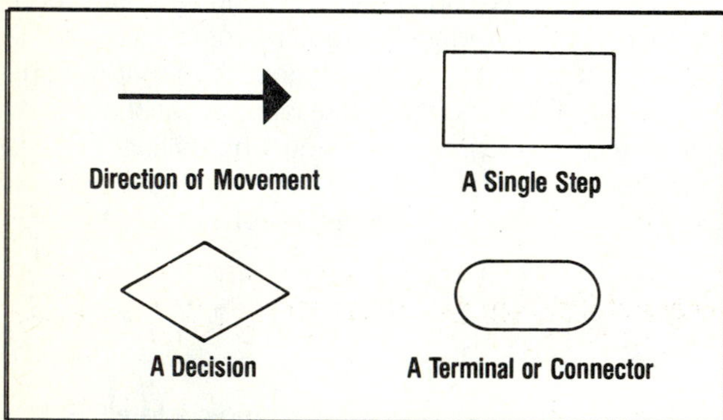

The *rectangle* represents a single step in the process, such as the presentation of a sequence of information, the manipulation of data, or steps in performing a skill. A rectangle usually has one line flowing into it (input) and one line flowing out (output).

The *diamond* indicates a decision point at which a branch will occur. A diamond usually has only one input and up to four output points. Here are some examples:

- The computer may ask learners whether they wish to continue with the lesson. The choices may be: *stop, review, proceed.*
- The answers to a question lead to various video segments.
- The computer may judge the accuracy of a response to a question and then offer new instruction or recycle to view previous instruction on the tape.

The *oval* is used to indicate a terminal or connecting point. It marks the beginning and end of a flow chart and indicates where it connects with other flow charts or reconnects with itself at another point. Terminals usually have only one input or one output.

Develop a flow chart by first listing all of the steps in the instructional process. Then identify those steps that are decision points and will result in branches. Draw the steps (boxes) and the decision points (diamonds) in sequence on a sheet of paper and use lines with arrows to show how the program flows. The process will help you get a much clearer understanding of how the program should be constructed.

A flow chart, or a series of flow charts that fully treat the topic, can be drawn on paper. Templates are available for tracing the above illustrative symbols as needed. Flow charting by hand can be laborious, with any changes requiring erasure and redrawing.

Flow charting software for use with your computer can make the procedure much easier. With such programs as *Easyflow* for MS-DOS and *MacFlow* for Macintosh, flow charts can be created rapidly and items easily moved while sections are restructured.

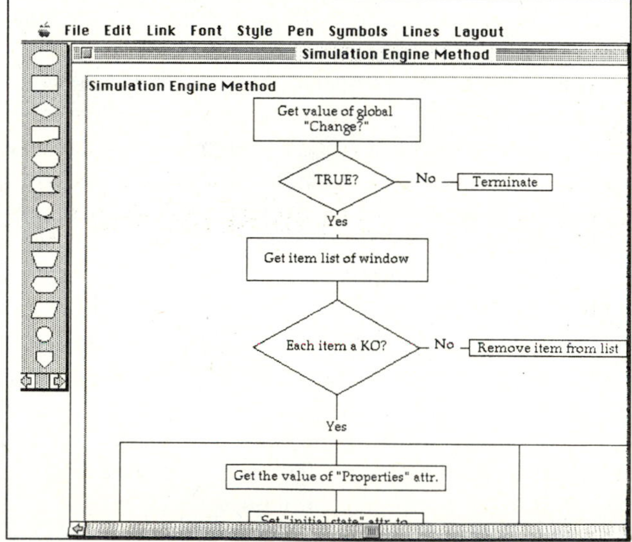

Source: MacFlow Program

Designing Frames (Storyboarding)

The detailed information that will comprise each *screen* or *frame* of the program must be specified. This may be printed textual information, a graphic display, or a combination of both (computer-generated sound also can be used). The best way to detail this information is to develop a **storyboard** illustration for each frame as indicated in the flow chart. Also, for decision or question frames, directions should be included about what frames follow, depending on learner responses.

You may find it useful to use a coding form such as that shown below. Such a form lets you specify the exact location of each character on the screen and provides you with additional information to simplify the programing process.

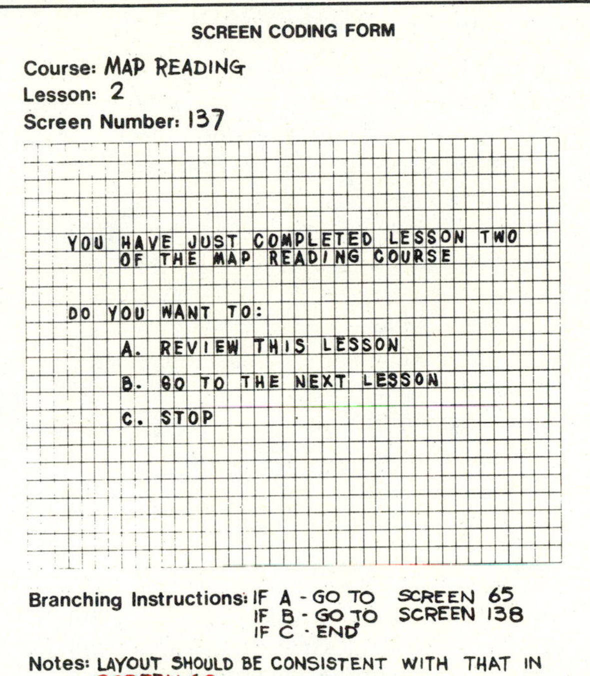

SCREEN CODING FORM

Course: MAP READING
Lesson: 2
Screen Number: 137

YOU HAVE JUST COMPLETED LESSON TWO
OF THE MAP READING COURSE

DO YOU WANT TO:
A. REVIEW THIS LESSON
B. GO TO THE NEXT LESSON
C. STOP

Branching Instructions: IF A - GO TO SCREEN 65
IF B - GO TO SCREEN 138
IF C - END

Notes: LAYOUT SHOULD BE CONSISTENT WITH THAT IN SCREEN 62.

When writing the text for a screen, use short sentences and include only that information required to meet the learning objectives. Be certain to maintain the flow from one screen image to the next, and consider the continuity for all possible branches of the program. See page 122 for further information about screen design.

As with flow charting, computer graphics software programs are available for storyboarding. *Canvas* for Macintosh and *PC Paintbrush* for MS-DOS computers allow the creation of text and graphic images in color, and permit adjusting their arrangement on the screen. In some cases, a computerized set of storyboard frames can be transferred to the final program as it is created. This can reduce programing time.

Programing with Authoring Tools

When you feel satisfied with your planning, including flow charts and storyboards, you are ready to create the instructional software. This is done by instructing the computer with all the details of the program. The procedure anyone can use involves applying an **authoring system.** This method requires no prior computer programing experience.

By replying to a series of options or "prompts," presented as questions, you are guided to develop a new program. For example, if a user decided to present a question, the system asks if the question is to be multiple choice, true or false, or short answer. Once this is determined, the system asks the user to specify the question, the correct answer, possible incorrect answers, and what should occur when each response is

Sample Authoring System Programing Sequence

Prompt by Computer	Response by User
Type your text.	This is a short math program.
Type your question.	How much is 8 + 2 + 4 – 3?
Is the question A. Multiple choice B. True/false C. Short answer	C
Enter the correct answer.	11
Enter the response to a correct answer.	That is correct.
Enter the response to an incorrect answer.	That is incorrect. The correct answer is 11.

given. Upon receiving this information, the system generates the segment of the computer program required to ask the question.

Here is a typical set of prompts that would be used in an authoring system:

- What is the name of this lesson?
- Type of text to be displayed.
- State question number 1.
- Provide correct answers.
- How many tries for a correct answer are acceptable?
- What hint should be given after each wrong answer?
- Indicate expected wrong answers.
- Provide feedback for expected wrong answers.
- Provide feedback for any unexpected answers.
- Do you have any questions that are unanswered?

Instead of being prompted by a set of verbal instructions or questions, an **icon-based** authoring system can be used. It consists of sets of small graphic images or symbols in the form of a flow chart on the screen. Text, graphics displays, sound, and even animated images can be specified by clicking on the appropriate icon. Pull-down menus contain commands for various authoring functions. A display, a question, a set of branches, feedback, and other required lesson components can be created.

Icon-based systems, such as *Course Builder* or *Authorware Professional* for the Macintosh and *Icon-Author* or *ProPi* for MS-DOS computers, are relatively easy to use. This programing procedure is applied in more sophisticated forms when interactive programs include video and other media. Refer to page 293 for the use of authoring tools in designing multimedia programs and page 264 for their use with desktop video procedures.

A good authoring system should have these characteristics:

- Easy to learn and use with clear instructions and explanations in accompanying manuals (the *documentation*)
- Provides flexibility for using whatever instructional design strategy is appropriate for learning needs that are to receive attention
- Provides flexibility for adjusting the program flow to individual learners
- Allows for flexibility by accepting more than one correct response to a question, as would be appropriate
- Recognizes and responds to incorrect answers, including both logical and unanticipated responses
- Provides for full use of computer's capabilities, including color, graphics, sound, highlighting, and pausing as words or graphics are being presented
- Includes program management and record-keeping capabilities for monitoring learner progress and for instructional analysis

In addition to the authoring software, other programs such as word processing (page 182) and graphics design (page 121) can be used when preparing CBI. Preliminary materials can be prepared with these programs and then "imported" through the authoring tool to the CBI program.

Accompanying Materials

If extensive reading material, complex diagrams, or other items are to accompany the program, they should be gathered or prepared, and duplicated. They could be packaged separately or included as "documentation" for the learner.

The guidebook or manual should contain the following:

- Program objectives
- Computer equipment and resources (including program disks) required
- Startup procedure
- Materials for use with the program
- Followup activities

Testing the Program

At various stages of program development, review and evaluate the progress with colleagues and a subject expert. This is **formative evaluation** referred to on page 174. It can take place when objectives, subject content, specifications, sequence identifications, flow charts, and storyboards are specified.

Unlike human beings, computers are very particular about the accuracy of the instructions they receive. A single misplaced letter or symbol can render a computer program useless as an instructional tool. Therefore it is very important that CBI materials be thoroughly tested before they are released for broad use.

Errors such as these are called "bugs" and the process by which they are located and removed is called **debugging.** This is best accomplished by letting a variety of people try the materials to see what types of problems might occur. Ideally these people should be representative of the learners for whom the materials are designed and should go through the materials under the anticipated circumstances for their use. They should be asked to work through the program several times, trying all of the options, so that each branch can be tested.

Evaluate these features:

- Use of accompanying materials
- Correlation of program with objectives

- Content sequencing
- Clarity of screens
- Suitability of interactions, feedback, branches
- Mechanical features, including grammar, spelling, etc.
- Time for learner to complete program
- How well program holds interest

What You Have Learned About Computer-Based Instruction:

1. To which instructional use for computers is each situation related?
   a. Guiding a learner through a basic electronics program with readings, answering questions, giving feedback on answers, reviewing as necessary, and allowing the student to progress successfully.
   b. Learning chemical formulas for pharmaceutical products by having to identify many examples that are shown repeatedly.
   c. Presenting a realistic financial planning problem in which numerous variables are introduced and have to be considered in reaching a solution.
   d. Engaging in competition as a history lesson is studied with points being awarded as the student proceeds through the program.
   e. Becoming competent in driving an automobile is preceded by learning how to respond to instructions and react to instrument settings shown on a computer screen.
   f. Reaching satisfactory conclusions in overcoming difficulties encountered with poorly operating construction equipment by using a program in which persons with special knowledge guide the user with answers to a series of questions.
2. What is the purpose of a flow chart?
3. What do the four basic symbols in flow charting illustrate?
4. How is *storyboarding* used in CBI planning?
5. To what phase of CBI development do the terms *prompts* and *icon-based* refer?
6. What items should be included in documentation accompanying a CBI program?
7. When is *formative evaluation* used in CBI development?

See answers on page 383.

COMPUTER/VIDEOTAPE

When subject content requires visual treatment with motion or the need to show complex relationships, then the video medium should be used. If interactive aspects of learning are desired, then the videotape player can be interfaced with a computer, resulting in **interactive video.** The computer provides to the learner directions and textual information, and manages testing of learning. The videotape player presents audiovisual material in short segments as directed by the computer. The two units of equipment function in coordination, rather than as separate entities.

As will be pointed out, there are some limitations in using a videotape player for this purpose as compared with a videodisc or CD player. But for many uses, the videotape player can be satisfactory. Also, by planning and producing a video recording for interactive learning, you would be well prepared then to work on a more complex laserdisc project.

Equipment

In order to utilize an interactive videotape system, four (or five) pieces of equipment are required:

- ***Microcomputer***—The **microcomputer** serves as the controlling component of the system since it receives input from the learner, processes the information, and outputs a display on the monitor, or directs that a certain video segment be shown.
- ***Videocassette player***—This is the unit on which the subject recording is played and controlled by the computer program.

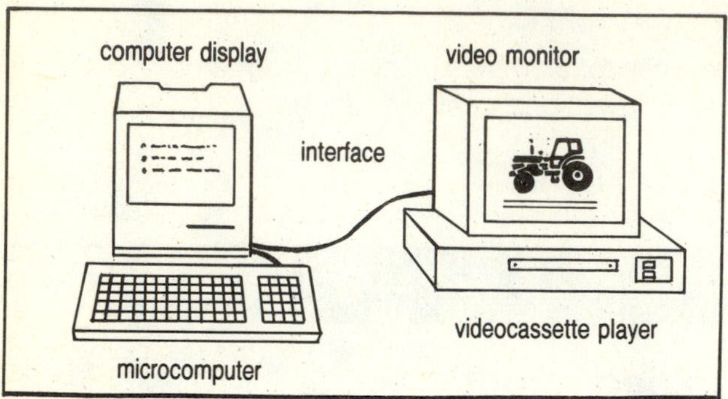

- ***Interface***—This unit consists of an accessory printed circuit board that fits into an expansion slot in the computer and through its electronic cable is connected to the videocassette player so it can transmit signals from the computer to locate segments of the videotape recording and control tape movement.
- ***Video monitor(s)***—The computer screen displays computer program information (directions, text, questions, answers) and the video monitor shows video images with sound. It is possible to use the computer display screen for both sets of images if a **video overlay controller card** is put into the computer's system unit. This will make the video perform to the computer display's specifications.

Some videocassette players include a built-in or hand-held touch pad accessory that contains a microprocessor that can be used as a controller for limited video branching program functions. The greater capacity and flexibility of a separate microcomputer with interface to the videocassette player is required for more sophisticated programing.

Program Planning

Planning an interactive video recording requires the same procedures used to design a conventional video recording. Consider this planning checklist:

- Have you considered the **audience** that will use the material and its characteristics (page 42)?
- Have you expressed your **ideas** clearly and limited the topic (page 41)?
- Have you stated the **objectives** to be served by your production (page 43)?
- Have you prepared a **content outline** (page 45)?
- Have you considered whether a computer/videotape **is an appropriate medium** for accomplishing the objectives and handling the content (page 58)?
- Have you written a **treatment** to help organize the handling of the content (page 64)?
- Have you sketched a **storyboard** to assist with your visualization of the content (page 65)?
- Have you prepared a scene-by-scene **script** as a guide for your shooting (page 67)?
- Have you, if necessary, **selected other people** to assist with the production and required related services (page 44)?
- Have you considered the **specifications** necessary for your production (page 70)?

You may find that a video recording already exists that contains most, if not all, of the contents you plan to treat. If such a recording is available, and proper copyright clearance is obtained, you can start with it and avoid much of the production phase. You may have to add some scenes or sequences as you identify needs while carrying out the following planning. The procedure of using existing video material and adapting it for interactive learning is called **repurposing** a videotape recording. See further discussion of this technique with videodiscs on page 291.

As you know, an important difference between conventional video and interactive video is that with the latter the visual sequences are not viewed necessarily in linear order. Ask yourself: "What should be shown and in what order?" Then, there will be a series of optional paths, depending on a learner's choice, decision, or answer to a question. The need to carefully plan, in detail, the flow of action with branching alternatives is the new ingredient you must manage. In order to do this, first

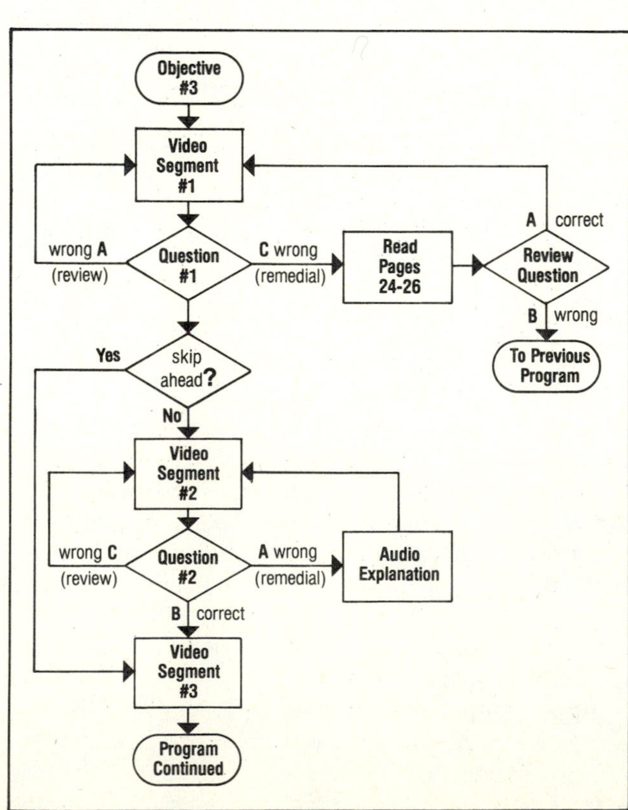

study the different branching patterns described in the CBI section on page 274.

Now, analyze each instructional segment of the content. Apply the flow charting procedure explained on page 280. Consider the questions raised there in your planning.

The flow chart, or a series of charts for the complete interactive program, should be reviewed and revised until you and other members of the planning team are satisfied that the content is being handled successfully. The next step is to write the script for the video recording (page 67). While you do this you may have to decide in detail what should be shown on the computer screen and also what will be on paper. Remember that any printed information (text, diagrams, questions, or answers) put on videotape requires "real" time (2 minutes or whatever time is needed) for reading and study.

Because segments of the video recording may be viewed in a different order by different individuals, be careful to plan continuity among scenes that could have a relation, even though not always logically so. This matter also will be important when videotaping scenes (showing same clothing, location of props in a scene, matching action, and so forth).

Program Production

Once the script is approved, move to production. The video segments are recorded and narration is added. As necessary, review video production topics in Chapter 15. Editing the tape requires special attention because of the branching feature. When a learner selects a segment to view, or chooses an answer for a question, the computer directs the videocassette player to advance or rewind the tape to the appropriate location. If two segments to be viewed sequentially are widely separated, then the "shuttle" time can take a few minutes and a learner may become restless, resulting in some loss in attention. Therefore, when editing, try to anticipate segments that should be in close proximity to reduce search time. Some systems interface two videocassette players with the computer so one can be searching for a sequence while the learner is viewing something on the other player.

You should already have chosen an authoring system that has the necessary features you will require for programing the computer (page 293). However, be aware that some authoring systems give emphasis to computer-based instruction as the primary instructional source and treat the video as an illustrative afterthought. Evaluate available systems thoroughly before deciding on the one to use. For example, consider these questions:

- Does the system allow for separate control of audio and video?
- Might you want the learner to operate the videocassette player separate from computer control?

These and other features should be considered as an authoring system is chosen.

Now proceed to carry out the programing function. Also, prepare accompanying printed materials (directions, readings, etc.).

Programing the Video Recording

An important feature of the authoring system you select is the capacity to control video segments by directing the videocassette player to access them. This means that the computer memory must hold information about the start and stop points for all video segments.

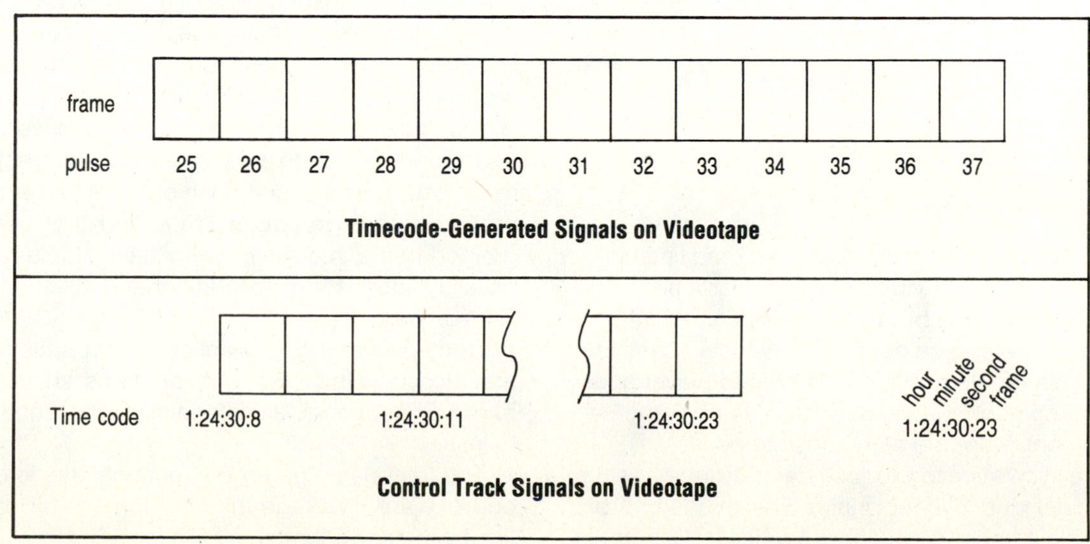

This can be accomplished in two ways:

- A *control track* can be recorded the full length of the videotape (page 285). Signals are placed every 1/30 of a second. Since the tape movement speed is 30 frames per second, there is a signal for each "frame." Through the interface connection, control-track signals are transmitted to the computer. Then the interface allows the computer to control the videocassette player via commands such as "find frame 479" or "play to frame 4356." Thus, by counting the pulses, the computer can be programed to locate any frame on the tape and command the tape to start or stop at that point. This movement may be by choice of the learner or automatically directed by the computer in response to a decision the learner has made. Unfortunately, videotape will slip somewhat as it starts and stops when advancing fast forward or rewinding. Therefore, with this method, errors in accuracy for locating specific frames can build up as the tape constantly moves back and forth.
- With a *timecode generator,* a signal is placed on an unused audio track (page 285) along the entire tape length. It is imprinted in hours, minutes, seconds, and frame numbers. The time code is read by the computer to locate specific start and stop points. This timecode method is more accurate than is the control-track method.

In practice, you must locate each video segment related to the proper program element. For help, refer to the flowcharts prepared during planning (and possibly revised when editing). For example, you locate a segment that would be viewed in response to an answer to a question, or to a segment selected by the learner that illustrates a specific concept. Note the timecode numbers for the beginning and end of the segment. Enter these data into the computer memory at proper program locations. Thereafter, the computer reads the numbers and directs the videotape to play the segment accordingly.

Barcode Software

An alternative to having the computer read timecode numbers and direct the video player to particular segments on tape is to use **barcodes.** A barcode contains start/end frame reference numbers. The user scans the barcode with a pen-like scanner. The video player goes to the exact point on the video and plays back the selected segment, stopping at the desired point.

Software allows you to produce barcode labels using your computer and a laser printer. The codes can be printed on plain paper or on adhesive-backed labels so the codes can be attached to lesson plans, text pages, frames of overhead transparencies, or any surface used during teaching and learning.

Topic	*Medium*	*Frame#*	*Barcode*
Brush types	Still	1459	
Brush strokes	Motion	12346-13649	
Results	Still	1532	

To make barcode labels, load the software disk into your computer and follow the prompts. You will first be asked about your equipment. This will be followed by a request for the frame number if a single visual is selected (as from a videodisc). If a motion visual sequence is needed you are asked to enter the beginning and ending timecode-generated frame numbers.

After you have entered all data needed, the program will allow you to preview the barcodes visually to ensure everything is correct. Then each barcode is printed with the laser printer. Once the barcodes are attached to the lesson materials, and the video player with its TV monitor is in place, it is a simple matter of scanning the barcodes using a hand-held barcode reader as described on page 355 in Chapter 19.

Completing and Testing the Courseware

In addition to having the computer program disk and the video recording, you may need to prepare or organize supporting printed materials. Also, directions for setting up the equipment to be used and for using the program components may all need attention. See suggestions for accompanying materials on page 282.

Test out the program with content specialists and some members of the potential audience. This could indicate any missing elements, unclear directions or inadequate explanations, program elements out of proper order, unsatisfactory branching path components, and such small matters as correct word spelling and proper use of expressions. Make corrections and retest until you can accept the program as ready for use by the learner group. You may find that certain programed paths through material have little use and can be eliminated. Refer to additional evaluation suggestions on page 282.

Once everything is checked out for satisfactory operation, duplicate copies of all items should be prepared. Protect original materials from potential damage or loss.

The total package for instructional use is called the **courseware.** Package the components for convenient use by learners.

Advantages and Limitations of Video Recording for Interaction

Now that you have an understanding of the procedures for using videotape to prepare an interactive learning program, you should recognize the advantages and limitations of this medium.

ADVANTAGES

- Project can be completed locally with available equipment.
- Duplicate copies are made locally.
- Sequences on videotape can be changed and reprogramed.
- Costs are comparable to other video productions but longer planning time is required.
- Available video equipment generally can be used.

LIMITATIONS

- Movement of tape from one segment to another may take a long time, thus reducing learner interest level.
- Still pictures to be viewed require full running time on tape.
- Locating specific frames on tape may be imprecise.
- With extensive use, videotape and player wear can become evident.

The limitations may outweigh the advantages for extensive use of videotape for interactive learning. The alternative is the videodisc.

COMPUTER/VIDEODISC

Of all media that are used to provide instruction, the videodisc, because of its unique features, offers the greatest potential for interactive uses. Full learner control, self-pacing, integrated still and motion images, branching, multiple paths, and instant feedback to the user are among the features that are conveniently treated on videodisc. Image quality and realistic action exhibited on a videodisc are combined with the versatility of the computer. Review the factors that contribute to interactive learning on page 271. We will examine how a computer-controlled videodisc program can be designed and produced to serve these factors effectively.

Advantages and Limitations of Videodisc for Interaction

While both videotape and videodisc units can be used for interactive learning, there are many practical benefits for the videodisc. Here are its advantages and limitations:

ADVANTAGES

- Can contain a large amount of material, namely, 54,000 still frames, 30 minutes of motion, or combinations of the two.
- Can combine both still images and motion sequences with precise, easy, and rapid access to any frame.
- Special features include flexible speed control, still picture and motion, frame freeze control, two audio tracks.
- Very little, if any, wear on disc or equipment during use.
- Low duplication cost for quantities of discs.

LIMITATIONS

- Because of the variety of features that can be used, planning is complex and time consuming.
- Needs careful attention to specific details and special requirements when organizing final materials.
- At present, videodisc preparation requires professional services.
- Cost for preparing the master disc is high.
- Changes or revisions cannot be made once master disc is produced.

Equipment and Videodisc Player Levels

Equipment similar to that listed for computer/videotape on page 283 is required here. The microcomputer, interface, and video display screen can be the same. The videodisc player may be one of three types depending on the level of interactivity desired for the program to be used with it.

- A **level I** videodisc player includes a manually operated *touch pad* or remote control unit that allows the user to have random access to program material on the disc. (Some home videodisc players are examples on this level.) Starting location for segments

(called *picture* or *chapter stops*) are defined by codes recorded on the disc during manufacture. The user can search for the start of a chapter and the section will play until a cue to stop is encountered. Touch pad use permits retrieval of single frames and movement of images forward and in reverse with slow or rapid motion. Level I videodisc instruction, controlled by the individual user, can be designed as semi-interactive. The barcode method for locating and viewing segments of a video recording (page 286) can be applied equally to videodisc use.

- A **level II** videodisc player has a built-in programable microcomputer capable of decoding and storing a limited amount of program information that was encoded on the disc. During use, the player is directed to perform certain playback sequences and to respond to viewer choices made through the touch pad. A videodisc designed for use on a level II player cannot be successfully used on a level III player.
- The **level III** videodisc player is interfaced with an external computer. This level of interactivity is the most versatile and the one usually meant when referring to an "interactive videodisc." All interactions are controlled through the computer program. Built-in features of some computers allow easy cable hookup to a videodisc player without adding a printed circuit board interface. The player will respond to commands from the computer and operate with fully programmed flexibility. By using a compatible interface device, computer images and video images can be viewed separately on the same screen. With other interfaces, computer-generated text and graphics can be overlayed on the display screen along with the videodisc images at the same time.

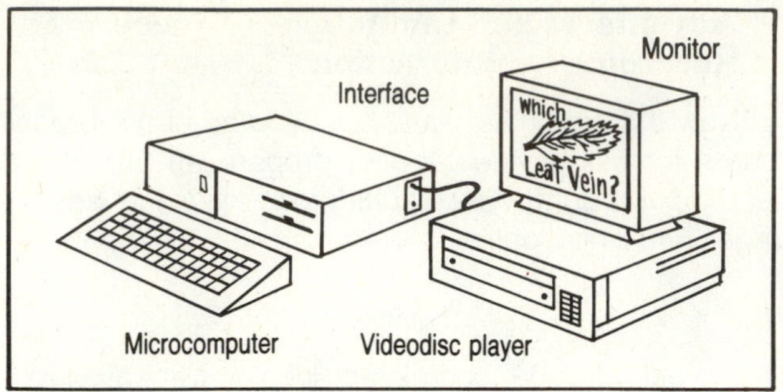

A level III program can include the capability to record every learner response to a question and even the time taken to respond. These data can give both the learner and the instructor feedback on need for remediation and opportunities for more advanced work.

Additionally, level III allows for excellent use of simulation and gaming techniques (page 279). The realism of well-designed and visualized situations in which a learner becomes involved in analyzing, synthesizing, evaluating, and solving problems can be most effective.

Program Planning

Planning an interactive program for a videodisc is similar to planning for an interactive video program. See the planning checklist on page 284. Although you should follow the same procedure, now you have more options—still picture sequences, still or freeze framing within a motion scene, almost instantly locating images, rapid response to answers for questions, and so on. Therefore, greater care needs to be taken in planning.

The questions raised and the flow-charting technique described on page 284 should receive detailed attention. Another suggestion is to develop a planning form like the one used in multi-image presentation design (page 231). It could be used to show what should be on the computer display screen, on the videodisc (visual and two audio tracks), and on accompanying paper. With these categories, the form could look like the one on the next page.

From the flow charts and the planning form, develop the scripts for the video and audio portions, for the computer program (using an authoring system), and for contents of printed materials. Review the scripts and flow patterns for proper order, to see that relationships are evident, and for smooth continuity results.

Program Production

According to the script, record all video segments on tape and collect or prepare other visual and audio materials. Because of the possible arrangements for video sequencing, care should be given to maintaining con-

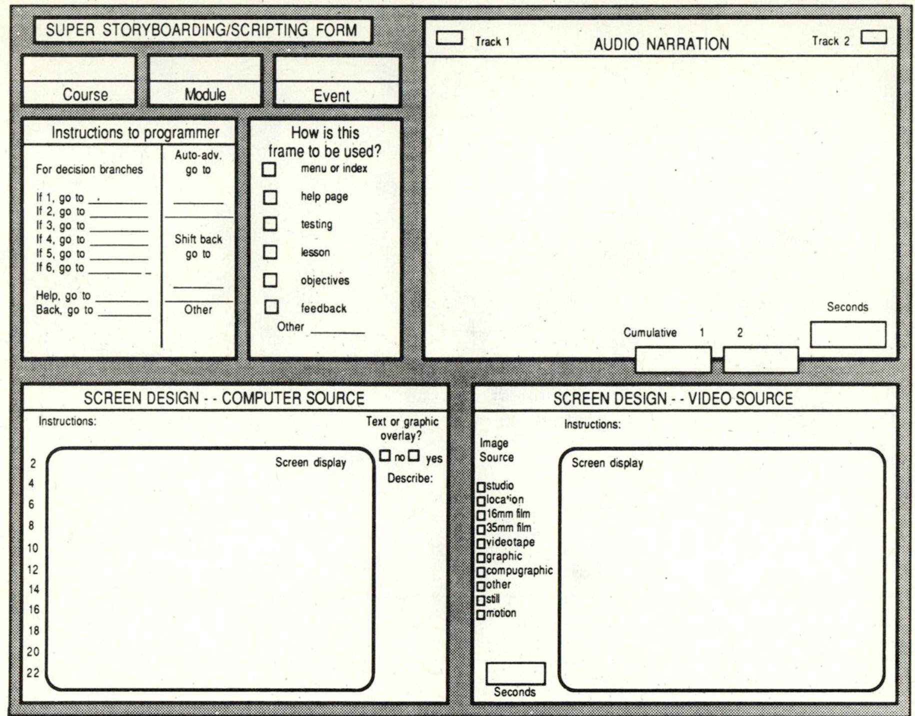
SUPER STORYBOARDING/SCRIPTING FORM

Course | Module | Event

Instructions to programmer

For decision branches — Auto-adv. go to ______

If 1, go to ______
If 2, go to ______
If 3, go to ______
If 4, go to ______
If 5, go to ______
If 6, go to ______

Shift back go to ______

Help, go to ______
Back, go to ______

Other

How is this frame to be used?
☐ menu or index
☐ help page
☐ testing
☐ lesson
☐ objectives
☐ feedback
Other ______

☐ Track 1 — AUDIO NARRATION — Track 2 ☐

Cumulative 1 2 — Seconds

SCREEN DESIGN - - COMPUTER SOURCE

Instructions:

Text or graphic overlay? ☐ no ☐ yes

Describe:

Screen display

2 4 6 8 10 12 14 16 18 20 22

SCREEN DESIGN - - VIDEO SOURCE

Instructions:

Image Source
☐ studio
☐ location
☐ 16mm film
☐ 35mm film
☐ videotape
☐ graphic
☐ compugraphic
☐ other
☐ still
☐ motion

Seconds

Screen display

Level III Videodisc Planning Form

Reproduced by permission from Michael DeBloois Corp., Logan, UT

sistent overall production style and image quality. Review information in Chapter 15 on the various aspects of video production.

If titles, menu (table of contents), questions, answers, and graphic materials will be put on videotape (as opposed to being generated by the computer and displayed on command or as requested), they should be prepared, using art techniques, a titler, or a character generator, and put on tape when slides and other still picture items are handled.

Premastering

In order to make a videodisc, a high quality videotape recording is prepared that contains all visual and audio materials. This is the **premaster.** Before it is prepared, the company that will produce the videodisc should be contacted so that all required specifications will be met. The details that will require attention when preparing the premaster are extensive. How well you accomplish them will greatly determine the quality of the resulting master videodisc. Review the introductory information (page 287) on videodisc formats, procedure for converting a video recording to the premaster, and then preparing the videodisc.

The premaster should be prepared on 1-inch videotape or other broadcast quality format, such as ½-inch Betacam. Most often, a video lab facility makes the premaster from your original or edited materials. Since a constant angular velocity (CAV) format videodisc will be prepared for interactive use, certain matters should receive special attention.

- Place the table of contents and other menu or index information close to the middle of the content on the disc so that access from any other point on the disc will take the shortest possible path and the least amount of time.
- Build from the middle of the disc. If you can predict that some options will be chosen more often than others, place these in the middle of your program, followed by the next most likely and so on.
- Put the expected least frequently used frames at the very beginning or very end of the disc, since access time is slowest to these locations.
- Still picture frames should be placed next to the motion scenes they precede or follow; do not group all stills together.
- Each still frame consists of two "fields" on the disc. In order to ensure there will not be a flicker when a still picture is shown, make sure the edits consistently start on the same field. Check with the laboratory for an explanation of this detail. If you repeat the still picture for three frames, the problem of different fields can be avoided.
- Avoid placing significant still frames, such as textual matter, within the first 3000 frames on the disc because this is the area of lowest resolution.

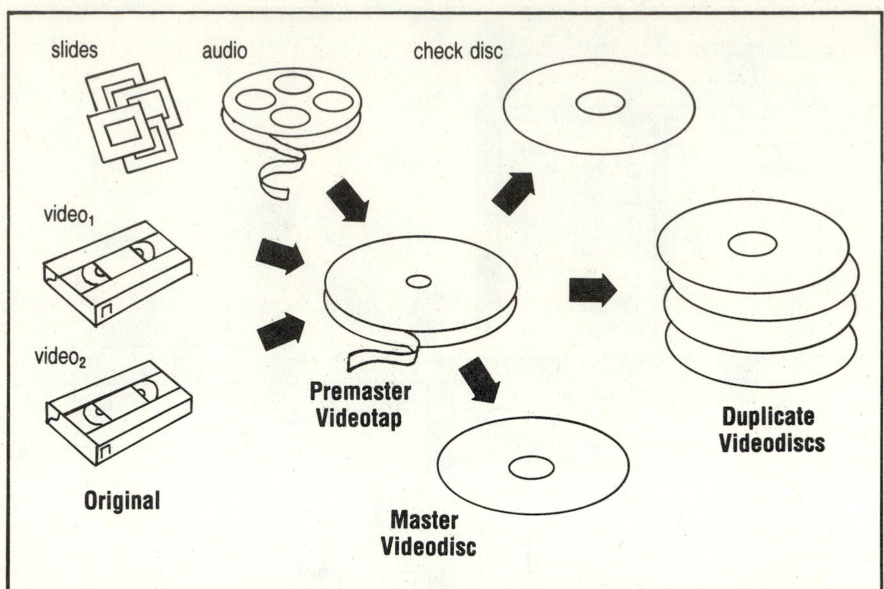

- Start each motion sequence with four to five freeze frames to ensure a steady image at the beginning. Repeat this at the end of the sequence.
- Add timecode numbers (page 286) for the full length of the premaster. These will be transferred to the videodisc as specific locations for each frame.
- Provide the facility that will produce the videodisc with your paper records of the flow charts, storyboards, and script, along with number assignments for frames, chapters, and still cue locations, and any other details that will help the technicians understand your plan for the videodisc.

When all the preceding steps have been completed and the premaster has been made, you have what is called a **formatted premaster.** A copy of the premaster should be examined carefully for accuracy, instructional flow, frame numbers for the computer program, and so forth. Cost of the videodisc master can be significantly reduced by presenting a high-quality, well-organized and carefully edited videotape to the videodisc production facility.

This is the time to complete the computer program since all frame numbers for assigned segments or still pictures can be entered.

Testing the Program

During the planning and video production phases, you should have periodically conducted a **formative evaluation** (page 174) as the project progressed. This would provide feedback and reactions that can lead to revisions for a better product.

Then, before the videodisc is actually made, as already explained, prepare a ½-inch copy of the premaster. Try the program out with some potential audience members. Although it cannot run as a completely smooth program, you can test whether it does work satisfactorily. This is the last chance to make changes before the costly videodisc master is made.

Preparing the Videodisc

At the videodisc production facility, the formatted premaster videotape is checked for its adherence to the required specifications. In the production process, the disc-mastering equipment scans all signals on the master tape, producing the master videodisc and entering frame code numbers and inserting cues. Then the master disc is replicated in quantity and checked for conformance with the specifications.

Frequently, a **proof disc** (also called a **check disc**) is prepared and played with the computer program to verify that every element of the program is included in the correct place. If there is a mistake, a change can be made before the duplicate discs are prepared.

Packaging the Courseware

When all materials have been completed, they should be assembled for use. This includes copies of the computer program disk, the videodisc, and the student manual or other printed material. The videodisc usually comes in its own folder. To this, envelopes can be attached to hold the other items so all courseware will be contained in a single package.

There will be continual developments and new innovations in interactive videodisc technology. These can be expected to modify the information and procedures described here. Watch for reports in the literature and developments in this potentially dynamic medium for instruction.

Repurposing a Videodisc

If the visuals and audio materials on an existing videodisc would prove useful for a new application program, the videodisc can be **repurposed.** This means that a computer program is developed to access sections or specific materials on the videodisc to serve a new set of objectives.

Repurposing can be a much less expensive way to make an interactive videodisc program than a full disc production project. A note of warning when an available videodisc is being considered for use—make certain the format of the disc is **CAV** and *not CLV* (page 267). The latter does *not* allow for use of many level III techniques.

Most repurposing is done from a **generic videodisc.** This type contains collections of slides as still frames and possibly video sequences, all relating to a subject area or a major topic. Once a videodisc suitable to the instructional purpose and topic objectives has been selected, the procedure to repurpose includes the following:

1. Carefully examine the images on the disc. Identify and document all still frames and motion sequences that could be used. It is helpful if a reference guide is available that describes the visuals, including frame numbers.
2. Develop a plan (flow chart, page 280) for instructional use of the materials. This should include planning similar to that required for any interactive learning program (page 272).
3. Videodisc audio is difficult to incorporate in the repurposing procedure. Digitized sound (page 154) can be stored on the computer hard disk and synchronized with videodisc images.
4. Monitors with both the computer and videodisc player, to show separate screen images, are preferable to a single monitor configuration.
5. Careful evaluation of the authoring system to be used is necessary since there can be shortcomings in what a tool can do for repurposing.

REVIEW

What You Have Learned About Computer/ Videotape and Computer/Videodisc Interactive Media:

1. What is an interface?
2. What term applies to the procedure of adapting an available recording or videodisc for microcomputer-controlled interactive learning?
3. When developing an interactive program, what detailed planning activity is now necessary that does not receive attention in conventional planning of a videotape recording?
4. What two important matters that receive little attention in conventional video production need attention when preparing and editing a videotape recording to be used for interactive learning?
5. What is done during production that allows the computer to locate beginning and end points of video sequences?
6. What is the value of applying the barcode procedure when planning an interactive lesson with a video medium?
7. Mark *T* (tape) for statements that are advantages for using videotape to produce interactive media and *D* (disc) for statements relating to videodisc advantages.
   a. Equipment for use generally available
   b. Production cost relatively low
   c. Can include large amount of information in a small space
   d. Sequences relatively easy to replace
   e. Rapid access to any picture or sequence
   f. Little wear on material or equipment
   g. Program can be completely produced within an organization
8. To which videodisc level does each statement apply?
   a. There is a limited number of times you can automatically make choices through the total

(continued)

program by selecting an option on the touch pad.
   b. Start a program. When a question is asked, refer to the frame number for each answer and call up your choice by using the touch pad.
   c. It can include a record of student responses to questions and time taken to respond.
   d. May permit overlaying graphic images on video images.
   e. Watch a program from beginning to end and have the opportunity to pause periodically for note taking.
   f. Allow for unlimited amount of interaction throughout the program.
9. What are six good practices when formatting a premaster tape?
10. What is the benefit of *repurposing* a videodisc?
11. Why is it important to conduct a formative evaluation of the premaster tape before having the master videodisc prepared?

See answers on page 383.

INTERACTIVE MULTIMEDIA

Technological advances lead to increasingly sophisticated ways for delivering instruction. For example, the development and use of videodiscs represents an entirely different dimension than does a conventional slide/tape program.

Now we can fully integrate still pictures, animation, high resolution graphics, motion video, and sound with text on a computer screen. Selected portions of each medium, controlled by the computer, are merged together sequentially, or considered in a non-linear order as necessary. The term **multimedia** is used when a variety of media is manipulated with the computer in control. The expression **media integration** is also applied in this instance. The result can be an on-screen presentation for use with groups or for individual user interactivity.

The two major aspects of media development—planning and production—as already described, require careful consideration relative to multimedia. Review these topics:

- Levels of interactivity (page 271)
- Factors contributing to interactivity (page 271)
- Media attributes (page 58)
- Media planning sequence (page 284)
- Branching and flowcharting (pages 273 and 280)
- Computer-based instruction (page 277)
- Computer peripherals (page 119)
- Video production (page 246)
- Desktop video production (page 264)
- Videodisc preparation (page 285)

Hardware Alternatives

As you know, a computer stores information in a + and − electronic code—the *binary system.* This is in

the form of digital signals. Therefore, for a computer to handle any media form, the analog format (page 154), in which most audio and visual media are prepared, must be converted to **digital** form. Once it is converted to digital, the media can easily be controlled and manipulated by computer equipment.

While various computer add-in boards can handle the conversion, laser storage systems are directly digital. Six major forms of digital optical disc technology are available today. Each one is based on the 4.72-inch (12 centimeters) diameter audio compact disc (CD):

- ***CD-ROM*** (Compact Disc Read Only Memory)—Used as a database for storing up to 300,000 pages of text, graphics, photos, and sound. (See page 296 for applications of CD-ROM for interactive learning.)
- ***CD-I*** (Compact Disc Interactive)—CD-ROM-based technology designed to play back up to 8,000 still images, including text, graphics, animation, and digital sound up to 34 hours on two channels. Includes a stand-alone playback unit that contains a built-in computer chip.
- ***DVI*** (Digital Video Interactive)—Uses standard CD-ROM disc to store up to 72 minutes of full motion video and audio (up to 44 hours on two channels), or any combination of text (650,000 pages) and still media (40,000 images) forms.
- ***CDTV*** (Commodore Dynamic Total Vision)—Similar to DVI with Amiga computer equipment running CD and CD-ROM programs.
- ***CD-ROM XA*** (Compact Disc Read Only Memory Extended Architecture)—Combines computer text and graphics with still images, video information, and high quality audio.
- ***CD-WORM*** (Compact Disc Write Once Read Many Times)—User can record data permanently on the disc mostly for archival purposes or mass storage of data.

Authoring Programs

With each major microcomputer group—Apple Macintosh, IBM and compatible MS-DOS computers, and Commodore Amiga—authoring systems are available for multimedia interactive applications. See introduction to authoring systems on page 281.

An authoring system provides guidelines that prompt you to input information or commands according to your instructional plan. Most often, the procedure or alternatives are in the form of a series of icon images or a menu pull-down that directs an information screen, a video or animation sequence, a set of still pictures, a sound component, or whatever media form is desired for selection. When a choice is made (often by action of a mouse), a blank screen template appears, to be filled in with necessary data, or the learner is directed to perform other chosen media functions.

With an authoring program, an individual with limited programing experience is able to create and link together textual, graphic, and other media-based infor-

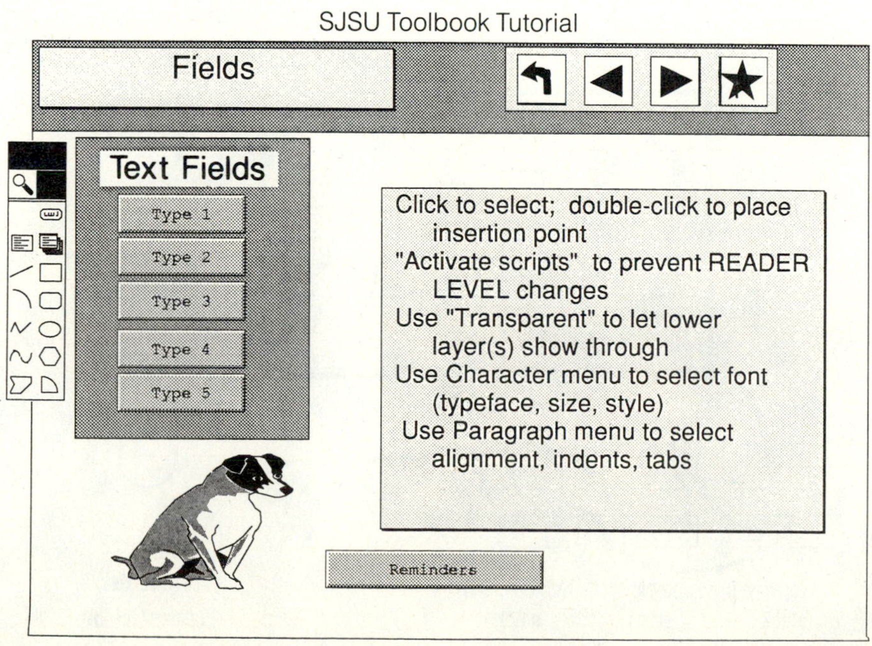

Source: Jim Carroll Authoring Project, SJSU

mation to create the multimedia program. Examples of authoring tools are:

- Macintosh—HyperCard, MacroMind Director, CourseBuilder
- MS-DOS—Multimedia ToolBook, IconAuthor, Quest
- Amiga—AmigaVision, The Director, Deluxe Paint III

Common features of HyperCard and ToolBook authoring systems include:

- Based on a metaphor of printed materials
  HyperCard—collection of "cards" forming "stacks"
  ToolBook—collection of "pages" in a "book."
- Information stored (including visuals) in networks of "nodes" which are connected together with "links."
- User can branch to any node for which there is a link.
- User can follow numerous paths, depending on specific needs or interests.
- User sees only information and program components related to one's need or interest; thus one extensive program can serve many audiences or individuals.
- Use concept of "layers," each consisting of a field with text, graphics, and "buttons" containing instructions to do something.
- Able to control external devices—videodisc and CD-ROM most often.
- Can include visual effects—dissolve, wipe, zoom.
- Program languages available (examples—HyperTalk and OpenScript) to add additional features or to create further applications.

These authoring tools allow you to create, store, and display data, text, images, graphics, and animation, in any combination, and also to control sound and images on a videodisc. The way the information is stored, manipulated, and presented makes this a special method of computer programing and use. The user can select and connect or sequence any parts of the stored information. The links of cross-references help a person to browse, locate specific information, and even develop one's own associations while navigating through large bodies of data. Rather than just acquiring a stream of facts, the results can be the conceptual understanding of a topic.

In addition to multimedia applications, these authoring tools are applicable in normal CBI programing. There are also many unique features with each programing system. For further details and specific operating procedures, refer to the references listed and literature available with each software package.

Another authoring tool is designed for courseware development directly applied to concepts in instructional transaction theory (page 17). The method consists of establishing instructional transaction shells. A shell consists of four primary components: (1) interaction management, (2) instructional parameters, (3) knowledge sequence, and (4) a resource database containing mediated representatives of the knowledge to be taught. Authoring with a transaction shell consists of selecting instructional strategies corresponding to a set of objectives, then supplying the content information required of these strategies.

An important strength of the transactional shell ap-

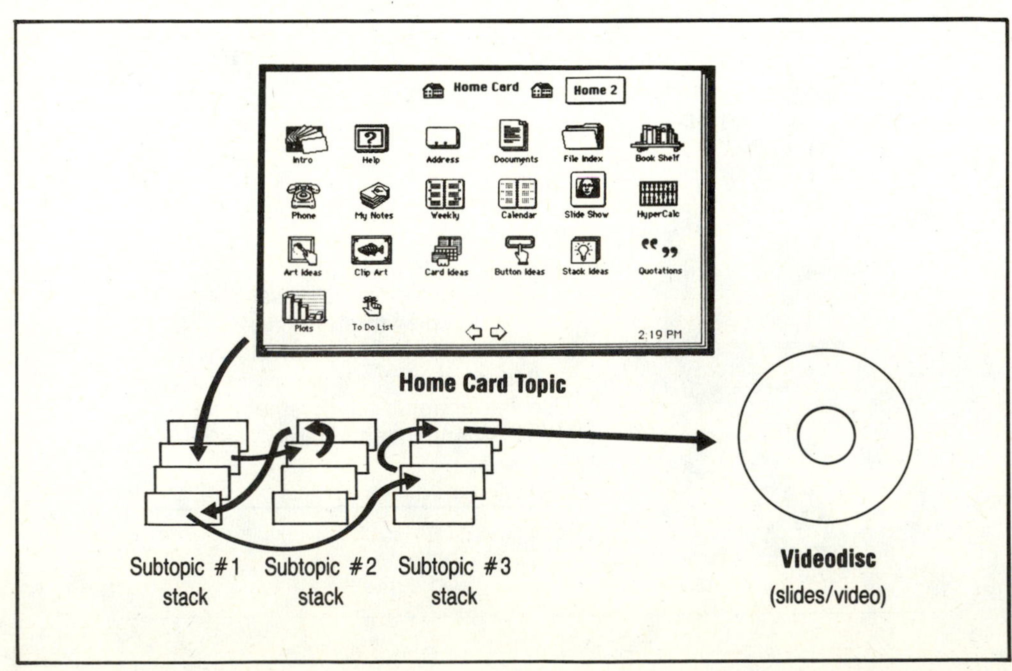

proach to programing for multimedia is that flexible and reusable instructional software can be designed. With availability of a range and large number of transactional shells, more efficient and possibly more effective development can take place than with other authoring tools.

Sample Multimedia Application

An application of HyperCard might be on the topic "Making a Presentation." It is designed to instruct a person who must plan, prepare, and present information to groups and audiences. The program starts with a *Home card.* This is the reference point from which to plan and execute your search. The Home card contains icons, which are components of the menu for stacks in the program—planning, analyzing audiences, selecting media, preparing media, presentation skills, and so forth. You can browse through the various subtopics by touching icons in order to decide where you want to start or what information you need. For example, if you choose *Selecting Media,* you will find reference to media attributes (with visualized examples to view, if desired), selection procedures according to the literature, and scenes on videodisc illustrating use of various media. By moving through these cards, you would become prepared to make a decision about media for your use. Then you would decide to move to another aspect of the Presentation topic, and so forth.

Factors to Consider When Selecting an Authoring Tool

Answer these questions when considering an authoring package for use in developing a multimedia program. The questions also indicate procedures you might use when designing a program.

1. Does the program you will design function satisfactorily with the equipment to be available to users (platform, memory requirement, peripherals)?
2. What user control interfaces are supported (keyboard, mouse, light pen, touch screen)?
3. Does the authoring tool provide for alternative ways to develop instruction, like using templates, scripting, or flowcharting?
4. Is the reference manual for the software understandable and convenient to use, containing examples, tutorials, help files, a reference section, and an index?
5. Does the program provide for various degrees of designer expertise by allowing for flexible use of features stated in the two previous questions?
6. Is the authoring mode the same as it will be in the final form, so as you proceed, you can see how the program will appear to the user?
7. Does the program accommodate all necessary media peripherals (CD-ROM, video player, audio player, etc.) and expansion circuit boards (full-motion video, video digitizer, audio, etc.)?
8. Does the program include necessary word processing features, including font variety, text composition and importation, editing capability, and so forth?
9. Are graphic features included for screen design, use of drawing tools, import ability from other graphic sources, and so forth?
10. Can you control audio signals, including handling of both analog and digital input, and visual editing by displaying a waveform of a sound file?
11. Can full motion video (tape and disc), possibly with multiple video inputs, be handled easily and not require additional equipment?
12. If you will include animation, does the program have the necessary capabilities, including various animation techniques with reasonable speed and compatibility with other animation programs you might use?
13. How can user performance records, such as amount of time spent on the program, time used to reply to a question, and number of questions answered correctly, be calculated conveniently and reported?
14. Do you need any special licensing arrangement from the authoring program owner to duplicate and distribute your resulting courseware?

What You Learned About Interactive Multimedia:

1. What is meant by the term *multimedia?*
2. Does a computer handle *digital* or *analog* media forms?

(continued)

3. Relate the items in the two columns.

_______	a. CDI	(1)	Stores great numbers of pages of text, graphics, and photos
_______	b. CD-WORM	(2)	Stores up to 8,000 images of text, graphics, animation, and sound
_______	c. CD-ROM	(3)	Stores up to 72 minutes of still, full motion, and audio in CD-ROM format
_______	d. CDTV	(4)	Runs CD audio and CD-ROM programs, controlled by Amiga computer
_______	e. DVI	(5)	Can record information in your facility

4. Which statements are *true* about multimedia authoring tools?

_______ a. Sequences of information are used in preset order.
_______ b. HyperCard is a program for Macintosh computer.
_______ c. A new authoring tool is transactional shells.
_______ d. There is no authoring tool for use with MS-DOS computers.
_______ e. Terms such as *stack of cards, book pages,* and *layers* are used.
_______ f. User selects sequences from stored information.
_______ g. Requires some programing experience to use.
_______ h. A Home card is like a Table of Contents for a book.

See answers on page 383.

MEDIA ADAPTABLE FOR REACTIVE LEARNING

Some conventional forms of instructional media can be modified or supplemented for reactive use. Three types are print media, audio recordings with print, and slide/tape programs with print. In addition, CD-ROM may be used. For someone with no experience in developing self-instructional materials, one of these forms of media might be a good starting point. The learner studies a sequence of the material, then replies to a question, solves a problem, or otherwise reacts to the information presented. The answer is given. With success, the learner advances to the next study segment. This linear arrangement is followed throughout the program.

Refer to the steps in planning on page 4 and the planning checklist on page 284. They guide the necessary planning for reactive materials. Then follow the procedures described for each reactive media form that follows here.

Printed Material

At times, individuals may need guidance in order to effectively study a textbook used in a course, or a manual used in preparation for a job. To fill this need, an accompanying workbook may be prepared. In it, learners can be directed to organize, review, and apply information, concepts, principles, and processes treated in the text or in the manual. Individuals may be prompted to answer questions, prepare outlines, complete exercises, and engage in other meaningful activities.

Another way to use printed material for reactive learning is to develop a self-instructional booklet that contains a sequential presentation of verbal information or a set of procedures. It may consist of small increments of information with periodic review exercises and application projects. The content may be treated with words supplemented by diagrams, other graphics, and even photographs. The information in Chapter 11 can be helpful in the design and preparation of printed media materials. See example on the next page.

To adapt or design printed media for reactive learning, carry through the planning steps previously outlined. The pretest results would indicate where individuals are prepared to start the program. Results of exercises would help to direct their progress through the program, leading to a better understanding of the printed media.

CD-ROM with Study Guide/Worksheets

CD-ROM discs (Compact Disc Read Only Memory) are commercially produced. Each one contains large amounts of textual material, and can include color graphics or photographs, as well as realistic music and sound effects. Animated sequences to illustrate concepts may also be on the disc.

Information on the 4.72-inch disc is assessed by a drive called a "reader." A computer reads the information selected, which is shown on the screen. Anyplace on the disc can be accessed in less than 1 second.

The large amount of storage and the interactive nature of the CD-ROM medium allow learners to browse

An *ideal* plan for study of each chapter is as follows:

1. Read the *Performance Objectives* given in the Guidebook.
2. Read the *Outline Overview* of the chapter in the Guidebook.
3. Read the chapter and study it actively.
4. Construct a more detailed outline from the skeletal structure given in the *Outline Overview.*
5. Work on the fill-in *Completion Exercise* and check your answers.
6. Go back to the text and clarify and fill in the gaps in your knowledge of the chapter content.
7. Take the *Self-Test* in the Guidebook.
8. Repeat step 6.
9. Select a *Project* in the Guidebook to help crystallize your newly acquired knowledge by putting it to work.
10. Look again at the *Performance Objectives* for the chapter to see how many you have achieved.

Recommended Study Sequence for Each Chapter of a Textbook with Accompanying Learner Guidebook

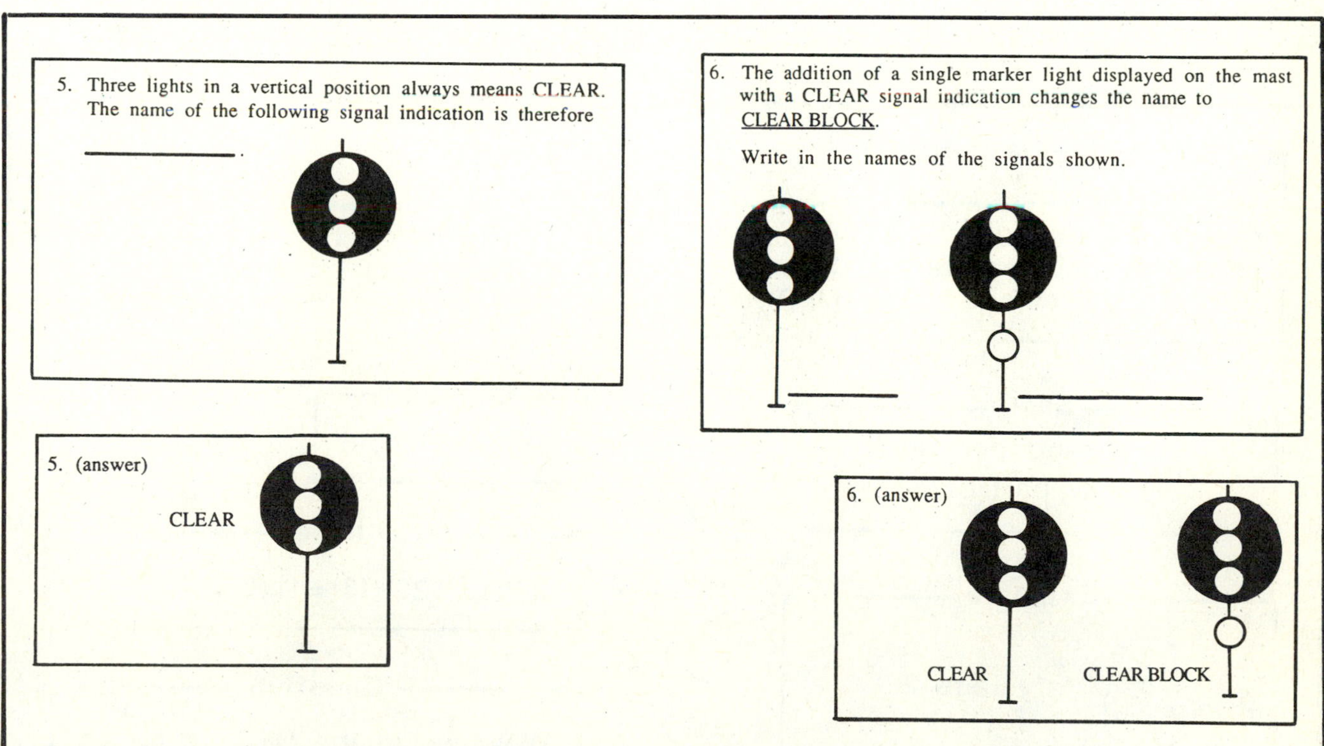

Part of a Self-Instructional Booklet on *Position Light Signals for Railroads*

or to conduct in-depth research on available topics. By developing a study guide and worksheets, or allowing individuals to select their own problem topic, CD-ROM resources can support reactive self-study activities. The result can be a written report or a visual presentation.

Audio Recording with Workbook

As compared with printed media described above, a more personal, flexible approach to interaction can be served by using an audio recording along with printed material. The recording guides the learner's progress through the topic. The instructor's voice provides directions, some information and explanations, feedback on exercise answers, a summary of the topic, and other useful verbal assistance. The printed material can include readings, graphics and other illustrations, and worksheets with review and application questions. See Chapter 13 for further suggestions on this topic.

Follow the planning steps listed previously. One additional key element in the planning process would be to script and record the narration for the audio recording. Use this procedure:

1. Outline the verbal introduction, directions, information, and explanations that should precede or follow the study of each content section and discuss answers for review exercises.
   Note: This narration is not a lengthy lecture. It may include a few minutes of explanation, but it should mainly provide directions, summaries, and feedback on answers.
2. Plan the content of the accompanying workbook so there is close correlation with the audio narration. It may include special reading material, visuals to accompany or supplement the audio, problems to solve, and a summary of the topic.
3. Write out the narration in an informal, conversational manner. Direct the learner to stop the tape to carry out an activity, namely reading, examining items, completing an exercise, and so forth. Five to six seconds of music can be used to indicate "stop" points on the tape. To ensure clarity of explanations, read over the scripted narration, referring to the materials being specified. Refine the narration so it will communicate effectively to the learner.
4. Record the narration. See suggestions for recording procedures in Chapter 9. If desirable, add low-level background music to the recording during lapses in narration. Then prepare a sufficient number of audiocassette duplicates for learner use.
5. Consider indexing the tape to provide learners

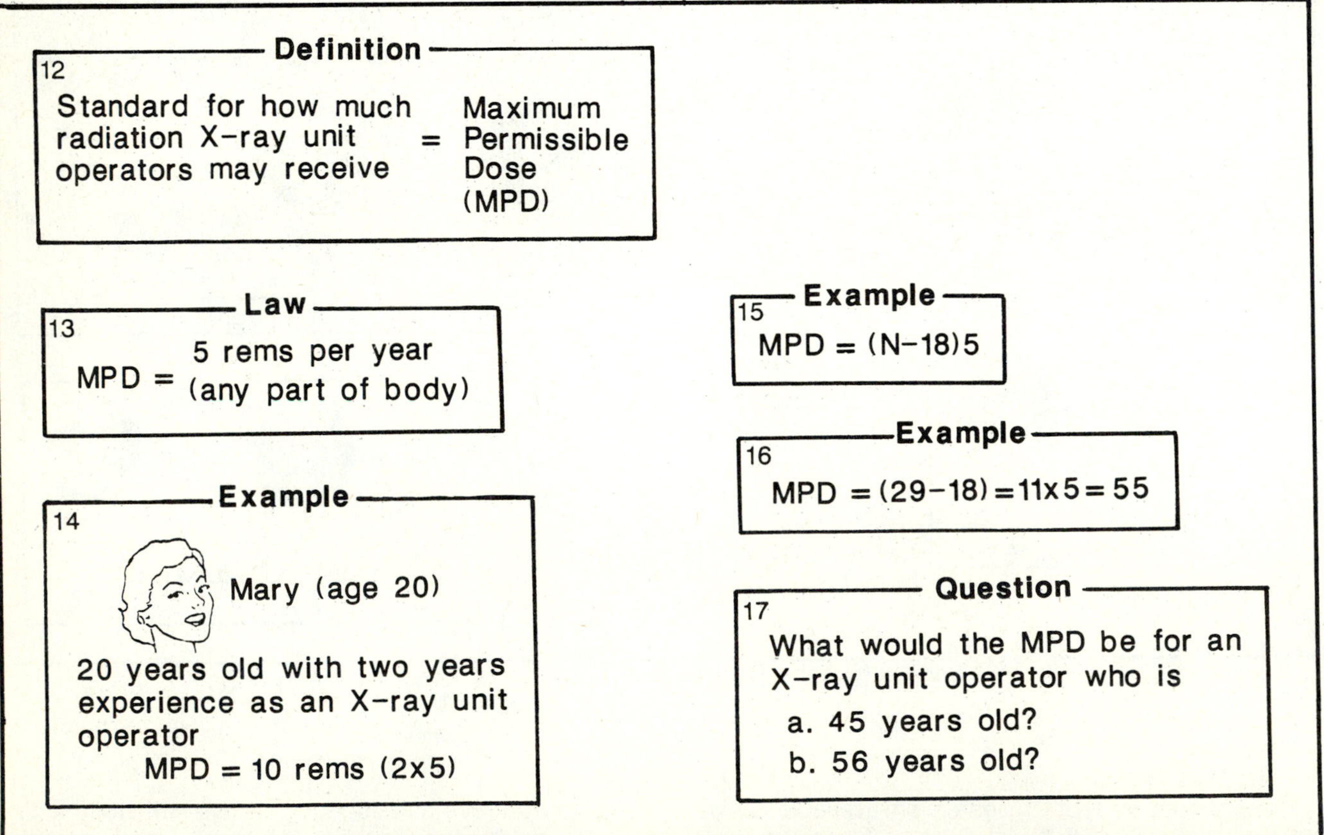

Section from Reactive Audiotape/Workbook Program on *Radiation Protection*

some flexibility or branching for individual use. This would allow a person to easily locate a desired section at any point on the audio recording. Indexing is explained on page 218. Include in the study guide or workbook a written explanation of how to use the index to locate the beginning of a specific section on the tape.

When all components are duplicated, package an audiocassette, study guide/workbook, and other material in a large envelope for learner use.

Slide/Tape with Workbook

If a topic requires the realism of color pictures for explanations and illustrations, or for demonstrating a procedure, then color slides with an audiotaped and synchronized narration might be the preferred medium. The procedure for preparing a slide series (Chapter 14), developing a storyboard and script (page 65), refining the narration (page 170), and making and synchronizing the recording (Chapter 9), should all be carefully studied and applied.

Although visual information requiring reading may be presented on slides, any material containing more than six to eight lines of text should be put on paper. Also, decisions need to be made about developing a pretest and including review questions, providing answers, and introducing related activities. Should these be on slides or in accompanying printed form?

Instructions on a slide, reinforced with narration, can direct the viewer to stop the tape and proceed to a worksheet or to a workbook page. Some recorders include a 150 Hz signal feature for automatically stopping the tape at predetermined spots. After completing an assigned activity, a button is pushed to restart the tape and the presentation proceeds.

One problem of working with two media forms, such as slides and audiotape, is the possible difficulty of

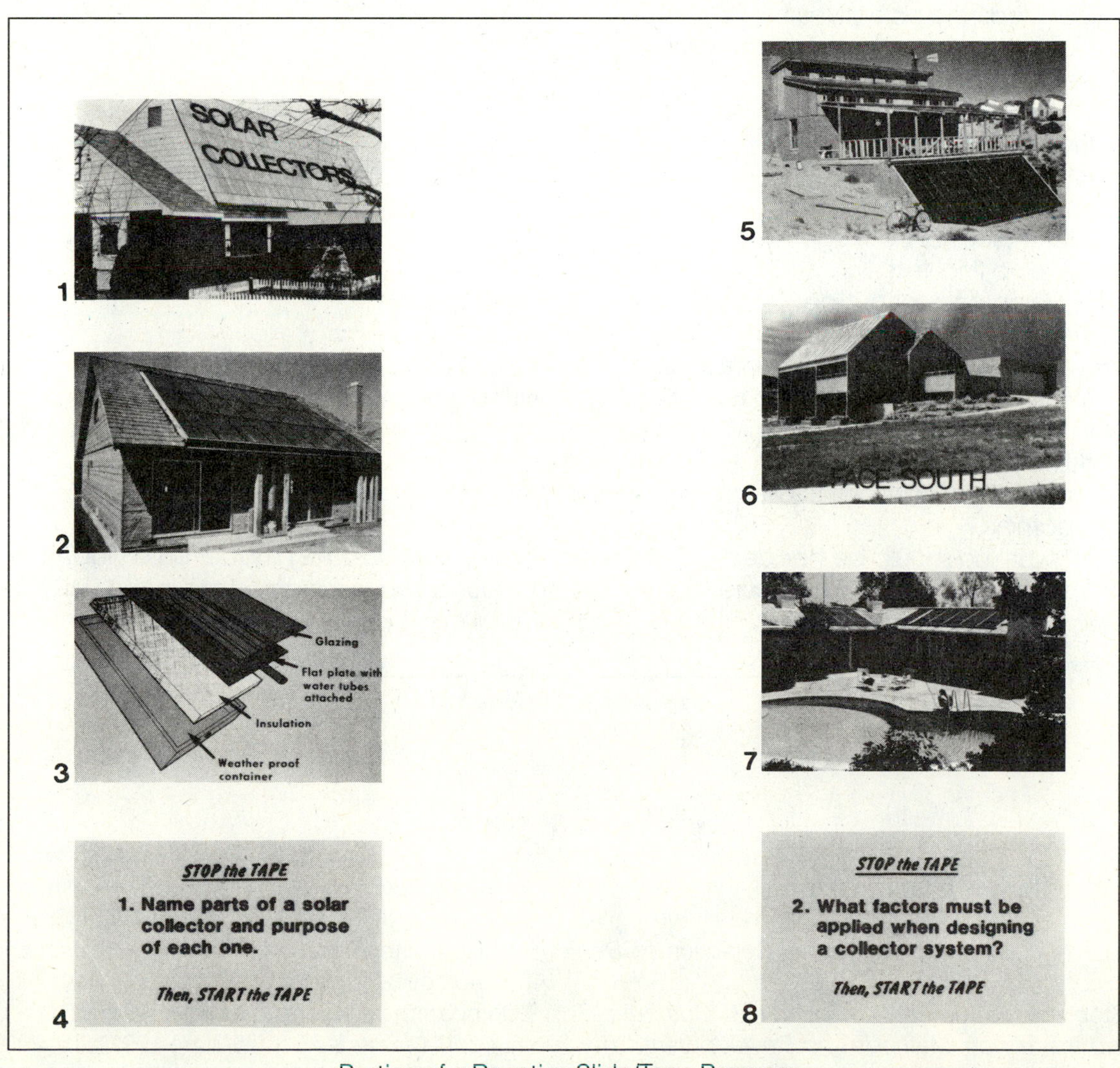

Portion of a Reactive Slide/Tape Program

maintaining synchronization between the slides and the recording. Typically, an inaudible signal on the tape (1000 Hz) controls the slide advance mechanism (page 161). If a malfunction causes the narration and slides lose their synchronism, then the user has difficulty in understanding the presentation.

Also, because you should want to provide as much flexibility as possible for learners to go back for a review, or as an alternative, to skip ahead, then other ways to ensure synchronization need to be considered. One way is to add a visible number to each slide and have verbal cues in the narration ("in slide 15 . . . ," "turn to number 17 . . ."). See page 162 for an explanation of this technique. Another method is to convert the completed slide/tape program to a videotape recording for ultimate use. This will guarantee the synchronism of picture and sound. See page 230 for an explanation of this method.

The resulting reactive program would consist of copies of the slides and audio recording, or the substituted video recording, and the necessary printed materials.

REVIEW

What You Have Learned About Media Adaptable for Reactive Learning:

1. What is a preferred order for developing each step when planning to adapt media for reactive learning? (Use numbers to indicate order.)
   a. State learning objectives
   b. Plan exercises and provide answers
   c. Select topic
   d. Write pretest
   e. Prepare directions
   f. Plan further activities
   g. Sequence content
   h. Assemble final package
   i. Develop final test
   j. Develop content outline
   k. Develop media
2. For what two reasons might printed media be adapted to an interactive format?
3. Why might you select an audio recording along with a workbook for self-paced learning?
4. What four elements, relating to learning content, can be provided by an audio recording and workbook?
5. When might you choose to use a slide/tape program correlated with printed material for reactive learning?
6. What warning should be heeded when you consider putting reading matter on a slide?
7. In what two ways can you ensure that picture and sound will be synchronized in the slide/tape program?

See answers on page 383.

REFERENCES

COMPUTER-BASED INSTRUCTION

Albin, Marilyn. "CBT Authoring System Selection." *CBT Directions* 4 (June 1991): 20–26.

Alessi, Stephen M. and Trollip, Stanley R. *Computer-Based Instruction: Methods and Development*. Englewood Cliffs, NJ: Prentice-Hall, 1991.

Borsook, Terry K. and Higginbotham-Wheat, Nance. "Interactivity: What Is It and What Can It Do for Computer-Based Instruction?" *Educational Technology* 31 (October 1991): 11–17.

"Comparing Authoring Systems: Where Do You Start?" *CBT Directions* 5 (May/June 1992): 15–29.

Criswell, Eleanor L. *The Design of Computer-Based In-*

struction. New York: Macmillan, 1989.

Franchi, Jorge. "CBT or IVD?—That's The Question." *Tech Trends* 37, ((2) 1992): 27–30.

McFarland, Thomas D. and Parker, Reese. *Expert Systems in Education and Training.* Englewood Cliffs, NJ: Educational Technology Publications, 1989.

Price, Robert V. *Computer-Aided Instruction: A Guide for Authors.* Pacific Grove, CA: Brooks/Cole Publishing, 1991.

Smith, Peter E. "Some Learning and Instructional Theory Considerations for the Development of Computer Related Instructional Materials." *Educational Technology* 29 (November 1989): 18–19.

Wilkens, Dennis A. and Cook, Paul F. "Instructor's Plan: A Computer-Based System for Lesson Planning." *Tech Trends* 36, ((2) 1991): 29–32.

INTERACTIVE LEARNING

Alessi, Stephen M. "Learning Interactive Videodisc Development: A Case Study." *Journal of Instructional Development* 11, ((2) 1988): 2–7.

Arwady, Joseph A. and Gayeski, Diane M. *Using Video: Interactive and Linear Designs.* Englewood Cliffs, NJ: Educational Technology Publications, 1989.

Bergman, Robert E. and Moore, Thomas V. *Managing Interactive Video/Multimedia Projects.* Englewood Cliffs, NJ: Educational Technology Publications, 1990.

Cooper, Rawley. "The Debate Over Learner Control." *CBT Directions* 4, (July 1991): 18–23.

Fraioli, Al. "Remediation in Interactive Media: A Requisite Element." *Performance and Instruction* 29 (August 1990): 32–33.

Gayeski, Diane M. "Software Tools for Interactive Media Developers." *Tech Trends* 36, ((2) 1991): 18–21.

Imke, Steven. *Interactive Video Management and Production.* Englewood Cliffs, NJ: Educational Technology Publications, 1991.

Iuppa, Nicholas V. *A Practical Guide to Interactive Video Design.* White Plains, NY: Knowledge Industry Publications, 1989.

——— and Anderson, Karl. *Advanced Interactive Video Design.* White Plains, NY: Knowledge Industry Publications, 1988.

Sayre, Scott and Montgomery, Rae. "A Selected Interactive Videodisc Bibliography." *Educational Technology* 31 (June 1991): 31–32.

MULTIMEDIA

Birkmaier, Craig. "QuickTime." *Videography* 16 (July 1991): C8–C-16.

Boone, Randall and Higgins, Kyle. "Hypertext/Hypermedia Information Presentation: Developing a HyperCard Template." *Educational Technology* 31 (February 1991): 21–30.

Galbreath, Jeremy. "The Educational Buzzword of the 1990's: Multimedia, or Is It Hypermedia, or Interactive Multimedia, or . . .?" *Educational Technology* 32 (April 1992): 15–19.

Heller, Neil. "The Story of CD-I, DVI, and Laser Interactive." *Video Systems* 16 (September 1990): 46–58.

———. "The Story of CD-I, DVI, and Laser Interactive, Part 2." *Video Systems* 16 (October 1990): 46–48.

"Hypermedia." (special issue) *Educational Technology* 28 (November 1988).

Iuppa, Nicholas V. and Wade, Marc. *The Multimedia Adventure.* White Plains, NY: Knowledge Industry Publications, 1992.

Jonassen, David H. *Hypertext/Hypermedia.* Englewood Cliffs, NJ: Educational Technology Publications, 1989.

Lanza, Antonietta. "Some Guidelines for the Design of Effective Hypercourses." *Educational Technology* 3 (October 1991): 18–28.

Lehtinen, Rich. "Multimedia Revisited: The IBM Multimedia Story." *Video Systems* 17 (October 1991): 78–83.

Leinfuss, Emily. "Multimedia not 'Muddle-Media' Is Goal of Authoring Software." *Computer Pictures* 9 (June/July 1991): 22–25.

Li, Zhongmin and Merrill, M. David. "Transaction Shells: A New Approach to Courseware Authoring." *Journal of Research on Computing in Education* 23 (February 1990): 72–87.

Magel, Mark. "An Introduction to Authoring Languages: Part 1." *AV Video* 14 (February 1992): 120–129.

———. "CD-I and DVI Delivery and Development." *AV Video* 13 (October 1991): 72–79.

———. "Interactive Design: Making Ideas into Multimedia." *AV Video* 13 (May 1991): 58–67.

———. "Up Close and Personal with Multimedia Authoring: Part 2." *AV Video* 14 (March 1992): 108, 117–126.

Milheim, William D. *Emerging Technologies and Instruction: Hypertext, Hypermedia, and Interactive Multimedia: A Selected Bibliography.* Englewood Cliffs, NJ: Educational Technology Publications, 1991.

Nelson, Laurie Y. and Nelson, Carole. "A Model for Instructional Multimedia Design." *CBT Directions* 4 (January 1991): 20–26.

JOURNALS FOR EQUIPMENT, MATERIALS, SOFTWARE

AV Video
Montage Publishing Co., 701 Westchester Ave., White Plains, NY 10604

AVC Presentation for the Visual Communicator

PTN Publishing Co., 445 Broad Hollow Rd., Melville, NY 11747

CBT Directions

Weingarten Publications, Inc., 38 Chauncy St., Boston, MA 02111

Computer Pictures

Montage Publishing Co., 701 Westchester Ave., White Plains, NY 10604

Directory of Multimedia Equipment, Software and Services Directory of Video, Computer, and Audio-Visual Services

International Communications Industries Association, 3150 Spring Street, Fairfax, VA 22031

New Media

Hypermedia Communications, Inc., 901 Mariner's Island Blvd., Suite 365, San Mateo, CA 94404

Presentation Products

Pacific Magazine Group, Inc., 513 Wilshire Blvd., Santa Monica, CA 90401

T.H.E. Journal

150 El Camino Real, Suite 112, Tustin, CA 92680

Video Systems

Intertec Publishing Corp., 9221 Quivira Rd., Overland Park, KS 66215

Videography

P.S.N. Publications, 2 Park Ave., Suite 1820, New York, NY 10016

PART 5

Using Instructional Technologies

CHAPTER

17

Achieves my objectives?

Up to date?

Accurate content?

Audience level?

No social bias?

Vocabulary level?

Production quality?

Guide/documentation helpful?

Other strengths?

Any Weakness?

When designing a teaching/learning activity, you have three choices for obtaining instructional materials. One is to plan and produce your own materials. The previous chapters of this book guide you in carrying out this choice. The second is to use commercially produced materials, and the third alternative is to adapt or modify existing materials to fit your unique needs.

To make successful use of any available material, attention needs to be given to three preliminary matters: *locating* appropriate materials, *evaluating* potentially suitable items, and *selecting* the best material for use. These three steps should be carried out within the context of your instructional planning. As described in Chapter 4, whenever instructional materials are being considered, a number of factors need attention in order to ensure that the selected materials will adequately fulfill their role. Let us review these planning elements before examining the three preliminary matters already mentioned.

Locating, Evaluating, and Selecting Instructional Materials

INSTRUCTIONAL PLANNING

Learner Characteristics

Unless you know your intended audience and something about their characteristics, it is difficult to select appropriate instructional materials. Being familiar with the educational background, experience levels, knowledge of subject matter, as well as other abilities and interests of learners, can be helpful in guiding you to the selection of suitable materials. See page 42 for additional characteristics of an audience group that should be considered.

Purpose and Objectives

The instructional situation within which you plan to use the instructional materials needs to be defined. For what major purpose will the materials be used? What specific objectives should be served? Answers to these questions give further directions for selecting materials.

The purposes for which instructional materials can be used relate to three categories of needs: to *motivate* an interest or action to be taken by the audience, to *inform* the audience about a topic, or to *instruct* the audience on a topic. See page 42 for further explanation of these three purposes. Choose the one, or the combination of categories, for which you want to select media for use.

It is a common practice for instructors to write learning objectives that specify what is to be accomplished in their instruction. The objectives definitely influence the selection of media for use. See page 43 for a description of what should comprise a properly stated learning objective. Once objectives are specified, examine them carefully. They indicate the elements of subject content—the facts, concepts, and principles—that should receive treatment in the instructional materials you will be evaluating for selection.

Modes of Instruction

Instruction can take place when members of an audience or a class are grouped in various ways. Sometimes it is in groups of average or large size. Another situation may require small discussion or activity groups. A third mode of providing instruction is for individual learners to study independently. These three patterns of organizing for instruction are described in detail on page 6.

It is important to recognize that some types of media may be suitable only, or preferably, for use in one mode of instruction. For example, overhead transparencies are more appropriate for showing to average-sized or large groups rather than for use by individuals. On the other hand, printed photographs are only satisfactory for study by individuals or for use with a small group. Also, other physical features within materials, such as the size of lettering or graphic illustrations in projected materials, can affect their suitability for audiences of different sizes, as they relate to legibility.

Media Attributes

Unique characteristics of certain media, beyond those described in the previous paragraph, are important considerations when choosing materials for instruction. Whether a medium can show motion, or be in color, or include sound will affect materials selection in terms of the required learning objectives. For example: "I need something to help in teaching scuba diving. Because of the importance of motion, I'll look for a suitable film or video recording, because I know both media can portray motion."

The capabilities of a medium to exhibit certain characteristics are known as **media attributes.** They are described in detail on page 58. It is important that you become aware of them. Media attributes are the basis for one form of media selection procedure, namely, a decision as to the appropriate *type or groups of media* you should consider in terms of your subject and objectives. Review the media selection procedure on page 58 and the selection charts that follow. They can help you decide on the categories of instructional materials within which you will want to locate appropriate titles for your own evaluation and selection.

Each one of these matters—learner characteristics, purpose, and objectives; mode of instruction; and media attributes—is an important criterion that can affect materials selection. Give them careful attention.

LOCATING INSTRUCTIONAL MATERIALS

A variety of sources is available as you start the search for appropriate materials. Use as many of them as is feasible.

Media Centers

A media center, whether located in a school, school-district, region, college, or training facility, will contain a range of media for use in the instructional programs the center supports. These may include commercial items that have been purchased or materials previously prepared locally for certain instructional needs. In addition, most media centers maintain up-to-date files of catalogs and other references mentioned next.

The media specialist in the center can advise you about instructional materials on hand, those items that can be obtained from other local or regional sources, and suitable references you can examine relative to your own materials interests and needs of your

students. Technical assistance is available for placing orders to obtain instructional materials from outside sources.

Indexes

Often the easiest and most systematic way to locate materials relating to a topic is to consult indexes. They contain lists of most types of instructional materials that have been produced and are commercially available.

The best known and most comprehensive references about instructional materials are the indexes published by the National Information Center for Educational Media (NICEM). They can be found in many libraries and media centers that purchase instructional materials. The NICEM indexes are organized by media format. These include videotape recordings, films, overhead transparencies, slides, and audio recordings.

American Treasure: A Smithsonian Journey **Gen-Edu '86**
History-US/Museums
Closed Captioned
91808 90 mins C B, V *HOME*
Narrated by Gene Kelly
A wide-ranging survey of American history from colonial times to the present, using artifacts from the Smithsonian Institution for illustration.
F — ED
Christopher Sarson — *Playhouse Video* **P**

America's Railroads--How the Iron Horse Shaped Our Nation **Gen-Edu '86**
History-US/Trains
95610 22 mins C V, 3/4U *SCHO, HOME, SURA*
For students, a historical survey of the role railroads have played in American history, from their inception to the present day.

American Tongues **Gen-Edu '87**
Speech/Language arts
96036 56 mins C B, V, 3/4U *SCHO, HOME*
Narrated by Polly Holiday
Americans voice their opinions on their own and others' accents and dialects. Speakers from all parts of the country are profiled and the development of regional and social accents is charted.
CINE Golden Eagle '87; National Educational Film & Video Festival '87: Silver Apple.
C,A — ED
Louis Alvarez and Andrew Kolker — *Center for New American Media* **R, P**

(From NICEM Index)

Within a volume, items are listed under topical headings. For each item, the information includes the title and any subtitle, physical description, length, brief summary of content, recommended audience, release date, Library of Congress catalog card number, and the producer's name. Entries do not include any evaluations of the item.

In addition to treating specific materials, NICEM indexes are also available for major subject areas. Some of the volumes are *Index to Health and Safety Education, Index to Vocational and Technical Education,* and so forth. All indexes are available in printed volumes, microfiche, and as computer on-line service.

Another major source of guides to media materials is Educators Progress Service. Some of the titles are *Educators Guide to Free Films, Educators Guide to Free Audio and Video Materials,* and so on. These guides list materials that have been produced by a business company or governmental agency and are available at no cost, or for a nominal service charge.

In addition to these reference sources, there are other major references that specialize in a single medium such as *The Video Sourcebook* for prerecorded videotapes and videodiscs. Other publications treat a single subject area such as the U.S. Department of Energy's *Index to Energy Films* and the *Business and Technology Videolog* from Video Forum. Check your library and other sources for the references listed at the end of this chapter.

Commercial Catalogs

Every company that distributes instructional materials sends out brochures announcing new materials and also prints a catalog of their products. These are called *current lists* and often describe items before they

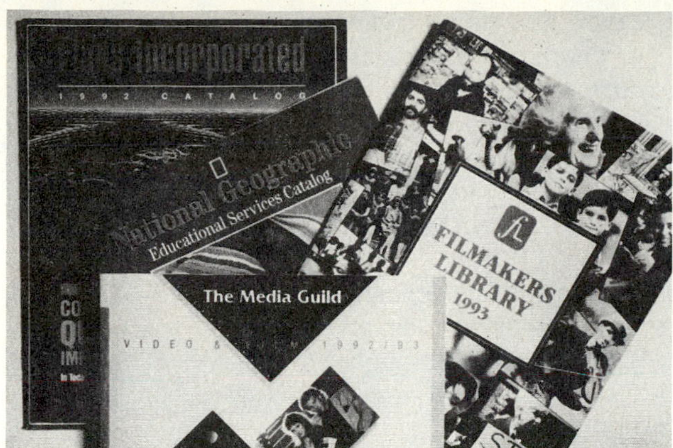

appear in an index. A media center will have a collection of commercial vendor catalogs. Often you will find advertisements in professional journals and subject-area magazines that advise of catalog availability.

University Media Catalogs

University media catalogs are classified as *retrospective* lists because they contain materials that were produced over the past several years. If your instruction on a particular topic is infrequent or only a one-time situation, it may be more economical to consider renting instructional materials for use. University media centers are a good source for a variety of potential materials. Many universities publish catalogs that list the instructional materials they have available for a rental fee.

Typically, the materials include 16mm films, video recordings, and in some cases filmstrips and slides. The catalogs describe the specific items including information on length, format, rental cost, suggested audience, and a brief content overview.

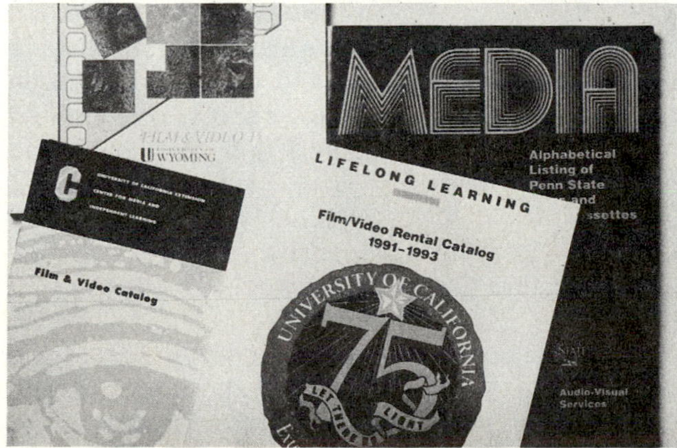

Journals

Many professional journals contain a column or a section devoted to lists and often reviews of newly released instructional materials. Check the annual index of a journal in your subject field for the issues in which instructional materials lists and reviews are included. The reviews can be of value when you are ready to evaluate and select materials.

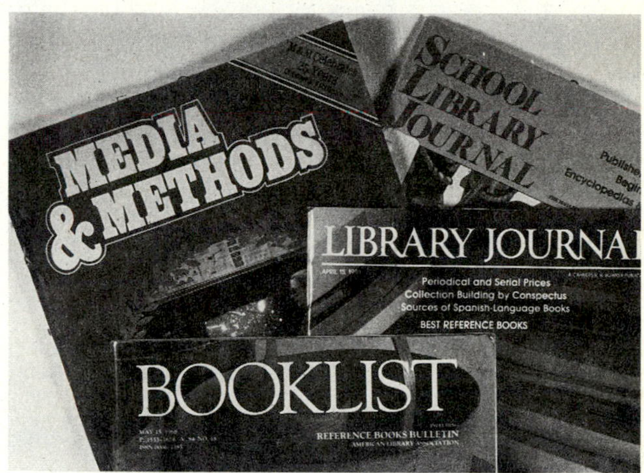

A detailed listing of references for locating all types of instructional media can be found at the end of this chapter on page 311.

PREVIEWING AND EVALUATING INSTRUCTIONAL MATERIALS

Based on your past experience and knowledge of the subject, *evaluation is a careful analysis* of the instructional material, preferably after previewing it. Evaluation of instructional materials should be done carefully and thoroughly to determine if the material will help you to achieve your instructional objectives.

Evaluation Procedures

Two options are available to you when evaluating materials. One is to rely on unbiased reviews published in journals or by professional review services. In addition to reviews in your subject-area journals, as indicated before, reviews of media materials are found in such publications as *Booklist, School Library Journal,* and *Library Journal.* Of much value is the *Media Review Digest* that indexes media reviews found in other publications.

The second option is for you to personally preview the material. In many instances this is preferable to relying solely on professional reviews. Whereas the latter reviews usually provide a general summary of content and an analysis of subject treatment, details important to you may not receive attention. Also, in terms of the definition of evaluation already stated, the personal experiences of the professional reviewer can influence his or her opinion, which may vary appreciably from your own when you see the material. Therefore, previewing the materials yourself can be quite important.

Evaluation Criteria

When you read a review or preview learning materials, take notes to gather information for making an eventual selection decision. This can best be done on a prepared form. The form should have space for both *objective data* and *subjective reactions and comments.*

Objective data include:

- Material form
- Program title
- Length, running time, number of components
- General subject area or topic treated
- Instructor's guide or program documentation available
- Production date
- Producer or programer (if name is important)
- Purchase or rental source
- Purchase or rental cost
- Recommended audience(s)
- Brief content overview

This information may be found in the papers accompanying the material. Certain items may have to be obtained when you observe the material itself. Objective data are helpful as comparisons are made among different media materials during selection.

Subjective reactions and comments include your own responses after reading about or previewing the material. These questions should receive attention:

- How well does the material achieve my learning objectives?
- How up to date and accurate is the content?
- Is it appropriate for the knowledge level of the audience?
- Is it appropriate for the experience level of the audience?
- Is it free from any social bias?
- What is the vocabulary level?
- What is the production quality?
- Is the instructional guide/documentation helpful for planning and material use?
- What are strengths or weaknesses?
- Do I recommend the material for purchase or rental and use?

In addition to answering each question directly, add general impressions and specific comments. Such subjective responses permit you to express and coalesce your thoughts. These, in turn, will justify your ultimate decision. See the sample materials evaluation form.

Because of the increasing use of computer software for instruction, special efforts should be made to evaluate the value of available CAI programs. A comprehensive checklist for software evaluation considerations has been prepared by Tolhurst. The following categories should receive attention:

- Implementation considerations
- Documentation and packaging
- Classroom management
- Curriculum considerations
- User interface

For lists of specific questions to answer under each category for evaluating a software package, refer to Tolhurst's article.

Please note that the term *evaluation,* used here in the context of judging the merits of instructional materials, should not be confused with evaluating the total learning experience after completion of instruction or training.

SELECTING INSTRUCTIONAL MATERIALS

Selection follows evaluation. After reviewing and previewing a number of materials on your subject or topic, your choice should have been narrowed down to a few usable titles. Now, **selection** means *choosing the one material that best fills your needs.* You are the person who will be teaching with the media, therefore in the end it is your decision as to which material to use.

Selection Criteria

When you engaged in the evaluation procedure, you considered a number of factors that helped you to weed out inappropriate materials and reach this selection point. Many of these same factors should be examined now. The following categories and questions need attention:

Learner—Does the material fit the age, experience, and knowledge level of the learners?

Purpose/Objectives—Does the treatment of the topic closely relate to the instructional purpose and learning objectives you want to accomplish without bias?

Content—Is the content suitable in terms of depth of treatment, accuracy, and being up to date?

Media Type—Is the medium used appropriate in terms of being capable to communicate the content

Sample Materials Evaluation Form

OBJECTIVE DATA (Nonevaluative)

Format ______________________________ Date of evaluation ______________________
(Video, computer program, slides, film, etc.)

Title ______________________________ Evaluator ______________________________

Running time (or length) ______________________________ Instructor's guide or documentation ❑ yes ❑ no

Subject area or topic ______________________________

Production date ______________________________

Producer/programer ______________________________

Purchase source ______________________________

Purchase cost ______________________ Rental fee ______________________

Recommended audience(s) ______________________________

Brief content overview (nonevaluative) ______________________________

SUBJECTIVE DATA (Evaluative)

Helps achieve instructional objectives: ❑ yes ❑ no

Content up to date and accurate: ❑ poor ❑ fair ❑ good ❑ excellent

Explain: ______________________________

____

Meets audience knowledge level: ❑ yes ❑ no

Meets audience experience level: ❑ yes ❑ no

Social bias evident: ❑ yes ❑ no

Vocabulary level: ❑ satisfactory ❑ unsatisfactory

Production quality: ❑ poor ❑ fair ❑ good ❑ excellent

Explain: ______________________________

____

Instructor's guide or documentation helpful:

❑ poor ❑ fair ❑ good ❑ excellent

Explain: ______________________________

____

Strengths or weaknesses of materials:

____

____

____

Recommended for purchase or rental: ❑ yes ❑ no

Remarks:

____

____

effectively? (See the discussion of media attributes on page 58.)

Active Learning—Is there provision for meaningful learner participation (page 300) as an integral part of the presentation and does it lead to beneficial followup activities?

Technical Quality—Is the production of acceptable technical quality in terms of photography or video imagery, color, sound, image legibility, continuity, packaging, and so forth?

Cost (if any)—Will the resulting learning be worth the expenditure of funds?

Validation—Does the producer provide satisfactory evidence from field tests that the material does contribute to an acceptable level of learning for individuals comparable to those comprising your group?

You should add other criteria to the preceding ones in order to make the selection of materials more specific to your unique instructional or training needs.

Once you have completed the selection process and made your choice, you are ready to plan for the instructional use of the material.

Finally, when you make use of media with your students, verify the value from the student viewpoint. Plan to discuss student perceptions about the quality and suitability of the materials. Such matters as the clarity of explanation, communication value of illustrations, soundness of conclusions, and motivation for further study can be the bases for questions. Then, testing and other evaluation activities can provide further evidence of the merits of the instructional materials.

What You Have Learned About Locating, Evaluating, and Selecting Instructional Materials:

1. List three choices you have for obtaining instructional materials.
2. What are the major elements of instructional planning that should precede the selection of materials?
3. What is meant by the expression "media attributes"?
4. List three major sources for locating commercial instructional materials.
5. What are the most comprehensive indexes of instructional materials?
6. Name two guides published by the Educators Progress Service.
7. What is a major reference for locating sources of available videotape recordings?
8. Where would you look for a source from which to rent media materials?
9. Define *evaluation* in respect to materials selection.
10. How does a *review* of media materials differ from a *preview* of materials?
11. List two media journals that publish media reviews.
12. Name a professional journal in your own subject field that reviews instructional materials.
13. What are the two categories of information for which notes should be made when previewing instructional materials?
14. Define *selection* with respect to instructional materials.
15. List the eight categories of information that should receive attention in material selection.
16. Choose a topic in your subject field. Locate, evaluate, and select one instructional material you would consider using. Keep a record of where you searched and what you do to arrive at a decision.

See answers on page 383.

REFERENCES

MEDIA SOURCES

Catalog of Audiovisual Materials: A Guide to Government Sources (ED 198 822). Arlington, VA: ERIC Documents Reproduction Service.

Catalog of Free-Loan Educational Films/Video. St. Petersburg, FL: Modern Talking Picture Service.

Educational Film and Video Locator. New York: R.R. Bowker.

Educators Progress Service, 214 Center Street, Randolph, WI.

Educators Guide to Free Audio and Video Materials
Educators Guide to Free Films
Educators Guide to Free Filmstrips and Slides
Educators Guide to Free Health, Physical Education, and Recreation Materials
Educators Guide to Free Science Materials
Educators Guide to Free Social Studies Materials

The Great Plains National Instructional Television Library Catalog. Lincoln, NB: Great Plains National Instructional Television Library.

National Information Center for Educational Media (NICEM), P.O. Box 40130, Albuquerque, NM.

Index to Educational Audio Tapes
Index to Health and Safety Education—Multimedia
Index to Nonprint Special Education Materials
Index to Psychology—Multimedia
Index to Educational Slide
Science and Computer Literacy Audiovisuals
Vocational and Technical Audiovisuals
Wellness Media Index
Audiocassette Finder
Film and Video Finder
Index to AV Producers

On Cassette: A Comprehensive Bibliography of Spoken Word Audio Cassettes. New York: R. R. Bowker.

Selecting Instructional Media: A Guide to Audiovisual and Other Instructional Media Lists. Littleton, CO: Libraries Unlimited.

The Video Sourcebook. Syosset, NY: National Video Clearinghouse.

MEDIA REVIEWS

Booklist. Chicago: American Library Association.

Curriculum Review. Chicago: Curriculum Advisory Services.

Educational Technology. Englewood Cliffs, NJ: Educational Technology Publications.

Library Journal. New York: R. R. Bowker.

Media & Methods. Philadelphia: North American Publishing.

Media Review Digest. Ann Arbor, MI: Pierian Press.

Performance and Instruction Journal. Washington, DC: National Society for Performance and Instruction.

School Library Journal. New York: R.R. Bowker.

TechTrends. Washington, DC: Association for Educational Communications and Technology.

Training: The Magazine of Human Resources Development. Minneapolis, MN: Lakewood Publishing.

Training and Development Journal. Washington, DC: American Society for Training and Development.

T.H.E. Journal. Tustin, CA: T.H.E. Journal.

Wilson Library Bulletin. New York: H. W. Wilson.

COMPUTER PROGRAM SOURCES AND EVALUATIONS

The Complete Directory of Public Domain and Shareware for Apple Macintosh Computer. Topeka, KS: Budgetbytes, Inc.

Computing Teacher: Journal of the International Council for Computers in Education. Eugene, OR: ICCE, University of Oregon.

Directory of Educational Objectives and Networkable Software. White Plains, NY: National Accounts Division, IBM Corp.

The Directory of Software Sources for Higher Education. Princeton, NJ: Peterson's Guides, P.O. Box 2123. 1988.

The Educational Software Locator. Seattle, WA; The Educational Software Center.

Educational Software Selector (TESS). Educational Products Information Exchange, P.O. Box 839, Water Mill, NY 11976.

Electronic Learning. Lyndhurst, NJ: Scholastic.

Guide to Free Computer Materials. Randolph, WI: Educators Progress Service.

Only the Best. The Annual Guide to Highest-Rated Educational Software. New York: R.R. Bowker.

Tolhurst, Denise. "A Checklist for Evaluating Content-Based Hypertext Computer Software." *Educational Technology* 32 (March 1992): 17–21.

VIDEODISC SOURCE

Videodisc Compendium. St. Paul, MN: Emerging Technology Consultants.

CD-ROM SOURCES

CD-ROM Directory. Detroit, MI: Omnigraphics, Inc.

CD-ROMs in Print. Westport, CT: Meckler Corp.

CHAPTER

18

Operating Media Equipment

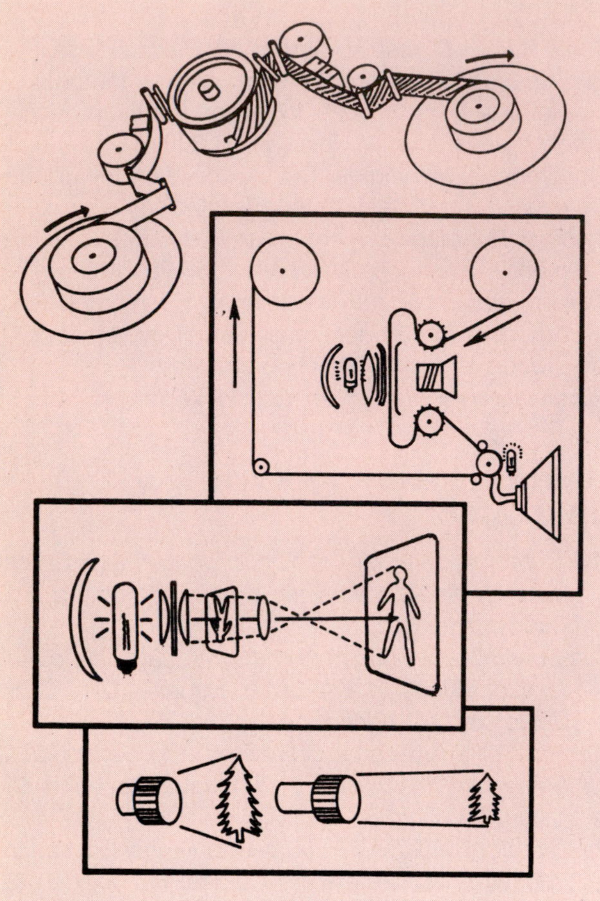

Still-Picture Projection

Motion-Picture Projection and Video Playback

Audio Players

Combinations of Equipment

Miscellaneous Items

Equipment Purchase

Equipment Maintenance

To be competent in any vocation, an individual must master and successfully apply the tools of the trade. This is true whether a person is a medical doctor responsible for cardiac examination, a technician using a drill, or an office worker preparing a document with a word processor.

In order to achieve instructional goals for effective communication with media, you should develop the ability to set up and operate various types of instructional media equipment. General principles can be applied to most brands and models of commercial media equipment.

In this chapter, technical features and standardized operating procedures for the most widely used categories of media equipment will be presented as outlined. Information on utilizing media for training and instructional situations follows in Chapter 19.

The successful operation of media equipment depends not only on your knowledge and understanding. A positive attitude is also important. The following procedures can guide you to competency and a satisfactory sense of accomplishment:

1. **Know the principle of operation.** By understanding the underlying principle, you should be able to operate various brands and models of projectors. Media equipment is designed to work in a logical manner. With some thought, what you learn can be transferred from one model to another.
2. **Never force anything on the equipment.** Equipment manufacturers design instructional equipment to be rugged and to be operated by ordinary people. Never force a part, but don't be afraid to experiment and explore until you master the operation.
3. **Always practice common sense when using equipment requiring electricity.** For example, use a three-wire grounded plug with equipment and avoid using light-duty extension cords. Pay attention to necessary precautions like these about which you are informed and that are indicated in operations manuals.
4. **Systematically investigate any problem encountered.** If a problem arises when using or preparing to use a piece of media equipment, don't panic! Review the principle of operation for that particular type of equipment. Then, step-by-step analysis will allow you to isolate the problem and find a solution.
5. **Practice operating the equipment you will use.** Practice the operating procedures until they become like reflex actions. In this way, you will be fully confident you can handle the equipment when ready to use it before a group. Then, you can even become the instructor and show others how to use the equipment!

STILL-PICTURE PROJECTION

With still-picture projectors, individual pictures, in various formats, may be shown for as long a time as desired.

Opaque Projector

Opaque materials are those through which light cannot pass. Book and magazine pictures, photographs, and handwritten sheets are examples of materials that can be used with an opaque projector. In this projector, light is *reflected off* the surface of the material. This is classed as an **indirect projection system.**

The opaque projector consists of a high wattage lamp surrounded by highly reflective surfaces and a mirror that allows an image of the object or material placed on the platen to be projected through a lens onto a screen. A highly efficient cooling fan is required to prevent heat damage to materials being projected.

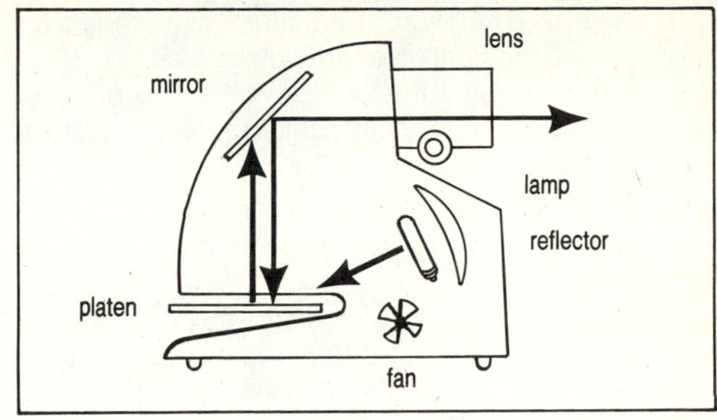

There are several features in an opaque projector that you should learn to operate. One is the roll-feed belt that can be inserted on top of the platen allowing the projection of a long item, such as a series of mounted pictures. Another useful feature is the optical pointer. This device projects onto the screen the image of an arrow, which can be manipulated by the instructor to point out details on the image being projected. The pointer knob is located on the side of the projector.

OPERATING INSTRUCTIONS

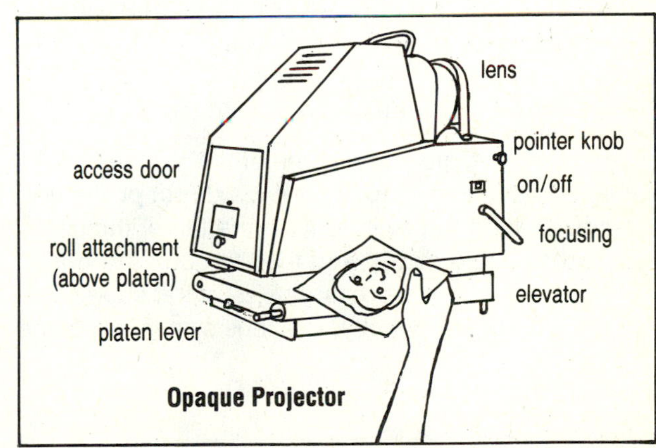

Opaque Projector

1. The opaque projector must be used in a totally dark room.
2. Place the projector on a suitable projection cart, preferably one 26 to 34 inches high.
3. Plug the projector into a grounded outlet.
4. Open the lens cover.
5. Turn on the LAMP/FAN switch.
6. Roll visual material into the machine using the ROLL FEED attachment or lower the platen using the PLATEN lever and place the material directly on the platen. Hold the material to be projected in a horizontal position with the front side

(readable side) up. The bottom edge should be toward the front (lens side) of the machine. Moving the lever to the left opens the platen, to the right closes it. To project thick materials, such as a page in a book, it may be necessary to remove the roll feed attachment.

7. Adjust the FOCUSING knob until the image is sharp.
8. Size the image to fill the projection screen by moving the projector closer to the screen to reduce the size of the image or farther away to increase the size. Refocus.
9. The ELEVATION knob or the elevation legs, on the lower front side, can be used to raise or lower the image on the screen.
10. To move the POINTER from left to right, or right to left, simply turn the knob clockwise and counterclockwise respectively. To move the projected image up or down, move the pointer knob toward the front or the rear of the projector.
11. A warning! With some older opaque projector models, prolonged projection may result in buckling or damage to the material due to heat absorption.
12. Open the access door on the back to reach the lamp and clean the reflecting mirrors.

Page 347 details the use of an opaque projector for instructional purposes.

Overhead Projector

The overhead projector is one of the simplest types of media equipment to operate. It is a **direct projection system.** Light is transmitted from the lamp, through a transparency, to a mirror, and then through the lens to the screen. Because of the large size of transparencies (up to 10″ × 10″) and the type of lens system used, the projector is placed near the front of the room, relatively close to the screen. A bright image is projected for viewing in a lighted room.

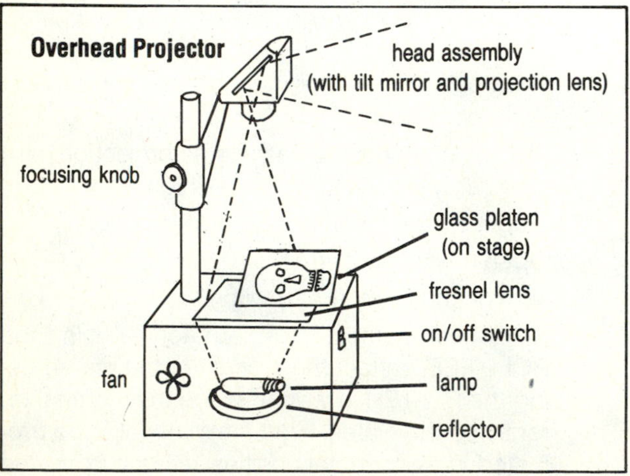

The primary controls include the on/off switch, the focusing knob, and the head assembly tilt mirror. Below the glass stage is a special lens called a **fresnel lens.** Its purpose is to spread out the light from the lamp below so it will project an evenly illuminated image of the transparency placed on the stage.

On some models there is a lever that is used to instantly shift an auxiliary projection lamp into place in case the lamp being used burns out. To prevent unnecessary lamp burnout, do not move the projector after use until the lamp is cool.

Operating Instructions

1. Connect to power with a properly grounded plug.
2. Stand beside the projector, usually on the left side, with the light shining over your right shoulder.
3. Hold a transparency as you would normally view or read it. Place the transparency on the STAGE of the projector face up, with the bottom edge toward the screen.
4. Turn on, size, and prefocus the projector on the screen using a test transparency. To raise or lower the image on the screen, move the HEAD ASSEMBLY at the top of the projector. To size the image, move the projector either closer to or farther away from the screen. The image should fill the screen. To focus the image, turn the FOCUSING knob, which is located on the post.
5. Adjust the projection screen to eliminate the *keystone effect* if it is a problem. See page 338 for information on correcting this effect.
6. Some projectors have a lamp-focusing device to eliminate the blue haze, which may appear on the edges of the screen when the placement of the overhead projector is not in proper relationship to the screen.
7. When transporting an overhead projector, carry it by the body. Lifting it by the post and head assembly will cause the image to align improperly.

Page 348 details the use of an overhead projector for instructional purposes.

Slide Projector

The carousel-type slide projector is the most commonly used today, although *single-slide carrier* projectors are found in some schools. The name **carousel** relates to the design of the circular tray that holds the slides for projection. Slides consist of transparent film in

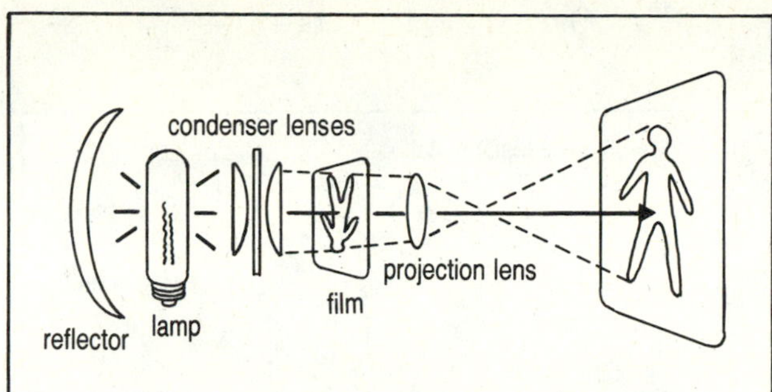

2 × 2 inch cardboard, plastic, or glass frames. As the diagram illustrates, light from the lamp passes through two condenser lenses and a heat filter to be concentrated on the slide. The projection lens then focuses the image on the screen. This projector is another example of a *direct projection system.*

The primary control on carousel-type projectors is the power switch, which generally consists of four positions: off, fan, low lamp, and high lamp.

Other adjustments that are important to a smooth operation include use of the elevation screw; the select bar, which releases the slide tray allowing you to rotate it; the forward and reverse control buttons; lens focusing knob; and, on the back, the receptacle for plugging in a remove-control slide changer.

Optional adjustments may include an autofocus switch for keeping all slide images in focus on the screen and a timer for automatic slide advance. A variety of lenses is available to adjust the size of the projected image so as to fill the screen when projecting from various distances in rooms of different sizes. Most popular is a lens with a 4-to-6 inch zoom capability.

OPERATING INSTRUCTIONS

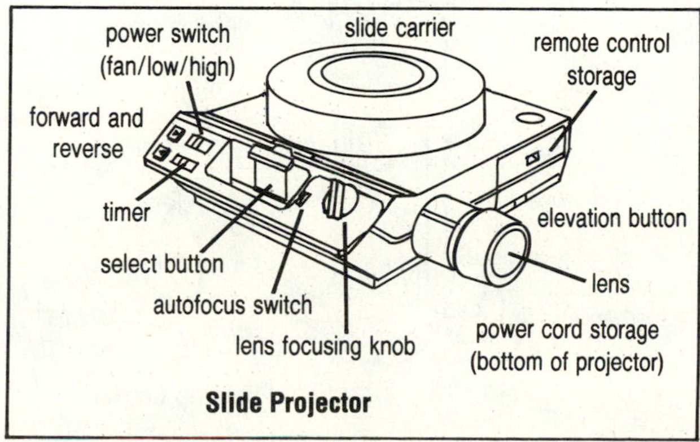

Slide Projector

1. Check the plate on the underside of an empty carousel slide tray. Make certain it is in the locked position so that individual slides cannot fall out.
2. Load your slides into the tray. Follow the arrow to unlock and remove the ring on top of the tray. As you face the screen, hold each slide in the normal viewing position. Invert the slide so the *image is upside down* (*not* backwards) and insert it into a numbered slot in the tray. Repeat this for each slide. If your slides have thumbspots (see page 351) in the lower left corner when viewed right side up, the thumbspot should be in the upper right corner for projection. Replace and lock the ring on top.
3. Remove the projector from its case and place it on a tall stand near the back of the room.
4. Connect to power using a properly grounded plug. The power cord is stored in a compartment in the bottom of the projector.
5. Turn the POWER switch to FAN position and firmly seat the slide tray at the zero position, then advance to a focus slide.
6. Turn on the LAMP, size and prefocus the image by moving the projector toward or away from the screen and adjusting the zoom lens as necessary. Raise or lower the image with the ELEVATION button.

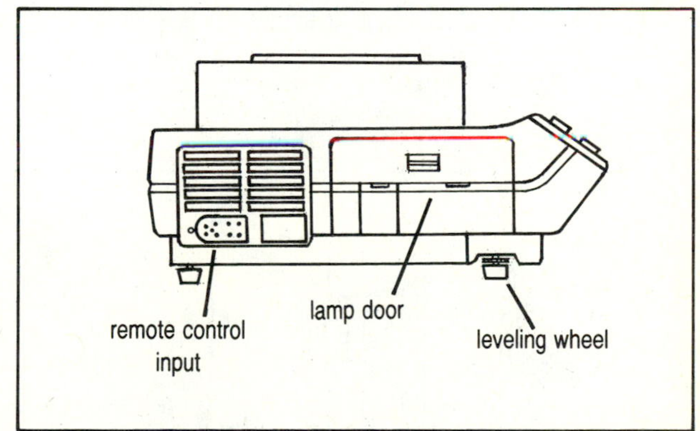

7. Plug in the REMOTE CONTROL on the back of the projector. (*Note:* An extension cord for the remote control may be available so you will have sufficient length to control the projector from the front of the room.) ADVANCE and REVERSE buttons are located on the slide projector if the remote control is not available. A WIRELESS remote control may be used instead of the cable one. It works like a remote control unit for opening and closing a garage door. The small, handheld controller is a transmitter, sending an electronic or infrared signal to a receiver plugged into the remote control attachment on the back of the projector.

8. Be certain the automatic TIMER is set at *manual* position unless you want slides to change automatically at a present rate (5 . . . 8 . . . 15 . . . seconds on some modes.).
9. The SELECT button can be held down to manually rotate the slide tray to a specific slide if needed. This button is also used at the end of a presentation to rotate the tray back to zero where it must be to remove it from the projector.
10. Following use, remove the slide tray. Most projectors must have the power on to activate the select button when removing the tray.
11. The power switch can be turned off immediately. Cooling the lamp is not necessary.
12. Remove the remote control, the lens, and store the power cord in the bottom before putting the slide projector in its carrying case.

Some slide projectors are actually filmstrip projectors that have a slide carrier that can be inserted into the projector replacing the filmstrip carrier. These are called *combination* projectors since they handle both filmstrips and slides. Many of these can still be found in schools but are gradually being replaced. The single-slide carrier is slow and awkward, and results in poor utilization because having to insert one slide at a time is inconvenient. Also, each slide must be checked for proper orientation before placement in the carrier for right-side-up projection.

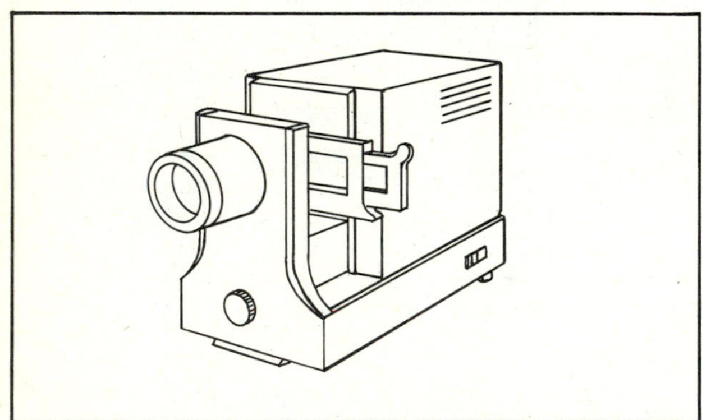

Page 350 details the use of the slide projector for instructional purposes.

Slide Viewer

For individual use, small viewers are available that allow one slide at a time to be viewed. These are usually battery powered. However, some operate from an AC electrical source. The slide is inserted into a slot on the top of the viewer in the same position as if you were holding it up to the light to view it.

Operating Instructions

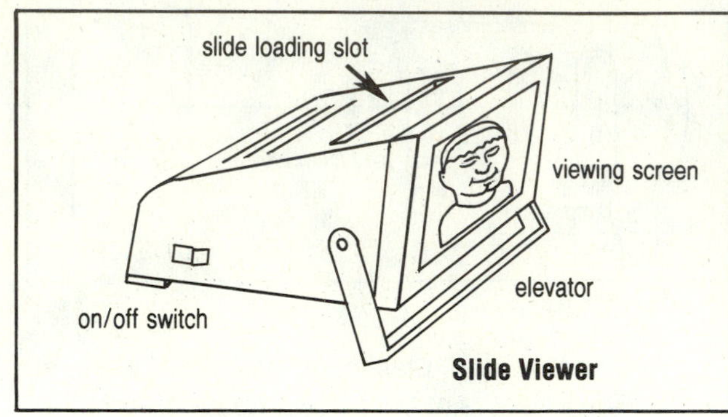

1. Prearrange slides into correct viewing order.
2. Insert first slide into the slot on the viewer.
3. Turn on the LAMP switch. (*Note:* Some slide viewers have a lamp switch that is activated when the slide is inserted. In such a unit, the slide must be held down in the slot or the lamp will not stay on.)
4. Focusing is not necessary on most slide viewers since the focal distance is preset.

Filmstrip Projector

Filmstrip projectors are available in a variety of brands and designs. They all have common operating principles and are comparatively small and lightweight. The lamp and cooling fan are housed at the rear. The filmstrip carrier is located between the lamp and the projection lens. This makes the filmstrip projector a *direct projection system.*

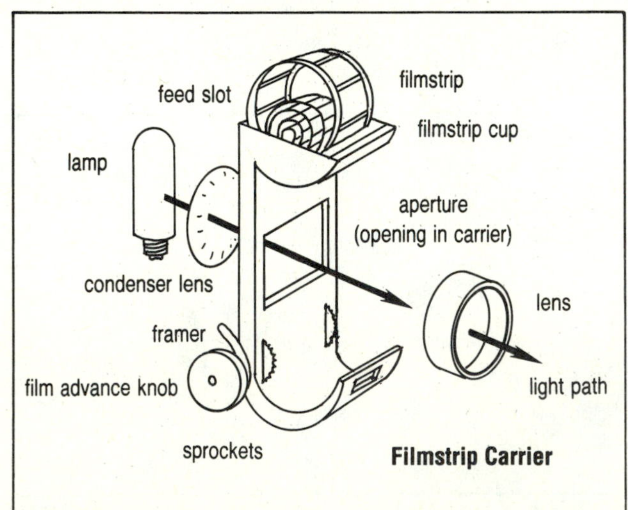

The filmstrip carrier on most projectors is removable and can be lifted out of the top of the machine for cleaning. It is important to keep the passageway for the film free from lint and dust. Use air pressure and a brush to clean the carrier periodically.

Two types of filmstrip projectors are commonly available. One has no audio capability and is called a *silent* filmstrip projector. The other, combining sound with the filmstrip, has a built-in audiocassette player synchronized to the projector for automatically advancing the filmstrip. The combination projector is discussed on page 333.

The silent filmstrip projector is used with captioned filmstrips or in support of verbal discussion led by the instructor. If you want to play an audiotape with a silent filmstrip projector, use any audiotape player and advance the filmstrip manually when you hear the audible beep, or follow marked script.

OPERATING INSTRUCTIONS

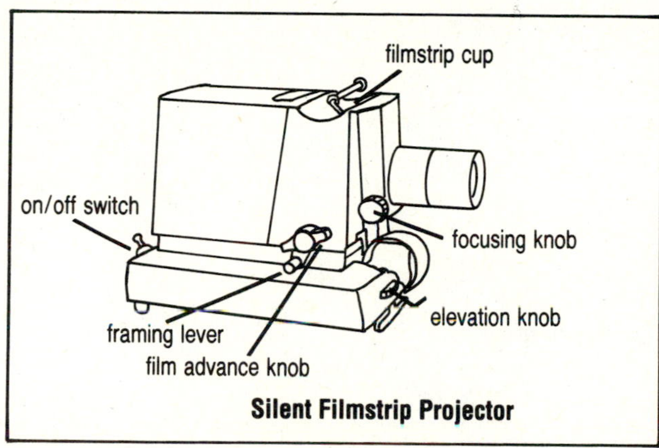

Silent Filmstrip Projector

1. Connect filmstrip projector to power using properly grounded plug.
2. Turn it on using the three-position switch (OFF/FAN/LAMP).
3. Hold the filmstrip so you can read the title. Then, for projection, invert the film (as you did with the slides) so the title is upside down.
4. Place the filmstrip in the cup at the top of the projector and insert its beginning edge into the slot of the carrier.
5. Push the filmstrip down into the slot until it stops, then advance the projector by turning the FILM ADVANCE knob *clockwise* until the sprocket teeth engage and pull down the filmstrip. Sprocket holes are damaged by turning FILM ADVANCE knob counterclockwise while filmstrip is being pushed down. Continue advancing the filmstrip until a focus frame appears on the screen. Use the FOCUSING knob and focus the image.
6. Using the FRAMING knob or lever, adjust the image so the entire area of a single frame is centered on the screen.
7. Size the image to fill the screen by moving the projector farther away from the screen to enlarge or closer to reduce the size of the image. Sharpen the image using the focusing knob.
8. To raise or lower the image on the screen, press the ELEVATION button to release the legs on the front of the projector. Some machines have an elevation screw that raises and lowers the front of the projector.
9. Advance the filmstrip to the proper beginning frame.
10. Start showing the filmstrip when appropriate.
11. After use, continue advancing the filmstrip so it completely exits the projector. Rewind it by handling the film at the edges. Turn off the fan/lamp switch and store the projector in its case.

Page 351 details the use of a filmstrip projector for instructional purposes.

Filmstrip Viewer

For individual use, small viewers are available. Silent filmstrip viewers are compact and lightweight.

OPERATING INSTRUCTIONS

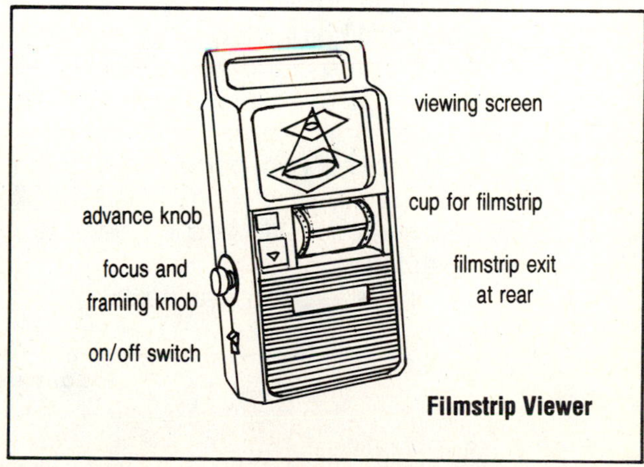

Filmstrip Viewer

1. Connect to power using a properly grounded plug.
2. Place the properly wound filmstrip into the filmstrip cup and insert the beginning end into the carrier slot.
3. Turn on the LAMP switch.
4. Continue pushing the filmstrip into the slot until it stops, then rotate the ADVANCE knob until an image appears on the screen. Focus the image if necessary.

5. Use the FRAMING knob or lever to adjust the image so the entire area of a single frame is centered on the screen.
6. Advance to the beginning frame and view the filmstrip.
7. After use, continue advancing the filmstrip so it completely exits the viewer. Rewind it by handling the film at the edges.

What You Have Learned About Practices for Successfully Operating Media Equipment and Still-Picture Projection:

1. What four practices should receive attention when learning to operate media equipment?
2. The following relate to *two different projection systems.* Place letter *A* before each item that relates to one system and letter *B* for items relating to the other system.
   a. Indirect projection
   b. Direct projection
   c. Transmitted light
   d. Reflected light
   e. Transparent material
   f. Opaque material
   g. Efficient projection
   h. Less than efficient projection
   i. Projects a picture found in a book
   j. Projects a 2 × 2 inch slide
   k. Projects filmstrip frames
3. To which type of still-picture projector does each statement refer?
   a. Uses carousel trays
   b. Can be used in a lighted room
   c. Materials for use placed on roll-feed belt
   d. Pointer in machine can indicate something in image on screen
   e. Includes a *framing* lever
   f. Uses a remote control accessory to change visuals
   g. Use from near front of room
   h. Has rear screen for viewing image
   i. Has select button
   j. Shows large-sized transparencies

See answers on page 384.

MOTION-PICTURE PROJECTION AND VIDEO PLAYBACK

In order to show moving images, either a motion-picture projector or a videocassette player may be used.

Motion-Picture Projector—Principles

For showing 16mm film, motion-picture projectors are available in a variety of brands and designs. The operating principles for all makes is the same. There are three subsystems within a motion-picture projector: **film transport, sound,** and **optical systems.**

Film Transport System The film first engages the film transport system. The film reel is attached to the feed arm at the front of the machine. The film comes off the bottom of the reel, which turns clockwise. The *sprocket holes* must be on the edge of the film toward the operator. The film is engaged under the *upper sprocket wheel.* A clamp keeps the film tight to the

Check Your Skills with Still-Picture Projectors and Viewers

Apply the details listed as you practice operating each projector or viewer. Each checklist can be used when your performance is evaluated.

Opaque Projector

_____ Connect to power
_____ Open lens cover
_____ Turn on lamp
_____ Show book page
_____ Use pointer
_____ Remove material
_____ Turn off lamp
_____ Retract lens and cover
_____ Store electrical cord

Overhead Projector

_____ Set projector on stand
_____ Prefocus and center image
_____ Stand (or sit) at projector
_____ Show transparency
_____ Fill screen with image
_____ Adjust screen to overcome keystone effect
_____ Show various transparencies (overlays, masking)
_____ Turn off lamp
_____ Store electrical cord

Slide Projector

_____ Load slides into tray
_____ Set up projector
_____ Connect to power
_____ Turn power switch to fan
_____ Place tray on projector
_____ Turn on lamp
_____ Focus image on screen
_____ Fill screen with image
_____ Use remote control with 5 or 6 slides (forward, reverse, focus)
_____ Remove slide tray
_____ Insert flat material
_____ Adjust focus
_____ Center image on screen
_____ Fill screen with image
_____ Unload slides
_____ Repack projector and cords

Filmstrip Projector

_____ Set up projector
_____ Connect to power
_____ Turn on lamp
_____ Thread filmstrip
_____ Focus image
_____ Frame image
_____ Fill screen with image
_____ Project 5 or 6 frames
_____ Remove filmstrip
_____ Rewind filmstrip
_____ Turn off lamp
_____ Repack projector

Slide Viewer

_____ Set up viewer
_____ Connect power
_____ Show slides
_____ Disassemble viewer

Filmstrip Viewer

_____ Set up viewer
_____ Connect power
_____ Thread filmstrip
_____ Frame image
_____ Show 5 or 6 frames
_____ Remove filmstrip
_____ Rewind filmstrip
_____ Repack viewer

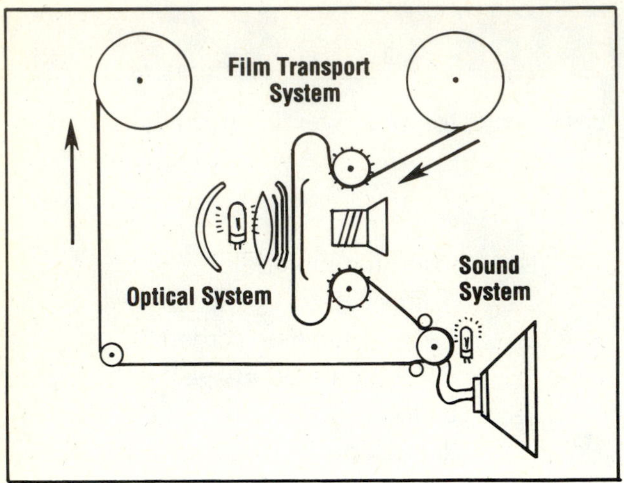

sprocket teeth. Then the *upper film loop* is formed. The film passes through the *film gate*, forms the *bottom loop*, and then passes around the top of the *second sprocket wheel*.

The two loops must be of proper size to ensure (1) that there will be a steady picture projected to the screen, and (2) that the sound will be properly synchronized with the picture. (See illustration above.)

Sound System After the film passes over the second sprocket wheel, it engages the sound system as it moves around the *sound drum*. To keep the film tight around the sound drum (which will ensure understandable sound), two *idler rollers* hold it taut. The sound drum has a shiny surface and close to it is a housing containing a small lamp called the *exciter lamp*.

When you examine the edge of a piece of 16mm sound film (opposite the sprocket hole side), you see an irregular pattern of dark areas. These dark areas cause varying amounts of light, coming form the exciter lamp, to be reflected off the sound drum to a *photoelectric cell*. This cell, in turn, converts the varying amounts of light into electricity. The electricity reaches the *sound amplifier* within the projector and sound is heard from the *speaker*.

Optical System The film is then projected through the optical system, which utilizes the direct projection principle. Light from the projection lamp is concentrated on the **aperture** opening of the film gate. As each frame of film is stopped momentarily (24 frames each second), the light transmits the image through the projection lens. The lens focuses the image on the screen.

Motion-Picture Projector—Threading and Operation

Depending on the make and model of a projector, there are three film threading options: **manual, slot-loading,** and **self-threading.** While the same film transport system described above is used with each option, different mechanisms are provided and different hand manipulations are required to place or guide film through the threading path.

Manual Threading In using a manual-threading projector (see illustration below), start with the sprockets on the film toward you. Attach the feed reel to the front arm and pull a length of film *clockwise* from the reel. Using your fingers, attach the film by following the threading path indicated on the projector: open the *clamp*, set film under *top sprocket wheel*, close clamp; form *top loop*; pass through the *film gate*; open and then securely close with a lever or pull projection lens toward you to expose the film path; and then secure the lens in its projection position. Now, open clamp, form *lower loop*, close clamp, and lead film tightly around the *sound drum* and secure to *take-up reel*.

Check to see that the film is set correctly at each point. Most projectors have a *hand-operated knob* that you can turn to move the film through the projector. This will show you whether the film is seated properly throughout the path and advancing smoothly through the projector.

Slot-Loading A slot-loading projector requires that you place the film into a long slot along the side of the machine. Before loading the film, the use of a lever opens the threading path. After the film is placed in the slot, reset the lever to engage the sprockets. Then lead the film around the sound drum and to the take-up reel.

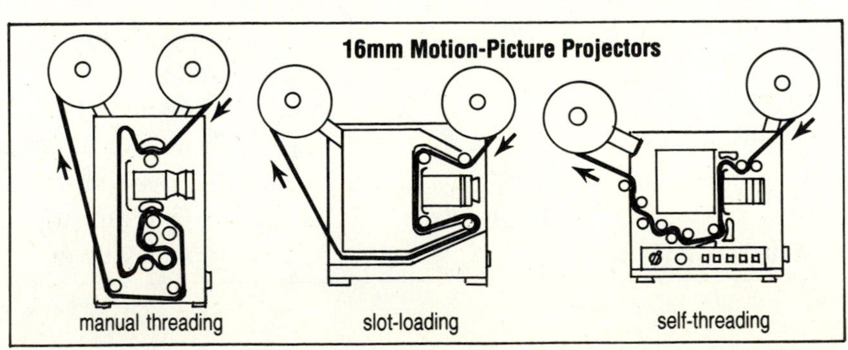

Self-Threading Self-threading projectors work like manual machines with one exception, that is, carefully placed guides channel the film through the transport system. The operator engages the *autothreading mechanism*. After making sure the film end is cut cleanly to facilitate movement of the film through the threading path, insert the film into a slot under the feed reel. Turn on the projector motor. When the film exits the projector, disengage the threading mechanism by pulling on the film. Attach the film to the take-up reel.

Study the threading diagram with your projector and follow the numbered steps.

OPERATING 16MM PROJECTORS

1. Open the projector and connect power cord.
2. Set up the feed and take-up arms. Place the film reel on the feed arm.
3. Thread the film, following the threading instructions on the projector being used.
4. Turn on the AMPLIFIER. This switch is generally part of the volume control, although on some projectors the amplifier comes on when the motor is turned on by using the MASTER CONTROL switch.
5. Start the MOTOR, then turn on the PROJECTION LAMP. This is generally on the same master control switch.
6. Size, position, and focus the image on the screen.
7. Set the sound level using the VOLUME control.
8. Frame the image if parts of two pictures show on the screen. The FRAMING knob is generally located near the top of the film gate.
9. Stop the projector and reverse the motor to return the film to the beginning. The reverse switch is part of the master control switch. You are now ready to show the film.

REWINDING FILM

1. Take the tail end of the film from the take-up reel and attach it to the feed reel by inserting the film in the slot. Rotate the feed reel counterclockwise a few revolutions to be certain the film is secured.
2. Lift take-up arm, or push or pull the REWIND button or lever, depending on the type of projector.
3. Turn the master control switch to the rewind position.
4. After the film has rewound to the original feed reel, turn off the projector and return the rewind mechanism to its original position.

Page 354 details the use of motion picture for instructional purposes.

Videocassette Player (VCR)

Video is a widely used medium in training and education. Commercially produced tapes are available in numerous content areas treating thousands of topics. Camcorders are used to locally produce video materials as described in Chapter 15.

VHS (including **Super-VHS**) and **8mm** formats are commonly used for instruction and training. VHS stands for Video Home System. The features and controls include the following:

- ***Tuning***—Knobs, pushbuttons, or a touch pad are the controls for selecting a picture channel.
- ***Multiple speeds***—One to three speeds may be available on a player. A recorded tape must be played at the recorded speed. A faster speed provides somewhat better picture and sound quality.
- ***Picture search***—Most players have controls for play; rewind; fast forward; scan, forward, or reverse at a speed faster than play control (allowing you to watch the picture); and still or freeze frame.
- ***Magnetic heads***—Standards VCRs have two video heads (erase/record and play) mounted on a drum that revolves at a high speed across the tape. Other players have extra heads for special effects, like slow motion and still pictures.

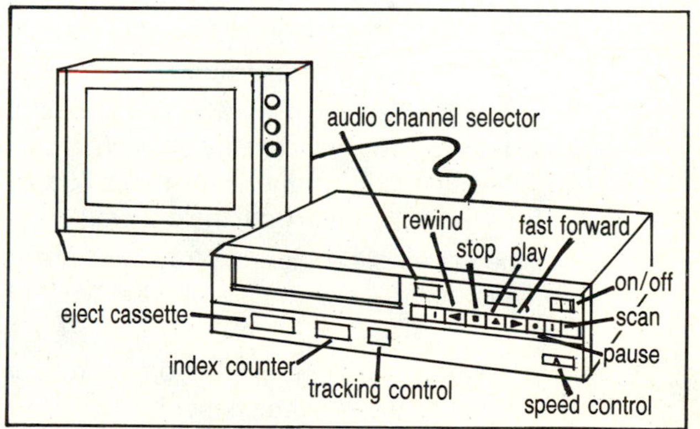

Videodisc Player

A videodisc player is relatively easy to operate because it has few moving parts. The disc is tracked by a beam of laser light that is converted into pictures and sound. A videodisc player can be used to show a complete program, just as a film is shown with a motion-picture projector. By using a built-in or separate control unit (**key** or **touch pad**), however, selected sequences anywhere on the disc can be viewed in any order.

Some videodisc players are stand-alone units, while other ones have built-in microprocessors (computer components) for more detailed picture control, and even more sophisticated ones can be connected to separate microcomputers for interactive learning. See the discussion of levels I, II, and III videodisc equipment and uses in interactive learning on page 287.

OPERATING INSTRUCTIONS

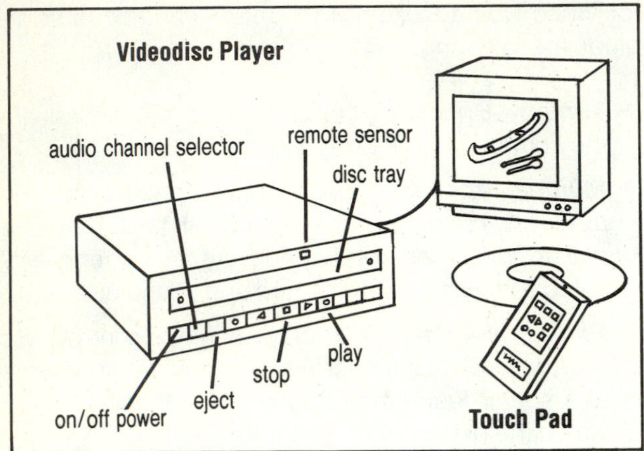

1. Connect the videodisc player to the TV receiver using an RF cable.
2. Plug the videodisc player and the TV receiver into a grounded outlet.
3. Turn on the POWER switch for both the videodisc player and the TV.
4. Push the COVER OPEN button or the EJECT button depending on the type of videodisc player.
5. Place the videodisc into the player being careful to have the side you want to play positioned correctly in relationship to the laser head. (Some read from the top, others from the bottom.)
6. Close the cover, slide the disc tray in or press the LOAD button depending on the type of player.
7. Press PLAY or LOAD. This is done on the front of the player or on the hand-held touch pad.
8. When a picture appears on the TV receiver, adjust for best COLOR setting and set the AUDIO level.
9. Assuming you have a menu of frame numbers, stop the videodisc by pressing the STOP button on the TOUCH PAD. Press FRAME DISPLAY to cause the individual frame number to appear in the upper-left corner of the TV picture. Punch in the frame number for where you would like to move next and push SEARCH. The videodisc player will instantly shift to the new location on the disc. Push the PLAY button if you want full motion. If you want one frame at a time, use the STEP button.

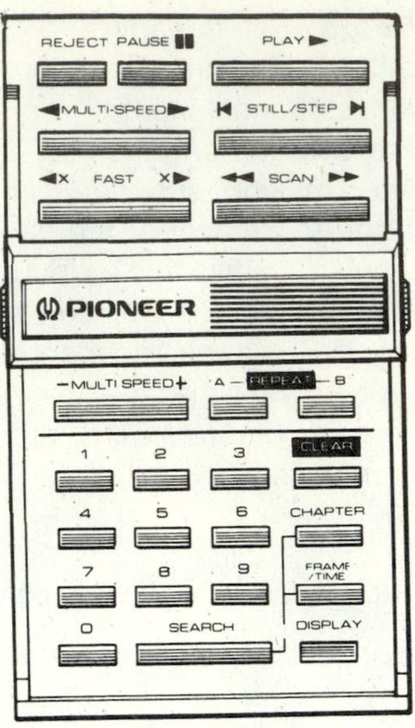

Touch Pad

10. After using the videodisc program, push the EJECT button to unload the disc. Reverse the loading procedure and turn off the player and TV receiver.

Read the specific operating instructions for the videodisc player you will use. They may contain further details and features in addition to those described above. Page 354 details the use of videodisc players for instruction.

Barcode Reader

The barcode reader is a popular device among instructors who use Level I videodiscs in their teaching and training. This equipment reads **pre-printed barcodes** that an instructor can produce using an inexpensive software package on a personal computer. The resulting barcodes are printed with a laser printer onto plain or adhesive-backed paper.

The laserdisc barcode reader is a small device. It has a pointed end that contains the SENSOR unit, with the TRANSMITTER unit on the other, blunt end. The unit can be connected by wire to the videodisc player or used in a wireless mode. If connected by wire, the unit will transmit the code to the disc player automatically as the scan is made. If it is used wireless, the instructor has about 60 seconds to point the blunt end (transmitter) at the videodisc player and press the SENDING key.

OPERATING INSTRUCTIONS

1. Set up the videodisc player and TV receiver, making certain the player is a model that will accept barcodes. (A Pioneer LD model player is commonly used with the Pioneer UC-V104BC laserdisc barcode reader.)

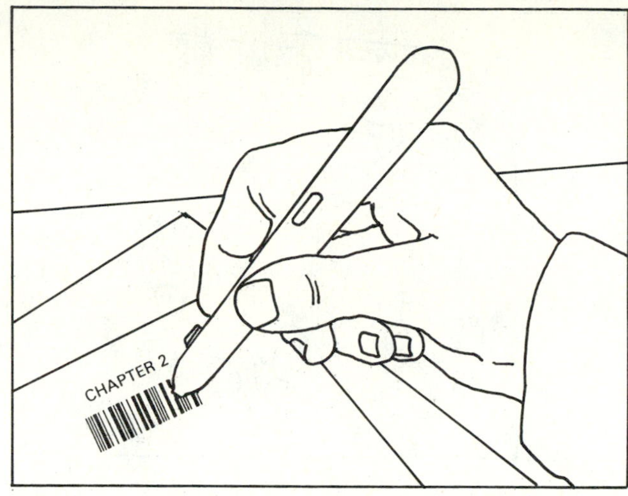

2. Be certain batteries are installed in the reader.
3. Set the SLIDE switch, located on the side of the reader, according to the format of code to be sent.
4. Press the READ key and at the same time pass the pointed tip across the barcode as follows: Hold the reader vertically to the barcode, and starting just outside the edges of the barcode, move it horizontally across the barcode (either left to right or right to left).
5. When the reading of the barcode is completed, a "beep" will sound and a small pilot light will come on. If the light does not come on, continue scanning until it does.
6. If you operate in a wireless mode, point the blunt end of the reader toward the videodisc player within 60 seconds and press the SENDING key. This will send a signal, which in turn carries out the command from the barcode. If using the direct wire mode, the videodisc player will move to the selected frame immediately after the scanning.
7. The videodisc player will carry out the instructions encoded onto the barcode.
8. After the lesson is completed, turn off the videodisc player and store the barcode reader. Remove batteries from the reader if the unit will not be used for a long period.

Videomonitor/Television Receiver

There is a difference between a videomonitor and a television receiver. A TV receiver has a built-in tuner to receive programs from television stations and cable channels. When a VCR is attached to a TV receiver, the latter must be tuned to either channel 3 or 4. A videomonitor does not include a tuner and is designed for direct attachment to a VCR, computer, or other device requiring video output.

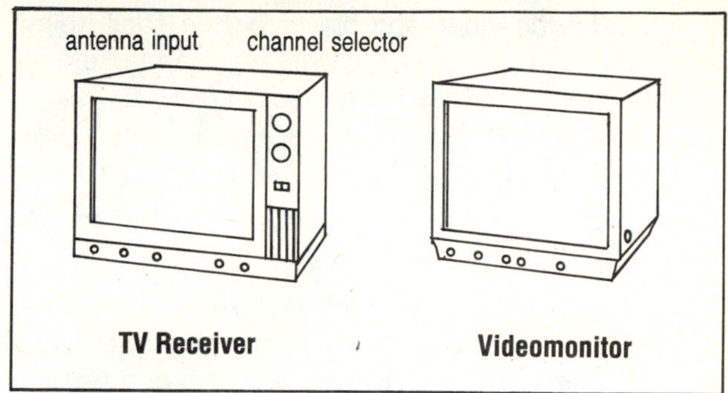

When sending video signals from a VCR player to a TV receiver, a single cable that carries both picture and sound is used. It is called an RF cable with F connectors at each end. A videomonitor requires two cables (for video and audio) to the videoplayer. The video cable uses BNC connectors on each end of the cable. The audio is carried on standard audio patch cords using one of the following connectors: RCA plug, miniplug, or ¼-inch phone plug.

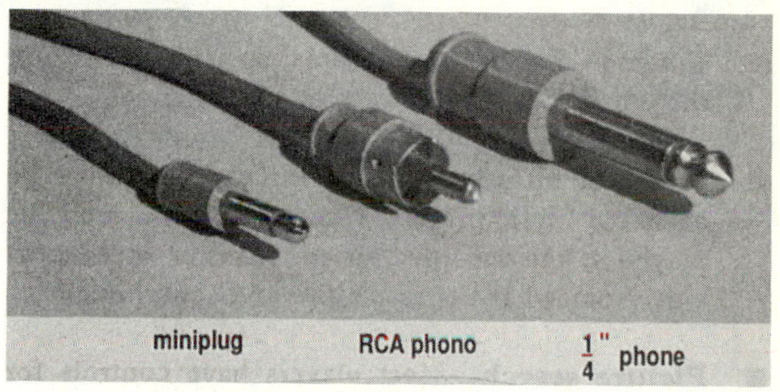

Audio Plugs

Video Connectors

OPERATING INSTRUCTIONS

1. Select a television receiver large enough for the size of your audience (23-inch screen can be used for a maximum group of 30 learners).
2. Place the TV receiver on a 52-inch projection cart. Secure the receiver to the cart to prevent accidents.

3. Place the videotape player on the shelf below the TV receiver. Use an RF cable and interconnect the player with the receiver.
4. Plug both the videotape player and the TV receiver into a grounded power outlet.
5. Switch on the TV receiver. Set to the proper channel (3 or 4).
6. Switch on the videotape player.
7. Push the EJECT button on the videotape player to open the cassette compartment or insert the tape into a slot, depending on the model of player being used.
8. Push the PLAY button. As the test pattern or image appears, make necessary adjustments on the TV receiver to perfect the image. On the videotape player, you may have to adjust the TRACKING CONTROL if the picture is distorted.
9. Set the AUDIO level after making sure you have the proper audio track (many players have settings for two audio tracks).
10. Then stop and rewind the tape to the point where you want to begin. Avoid showing color bars prior to the title to the audience. Use the FOOTAGE INDEX COUNTER if appropriate.
11. During use, you may find it desirable to control the tape with the FAST FORWARD, STILL FRAME, and REWIND buttons.
12. Following use, rewind the tape, turn off the videotape player and the TV receiver. Secure the equipment.

Video Projector

With large groups, or in an auditorium, a large-screen television may be used. A video projector throws a large image into a screen in a manner similar to that of a 16mm motion picture projector. However, since the TV system requires three cathode ray tubes (one for each of the video primary colors—red, blue, and green), adjustments of the projected image are very critical.

Less expensive video projectors based on liquid crystal display (LCD) technology are available (see page 354). While they cannot yet produce the same levels of resolution and brightness as the three-lens projection systems, portable LCD projectors offer a lightweight and affordable alternative. A variety of brands are on the market, which when connected to a video player, will project a very satisfactory image.

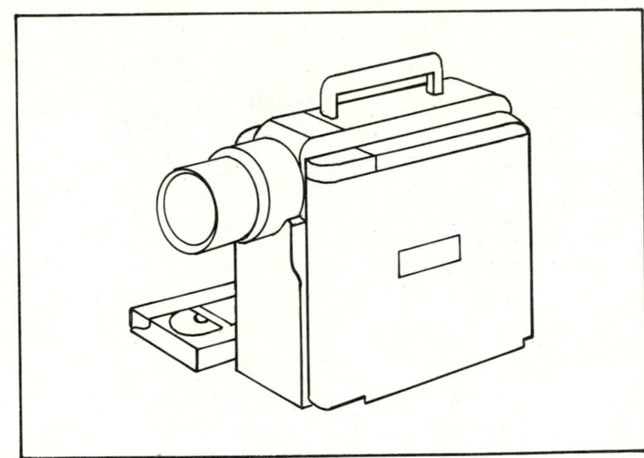

Consult the operating instructions with your equipment for other special features. Page 354 provides information on the use of video in instruction.

What You Have Learned About Operating Motion-Picture Projection and Video Playback Equipment:

1. To which *subsystem* in a 16mm projector does each relate?
   a. Sound drum

(continued)

Check Your Skills with Motion Picture Projectors and Videotape/Videodisc Players

Apply the details listed as you practice operating each projector or video unit. Each checklist can be used when your performance is evaluated.

16mm Sound Motion Picture Projector

____ Set up projector on stand
____ Connect power
____ Place film reel on feed arm
Thread film:
  ____ Manual path
  ____ Slot-loading
  ____ Self-threading
____ Turn on amplifier
____ Start projection
____ Focus image
____ Fill screen with image
____ Frame image
____ Set sound/tone levels
____ Prepare for showing
____ Show film
____ End showing
____ Rewind film
____ Turn off switches
____ Repack projector

Videocassette Player TV Receiver/Videomonitor

____ Set up player
____ Set up receiver/monitor
____ Connect the two units
____ Turn on receiver/monitor
____ Turn on player
____ Open player tray
____ Seat disc
____ Close tray
Use player controls:
  ____ Play
  ____ Scan
  ____ Adjust picture/sound
Use touch pad:
  ____ Play

____ Select channel
____ Turn on player
____ Open player cover
____ Insert cassette
____ Close cover
____ Play cassette
Make adjustments on receiver/monitor:
  ____ Sound level
  ____ Steady picture
  ____ Picture color/contrast
Use player controls:
  ____ Fast forward
  ____ Scan
  ____ Still frame
  ____ Rewind
____ Remove cassette
____ Turn off player
____ Turn off receiver/monitor
____ Repack equipment

Videodisc Player TV Receiver/Videomonitor

____ Set up player
____ Set up receiver/monitor
____ Connect the two units
____ Turn on receiver/monitor
____ Select channel
  ____ Scan
  ____ Fast forward/reverse
  ____ Slow forward/reverse
  ____ Step/still
  ____ Stop
  ____ Locate specific frames
____ Remove disc
____ Turn off player
____ Turn off receiver/monitor
____ Repack equipment

b. Projection lamp
c. Photoelectric cell
d. Feed arm
e. Aperture
f. Film loops
g. Exciter lamp
h. Lens
i. Sprocket wheels

2. What three methods of film threading are found in various 16mm film projector models?
3. Which statements are *true* about 16mm film projectors?
   a. Sprocket holes are on the film side toward the operator.
   b. Film winds off and on reels in counterclockwise direction during projection.
   c. Film moves continually through the projector at 24 frames per second.
   d. The sound track is visible on the film.
   e. Use the framer to center a single frame of film in the aperture.
4. What sequence of steps should be followed in operating a film projector?
   a. Thread film
   b. Set sound level
   c. Position, size, and focus image
   d. Start motor and turn on projection lamp
   e. Place film reel on feed arm
   f. Rewind film to beginning
   g. Frame image
   h. Turn on amplifier
5. Which video format is most commonly used? What is its tape size?
6. What are the common controls on a videocassette player?
7. What is the main difference between a TV receiver and a videomonitor?
8. Explain which cables are used with a TV receiver and which with a videomonitor.
9. What are three advantages of a videodisc player over a videocassette player?
10. What purpose does a barcode reader serve?
11. What is an LCD video projector?

See answers on page 384.

AUDIO PLAYERS

Most people are familiar with audio equipment because it has become so much a part of their everyday lives. Cassette and reel-to-reel audiotape players are widely available. Whereas cassette use dominates, professional studio production requires reel-to-reel units. The cassette format will be considered here because of its popularity and availability. Reel equipment, however, receives attention in Chapter 9. Furthermore, the recent addition to the audio family, the compact disc player, is examined.

Audiocassette Player/Recorder

Audiocassette equipment that has only playback capability can be purchased, but most units have both recording and playback features.

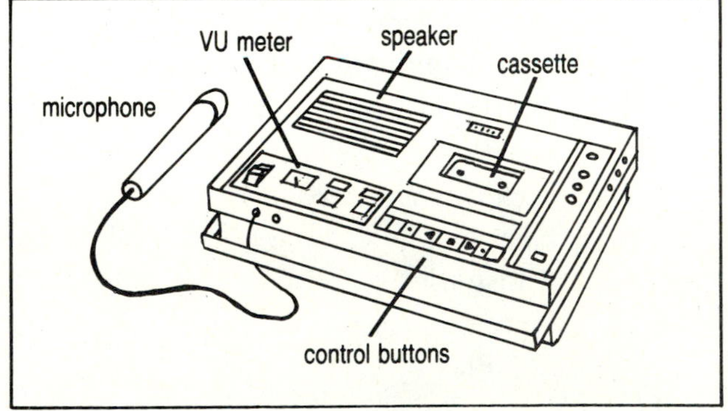

OPERATION FOR PLAYBACK

1. Turn power on. (When you push the start/play button on some machines, the power is automatically turned on.)

2. Load cassette and push the START/PLAY button. Adjust the VOLUME and TONE controls. The tone control only operates in playback mode.
3. Use the REWIND/FORWARD lever or buttons to return the tape to the proper beginning point or to skip to another section of a recording.
4. The INDEX COUNTER can be set at zero by pushing the RESET button.
5. Most recorder/players have a PAUSE button that can be pushed to temporarily stop the tape while the instructor of user engages in another activity. Depressing the pause button again will restart the tape.
6. After completing the audio presentation, stop the tape with the STOP button. Then rewind the tape using the REWIND button or lever.
7. Remove the cassette with the EJECT button. Turn off the power.

OPERATION FOR RECORDING

1. Plug the microphone into the *microphone (MIC) input jack* generally located on the side of the machine. If recording from another recorder, record player, or mixer, plug into the *line input jack.*
2. Turn power on and load a cassette.
3. Depress the RECORD button and hold in place, simultaneously depress the START/PLAY button. If the knockout tabs have been removed from the back corners of the cassette the recorder will *not* go into the record mode. This is done to protect a recording already on the tape from accidental erasure, which takes place as a new recording is made on the tape. If you wish to record on a cassette that has had the tabs removed, secure small strips of masking tape over the open areas where the two tabs were located.

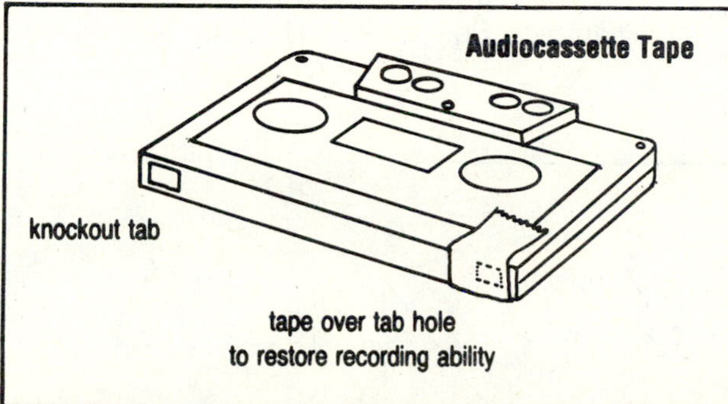

4. Some recorders have an *automatic volume recording level* (marked AGL, AVL, ALC) others require adjusting the level with the *volume control* knob. Several recorders have both and you set a switch to the option you want. The automatic setting, while convenient to use, has an important drawback. A hiss or extraneous sounds are recorded during narration pauses. If you manually set the recording level, a *VU meter* is provided to help you determine the correct setting. The level is set using the volume control, being certain that the VU meter needle moves in the proper range, according to instructions provided with the recorder.
5. While recording, the PAUSE lever or button can be used to temporarily stop and then restart the tape movement.
6. After recording, STOP the machine and rewind the tape using the rewind lever or button.
7. Activate the EJECT lever to remove the cassette.
8. Punch out the tabs on back of the cassette to protect the recording.
9. Turn off the power, if necessary.

Page 366 provides information on uses of audio players for instruction. Chapter 9 discusses in more detail how to produce an audio recording and Chapter 11 the preparation of recordings for instruction.

Record Player

The record player is a common unit of instructional equipment, although it is being replaced for many uses by audiocassette and compact disc players. Basic record players have a built-in speaker and operate at three speeds—33⅓, 45, and 78 revolutions per minute (rpm)—to accommodate different records.

A record player can be used as a public address system if it has a microphone input connection. A player may also include a tempo control lever, a pause control knob, external speaker and headphone output, and tone (treble and bass) controls.

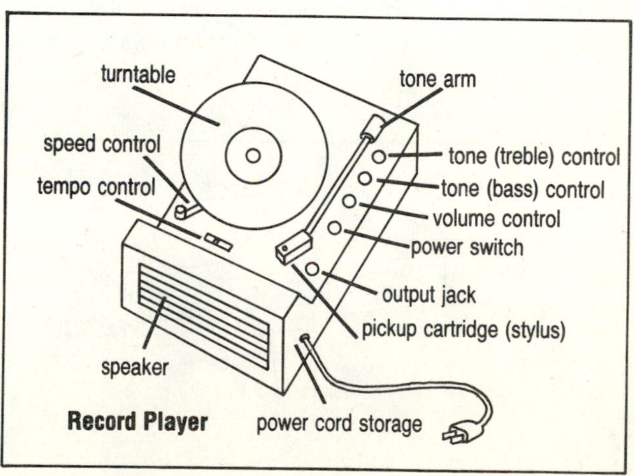

Operating Instructions

1. Remove the cover and plug the player into a grounded electrical power outlet.
2. Position the player so the speaker faces the audience.
3. Turn on the POWER to the amplifier and turntable.
4. Set the turntable at the SPEED appropriate to the record being used.
5. Set STYLUS on TONE ARM (fine point for 33⅓ and 45 rpm records).
6. Use the PAUSE control and stop the turntable while placing the record in position.
7. Release the pause control to start the turntable. If the player has a TEMPO CONTROL, fine tune the speed of the turntable.
8. Pause the record, unlock the tone arm, and gently position the needle at the desired starting point on the record.
9. Release the pause control and adjust the sound VOLUME. Make any needed adjustments in the bass and treble.
10. Pause the record, reposition the stylus, and you are ready to present.
11. After using the record player, remove the record, handling it by the edge.
12. Relock the tone arm to the post to prevent needle damage while transporting the player.
13. Turn off the power, store the power cord, and replace the cover.

Compact Disc (CD) Player

A compact disc player is about the size of an audiocassette player. Recordings are produced in 4¾-inch silvery discs that are played by a laser beam. Over 60 minutes of high quality sound may be recorded on one side of a disc. The sound is *digitally encoded* (known as digital sound). The laser beam neither causes record wear nor does it respond to flaws in the record surface that would normally be heard as noise.

Some CD player models include wireless, remove-control *touch pads* and may permit the random selection of any track on a disc. Also, compact discs containing printed information are available as library resources. They are known as CD-ROM and can be used with a regular CD player that has *single-frame* control. See page 154 for a further description of this media form.

In addition to the following general instructions, consult specific instructions for the particular compact disc player you intend to use.

Operating Instructions

1. Connect CD player into speaker system.
2. Plug into a grounded outlet.
3. Turn on power by depressing POWER button.
4. Load the compact disc by pressing the OPEN/CLOSE or EJECT button.
5. After positioning the disc, close the disc compartment by pushing the OPEN/CLOSE button.
6. Push the PLAY button located on the player or use the remote control pad.
7. After use, eject and remove the disc.

Dub Record to Audiotape

In addition to using each piece of audio equipment by itself, the music on a record can be transferred (called **dubbing**) to tape, and even combined with narration. To do this it is necessary to connect a record player to an audiocassette recorder.

Use a **jumper cord** from the **output** jack on the record player to a **line input** jack (*not* microphone input) on the tape recorder. Set volume on the recorder at a moderate level. Adjust volume setting on record player to a high enough level to obtain a quality recording.

Narration can be mixed with music by adding a microphone at the **mic input,** preferably in the record player. Volume levels must be balanced between music and the narration. See page 160 for further details.

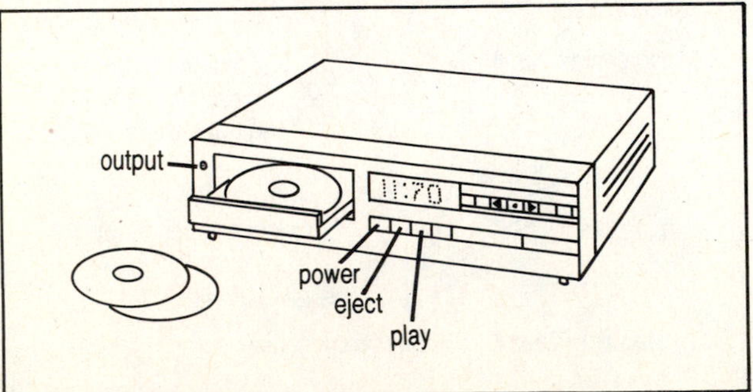

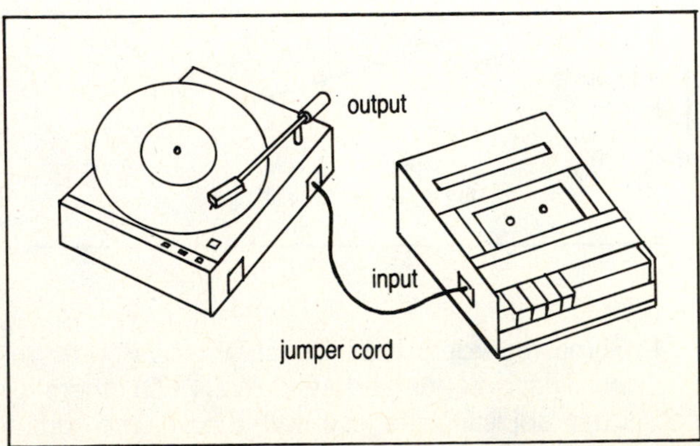

Check Your Skills with Audio Players

Apply the details listed as you practice operating each unit of audio equipment. Each checklist can be used when your performance is evaluated.

Audiocassette Player

Select power source:
- ____ Battery
- ____ AC adapter or cord

____ Load cassette
____ Play cassette
____ Adjust volume and tone

Use other controls:
- ____ Fast forward
- ____ Pause
- ____ Rewind

____ Remove cassette
____ Repack player

Audiocassette Recorder

Select power source:
- ____ Battery
- ____ AC adapter or cord

____ Load cassette
____ Attach microphone

Select volume control:
- ____ Automatic
- ____ Manual

____ Set index counter to 000
____ Make test recording
____ Check recording quality
____ Make any adjustments in settings
____ Make recording
____ Play back recording
____ Rewind tape
____ Remove cassette
____ Protect recording from erasure
____ Repack recorder and microphone

Record Player

____ Set up player
____ Connect to power
____ Turn on amplifier
____ Choose stylus
____ Select record speed
____ Place record on turntable
____ Start turntable
____ Fine tune speed
____ Set volume and tone levels
____ Pause record
____ Reposition stylus to start
____ Play record
____ End play
____ Lock tone arm
____ Remove record
____ Plug microphone into input
____ Use as public address system
____ Turn off power
____ Repack player

Compact Disc Player

____ Connect player to speaker
____ Connect to power
____ Turn on player power
____ Load disc
____ Play disc
____ Use remote control (if available)
____ Remove disc
____ Disassemble equipment

Dub Record to Audiotape

____ Set up record player
____ Set up audiocassette player
____ Connect two units with jumper cord
____ Play record
____ Record on cassette
____ Adjust volume on each unit
____ Listen to recording
____ Mix music with voice
____ Listen to recording
____ Repack equipment

REVIEW

What You Have Learned About Operating Audio Players:

1. What purpose is served by the *pause* control on an audiocassette player and how is it used?
2. What is the difference between a *line input jack* and a *microphone input jack* on an audiocassette recorder?
3. What is the function of the knock-out *tabs* on audiocassettes?
4. What is the purpose of a *tempo control* on a record player?
5. What is the most widely used rpm recording?
6. What two main factors make a compact disc and its player different from a conventional record player?
7. What setup is used to transfer music properly from a record to tape?

See answers on page 384.

COMBINATIONS OF EQUIPMENT

Motion picture projectors and videotape players show pictures and also play back sound. Although in a single housing, we consider them combinations of media equipment. Several companies manufacture equipment that either combines the functions of separate pieces of media equipment into a single unit, or allows for interconnection between two units for synchronous use. The most common combinations are for slide/tape, filmstrip/tape, and video monitor/player units.

Synchronized Slide/Tape System

An audible signal, such as a "click" or a "beep," can be recorded on tape along with the narration to indicate slide changes. For a more professional production, some audiotape recorders contain special features for synchronizing slides with the audio narration of a slide program. These machines allow you to record an inaudible cue on the second track of the audiocassette tape; on playback, this cue activates a relay to advance slides. A further explanation of this technique is on page 161.

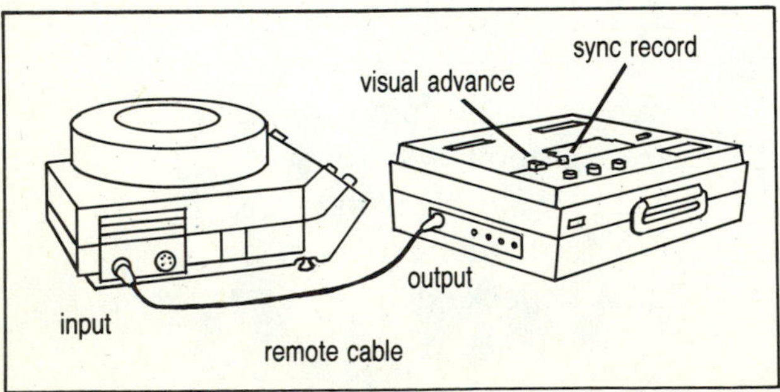

OPERATING INSTRUCTIONS

1. Complete the audio recording.
2. Connect the remote cable from the slide projector to the PROJECTOR OUTPUT on the audiocassette recorder/player.
3. Place the carousel slide tray on the projector with slides loaded in the correct order. Turn on the lamp. Begin with a blank slide in slot number one and the projector advanced to the number one position. This prevents white light from reaching the screen. Some projectors have an automatic shutter eliminating the need for a blank side.
4. Put recorder in synchronization mode by holding the SYNC mode switch in record position while pressing the START/PLAY button. *Do not press* the audiorecord button!
5. Follow the narration with a script marked to show where slide changes should take place. Press the VISUAL ADVANCE or SYNC button on cue. This records an advance signal on the second track of the audiocassette tape. At each press of the button, the projector will advance, ensuring that the sound and the slides are in perfect synchronization. Record the advance signal for the entire program.
6. Rewind the audiocassette tape and, using the SELECT button on the slide projector, rotate the slides to the beginning point. Put the sync mode switch into PLAY position and start the tape to test the program for proper synchronization. If all slides advance automatically and at the appropriate time, stop the tape, rewind, and return the slide tray to the beginning point.

7. If any slides do *not* correctly change with the narration, you need to erase incorrectly placed signals, rerecord them properly, and add any that were missed. To do this:
   a. Rewind and play the tape until you find a place needing correction.
   b. Wind the tape back to a point shortly *after the last correct signal.* Check this location a couple of times by listening to the recording and watching the slide changes while following the script.
   c. Then, start playing the tape and immediately switch the SYNC MODE switch to *record position.*
   d. Put one or more new advance signals on the tape according to the script.
   e. Be certain to stop the playback or remove the sync mode switch from record position *before* you reach a properly located signal. Using this procedure, the improper signals are erased at the same time that new ones are added.
8. Use the equipment to make your slide/tape presentation.
9. Following the presentation, rewind the audiocassette tape and remove the slide tray.
10. Turn off all power on both the slide projector and audiocassette tape player.
11. Store power cords, replace covers, and/or return to proper case.

Dissolve Unit for Slide/Tape

A synchronizing audiocassette recorder/player can also control a dissolve unit that links two carousel-type slide projectors that are focused on the same screen. The dissolver blends slides as they are shown by eliminating the sudden black screen normally seen between slides as a series is projected. As the light from the first projector fades out, the light from the second projector fades in, thus dissolving one image into the next one.

Some dissolve units allow for dissolves to take place at various rates to give variety to a slide program. Other, more complex, units not only have multiple dissolve speeds, but also can provide special effects such as flashing and overlay capability. See page 231 for a further explanation of dissolve control functions with slide/tape presentations.

OPERATING INSTRUCTIONS

1. Load slides into two trays alternating the numbered slides. Tray A will have slides 1, 3, 5, 7, . . . and tray B will have slides 2, 4, 6, 8, and so on.
2. Always use a multiple outlet power box or power bar so all equipment is operating from the same electrical source. Failure to do this may result in erratic slide changes.
3. Plug the two carousel projectors into the outlet bar. Plug the synchronizing audiocassette recorder/player into the same power source and attach the "A" cable from the dissolve to the left projector, and "B" cable to the right projector.
4. Plug the dissolve unit into the power bar and, for recording pulses, attach the sync cable from the *sync output* jack on the dissolve unit to the *sync input* jack on the cassette recorder. (Reverse this setup for playback after the initial synchro-

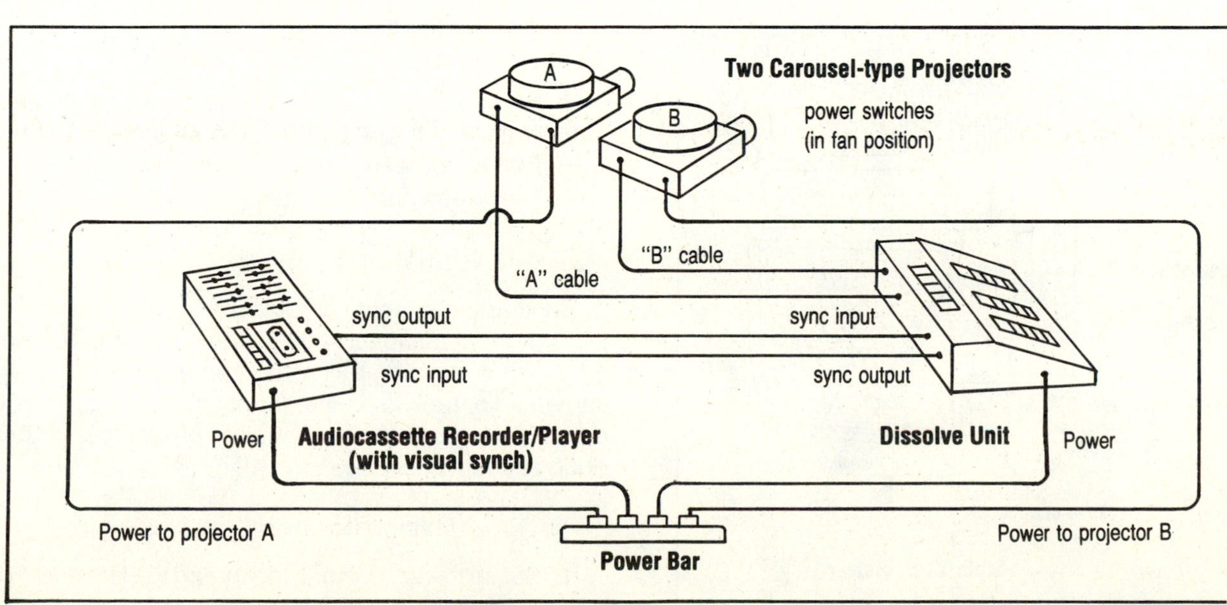

nization is made, that is, plug the cable into the *sync input* on the dissolve unit and the *sync output* on the audiocassette player.)

5. Put the projector switches into FAN position and place the prerecorded cassette into the tape recorder. Hold the sync lever in *record mode* while depressing the START/PLAY button.
6. Following a marked script, push the appropriate buttons on the DISSOLVE console depending on the effect wanted. This records an inaudible pulse on one track of the audiocassette tape. If a mistake is made, just rewind the tape to the position just prior to the mistake and rerecord with a new sync pulse.
7. Rewind the tape and return the slides to the starting point.
8. Reverse the sync cable hook up as described in step four.
9. Push the PLAY lever when ready to present the program and all slides will change in correct order and at the speed for which they were preprogrammed. (Remember to put projector switches into FAN position, *not* lamp position.)
10. After the presentation, rewind the audiocassette tape and store all equipment.

Page 352 details the use of multi-image programs for instruction.

Rear-Projection Slide/Tape Unit

Several slide/tape units with built-in rear-projection screens are available. These generally have a modified carousel slide projector synchronized to an audiocassette tape recorder/player, with both units being integrated into a single compact case. Some have a rear screen that collapses to form a briefcase. Other units are less portable, but function well for individualized or small group viewing.

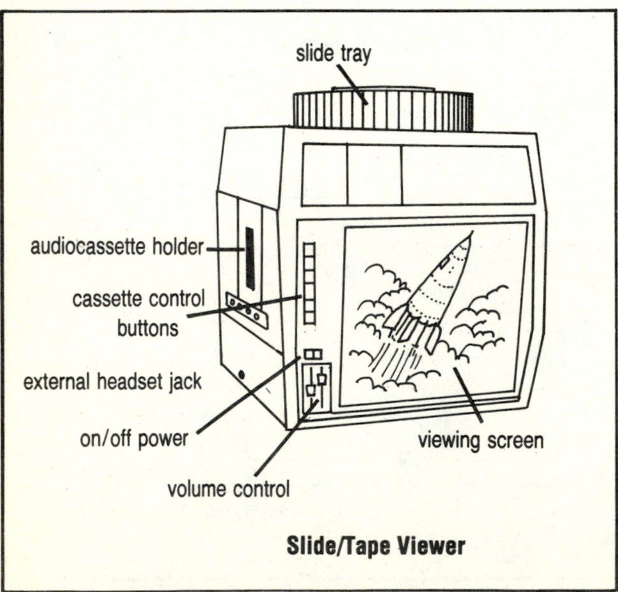

Slide/Tape Viewer

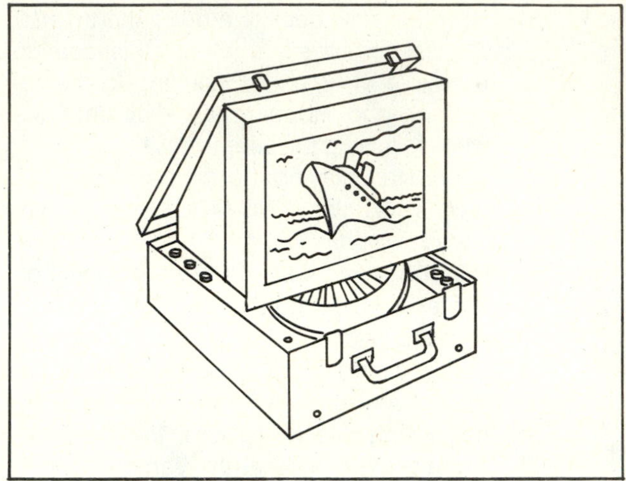

Operating Instructions

1. Follow setup procedures as outlined in the instruction manual or on a diagram attached to the rear-projection unit.
2. Plug the unit into a grounded electrical outlet.
3. Load slides, turn on power, and position the slide tray onto the projection unit.
4. ADVANCE to a slide and FOCUS the image.
5. Insert the audiocassette tape. If necessary, start the player and adjust the VOLUME. Test it to be certain the slides are advancing.
6. Return the slide tray and audiocassette tape to the beginning.
7. View the presentation.
8. Following the presentation, remove the audiocassette tape and slides. Turn off all power. Collapse the rear screen or place a protective cover over the screen and store the power cord.

Sound Filmstrip Projector

Another equipment combination is the filmstrip projector with an audiocassette player. The synchronizing signal for advancing a filmstrip frame is placed on the same audio track as is the narration. This is difficult to do, and for this reason, most sound filmstrips are produced commercially.

Operating Instructions

1. Set up the equipment and thread the filmstrip. Follow the steps outlined on page 317.

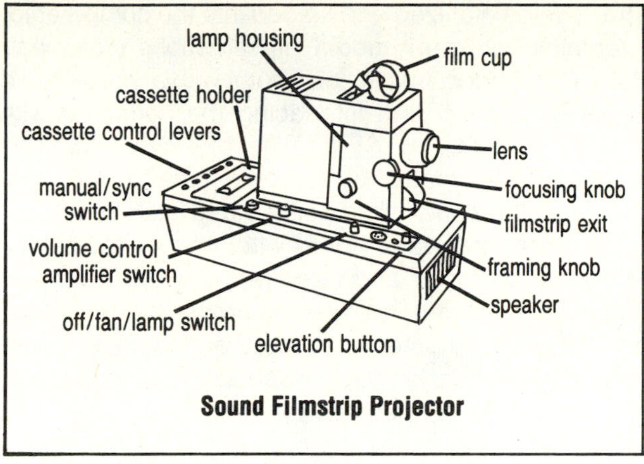

Sound Filmstrip Projector

2. ADVANCE the filmstrip to the proper beginning frame.
3. Insert the audiocassette tape in the cassette holder by pressing the STOP/EJECT button. Turn on the AUDIO AMPLIFIER. Some projectors have a separate switch and others combine the amplifier switch with the VOLUME control. Press the PLAY button and adjust the sound level with the volume knob.
4. As the tape plays, check to be certain that the filmstrip advances automatically. Some model machines have a MANUAL ADVANCE/SYNC switch. Make certain it is in the proper position.
5. After testing, return the filmstrip and audiocassette tape to their beginning.
6. Other audio adjustment buttons generally include REWIND, FAST FORWARD, and PAUSE, depending on the specific brand of sound filmstrip projector.
7. Refer to the operating instructions for the equipment you have for details on using special accessories.
8. After use, remove and rewind the filmstrip and/or cassette. Turn off all switches and store the projector in its case.

Page 351 details the use of sound filmstrips for instruction.

Sound Filmstrip Viewer

Sound filmstrips can be studied by individuals or small groups when used with rear-screen viewers. The filmstrip is either advanced manually, following an audible tone, or responds automatically to an inaudible cue.

OPERATING INSTRUCTIONS

1. Turn on the power.

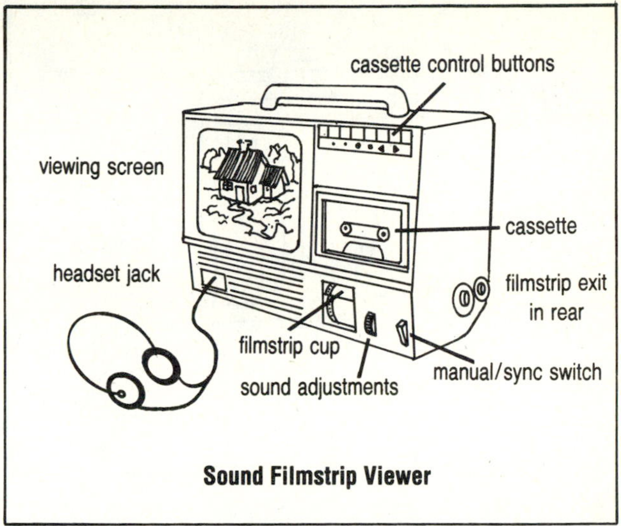

Sound Filmstrip Viewer

2. Insert the filmstrip and advance it to the beginning frame.
3. Insert the audiocassette tape.
4. Press the PLAY button to test the audio level. (Some sound viewers have a separate audio switch. Others are activated by pressing the play button.)
5. Adjust the audio level. Many sound filmstrip viewers are only equipped with a *headphone jack* and no speaker since they are designed for individual use. If this is true, a set of headphones must be plugged into the viewer and used to set the audio level.
6. If the viewer is equipped with an automatic filmstrip advance, make sure the MANUAL/SYNC switch is in the proper position. Test to be certain the tape and filmstrip and synchronized properly.
7. View the filmstrip.
8. After use, remove and rewind the filmstrip and/or audiocassette tape. Turn off all power.

Video Monitor/Player Combination

A unit that combines a video monitor and a video player as a combination piece of equipment is the compact monitor/player. It is designed for self-instructional use or small group viewing. Several companies manufacture these units. They are not only for general use, but are also placed in laboratories where learners can view videotapes as they proceed through an experiment or another assignment.

OPERATING INSTRUCTIONS

1. Follow the setup procedure as outlined in the instructional manual.

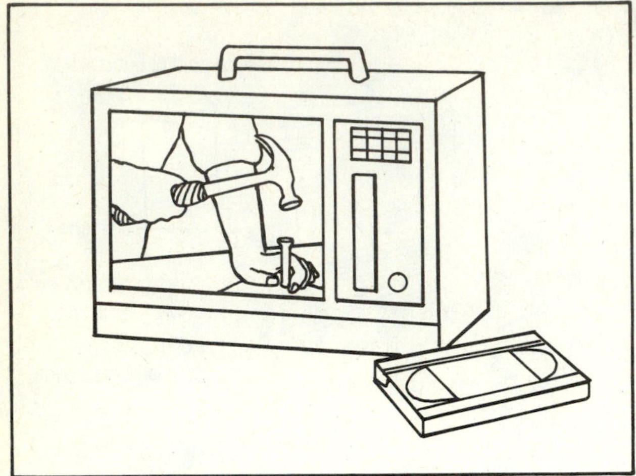

2. Push the POWER ON button, generally located on the front panel.
3. Insert the videocassette into the holder, which is usually located to the right or below the video screen. Be certain the cassette is inserted according to the symbol on the cassette holder.
4. Most units will begin playing the tape as soon as the cassette is inserted. Other units have a separate PLAY button.
5. Following the completion of the program, press the STOP button.
6. Press the REWIND button to return the tape to the beginning.
7. Press the EJECT button to remove the cassette.
8. Press the POWER ON button to turn power off.
9. Unplug the unit and store the electrical cord.

Monitor/player units have other features that allow for creative use of a video recording. An example is the REPEAT PLAYBACK feature. It is used if you need to leave the unit unattended as part of a display. It will automatically rewind the tape and start playing it again. Other features may include a headphone jack for private listening, and both audio and video input/output terminals.

Computer/Videodisc or Videotape Player

Computers combined with a videodisc or a videotape player allow for group use or for self-instructional learning. With digital technology, materials from such sources as a video recording, a videodisc, or still pictures can be digitized and loaded into the computer for integration into **multimedia** presentations (see page 292). The learner uses the computer with a monitor, and is not concerned with interfacing the computer with other equipment.

Those who already have a computer and would like to explore the world of interactive video instruction must purchase an **interface board** with appropriate cables to link the computer and video player. Be certain your computer and video unit have the proper external ports, and that the computer will accept an interface board. The interface needed for a videodisc is different from one required for a videotape player.

Operation of interfaced computer/video equipment requires planning for interactive program development. Video segments must be identified by frame number and integrated with the computer software. See page 284 for information on designing interactive instruction and page 283 for using computer/video equipment.

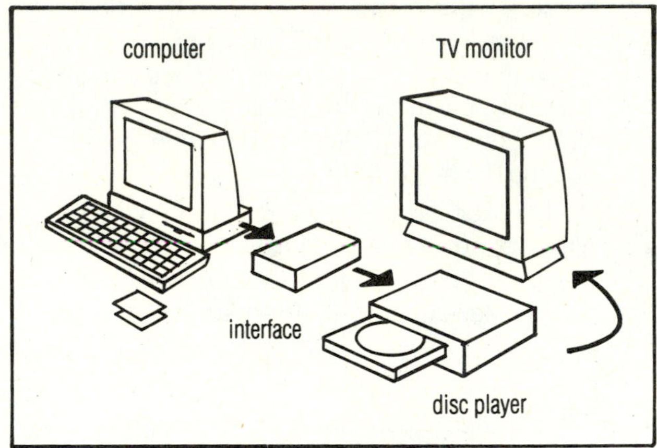

OPERATING INSTRUCTIONS

1. Position the computer, monitor, and video unit in a comfortable position for use.
2. Plug in power cords and connect the INTERFACE cable between the computer and video player.
3. Turn power ON to both computer and player.
4. Boot the computer and load the cassette or disc into the player.
5. Follow procedures to carry out instruction.
6. After completing instruction, remove all course materials, turn power OFF to both units, and if required, disconnect cables and store equipment.

Check Your Skills with Equipment Combinations

Apply the details listed as you practice operating the combinations of media equipment. Each checklist can be used when your performance is evaluated.

Synchronize Slide/Tape

____ Prepare audio recording
____ Load tray with slides
____ Connect cable between projector and recorder
____ Put recorder in sync mode
____ Synchronize all slides to narration
____ Check synchronization
____ Correct improper signals
____ Present program
____ Rewind tape
____ Remove slides
____ Repack equipment

Sound Filmstrip Projector

____ Set up projector
____ Connect to power
____ Thread filmstrip
____ Prepare filmstrip for showing
____ Load audiocassette tape
____ Check sync switch setting
____ Test program
____ Reset filmstrip/tape to start
____ Make presentation
____ Rewind tape
____ Remove/rewind filmstrip
____ Repack projector

Dissolve Slide/Tape

____ Load trays with slides (alternating numbers)
____ Set up two projectors
____ Set up audiocassette player (with sync feature)
____ Set up dissolve unit
____ Connect all power cords to bar
____ Connect dissolver to audio player (for recording advance signal)
____ Connect projectors to dissolver
____ Set power switches on projectors to FAN
____ Load cassette with narration
____ Record advance signals on tape
____ Check sync/dissolve program
____ Correct errors
____ Reverse sync cable, dissolver-player hookup (input/output jacks)
____ Present program
____ Rewind tape
____ Remove slides
____ Repack equipment

Slide/Tape Viewer

____ Set up viewer
____ Connect power
____ Load slides into tray
____ Position tray in viewer
____ Insert audiocassette tape
____ Turn on power
____ Check synchronization
____ Return slides/tape to start
____ Make presentation
____ Rewind tape
____ Remove slide tray
____ Repack viewer

Sound Filmstrip Viewer

____ Set up viewer
____ Connect power
____ Thread filmstrip
____ Prepare filmstrip for viewing
____ Load audiocassette tape
____ Check sync switch setting
____ Test program
____ Return filmstrip/tape to start
____ Make presentation
____ Rewind tape
____ Remove/rewind filmstrip
____ Repack viewer

What You Have Learned About Operating Combinations of Equipment:

1. What feature must an audiocassette recorder have to allow it to synchronize with slides?
2. Describe how you would correct an improperly placed slide-advance signal on an audiotape recording.
3. What is the function of a dissolve unit in a slide/tape presentation?
4. Why is the use of a multiple electrical outlet box or bar recommended with multimedia program equipment?
5. To what matter should you give attention if a filmstrip does not advance in synchronization with the narration when you are testing it?
6. What equipment and accessories are required, in addition to a computer, for presenting interactive instruction involving various forms of media?

See answers on page 384.

MISCELLANEOUS ITEMS

Projection Screens

There are two categories of projection screens for use with media equipment: **front projection** screens and **rear projection** screens. Rear screens are translucent, with projectors placed behind the screen so images can be transmitted *through* the screen. There is no equipment in the room in which the audience watches the presentation. Rear screens are often found in special lecture halls and auditoria.

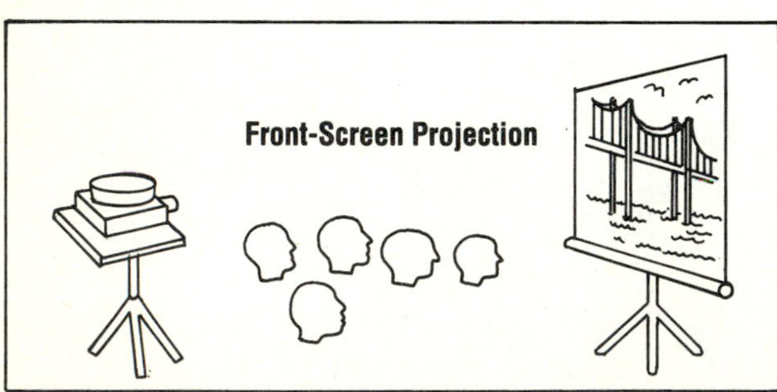

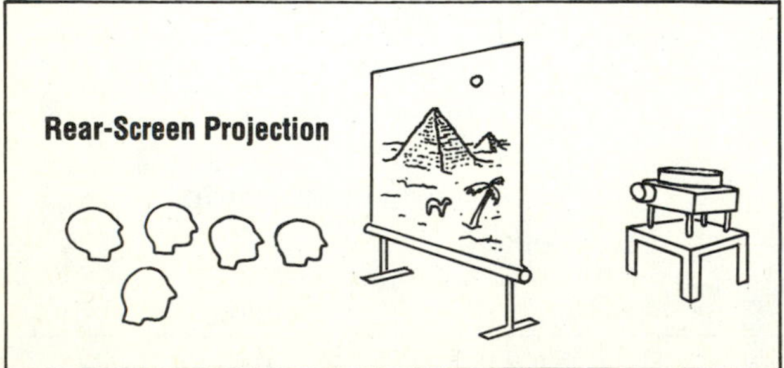

The most widely used screens are front projection types. They *reflect* images of visual media back to the audience, with projectors in the same room. As a substitute, a flat, white-painted wall could serve as a satisfactory projection surface.

Reflected-Screen Surfaces

Reflected-screen surfaces are manufactured for different viewing conditions and are of three basic types: *beaded, matte,* and *lenticular.* A simple way to select a screen is to remember that for long narrow rooms, a glass-beaded screen is best. For wide shallow rooms, a matte screen is preferred. The lenticular screen combines the brilliance of the beaded screen with the viewing angle of the matte screen area. The surface of a lenticular screen is silver rather than white as is the beaded and matte screen surfaces.

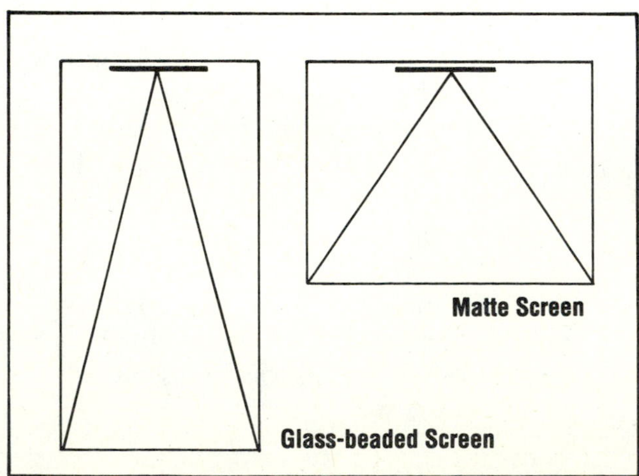

Screen Styles

Wall screens and portable free-standing screens are two major types of projection screens. Wall screens are permanently mounted on the wall in the instructional facility. Some are lowered by hand, others electrically. A wall screen should be mounted high enough to allow the audience an unobstructed view of the images being projected. The type of surface is selected on the basis of the room's dimensions and the viewing angle of the audience, as previously described.

Tripod and other free-standing screens are available in a variety of sizes and should be selected according to the intended use. Tripod screens are popular because they can be collapsed for convenience in storing and carrying. Glass-beaded, matte, and lenticular surfaces are all available in tripod screens.

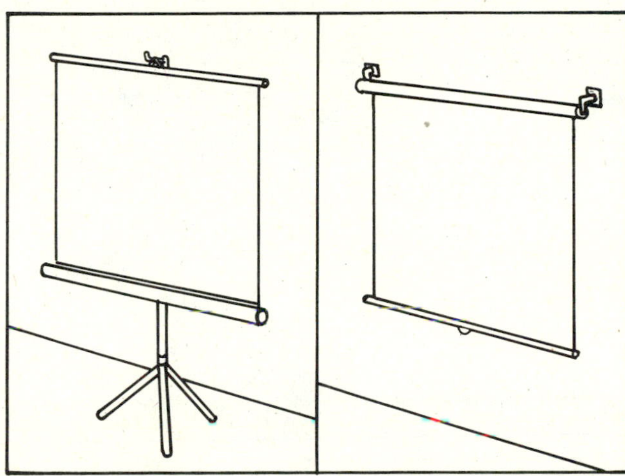

SETTING UP A TRIPOD SCREEN

1. Hold the screen in a vertical position and use your foot to release the leg lock.
2. Spread the legs so they extend out to their maximum distance to ensure stable support of the screen.
3. Next, release the upper extension rod that is inserted into the end of the metal case.
4. Rotate the metal case from vertical to a horizontal position.
5. Rotate the keystone correction bar into place if you intend to use it (see page 338 for an explanation of keystone effect). If not, proceed to the next step.
6. Grasp the handle on the edge of the screen and pull the screen up and hook the handle into the extension rod or keystone correction bar.
7. Raise the extension to the desired height. This pulls the screen out of the metal case.
8. To collapse the screen, reverse the procedure.

Another type of screen, used frequently, is a table-top screen. This screen is used in situations where space is limited and a table is available. It is generally in a wood or metal box, which is placed on a table at the front of the room.

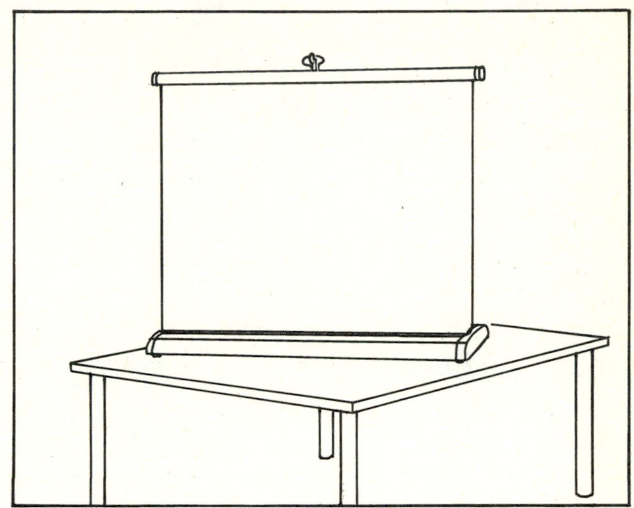

SETTING UP A TABLE-TOP SCREEN

1. Table-top screens have a support board or rod that hinges from the box that contains the screen. Raise the support to its vertical position and lock it into place.
2. Lift the lid of the box and grasp the handle on the top edge of the projection screen and lift.
3. Raise the screen to the top of the vertical support and attach the handle to the hook.
4. To take down and store, simply reverse the procedure.

For information on other specialized screens, consult the ICIA *Equipment Directory* (page 374) or a local media equipment dealer.

Screen Placement

Use common sense when deciding the best location for the screen. Consider your audience, the size of the room, and location of windows. Some windows cannot be totally darkened so you must locate the screen so the least extraneous light hits its surface.

In long narrow rooms, the screen is generally placed at the front in the center of the room. A second location is at the front in one corner, at an angle.

In planning both the screen placement and audience seating, it is best to follow the *two-times-eight rule.* This means that no viewer should be closer than two screen

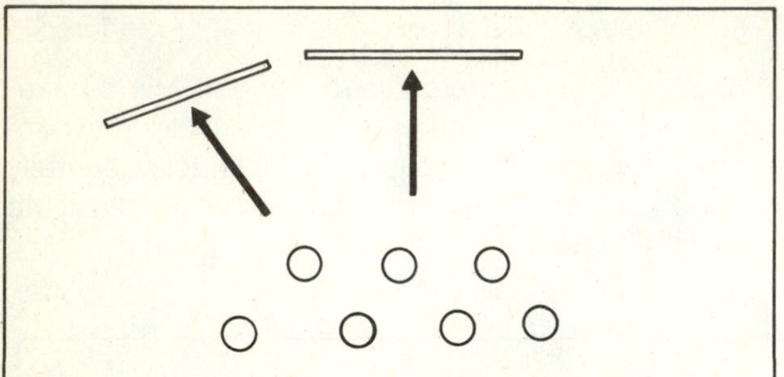

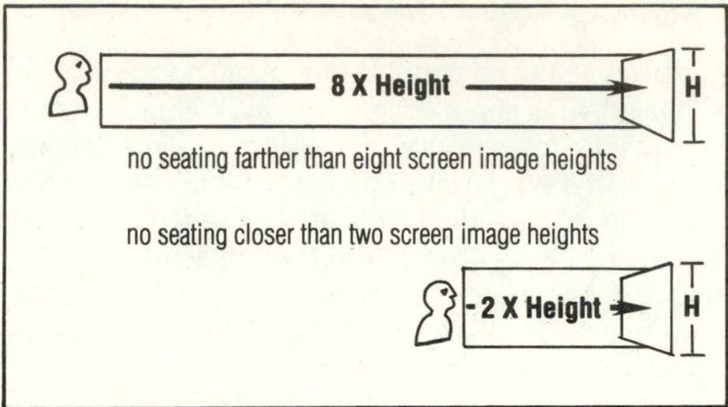

widths or farther than eight screen widths from the screen. An assumption is that the projected image will totally fill the screen. When this rule is followed and materials are designed with the rule in mind, then the readability of printed materials will be adequate for all members of the audience, whether seated near or far from the screen.

Keystone Effect

A keystone is the last stone used to complete construction of a stone arch. Its shape is *wide at the top and narrow at the bottom.* A projected image will have a **keystone effect** (appear distorted) if the projected beam of light is not at a right angle to the screen. Ordinarily, the amount of keystone effect produced does not seriously affect good viewing by the audience.

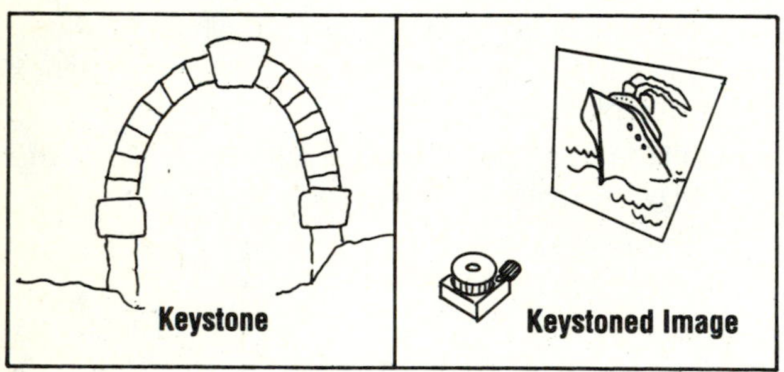

If raising the projector (for example, an overhead projector whose image is susceptible to keystoning) high enough to eliminate keystoning will block the view of the screen for the audience, then a keystone correction device should be used with the screen. It will extend the top of the screen to better form the 90-degree right angle with the projector lens to reflect undistorted images.

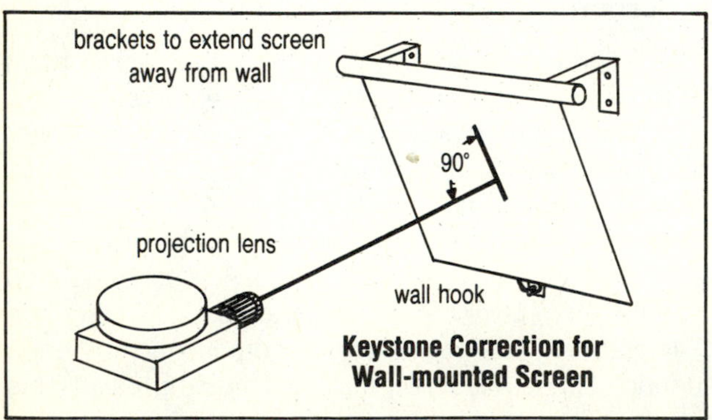

Keystone Correction for Wall-mounted Screen

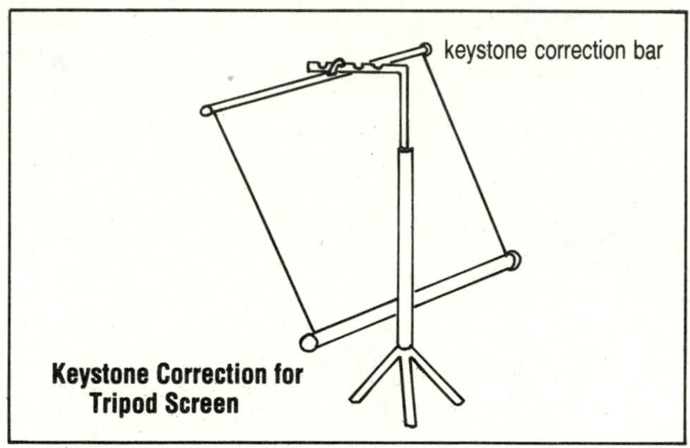

Keystone Correction for Tripod Screen

Projection Carts and Stands

Projection carts have wheels and projection stands have legs that are either detachable or permanent.

The prime consideration for carts and stands is stability. Safety is a concern because many media devices are very heavy and can cause serious injury if they fall on someone. Large TV monitors are especially heavy and, when placed on a 54-inch high cart or table, must be secured. A strap securing heavy pieces of equipment to high projection tables and carts is a good safety precaution.

Grounded electrical outlets and attached extension cords are important features to have on projection carts. A method to store the extension cord should be provided so the cord does not get under the wheels when moving the cart and cause an accident.

Most projection carts are constructed from either metal or heavy plastic. The material is not as important as stability, so select carts based on an evaluation of their merits. Locking wheels are important to secure the cart when projecting in auditoria with inclined floors.

See the reference on safety by Whiting and Kuchta (page 374).

There are dozens of uniquely designed projection carts and stands for many special purposes. Consult equipment catalogs and dealers for information on special purpose projection carts and stands.

Projection Lamps

Projection lamps differ from projector to projector. It is imperative that replacement lamps be the same size as recommended for a given machine. Most projectors have a printed label, attached to the lamp housing or close to it, giving the exact size and code number of the appropriate lamp. Manufacturers of projection lamps supply catalogs listing lamps that are interchangeable between brands.

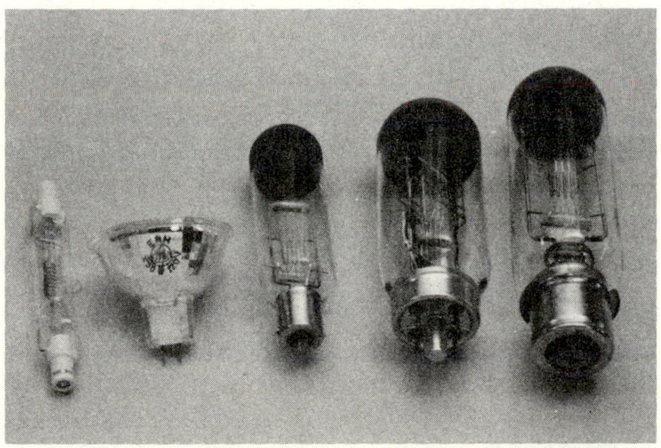

single contact | two pin | bayonet | four pin | medium prefocus

Projection Lenses

The projection lens expands the image to fill the screen and is used to achieve a sharp, clear picture. A variety of lenses is available with different focal lengths. The *higher* the focal length number, the *smaller* the image it projects.

With the right lens, a projector can be placed in almost any location in the room and still fill the screen with the projected image. Zoom lenses (for example, a 4-to-6 inch lens for slide projector) are popular because of their flexibility. Charts are available from lens manufacturers that will assist you in selecting and purchasing the appropriate lens for a specific need.

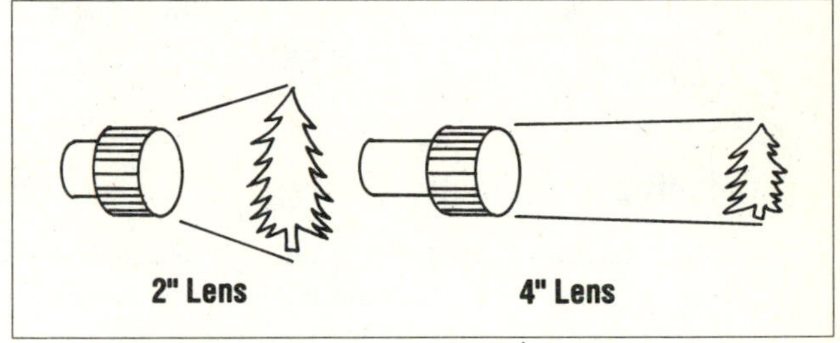

EQUIPMENT PURCHASE

Two specific references are important if you intend to purchase media equipment. The first is the International Communications Industries Association's (ICIA) publication, *The Equipment Directory of Video, Computer, and Audio-Visual Products.* This directory is published each year and is considered the single most comprehensive source of specifications for media equipment. This is not a catalog for ordering equipment, but is a directory of what is available with enough technical information to determine the piece of equipment that should be purchased to do a specific job. The directory does not include evaluations of the equipment listed.

The second reference of value when making equipment purchase decisions are the reports from the Educational Products Information Exchange (EPIE) Institute. EPIE does evaluations on some media equipment and publishes them as reports.

Many equipment dealers are willing to bring equipment to you organization for review and tryout to see if it meets your needs and specifications prior to purchase. You may want to create an equipment evaluation form listing important criteria and specifications with a rating scale and space for written comments. The equipment salesperson is an excellent source of help in learning how to operate and do simple maintenance on equipment. Good equipment dealers will generally insist on teaching you how to properly operate the equipment you purchase from them to ensure customer satisfaction. Be certain that an operator's manual is included in all equipment purchases. When reading the manual, have the piece of equipment at hand and practice with it as you go through the operator's guide.

EQUIPMENT MAINTENANCE

Periodically, all media equipment requires preventive maintenance, service, and possibly repair. The responsibility for matters that require technical or specialized skills should be left to qualified technicians. But such matters as replacing a burned out lamp, cleaning recording and playback heads, and keeping parts or surfaces clean are details of good practice when preparing to use media equipment.

You should become familiar with the following simple maintenance procedures for the appropriate kinds of equipment.

Replacing a Projection Lamp

If a lamp burns out in some projectors, a spare one can be easily switched into position. When it is necessary to remove and replace a lamp in a projector, follow this procedure:

1. Unplug the projector from the power source.
2. Open the housing containing the lamp.
3. Make certain the lamp to be removed is cool.
4. Remove the lamp. Some lamps easily come out of their receptacle when a restraining bar is released. Others require some downward pressure against a spring and a counterclockwise turn to loosen them from their receptacle.
5. Handle a new lamp by its base or with a piece of paper or a cloth. This prevents getting oil from fingers on the glass and thus reducing lamp life.
6. Secure the lamp by reversing the procedure you used to remove it.

Cleaning Record and Playback Heads

The magnetic heads found in audiocassette and videocassette players tend to pick up small amounts of oxide from the tape as it passes over them. In time, the accumulation of oxide can interfere with the recording and playback quality (spots and streaks in videopictures). After about 10 to 12 hours of use, heads should be cleaned.

Cleaning can be done in two ways. If the heads are easy to reach, dip a cotton swab in methyl alcohol and gently rub the cotton tip over each head. Rotate the tip so clean cotton is used and repeat the procedure until no further deposit appears on the cotton. While cleaning the heads, also clean the rollers in the audioplayer around which the tape passes.

The second method of cleaning heads is to use a special cleaning tape cassette that is designed for this purpose. Such a cassette can be purchased for use with either audiocassette or videocassette players. A cleaning cassette can be either a dry or wet type. The dry cassette is easier to use, but may cause wear on the heads.

Cleaning the Film Path

Motion picture film and filmstrips tend to pick up foreign particles relatively easily. Scratches then result in projectors and viewers when the film passes between tight-fitting plates near the aperture, or when film rubs on itself.

With most projectors, covers and film gate can be either opened or removed. Use a soft brush or lint-free cloth to clean the gate surfaces periodically. When an appreciable amount of dirt has accumulated, you will see material around the edges of the projected picture on the screen. Before dirt becomes this apparent, the gate surfaces should be cleaned.

To help avoid dirt on film, keep your fingers off its surface. Handle film by the edges.

Cleaning Lenses, Reflecting Mirrors, and Other Surfaces

A projection lens and all surfaces in or on projectors tend to accumulate dirt. Again, try not to touch any surfaces with your fingers as the oil you transfer to a surface will easily hold dirt particles. If a lens or surface seems dirty, use a soft brush or lint-free, soft cloth to gently clean the surface.

Overhead projectors and other equipment used near chalkboards will pick up chalk dust. Clean not only the exposed surfaces, like the horizontal glass stage on an overhead, but open the machine (after unplugging the power cord) to dust other exposed parts.

By keeping equipment clean, images will appear brighter and the machine will give better service.

What You Have Learned About Using Miscellaneous Items and Purchasing and Maintaining Equipment:

1. What type of projection screen is recommended for a very long, narrow room?
2. Group the terms having similar relationships.

(continued)

Check Your Skills with Miscellaneous Items

Apply the details listed as you practice the following set-ups and maintenance operations. Each checklist can be used when your performance is evaluated.

Set-Up Tripod Screen

____ Release leg lock
____ Spread legs
____ Release extension rod
____ Rotate metal case
____ Pull screen up and hook on extension rod
____ Raise rod to desired height
____ Repack screen
____ Correct projection for keystone effect (using overhead projector)

Change Projection Lamp

____ Disconnect power cord
____ Open lamp compartment
____ Release and remove lamp
____ Handle new lamp (by base, with paper or cloth)
____ Reinsert and secure lamp
____ Close compartment

Clean Recorder Heads (Audio and Video)

____ Locate heads
____ Dampen cotton swab with alcohol
____ Rub over heads until clean
____ Clean rollers
____ Use cleaning-tape cassette

Clean Film Path

____ Open film gate
____ Examine film path surfaces and aperture
____ Clean with brush or cloth
____ Close film gate

Clean Lens and Other Surfaces

____ Examine projection lens for fingerprints and dirt
____ Inspect mirrors and other surfaces for dirt
____ Clean with brush or cloth
____ Close compartments

a. Front projection
b. Translucent surface
c. Rear projection
d. Reflected light
e. Projector in the room
f. Projector not in the room

3. If there are windows along one wall of a room that cannot be fully darkened, where should a screen be placed?
4. What is the *keystone* effect? With the use of what equipment is it often seen?
5. What is the recommended maximum distance from a screen at which members of an audience should be seated?
6. What are two safety matters requiring attention in using projection carts and stands?
7. When choosing a projection lens for equipment to be used from the rear of a large room, which focal length would be appropriate?
   a. 1.5 inch
   b. 3 inch
   c. 7 inch

(continued)

8. How should a new projection lamp be handled when inserting it in place?
9. What two methods can be used to clean the heads in a recorder?
10. What main part of a motion picture projector needs cleaning periodically?
11. How should film be handled to avoid the collection of dirt on it?
12. What reference source can be used for finding out what specific models of a type of equipment are on the market?

See answers on page 384.

CHAPTER

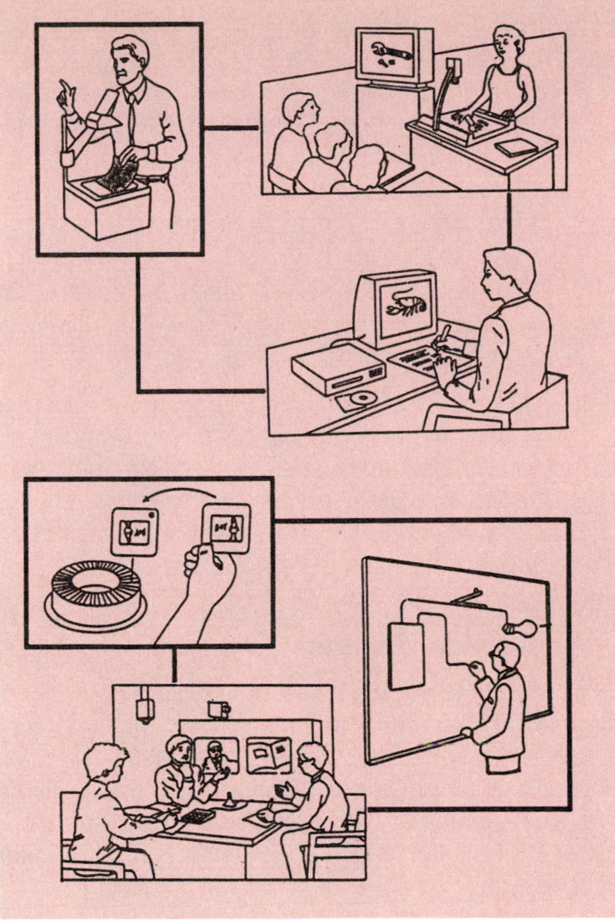

PREPRESENTATION

PRESENTATION

USING STILL PROJECTED MEDIA

USING MOTION PROJECTED MEDIA

USING NONPROJECTED MEDIA

ELECTRONIC DISTANCE LEARNING

POSTPRESENTATION

EVALUATE RESULTS

SUMMARY

Now you are ready to use your instructional media with the intended audience. This is the final activity as a result of your work relating to the content of all previous chapters. Let us briefly review how you have reached this point.

In Part One of this book you gained an understanding of the role of instructional media for education and training. Hopefully, you developed an appreciation of the perceptual and theoretical bases for using media. Then from research findings, you also learned about production factors that can affect the quality and effectiveness of materials design and production.

In Parts Two, Three, and Four you were informed of the planning and production aspects for making instructional materials. Several elements were examined: first, the planning stages, then production skills fundamental to all media types, and, finally, specific production procedures for various instructional materials.

Integrating Technologies with Instruction

Part Five acquainted you first with additional media support matters, namely, locating, evaluating, and selecting commercially produced materials. These activities have been of importance in connection with your production planning and they guided you to choose available instructional materials in direct support of your instruction. Second, you learned the principles of operation for many types of media equipment. And now, we will prepare you to use your media in a communications or learning situation.

On page 4 you were introduced to the instructional design concept in which ten interrelated components receive attention in an effective instructional design plan. Planning for media use builds on these components; therefore, you should have carried out these steps:

1. Considered characteristics of the audience or learners who will experience the materials
2. Identified the objectives the media will serve
3. Outlined instructional activities and decided how the media will be used
4. Selected media type or combination for use
5. Designed and produced materials or located, previewed, and then selected appropriate materials

It may also be beneficial to review the evidence that has been derived from research on the instructional uses of media. These guidelines are summarized on page 32. You should now be ready to prepare and carry out the final arrangements leading to the use of media. These details fall within three phases: *prepresentation, presentation,* and *postpresentation.*

PREPRESENTATION

You no doubt are familiar with your materials, perhaps by your having produced them or having selected items after previewing commercial sources. Now, in preparation for using the materials with the intended audience, review the materials to familiarize yourself with sequencing and details. Keep in mind the audience, objectives, and instructional context within which the materials will be used.

Develop a Plan

Develop a plan that answers the following questions:

1. What preparation should the audience have before experiencing the materials? (Reading, activity, etc.)
2. How will you introduce the materials to the audience, class, or individuals so they are properly alerted as to what is coming? (Outline, questions, problem situation, etc.)
3. What will you be required to do during use of the material? (Show items, stop/start VCR, raise questions, etc.)
4. What will be required of the audience during use of the materials? (Take notes, answer questions, practice a skill, etc.)
5. What should be done after use of materials? (Answer questions, encourage discussion, complete followup activities, etc.)

While explaining the planning stages in Chapters 4, 5, and 6, prior to media production, the subject of solar collectors was used to illustrate an application of each step. The same subject now serves to demonstrate the final phases of integrating media with instruction. See the prepresentation plan that follows on page 346.

Arrange Facilities and Equipment

In addition to making plans for using the media, give attention to the room or other facility in which your materials will be shown or otherwise used. Many technical details may need consideration for successful media use. This applies to both group and individual use of materials. Refer to the operating instructions in Chapter 18 for the specific equipment you will be using.

Group Use

If you are familiar with the room in which the media will be used, it should be relatively easy to get ready. However, if you know little or nothing about the room, or are not experienced with the use of the projection or video viewing equipment, you probably can obtain some assistance. If you must take responsibility for arranging a room and showing the materials yourself, here are some pointers that may make this and subsequent uses of your instructional media successful:

- Visit the room in which the materials will be used. Check for electrical outlets, best location for screen placement, seating arrangements, viewing distances, appropriate placement for the projector and other equipment. See suggestions on page 336. Also find out how the room lights are controlled and, if room speakers are available, how to connect the audio into them.
- Arrange for necessary equipment—projector(s), audio- or videoplayers, microphone, stands, screen, videomonitors, speakers, extension cords, and extra projection lamps.
- If necessary, find out who will assist you with projection, audio, lighting, and other services. Give instructions accordingly.

- ▸ Provide for distribution of handout materials, if appropriate.
- ▸ Provide for the proper physical comfort of the group—ventilation, heat control, light control, and other conditions.
- ▸ Check the scheduled use for the room to be certain you have sufficient time to get everything set up and ready.

Individual Use

When instructional media are designed for individual, self-paced learning, their successful use will be better guaranteed if attention is given to the following:

- ▸ Make sure the media are packaged for convenient use and correctly labeled. Color coding packages and individual items for quick identification is worthwhile.
- ▸ Prepare instruction sheets and guides for media use unless the media are part of a packaged unit of instruction, for example, a study module.
- ▸ Provide a convenient method to assign or check out the materials for learner use.
- ▸ Make available the necessary equipment with which to use the media in a convenient study area.
- ▸ Introduce learners to use of the equipment.
- ▸ Have a qualified person available who can answer questions and give assistance, either while learners are studying or on an assigned-time basis.
- ▸ Plan for each item to be checked after learners finish using the materials, to ascertain its condition and proper placement in the package.

Rehearse

Finally, if you will be using your materials for the first time before an audience, or if you are unfamiliar with the equipment or the presentation room to be used, arrange to rehearse your presentation. Preferably this should be done in the scheduled location, although you might have to practice in another room. In any case, arrange materials for use, and run through your program. This will reveal any details relating to the materials, the equipment, or the facility which may still need attention. Also, by rehearsing you will develop a personal sense of confidence and a smoothness in carrying out the presentation.

What You Have Learned About PrePresentation Preparation:

1. What advantageous knowledge can be gained in developing a plan for your presentation?
2. Why should you be concerned about the facilities in which you will be making a presentation to a group?
3. Which items are important to consider when preparing the room for a group media presentation?
   a. Check room temperature.
   b. Locate room light switches.
   c. Locate where media equipment should be placed.
   d. Know location of electrical outlets.
   e. Find input jack to room audio system.
   f. Check arrangement of chairs for audience.
   g. Ascertain room darkening capability.
   h. Determine place in the room where you will be located as the presenter.
4. Which items are important to consider when using media for self-paced learning?
   a. Easily understood checkout procedure
   b. Instructions for the learning tasks clearly defined
   c. Clearly labeled media materials
   d. Readily available instruction sheets
   e. Information on where to obtain help if necessary readily accessible
5. What are two things that a rehearsal of your presentation will do for you?

See answers on page 384.

Plan for Media Use

Topic:

Construction and use of solar collectors

Learners:

Adults in energy conservation workshop

Introduction:

Instructor introduces topic at first session

Present objectives:
1. To explain how four scientific principles are applied for creating heat in a solar collector
2. To identify four parts of a solar collector and the functions of each
3. To assemble a solar collector when provided with the four essential parts

Show model of solar collector and discuss application of scientific principles for making hot water

Prepare for visitation

Preparation:

Visit two homes to observe solar collectors being used to heat water for house uses and for a swimming pool

Premedia use preparation:

Since small groups of learners will view video recording program when they are ready, equipment and materials will be available on request. Handouts with instructions are prepared and will be used when program is viewed.

Use of materials:

Groups view video recording program and complete worksheets as they move through sections of the program. Discuss answers within group. Instructor available for questions.

Follow-up:

Each group makes plan for constructing a solar collector, carries out construction, and tests it for heating water.

PRESENTATION

Everyone feels a certain sense of excitement and anticipation when he or she is about to make a media presentation to a class or other audience. You may experience similar feelings when individuals start to use your materials on their own. Now, the communication effectiveness of the materials will be realized and can be observed. Two important activities can contribute to successful outcomes:

1. Prepare the learners.
2. Properly utilize the media.

Prepare the Learners

Unless media are designed for casual use (for example, a display) or for entertainment, the learners should be prepared for the experience. During your prepresentation activity, you developed a plan for using the media. Now implement the plan. This should include the following:

1. Introduce the topic or subject the media treats.
2. State the objectives to be served.
3. Point out new vocabulary or concepts that will be used.

4. Indicate what each person may or should do during the presentation.
5. Relate the materials to other activities or course work, helping the learners integrate the concepts to be presented.
6. Describe activities that will follow media use.

The plan for the solar collector topic on page 5 illustrates activities, relating to the preceding items, that would prepare the learners for using the video recording. Review it to see the preparation made for using the materials.

Utilize the Materials

Present the materials and carry out the participation activities you have planned. As you proceed, give attention to two essential matters for successful use.

Your first concern should be your own appearance and behavior before the group. Establish a rapport and hold your audience's attention by employing these public speaking practices:

- ▶ Speak from notes but do not actually read your introduction.
- ▶ Show enthusiasm for the subject.
- ▶ Speak clearly with some facial animation.
- ▶ Control your posture and body movements.
- ▶ Maintain eye contact with various members of the audience.
- ▶ Use gestures purposefully.
- ▶ Project your voice so all can hear, using variety in pitch and emphasis.
- ▶ Use humor and personal references if appropriate.
- ▶ Be brief in your remarks; let the media carry your message.

If necessary, during prior rehearsal, practice these suggestions. Have a colleague evaluate your actions and presentation. Better yet, have someone videotape your trial presentation so you can see and judge your own behaviors. Remember, you need to exhibit some degree of showmanship before the group, especially when you are competing with your own high quality media!

Second, for further success in front of the audience you must handle your materials and operate the media equipment properly and smoothly. This means you are to display items in a natural way; show materials so that images are properly focused, clearly visible to viewers, and with sound volume and tone properly set; and so forth.

See the following sections of this chapter for good utilization practices with specific media.

What You Have Learned about Presentation Techniques When Using Media:

1. What two major activities can contribute to a successful presentation of media?
2. What five matters should receive attention when preparing an audience for a media presentation?
3. What two personal sets of behaviors can help you to make a successful media presentation?
4. What are two ways you can get feedback on your performance during a rehearsal of a media presentation?

See answers on page 385.

USING STILL PROJECTED MEDIA

Each type of media is unique when utilized. In Chapter 18 you were introduced to the basic operating principles of various types of media equipment. In this section, we examine utilization features of the still projected media forms. The following section will treat the motion, nonprojected, and audio forms. Read through the descriptions and practical suggestions for the types of media you will use. Practice the skills as you rehearse your own presentation.

Opaque Projector

Because reflected light is used, the chief advantage of the **opaque projector** is that no special preparation of materials is necessary to show with it. Most opaque projectors are bulky, although manufacturers continue

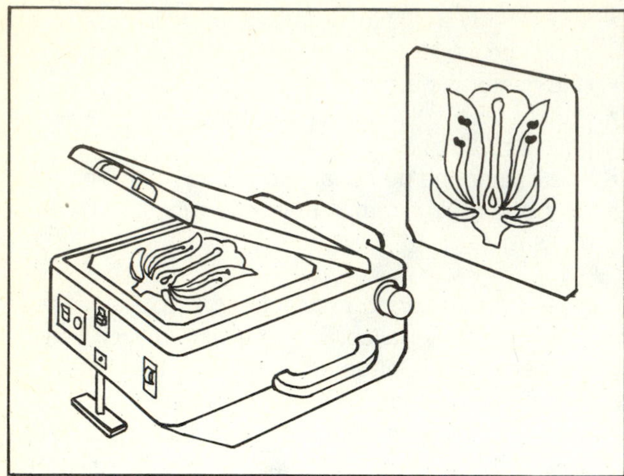

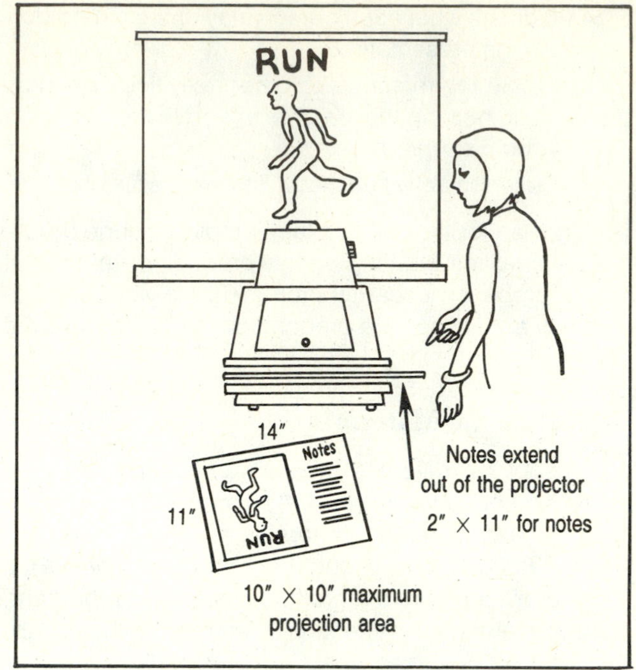

to reduce their size and weight, while improving the design. With some newer units, the visual to be shown is loaded from the top. Older, more common design models require that materials be inserted at the lower backside of the machine. The opaque projector does not project as bright an image as do transmitted-light projectors (overhead, slide, filmstrip, motion picture).

Review the operating instructions for the opaque projector on page 313. The following points should receive attention when you use an opaque projector in an instructional or training situation:

- The opaque projector is often placed in the area where learners are normally seated. You must prefocus and arrange the seating accordingly.
- Because of the excessive heat from the reflected-light source, a sizable cooling fan is necessary. The effect of heat on materials being projected must be considered. You must also decide if the noise level is acceptable for your presentation situation.
- The room must be capable of total darkness since the light output of an opaque projector is relatively low.
- The order of materials you intend to project must be prearranged. If you are using still pictures, they should be mounted on 11 × 14 posterboard to avoid flutter from the cooling fan. Materials can be stacked in order and placed in the projector with the bottom of the visuals toward the screen. The visuals are changed by pulling each one off the top of the stack as the presentation is made.
- The instructor faces the screen. Light from the lamp allows the reading of notes on the edge of materials.
- Most opaque projectors come with a roll-feed device that can be used to roll long materials through in the prearranged order.
- An opaque projector can be used before the audience arrives to project a drawing or map onto the chalkboard. Trace the image using colored chalk. See page 126 for an explanation of this illustrating technique.
- Consider using the lighted pointer that comes as standard equipment on most opaque projectors. This can be a great help in pointing out various aspects of the item being projected.

Overhead Projector

The **overhead projector** is a popular device in support of classroom instruction and other presentations to groups. The primary reason for its popularity is that you, the presenter, can face the audience from the front of the room and maintain eye contact, while projecting transparencies in a lighted room.

Another advantage of the overhead projector is the simplicity of its operation, which allows the presenters total control of their materials without requiring assistance. Most prefer this to their having to coordinate projection with another person. With careful rehearsal, following the operational suggestions on page 314, a smooth, professional presentation can be competently made.

There is a number of ways to make a presentation with the overhead projector dynamic and memorable.

- You can control the rate of presenting information by covering a transparency with paper or cardboard and then exposing the data when you are ready to discuss each point.

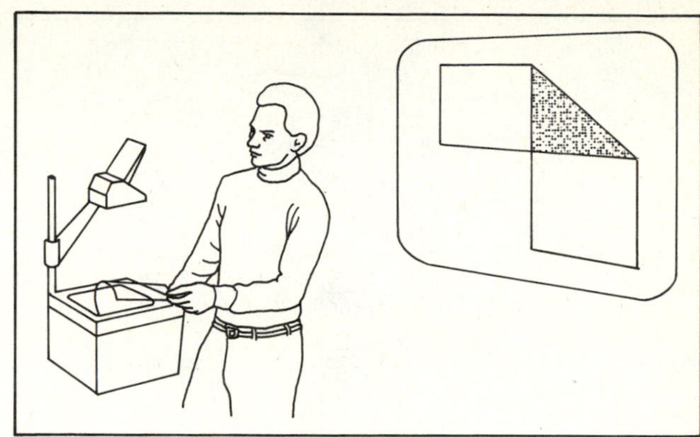

► You can show pictures and diagrams, using a pointer on the transparency to direct attention to a detail. The silhouette of your pointer will show on the screen.

► You can show three-dimensional objects from the stage of the projector—in silhouette if the object is opaque, or in color if an object is made of a transparent color plastic.

► You can use a felt pen or a special pencil to add details or mark points on the transparency during projection.

► You can duplicate on paper the material to be presented as transparencies. Distributing copies to the class or audience will relieve them of the mechanics of copying complex diagrams and outlines.

► You can superimpose additional transparent sheets as overlays on a base transparency so that you separate processes and complex ideas into elements and progressively present them.

► You can simultaneously project other visual materials that illustrate or apply the generalizations shown on a transparency.

Here are some key points to remember when using the overhead projector:

- Select a projection screen large enough for the room and position it so the audience can easily see your visuals.
- Place the overhead projector on a low stand and far enough from the screen so the projected image completely fills the screen.
- Prefocus and size the image on the screen before the audience arrives. Allow for both vertical and horizontal transparencies if needed.
- Preadjust the room lights to turn off front lights that reflect directly off the screen and reduce image brilliance.
- Check to be certain your transparencies are arranged in proper order.
- Transparencies should be mounted in frames for a professional look to your presentation. Frames help prevent damage to visuals and extends their life.
- Framing helps you to position the visuals on the overhead projector stage accurately. Tape a strip of heavy cardboard to the lower edge of the stage and set each transparency against it to further ensure alignment.
- On the frame, write notes, details, and cues that will be useful in your presentation as you show the transparency.
- Do not block the projected light with your shoulder.
- Avoid annoying hand movements over the stage causing distractions on the screen.
- Use a pointer device when making reference to items on the transparency (a pencil works well).
- Turn off the overhead projector while changing the transparencies thus avoiding annoying movement on the screen.
- Do not walk in front of the projected image; you will cast shadows of yourself on the screen.
- Remain at the projector rather than walking back to the screen to point out specific parts on a transparency. If your body is blocking the view of the screen for some of the audience, you may need to make an exception and step back to the screen. If this is necessary, you should use a long pointer, being careful not to touch and damage the screen.

Liquid crystal display (LCD) panels have proven to be effective for use on an overhead projector in conjunction with a computer. This is discussed in Chapter 12 on page 206 and also in this chapter on page 356.

Slide Projector and Slide/Tape Equipment

Slides are very popular for instruction and training because of the realism with which they can depict an object or event, their flexibility, and their relative low cost. Presentations can be updated easily by inserting a new slide to replace outdated content. Many instructors use slides as support for their verbal presentations and prefer to advance slides for themselves using a remote changer.

The 2 × 2 inch slide used in a carousel-type tray is the most popular slide projection system. Slides are often used in conjunction with an audiotaped narration that has been synchronized to the slides. Operation of the slide projector is described on page 315; the synchronized use of an audiocassette recorder with a slide projector is explained on page 330. Following are practices that are essential when using slides in presentations:

- Arrive early and arrange the room so all members of the audience can view the slides without obstructions.
- Set the screen at a high position and the projector on a tall stand behind the seats.
- Fill the screen with the image. Some slide projectors have a zoom lens. If not, physically move the projector until the screen is fully utilized.
- Locate the light switches in the room and prearrange for someone to lower the lights on cue.
- If the slide presentation has a prerecorded and synchronized audiotaped narration, check to be certain the cable connections are working and the slides are advancing on cue. Have a prearranged signal for a projectionist to turn on the slide projector and start the tape player at the appropriate time during your presentation. Try to make this smooth and avoid calling attention to the procedure.
- If the slides are designed to accompany your live presentation, use an extension with remote control so you can change your own slides. Some projectors have a shutter that prevents the glare of white light on the screen at the beginning and end of the pre-

sentation. If your projector does not have a shutter, cut pieces of 2 × 2 poster board to serve as blank slides to block the light and place one at the beginning and the other at the end of your presentation. Leave the projector switch in ON position so you can begin showing your slides without having to ask someone to turn on the projector. You may insert blank slides at any point in your presentation where you want to bring the attention of your audience back to yourself.

- Check to be certain the slides are in correct order and not loaded in the tray so they project upside down or backwards. If a **thumbspot** is placed in the *lower left* corner (when the slide is viewed correctly), then it will be in the *upper right* corner when placed

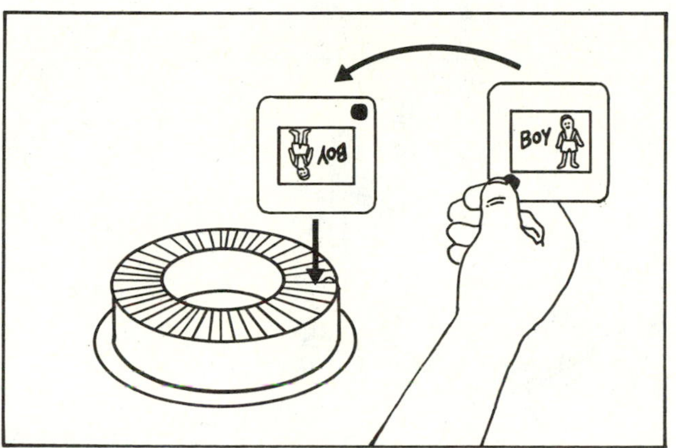

in the tray for projection. Glance around the tray to check the thumbspots. Another technique can ensure that slides are placed properly in the tray. With all slides upside-down, draw a diagonal line across the top edge of all slides. Then, if you find a break in the line, look for a missing or improperly positioned slide. Make certain the ring on top of the slide tray is locked in place if the tray is overturned.

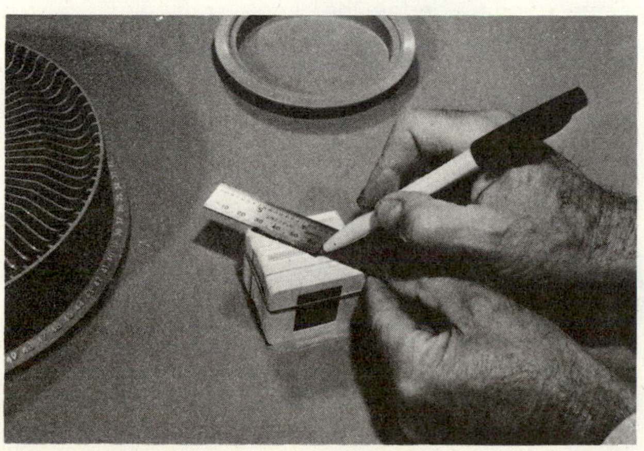

- Don't leave a slide on the screen too long (10 seconds is usually sufficient). If you are not discussing information related to the slide, advance to a blank slide as suggested previously. If you use this technique frequently, provide for subdued room lighting so you can have some visual contact with the audience.

Filmstrip Projector and Sound Filmstrip Equipment

Some filmstrips have the narrative overprinted on each frame, and the learner reads the message as each frame is projected. Other filmstrips have a printed script from which the instructor reads or lectures. The script should be marked with change cues so the instructor knows when to advance to the next frame. Many filmstrips are accompanied by an audiocassette with a professionally produced sound track. One side of the cassette has audible cue beeps for use with a separate projector and audiocassette player. The other side of the cassette has a prepulsed inaudible cue for use on combination sound filmstrip projectors.

The chief advantages of filmstrips over slides are that the pictures are in a set order and the reproduction costs for mass distribution are less. The storage space required for filmstrips is minimal especially when compared to slides that are loaded into carousel trays.

A filmstrip projector is easily threaded. See page 317 for threading instructions and details on how to operate a filmstrip projector. Combination audiocassette and filmstrip machines are common and preferred by many presenters since most commercially available filmstrips come with a prerecorded audio tape. Following are some considerations when using filmstrips:

- Position the filmstrip projector to fill the projection screen through a patch unobstructed by the audience. The lens on most combination audiocassette and filmstrip projectors require that the machine be

placed closer to the screen than the conventional slide projector.
- Prefocus and frame the image on the screen.
- Test the audio to be certain the filmstrip is advancing properly.
- Preset the audio level and be certain the audio synchronizes with the visual. This should be done before the audience arrives to ensure a smooth presentation.
- If the filmstrip has to be manually advanced, be certain the remote advance button is easily accessible. If you advance frames by following a marked script, provide a lamp, or other light, so you or the projectionist can see the marks on the paper.

Laser Pointer

When you want to direct learners' attention to specific aspects of a projected slide or opaque image, use a laser pointer. This device is small, but delivers a powerful laser beam to highlight a part of a subject being shown. It is used by pressing a button after pointing the unit at the screen. When you release the button, the beam goes off. Most units are powered by three or four AAA alkaline batteries that provide at least 8 hours of use.

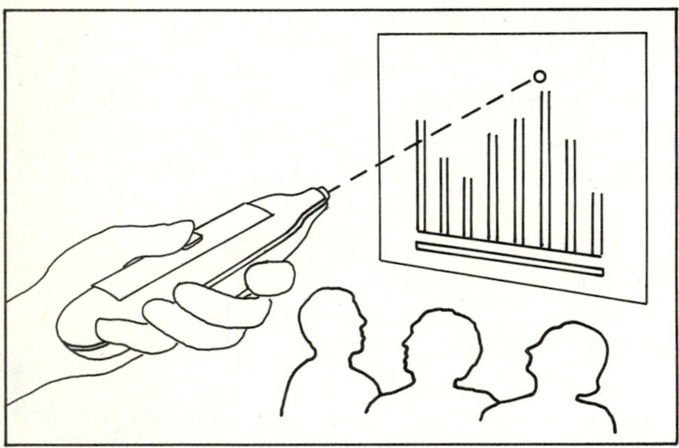

A laser pointer eliminates the need for using a stick pointer or your moving to the screen. Thus, it keeps the presenter from appearing in the beam of the projected light or casting the shadow of a finger on the screen when attempting to point to something.

Multi-Image Equipment

When more than one slide projector is used for a presentation, along with a synchronizing audiocassette player and a dissolve unit, the complexity of the setup requires special care. On page 331 the operation of multi-image equipment is explained. More attention is required for preparing the facility and the equipment when a multi-image program is being used.

Ideally, the use of a facility specially designed for multi-image media could avoid many difficulties. Usually, the equipment is hidden in a projection booth so the audience is not distracted by the sight and sound of it during the presentation. However, if a regular auditorium or room is to be used, give yourself plenty of time for setting up and checking all equipment. There are many details that require attention.

- Preferably, place the programing and projection equipment at the back of the room so the audience does not have to look around or over it. This may require projection lenses with long focal lengths so images will properly fill the screen. If, because of projection distance and size of audience this is not possible, consider locating the equipment in a wide center aisle within the room.

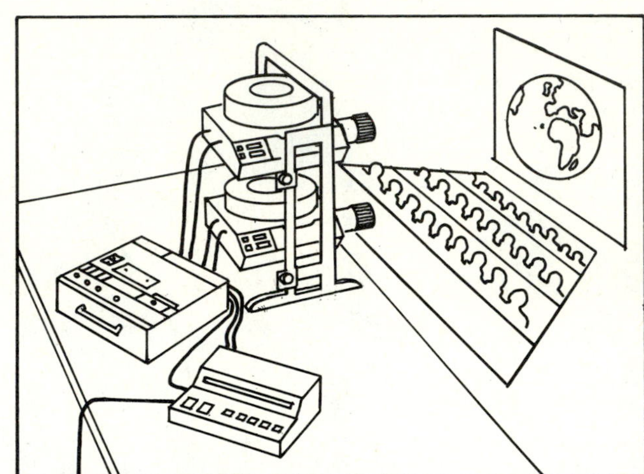

- Place the projectors on very high stands or on the upper of two banquet tables stacked one on top of the other. Special racks can be used to hold projectors securely in position. Having the projectors at this height eliminates keystoning (page 338) and having images blocked by the heads of the audience.
- Check the electrical power requirements of all equipment and be certain the circuit for the electrical outlets can handle the load. Frequently, power from two electrical circuits is required. Use heavy-duty grounded extension cords and multiple outlet boxes to bring power to the location of the projection and programing equipment. Either tape electrical cords to the floor, run them along the wall, or cover them with throw rugs or plastic carpet runners.
- When you plug equipment into an electrical source, make certain that the programer and projector control units (dissolvers) are hooked into the *same* grounded electrical outlet so that any current fluctuations are the same for all equipment. This can pre-

vent one potential cause of miscued slide change signals.

- Use a single wide screen, two or more large tripod screens of the same type (matte, lenticular, beaded) placed side by side, or even a light-colored wall as a projection surface. Another possibility is to use a roll of photographer's white background paper and cut a screen proportionate to the desired projection area. If the latter material is to be used more than once, cover the edges with cloth book-binding tape to extend the life of the screen. Hang the paper by pinning it to the drapes on a stage or tape it to a side wall if movable seating is available.
- Obtain similar model projectors and lenses so the brightness of images will be the same.
- If a room sound system is available, use connecting cords to feed the sound from the tape player to the system's amplifier or directly into the built-in speakers. If a room system is not available, arrange for one or two 12–inch portable speakers that can be placed adjacent to the screen and connected to the output of the tape player. Be sure to secure the speaker cables to the floor.
- Make certain that the room can be adequately darkened, if it has windows. Check the location of all light switches in the room and assign someone to switch them off just before the presentation starts.
- Consider ventilation and temperature control of the room to be used for a multi-image presentation. Multiple slide projectors give off considerable heat and when combined with a large audience may raise the room temperature above what is normally expected.
- Be sure to check yourself and any assistants on the operation of all equipment and rehearse the presentation before the first showing.

What You Have Learned About Using Still Projected Media in Presentations:

1. What are three limitations when using an opaque projector?
2. What can be two advantages for using an opaque projector?
3. For what two main reasons is the overhead projector so popular for use in presentations?
4. Describe at least five ways of using transparencies on the overhead projector.
5. What statements are *true* when using an overhead projector?
   a. Use your hand to point out parts on a transparency.
   b. Have the projector light pass over your shoulder.
   c. Turn off the projector when changing transparencies.
   d. Mounting transparencies in cardboard frames is an unnecessary expense.
6. Why are slides so well accepted as a media option?
7. What can you use to eliminate light from a slide projector reaching the screen when you want to make comments and shift audience attention away from the screen at certain predetermined points in a slide presentation?
8. Where is a thumbspot placed on a 2 × 2 inch slide? Where is the thumbspot when the slide is being projected?
9. Among all still-picture projected media, which type is often available as a commercial product? With what other medium is this form frequently used?
10. Why is a laser pointer useful?
11. Which statements are *true* concerning multi-image equipment use?
    a. Connect projectors to separate electrical outlets to prevent circuit overload.
    b. Connect the sound system from the audio player to room speakers for best sound quality.
    c. Always rehearse a multi-image program before showing it to an audience.
    d. Place the equipment close to an audience so members can feel they are a part of the program.

See answers on page 385.

USING MOTION PROJECTED MEDIA

Film Projector and Videocassette Player

When motion is a significant factor for a subject, then a film or a video recording should be considered for instruction. Chapter 15 is devoted to video production. If you intend to use commercially produced films or video recordings, refer to Chapter 17 for procedures on locating, evaluating, and selecting instructional materials. See page 318, in Chapter 18, for the discussion on operation of film and video equipment.

Films and video recordings have several unique features. They can do the following:

- Overcome time limitations
- Speed up processes
- Slow down processes
- Overcome distance
- Recreate the past
- Stop action
- Provide access to things not normally viewable
- Bring still objects to life through animation

If you intend to use a film or video recording in a presentation, consider the following:

- Never use a film or video without first previewing the material to be certain it fits your instructional objectives.
- Make notes during the preview so you can properly prepare the learners and tell them what to look and listen for during the viewing. Also consider followup activities.
- Provide a sufficient number of videomonitors so no member of the audience will be seated beyond the anticipated legibility limit of words and numbers on the screen—generally 8 feet distance for a 21-inch picture tube or 30 feet for a 4-foot screen.
- Make sure each person in the audience has a clear, undistorted view of the monitor or screen and can hear the sound. This may require that monitors be placed on tall stands and, for a film, a loudspeaker be located adjacent to the screen.

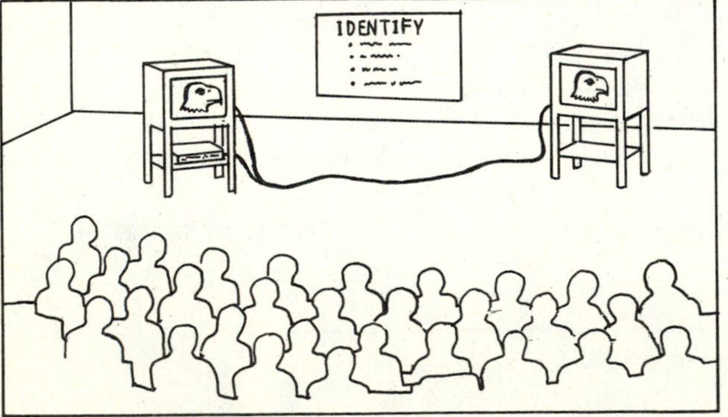

- Control stray light that may fall on the monitor or screen by closing window drapes. If necessary, turn the monitor slightly so that any stray light that cannot be controlled will be reflected away from viewers.
- If you are using a film, be certain you have the matching size take-up reel to receive the film. Before your audience arrives, prethread, focus, and set the sound level on the projector. For videotape, be certain to load the cassette into the player and test the audio level. Adjust controls on all monitors to obtain good quality pictures (steadiness, color, contrast). Have the videotape or film set so once you start the projector or videocassette player, the visual appears immediately. Showing color bars or numbered leader is distracting.
- Locate the light switches and test the desired light level for viewing.
- Check room temperature and ventilation for proper comfort level.
- If someone other than you will operate the videocassette player, meet and instruct the person as to your plan for use.
- After the learners arrive and you are ready to show the film or video, take a few minutes to introduce the material and outline the points to consider on the chalkboard or flip chart, or provide a handout.
- Dim the room lights and start the projector or videocassette player. Make slight adjustments in the audio volume if needed. A roomful of people will absorb a great deal of sound.
- Never leave the room during the film or video. You are communicating a message of disinterest to your learners if you leave.
- Make additional notes during the viewing for followup discussion or activity to ensure comprehension of the concepts you are intending to communicate.
- After the viewing, immediately ask questions and seek discussion on the concepts to determine comprehension and to see if your objectives have been met. You may want to assign followup activities based on the material viewed.
- After the training session or class, rewind the videotape. (Many media rental libraries prefer that you do not rewind films.)

Video Projection System

When using video format learning materials, it is important to provide the learner with an image large enough to allow for proper study of what is being presented. In many situations, a standard TV receiver or monitor is *not* suitable for the size of the audience expected to view the material. Ideally, it would be preferable to use a **CRT** (cathode ray tube) video projector that has three lenses that can deliver a high quality image to a large screen.

Some CRT models are mounted permanently to the ceiling of the training room and are always prefocused and ready to use (see page 324). Other models are placed on a cart that can be moved into any instructional area and aimed onto a standard projection screen. Other video projection systems feature a built-in screen. However, the screen size is generally limited to a width of 4 or 5 feet.

A less expensive alternative to the CRT model is the small, lightweight **LCD** (liquid crystal display) projector. While it may not produce the same level of resolution and brightness, it does offer large video images with acceptable quality. LCD video projectors are portable; some are small enough to be carry-on airplane luggage.

No matter which video projection system is selected, follow good utilization practices when integrating video into your instruction. Be certain to place the projection screen in a location that can be easily seen by the entire audience. Locate the video projector so the entire screen is filled.

Videodisc Player

Videodiscs are a significant medium for instruction and training. Three levels of videodisc are used, and levels I and III more commonly so. Refer to page 287 for information on the disc levels.

A level I videodisc is instructor- or learner-controlled using a touch pad similar to a home television remote channel changer. If you use a well-designed level I videodisc in an instructional situation, it requires that you change your role, from that of a presenter to one of a facilitator of the learning experience, as you work with the learners.

The design for instruction will have been embedded

in the disc as based on extensive preplanning and formative evaluation during the development of the lessons. The power of videodisc is in its branching capability, freeze frame, instant random access to 54,000 frames, dual-sound track, motion, frame step, and other features. The primary instruction is delivered by videodisc freeing the instructor to move among the learners to help with individual problems.

Videodisc levels II and III are primarily used for self-instruction and incorporate a microprocessor in the player, or an interface with an external computer.

Some considerations for effectively using videodisc follow:

- A well-developed videodisc will have documentation and instructor guides. You should study these materials to learn how to use the disc effectively. Not only will your role as instructor be outlined, but instruction for the learner will also be provided. Some videodiscs will have prompts for the instructor and learner incorporated in the disc lessons making them very easy to manage.
- Many videodisc materials can be purchased as a kit, which, in addition to the discs, includes workbooks for the learners, instructor guides, and tests. Using these materials effectively requires that you study all materials in advance and plan your approach.
- Arrange the instructional area so all learners can view the television screen in an unobstructed manner. Be conscious of your body placement when using level I videodiscs because you are among the learners and you do not want to block anyone's view of the TV receiver.

Barcode Reader

This is a device that improves the utilization of videodiscs. With the barcode reader, the integration of videodisc materials into instruction is convenient, smoothly carried out, and can be enjoyable for both instructor and learners. The barcode reader is programmed by scanning a preprinted barcode that loads commands, which in turn can activate the videodisc player. For information on how to create barcodes, see page 286.

Once prepared, the barcodes should be adhered to your lesson plan outline so you can scan them at the appropriate point in your instruction. Some instructors adhere the barcodes in the margins of textbook pages containing information they want to reinforce with visuals from a videodisc. Barcodes can be adhered to the frames of overhead transparencies if you are making a presentation and want to shift to a videodisc-based motion sequence at a certain time.

The barcode reader frees the instructor from using the videodisc touch pad and referring to a list of frame numbers. This can be awkward and cumbersome during a presentation. To learn how to operate the barcode reader, refer to page 322 in Chapter 18.

Video Presentation Stand

A video presentation stand allows you to show real objects, still pictures, 2 × 2 slides, overhead transparencies, and even external video materials on a TV monitor. The presentation can be shown on a large screen providing the unit is connected to a video projection system.

This device looks like an overhead projector except it has a small video camera where the mirror and lens assembly is normally located. A pair of auxiliary lights is available to improve the quality of opaque items being transmitted. The zoom lens provides flexibility for closeup shots when placing pictures or real objects under the camera. The stage has a built-in illuminator for use with 2 × 2 slides or transparencies. For other features of this device, refer to the equipment manual.

A video presentation stand can be used in electronic distance education (page 367) by incorporating it into a video-based teleconference system. It also may be used in large classrooms or an auditorium, allowing the instructor to visualize concepts with ease. To integrate the variety of resources this device is capable of transmitting one must be organized, being certain materials are in proper order for use.

Computer, Electronic Data Display, and Video Projection

Computer-generated images can be displayed with both a still-picture projector and a video projection system.

Electronic Data on Overhead Projector It is possible to have information that is stored in computer memory, or data instantly prepared at a computer terminal, displayed before a group. One method is to use a *liquid crystal display* unit (LCD), connected to the computer output and placed on the stage of an overhead projector. See page 206 for a description of this application.

Planning meetings can be expedited by using a computer and an LCD panel on an overhead projector. As points are made by the participants, a typist inputs the material for all persons in the room to see, thus allowing reactions and more input on the subject being discussed. Changes are easily made as new suggestions are considered. Enlarged copies of key items can be made using a poster maker (page 360) and then displayed on the wall for later reference. If a plain paper copier is available, at the end of the meeting the participants can have copies of the proceedings for further use and study.

Electronic Data with Video Projection Another technique that can be used to support a presentation utilizes a microcomputer connected to a standard videoprojection system. Video projection makes it possible to project large video images that allow sizable audiences to view visuals that have been created and stored on computer disks. This communication procedure is often called a **desktop presentation.**

To use this presentation technique, the presenter loads the disk into the microcomputer prior to the beginning of the presentation or training session. The presenter simply calls up the needed visual support materials by typing commands into the microcomputer or selecting from a menu using a mouse, as the presentation progresses. Full-color still pictures, lettered outlines, charts, and graphs appear as needed on the screen. Animated sequences can be called up to support a presentation. The computer can also interface with videodisc or videotape sequences, creating a very convenient and impressive experience for the learners.

This presentation method does require extensive preplanning, including storyboarding (page 65) or flow charting (page 280) the information to be presented. Moreover, the careful selection of examples, illustrations, and applications is necessary.

Dedicated Presentation Device with Video Projection

A presentation can be created on a home or office computer and the data stored in a *dedicated* presentation device (designed only for a specific application, such as 2 × 2 slides) for later delivery in the form of an electronic "slide show." Such a unit reduces the size and amount of equipment needed when traveling to a distant location for making a presentation. The device is connected to TV monitors or used with a video projector.

Some LCD panels have a built-in microprocessor that can store computer-generated data. This eliminates the need for a separate computer during your presentation.

When using any of these devices, be certain to apply good utilization practices as previously stated.

High Tech Teaching Stations

Ease and convenience are key factors in helping instructors to use learning resources when teaching. Many training departments and universities are equipping classrooms and training centers with technology-based podiums that may be called **High Tech Teaching Stations.**

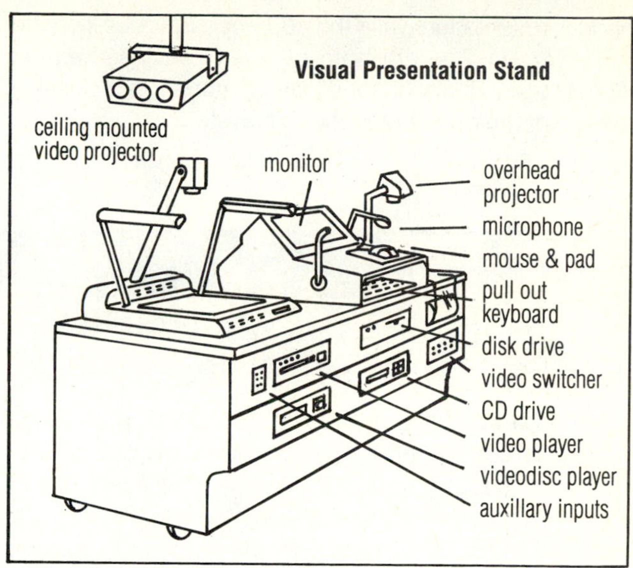

These teaching stations range in cost depending on the capabilities built into the system. Most have a computer connected to a video projection system mounted on the ceiling of the room. Other stations may include a videotape player, videodisc player, visual presentation stand, and a compact disc player. Also, an overhead projector may be mounted on the stand.

The high-end system has a **wireless touch panel,** which allows the instructor to simply press the appropriate label on the panel to control room lights, and to start or stop a specific piece of presentation equipment located on the stand or elsewhere in the room (like a slide projector at the rear of the room).

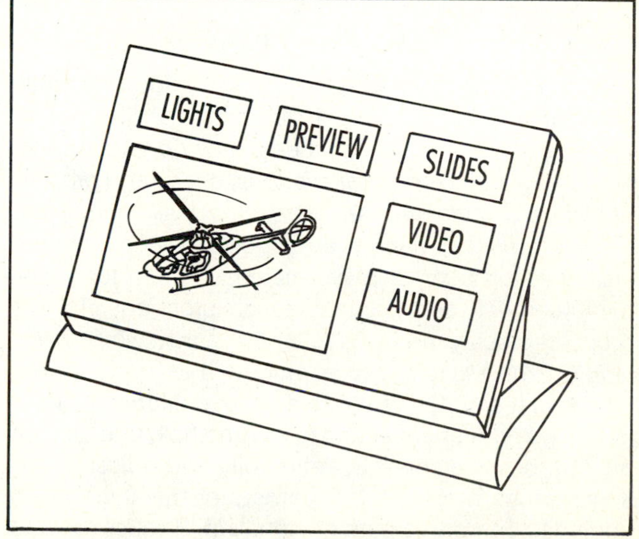

Some panels include a video monitor built into the touch panel so the instructor can control and view his or her presentation while the audience watches it on the room screen. The ability to privately preview the next visual segment on the touch panel monitor is a positive feature of the more sophisticated systems.

As systems of this type become more common, and the ease of integrating multiple learning resources into instruction is simplified, the quality of instruction and training should improve.

What You Have Learned About Using Motion Projected Media in Presentations:

1. List five unique features of motion-picture film and videotape recording.
2. Which statements indicate good practice when using a film or videotape recording?
   a. It is a good practice to introduce a film to the group before starting to show it.
   b. If you have read a review of a film, it is probably not necessary to preview it.
   c. Probably two TV receivers are suitable for an audience filling a room 40 feet long.
   d. Have the film or tape run to the point where the visual starts when you turn the equipment on to show it.
3. What do you communicate to an audience if you leave the room during the showing of a film or videotape recording?
4. Differentiate between an LCD and CRT video projector.
5. Describe the difference between using a videodisc and a video recording in a classroom.
6. How does a barcode simplify the choice of sequences on a videodisc?
7. What is the most unique feature and advantage of a video presentation stand?
8. How would you show data from a computer program to a large group so everyone can see the information as you discuss it?
9. If you are conducting a meeting in which information is presented, discussed, and revised, with what technological resources can you conduct and conclude an efficient meeting?

See answers on page 385.

USING NONPROJECTED MEDIA

When an instructor or speaker is to address a small class or an audience (up to 25 persons), the use of some type of nonprojected media may be appropriate. This category includes *still pictures*, *charts* and *graphs*, *chalkboard*, *multipurpose board*, *other wall boards*, and *cloth boards* (felt, flannel, and hook-and-loop). In each instance, the user displays materials, often for visual reinforcement, as the presentation proceeds. To this group of display media used by a speaker, we add *bulletin boards*, *exhibits*, *realia*, *models*, and *mock-ups*.

These media forms may be used in informal yet dynamic ways. A speaker can focus and hold attention on an item being displayed, yet modify and adjust a presentation as it proceeds. Learners or members of an audience can participate by handling, discussing, and showing materials.

Many of the skills described in Chapter 8 can be utilized when preparing nonprojected materials. Particular reference should be made to these sections:

- Illustrating, including enlarging and reducing techniques (page 124)
- Procedures to ensure satisfactory legibility of lettering for nonprojected materials (page 132)
- Lettering techniques and aids suitable for preparing non-projected materials (page 136)
- Dry mounting techniques to preserve and display pictorial materials (page 143)

Another group to be discussed include *simulations* and *games*, which are more time consuming and require preplanning.

The last medium to be reviewed in this chapter is *audio*, a powerful but often underestimated instructional resource.

Still Pictures

Well-mounted still pictures continue to be a fine medium for instruction. Size is a factor that should be taken into consideration when using them since the audience must be able to see the detail depicted. Still pictures are used with small groups of learners and also are excellent for display purposes. Page 141 provides detail on mounting flat pictures.

Commercial sets of still pictures are available, but should be carefully evaluated to ensure they meet your instructional objectives.

Following are some things to consider when using still pictures:

- Be certain the pictures are large enough for the group viewing them if you intend to display them at the front of the room.
- Acquire an easel to display the pictures. Free-standing or table-top easels are available. Be certain the easel is high enough to allow for unobstructed viewing by the learners.

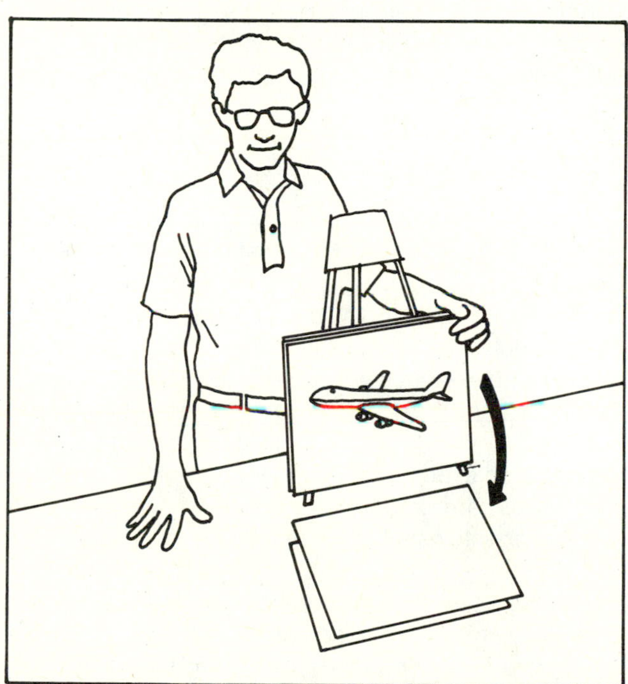

- It may be a better use of still pictures to pass them around among the learners for close inspection if the pictures are small. Consider, however, the potential distraction from your presentation that this will create.
- A good utilization technique for a series of still pictures is to mount them all on a standard-sized posterboard. Stack them in correct order and place all of them on an easel. As you finish discussing a picture, simply flip it down onto a table in front of the easel.
- Some commercial, still-picture sets come with printed information mounted on the back of each picture to help you in discussing the content. You can

add your own notes to the backside of locally collected or produced still pictures. As you instruct, hold the picture up high, to your side but out in front of you enough so you can read the notes on the back. This technique contributes to a professional presentation and eliminates holding notes or glancing down to see them.

Charts and Graphs

Charts and graphs have proved very useful for explaining technical information. Page 127 has details for producing charts and graphs. Graphs and charts can be mediated through slides and transparencies or prepared on large paper, poster, or cloth-based material. The latter method of using charts and graphs will be discussed here. Flip charts mounted on large easels are very useful for both preprepared outlines and for spontaneous lettering using felt pens.

The following tips for making effective use of charts and graphs may be helpful:

- Stand to the side of the easel facing the audience when you use a flip chart. As you write on the flip chart, practice standing to the side and reaching across so your body blocks as little of the writing areas as possible. Talk to the audience, not to the easel, when using charts and graphs.

- Lettering on flip charts and graphs should be large, legible, and kept to a minimum. Printing is preferred to cursive writing.
- Use felt pens with a broad tip to ensure legibility.
- Consider color felt pens to design your message so the audience can follow it with ease.
- If reference needs to be made to charts already shown, tear them from the pad and tape them to the wall at the side of the room as you move through your presentation.
- Flip charts, prepared in advance and then shown as each is needed, will save time. This may be more efficient than writing on a sheet as the presentation proceeds.
- Small, lightly penciled lecture notes can be written on the edges of the charts, which can be seen by you but not by the audience. This frees you from having to hold notes in your hand and gives a more professional look to your presentation.

Poster Maker

Electronic devices that create 23 × 33 inch posters from originals on 8½ × 11 inch sheets of paper are available to speed the process of creating posters and flipcharts for display on the wall or for use on an easel. Prepare the original by hand or with computer software on paper, being sure to use bold, legible printing or type fonts.

A choice of several color combinations of receiver paper is available in 23-inch rolls. Load the receiver paper into the poster maker. Place the original face down into the slot provided, turn on the power, and press the print button. The original is scanned and an enlarged poster-size copy emerges in seconds. Banners can also be produced by following instructions.

Some receiver papers are heat sensitive and should not be mounted using a heat process (page 143). Also, heat sensitive papers should not be displayed in direct sunlight.

Chalkboard

Chalkboards are familiar to all of us; however, many instructors do not use them to their full potential. With a little preplanning, a number of techniques and tools can be developed to assist you in utilizing the chalkboard more effectively. Key words, outlines, lists, diagrams, graphs, and sketches are some of the visual and verbal items that can be written or drawn on the chalkboard.

For success in using the chalkboard, planning what will be displayed and employing simple preparation techniques are important considerations. Here are some suggestions:

- Plan to build explanations on the board, point by point, as the presentation proceeds.
- Prepare by writing or drawing lengthy materials on the board before the class or meeting is to start. Cover with a pull-down projection screen or paper held with tape; remove when ready to use.
- Place a few dots across the board in advance of use so that a line of writing will appear level.
- Use light chalk marks to place lines for guidance in drawing complex diagrams.
- Use templates made of plywood or heavy cardboard for tracing frequently used shapes.
- Use colored chalk, with a strong and intense color, to highlight parts of a diagram or important words.
- Be considerate of your audience and write large enough so those at the back of the room can read the material. Be sensitive to keeping lines straight and write slowly enough to be legible.
- Work on your body position in relation to the chalk-

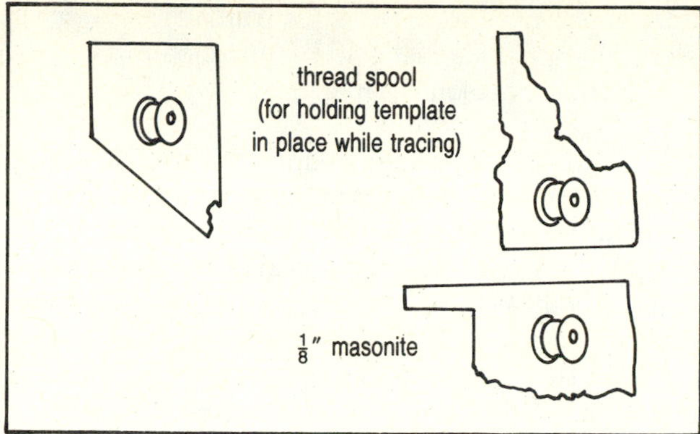

board and your audience. Avoid excessive blocking of the board.

- A fun and effective chalkboard technique is called the **pounce pattern.** It is used to improve the quality of your drawings on the chalkboard. If you anticipate needing a chalk drawing during a presentation, make a pounce pattern by enlarging the drawing (using the opaque projector) on a piece of thin posterboard or oak tag, then punch holes with a sewing pattern wheel all along the lines. Before class, place the pattern on the chalkboard and pounce chalk dust through the tiny holes using a dusty eraser. This method leaves a very light pattern on the chalkboard that you can see but the audience doesn't know is there. When you need the drawing, simply connect the dots and you have prepared a neat, professional drawing.

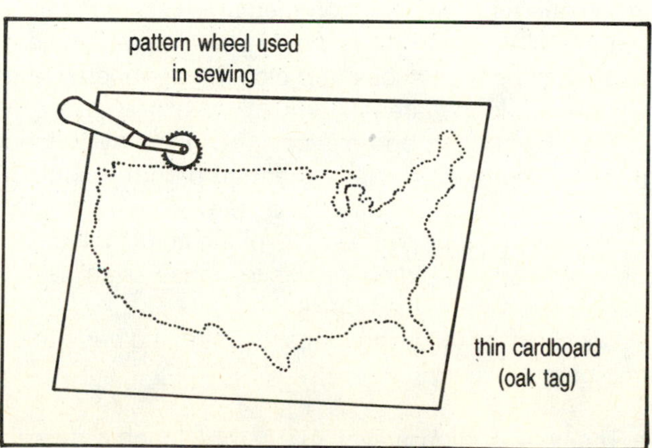

- Some chalkboards are constructed for multiple use. They have a metal base and will hold small magnets. Pictures, word strips, and other visual materials can be displayed with a magnet glued to the back, which will hold the material on the chalkboard. Chalk can be used to write additional material or lines can be drawn to interconnect the magnetic materials. This board often is called a **magnetic chalkboard.**

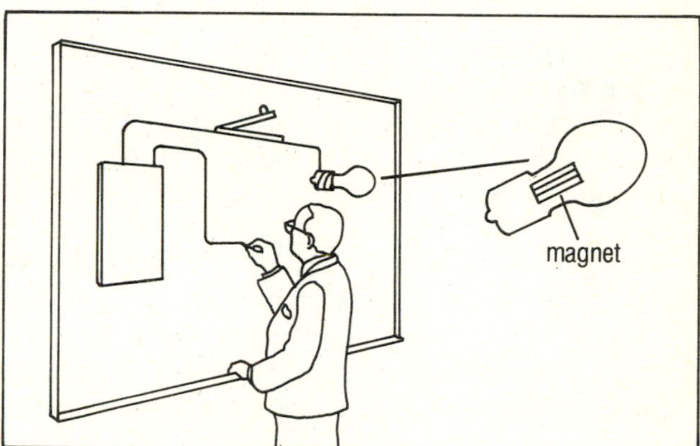

Multipurpose Board

Sometimes called whiteboard or markerboard, a **multipurpose board** is used with special felt pens. It is especially important in computer laboratories or other areas where chalk dust would be a problem. These boards can be erased just like chalkboards but have the added advantage of displaying bright, colorful lines with no dust residue. Some special considerations for multipurpose boards follow:

- Special semipermanent pens can be used to put a base illustration, such as a map, on the board that can only be removed with a special solvent. The standard markers can then be used to add information to the map. You erase the information without disturbing the base map. This technique is excellent when teaching music. The staff can be put on the board using the semipermanent marker and the notes using the standard erasable marker.
- Magnets can be used on many multipurpose boards that have a metal base.
- When writing on a board, print large and legible letters.
- Use colored felt pens to your advantage as an effective communication tool.

- Place the board high enough and in a good position, so it is easily seen by all members of the audience.
- Keep your message simple. Limit the information to one concept at a time.
- Use tracing templates as suggested for the chalkboard and described on page 360.

Other Whiteboards

There are several variations of the conventional whiteboard that you may find useful. One consists of thin sheets of a white "plastic-like" material that is torn from a pad and adhered to most walls by rubbing the surface to create static electricity. You use conventional whiteboard markers to write on the surface. Marks are erased normally, and the sheet is reused. A prepared display can be rolled and saved for future use. Several companies make this material and it can be purchased at office supply stores.

Entire walls can be converted to writing space by purchasing modular, dry-erase panels that fit together to create an expanse of writing area for use in training, planning meetings, and research development.

Electronic whiteboards are available with a component that, at the press of a button, prints out an 8½ × 11 inch paper copy of the information written on the board. A scanner traverses the surface of the board, digitizing the content, and reducing it to standard paper size. A copy emerges at the bottom or side of the board. Copies can then be duplicated for those in attendance at the meeting.

Cloth Boards

Felt and Flannel Boards The fuzzy surface of a **felt,** or **flannel, board** allows visual materials with appropriate backing material to adhere. A variety of materials will hold to felt and flannel boards, including the following:

Sandpaper	Felt	Yarn
Pellon	Flannel	Styrofoam
Pipe cleaners	Blotter paper	

Some materials adhere better than others, and it does help to lean the felt, or flannel, board back at a slight angle when presenting. It is best to cover the entire back surface of items to be displayed, so maximum friction is created when the materials are placed on the board.

The ability to move visual materials around on the surface of a felt or flannel board makes this medium popular for storytelling. Felt and flannel boards are also excellent for displaying word strips and can be used with audiences of any age, even though many people think of it as a medium used only with children.

Consider these ideas when using felt and flannel boards:

- Position the board so the audience can see it and provide a comfortable place for yourself to stand or sit.
- Felt and flannel boards are small group media so you may want to sit down as you present, with learners seated on the floor or on chairs in a semicircle.
- Secure the board on an easel or lean it against a solid surface so it will not move during your presentation.
- Have your display materials prearranged in proper presentation order.
- As you place items on the board, press them against the cloth and shift the materials slightly to cause the two surfaces to interact and adhere.
- Talk to the audience, not to the board, and maintain eye contact as much as possible.
- When not in use, store materials in a marked box to keep them clean and prevent them from being damaged.

Hook-and-Loop Board **Hook-and-loop boards** are used in similar fashion to felt and flannel boards but are unique as a presentation medium. This material is also called Velcro and has many commercial applications. Fasteners on shoes and clothing are often made of hook-and-loop material.

A hook-and-loop board is covered with a nylon loop material. The nylon hooks are adhered on the back of the instructional materials to be displayed on the board. It only takes a small piece or two of the hook material to provide enough holding power to cause even heavy materials to stay on the board.

Consider the following ideas for using the hook-and-loop board:

- The hook portion is available in rolls 1 inch wide with

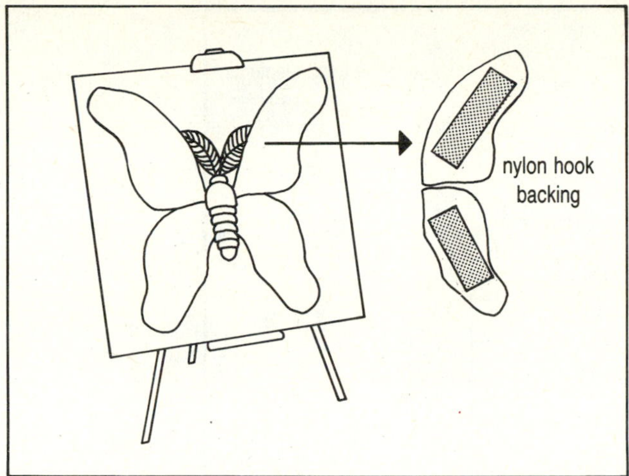

adhesive on the back. Cut a small piece, peel off the protective paper to expose the adhesive, and stick it to the back of the item you want to place on the board. Surprising amounts of weight can be placed on a hook-and-loop board.

- Consider real things, not just pictures and poster-board items. As an example, hook-and-loop is used to teach the proper way to set a table. Dishes, glass, knife, fork, and spoon can all be placed on the board in proper arrangement. Tools being discussed in shop classes can be displayed.

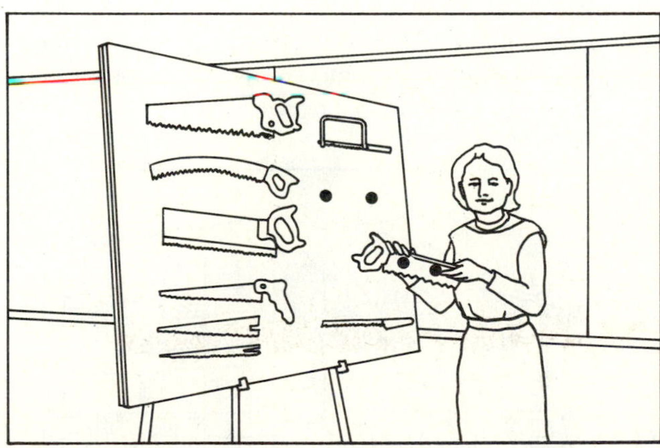

- The same suggestions outlined for using felt and flannel boards should be considered when presenting with a hook-and-loop board.

Bulletin Board

Bulletin boards are generally not used directly in instruction but tend to be a supplement. They often serve to introduce or follow up content presented in the classroom. Bulletin boards are also commonly used as self-instructional devices designed to carry a message without the presence of a live instructor.

The term bulletin board came from their early use as a place to post announcements and other informational items. This is still a good use of bulletin boards, but in an educational setting they can be used as a more direct instructional medium.

Placement of a bulletin board is critical. Opposite a door entering a classroom or training center is a good location. The best way to catch the eye of the learner is to use good design and appealing graphics. It is also important to change the board at least every two weeks as it does lose its attraction after people become familiar with the display. It is appropriate to leave a board blank for a period of time, so when you do display something it will be noticed.

The following list may give you some ideas on how to effectively use bulletin boards. See example, page 364.

- Try to make your bulletin boards informative. Some people consider them as decorative and in one sense of the word they are, but they should still carry a message that impacts the learner in some way.
- Some boards are designed to motivate the learner to seek additional information on a subject. You may want to use a motivational board prior to beginning a unit of instruction to create curiosity about the topic.
- Production of a bulletin board is time consuming, so you should preserve the materials so they can be used again. Between uses, devise a good storage and filing system so the life of the material is extended.
- Refer to Chapter 8 for information on visual design, layout, and production techniques that will help you create quality bulletin boards.
- Select three-dimensional objects or create a three-dimensional appearance from flat pictures by raising them from the surface with blocks of supporting wood.
- Involve the spectator with a question, a guessing game, a contest of skill, or by offering something to be picked up and taken away.
- Use attention-getting devices such as an unusual design, striking color combinations, a startling or unusual leading statement, or moving parts on the board (operated by a motor run by small batteries).
- Use pictures to illustrate the heading, thus reducing the time needed to read words.
- Finally, as you assemble the bulletin board, ask yourself these questions:

How will attention be captured so that interest is stimulated?

How will attention be held until the message has been read completely?

Can the message be easily understood in one reading?

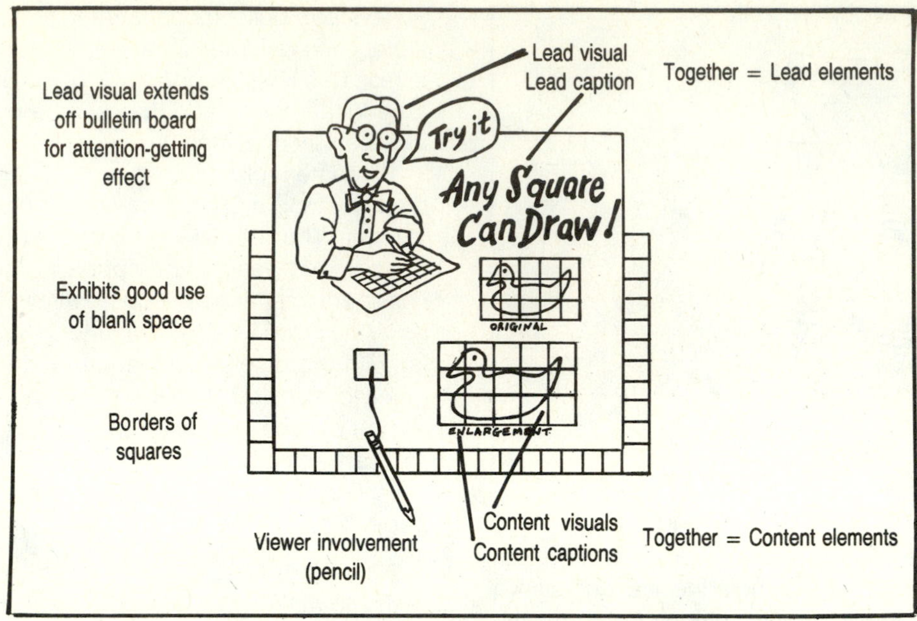

Bulletin Board Showing Squaring or Grid Enlarging Technique

Exhibits

Exhibits differ from bulletin boards because they are considered permanent. Display materials are attached to a backing surface called the *vehicle.* Attachment can be with screws, glue, or nails. The vehicle can be almost anything, although common exhibit vehicles are materials such as masonite, plywood, cellotex, foamcore, paneling, and formica. Unique exhibit vehicles could be made of rope, fish line, mesh wire, screening, or plexiglass. Many commercial exhibit vehicles can be purchased. These are generally made to be taken apart and put into a shipping case for traveling exhibits.

Consider the following uses for exhibits:

- Exhibits should be considered in situations in which the content has continuing value but the audience changes.
- Exhibits can be motivational, causing viewers to ask questions and seek answers.
- Use exhibits to teach procedures that seldom change. The exhibit can be placed in the area where the procedure is performed.
- If the exhibit is not a free-standing type, attach it to the wall at a height proportionate to the height of the viewers.
- Exhibits are excellent for displaying real objects and specimens. Objects can be attached to the vehicle using a variety of fasteners. Objects that would be damaged by fasteners can be placed on shelves or in specially constructed plastic boxes.
- Illuminate the exhibit carefully with one or more floodlights, or highlight a key part that can create a feeling of excitement.
- Make sure the exhibit will be located where there is a good flow of viewer traffic.
- Allow the exhibit to remain in place for an amount of time that is suitable to attract widespread attention.
- Project slides on a small rear screen as an integral part of the exhibit.
- Include sound, if appropriate, by having the visitor push a button to operate an audiocassette player containing a continuous-loop tape.

Realia

You might not be aware that **realia,** or real objects, can be instructional media. Historically, they are probably the original instructional materials. Instructors have always used objects to illustrate and teach. Whether rocks used by a geology professor teaching at a university or a pipe valve used by a training instructor teaching at a natural gas company, realia make useful instructional materials. Here are some things to consider when using realia in teaching:

- Does the real object truly show the concept being taught or would some other form of media be better?
- Some real objects are too heavy and cumbersome to carry and hold. Be certain proper safety precautions are used to secure the object.
- Arrange the real object so your audience can see it. If the item is small and durable consider passing it among the audience.
- Some real objects can be enlarged by using an opaque projector.
- Some real objects can be improved for instructional purposes by doing a *cut-away.* The item may be cut in half exposing the internal make up of the object.
- You may want to attach real objects to a display board and label the parts or salient points. Color coding, labels, and arrows may be useful.

Models and Mock-ups

Models and mock-ups are fascinating instructional materials and offer great learning potential. With models and mock-ups, you can allow the learner to examine things often not easily seen in the real thing. Models differ from mock-ups in that a **model** is an exact recreation of the real thing, only smaller or larger for handling or examination ease. A model may be constructed of clear plastic so the learner can see the inner workings of the item being studied.

A **mock-up,** on the other hand, exaggerates certain aspects of the real object to better show parts and how it functions or operates. A good example of a mock-up is a working cut-away made out of wood showing how a piston moves.

Some excellent models can be purchased at toy and hobby shops rather inexpensively. Professional models and mock-ups are very expensive but highly accurate in technical detail. This is especially true of anatomical models used in the medical and health professions.

When using models or mock-ups in instruction, the following points should be considered:

- Because models and mock-ups are expensive, care should be taken to store them properly. When using them be sure they are secured to a surface and placed so they can be seen by the audience and be shown, or operated, comfortably by you.
- You will need to ask the learners to gather around the model or mock-up unless it is extremely large. Prearrange an area for this activity to avoid unnecessary confusion and distractions. An alternative is to aim a videocamera at the object and see it enlarged on a monitor.

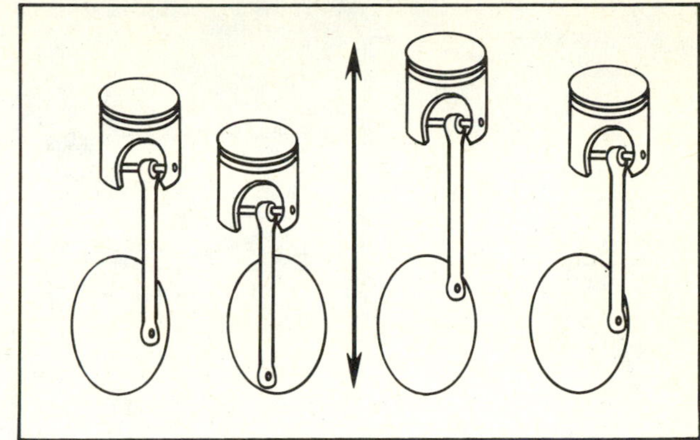

- If the model or mock-up is a functioning one, you may want to allow the learners to handle and operate it. This creates high interest and permits a close-up observation of how it works.
- After your formal presentation, it may be appropriate to leave the model or mock-up on display for a period of time, allowing learners to independently study the item.

Simulations and Games

A **simulation** recreates or represents an actual event or situation that causes the learner to act, react, and make decisions. Simulation allows learning to occur without putting participants into the actual situation. In some cases, the actual situation could be life threatening or simply impossible to experience. Simulation is a technique used in interactive videodisc instruction and computer-based instruction (page 279).

Instructional *games* are formalized simulations that follow rules and procedures. They are designed to be not only enjoyable but also informative, causing the learner to gain insight, experience, facts, and knowledge concerning events and processes. Many games sold for home entertainment purposes have definite instructional uses.

Companies marketing educational materials offer a variety of instructional games that should be considered as resources if they meet learning objectives. Careful evaluation and selection procedures should be used as discussed in Chapter 17.

Games are difficult to design and produce locally. Simulations, however, are often designed and developed by individual instructors to meet specific instructional objectives.

An example of effective use of simulation is in training ski patrol personnel *to conduct a search and rescue avalanche operation.* A large rear projection screen is set up in front of a table where the ski patroller is seated with a radio. An aerial view or drawing of the ski mountain showing the base buildings and all lifts is projected

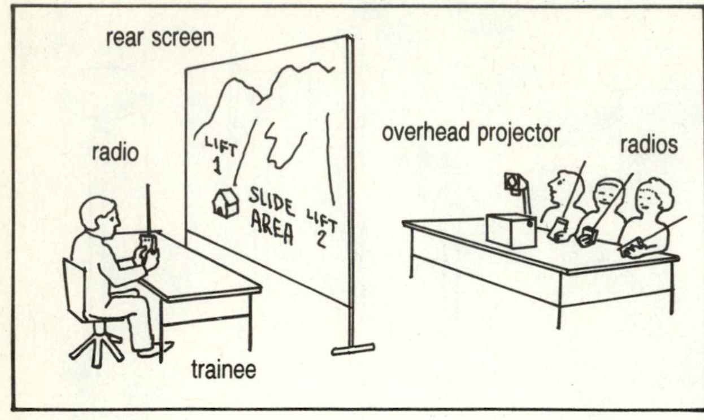

on the screen. Behind the screen is an overhead projector with overlays depicting a variety of scenarios depending on the decisions made by the patroller at the table who is put in charge of the rescue operation. Four other individuals are behind the screen, each with a radio waiting for instructions from the trainee patroller in charge. One person represents area management, another, the ski patrol director, a third, the county sheriff, and the fourth, the hill operations manager.

The trainee patroller at the table is given the following note:

> You are across the valley on a mountain opposite the ski resort doing snow depth checks when you witness an avalanche breaking loose and burying three skiers at the resort. You have a radio but have just broken a ski so you cannot return to the area. You are in charge of the rescue!

This is an example of a simulation that creates many of the same pressures of a real event but is safe for the participants and yet very informative. As the patroller makes decisions and gives instructions, overlays are placed on the screen to depict the results. A wrong decision may result in more skiers being injured or the loss of rescue patrollers. Following the simulation, the participants are debriefed. If wrong decisions were made, endangering other people, these are discussed and correct solutions given.

Utilization considerations for simulation and games include:

- Simulations and games are time consuming to use. You must decide if the instructional time is worth the anticipated outcomes in terms of your objectives.
- When using simulations or games, it may be necessary to divide your class into small groups. Many instructional games have a competitive aspect and you can have the groups compete against each other. Handle this matter carefully so feelings are not hurt.
- Before meeting the learners, review the game or simulation to be confident you know how to manage it.
- Check to be certain all the game parts or simulation materials are on hand. It is very embarrassing to discover materials are missing once the process has started.
- Following the use of the materials, collect each game or simulation part and return it to its proper envelope or box so it will be ready for the next use. Materials for simulation and games have to be managed properly to ensure they will be available for many future uses.

Audio Media

Audio experiences for learning can be provided through audio recordings and records. Operation of the three main types of audio equipment—*audiocassette recorders/players, record players,* and *compact disc* (CD) *players*—is described on page 326. Chapter 9 presents techniques for producing audio materials, and Chapter 13 provides information on the design and use of audio materials for both groups and individuals.

Commercial audiotapes and compact discs are available from a variety of sources. Follow the suggestions in Chapter 17 and do a careful job of evaluating and selecting your audio materials. Never use audio materials to which you have not listened.

Actual use of audio materials involves the following considerations:

- Prepare the audience. You may want to list major points to listen for on a flip chart or chalkboard.
- Have the tape or disc cued to the exact starting point to prevent long pauses in your presentation.
- Preset and check the sound level to avoid embarrassing loud bursts of sound.
- Encourage good listening by asking students to (1) listen quietly, (2) concentrate on the audio, meaning: what is said, how it is said, and what it means, and (3) relate what is heard to prelistening preparation.
- Be attentive yourself. It is important that your audience know you are interested and listening.
- Some audio materials can be used effectively by stopping at certain predetermined points and leading a discussion on salient points. Then, resume the presentation.
- Following the audio instruction, it is important to summarize and discuss what was heard. Having a prepared list of discussion topics or questions for this purpose might be useful to you. Then, it may be appropriate to make assignments for followup activities.
- After the lesson ends, repack and store the materials and equipment.

REVIEW

What You Have Learned About Using Nonprojected Media in Your Presentations:

1. List five graphic-type (uses diagrams, photographs, lettering, and so forth) nonprojected media an instructor might use in a presentation to a small class or group.
2. List five nonprojected media that are used for display purposes.
3. To which type of display media does each statement relate?
   a. Revealing, in turn, a sequence of related items on a portable display surface
   b. Flexible, in that both displaying objects and writing on the surface can take place
   c. Commonly found in most classrooms
   d. Including three-dimensional objects as part of a long-term display
   e. Displaying heavy, three-dimensional objects suspended on a board
   f. Various techniques can be employed: using templates, preplanning with guide marks or lines, and writing in color
   g. A flat surface on which information can be displayed to attract persons passing by
   h. A *pounce pattern* used as a guide for drawings
   i. Using special felt pens eliminates chalk dust
   j. Using readily available materials to make this type of cloth board
4. To which items would you give attention when designing and preparing any display media?
   a. Plan to display each piece of material when it will support the verbal presentation, then remove or cover the item.
   b. At one time, show all the details required for the total presentation so the audience will see everything in relationship.
   c. By employing such eye-catching techniques as bright colors and unusual shapes, and by manipulating objects or writing on the surface, the use of display materials can be enhanced.
   d. Give attention to the size of objects and to printed words so all can be seen by the audience.
5. Why is a *poster maker* such a useful device?
6. What is the advantage of using an *electronic* whiteboard?
7. Define *realia, model,* and *mock-up.*
8. What is the difference between a *simulation* and a *game?*
9. What are four practices that can contribute to the instructional effectiveness of audio materials?

See answers on page 385.

ELECTRONIC DISTANCE LEARNING

In recent years, more opportunities are being provided for young learners and adults to take courses outside of a regular school or campus environment. People may choose to take such a course because of a schedule conflict, travel difficulties, local unavailability of advanced or specialized courses, or the need to conveniently complete continuing or professional education requirements. To overcome these barriers, instructions may be delivered by television from a central site to one or more other locations. All learners, at nearby or distant locations, see and hear the instruction as it is presented. Today, virtually every state and Canadian province has some type of educational plan for distance learning.

Planning Courses

The same principles of instructional design (page 4) that are important in planning and designing other instructional programs are applicable to distance learning courses. Even more attention to careful planning may be necessary because of these special circumstances:

- Instruction provided at many sites
- Requires instructor, local facilitators, and learners to adapt to new teaching/learning environment and use of complex technology
- Must help learners assume more responsibility for their own learning
- Requires understanding and cooperation of facilita-

tors at sites so they encourage and assist students

- Limited, if any, personal contact between instructor and students at outlying sites
- Need to make special efforts to maintain communication (verbally, through materials, with assignments)

Because of these and other circumstances, lesson plans should give careful attention to motivating learners, promoting for *reactive* viewing, and involving learners in a variety of followup *interactive* activities with feedback. See Chapter 17 for suggestions relative to reactive and interactive learning.

Producing and Transmitting Courses

For realism, the instructor usually teaches before an actual class of learners. Video cameras pick up long shots and close-ups of the instructor speaking, writing on the chalkboard, demonstrating, and showing images from overhead transparencies, slides, video recordings, or other visuals. Through an electronic switcher, the instructor, or more often a technician, selects and controls the specific images to be transmitted to receiving sites. Because of the ease of using a variety of resources, more sophisticated instructional strategies than are conventionally used can be effected in distance learning courses.

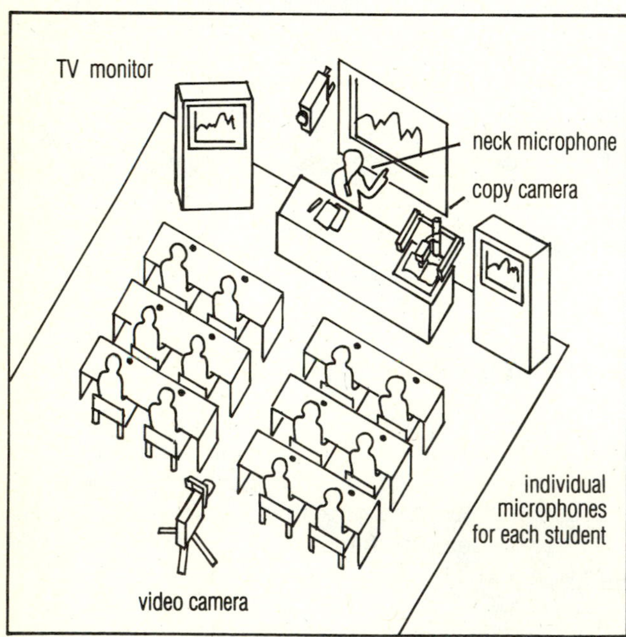

Depending on transmission capabilities, signals may be originated and sent through a network via closed circuit coaxial cable or fiber optics cable, microwave (ITFS—Instructional Television Fixed Service) beamed from a transmitting tower to receiving sites, or by means of satellite transmission.

Copyright Permission When planning and producing courses for distance learning, pre-existing materials (print, video, slides, and other media forms) may be selected and incorporated into a program. If such materials are protected by copyright, then permission for their use *must* be obtained from the copyright owner. This means that clearance is required before including the material in the course program and also for the right to transmit it to other locations.

Most producers and distributors of commercial materials have licensing policies that indicate the costs for using their materials. Cost may relate to the size of the anticipated viewing audience, number of planned uses, and rights to record a program containing the copyrighted materials off-the-air. Obtaining copyright permission will take time, so plan correspondence as soon as materials for a program have been selected.

An alternative to using copyright materials is to select "public domain" items. These may be available from governmental or other non-profit courses, or as items for which the copyright period has run out (life of author plus 50 years). See sources for materials on page 73.

Receiving Courses

Each classroom or meeting area is equipped with one or more television monitors to receive the instruction. But distance learning is more than just a one-way lecture. Two-way communication links provide either return television pictures and sound, or telephone conversation from each outlying facility.

If video is used for feedback from receiving locations, it may be via telephone lines using a *slow scan* technique (image scanned electronically more slowly than normal to produce images that can be transmitted economically). *Compressed video* (converting the wide analog video signal into a narrow digital signal; then reconverting to analog video signal at the receiving end) is also starting to be used. A video camera shows the local class or individual learners. The instructor, at the originating base, as well as learners at other locations, can see who asks or answers a question, or engages in discussion.

Due to costs, it is more common today to have microphones installed for input by learners than to have a video camera in receiving rooms. Sound is transmitted by means of an amplified telephone connection.

A statewide or multi-state satellite network may be used for providing effective distance learning to numerous sites at one time. A satellite dish *uplinks* the live instruction to a specific satellite channel where a *transponder* automatically transmits the signal back to earth on a designed frequency. A school receives the

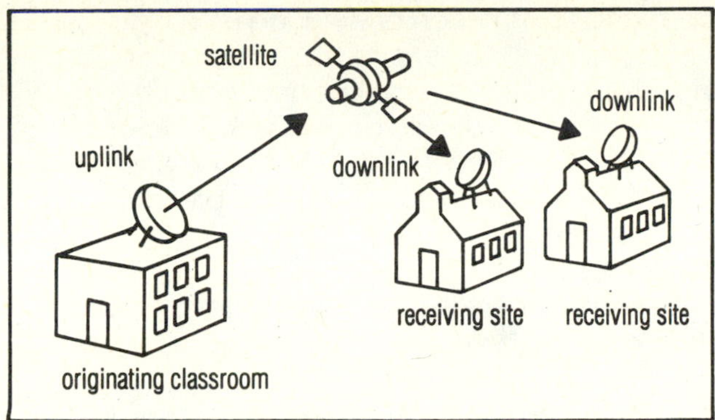

broadcast via a satellite reception dish, installed on the building as a *downlink*. The signals are carried through building cable to participating classrooms. Usually a telephone in the room (often with a toll-free 800 number) allows for return questions and comments by learners.

With multiple classrooms interconnected, every learner can either see and hear, or only hear every other participant—just as they would if everyone were in the same room. The instructor can call up the image or voice of any learner being asked to answer or who may raise a question.

An instructional assistant (often called a facilitator) coordinates activities at each receiving site. When distances are not too great, the instructor may visit with learners periodically at receiving sites for in-person discussion. Also, it is common practice to videotape each class session. The recording is made available to learners who miss a class or want to review what was presented.

Study guides contain outlines of lessons, homework assignments, topic assignments, copies of visuals, project activities, and other information. During a course, facsimile (fax) machines may be used to deliver class materials and tests more conveniently than by courier service.

In addition, communication can be enhanced through microcomputers linked by modem (page 120). Information input by the instructor simultaneously appears on all remote screens. Thus, the computer screen becomes an "electronic chalkboard." Information can then be saved and printed out locally for further study and use.

Teleconferencing

In order to reduce travel costs and also to save time, many organizations use teleconferencing as a substitute for face-to-face meetings and conferences. The procedure provides two-way communication with live video so that personnel at various sites are able to see, hear, and interact with each other. This allows participants at different locations to take part in a meeting while remaining at their offices or going to a nearby teleconference center, often in a hotel that has uplink and downlink connections.

Each room is equipped with at least two video cameras and microphones. One camera is focused on the conference participants in the room, while the other one is adjusted for close-up of materials as they are shown. Television monitors at the location show images from other places as persons there talk and show their materials. A small control unit allows a member of each group to switch and zoom cameras for sending images. Often a fax machine at each site is used for sending and receiving information on paper.

Transmission between or among locations can be via telephone lines, microwave signals, or through a space satellite channel. Numerous corporations and public agencies have installed their own videoconferencing network and many hotel chains provide teleconference viewing facilities. These services indicate the value of distance learning in corporate communications and training programs.

REVIEW

What You Have Learned About Electronic Distance Education and Teleconferencing:

1. What are five factors that need careful consideration when planning a distance learning course?

(continued)

2. Which statements are *true* concerning the production and transmission of distance learning courses?
   a. It is convenient to include a variety of visual materials in addition to chalkboard writing.
   b. Because of the nature of a distance learning course, provisions should be made for involving learners in reactive and interactive activities.
   c. Communication from distant sites to the instructor is limited to sending in written materials.
   d. The instructor usually conducts the course from a TV studio.
   e. A technician selects the pictures to transmit to other sites.
   f. Because of the memorable dynamics of a live video class, there is little advantage to providing recordings of sessions for learners to view after class.
3. Fill in the blanks with the proper words:
   A video signal is __(a)__ to a satellite channel and then __(b)__ to receiving sites where the signal is received by a __(c)__ __(d)__.
4. In what ways do the activities of a teleconference differ from those in a distance learning course?

See answers on page 386.

POSTPRESENTATION

In some teaching situations, media use is incidental to instruction. The instructor may show a videotape recording or some slides not directly related to the unit of study that is underway. This would be an unfortunate situation since the learners could find no learning value in such an experience. The media are treated as entertainment or used just to fill time.

Integration with Instruction

Any media use should relate to the instruction taking place in an integral way. First of all, the material was selected or prepared to serve learning objectives you established or accepted from another source. The concepts treated in the materials support the objectives and you developed a prepresentation plan (page 344) that prepared the group for using the materials. Then, during use, you have included specific participation activities for the learners.

Now, after use, invite questions and use discussion topics you have prepared, allowing learners to openly discuss the concepts presented. The learner's experiences with the materials and misunderstandings will thus be revealed. Discussions also allow for the expression of opinions and attitudinal positions.

Carefully integrate the content presented to related instructional activities—a lecture, a textbook topic, a guest speaker, a class exercise, and so on. Also, you may find it beneficial to use a review test at this time.

If you have used materials that you prepared, for example, overhead transparencies, slides, or nonprojected materials, this integration will be easier than if a commercial product (a sound filmstrip, a film, or a video recording) had been used. Because the latter may have a more generalized treatment of the subject, it probably requires more thought and planning to provide for the necessary integration with your instruction.

Follow-up Activities

The media use should lead to other activities. Some may relate directly to the materials, like follow-up readings and written assignments. In addition, laboratory activity, field work, a field trip, and group or individual projects can supplement or apply what was seen and heard. To reinforce learning, it is always necessary to have some related activity as follow-up to media use.

Note the follow-up activity for the Solar Collector topic on page 346.

EVALUATE RESULTS

A final matter should be considered as media are integrated with instruction. How well have the media served the objectives? You may recall that a suggested checkpoint during the formative evaluation stage of media production was to gather reactions from colleagues and from a learner group for improving the materials before they were put into final form. Now, to determine the effectiveness of your instructional materials, after use, you should want to evaluate two types of results—learning effected and audience reaction.

Learning

First, assess the level of individual learning or performance skill attained as the result of experience with the media. Accomplish this by giving a written or a performance test at an appropriate time. Tests may be in the form of multiple choice, true-false, matching, short answer, or essay. See references for help in developing various types of written tests and performance measures. The results of such a test will allow you to answer the question, "How well have the materials done the job for which they were designed?"

For the adult learner, for example, the test to measure successful learning with the solar collector slide/tape program would be the quality of solar collectors constructed as the followup activity. The instructor might use a rating scale like the one below. This would be more appropriate for these learners, in this learning situation, than a pencil and paper test.

Opinions and Attitudes

The second area of evaluation is to obtain reactions and opinions from audience members as to their likes and dislikes relating to the materials. Answers may be obtained to questions such as the following:

- Did the materials meet your expectations in terms of the objectives?
- Were the materials appealing?
- Was the time period used to present the information adequate?
- Are any revisions or rearrangements suggested?
- Were the physical arrangements for use satisfactory?
- Was the instructor skillful in using the media equipment?
- Did the instructor do a satisfactory job of introduction? or follow-up?

See the example of the opinionaire for students treating the solar collector topic previously developed on page 177.

Solar Collector Project Rating Scale

A. Applying scientific principles

____
poor — excellent

B. Assembling four parts of collector

(1) Glazing

____
unacceptable — acceptable

(2) Flat plate

____
unacceptable — acceptable

(3) Insulation

____
unacceptable — acceptable

(4) Container

____
unacceptable — acceptable

C. Quality of workmanship

____
unacceptable — acceptable

D. Completion time

____
unacceptable — acceptable

E. Summary evaluation

____
unacceptable — acceptable

Furthermore, you should be a part of the evaluation process. Ask yourself (or more formally, prepare on paper) questions similar to these:

- Did the materials meet the objectives I set?
- Am I satisfied with the materials now, or should some revisions be made?
- Was I comfortable in using the media equipment?
- Was learner interest in the topic increased?
- Has learner behavior changed in ways I expected?
- Was my introduction to the materials satisfactory?
- Did the follow-up activities serve their purposes?

When seeking answers to opinion-type questions such as those preceding, it will be necessary to design appropriate evaluation instruments to gather data. The instruments may take any of a number of forms, depending on the nature of the questions. It may be a checklist, a rating scale, or a questionnaire consisting of either open-ended or alternative-response questions. See references for assistance in test and opinionaire construction.

On the basis of the results of all evaluations, revise the materials as necessary. Repeat the evaluation periodically to maintain a standard of effectiveness. Keep the materials up to date by adding or substituting new content when appropriate and eliminating that which is obsolete. With rapid changes in technologies, you may find that alternative media resources are needed. Only by revision will your instructional media be kept timely and maintained at your standard of quality and effectiveness.

SUMMARY

Integrating media with instruction requires attention to three areas of activity: prepresentation, presentation, and postpresentation.

Prepresentation starts with the development of a plan that includes preparatory learner work, decision making as to how the materials will be introduced to learners, participation activities by learners and for yourself during use, and follow-up activities. At the same time, facility and equipment arrangements need to be considered for using the materials with groups and by individuals. If you will use the materials before an audience, rehearse their use so you will be more certain that everything will go smoothly.

The presentation component includes preparing the audience for seeing and hearing the materials, and then the actual use of the materials with the audience. During the presentation, give attention to your own appearance and behavior as well as to the proper use of the media equipment. Different types of equipment require special methods of use.

After the presentation, use the questions, discussion topics, and activities that were developed for integration with instruction and for follow-up.

Finally, evaluate individual student learning and the value of the materials. This should include a written or performance test of learning and an opinion questionnaire completed by persons experiencing the media. Also, question yourself as to the value and suitability of your instructional media. Consider all results to improve media use the next time.

What You Have Learned About Postpresentation and Evaluating Results of Media Use:

1. What is the most important activity you must do with the learners immediately after a media presentation?
2. What are three potential postpresentation activities you could require of learners?
3. What are two outcomes of media use that should be evaluated?
4. What are some types of tests that could be used to measure learning?
5. What are three questions that could be asked in an opinion questionnaire?

See answers on page 386.

REFERENCES

USING MEDIA

Heinich, Robert et al. *Instructional Media: The New Technologies of Instruction.* New York, Wiley, 1988.

Koontz, Franklin R. *Media & Technology in the Classroom: Student Workbook.* Dubuque, IA: Kendall-Hunt, 1990.

Locatis, Craig and Atkinson, Francis. *Media and Technology for Education and Training.* New York: Macmillan, 1984.

Price, Robert V. and Johnson, Bettye. *Basic Skills for Audiovisual Instructional Technology.* Dubuque, IA: Kendall-Hunt, 1990.

Satterthwaite, Les. *Instructional Media: Materials Production and Utilization.* Dubuque, IA: Kendall-Hunt, 1990.

Whiting, Ralph and Kuchta, Roberta S. *Safety in the Library Media Program: A Handbook.* Washington, DC: Association for Educational Communications and Technology, 1988.

DISTANCE EDUCATION

Barker, Bruce O. et al. "Broadening the Definition of Distance Education in Light of the New Telecommunications Technologies." *American Journal of Distance Education* 3 (3): 20–29, 1989.

Bender, Ivan H. "The Copyright Side of Distance Education." *TechTrends* 38 (1): 15–17, 1933.

Clark, Thomas A. and Verdium, John R. Jr. "Distance Education: Its Effectiveness and Potential Use in Lifelong Learning." *Life Learning* 12 (January 1989): 24–27.

Giltrow, David. *Distance Education.* Washington, DC: Association for Educational Communications and Technology, 1989.

Holloway, Robert E. and Ohler, Jason. "Distance Education in the Next Decade." pages 259–266 in *Instructional Technology: Past, Present, Future.* edited by Gary J. Anglin. Englewood, CO: Libraries Unlimited, 1991.

Moore, Michael et al. *Contemporary Issues in American Distance Education.* Elmsford, NY: Pergamon, 1990.

——— and Thompson, Melody M. *The Effects of Distance Education: A Summary of Literature.* University Park, PA College of Education, Pennsylvania State University, 1990.

Willis, Barry. *Distance Education: A Practical Guide.* Englewood Cliffs, NJ: Educational Technology Publications, 1993.

———. *Effective Distance Education: A Primer for Faculty and Administrators.* Fairbanks, AK: University of Alaska Statewide Academic Affairs, 1992.

Wise, Kenda C. *Distance Education: Selected References.* Maxwell, AL: Air University Library, 1990.

WRITTEN/PERFORMANCE TESTS

"Constructing Multiple Choice Test Items"
"Constructing True-False Test Items"
"Constructing Matching Test Items"
"Constructing Matching Test Items"
"Constructing and Scoring Essay Tests"
"Performance Testing"
in *Instructing and Evaluating in Higher Education.* edited by Ron J. McBeath. Englewood Cliffs, NJ: Educational Technology Publications, 1992.

Gronlund, Norman. *How to Construct Achievement Tests.* Englewood Cliffs, NJ: Prentice-Hall, 1987.

Morris, Lynn et al. *How to Measure Performance and Use Tests.* Newbury Park, CA: Sage, 1987.

Popham, W. James. *Modern Educational Measurement.* Englewood Cliffs, NJ: Prentice-Hall, 1990.

PROGRAM EVALUATION

Bingham, Richard D. and Felbinger, Claire L. *Evaluation in Practice.* New York: Longman, 1989.

"Developing Opinion, Interest, and Attitude Questionnaires." in *Instructing and Evaluating in Higher Education.* edited by Ron J. McBeath. Englewood Cliffs, NJ: Educational Technology Publications, 1992.

Fitz-Gibbon, Carol and Morris, Lynn I. *How to Design a Program Evaluation. Volume 3.*

Henerson, M. E. and others. *How to Measure Attitudes. Volume 6.*

King, Jean A. and others. *How to Assess Program Implementation. Volume 5.* Newbury Park, CA: Sage, 1987.

SOURCES FOR EQUIPMENT CITED

AMX Corp., 11995 Forestgate Drive, Dallas, TX 75243 (Equipment Remote Control).

Crestron Electronics, Inc., 101 Broadway, Cresskill, NJ 07626 (Wireless Touch Panel).

Dennison Stationery Products Co., Framingham, MA 01701 (Static Plastic Sheets).

Elmo Manufacturing Corp., 70 New Hyde Park Road, New Hyde Park, NY 11040–9980 (Video Presentation Stand).

General Parametrics, 1250 Ninth Street, Berkeley, CA

94710 (Dedicated Presentation Device).

Plus Corporation of America, 80 Commerce Drive, Allendale, NJ 07401 (Laser Pointer).

Quartet Ovonics, 5700 Old Orchard Road, Skokie, IL 60077 (Electronic and Modular Whiteboards).

Varitronics, 600 Highway 169 South 300, Minneapolis, MN 55440 (Poster Maker).

Equipment Directory of Audio-Visual, Computer and Video Products. Fairfax, VA: International Communications Industries Association. Pioneer Electronics Corp., 2265 East 220th St., Long Beach, CA 90810–1720 (Laserdisc Barcode Reader).

Answer Key

Chapter 1

Introduction (Page 10)

1. (a) 8, (b) 3, (c) 5, (d) 4, (e) 1, (f) 2, (g) 7, (h) 9
2. Nature of learners
   Objectives to be accomplished
   Teaching/learning methods and activities
   Evaluation procedures
3. Selection of media and its development is influenced by such instructional planning elements as nature of learner group, objectives to be served, content to be treated, and methods of instruction.
4. Presentation to groups
   Individualized or self-paced learning
   Instructor-learner interaction
5. a. Individualized learning
   b. Instructor presentation
   c. Group interaction
   d. Instructor presentation
   e. Individualized (self-paced) learning
6. Mechanical level—simple preparation
   Creative level—production of complete instructional materials
   Design level—selection and production of materials within an instructional design framework
7. a. Mechanical
   b. Design
   c. Creative
   d. Mechanical
   e. Creative
   f. Design
8. Developing skills in interpreting, judging, responding to, and using visual representations of reality
9. Take responsibility, share within a group, become perceptive and analytical of visual world, become fluent in expressing ideas verbally and visually

Chapter 2

Perception, Communication, and Instruction/Learning Theories (Page 22)

1. Perception—the internal awareness a person develops for recognizing an event or object in the environment. Gaining a person's attention, holding his or her interest, and making sure the correct message is received are important considerations in designing audiovisual materials relating to perception.
2. Fleming and Levie, *Instruction Message Design*
3. a. Perceptual element
   b. Basic principle
   c. Perception and cognition
   d. Attention
   e. Perceiving picture and worlds
   f. Perceptual capacity
   g. Basic principle
   h. Perceptual distinguishing
4. The transmission-channel step
5. a. Information-processing
   b. Operant conditioning
   c. Motivation
   d. Social learning
   e. Instructional transaction
   f. Information-processing
   g. Conditions of learning
   h. Operant conditioning
   i. Constructivism
   j. Motivation
   k. Social learning
   l. Attribution
   m. Conditions of learning
   n. Attribution
   o. Instructional transaction
   p. Elaboration
   q. Information-processing
   r. Component display
6. a. Instructional resources
   b. Learning objectives
   c. Feedback
   d. Participation
   e. Individual differences
   f. Prelearning
   g. Practice
   h. Application
   i. Reinforcement
   j. Organization of content
   k. Motivation
   l. Learning sequence
   m. Motivation
   n. Organization of content
7. Cognitive, affective, psychomotor; affective domain most difficult to serve
8. a. Psychomotor
   b. Cognitive
   c. Psychomotor
   d. Affective
   e. Psychomotor
   f. Cognitive
   g. Affective
9. a. Higher
   b. Low
   c. Low
   d. Higher
   e. Higher
10. a, d

Chapter 3

Research Findings for the Design, Production, and Use of Instructional Technologies (Page 33)

1. Agree
2. Disagree (depending on value you attribute to finding 25)
3. Agree
4. Agree
5. Agree
6. Agree
7. Disagree
8. Disagree
9. Disagree
10. Agree
11. Agree

12. Agree
13. Agree
14. Agree
15. Disagree
16. Disagree
17. Disagree
18. Agree
19. Agree
20. Disagree
21. Agree
22. Agree
23. Agree
24. Agree
25. Agree
26. Disagree
27. Agree
28. Agree
29. Disagree
30. Agree
31. Disagree
32. Disagree
33. Disagree
34. Disagree
35. Disagree
36. Agree
37. Agree
38. Disagree
39. Disagree
40. Agree
41. Disagree
42. Disagree
43. Agree
44. Agree
45. Disagree
46. Agree
47. Agree
48. Disagree
49. Disagree
50. Disagree
51. Agree
52. Disagree
53. Agree
54. Agree

CHAPTER 4

PRELIMINARY PLANNING (Page 48)

1. Purpose or idea, audience, objectives, content outline
2. Subconscious thoughts
3. a. Objective
   b. Content outline
   c. Purpose
   d. Objective
   e. Audience
4. Motivation, information, instruction
5. a. Information
   b. Instruction
   c. Motivation
   d. Information
   e. Instruction
   f. Motivation and information
6. Age, education, maturity level; skills in reading, writing, math computations; attitude toward topic; present knowledge or skill relative to topic
7. Action verb, content reference, performance standard
8. b, c, d, g, h, i
9. a. (1) Cognitive
   (2) Cognitive
   (3) Cognitive/affective
   (4) Psychomotor
   (5) Affective
   (6) Affective
   b. (3) To *understand* their role . . .
   (reword) To *explain* to other employees their role . . .
   (6) B. To *know* how youth activities help . . .
   (reword) To *cite* four instances of how youth activities help . . .
10. Subject specialist, communications specialist, technical staff
11. May offer useful ideas.
    Materials already produced might serve objectives and be suitable for use.
12. Write information on cards and display cards on a planning board.
13. Reader's activity

CHAPTER 5

KINDS OF INSTRUCTIONAL MEDIA AND TECHNOLOGIES (Page 60)

1. a. Overhead transparencies, multi-image presentations
   b. Printed media, interactive learning media
   c. Audio recordings, slide series, video recordings
2. (1)—b (2)—f (3)—a (4)—e (5)—d (6)—h (7)—c (8)—f (9)—b (10)—a (11)—i (12)—d (13)—c (14)—d, e (15)—i (16)—f (17)—e (18)—g
3. a, b, d, f, g
4. (Note: alternative answers for following are possible)
   a. Media required?—yes
   Visual form only?—yes
   Graphic only?—yes
   Overhead transparencies
   b. Media required?—yes
   Audiovisual technique?—yes
   Still only?—yes
   Videodisc (preferable to slides as costs lower for multiple copies required to serve 2000 learners)
   c. Media required?—yes
   Audiovisual technique?—yes
   Motion necessary?—yes
   Interactive video or videodisc (latter for extensive uses)
   d. Media required?—yes
   Audiovisual technique?—yes
   Motion necessary?—yes
   Videotape recording
   e. Media required?—yes
   Multi-image technique?—yes
   Multi-image—slides
   f. Media required?—yes
   Audiovisual technique?—yes
   Still only?—yes
   Paper/tape (audio-notebook)
5. a, b, c, e, f

CHAPTER 6

DESIGNING INSTRUCTIONAL MATERIALS (Page 72)

1. **Treatment:** a verbal description or approach to how the content will be sequenced. The treatment starts you toward visualization of the content. Thus, you are moving from verbal to visual, a normal thought-process sequence.
   Storyboard: a series of pictures with narration notes that illustrate how each sequence will be treated. The storyboard shows visual situations that prepare you mentally for the specifics you will need when making actual pictures.
   Script: the plan that describes each scene to be photographed or drawn along with necessary sound. This is the map or blueprint that indicates the details of the instructional material to be produced.
2. Move from things known to the unknown or new.

Start with an introduction, then develop the details, finally summarize or review.
3. The learner or trainee has to either mentally or actively respond to a part of the content or to a situation presented. This may require answering questions, other written or verbal activity, or some type of physical performance.
4. Allows for more effective learning of content
5. Expository, personal involvement, dramatic
6. Simple sketch, detailed sketch, 2 × 2 color slide or photographic contact print, instant photograph
7. Frame or sequence number, visual, narration information, special notes
8. (a) False, (b) True, (c) True, (d) False, (e) False, (f) True, (g) False, (h) True
9. Allow sufficient time to develop the subject and for the audience to comprehend it, but not so long that interest will be lost.
10. They allow you to see what will have to be done to produce the materials, as well as the assistance needed, the probable costs, the time required, and so forth.
11. Type of media, materials required, sound features, length, timeliness, facilities and equipment, special techniques, special assistance, budget

12–16. Reader's activity

CHAPTER 7

CAMERA TYPES (Page 79)

1. Reader's activity
2. Reader's activity
3. a. Self-processing film camera
   b. Twin-lens reflex camera
   c. 35mm camera
   d. Electronic still camera

CAMERA LENSES (Page 81)

1. Reader's activity, page 80
2. Millimeters
3. Wide angle, normal, telephoto
4. (a) Normal or macro, (b) wide angle, (c) telephoto, (d) telephoto
5. Reader's activity

CAMERA SETTINGS (Page 85)

1. Twice as much
2. (a) 1/500 second, (b) 1/250 second, (c) 1/125 second
3. *f*/22 and 1/30 second
4. 3½–5 feet
5. Less

FILM (Page 88)

1. Type of light source (daylight or tungsten light)
2. Kodacolor negative or color reversal film
3. Indicates the relative light sensitivity of the film; higher number for greater sensitivity (faster film)
4. For use under lower light levels or to film faster action
5. A filter passes light of its own color, while blocking out light of the complementary color.

DETERMINING EXPOSURE (Page 92)

1. Film speed, *f*/stop, shutter speed; *f*/stop and shutter speed; film speed
2. *f*/32 at 1/15 second
3. Film speed and light level indication
4. *f*/stop and shutter speed
5. When light is coming toward the camera, not over your shoulder; when photographing an unusually bright or dark area that is not important to the subject in the picture
6. *f*/32 and 1/8 second
7. Incident-light meter

LIGHTING (Page 97)

1. Small areas
2. *f*/16
3. Flat shadowless lighting on the subject with heavy background shadows
4. Incident meter reading of key light, measured at the scene, is four times that of the fill light. No, the ratio is too high.
5. Describe use of either a reflected or incident light meter.
6. a. Key—main light on subject; 45° to side of camera and placed higher than camera
   b. Fill—lighten shadows created by key light; at camera position on other side from the key
   c. Background—lighten background, reduce shadows on background and give some depth to scene; aimed at background from side
   d. Accent—highlight or outline the subject and separate it from background; above the subject, aimed down
7. To avoid reflections

CAMERA SHOTS AND PICTURE COMPOSITION (Page 102)

1. (a) Low angle, (b) high angle, (c) subjective, (d) objective, (e) either high or low angle
2. Long shot
3. (a) MS, (b) XCU, (c) LS, (d) LS, (e) CU high angle, (f) CU, (g) MCU low angle, (h) MS low angle
   Sequence: c-a-g-b-h-e-f-d (Your sequence may vary and still be acceptable to an audience.)
4. Generally (c) or (e) would be preferable because of the careful framing.

CLOSE-UP AND COPY WORK (Page 106)

1. All cameras that have separate window-type viewers
2. No. Calculation is necessary if a bellows is used.
3. Macro lens
4. Larger number (that is, smaller opening); slower; tripod essential
5. Divide 160 by 5. Set meter at film speed of 32.

PROCESSING FILM AND MAKING PRINTS (Page 112)

1. Developer—causes chemical change to form black silver image on film
   Rinse—stops action of developer
   Fixer—sets the image on the film

Wash—removes all chemicals
Dry—hardens film surface and natural curl

2. See list on page 107.
3. Paper developer instead of film developer in first step, others the same
4. You can examine photographs to select best negatives for enlargements.
5. Faster processing and requires less print handling and darkroom space
6. A single-developer step is used in color negative processing, while with color reversal processing, after the first developer, a color developer is used that brings out the positive image. Eventually the negative image is bleached out.
7. Either shoot color negative film or color slide film of the operational steps. Either the negatives or positive slides can be printed on paper as color photographs.
8. a. Enhance
   b. Capture
   c. Display
   d. Display
   e. Enhance

CHAPTER 8

PLANNING ART WORK (Page 118)

1. 6 × 9 inches or 9 × 12 inches
2. To allow sufficient "bleed" space when filming because a camera may record a larger total area than is seen through viewfinder
3. 8 × 10 inches—photographs and overhead transparencies; 12 × 18 inches—35mm slide; 9 × 12 inches—video
4. When a number of layers comprising a visual must be accurately aligned
5. (a) space, (b) formal balance, (c) simplicity, (d) color, (e) emphasis, (f) unity
6. (a) simplicity and line; (b) balance and space

COMPUTER GRAPHICS SYSTEM (Page 124)

1. Art on paper, 35mm slides, overhead transparencies, video
2. Increased speed of production, ease of making revisions, increased emphasis on design
3. Input device: a, d, e, h, i, j
   Output device: b, c, g
   Storage device: f
4. a. Paint and enhancement creation program
   b. Preformatted creation program
   c. Object-based/free form creation drawing program
5. Screen design and layout, coloring, lettering
6. a. Pixel—rows of dots that make up the computer-generated image
   b. Mouse—an input device, which when moved on a surface, causes actions to appear on the display screen
   c. Formatted program—a program containing standard graphic visuals that are selected and into which data are entered to design a visual
   c. Modem—a device that permits transmission of output from computer via telephone to another location
7. Laser printer
8. Resolution (sharpness of image)
9. Partial system—design materials on your own computer, transmit to a production center, receive completed visuals
   Production services—visual total designed and produced by a commercial company

ILLUSTRATING TECHNIQUES (Page 126)

1. Opaque projector
2. Ready-made pictures (tearsheets)
3. Computer graphics program
4. Reverse projection with overhead projector
5. Office photocopy machine

VISUALIZING STATISTICAL DATA (Page 128)

1. Bar or column
2. Circle
3. Line
4. Bar or column
5. Surface

USING GRAPHIC TOOLS AND BASIC MATERIALS (Page 129)

1. 14-ply cardboard
2. Dividers
3. T-square
4. Technical drawing pen
5. Compass or template containing circles
6. X-acto knife
7. Triangle
8. 4H–9H pencil
9. Tracing paper

COLORING AND SHADING (Page 131)

1. Emphasis, legibility, and clarity
2. Background and content (lines, text, design areas)
3. Spray paints are quicker to use and provide a more even coloring, but time is required for masking and protecting areas not to be sprayed with a color.
4. It is too hard to separate the color sheet from the backing sheet unless a "lip" remains for insertion of a blade. If a piece is cut to exact size it is very difficult to line it up exactly over area to be covered. Cutting it larger allows some margin when placement is made.
5. Airbrushing
6. a

LEGIBILITY STANDARDS FOR LETTERING (Page 135)

1. So the lettering can be read easily by audience at an anticipated maximum distance
2. Legibility decreases as quantity of information increases.
3. Check guidelines starting on page 132.
4. 1 inch
5. About 1/5 inch high
6. Larger
7. Larger
8. 6 feet
9. Use large, bold lettering

Lettering Methods (Page 139)

1. Hold pen firmly in hand, make only arm movements
2. Against a T-square or a lightly ruled line
3. Protects back of letter sheet from dirt and inadvertent pressure that may transfer letters
4. Preferably a special burnishing tool, but any blunt object like the rounded edge of a pen can be used
5. Pressure machine or computer
6. Computer word processing or graphics program
7. Pressure machine (Kroy or Merlin)
8. Fine-tipped
9. Reader's activity. Then see Table 8–3 on page 139. Background for titles: (1) color overlay title, (2) black overlay title, (3) white overprint title

Mounting and Surface-Protection Methods (Page 146)

1. Coat only one surface and put two surfaces together for temporary mounting while cement is still wet.
   Coat both surfaces and allow them to dry for permanent mounting.
2. You can see guide marks through it; it does not adhere to rubber cement.
3. It is faster and somewhat cleaner.
4. A heat-sensitive adhesive is coated on both sides of tissue paper.
5. So both picture and tissue can be accurately trimmed together.
6. Puncture bubble with a pin, reapply heat and pressure
7. Reader's activity
8. It allows dry-mount tissue to be adhered to the back of a picture so the cutout can be made without the tissue shifting.
9. For cardboard or cloth, size is the deciding factor. Choose rolling or folding on the basis of convenience of use.
10. So there is no exposed adhesive that might stick to the working surface or to the dry-mount press
11. Seal laminating film over the surface.

Making Pasteups (Page 147)

1. Each item is adhered separately to a surface, rather than preparing all items on the surface at one time.
2. Rubber cement, spray mount, stick-glue, and heated wax
3. Use an office copy machine.
4. Apply desktop publishing procedure with a computer.

Chapter 9

Equipment, Tape, and Facilities for Recording Sound (Page 156)

1. a. Unidirectional
   b. Omnidirectional
   c. Bidirectional and dynamic
2. Remove oxide from heads, capstan, and rollers; demagnetize the heads
3. a. Open reel two-track stereo
   b. Open reel multitrack
   c. Open reel or cassette two-track monophonic
   d. Four-track stereo cassette
4. Volume level, tone, fading sound, blending sound
5. See explanation and diagrams on page 154.
6. a. 1 mil, 7-inch reel (7½ ips)
   b. 1.5 mil, 7-inch reel (7½ ips)
7. C-60 cassette (full recording on one side); or C-30 cassette (14.30 minutes side 1, 10:30 minutes side 2)
8. Soundproofed room, eliminate ambient noise, avoid equipment that may generate 60 cycle electrical interference

Sound Recording Procedures (Page 163)

1. Uses conversational tone; gives emphasis to certain words; changes rate of speaking; delivery fits mood and intent of words; provides suitable pauses and pacing
2. Proper microphone placement; select recording tape speed; avoid using AGC; make volume level check on voice with moderately high setting; provide comfortable position for narrator; run test on equipment; have a glass of water at hand
3. Use a mixer into which both the microphone and record player input in order to combine the sounds before going into the recorder, or record the narration on tape and then mix the recorded narration and the record as they go onto the tape.
4. Return to the last correct sentence and rerecord from then on; or, continue recording by repeating the material correctly, preceded by a verbal indication such as "take 2."
5. Advantages: Allows setting volume level at start of presentation and as a background creates a mood while providing continuity for presentation.
   Drawback: Musical background, if too loud or recognizable, can interfere with narration.
6. Physical editing is cutting and splicing a copy of the original tape, thus eliminating and reordering sections as necessary.
   Electronic editing is omitting and reordering parts of the original recording as a copy is being made by dubbing to another tape.
7. Review page 159.
8. It shortens listening time, reduces boredom, keeps listener alert, may increase learning.
9. Either create an actual sound—musical note, chime, buzzer, or bell—or use a tone generator and select a tone between 100 and 440 cycles per second
10. Use only side of the cassette for narration with audible signal and repeat the same recording, with signal, on other side; have narration on one side and inaudible signal on second track.
11. Reader's activity, see page 162.
12. Reader's activity

Chapter 10

Producing Materials (Page 178)

1. (a) 7, (b) 4, (c) 10, (d) 1, (e) 3, (f) 12, (g) 11,

(h) 6, (i) 9, (j) 2, (k) 13, (l) 5, (m) 8
The sequence for production may vary as some of the minor elements are handled at different times.

2. (a) True, (b) True, (c) False, (d) True, (e) True, (f) True, (g) False, (h) True, (i) False, (j) False, (k) False, (l) True, (m) False, (n) False, (o) True, (p) True, (q) True, (r) True
3. Positively: a, b, d, g
4. Does the material serve the objectives?
   Does it exhibit a smooth continuity?
   Does the narration support the visuals?
   Is the material of suitable length?
   Has anything important been left out or unnecessary material be included?
   Are all pictures satisfactory for communicating the content?
   Is the material technically acceptable?
5. a. To obtain reactions, suggestions, and help that might improve your instructional materials
   b. Checkpoints: content outline, storyboard review, script, formative evaluation, or tryout time
6. Reader's activity
7. Reader's activity
8. Reader's activity

CHAPTER 11

PRINTED MATERIALS (Page 198)

1. Learning aids: guide sheets, job aids, picture series
   Training materials: handouts, study guides, instructor's manuals
   Informational materials: brochures, newsletters, annual reports
2. a. Graphics program
   b. Text-based word processor
   c. Desktop publishing program
   d. Text editor
3. a, b, d, e, g
4. a. Nonimpact—Thermal
   b. Impact—Dot matrix
   c. Nonimpact—Ink jet
   d. Nonimpact—Laser
   e. Impact—Daisy wheel
5. Syllables per 100 words; sentences per 100 words
6. 12th grade level (4 sentences, approximately 164 syllables)
7. By only counting numbers of syllables, words, and sentences you do not consider how matters of content organization, page layout, and personal ways of processing information affect clear understanding of printed materials.
8. Thumbnail, rough, comprehensive
9. (a) False, (b) True, (c) False, (d) False, (e) True
10. Underline, capitalize, boldface, italics, box-in
11. a. Electrostatic (xerography)
    b. Laser
    c. Spirit
12. a. Guide sheet
    b. Study guide
    c. Brochure
    d. Handout
    e. Newsletter
    f. Picture series
    g. Instructor's manual

CHAPTER 12

DESIGNING TRANSPARENCIES (Page 205)

1. Horizontal, because in rooms with low ceilings the lower portions of a vertical transparency cannot easily be seen by all members of an audience
2. $7\frac{1}{2} \times 9\frac{1}{2}$ inches
3. Check answers against suggestions on page 201.
4. Vertical format rather than horizontal, quantity of information included, size of lettering, need for copyright clearance
5. Eliminate unnecessary details; modify visual elements; replace lettering with larger size type; divide a complex diagram into sections; consider using masking and overlay techniques
6. Clarify elements, give emphasis, increase interest
7. $\frac{1}{5}$ to $\frac{1}{4}$ inch (page 132)
8. Most suitable would be dry transfer, computer word processing/or graphics program, and pressure-machine lettering (Kroy, Merlin)
9. Register each overlay drawing with the master drawing by use of guide marks in two corners.

PREPARING TRANSPARENCIES (Page 209)

1. a. Object-based system
   b. Paint and enhancement system
   c. Preformatted system
2. See list on page 206.
3. Use a printer that will develop the transparency in black-and-white or in multiple colors.
4. Computer attached to LCD unit, which is set on overhead projector stage.
5. Electrostatic process
6. The writing material used to make the image on the paper must have a carbon base.
7. No
8. Underexposed. Slow down the machine.
9. With felt pen or colored adhesive
10. Full-color electrostatic process
11. No. Marks made by some do not adhere to acetate.
12. Use a solvent, such as lighter fluid.
13. No
14. Cover with a sheet of clear acetate.
15. Enlarging electrostatic machine; photographic process with high-contrast (lithographic) film
16. Use special full-color electrostatic-type machine.

COMPLETING AND FILING TRANSPARENCIES (Page 212)

1. On the underside
2. Base on underside; overlays on separate sides, top of mount
3. Sliding mask and hinged section masks
4. Reader's activity, page 211.

CHAPTER 13

AUDIO RECORDINGS (Page 219)

1. With an informative recording the listener only receives information. With an instructional recording the listener also should have opportunities to interact with the material presented.
2. See the list on page 215.
3. See the list on page 215.
4. Audio-notebook or audio-tutorial system
   The audio-notebook generally is limited to correlated printed material, whereas the AT system includes a variety of other activities and resources for learners in addition to pencil and paper work.
5. Refer to the list on page 217.
6. Answering questions, solving problems, completing readings, applying the information, making observations, receiving answers to the questions, and so on
7. Informal, conversational, one-to-one
8. Not over 10 minutes
9. Reader's activity
10. See the discussion on page 218.

CHAPTER 14

PREPARING SLIDE SERIES (Page 232)

1. See explanations on page 222.
2. See Table 14–1, page 223. Many other 35mm reversal color films are available. Justify your answer.
3. To block out unwanted areas; change proportion of a slide; create an unusual shape
4. a. See slide example 4 on page 225.
   b. See slide example 2 on page 225.
   c. See procedure for progressive disclosure on page 225.
5. A film recorder containing 35mm color film
6. Script is prepared *after* the picture taking of the event is concluded.
7. E-6
8. How well the slide treats the subject and technical quality (exposure, focus, composition)
9. Cardboard, plastic, glass; see discussion on page 227.
10. Reader's activity. See methods starting on page 229.
11. Increase in contrast and shift in colors. Use a film that will control contrast (film designed for duplication); balance colors with color correction filters.
12. Reader's activity. See page 230.
13. An image is always on the screen, even when one is being removed (fading out) and the next one starting to appear (fading in).
14. Reader's activity, page 231.

MULTI-IMAGE PROGRAM (Page 236)

1. Provide a motivational experience for the viewer; process large amounts of information effectively in a short time.
2. Sweeping panoramas, comparing or contrasting objects and events; illustrating verbal information with supporting visuals. In addition other concepts can be treated in a multi-image presentation: showing subject from different camera angles or distances; presenting sequential time segments relating to an event; simulating motion of a still subject across multiple screen areas; giving meaning to an abstract idea with several supporting visuals; illustrating steps in a process; relating parts of a subject to the whole; combining motion and still pictures.
3. (a) False, (b) False, (c) True, (d) True, (e) False, (f) True
4. Put narration on one track and slide-change cues by voice on second track.
5. Reader's activity, page 234.
6. Dissolver
7. Real time—programing in actual clock time required to present the program
   Leisure time—taking as much time as you wish while programing each image in turn
8. (a) Flash, (b) freeze, (c) fade-out, (d) wipe

CHAPTER 15

VIDEO EQUIPMENT AND VIDEOTAPE (Page 245)

1. See list of eleven items on page 240.
2. Videocamera, microphone, videotape recorder
3. Outdoor/indoor filter adjustment and white balance
4. Picks up unwanted extraneous sounds and it is better to locate microphone closer to subject for many scenes.
5. ½ inch VHS and 8mm
6. b and c
7. NTSC
8. a. Videocassette—tape reels inside a sealed cassette
   b. Control track—signals recorded along lower edge of tape to regulate tape speed
   c. Glitch—discontinuity in recorded picture between scenes due to stopping and restarting the recorder
   d. Dropouts—momentary sound loss on tape or horizontal flashes on videoscreen

RECORDING THE PICTURE (Page 249)

1. Motion; time
2. *Scene* describes the location of the subject; *shot* specifies the action to be recorded; *take* refers to a number assigned each time the same scene is filmed; *sequence* is a series of scenes all related to the same idea or concept.
3. (a) Tilt, (b) zoom, (c) pan, (d) pan, (e) dolly
4. Look through the camera viewfinder.
5. A scene that orients the viewer to the subject after a number of close-up scenes
6. (a) MS, (b) CU, (c) LS, (d) MS low angle

PROVIDING CONTINUITY (Page 254)

1. Carefully relating the action at the end of one scene with that at the start of the next scene
2. To keep the audience properly oriented
3. Show direction of movement changing or a head-on shot directly toward the camera; cut-away to related action or an observer
4. Close-up of the person's face; spool with thread coming off;

or other scene you may think of

5. (a) Hour hand of clock moving or title "Allow paint to dry"; (b) few seconds of closed house door, traffic on street; (c) fade-out/fade-in
6. As bridges for time and space
7. Fade-out/fade-in; dissolve; wipe

SPECIAL VIDEO TECHNIQUES (Page 257)

1. Keeping in mind what has already been recorded and anticipating what might be coming next
2. Because a glitch or discontinuity of image appears on the tape each time the recorder is stopped and then started again
3. A discontinuity that appears between scenes when the recorder is stopped and then started to record the next scene
   Overcome by using a recording having a *flying erase head* that ensures a clean break from one scene to the next
   (Avoid glitches by putting the recorder *briefly* on the PAUSE position between shooting scenes.)
4. Carefully follow scripted series of scenes.
   Rehearse scenes and control action when recording.
   Have titles and any graphics ready to record as you proceed.
   Check lighting conditions and camera use for each scene.
5. It accelerates action that takes place slowly.
   It is used by single framing or exposing short amounts of tape (about 1 second) of lengthy action at repeated time intervals over a long period of time.
6. $\frac{\text{360 minutes}}{\text{20 seconds}}$ = every 18 minutes for the 6 hour period

OTHER PRODUCTION FACTORS AND RECORDING SOUND (Page 255)

1. Used as a reference when adjusting video players and receivers in order to show the best color images
2. Word titles briefly; use simple, bold lettering; adhere to legibility standards; proportion the lettering in 3 to 4 ratio; record title for a period of time that allows title to be read twice; provide for one-sixth marginal loss on video screen.
3. Use a titler or character generator; create titles with a computer using word processing or graphics software, then transfer the stored images to videotape.
4. Synchronous voices or sounds, narration, sound effects, music
5. Important for use during editing so that a recorder or player can be backspaced and stabilized before the transfer of a scene takes place

EDITING VIDEOTAPE (Page 263)

1. To select, rearrange, and shorten scenes, as well as to insert scenes or sound in place of a portion of a scene
2. Assemble-mode editing
3. a. Manual assemble edit: One source player VCR, one recorder VCR
   b. Automatic assemble edit-mode: One source player VCR, one edit/record VCR, an edit controller
4. Automatic assemble-mode edit method
5. Putting a brief picture or sound, or a complete scene on tape to replace part of a scene that has already been transferred to the master tape
   Most commonly, insert editing is used to add a cut-in or cut-away shot, also to replace synchronous sound with narration or a sound effect.
6. a. Control track—pulse along lower edge of tape that determines tape playback speed and is used to locate specific places on the tape
   b. Edit-in point—initial frame of a scene at which transfer from the player tape starts to the master tape being recorded
   c. A and B rolls—original videotapes that are to be combined or used in special effects (dissolve or wipe) when transfer is made to the master tape
   d. Time code—a series of eight-digit code numbers recorded to indicate each frame on the videotape and used in editing
7. a. Adjusts picture quality of scenes on A and B rolls
   b. Creates titles and graphics
   c. Creates fades, wipes, and other effects of scenes on the master videotape
   d. Records an eight-digit code number on an audio track of the tape to identify and locate each frame when editing

DESKTOP VIDEO (Page 266)

1. Desktop video, with a computer, can integrate a number of audio and visual components along with live video into a complete program.
2. See list on page 264.
3. See programs on page 265.
4. a, b, d
5. See list on page 265.
6. Result can be a poor quality recording that may be a sixth or higher generation copy.

DUPLICATING VIDEO RECORDINGS AND PRODUCING A VIDEODISC (Page 268)

1. Image quality, including sharpness and color fidelity, would be best
2. As videodiscs (if equipment available for use). The content is firm and will not be changed for a long period of time. If videodisc not available, use videocassette.
   Use high quality master such as S-VHS. Also, must have balanced colors and careful sequencing and framing of visuals.
3. Image and sound read by a laser stylus.
4. A large quantity of information can be stored.
   Images and sound are of high quality and hold up well.
   Any location on a disc can be found easily and quickly.
5. Constant angular velocity (CAV) and constant linear velocity (CLV) formats; CAV is used for instruction, especially when the learner must choose among alternative visual sequences and optional paths are followed.
6. Make original videotape recording and collect film footage, slides, and audio recordings, and other media for program.
   Premaster on broadcast quality videotape equipment such as ½-inch Betacam or 1-inch videotape.
   Produce master videodisc.
   Prepare check disc.
   Make duplicate discs for use.

CHAPTER 16

THE FACTORS CONTRIBUTING TO INTERACTIVE AND REACTIVE LEARNING, PLANNING, AND LINEAR AND BRANCHING FORMATS (Page 276)

1. Interactive learning—individual has control over sequence and pace of instruction
   Reactive learning—individual follows set sequence of instruction, varying pace of study
2. a. Structure the content
   b. Give specific directions
   c. Develop a pretest
   d. Provide for higher levels of learning
   e. Provide feedback on answers
3. See list on page 272
4. See list on page 272
5. Suggested order (there can be alternatives): c, h, b, i, k, d, j, a, f, m, g, l, e
6. (a) Single remedial branch, (b) pretest and skip, (c) linear, (d) multiple remedial branch, (e) compound branches

COMPUTER-BASED INSTRUCTION (Page 283)

1. a. Tutorial
   b. Drill and practice
   c. Problem-solving
   d. Game
   e. Simulation
   f. expert system
2. Illustrates how a program presents information, indicates decision points, and shows alternative paths
3. Arrow—shows direction of movement
   Rectangle—step in the process
   Diamond—decision point at which branching will occur
   Oval—beginning or end of a sequence or connecting point to a continuation
4. Illustrates the content and its appearance on each screen
5. Use of an authoring system
6. See list of five items on page 282.
7. To evaluate the acceptance or success of various development stages—objectives, subject content, specs, sequences, flow charts, and storyboards

COMPUTER/VIDEOTAPE AND COMPUTER/VIDEODISC INTERACTIVE MEDIA (Page 291)

1. A connection between the microcomputer and a videocassette or videodisc player
2. Repurposing the videotape recording or videodisc
3. Flow charting with branching paths
   More detailed storyboard preparation
4. Plan continuity among scenes that could have a relationship, even though not logically so
   When editing, place scenes that may be viewed sequentially close together to reduce shuttle time
5. Record control track on videotape recording
   Place signals on unused audio track with timecode generator
6. Allows the user to quickly locate and view specific frames or motion segments on tape or disc without computer interface
7. (a) T, (b) T, (c) D, (d) T, (e) D, (f) D, (g) T
8. (a) II, (b) I, (c) III, (d) III, (e) I, (f) III
9. See list on page 289.
10. Less expensive and less time than producing a videodisc
11. This is the last chance to make any changes before the costly step of preparing the videodisc.

INTERACTIVE MULTIMEDIA (Page 295)

1. Using a computer to control and manipulate a variety of media forms
2. Digital forms
3. (1) b, (2) f, (3) a, (4) d, (5) c
4. a, c, e, f, h

MEDIA ADAPTABLE FOR REACTIVE LEARNING (Page 300)

1. (a) 2, (b) 5, (c) 1, (d) 8, (e) 9, (f) 6, (g) 4, (h) 11, (i) 7, (j) 3, (k) 10
2. Guidance in studying a textbook
   Self-study or sequences of verbal information or sets of procedures
3. Can be a personal, flexible method of learning
4. Directions, information or explanations, feedback on answers, summary of content
5. Treatment of topic requires realism of color pictures.
6. Only 6–8 lines of text should fill a slide for ease of reading.
7. Use verbal cues for slide changes.
   Copy the slide/tape program to videotape.

CHAPTER 17

LOCATING, EVALUATING AND SELECTING INSTRUCTIONAL MATERIALS (Page 310)

1. Produce your own, use commercial materials, adapt existing materials
2. Learner characteristics, purpose and objectives, mode of instruction
3. Certain features that are characteristic of a type of media: motion, color, sound, media size, synchronized picture and sound, both still pictures and motion in any arrangement with random selection, graphic or photographic form, and so forth
4. Media centers, indexes, catalogs, journals
5. NICEM
6. See list under its name on page 311.
7. *The Video Sourcebook*
8. A university media catalog
9. A careful analysis of instructional materials
10. Review is a published report on a media material; preview is your own report after viewing the material.
11. See list in References, on page 311.
12. Reader's activity
13. Objective data and subjective reactions and comments
14. To choose the best material for use
15. Learner, purpose/objectives, content, media type, active learning, technical quality, cost, validation
16. Reader's activity

CHAPTER 18

PRACTICES FOR SUCCESSFULLY OPERATING MEDIA EQUIPMENT AND STILL-PICTURE PROJECTION (Page 318)

1. Know the operating principle.
   Never force anything.
   Investigate a problem through step-by-step analysis.
   Practice the operation.
2. (a) *A*, (b) *B*, (c) *B*, (d) *A*, (e) *B*, (f) *A*, (g) *B*, (h) *A*, (i) *A*, (j) *B*, (k) *B*
3. a. Slide
   b. Overhead
   c. Opaque
   d. Opaque
   e. Filmstrip
   f. Slide
   g. Overhead
   h. Either slide or filmstrip
   i. Slide
   j. Overhead

OPERATING MOTION PICTURE PROJECTION AND VIDEO PLAYBACK EQUIPMENT (Page 324)

1. a. Sound
   b. Optical
   c. Sound
   d. Film transport
   e. Optical
   f. Film transport
   g. Sound
   h. Optical
   i. Film transport
2. Manual, slot-loading, and self-threading
3. a, d, e
4. a. (2)
   b. (6)
   c. (5)
   d. (4)
   e. (1)
   f. (8)
   g. (7)
   h. (3)
5. VHS; ½ inch
6. Play, rewind, fast forward, scan, and still frame
7. TV receiver includes a tuner for selecting broadcast and cable channels. Monitor does not contain a tuner.
8. TV receiver: RF cable with F connectors
   Videomonitor: Video cable with BNC connectors and audio patch cord
9. No wear on the video material
   Opportunity to move to any location on the disc almost instantly
   Able to hold a still frame picture for long period
10. Scans across a pre-printed barcode to rapidly locate a frame or sequence on videodisc
11. Portable video projector that uses liquid crystal display technology in place of larger, three-lens video projection system.

OPERATING AUDIO PLAYERS (Page 330)

1. Stops the tape movement when it is depressed; depressing the button or lever again starts the tape.
2. Line input is a connector from other sources having an already prepared recording (another tape recording, a record). Microphone input is just for recording sound being created through the microphone.
3. To prevent accidental erasure of a recording
4. Fine tune the speed of the turntable
5. 33⅓ rpm
6. A laser beam is used to read digitally encoded signals on a disc.
   Nothing touches the disc while playing, so no wear results.
7. Jumper cord from output jack on record player to line input jack on tape recorder

OPERATING COMBINATIONS OF EQUIPMENT (Page 336)

1. A control to activate an electronic signal that is placed on the second audio slide changes
2. Wind tape back to *after* last correct signal. Play audiocassette tape and activate sync mode switch to record position. Add signal at proper point. Stop playback.
3. Eliminates sudden blackout between slide changes
4. Avoids possible current variations from reaching media equipment components that may cause erratic slide changes
5. The sync mode switch may be in the *manual advance* position.
6. Video player, interface board in computer, and linking cable

USING MISCELLANEOUS ITEMS AND PURCHASING AND MAINTAINING EQUIPMENT (Page 340)

1. Glass-beaded
2. a, d, e, b, c, f
3. In front of the windows to avoid extraneous light from reaching the screen
4. Distortion of a projected image due to improper 90-degree alignment of projector with the screen; often, a problem with overhead projector
5. Six times the width of the screen
6. Stability and locking wheels
7. 7 inch
8. By its base or with paper or a cloth to avoid getting finger oil on the glass
9. Swab with a cotton tip coated with alcohol
   Run a cleaning tape cassette through the machine
10. Film channel behind the lens
11. By its edges
12. *The Equipment Directory of Video, Computer, and Audio-Visual Products* from International Communications Industries Association

CHAPTER 19

PREPRESENTATION PREPARATION (Page 345)

1. You will know:
   Preparation learners had for using materials
   How to introduce media to audience
   What you should do during presentation
   What learners should do during presentation
   How to followup after presentation
2. In becoming familiar with the location, technical matters and audience comfort needs can be anticipated; also, pos-

sible problem areas may be revealed and can be addressed to ensure a smooth presentation.
3. All items are important.
4. All items are important.
5. Reveals any problems with materials, equipment, and facilities
   Gives you a personal sense of confidence in your presentation

PRESENTATION TECHNIQUES WHEN USING MEDIA (Page 347)

1. Prepare the audience for using the materials.
   Use the media effectively.
2. Introduce the topic.
   State objectives.
   Point out new vocabulary or concepts treated.
   Indicate learner activity during presentation.
   Relate media to other program or course activities.
   Indicate followup activities.
3. Personal appearance and public speaking skills
   Handling media and operating equipment properly and smoothly
4. Have a colleague evaluate your presentation skills and handling of media.
   Have a videotape recording made so you can critique yourself.

USING STILL PROJECTED MEDIA IN PRESENTATIONS (Page 353)

1. Machine is bulky, often needs to be placed in middle of room and has noisy fan.
   High wattage lamp creates excessive heat close to material.
   Image projected is not particularly bright.
2. Can project readily available material with no or little preparation
   Useful for enlarging a diagram onto chalkboard or cardboard
3. You face the audience and maintain eye contact.
   Room lights are on at a comfortable level.
   You, the instructor, control the materials.
4. Point to items.
   Make marks on transparency.
   Uncover parts of transparency.
   Use overlays as layers of a transparency.
   Show 3-dimensional objects.
   Handout paper copies to accompany use of transparency.
   Project other materials, such as slides along with a transparency.
5. b and c
6. Flexible for rearrangement
   Realistic portrayal of reality
   Low cost
   Easy to use
7. Insert blank 2 × 2 inch posterboard at appropriate places in slide tray.
8. Lower left corner slide
   Upper right corner
9. Filmstrip
   Combined with audiotape recording
10. Allows you to highlight an aspect of a projected image on the screen easily
11. b and c

USING MOTION PROJECTED MEDIA IN PRESENTATIONS (Page 358)

1. Overcome time
   Overcome distance
   Speed up a process
   Slow down a process
   Recreate the past
   Stop action
   Provide access to the inaccessible
   Bring life to still objects through animation
2. a and d
3. Disinterest in the materials
4. CRT has three lenses and delivers a high quality image. LCD has one lens and microprocessor; is smaller with acceptable projected image.
5. With a videodisc, instructor can easily freeze an image, branch to another picture or action sequence, and use other features not convenient or even possible with a videocassette player.
6. The reader scans a preprinted barcode, reading the code, which activates the videodisc player to locate the required frame number on the disc, thus showing the start of the sequence.
7. It permits showing all types of small 3-dimensional objects, opaque still pictures, slides, transparencies, and video material.
8. Use a display unit (LCD) attached to the computer and set on overhead projector; connect computer to a video-projection system.
9. Use equipment in answer to question 8 plus prepare paper copies at end of meeting.

USING NONPROJECTED MEDIA IN YOUR PRESENTATIONS (Page 367)

1. Still pictures, charts/graphs, chalkboard, multipurpose board, cloth board, exhibits
2. Bulletin board, exhibit, realia, model, mock-up
3. a. Flip chart
   b. Multipurpose board
   c. Chalkboard
   d. Exhibit
   e. Hook-and-loop board
   f. Chalkboard
   g. Bulletin board
   h. Chalkboard
   i. Multipurpose board
   j. Felt or flannel board
4. a, c, d
5. A handmade or computer-generated poster on 8½ × 11 inch paper can be enlarged immediately to about 2 × 3 feet for display.
6. Material written or drawn on the board can immediately be printed out on paper.
7. Realia—real objects

Model—recreation of a real object only smaller or larger for handling and examination ease
Mock-up—exaggeration of aspects of a real object to better show parts, functions, and operations

8. Simulation—recreates a real situation in a protected environment, causing a person to act and make decisions
   Game—formalized simulation that follows rules and procedures to provide experiences and have players gain insights
9. Prepare the audience.
   Cue tape to starting point.
   Preset sound level.
   Show interest in the recording yourself.
   Stop audiotape recording at appropriate points for discussion.
   After listening, summarize and discuss concepts heard.

ELECTRONIC DISTANCE EDUCATION AND TELECONFERENCING (Page 369)

1. See list on page 369.
2. a, b, e
3. (a) uplinked; (b) downlinked; (c) reception; (d) dish
4. Teleconferencing more commonly provides two-way video than may be available in a distance learning course. Participants in a teleconference usually control switching and zooming cameras themselves, while a technician does this in a distance learning course.

POSTPRESENTATION AND EVALUATING RESULTS OF MEDIA USE (Page 372)

1. Consider questions and have a discussion to determine if objectives have been met, to clear up misunderstandings, and to reveal attitudes.
2. Readings, written assignments, lab or field activities, field trip, projects
3. Level of learning
   Opinions and attitudes by learners about the media
4. Multiple choice, true-false, matching, short answer, essay
5. See page 372.

Glossary

ASA film rating (see *exposure index*)
accent light a light that accentuates and highlights an object in a scene
acetate (clear) a plastic sheet that permit a high degree of light transmission, resulting in a transparent appearance
activator bath that starts action of developing agents built into photographic paper in photostabilization process
advance organizer element in information-processing learning theory that builds on already learned knowledge through examples and analogies
affective domain category of instructional objectives relating to attitudes, values, and appreciations within human behavior
airbrush compress-air controlled, small area spray painting device
analog any system operating over a continuous range of values
analog sound sinelike wave caused by compression and expansion of air, or movement of needle in a record, or varying magnetic fields created on audiotape
andragogy considering the uniqueness of adults when learning is to take place
animation a filming and video technique that brings inanimate objects or drawings to apparent life and movement by very brief or single-frame exposure
aperture rectangular opening in film channel behind the lens so a single frame is illuminated by the lamp
artificial intelligence humanly formulated method of using computer technology for problem solving
aspect ratio proportion or format of an instructional media, such as 2 to 3 for slides, or 3 to 4 for video
assemble editing putting scenes of a video program in 1–2–3 order according to the script
attributes of media capabilities of an audiovisual medium to exhibit such characteristics as motion, color, sound, or simultaneous picture and sound
attribution learning theory explains ways individuals seek understanding of events taking place in their world
audible picture advance signal a signal on tape that is heard (bell, buzzer), thus informing the user to change the slide or filmstrip to the next picture
audio-notebook study guide and/or workbook with audiotape recording to guide learner in studying a topic
audio track portion of a video recording on which sound is recorded
audio-tutorial system (AT) audio recording provides information and directs learner to learning activities with various resources
audiocassette recorder a recorder that uses magnetic tape on spools that are enclosed in a plastic case
authoring language a computer language designed specifically for CBI
authoring system computer software that takes you, step by step, through the process of developing CBI
automatic volume level control (AVL) a circuit in an audiotape recorder that automatically controls a uniform level of recorded sound intensity
background light the illumination thrown on the background to lighten it; giving the scene depth and separating the subject from the background
barcode reader scans patterns of printed vertical lines for transmitting the code to play a chosen segment of a video program
behaviorism (see *operant conditioning*)
Betacam ½-inch video format of high picture quality
bidirectional microphone one that picks up sounds only on two opposite sides
bit smallest unit of information a computer can handle electronically
block-format script directions for producing media that consist of visual descriptions of scenes written full-width across page with narration and other sounds indicated in narrow column, centered below visual description
bounce light in photography aimed at ceiling or other surface to illuminate subject indirectly by reflection
branching program instructional program containing options, either selected by the learner or to which the learner is directed, thus consisting of sequences that may be different for each learner

CAV (see *constant angular velocity videodisc*)
CBI (see *computer-based instruction*)
CCD charged-coupled device microchip with light receptors used in video cameras
CD (see *compact disk*)
CD-I compact disk interactive uses CD-ROM disks with added ability to respond to computer commands
CD-ROM compact disk read only memory stores great amounts of information as text, graphics, photos, and sound
CD-WORM (see *WORM*)
CDTV Commodore dynamic total vision uses Amiga computer equipment for running CD and CD-ROM programs
CGA Color graphics adapter board for use in a computer
CRT abbreviation for cathode ray tube used to show images in TV receivers, videomonitors, and computer display screens
CU (see *close-up*)
camcorder videocamera and video recorder as a single, compact unit
camera ready paste-up copy of pages that are ready for reproduction with a process camera
captions the printed explanations to accompany visuals
cardioid microphone instrument that picks up sounds in a heart-shaped pattern, namely, with major sensitivity from one side, some sensitivity on adjacent two sides, and almost none from back side
carousel term generally applied to slide projector using a circular tray that holds slides for projection
cassette (see *audiocassette recorder* or *videocassette recorder*)
central processing unit (CPU) component of a computer that receives, decodes, and executes instructions

chapter major search location on a videodisc at start of a new section
character generator electronic device used to create titles and simple graphics that can be translated into video signals on videotape
check disc test videodisc prepared from master videodisc used to verify placement of all program elements
checkpoint periodic stages during media planning and production when work should be read or viewed by persons outside the project for reactions and comments
clearance form (see *release form*)
clipbook a printed booklet containing a variety of commercially prepared black-and-white line drawings (**clipart**) on various subjects
close-up a concentration of the camera on the subject, or on a part of it, excluding everything else from view
cognitive domain category of instructional objectives relating to knowledge, information, and other intellectual skills within human behavior
color adhesive a translucent or transparent color printed on a thin acetate sheet having adhesive backing for adherence to cardboard, paper, acetate, or film
color bars color pattern put on the beginning of a video recording that serves as reference for adjusting players and receivers for maximum color quality when a videotape is played
color processor (video) device for correcting colors in scenes and used when copying a recording to make the master videotape
compact disc (CD) 4¾-inch disc on which sound is recorded with laser beam as series of digital patterns (0s and 1s or low/high voltage); laser reads digital pattern on playback
component display theory learning theory that gives attention to content and learning performance with delivery of instruction in terms of prerequisites and expository presentations
compressed video using telephone line to transmit video signals
computer-based instruction any application of computer technology for instruction
computer display screen (see *videomonitor*)
condenser microphone one that transmits sounds when a plate that receives direct current is caused to vibrate with respect to an adjacent fixed plate
constant angular velocity videodisc (CAV) each video frame occupies one track, permitting still pictures, slow motion, and rapid movement to any section of disc for branching programing
constant linear velocity videodisc (CLV) each video frame occupies one half of track and is used for continual running program
constructivism learning theory with the premise that learning is derived mainly from one's individual experiences
contact print a photographic print the same size as the negative, prepared by exposing to light the negative and paper, placed together
continuity the logical relationship of one scene leading to the next one and the smooth flow of action and narration within the total instructional media
continuous-tone subjects illustrations consisting of shades of gray, varying from black to white
control track continuous series of signals placed along lower edge of videotape when recording to regulate tape speed during playback, used during editing for locating scenes, and referred to by computer for locating specific frames in a program
copyfitting adapting text to fit available space on a page
copy stand a vertical or horizontal stand for accurately positioning a camera when photographing flat subjects very close to the lens
courseware total instructional package including computer software, visual and audio media, and printed material
crawl titles or text moved slowly across a video display screen
credit title a listing of those who participated in or cooperated with the media project
cropping marking the edges of a photograph to indicate visual area to be printed
crystal microphone contains crystals or granules that produce electricity when pressure from a sound wave is applied
cursor flashing or nonflashing line, square, or arrow that appears on computer screen to indicate where next text character, data, or graphic element will appear or start
cut instantaneous change from one image to another within a sequence of projected visuals
cut-away shot scene of a subject or action taking place at the same time as the main action, but separate from it, and placed between two related scenes that have a discontinuity of action
cut-in shot a close-up feature of a subject being recorded on videotape and usually placed between two scenes that have discontinuity of action

DVI digital video interactive uses CD-ROM disks to store full motion video and audio
daisy wheel printer spinning wheel with spokes that contain raised letters and numbers; when desired character is positioned, hammer presses spoke against ribbon to impress image on paper
debugging testing a computer program and correcting any deficiencies
dedicated presentation device stores computer data, usually as slides, for video projection
depth-of-field the distance within a scene from the point closest to the camera in focus to the farthest in focus
design principles factors of simplicity, unity, emphasis, and balance, along with visual tools to be considered when designing art work
desktop presentation a presentation technique using a microcomputer connected to a video projection system with the computer storing all instructional resources for the unit of instruction in digital format
desktop publishing preparation of printed materials using a personal computer, with word-processing and graphics software, and a high resolution printer
desktop video allows creation of video materials without investing in expensive and complicated equipment nor-

mally associated with video production

developer a solution that chemically sets the photographic image by acting on silver salts, which have been affected by light during picture taking, in exposed film

digital information or graphic data that have been translated into discrete numerical values and can be manipulated or reproduced without loss of quality

digital audiotape (DAT) (see *digital sound*)

digital photography an electronic image as a series of numbers that can be manipulated by a computer into a photographic image

digital sound binary signals of low or high voltage level pulses recorded on tape or disc

digitize transforming an image into a dot pattern (pixels) so it can be stored in computer memory

digitizing pad (see *graphics tablet*)

direct projection system used when list is transmitted through a transparency being projected

disc refers to videodisc and compact disc; differs from *disk* (see below)

disk (also *diskette*) electronic storage medium for computer data consisting of thin magnetic mylar sheet that revolves in a jacket and from which a disk drive reads data and to which it writes data

disk drive device that operates a disk, rotating it at high speed to read stored information or to add new information

disposable camera box with lens and shutter containing roll of 35mm film; after film removed, camera discarded

dissolve effect involving two superimposed scenes in which the second one gradually appears as the first one gradually disappears

dissolve unit a device that activates one or more projectors to fade out an image on the screen while an image projected by another projector begins to fade in as a superimposed image over the first one

documentary approach a method of taking pictures or recording images without detailed script preparation

documentation descriptive material accompanying a computer program that tells the user how to use it

dolly shot a videotape scene recorded as the camera is moved toward or away from the subject

dot matrix printer device that through use of pins that form letters, numbers, and lines impacts coarse dot pattern on paper

dramatic treatment mediated program that evokes an emotional response

drill and practice a computer program consisting of questions and exercises for the user to complete

dropouts momentary loss of sound on an audiotape recording or horizontal flashes on a videoscreen due to dirt on the tape or loss of head-to-tape contact

dry-mount press device that uses heat and pressure to seal flat materials to cardboard with a heat-sensitive adhesive placed between the two surfaces

dry mounting sealing a picture to a cardboard or cloth backing with a heat-sensitive adhesive material

dry-transfer commercially prepared symbols for transferring from a sheet to the working surface by rubbing with a blunt tool

dubbing the transfer of a recording from one unit to another; commonly from record to tape, audiotape to audiotape, or videotape to videotape

dummy final layout of all elements for a page that serves as guide for paste-up

duplication making a few copies (less than ten) of original pages

dynamic microphone one that employs a moving coil in a magnetic field to generate an electrical signal from sound waves

edit controller a machine that permits the precise location of a videotaped scene's beginning and end points for cueing VCR player and recorder

editing the selection and organization of visuals after filming and the refinement of narration or captions; or, the procedure for rearranging elements of an audio recording or video recording, removing bad-sound takes, and lengthening pauses

editing VCR a recorder that can record video and audio tracks separately or simultaneously, and will smoothly and accurately record scenes without distortion on a master videotape or videocassette

editing-in-the-camera technique recording scenes in sequence according to their listing on the script

8mm video format with 8mm wide tape

elaboration theory learning theory in which instruction is ordered in terms of increasing complexity

electronic distance learning providing instruction from a classroom to remote sites by means of video transmission with two-way audio and possibly return video

electronic imaging process for capturing, enhancing, and displaying subjects through digital methods as compared with conventional photographic procedures of exposure, development, and printing

electronic microprocessor programer commands stored as digital "bits" direct multi-image projectors to carryout operations

electronic publishing (see *desktop publishing*)

electronic still camera still camera in which subjects are recorded as video signals on a disc with images viewed through videoplayer

electronic whiteboard prints out 8½ × 11 inch copy of whatever is written on the large display board

electrostatic process a process that uses an electric charge and powdered toner to create copies on paper or acetate

enlarging process of photographically printing a larger image from a negative onto paper or film

equalizer a device for boosting or subduing certain audio frequencies to improve the tonal quality of a recording

establishing shot a medium or long shot that establishes the whereabouts of a scene and serves as orientation

evaluation careful analysis of an instructional material

exciter lamp small lamp in sound motion picture projector whose light shines through the film's sound track, and is then converted, by a photoelectric cell, to electrical impulses for sound

expert system information from knowledgeable experts, embedded into computer software, used to guide learner to become competent in a subject or task

expository treatment straightforward informational presentation of a mediated program

exposure index a number assigned to a film by the manufacturer that indicates the relative emulsion speed of the film for determining camera settings (*f*/number and shutter speed) according to American Standards Association (ASA) and International Standards Organization (ISO) in terms of required light conditions

exposure meter (see *photographic light meter*)

fade-in a visual effect in video recording in which a scene gradually appears out of blackness

fade-out a visual effect in video recording in which a scene gradually disappears into blackness

feedback informing a student of success or progress in learning

fill light the secondary light source illuminating a scene, which brightens dark shadow portions created by the key light

film recorder a special camera to reproduce colored images on photographic film as output of a computer

film speed (see *exposure index*)

film transport system path film takes as it moves through 16mm projector; includes upper sprocket wheel, upper loop, film gate, bottom loop, and second sprocket wheel

filmograph a sequence of still pictures on a videotape or motion-picture film

fixed microphone type attached to a stand and placed on a table or suspended above the scene being recorded

fixer a solution in which the chemicals desensitize the developed film image to light and change all undeveloped silver salts so they can be removed by washing

flannel (felt) board a presentation board consisting of a flannel or felt surface to which objects backed with flannel, felt, or sandpaper will adhere

flash an effect used in multi-image presentations consisting of on–off changes of a lamp while a slide remains in projection position

floppy disk flexible plastic disk, protected by pocket cover, stores information generated by computer

flow chart a diagram that illustrates the sequence(s) of steps that a learner might follow in a computer-based or interactive instructional program

flying erase head element in a VCR that allows a "clean cut" between adjacent video scenes

***f*/number (*f*/stop)** the lens setting selected from a series of numbers consisting partially of . . . 2, 2.8, 4, 5.6, 8, 11, 16, 32 . . .

focal length a classification of lenses, being the distance from the center of a lens to the film plane within the camera when the lens is focused at infinity

formative evaluation testing effectiveness of media with a potential audience before being put into final form

formatted premaster (see *premaster*)

frame an individual picture in a filmstrip or video recording

frame grabber (see *video digitizing camera*)

freeze holding a single image on the screen during a multi-image presentation, videotape, or film sequence

fresnel lens large lens under the glass stage of an overhead projector that spreads light evenly over transparency placed on stage

f/16 rule general camera setting for exposing film by using f/16 and setting shutter speed at film speed rating

galley proof first copy of the press run of typeset material to be proofread

game a computer program built on competition to motivate the user to learn

generation of video recording designation indicating levels of removal, from the original recording, of a tape copy (original—1st generation, edited master or copy—2nd generation, copy of master for use—3rd generation, and so forth)

generic videodisc disc containing unprogramed, still pictures and motion sequences as a resource file

genlock device that synchronizes computer data with video signals from sources like a video camera and a VCR to produce a recordable composite picture

glitch interference in the video image that appears on the screen when, during recording, the recorder is stopped and then restarted for the next scene

graphics printer mechanism that reproduces, in printed form, information entered into or generated by a computer

graphics tablet includes electronic pen connected by wire to computer and moved on sensitive surface to create graphic shapes that can be seen on a screen and stored in computer memory

guide number (exposure guide number) a number assigned to a film for the purpose of calculating exposure when electronic flash units are used; it is based upon the film speed, the power of the electronic unit, and the shutter speed

half-frame camera a camera used for making filmstrips that has an aperture one-half the size of a regular 35mm slide and oriented horizontally across the film width

halftone printed illustration consisting of uniformly spaced dots of varying size, which blend together and convey shades of gray

hard copy information generated by computer and printed on paper or film

hard disk magnetically coated metal disk capable of storing large quantity of information for computer memory

Hi8 8mm video format that records a picture superior to that on VHS tape

high-angle shot a scene photographed or recorded with the camera placed high, looking down at the subject

high-contrast film used to photograph paste-up or other line drawn or printed subjects to produce clear lines on opaque background (Kodalith film or equal)

high-contrast subject an illustration consisting solely of black lines or marks on white paper

high tech teaching station consists of media equipment mounted on a stand at front of room for instructor use

hook-and-loop board a presentation board consisting of a cloth surface textured with minute nylon loops with which display materials backed with strips of tape having nylon hooks will intermesh and hold firmly

HyperCard information presentation system used with MacIntosh computer that allows the creation and storage of data in any form and its display in any order or with any connection

ISO (see *exposure index*)

icon small pictures on a computer screen that represent applications, options, or documents in computer memory

inaudible picture advance signal an electronic signal placed on tape and not heard, but which automatically activates a projector to change the picture

incident-light method the measurement of light falling on a scene by the use of an incident-light meter held in the scene and aimed at the camera

indirect projection system used when light is reflected off the opaque surface of material being projected

individualized learning the procedure in which each learner assumes responsibility for learning through independent use of appropriate materials and study at a preferred pace

information material item about an activity of organization in form of a brochure, newsletter, or report

information processing theory learning theory related to mental processes whereby humans perceive, organize, and remember information within short- and long-term memory

infrared light source heat lamp used in processing thermal film transparencies

ink jet printer tiny nozzles spray drops of ink to form letters on paper or film

input a receptacle or other connection through which an electronic signal is fed into an amplifier

input device a keyboard, graphics tablet, light pen, or other device used to put information into a computer

insert edit adding a scene, replacing a scene, or adding sound within a recorded videotape

instructional-design plan procedure for instructional planning that involves application of a number of interrelated steps pertaining to objectives, instructional strategies, and evaluation of learning

instructional designer or developer a person having broad knowledge of audiovisual media and capable of organizing the content of instructional media to be produced so that the stated purposes will best be served

instructional development process of designing an instructional program employing an objective, systematic procedure, such as an instructional-design plan

instructional media audiovisual and related materials that serve instructional functions

instructional technologies audiovisual, electronic media, and related resources that serve instructional functions in education and training

instructional transaction theory learning theory represented as entity, activity, and process structures called frames that form transaction shells for designing instruction using electronic databases and applied as expert systems

interactive learning interplay between a person and any media wherein the learner controls the pace and sequential use of the media for instruction

interactive video combining video images with computer programing, such that the sequence of the program will depend on user choices, answers to questions, and so forth

interface interconnection device between a microcomputer and video player, or other media equipment, which translates computer commands into signals that direct the media to start, stop, skip ahead, or back up

job aid (see *learning aid*)

jumper cord (see *patch cord*)

justify changing spacing between letters and words of printed lines comprising columns on a page so that each line is of the same length at both right and left margins

kerning adjusting the relative spacing between adjacent letters

key light the brightest light source on a scene, forming a large portion of the total illumination

keyboard device consisting of individual controls for letters, numbers, and symbols to input data into computer memory

keypad (see *touch pad*)

keystone effect distortion of a projected image on a screen, wide at top and narrow at bottom

LS (see *long shot*)

laminating applying a thin adhesive-backed clear acetate coating over a picture or other graphic material

laser pointer delivers a laser beam to highlight part of a projected image on the screen

laser printer electronic beam "etches" images onto photoelectric drum, which transfers the high quality image to paper as in a photocopy machine

laserdisc (see *videodisc*)

lavalier microphone type clipped to a speaker's clothing or hung around the person's neck

layout a design on paper illustrating how all elements that comprise the visual, or a page, will appear

learning aid a checklist of steps or procedures, with or without line drawings and photographs, to be used by a person when assembling, operating, or maintaining equipment

legibility the requirement for lettering size and style so that the farthest seated member of a potential audience can see and read projected or nonprojected material satisfactorily

leisure-time programing pressing keys on a microprocessor to store control signals for a multi-image presentation at one's own pace or convenience, and then playing back the commands for operating the program at regular showing pace

lens diaphragm the opening through which light enters a camera; its size is controlled by an adjustable diaphragm consisting of metal blades

letter quality printer device that generates documents of typewriter quality from data in computer memory

light pen electronic pen connected to computer and touched directly to display screen to call up program elements and draw graphic images

lighting ratio the relationship between the intensity of the key light and the intensity of the fill light as measured with a light meter

line copy (see *high-contrast subject*)

linear program information and instruction presented in a fixed sequence that is the same for all learners

line input electrical connection so that electronic signals from a piece of audio equipment can be fed into an amplifier

liquid crystal display (LCD) a device for direct overhead projection of computer-generated data

litho film (see *high-contrast film*)

log sheet a written record of all pictures taken, including scene numbers, takes, camera settings, and special remarks

long shot a general view of a subject and its setting

low-angle shot a scene photographed or recorded with the camera placed low, looking up at the subject

macro lens one specially adapted for close-up and copy work that does not distort lines in a subject

magnetic chalkboard a multipurpose display board consisting of a metal sheet, covered with chalkboard paint, to which magnetic-backed objects will adhere and on which chalk marks can be made

magnification amount of enlargement of a subject when viewed or recorded through a lens

main heading title in printed material for overall subject treatment that follows

main light (see *key light*)

main title the name of the production, shown at the start of instructional media

master any audio, visual, or audiovisual media prepared from original material and then from which duplicate copies are made

master videodisc high quality disc made from premaster videotape as laser beam etches image on glass surface

master videotape finished product that results after editing all original recorded materials

matched action the smooth continuation of action between two adjacent, related video scenes

mechanical term applied to the completed paste-up ready to be reproduced on an offset press

media attributes (see *attributes of media*)

media integration (see *multimedia*)

medium shot a view of a subject that eliminates unnecessary background and other details

menu list of content or options within a computer or videodisc program from which the user makes a selection

microchip an integrated microprocessor circuit etched onto a silicon chip

microcomputer a self-contained computer including a keyboard and memory, and attached to a display screen or a printer

microphone device that converts sound to electronic signals for use in other audio equipment

microphone input connection so signals from a microphone can be fed into an audio amplifier

microprocessor single integrated circuit chip as central processing unit of a computer, containing all essential elements for processing data

microprocessor programer uses computer commands to control a number of slide projectors and dissolve functions for multi-image presentations

mixer a control mechanism through which a number of sound-producing units can be fed in order to combine voice, music, or sound effects at desired recording levels onto a single audiotape

mock-up an exaggeration of aspects of a real object

model a recreation of a real object, may be smaller or larger

modem a device that permits information to be transmitted between computers using telephone lines

module a study unit or program designed for self-paced learning

monitor (see *videomonitor*)

monophonic tape recorder a tape recorder with a single recording head, capable of only recording on one channel at a time

monopod a one-legged device for supporting a camera like a tripod does

montage a series of short scenes in a video recording used to condense time or distance or to show a series of related activities or places

mouse computer input device with which actions can be performed by movements on a surface that are then shown on the display screen

multicamera technique recordings of the same action with two or more cameras operated at the same time and located at different positions in relation to the subject

multi-image simultaneous projection of two or more pictures on one or adjacent screens for group viewing

multimedia variety of media materials that have been digitized and stored in computer memory, then merged together, shown sequentially or in variable arrangements

multipurpose board display surface that can be written on with special felt pens and that has metal backing for displaying magnet-backed objects

multitrack recorder a recorder with 4, 8, 16 or more tracks, which allows a separate recording to be made on each track and played back in any combination

NTSC video standard used in United States, Japan, and most of South America

narration the verbal comments made to accompany the visuals

normal lens most often used lens of a specific focal length for a camera (example 50mm lens for 35mm camera) (see also *focal length*)

object-based drawing program computer software that allows design of nonformatted visuals from various building blocks

objective scene a scene recorded with the camera aimed toward the subject, from a theater audience point of view
omnidirectional microphone instrument that picks up sounds coming from all directions
opaque projector a projector that can enlarge information from paper, pages from a book, or other nontranslucent or nontransparent materials
open reel recorder a tape recorder that uses magnetic tape on separate reels
operant conditioning stimulus-response (S-R) pattern of behavioral psychology identified by B.F. Skinner
optical disc (see *videodisc*)
optical system path that light takes in direct projection to reach the screen; emanating from a lamp, light is reflected to pass through condenser lenses, a heat filter, the aperture opening, a frame of film, and the projection lens
output a connection on an electronic device at which the signal leaves the unit
output device video screen, plotter, or printer to display the information provided by a computer
overhead projector a projector that accepts transparent and translucent sheets and projects the information prepared on them onto a screen
overlay one or more additional transparent sheets with lettering or other matter that can be placed over a base transparency or an opaque background
overprint the superimposition of one scene over another; generally titles, captions, or labels over a background scene or a specially prepared background

PAL video standard used in England and parts of Europe
page proof a trial copy of final pages for checking before the press run
paint and enhancement graphics program computer software allowing the design of original visuals
pan (panorama) the movement of a videocamera, while shooting, in a horizontal plane (left and right)
parallax the difference between the vertical position of an object in a filmed scene as viewed through a viewfinder and as recorded on film through the camera lens
paste-up the combination of illustrations and lettering, each unit of which is rubber-cemented in position on paper or cardboard
patch cord an electrical wire used to connect together two pieces of sound equipment (such as tape recorders and record players) so that electrical impulses can be transferred between the units in order to make a recording
pen plotter computer output device that draws lines and prints characters with pens for graphic representations on paper or film
perfect binding gluing sheets to form a spine when assembling printed pages
permanent mounting use of dry-mount tissue placed between the material and the mount surface, with heat and pressure being applied to seal the layers together
photoelectric cell electronic element of sound system in motion picture projector that converts varying amounts of light from the exciter lamp to electrical impulses for sound
photographic light meter a device for measuring light levels, either incident upon or reflected from a scene
photo modifier a large-size camera used to enlarge or reduce art work
photostabilization a two-step rapid processing method for photographic paper
picas a printing measurement in which 6 picas equals 1 inch of line length
pinboard (see *register board*)
pixels arrangement of dots or picture elements that comprise a computer-generated graphics image
planning board a board with strips of acetate channels holding storyboard cards
points a printing measurement in which 72 points equal 1 inch of line length
poster maker a device that creates approximately 2 × 3 foot posters by scanning an original prepared on 8½ × 11 inch paper
pounce pattern use of a sewing pattern wheel to punch holes in thin cardboard while following lines on a drawing; cardboard is dusted with chalk to create a light pattern on the chalkboard for tracing
preformatted graphics drawing program software program containing prepared, standard graphics to which a user enters data to design a visual
premaster high-quality, edited video recording from which master videodisc is prepared
pressure machine lettering Kroy or Merlin-type machine in which pressure is applied to a character, causing an impression on carbon film that transfers to paper or film as lettering
pressure zone microphone captures direct and reflected sound waves so they reinforce each other to clearly reproduce regular, distant, and low level sounds
printer (see *graphic printer*)
process camera a large-sized, cut-film camera, used by a graphic artist or a printer to convert paste-up, or other original material, with necessary size change, to a high quality paper or film copy
programer a control unit to activate one or more projectors to change images on screens according to scripted sequencing
progressive disclosure exposing a series of items on a transparency or slide by moving an opaque mask during use or preparation
proof disc (see *check disc*)
proof sheet printing photographic negatives by placing negatives on photographic paper to prepare same-size print
psychomotor domain category of objectives for learning that treats physical skills and coordination of skeletal muscles

RAM random access memory in a computer with content that can be altered and which vanishes when power is turned off
RGB monitor a high resolution color video display screen used as output device for computer-created data or videoplayer
ROM read only memory of a computer with content that

cannot be altered

radio microphone (see *wireless microphone*)

rangefinder a camera attachment that, upon proper setting, indicates the distance from camera to subject or sets the lens in focus at that range

rapid-process method (see *photostabilization*)

reactive learning self-paced learning as an individual moves through a program following a single track

readability formula procedure to count the number of syllables and sentences for a certain number of words on a printed page in order to determine a grade level of difficulty for reading material

realia real objects

real-time programing putting control signals on audiotape in actual clock time required to run the program when synchronizing a multi-image presentation

rear-screen projection projecting on the back side of a translucent screen with the projector placed behind the screen

reflected-light method the measurement of light reflected from a scene by the use of a reflected-light meter aimed at the subject

register board a surface with two or more small vertical posts for holding paper, cardboard, or film materials all correctly aligned when more than one layer must be assembled for picture taking

register marks cross symbols placed on a base sheet and also on each overlay sheet to register (match) colors when reproducing multicolor pages or transparencies

reinforcement the result of success in learning that builds confidence in an individual to continue learning

release form the form used to obtain written permission for use of pictures taken of persons or of their copyrighted materials

release paper silicon-treated paper used in dry mounting to ensure materials being mounted to not adhere to a surface in the dry-mount press

reproduction making many copies (ten or more) of printed material

repurposing adapting an available video recoding or videodisc for interactive use

reversal film film that, after exposure, is processed to produce a positive image on the same film

SECAM video standard used in France, Russia, and part of Europe

S-VHS (see *Super VHS*)

sans-serif style of lettering lacking small barlike strokes on top and bottom edge of letters

scanner converts material on paper into an electronic image in computer memory

scene indicates description of subject for each element in a script

script the specific directions for picture taking or art work in the form of a listing of scenes with accompanying narration or captions

scroll slow movement of titles or text up and down on a display screen

selection process that leads to choice of material that best fits identified instructional need

self-paced learning an instructional method whereby each student assumes responsibility for independent study at a preferred rate of study while using required materials

self-threading projector motion picture projector with a guided channel for automatic film threading

semipermanent mounting the application of rubber cement to the back of a flat material to be mounted and also to the mount surface, then permitting the two surfaces to dry before adhering them together

sequence a section of instructional media, more or less complete in itself, and made up of a series of related scenes

serifs style of lettering with small, bar-like strokes on top and bottom edges of letters

shading film textures and patterns printed on acetate sheets having adhesive backing for adhering to cardboard, paper, acetate, or film

shot action in a scene recorded each time videotape moves past the recording head

shotgun microphone a unidirectional type microphone that accepts only a narrow angle of sound and rejects most other noises

shutter speed the interval between opening and closing of the shutter of a camera, measured in fractions of a second

simulation a program that attempts to emulate a realistic situation

single-framing exposing one frame at a time or very brief recording with a videocamera, as opposed to continuous exposure

single-lens reflex camera a compact camera employing a mirror or prism for accurate viewing directly through the camera lens

slate a record of a scene and take number for a shot in video recording

slot-loading projector motion picture projector having a long slot along the side for film threading

slow scan video subject scanned more slowly than normal to produce images that can be transmitted economically via telephone line

social learning theory attention given to personality factors and interactions among people

software a program for use with a computer

sound effects realistic sounds (street traffic, machinery, animals, and so on) that can be added to an audio or video program

sound system parts of motion picture sound projector that create the sound as the film moves, including sound drum, idler rollers, and exciter lamp

special-effects generator a device that allows the addition of various effects to visual images as they are selected and recorded on videotape

specifications the framework and limits within which instructional media are produced; may include such factors as length, materials, special techniques, assistance required, completion date, and budget

split-field image upper and lower halves of subject appearing in camera viewer and aligned as a proper, matched position at focus point

spot meter a reflected-type light meter that accepts only a narrow angle of light; used to measure accurately the light level from a small portion of a scene

stabilizer bath that acts on exposed photographic paper in stabilization process to stop development and set the image

stencil lettering lettering made by using a special pen to fill in the outline of a letter or number cut into a piece of plastic

stereophonic tape recorder a recorder on which a recording is made on two tracks simultaneously and then played back together

still-picture videocamera *see* electronic still camera

stop bath a solution in which the chemicals stop the action of a developer on exposed film

storage device disk drive with magnetic floppy or hard disk, or other device for storing computer information

storyboard a series of sketches or pictures that visualize each topic or sequence in instructional media to be produced; generally prepared after the treatment and before the script

subhead titles in printed material that introduce elements of a subject

subjective scene a scene recorded with the camera placed in the subject's point-of-view position (over the shoulder) and aimed at action being performed

subject matter expert (SME) a person having broad knowledge of the subject content for instructional media to be produced

summative evaluation judging results of a program after instruction or other use is concluded

super-imposed image two images of subject appearing in camera viewer and overlapping to match at focus position

Super VHS form of ½-inch videotape format that produces higher quality images than conventional VHS

synchronized sound sounds on audio or videotape that correlate in proper relationship with pictures

take (of a scene) one exposure among two or more for the same scene; successive takes of the same scene are numbered from 1 upward

tape cassette (see *audiocassette recorder* or *videocassette recorder*)

tape recorder device in which magnetic tape moves and on which sounds are recorded or from which magnetically recorded sounds are heard

tearsheets collections of pictures from magazines and other sources

technical staff a person or persons responsible for the photography, graphic-art work, video and sound recording in producing instructional media

teleconference using two-way live video to hold a meeting with participants at various locations so each group or individuals can see, hear, and interact with each other

telephoto lens a camera lens that permits a closer view of a subject than would be obtained by a normal lens from the same position

television receiver a device that receives signals through an antenna or cable connection and then converts these signals into video and audio impulses

template guideline in computer graphics program for consistent application of features like color schemes, fonts, and layout treatment

temporary mounting the application of rubber cement to the back of an illustration or lettering, which is immediately placed on a mount surface while the cement is still wet

thermal film a film sensitive to infrared heat for producing overhead transparencies from carbon marks made on ordinary paper

thermal transfer printer a device that uses heat to create colored impressions on heat-sensitive paper or film as output from information generated by a computer

thumbspot a visible mark placed in the lower left corner of a slide to indicate the proper position for correctly viewing the slide

tilt the movement of a videocamera in a vertical plane (up and down)

time-base corrector a device used to ensure acceptable picture and sound quality when combining videotaped materials from various sources

time-code generator electronic device that records eight-digit numbers on each frame of a videotape and is used during editing

time-lapse recording the exposing of individual frames at a much slower rate than normal, for projection at normal speed; the method accelerates action that normally takes place too slowly for motion to be perceived

titler electronic device that creates lettering in a videocamera that is recorded on videotape while a scene is being taperecorded

tone-control programer uses audio frequency tones to control a number of slide projectors or different dissolve functions for a multi-image presentation

toner a black powder used in the electrostatic duplicating process to deposit on the paper or film and provide the visible, opaque image

touch pad remote controller for use to send instructions to a videocassette or videodisc player

touch-screen technique user touches a finger or light pen to item on computer screen and computer responds accordingly

tracking control a setting on videocassette recorders to adjust video head speed to overcome minor variations that affect picture quality of a tape during playback

training material item for instructor or learner used during instruction that provides directions, information, and activities

transitional devices the use of such techniques as fade-out, fade-in, and dissolves to bridge space and time in video recordings

transponder transmits signals received on a satellite channel back to earth-based receiver

treatment a descriptive synopsis of how the content of instructional media can be organized and presented

truck shot video scene as camera is moved parallel to the subject

tutorial a computer program that presents information followed by a question or problem, then, based on user's answer, the next block of instruction is presented or remedial instruction is provided

twin-lens camera includes a lens for viewing the subject and second lens for picture-taking

two-column format script for producing media that consists of visual description of scenes along left-side of page and narration with other sounds on right side, opposite scene description

typeface specific design of a set of letters and numbers

unidirectional microphone (see *cardioid microphone*)

VHS a ½-inch video format

vellum a high grade translucent paper or film on which drawings are prepared

videocassette a sealed, rectangular container holding reels of videotape

videocassette recorder (VCR) a video unit that records and plays back visual images and sound as magnetic tape, on reels in a sealed container, passes by the record or playback head in the machine

video digitizing camera (scanner) input device that transforms an image of a picture or object into a dot pattern (pixels) so it can be stored in computer memory

videodisc similar in appearance to a long-play audio record containing up to 30 minutes of video and sound or 54,000 still frames, in any combination, and played with a laser stylus

videodisc player level I unit with manually operated controls used to locate materials on videodisc for limited interactive learning

videodisc player level II unit with built-in microprocessor to program limited amount of information for interactive learning

videodisc player level III unit with interface connecting microcomputer and player for extensive interactive learning

videomonitor receives video signals from a videotape player directly into video and audio circuits; also, display screen that receives images from a computer

video presentation stand a small videocamera mounted over a flat surface on which objects, pictures, slides, and transparencies can be shown through video projection

videotape recorder (VTR) a video unit that records and plays back visual images and sound as magnetic tape from one reel passes by the record or playback head in the machine and takes up on another reel

video toaster commercial product that, with a compatible computer, represents a method for integrating digital video effects, titling, transitions, and other techniques for extending the operational capacity of desktop video

visual literacy skills an individual develops in interpreting, judging, responding to, and using visual representations of reality

visual tools factors of line, shape, space, texture, and color to consider, along with design principles, when designing art work

WORM write once read many videodisc that can be prepared locally and used for mass storage of data

white balance a videocamera setting to fine-tune the camera for the particular light conditions under which the scene will be recorded

white letter overprint clear letters that appear over a scene in any visual material

wide-angle lens a camera lens that permits a wider view of a subject and its surroundings than would be obtained by a normal lens from the same position

wipe a visual effect in videotape recordings in which a new scene seems to push the previous scene off the screen

wireless microphone a microphone that acts as a radio transmitter, broadcasting the audio signal to a receiver

wireless touch panel exhibits labels for items of media presentation equipment in a room, which, when pressed by an instructor, start or stop equipment operation

word processing entry, manipulation, editing, and storage of text using a computer program

xerography (see *electrostatic process*)

Y jumper cord (see *patch cord*)

Zimdex a method of placing index numbers on tape to facilitate locating specific parts of a recording on the other track

zoom lens a camera lens of variable magnification that permits a smooth change of subject coverage between distance and close-up shots without changing the camera position

Index

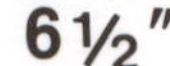

8½″

MASK FOR VIDEO FORMAT

The area enclosed within the rule is the area within which titles, art work, and other visuals for a video recording should be composed (proportion 3 × 4).